THE SMALL GROUP IN POLITICAL SCIENCE

The Small Group
in
Political Science

The Last Two Decades
of Development

EDITED BY

ROBERT T. GOLEMBIEWSKI

THE UNIVERSITY OF GEORGIA PRESS

ATHENS

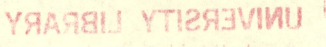

Library of Congress Catalog Card Number: 75-36688
International Standard Book Number: 0-8203-0405-0

The University of Georgia Press, Athens 30602

Copyright © 1978 by the University of Georgia Press
Printed in the United States of America

Contents

Introduction

This volume is a period piece, but hopefully one with a future as well as a past. More plainly this volume is an interim report on the progress that has been made over the last two decades by approaching the subject matter of Political Science from a group perspective. This volume deals somewhat pridefully with some results of this first-generation empirical inquiry, and it also looks forward to much more progress in the future. Like all period pieces, this volume must establish a time-frame. That is easy enough to do. For most practical purposes, the current wave of interest in the relevance of group phenomena in Political Science can be traced directly to David Truman's *The Governmental Process* (1951).

Truman's contribution was made in the context of a broad range of demonstrations of the usefulness of a microorientation in understanding broad ranges of phenomena of social and political interest. Perhaps the most massive impact came from seminal works by Homans (1950) and Whyte (1952). And Truman's genealogy goes back to classic sources in Political Science, to Aristotle's rooting of political analysis/philosophy in the crucial but unspecific observation that man is a social animal; to Rousseau's clear perception of the cohesive power of small social aggregates in *Du contrat social;* and through Kaufman's (1964) observation that a family of common theoretical notions underlies all social, political, and organizational theories.

Most immediately Truman's popular volume redirected attention to a great book, often cited and usually the center of controversy, and a volume that has experienced several cycles of discovery/neglect/rediscovery (Golembiewski 1960, 962-964). Specifically Truman's *The Governmental Process* served as a third-generation booster for Arthur Bentley's *The Process of Government* (1949). Thus in a volume originally published in 1908, Bentley had tried to redirect political inquiry in at least two major ways. He sought to complement the individualistic bias of most political analysis by emphasizing the role of both very small and very large groups. Moreover Bentley urged on political analysis the major significance of a critical distinction and differentiation. He stressed the profound usefulness of distinguishing the development of intellectual or philosophic ideas about what the world could or should be like, as well as the corresponding need to differentiate this kind of intellectual activity from piecing together increasingly broad scientific theories that seek to describe the world as it is. Bentley did not hide his feelings as to which of these two basic endeavors he accorded priority. He sought "hard data" and shunned "soul stuff."

In today's context these aims of Bentley seem pedestrian enough. From the most important analytic perspectives, Bentley only sought to emphasize what illustrious others before him had sought to establish, men like Aristotle and Francis Bacon, for example (Golembiewski, Welsh, and Crotty 1969, 49-58). In Bentley's day and time, however, all hell broke loose. In part the outcome was foreordained: too many oxen were being gored. In some part, also, the outcome was due to Bentley's self-confessed reliance on hyperbole, which could be interpreted as taunt or even ridicule. Consider his denigration of the intellectual search for "soul stuff" and its senseless (to him) preoccupation with the fluff of ideas and ideology, as distinguished from an emphasis on the hard data of activity and behavior. It was clearly a case with Bentley of friend versus foe, of useful versus preposterous, of essence versus nit picking.

Bentley did not leave much middle ground if any. His central conceptual thrust was as one with his strategy of presentation: both encouraged polarization. Scholars tended to be either for him, or against him, and intensely so in both cases. When he first wrote, only a small remnant was with him. They proved to be an influential and a resilient remnant. But these scholars were not able to gain in-depth acceptance of Bentley's central ideas, although they kept them center stage at recurring intervals over a half century, more or less.

Thus Bentley highlighted several massive themes that kept surfacing, often as reincarnations of interest in Bentley presented as periodic rediscoveries of his seminal work. Before Truman redirected attention to *The Processes of Government,* to summarize a very long story, two earlier and more or less distinct waves of interest in Bentley's work had established only a narrow beachhead on the traditional turf of Political Science (Rothman 1960). Applications of the group concept were basically restricted to pressure groups or interest groups (Odegard 1958); and Bentley's basic methodological concerns received little fruitful attention (Golembiewski, Welsh, and Crotty 1969, 129-139). As a major by-product, however, many academic blood pressures were elevated by the common interpretation of Bentley's message as reductionist, materialist, and determinist (Loveday 1962).

Truman's third-generation boosterism about Bentley's group emphasis was unique in a critical sense. It roughly coincided with the emergence of some two decades of growing development of the group concept within Political Science. Thus Truman helped induce what Bentley and two other generations of boosters could not. The "group orientation" quickly spread to numerous areas of traditional concern within Political Science and influenced much thinking and even some research. The dimensions of this diffusion can be suggested briefly in outline form.

1. Two major efforts by political scientists, both of which originated in doctoral research, sought to comprehend large bodies of group research and to identify their relevance to traditional concerns in Political Science (Golembiewski 1962A, Verba 1961).

2. The justices of the Supreme Court were analyzed as an interacting group (Snyder 1958, Ulmer 1965).

3. Group-level constructs were used to describe and explain the behavior of legislators and legislatures (Matthews 1959, Fenno 1962, Francis 1962, Manley 1965, Dodd 1972).

4. New and more sophisticated attention was given to a ubiquitous

grouping, the family, as an agency of socialization in the development of political attitudes and behaviors (Maccoby et al. 1954, McClosky and Dahlgren 1959, Siegel 1965).

5. Group-level constructs enriched the analysis of politically relevant decision making in both experimental (Snyder 1955, March 1956, Bloomfield and Paddleford 1959, Barber 1966) as well as natural-state contexts (Shils 1951, Gore 1956).

6. The value of group-level analysis was demonstrated for a range of administrative issues and situations historically dealt with by political scientists, as in Public Administration (Blau 1955, Golembiewski 1959, 1962), International Relations (Gordenker 1959, Galtung 1968, Toma 1968) and related areas (Commons 1950).

7. Two increasingly popular kinds of research in Political Science —simulation and experimentation—typically generate and require group-level analysis (Riker 1962, LaPonce and Smoker 1972).

8. Groups were shown to be major, indeed apparently massive, determinants of such critical political processes as the climate of decision making (Lewin, Lippit, White 1939), patterns of forming consensus/conflict (Deutsch 1949, Sherif and Sherif 1953), the formation of opinions deviant from group standards or norms (Asch 1956), and in the broader processes of developing public opinion (Baur 1960).

9. Group analysis was extended to such politically central areas as jury behavior (Strodtbeck, James, Hawkings 1957).

10. Political scientists have become conversant with the techniques of group analysis and have even innovated such techniques (Madron 1969, Walcott and Hopmann 1974).

11. Attempts have been made to build into Political Science methodological concerns and lessons that are derived from empirical research on groups (Golembiewski, Welsh, Crotty 1969).

This diverse outpouring of concern and research did not merely rest on the persuasiveness of Truman's development of Bentley's argument for a group orientation in political analysis, of course, although Truman's popular volume was patently important in helping to legitimate research on group phenomena. More centrally, Truman's volume coincided with the early stages of a truly monumental expenditure of effort in several disciplines that focused on small-group phenomena (Strodtbeck 1954). The growth curve of small-group analysis was the most prominent one in the burgeoning behavioral sciences, in fact. That growth curve was buoyed by two dominant factors: the growing awareness of the potency of group contexts for influencing behaviors, values, and attitudes of individuals; and the convenient research opportunities implicit in a unit composed of perhaps three-fifteen individuals, a convenience manifest not only for laboratory experiments but also for field research. Truman's third boost for research emphasizing a group orientation, in a very real sense, was caught up in the great whoosh of work in small-group analysis. A very real coattail effect was involved.

In its broadest and simplest scope, this collection seeks to serve as both yardstick and carrot, to objectify its intent. On the one hand, this volume seeks to provide some measure of the progress toward exploiting the group orientation that was induced within Political Science under the cumulative goading of Bentley/Truman/small-group analysis. Additionally, this volume seeks to motivate further work, to sustain and increase the momentum built up over the past two decades. Beyond those elemental intentions, this book rests on a compound rationale. Six factors in that rationale deserve highlighting.

First, the present volume seeks to illustrate the relevance of group-oriented research to major common concerns within Political Science. The word "illustrate" is used advisedly, for the focus below is on small-group analysis; the broader task of dealing with group-oriented research would take several volumes.

But the present focus provides scope enough, especially since the traditional concerns in Political Science have basically centered around macrolevel phenomena. Thus establishing the relevance of small-group analysis to Political Science will not be easy, given the latter's historic thoughtways. Making the point will require varying degrees of several kinds of demonstrations, including those (1) which establish or suggest that concepts for describing dynamics in small groups are analogous to or the same as those useful for describing larger aggregates, (2) which establish or suggest that lawful regularities in small groups may also hold in larger aggregates, (3) which establish or suggest linkages between microlevel and macrolevel phenomena, even though different concepts and lawful regularities are applicable at the two levels, and (4) which establish or suggest that macrolevel issues can be dealt with via small-group techniques or approaches, whether in analytical or in practical senses.

In addition this volume tries to locate such demonstrations in diverse areas of traditional concerns to political scientists. For example issues in international affairs, police-community relations, and organization behavior, plus others, receive attention below, by way of illustrating how macrolevel issues can be approached via a small-group technology. Moreover the emphasis will be on empirical research as well as on applied interventions in complex systems in ways intended to produce specific effects.

The thrust of these several kinds of demonstrations of the relevance of small-group analysis to Political Science is toward two conclusions. Thus the direct relevance of group-oriented work to disciplinary concerns in Political Science can now be established with some certainty. Moreover, that relevance is likely to increase, and at a rapid pace.

Second, the reasons for highlighting small-group research in Political Science are direct, if compound. Consider only two reasons/goals underlying this focus on the group orientation. One patent goal is to encourage research and its applications that extend the boundaries of existing knowledge and research. Perhaps the more central goal is to further legitimate a microlevel approach, in a consciousness-heightening sort of way. The first reason/goal requires no elaboration, but the second will profit from further specification.

The consciousness-raising rationale of this volume implies two basic motivations. For one, much of the research by political scientists focusing on group phenomena is scattered over a broad range of research loci. Relationships and identifications with political scientists interested in groups consequently have been hard to build and harder still to maintain. Such viable interfaces are critical to collaborative research efforts, grant proposals, etc. Hopefully this volume will provide one further impetus to collective attack on common concerns.

Moreover the consciousness-raising reason/goal of this volume is motivated by the current stage of the development of Political Science as a discipline. Directly, if the experience of other disciplines is any guide, panels or divisions within the American Political Science Association may soon begin to evolve in earnest. Such division is traditionally vertical, as in identifying International Relations and Public Administration as different fields. Vertical division can be fragmenting for some purposes, however. Just as it is useful for heightening a sense of identification and for focusing traditional inquiry, vertical division also may impede the development of new lines of inquiry and new identifications. Hence it is, particularly in times of change and ferment, that there is an especial value to horizontal ways of integrating/dividing specialists. The two approaches to differentiation generate a matrix whose cells have some common members and some unique ones. For example, if Political Science horizontally distinguished Micropolitics from Quantitative Politics, both areas could include members from all or many vertical divisions such as Public Administration or International Relations. In a small way this volume can be seen as providing one further stimulus to a formal horizontal structuring of Political Science, which is much needed.

Third, consistent with its integrative thrust, this volume brings together a range of variously differentiated efforts. Thus perhaps 50 percent of the selections have been published elsewhere; the rest were specifically commissioned for this volume. The selections which have previously been published fall about equally into two classes: they appeared in well-known sources within the normal reading limits of political scientists; or the selections were published in out-of-the-mainstream sources, as judged from the perspective of most political scientists. Similarly, many of the selections below are the products of professionals who identify themselves as political scientists. However, several come from fellow professionals who have dealt with phenomena of political relevance.

Fourth, this volume seeks to emphasize what is taken to be a basic reality. Directly the traditional concerns of Political Science cannot merely be seen as a set of loci for the application of group methods or approaches for analysis, however reasonable this posture was as a starting point. Political scientists must come to be seen increasingly as contributing to the development of group methods and approaches, as contrasted with merely applying those methods and approaches. The failure to achieve increasingly such a disciplinary daily double is likely to have one or both of two major consequences, which are about equally unattractive. Thus failure by political scientists to contribute to, as well as apply, the group technology is likely to result in research designs and results that are not sensitive to the inputs, issues, and perspectives that are central to Political Science.

In this sense, whether individually or as members of cross-disciplinary teams, political scientists must really rather do it themselves to a growing degree. The crux, of course, is to become increasingly producers as well as consumers of group-oriented research. If not, some important somethings may not get done at all, or at least they may not get done at an appropriate time. The track record is quite convincing on this point (Lazarsfeld, Berelson, Gandet 1948). Moreover (alternative to some relevant things not getting needed or timely attention) a kind of disciplinary poaching may occur unless political scientists go beyond providing a convenient locus for group-oriented research/applications. An academic discipline may appropriately decide that some approaches or technologies are not its thing, of course. But it is equally clear that there are practical limits on how many traditional foci or concerns can be left open for homesteading by others before disciplinary values may be affected. Indeed, beyond some point of benign or aggressive neglect, poaching not only may occur, it should occur. For such reasons, to use a convenient simplification, political scientists must increasingly become producers as well as consumers of basic group-oriented research and applications. The distinction is a rough one, but a useful one nonetheless.

Fifth, one of the present goals is to suggest how group-oriented research and applications of its findings can be mutually reinforcing. The basic thrust here is that the best test of an empirical theory is whether it works, to paraphrase Kurt Lewin. And the best way to test whether a theory works is to apply it to determine whether it leads to the expected consequences under specified conditions. The notion is simple but profound in its implications.

Political Science has generally been slow to acknowledge this reinforcing of research ⟷ application. Hence it is, for example, that experimentation has been rare in Political Science (LaPonce and Smoker 1972), even in those areas where it is clearly of central significance. To be sure, there have been some major efforts to emphasize the centrality of the research ⟷ application interface, as in some of what are known as the policy sciences. But such efforts have been exceptional in Political Science and are not highly developed even when they do attract attention.

The purpose here is not to force fit some rose-colored spectacles through which to view the world of scientific analysis. There are problems with research ⟷ application interaction, to be sure. But it is not reasonable to avoid the problems by acting as if substantial benefits do not exist. For example political scientists might become the handmaidens of some establish-ment which applies hard-gained knowledge for its own ignoble purposes. But this possibility is clearly a generic one. All knowledge is subject to im-provident or even immoral use. Such possible outcomes, however, hardly constitute a rationale for ignorance or neglect. Rather they imply a central dilemma that requires constant and conscious attention.

Sixth, overall this volume seeks to emphasize two related themes. Thus the group-orientation has an across-the-board relevance to a broad range of concerns in Political Science. This relevance will have to be established, and it is patently incomplete even if growing.

Moreover, and more centrally, this volume stresses the strategic methodological advantages of small-group analysis in supporting the early stages of the full-scale development of a scientific approach to political phenomena. Specifically, focus on small-group phenomena forces the analyst to deal with basic concerns of scientific analysis—conceptual and operational definition, research design, etc. These concerns can then be transferred to other problems, perhaps less amenable to scientific inquiry. From this perspective, small-group analysis is a convenient jumping off point, not some end of the line. The point too often goes unappreciated in Political Science.

REFERENCES

Asch, S. E. 1956. Studies of independence and submission to group pressure: A minority of one against a unanimous majority, *Psychological monographs* 70: whole no. 416.

Barber, J. D. 1966. Power in committees. Chicago: Rand McNally.

Baur, E. J. 1960. Public opinion and the primary group. *American sociological review* 25: 208-218.

Bentley, A. F. 1949. *The process of government.* Bloomington, Ind.: Principia Press.

Blau, P. M. 19955. *The dynamics of bureaucracy.* Chicago: University of Chicago Press.

Bloomfield, L. P., and Padelford, N. J. 1959. Three experiments in political gaming, *American political science review* 53: 1105-1115.

Commons, J. R. 1950. *The economics of collective action.* New York: Macmillian.

Deutsch, M. 1949. A theory of cooperation and competition, *Human relations* 2: 129-152 and 199-231.

Dodd, L. C. 1962. Committee integration in the senate, *Journal of politics* 34: 1135-1171.

Fenno, R. F. 1962. The house appropriations committee as a political system: The problem of integration, *American political science review* 56: 310-324.

Francis, W. L. 1962. Influence and interaction in a state legislative body, *American political science review* 56: 953-960.

Galtung, J. 1968. Small group theory and the theory of international relations. *New ap-proaches in international relations,* ed. Morton A. Kaplan, New York: St. Martin's Press. 270-302.

Golembiewski, R. T. 1959. The small group and public administration, *Public administration review* 19: 149-156.

Golembiewski, R. T. 1960. The group basis of politics: Notes on analysis and development, *American political science review* 54: 967-971.

Golembiewski, R. T. 1962. *Behavior and organization.* Chicago: Rand-McNally.

Golembiewski, R. T. 1962A. *The small group.* Chicago: University of Chicago Press.

Golembiewski, R. T., Welsh, W. A., and Crotty, W. 1969. *A methodological primer for political scientists.* Chicago: Rand-McNally.

Gordenker, L. 1959. *The United Nations and the peaceful unification of Korea: The politics of field operations.*The Hague: M. Nijhoff.

Gore, W. J. 1956. Decision-making in a federal field office, *Public administration review* 16: 281-291.

Homans, G. C. 1950. *The human group.* New York: Harcourt.

Kaufman, Herbert 1964. Organization theory and political theory, *American political science review* 58: 5-14.

La Ponce, J., and Smoker, P. eds. 1974. *Simulation and experimentation in political science.* Vancouver, B. C.: University of Vancouver Press.

Lazarsfeld, P. L., Berlson, B., and Gaudet, H. 1948.*The people's choice.* New York: Columbia University Press.

Lewin, K., Lippit, R. and White, R. K. 1939. Patterns of aggressive behavior in experimentally created 'social climates,' *Journal of social psychology* 10: 271-299.

Loveday, P. 1962. Group theory and its critics. *Groups in theory and practice*, ed. P. Loveday and Ian Campbell, pp. 1-24. Sydney, Australia: F. W. Cheshire.

Maccoby, E. E., Matthews, R. E., and Morton, A. S. 1954. Youth and political change, *Public opinion quarterly* 18: 23-39.

Madron, T. 1969. *Small group methods and the study of politics.* Evanston, Ill.: Northwestern University Press.

Manley, J. F. 1965. The house committee on ways and means, *American political science review* 59: 927-939.

March, J. G. 1956. Influence measurement in experimental and semi-experimental groups, *Sociometry* 19: 260-271.

Matthews, D. R. 1959. The folkways of the United States Senate: Conformity to group norms and legislative effectiveness, *American political science review* 53: 1064-1089.

McClosky, H., and Dahlgren, H. E. 1959. Primary group influence on party loyalty, *American political science review* 53: 757-776.

Odegard, P. H. 1958. A group basis of politics: A new name for an old myth, *Western political quarterly* 11: 689-702.

Riker, W. H. 1962. *The theory of political coalitions.* New Haven: Yale University Press.

Rothman, S. 1960. Systematic political theory: Observations on the group approach, *American political science review* 54: 15-33.

Sherif, M., and C. 1953. *Groups in harmony and tension.* New York: Harper.

Shils, E. A. 1951. The study of the primary group. In *The policy sciences*, ed. Daniel Lerner and Harold D. Lasswell, esp. pp. 43-48. Stanford, Calif.: Stanford University Press.

Siegel, R., 1965. *Political socialization: Role in the political process.* Philadelphia: American Academy of Political and Social Science.

Snyder, E. 1958. The Supreme Court as a small group. *Social forces* 36: 232-238.

Snyder, R. C. 1955. Game theory and the analysis of political behavior. In *Research frontiers in politics and government*, ed. R. C. Snyder, pp. 76-95. Washington, D. C.: Brookings Foundation.

Strodtbeck, F. L. 1954. The case for the study of small groups, *American sociological review* 19: 651.

Strodtbeck, F. L., James, R. M., and Hawkins, C. 1957. Social status in jury deliberations, *American sociological review* 22: 713-719.

Toma, P. A. 1968. Sociometric measurements of the Sino-Soviet conflict: Peaceful and nonpeaceful revolutions, *Journal of politics* 30: 732-748.

Truman, D. B. 1951. *The government process.* New York: Knopf.

Ulmer, S. S. 1965. Toward a theory of sub-group formation in the United States Supreme Court, *Journal of politics* 27: 132-152.

Verba, S. 1961. *Small groups and political behavior.* Princeton: Princeton University Press.

Walcott, C., and Hopmann, P. T. 1976. *Interaction analysis and bargaining behavior.* This volume.

Whyte, W. F. 1952. *Street corner society: The social structure of an Italian slum.* Chicago: University of Chicago Press.

I. Methodological Contexts

The Small Group's Central Role
in Political Science

The ideal central focus for any knowledge-seeking discipline will have two major characteristics or will contribute substantially toward two ends. It will diversely relate to traditional major concerns and perspectives in the discipline, for openers, hopefully in novel and revealing ways. Such an ideal focus will permit making use of knowledge accumulated in the past, while ordering it in more convenient or newly revealing ways. In addition an ideal focus will provide a cutting edge that orients traditional concerns and perspectives into new disciplinary territory, or which permits more intensive and systematic study of hallowed areas.

The burden of this volume is that small-group analysis provides just such an ideal central focus for Political Science. As a supporting theme, the volume also implies that now is an opportune time to press this advantage. Much of the early developmental work is behind us, and the small-group emphasis is in a kind of a parking orbit in Political Science or, to use an alternate metaphor, it is on a developmental plateau. Relatively small amounts of resources, if this gross picture is accurate, should consequently trigger relatively large increments in knowledge and development. Hence the value of looking backwards as a way of attempting to encourage a more substantial future commitment to the group approach in Political Science.

A PREVIEW OF THE VOLUME

Five emphases in this volume seek to provide skeletal but convincing proof of the broad contention that small-group analysis provides a useful central focus for Political Science. Note that the five emphases relate to a central focus, not the focus. This volume is happy to let many flowers bloom, as it were. These five emphases are detailed here by way of previewing what is to come.

Chapter I seeks to develop a methodological context which supports this volume's basic contention. Essentially, small-group analysis has certain methodological strengths which happen to fit closely major current developmental needs of Political Science as a discipline. How students go about studying small groups can provide valuable models to political scientists as to how they should go about studying other phenomena of concern to them in a descriptive or scientific way. Moreover, strategically, the small group is a powerful unit of social control; and this elemental fact also encourages intensive attention by political scientists to group phenomena.

Chapter II provides detail about how political scientists became increasingly aware of and specific about the relevance of the small group to their traditional concerns. This chapter seeks, as it were, to provide a picture of an unfolding conceptual context, of how a broad core-insight came to be seen as more precisely relevant to a broadening disciplinary range of issues.

Chapters III through V provide illustrations of the small group as ubiquitous, and of its dynamics as momentous. Specifically the chapters individually focus on natural-state contexts, experimental contexts, and simulation contexts. The common goals are to show the ubiquitousness of the powerful effects of a small group on its members, and to highlight the flexibility of the small-group level of organization for research in natural as well as contrived settings. Cumulatively the three chapters document the relevance of small-group dynamics to a broad range of concerns in the behavioral sciences generally, as well as documenting their relevance to an impressive spectrum of central issues in Political Science specifically.

Chapters VI and VII concentrate on what may be called social engineering, on illustrations from evolving goal-based, empirical theories that illustrate how small group dynamics can be put to a critical test. That test is whether empirical knowledge about small groups—the "pure science," if you will—is sophisticated enough to permit interventions in nature that have the desired effects. One chapter focuses on political actors and systems, with the goal of showing how it is possible to intervene in conflicts between nations as well as between historic enemies. The second chapter deals with applications of small-group dynamics in large organizations, especially as they relate to Public Administration, which is generally thought of as a field of Political Science. These two chapters are critical ones in two basic senses. They demonstrate what it means specifically to note that the test of a good empirical theory is that it works. Moreover these chapters demonstrate how an appropriate methodology can help a knowledge-seeking discipline grow even on its own failures. This is a delightful attribute in any area of human endeavor, of course, where failure is common.

The argument in Chapters VII and VIII is hardly that comprehensive goal-based, empirical theories have been developed and are on the shelf, as it were. The point is at once more limited and yet more exciting. That is, some fragments of goal-based, empirical theories are coming along nicely, thank you. Moreover it is still early enough in the game for large numbers of students/practitioners to make major contributions at the relative frontiers of knowledge in this area. This is an attractive combination.

Chapter IX seeks help and guidance for Political Science from the experience of two disciplines which have given much attention to the small group from their own perspectives. These two disciplines are Psychology and Sociology. Essentially the chapter seeks answers to a simple question: Given your experience with research on small groups, what can political scientists learn that will help avoid dead ends? And what can they learn from the earlier experience of researchers that will help them more successfully cope with problems involved in dealing with that level of social organization?

A PREVIEW OF THIS CHAPTER

Two selections constitute the present sketch of the contributions of small-group analysis to enhancing the capacity of Political Science as a discipline to deal with its traditional subject matter. Broad perspective is provided by

Robert T. Golembiewski in "Small Group Analysis and the Development of Political Science: Two Perspectives on the Interface." Basically he seeks to demonstrate how an emphasis on the small group requires working with the full range of phases of a simple paradigm of empirical research. The derivative benefits to Political Science can be great, for it is in the second decade or so of its own substantial commitment to developing a natural-science approach to much of its own subject matter, the enthusiasm for which has at least stabilized and may even be beginning to fade somewhat. In part this leveling off is due to the overexuberance of early advocates of empirical or behavioral work, whose salesmanship generated a kind of scholarly backlash. In part, also, the perhaps-waning enthusiasm derives from the intractability of the usual units or levels of analysis in Political Science, such as the nation-state or other macrounits.

The several components of this paradigm for empirical science also require confronting a broad range of concerns and issues that have long been at the heart of Political Science. For example small-group analysis requires a melding of descriptive and prescriptive approaches at certain stages of its development. Just such an interaction has been a major stumbling block in the recent disciplinary development of Political Science. The small group thus can well serve the development of Political Science in both senses, Golembiewski argues. This is the central proposition of this volume.

Thomas Madron provides detailed counterpoint to this central proposition from the standpoint of a scholar familiar with the developmental history of a wide variety of areas of inquiry, and from the perspective of a major actor in one of the few laboratories for observation of politically relevant phenomena. Madron's "Some Costs and Benefits of Small Group Analysis in Political Science" builds around the theme that political scientists "do have something of a commitment to pursue the goal of finding either the 'laws' of human political behavior or, alternatively, of substantiating their probable non-existence." Essentially, for Madron, this commitment implies that political scientists must devote major resources to the two types of analysis capable of permitting the required judgment about possible laws of human political behavior: experimental research and time-series research. The small group is a central vehicle for experimental research, and Madron also suggests how the small-group focus might be useful in some kinds of time-series research, illustratively in studies of political parties.

If Madron implies that political scientists can neglect the small group only at the expense of incomplete understanding of political phenomena, he also is clear that the required attention is costly. Consistently Madron stresses the kinds of investments of time, resources, and intellectual power necessary to exploit the group concept. The difficulties and costs are not trivial, and they derive from multiple sources. Practically Madron notes that one need is to convince "those who control funds . . . that political scientists—as well as physicists, chemists, psychologists, and others—require sometimes elaborate laboratory facilities and instruments." Conceptually, in addition, the difficulties and costs (as well as the opportunities) of small-group analysis derive from its pure and applied features. Thus, to deal with the small group forces attention to two kinds of questions: (1) What exists? (2) How can knowledge of what exists be used to approach more closely some working definition of what is desirable?

Small Group Analysis
and the Development of Political Science:
Two Perspectives on the Interface

ROBERT T. GOLEMBIEWSKI

Two themes dominate this paper. First, the focus on the small group can contribute substantially to the development of Political Science in encouraging and facilitating a natural science and experimental orientation. In this sense, the focus is tactical. The small size of the research unit implies a variety of advantages in focusing attention on and permitting the development of skills necessary for empirical science.

Traditional focal concerns in Political Science have been less benign in this matter, to put it mildly. The nation-state, in sharp contrast, is a very intractable research unit, and has stood as an obstacle to the development of interests and skills neccessary to study empirically the processes central to the formulation of public policy and its implementation. The reasonable fixation on the nation-state implies a major cost. Directly, that level of organization exacerbated the real difficulties of developing orientations and skills required to permit intensive exploration of those areas of Political Science initially more open to empirical analysis. Epigrammatically, that focus was like opening a Ballet I class with a pas de deux exercise.

However, the value of the small group is not only tactical. Second, that is, the present position is not simply that the group focus is a temporary convenience for developing skills and interests appropriate for empirical analysis, which would be abandoned when a suitable cadre of resource persons with natural science skills and orientations had accumulated. To put the point positively, an emphasis on the small group is also strategic. That level of social organization has a critical significance in itself, in short, as well as for the skills and interests it can help develop. These two themes deserve separate elaboration, which will follow.

Scientific inquiry may be described as a kind of complex percolator, whose basic subprocesses are sketched in Figure 1. The juices of scientific inquiry bubble away for long periods at the perceptual level, as reality is experienced and tentatively and laboriously classified in terms of concepts as well as of valid and reliable ways of operationalizing them. After some time, theoretical statements of the relationships of these conceptualized /operationalized somethings evolve, either as statements of probability or as "if . . , then . . ." statements. The adequacy of these theoretical statements will be variously tested, as by observation, but experimental interventions into nature typically provide the most powerful test. A good theory will permit many observers to intervene in ways that will have similar consequences under similar conditions.

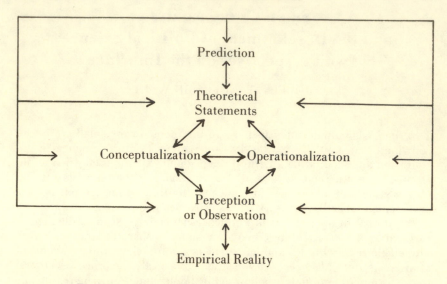

Figure 1. A simplified paradigm for empirical science

The total sense of the natural science effort is perhaps best suggested as bubbling and recycling to ever greater comprehensiveness in an expanding spiral that seeks to encompass more and more of reality. There will be resting orbits in this expanding spiral, and the spiral will sometimes collapse into itself toward some lower developmental level. But the game literally cannot be lost as long as the players are willing and able, for such is the scientific enterprise that even gross failures can be helpful. Failure to verify predictions can be especially learningful, in fact. If predictions derived from any theoretical statements, or consistent with them, are verified, to that degree do the statements provide a framework for more comprehensive efforts to provide a model of nature. As such predictions are found variously wanting, the scientific subprocesses must recycle in complex ways. Thus the failure may be remedied by more extensive observation, by conceptualizations that are more nearly unidimensional, by operations that more validly and reliably measure variation of conceptual domains, as well as by more sensitive theoretical statements.

Success in verifying predictions may have less impact, and indeed may create an illusion that all is known that needs knowing. But nature typically cooperates in this regard, and usually sooner than later. Even the theoretical statements in which we have the greatest confidence today—let us say, those in atomic physics—are likely to have a short half-life.

The situation has been substantially different in the social sciences generally, and in Political Science specifically. Crudely, Political Science has been concept-rich and theory-glutted, but it has been weak in observation and poor in prediction. No small part of this record is due to the scarcity and difficulty of experimentation in Political Science, even today. In turn, no small part of the lack of experimentation is due to the fixation in Political Science on the nation-state. Hence the half-life of a political theory is likely to be a long one, once it somehow catches hold.

Here small-group analysis can help fill a critical need. For a focus on that level of social organization simultaneously forces a major distinction between types of theories that are often confused in Political Science, and also helps relate two kinds of work in Political Science—the descriptive and the prescriptive—whose complex interactions still bedevil political scientists. Attention will be devoted to these two key topics, in turn.

Three Kinds of Theory. It has lately become fashionable to note that there is nothing so practical as a good theory, and that position inspires no argument here. But it is also true that there may be nothing worse than an inept theory, especially one that is self-fulfilling and defies testing or is untestable.

Overall, Political Science has more of the worst than the best of it in the matter of theory. The role of theory in Political Science often has been mischievous, at least, and largely because of a confusion about several kinds of theories, each of which has its own usefulness and limits. Three types of theory will receive attention here. The purpose is to specify with some precision the boundaries of the practicality of each type, as well as to stake out the limits of each. The goal is to illustrate how small-group analysis will help in effectively distinguishing types of theories, and hence how it will help in the development of Political Science. The argument rests heavily on an earlier presentation (Golembiewski 1962; 49-52, and 54-57).

The first type may be called empirical theory. Empirical theory has as its purpose the statement of the relations which exist in the physical or social worlds, that is, the statement of what is related to what. Hence one proposition from an empirical theory is: The earth revolves around the sun. This proposition is a commonplace. But it was not very long ago—an instant, measured in terms of man's history—when men were called fools (and worse) for supporting this proposition. The nature of empirical theory, then, can be illuminated by describing how we made this journey from ignorance to knowledge, and how we in the process developed some useful distinctions about types of theories.

What we now know as elementary empirical theory dealing with the relationship of sun and earth—indeed what we have only just recently observed in the NASA space flights—contrasts sharply with early beliefs on the relation of sun to earth. Thus it was believed that the earth must be the center of the universe. The rationale is straightforward and, granted certain assumptions, plausible. Man was made in God's image; thus man had to be the focal point of creation; and therefore earth, man's home, had to be the focal body of the universe. While satisfying at one level, such ideational networks left much to be explained or, rather, their explanations were of the residual category variety. For example the networks did not explain or predict eclipses except that the sense of theoretical failure was reduced by viewing eclipses as unpredictable acts of God.

Empirical theory started from quite a different base, one rooted in observation rather than speculation or derivation, as well as one rooted in the verification of predictions rather than in arbitrary acts of some intrusive deity. Much information on eclipses, phases of the moon and the like, had convinced a few early scientists that the earth revolved about the sun, rather than vice versa. This implied quite a different explanation of eclipses. Interestingly, and perhaps frighteningly, quite sophisticated lunar and solar understanding was available as early as 5000 B. C., reflected in monuments to knowledge such as Stonehenge that long puzzled ages of observers who somehow lost what their ancestors knew, and only regained by centuries of search and study (Hawkins 1973).

But the choice between theories was not straightforward, for the early scientists could not be certain that their sun-center conclusion was correct although it was consistent with available information. Logically their theory had no firmer footing than the theory they challenged. Indeed both theories were of this form: "If A, then B." More fully: (1.) If (A) God wills, then (B) an eclipse will occur; and (2.) If (A) the moon is in a certain position with respect to the earth as the earth revolves about the sun, then (B) an eclipse with predictable characteristics will occur at a predictable time. Good enough. But only the B's of the argument can be observed, for God's will cannot be observed directly, and only impossible space travel would have permitted the direct observation of the movement of the moon around the earth and the earth around the sun. Thus propositions of the type "If A, then B" must be handled gingerly. Moreover it is illogical to argue that, because B is the case, A also must be the case. This unacceptable style of argument is known as the "fallacy of affirming the consequent."

Empirical theory often faces such a proof. The observer must determine which of many possible explanations for a particular event is appropriate. Sometimes both A's and B's may be observed, as in a controlled experiment in which an attempt is made to see that other factors do not affect the relations. But it is very difficult to control many factors, especially in the study of behavior. Unlike the atom, humans can change their behavior when, for example, they read the results of a previous study about what their behavior is predicted to be.

All is not chaos, however. Theories may predict accurately for the wrong reasons, and there may be many explanations of a particular event. But there is a generic way of choosing between theoretical propositions. Essentially, the utility of any empirical theory depends upon its ability to predict accurately the outcomes of similar events; and that utility also depends upon the continual, indeed relentless, extension of the theory to cover related phenomena. Thus any empirical theory is held tentatively, and only so long as it meets these two tests. Failing this the theory must be modified or discarded. The earth-center theory about eclipses, for example, could not predict the time of eclipses. It did explain eclipses, of course. Thus this theory was inferior to that based upon the earth's rotation about the sun. This is the case in the senses that the latter theory not only offered a plausible explanation of eclipses, but especially in that it permitted the precise prediction of the time of eclipses. The sun-center theory also explained and predicted related phenomena.

A good empirical theory, then, should be a central concern in Political Science. And determined efforts have been made to make it so, not only recently but extending back in time at least to political philosophers of such ancient repute as Plato and Aristotle. But no doubt exists that the development of empirical theory in Political Science has suffered because of the lack of a research focus that requires an unrelenting focus on natural science skills and orientations. And here small-group analysis can be of major service to the development of the discipline.

A substantial part of the difficulty in isolating a distinctive role for empirical theory in Political Science derives from its confusion with two other types of theory. And this recurring confusion, in turn, is aided and abetted by certain recalcitrant features of typical research loci in Political Science, which an emphasis on the small group can help avoid.

To begin an explanation, consider a second type of theory—goal-based empirical theory. It is built upon empirical theory, but it is quite distinct from it. The point of distinction may seem minor, but it is crucial. Empirical theory describes what is; goal-based empirical theory prescribes what must be done to attain what is desired, based upon knowledge of reality. In contrast to empirical theory, then, goal-based empirical theory takes a conditional form. Thus such a proposition would state: If you want to accomplish purposes 1 and 2, then you must do A, B, and C. Patently there can be many goal-based empirical theories, one for each of the innumerable sets of goals or values that can be imagined. In contrast there will be but one general empirical theory for any problem area. As in modern genealogy, of course, there may at any point in time be several contenders touted as providing that general theory.

Such central distinctions can profit from a reinforcing illustration. Assume that a tolerably comprehensive empirical theory has been developed: we know what is related to what under which conditions in a nation-state or other political unit. Such a theory does not directly prescribe, let us say, a pattern of governance. Only a goal-based empirical theory can fill this bill, and such a theory develops in two stages. First, decisions must be made concerning what is desired. Normative or value choices, in short, are the foundation of goal-based empirical theory. Second, empirical theory must be surveyed to determine which conditions must exist if the normative choices are to be achieved in practice. One of these stages alone cannot do the job of goal-based empirical theory. For example it is one thing to desire that men were angels. It is quite another to determine those empirical conditions under which men can (and will) become angels. Specifying those conditions is the basic burden of goal-based empirical theory.

Goal-based empirical theory, then, must have a prominent place in the priorities of Political Science. A good theory of this second type will be very practical. Indeed the development of goal-based empirical theories may be taken to be the central traditional concern of the discipline, as in the fundamental question: What is the good civic life, and how can it be attained? Such questions of the interaction of descriptive and prescriptive perspectives also are convenient ones to pose, given some unfortunate immediate-past history in Political Science. Much scholarly ink has been poured into the fact-value controversy, for example, which more or less sharply distinguished the two foci and tried to drum the latter out of the discipline. This procrustean exercise had the awkward consequence of developing far more heat than light.

The development of any goal-based empirical theory is a fantastically difficult enterprise as well as an enormously rewarding one. Specifically any such theory must be evaluated in terms of affirmative answers to two questions: (1) Are the goal-bases of any theory normatively acceptable? (2) Does the theory reflect a knowledge of the empirical world sufficient to warrant a reasonable expectation that following the theory will achieve the desired purposes? The first question, of course, poses a host of difficult judgments about which sincere men may differ, but which they cannot avoid. This feature does not make the development of a goal-based empirical theory a simple matter. In addition, a "yes" answer to the second question presumes an empirical theory of some comprehensiveness. The problems of the development of empirical theory have been outlined above. Goal-based empirical theory falls heir to them. On two counts, then, this second type of theory is an analytical bearcat to handle.

Because the human spirit has seldom been sanguine enough to wait until such dual answers are substantially available, and because the rush of events has been so coercive, little dispute about goal-based empirical theories in Political Science has been disciplined by a knowledge of major empirical regularities. Small-group analysis can be of major aid in this regard, generating as it does empirical regularities relevant to many central value concerns in Political Science, including participation, deviance, commitment, etc.

A third type of theory will be called utopian theory. This type must be distinguished carefully, for it is both similar to and unlike the two types of empirical theory. The failure to respect the senses in which utopian theory is unlike the two types of empirical theories, in addition, has caused much grief in the study of social organization broadly, as well as in Political Science specifically. There are, then, substantial reasons for emphasizing the character and role of utopian theory. Two properties suffice to distinguish utopian theory from the two empirical types. First, utopian theory deals with (or is applicable to) aspects of the empirical world. Thus it is not ethical or value theory. Ethical theory deals only with desirable relations which ought to exist between man and man and between man and his Maker, rather than with the actual relations which do exist. The Ten Commandments, for example, are an ethical theory. Nor is utopian theory the same as logical theories, such as some mathematical structures, which are not testable because their properties have no empirical referents. Such differences, however, should not be interpreted in too strict a way, for a utopian theory may—and often does—imply or state some ethical preferences. And utopian theories can be tight logical structures.

In this first sense, then, utopian theory is like the two types of empirical theories, for all three types of theories deal with the empirical world. And they all may be characterized by a high degree of logical rigor in their development. In addition, utopian theory and goal-based empirical theory are alike in the respect that both may be based upon a set of ethical preferences to be attained.

Second, and paradoxically, utopian theory is insensitive to empirical data at the same time that it deals with, or is applicable to, empirical relations. This is the case in two possible senses. Either the properties of a utopian theory will not have been tested, even though it is possible to do so. Or the properties of a utopian theory will not be changed, even when evidence demonstrates their inadequacy. In this second sense, utopian theory is unlike the two types of empirical theory. Indeed they could not be two more different kinds of animals. The major dimensions of this difference may be touched upon. The properties of a utopian theory are fixed and unchanging. The properties of an empirical theory are provisional and subject to continuous challenge. Relatedly, propositions of both empirical types of theory depend upon their development from and their test against physical or social reality. But the propositions of a utopian theory are constructs of the imagination which do not require empirical counterparts. Thus a utopian theory might be developed from these two properties: that people have three hands, and that they obey orders instantly.

Utopian theories do not just grow, willy-nilly. The choice of propositions for a utopian theory, to be sure, is limited only by the imagination of the developer. But these propositions ideally are developed into a comprehensive and consistent system. Thus utopian theory plays a wide field in its choice of basic propositions, but it can treat these propositions strictly.

If utopian theory seems uncommon, a few examples will serve to dispel the illusion. The early theory of eclipses, for example, was a utopian theory. Plane geometry also is. Thus both systems are based upon certain assumptions which are taken as given (e.g., a straight line is the shortest distance between two points). Logically consistent systems are then developed from these propositions. Illustratively there are many possible geometries. Indeed their number is limited only by man's ingenuity in developing sets of properties which are taken as the basic dimensions of any geometry's space. Thus plane geometry conceives of space with two dimensions, length and width. Solid geometry builds upon three dimensions; other geometries endow space with four, five, and more dimensions. With it all, the properties of empirical space (whatever number there are) are incompletely known.

It might seem strange to argue that utopian theory is practical, but it has its several uses. First, utopian theory (e.g., plane geometry) serves the function of developing reasoning skills. Second, utopian theorizing permits the development of models of the nature of things were certain conditions to exist, whether or not these conditions ever existed or ever will exist. Such models are useful in suggesting the end results of what appear to be developmental trends, in isolating possible problems, and the like. Third, utopian theory may aid the development of empirical theory. Thus it may suggest certain relations which can be tested empirically, although these relations were derived from propositions which were originally only convenient or interesting or even flagrantly improbable. Fourth, the properties of a utopian theory may approximate reality closely enough to be useful for certain purposes. For example there is no "space" corresponding to that assumed by plane geometry. Space in the real world, whatever its complete properties, is not restricted to length and width; and the shortest distance between two points is hardly ever, perhaps never, a straight line. But plane geometry is useful for certain purposes, such as making a picture frame.

The use of any utopian theory must be monitored carefully, consequently. Two types of tests should be applied to theories of this type before they are used as patterns after which to model empirical relations: an empirical test and a normative test. Empirically the use of plane geometry to plan a transoceanic flight would be ill advised. Events would sharply demonstrate that the shortest distance between those two points is most definitely not a straight line, no matter how convincing the logical argument of plane geometry. Moreover the propositions of any theory should be checked normatively before an attempt is made to pattern relationships after the utopian system. That is, are the propositions as well as the anticipated end states of the utopian theory desirable?

Let's make a long story very short and simplify it. The emphasis on the nation-state and other macrounits encourages utopian theorizing in Political Science. Data are hard to come by, and experiments are difficult to run and harder to evaluate even when they happen by design or natural happenstance. To put the point another way, a focus on the small group will facilitate the development of empirical theories as well as goal-based empirical theories. The possibility of contrived or natural-state experimentation is the central attraction of small-group research.

Interfaces between Prescriptive and Descriptive Issues. One main point of the discussion above involves the significant interaction between the prescriptive and descriptive in Political Science. From one point of view political scientists reflect a strong ethical tradition, and small-group analysis provides ample room for such concerns. Patently, goal-based, empirical theories build upon value bases. In this sense application of empirical theory should be disciplined by value concerns.

From another point of view, small-group analysis and the experimentation it permits can be an effective discipliner of even true believers. Take any such system as Marxism, for example. It purports to describe an ideal state and how mankind will arrive there. Now there may be no way that an empirical orientation can successfully dispute tastes in regard to desired forms of governance. But it is clearly fair game to question whether key assumptions in any theory seem to be consistent with what we know about existing relationships in nature. Moreover it is also clearly fair game to inquire as to the probable adequacy of the dialectic Marx prescribed for getting there. Finally the application of prescriptions in the real world may generate consequences that are unexpected and which may even be contrary to the prescriptions. Our experience with Prohibition provides a convenient example. Empirical analysis can help isolate and even anticipate such consequences, and thus description again has an important interface with prescription. Figure I.2 sketches the sense of these three major interfaces of empirical inquiry and normative concern.

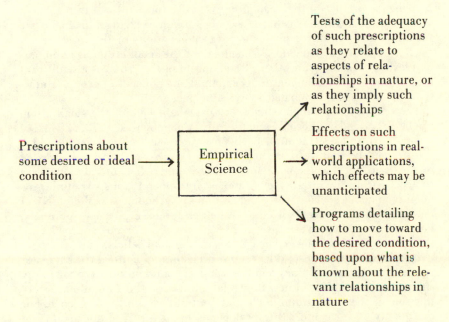

Figure 1.2. Interfaces of normative and empirical issues

The illustrations might be extended, but the point should be patent. Small-group analysis can contribute to the development of Political Science in its concern with values and prescription as well as in natural-science description. The small group's thrust toward empirical science can at once serve to define some limits for exuberant prescriptions, as well as to force fundamental questions on whether or not we should try to utilize some regularity that seems to exist in nature.

The small group also has a strategic value in the development of Political

Science. This both reinforces and yet transcends its substantial tactical value in encouraging a natural-science orientation to research units of convenient size. Ample evidence supports the kaleidoscopic power of small social units over a wide spectrum of life (Janis 1972). Specifically small groups have been shown to be critical elements in socialization, in the development of norms for behavior, in conforming and deviant behavior, in the formation of opinions, etc. Since these elements are variously central to traditional concerns of Political Science, it follows that the small group can play a strategic role in the development of that discipline.

The strategic status of the small group is usefully elaborated in the broadest sense in terms of three phases of its perceived importance in the behavioral sciences generally. More or less, the three phases were historically sequential, and each phase of understanding implied the increasing importance of the small group as both a focus for research and as a vehicle for applications of that knowledge to induce change, to ameliorate suffering, etc. The three phases are: (1) perceptions of the influence of small groups on the behavior of members of the small group as an important level of social organization, (2) a concept of the group as a significant locus within which change can occur, and (3) a concept of group interaction as a basic agent for change as well as a locus for it.

The sense of these increasingly expansive concepts of the small group can be elaborated both briefly and usefully (Golembiewski 1972, 320-322).

Small group as influential. Early observers—including Aristotle in his *Politics* and Le Bon in his influential *The Crowd*—often were impressed by the basic fact that the behavior, attitudes, and beliefs of individuals are rooted basically in interpersonal and intergroup relations. Aristotle saw nobility in man's social nature, and Le Bon saw groupiness as the source of much mischief, perhaps all of it. Whether for base purposes or noble, however, many observers agreed that groups are a major source of influence over their members' behavior, attitudes, and beliefs.

In this elemental sense, the group is a medium of control. It is a major context in which people develop their concepts of who they are, or to say almost the same thing, of how they relate to others. If for no other reason, this role of the small group implies its centrality in Political Science. For the quality of civic life basically depends upon the kind and quality of behavioral control.

Small group as target for change. The 1930s and 1940s contributed significantly to the evolution of the basic observation that groups influence behavior. Substantial research provides ample detail underlying that developmental notion, but the core insight is as simple as it is powerful. If groups can influence or control behavior, attitudes, and beliefs—goes this core insight—then it is expedient to think of the group as a target of change (Cartwright, 1951).

A variety of theoretical and applied work leaped at the challenge of gaining the leverage inherent in a group's influence over its members so as to change either individual or group behavior. Thus group contexts were used

to induce mothers to feed orange juice regularly to their babies, to encourage industrial workers to raise output, or to get housewives to use uncommon cuts of meat so as to ease wartime shortages.

The first conceptual extension of the basic group insight generated considerable research and applied activity, usually called group dynamics.
Several basic regularities in nature were unearthed by this research and
have had a wide impact. Illustratively, the following derivative principles
have been applied in a broad range of teaching, healing, and work contexts:
(1) the greater the attractiveness of a group for its members, the greater
the influence it can exert over its members, and the more widely shared are
a group's norms by its members, (2) the greater the attractiveness of a
group for its members, the greater the resistance to changes in behavior, attitudes, or beliefs which deviate from group norms, and (3) the greater the
prestige of an individual group member, the greater the influence that
member can exert.

There is one particular weak link in such principles of group dynamics.
Although they are often criticized as mere uses of science to serve the purposes of some manipulative elite, whether bureaucratic or therapeutic,
there is no guarantee in the principles that groups will do the right thing as
far as formal authorities are concerned. For example if workers view their
group as attractive on social grounds, that group will not necessarily be a
useful medium for raising output levels as management desires. A more attractive group might only be able to mobilize better its resources to resist
management, in fact.

Small group as agent of change. Consequently it became increasingly
clear that other principles of group dynamics were necessary to predict
whether and in what direction a group's influence would be applied in
specific cases. Some significant "other principles" illustrate the broader
field: (1) the greater the sense of belonging to a common group that is
shared by those people who are exerting influence for a change and those
who are to be changed, the more probable is acceptance of the influence,
and (2) the more relevant are specific behaviors, attitudes, or values to the
bases for attraction of members to a group, the greater the influence a
group can exert over these behaviors, attitudes, or values. Such principles
imply a second and profound conceptual development of the primal observation that groups influence behavior. Directly, much of the resistance inherent in the use of the group as a target of change could be avoided by using the group as the agent of change.

The radical implications of the concept of a group as the agent of change
are reflected in a number of behavioral science approaches, such as treatment of delinquents, but its implications were nowhere so clearly realized
as in the T-Group (Golembiewski and Blumberg 1973). Within very wide
limits, in fact and by intention, members of a T-Group can determine their
own destiny as a temporary social system. T-Group members early "begin
to focus upon their relationship to each other, the problems of intimacy
and closeness," one observer notes, "and learn from this emphasis on peer

relationships about their characteristic models of interaction" (Horwitz 1964).

The great scope for self-determination in a T-Group enhances the probability of undiluted group influence. Crudely the T-Group needs to apply fewer of its resources to resisting outside authority and, consequently, can direct more of them to the learning or influence process. The experience with T-Groups, in sum, implies the significance of several other major principles of group dynamics: (1) the greater the shared perception by group members of the need for change, the more the pressure for change that will originate within the group, and the greater the influence that will be exerted over members, (2) the more widely information about plans for change and their consequences are shared among group members, the greater is member commitment to the change and to its implementation, and (3) the strains deriving from change in one sector of a group will produce systemic strains in other sectors, which can be reduced by negating the change or by readjusting the several sectors of a group.

A basic conclusion inheres in these considerations. In sum the three concepts of the small group imply its strategic significance to a variety of areas of scholarly and applied activity, including Political Science. For example political scientists have a substantial interest in what is called political socialization. The three concepts above imply a major relevance of the small group in exploiting this interest. This is the case if the goal is to understand a socialization process—to develop an empirical theory; it is equally the case if the goal is to ameliorate some lack or deficiency in socialization—to develop specific goal-based, empirical theories.

There is much further impetus for the development of Political Science implicit in these three developmental phases. Consider only two. Thus Political Science has clearly accepted the group as influential; there is some awareness, especially in Public Administration, of the group as a target for change; but little work in the discipline specifically extends the concept of the group as a vehicle for change. In sum some likely-looking bases have not been touched, and they may be critical bases in the contemporary search for representational vehicles to supplement and reinforce available ones, such as the vote and mass demonstrations. The interest in kibbutzim and neighborhood control suggests the perceived relevance of such alternative units of representation/socialization/control.

Moreover the three concepts of the small group also imply a major lesson for the development of Political Science. Directly, every viable area of inquiry should have both pure and applied emphases, although those labels are more convenient than revealing. The rationale is elemental. Successful applications will help establish the adequacy and comprehensiveness of the existing empirical theory from one perspective. And comprehensive theory will generate more pervasive and effective applications of that theory. Hence the two-way street between pure and applied approaches is not merely convenient, it is critical and perhaps unavoidable. Political Science has been more or less a one-armed paperhanger, in this regard.

REFERENCES

Cartwright, D. 1951. "Achieving change in people," *Human relations* 4: 381-392.

Golembiewski, R. T. 1962. *Behavior and organization.* Chicago: Rand McNally.

Golembiewski, R. T. 1972. *Renewing organizations.* Itasca, Ill.: F. E. Peacock, 320-322.

Golembiewski. R. T., and Blumberg, A., eds. 1973. *Sensitivity training and the laboratory approach.* Itasca, Ill.: F. E. Peacock.

Hawkins, G. S. 1973. *Beyond Stonehenge.* New York: Harper & Row.

Horwitz, L. 1964. "Transference in training groups and therapy groups;" *International journal of group psychotherapy* 14: 208.

Janis, I. 1972. *Victims of groupthink*, Boston: Houghton-Mifflin.

Some Costs and Benefits of Small-Group Analysis in Political Science

THOMAS WM. MADRON

In the preceding section Robert Golembiewski has placed small-group studies in Political Science in a necessary theoretical context. In this section we will explore some of the costs and benefits implicit in attempting to make small group perspectives operational in the discipline. In looking at the operational problems involved we can approach the discussion from a variety of perspectives. Whereas Golembiewski has introduced the impact small groups have on individual behavior, we might ask the more structural question: what impact do small political groups have on systemic behavior? Such a question can focus either on the development of a behavior theory of political structure or on efforts to effect change in that structure. In this context the word "change" might apply to bureaucratic needs for reorganization or to the social reformers' zeal to alter fundamental characteristics of our political system.

THE STUDY OF SMALL GROUPS IN POLITICAL SCIENCE

Several years ago (1969), writing on a similar topic,[1] I suggested that a question facing the discipline is this: Why should political scientists be concerned with small-group studies? At that time I suggested that we needed to look only to committees in legislatures, to city councils, to formal and informal party groups to recognize the importance of small groups (Madron 1969, xii). Save for a very few books (three to be exact), Political Science through the decade of the 60s produced few extended works of either a theoretical or methodological character concerning small groups.[2]

Beginning with the 1970s, however, the pace quickened. Prior to 1970 a few articles appeared in the journal literature interpreting certain political groups, most notably courts, in a small-group context. In 1970 Heinz Eulau brought together a group of young political scientists interested in small-group research, and together they conducted a two-week seminar. From that time almost every yearly meeting of the American Political Science Association has had a panel devoted to small groups and Political Science. In addition, in 1972, James Dyson at Florida State, along with some collaborators, started a journal called the ***Experimental Study of Politics (ESP).*** While ESP is not devoted entirely to small-group studies, a considerable proportion of its pages have contained such investigations. The total number of political scientists currently involved in small-group research is still apparently small, but it is a facet of Political Science which, if not completely established, is at least recognized.

OPPORTUNITIES AND PROBLEMS
IN SMALL-GROUP RESEARCH

The opportunities for Political Science from the study of small groups are diverse. First, because of the physical size of small groups—and we all weasel about what size a small group really is—and because of some of the hypotheses to be tested, some small-group studies can be carried on in controlled laboratory or experimental situations. If one of our objectives as political scientists is to develop one or more systematic empirical theories of politics, then we must look toward causal explanations (in addition to probablistic explanations). In a research context, causal explanations can likely be produced only through the testing and verification of hypotheses in one of two ways: through experimental research or through time-series research. Although we can adduce arguments in favor of a proposition with cross-sectional data, and although we can gain some interesting insights through the use of statistical techniques such as causal modeling, we cannot nail down causal relationships other than by experimental or time-series analysis. There are a number of consequences relative to the propositions above.

One consequence is that we may never be able to provide causal explanations for certain political behaviors simply because our research technology or our values concerning the political system preclude the appropriate studies. Where our technology is adequate, and when our moral scruples do not impede us, however, we do have something of a commitment to pursue the goal of finding either the laws of human political behavior or, alternatively, of substantiating their probable nonexistence. Both experimental research and time-series research pose problems. One such problem is that aside from any direct monetary expenditure those involved in such research will have to lead more disciplined research lives for the accumulation of information in either context. Such work is manifestly not the work of a single person.

A second opportunity to be derived from small-group research in Political Science should be the acquisition of knowledge needed to modify behavior. As noted earlier, this objective may be useful in either a reform or a bureaucratic context. One technique of small-group research —sociometry—developed by one of the early pioneers, J. L. Moreno, was invented primarily as a means for behavior modification and is used that way today in education and in other group situations. Sociometric techniques can be used in a research setting to develop time-series data on group behavior, and they can also be used for data collection in experimental conditions.

There are, however, at least two major costs associated with techniques which lead to behavior modification. The first is simply the cost in time, money, and energy involved in collecting the necessary data. The reason for this is that the target groups are usually existing groups rather than experimental groups, and major problems are posed by either field experiments or extended observational periods. A second cost is more value laden: should we be able to modify the behavior of political groups? Obviously the answer to the last question is: "sometimes yes, sometimes no." Social science techniques are already extensively used to alter political outcomes—for example in the use of survey research during election campaigns. In some major litigations law firms have used survey research to find out what classes of people are most responsive to their clients, and this data provides guidance in jury selections. Although we may not wish to acknowledge it, the use of scientific technique for private gain is a problem with which we must reckon.

THEORETICAL GOALS AND
RESEARCH TECHNIQUE

One of the problems confronting those doing small-group studies and those reading the results of such studies is that limited continuity exists in the theoretical objectives inherent in the research. On the one hand considerable theorizing and research has gone into explaining individual behavior by reference to the small-group environment in which the individual works, lives, or plays. Illustrative of this approach are all three concepts of small groups identified by Golembiewski above: the small group as influential, as target for change, and as agent. In each of these concepts the essential objective would be to say something about individual behavior. An alternative to small-group study as an agency of individual behavior, on the other hand, would be to interpret small groups as an essential element in the building of a social or political system. Wherein are the groups per se the building blocks of a social order, and how do they relate to one another? Each of these goals—small-group study for the explanation of individual behavior and/or small-group study for the explanation of systemic behavior—are characterized by peculiar methodological and technical problems and opportunities.

Individual, small group, and systemic behavior. The problem is not, of course, so neatly trichotomous as it was portrayed above. It is sometimes difficult to distinguish among individual behavior, small group behavior, and systemic behavior. For analytical purposes, however, the trichotomy makes some sense. As political scientists we are presumably in search of an integrated body of knowledge concerning political behavior. If we fixate only on individuals or small groups, we tend to fall into the philosophical trap of reductionism. A focus on systemic aspects only may encourage theory that is insufficiently grounded in observables. These problems might best be illustrated by reference to what we know and don't know about political parties.

Of all the political institutions in the United States, political parties have probably received as much study as any. The literature on political parties is peculiar in that there is an enormous quantity of empirical data on the impact parties have on individual voting behavior of citizens, or even of members of Congress or state legislatures. There are also considerable quantities of information available about the organization of political parties at the national level. As a discipline we have executed relatively few studies, however, which seek to relate the national party system down through channels finally ending in the voting behavior of individuals. Much lip service has been given, for example, to the notion that even in Presidential elections it is the party at the local level which translates (or fails to translate) the national or state-wide party goals to actual votes in the precinct. However, little empirical data exists other than in anecdotal form.

A hypothetical research design. In a paragraph we might try to spin out a research design which would remedy the lack of integrated knowledge about political parties, while also illustrating the point at which small-group studies could be important. Should we wish to start with individual voters, we might first identify actives and inactives. The inactives might be influenced by the actives as a function of several things, including behaviors implicit in the opinion leadership theories of Katz and Lazarsfeld[3] or some other more or less mundane explanation. The opinion leadership notion is itself a small-group perspective. The actives might then be identified as members of factions. Factions within a party might be described in terms of power and/or friendship relations and/or in terms of the formal party machinery. The factions within a county constitute an assemblage of small groups, probably with overlapping memberships. These small groups may interact with one another during state-wide or national campaigns in terms of what support of their favorite candidate might do in the context of competition for local power and privilege. When overlapping memberships in different factions occur, a lessening of group cohesiveness occurs, and a lessening of group cohesiveness will likely reduce the bargaining power of the faction. The outcome of the broader election might well determine factional relationships with both the broader system (i.e., who becomes the patronage officer in the county) and with the competition for control of the formal party apparatus at the local level. If this outline of party behavior were taken as the basis for research, we might find one or all of the assumptions correct or incorrect.

There are two primary points to be made from the foregoing. First if we were to work out a full-fledged research design to test the assumptions, we would be putting together a project which would seek to integrate individual, small group, and systemic behavior. Second the importance of small-group research is manifest in assumptions about the relationship of the individual to the party on the one hand, and about the relationship of the county-level party to the larger system on the other hand. Implicit in the set of assumptions was the notion that the backbone of local politics is the interactions among factions (i.e., small groups).

Research goals and research techniques. Our research goals also tend to influence our choice of research techniques. If we are intent on explaining individual behavior as a function of small-group membership, we would then tend to elect techniques which would retain the individual as the primary level of observation. If we were seeking to use small-group research to explain systemic behavior, we would likely focus on subdivisions of small-group research such as leadership studies or the relationship of groups or factions to larger organizational elements. For this purpose we might tend to use the faction or group as the basic unit of observation and to create data-collection techniques which would result in aggregate or group measures. A fully integrated body of knowledge about political parties would provide the stepping stones from individual to small group to system and back again. It would seem apparent, however, that the small group (faction in a political party) simultaneously would be the primary social unit in which individual behavior might take place while it also provided the basis for the behavior of political parties as a system. We might go so far as to suggest, without wishing to take the analogy too far, that small groups should be for political scientists what atoms are for physicists—neither the smallest nor the largest unit of observation but one which is nevertheless important for understanding selected behaviors.

For political scientists, the payoff for small-group research could well be the opening of the door for a more integrated understanding of politics. The problems and costs associated with such efforts are substantial, however. For one thing we might have to move away from substantial demands for individuality in research and move to a point where we encourage widespread adoption of similar or identical research designs across broad areas of both time and space. If the assumptions about party behavior given above were turned into a detailed research design, for example, it would not suffice to execute that design in a single county in the United States. Rather the design would have to be repeated in a large number of counties and across a number of time periods. In a sense this would amount to a large number of systematically organized case studies, each of which would bring forth yet another set of measurements on the same variables for another observational unit or set of units. This technique has long been used in the physical sciences and is essentially the process of replication.

THE TECHNOLOGY OF SMALL-GROUP RESEARCH

Both Golembiewski and I have pointed to a number of the theoretical problems implicit in the methodology of small-group research. Given the assumption that we can overcome the theoretical problems, some technological problems clearly confront us. Like all social research, the study of small groups requires the elaboration of appropriate measuring instruments. Often such instruments pose no problems beyond the usual ones endemic to social science. With small-group research, however, there exists the potential for a technology involving recording instruments such as video or audio equipment or instruments capable of measuring physiological stress—instruments with which the political scientist is generally unfamiliar and which he may have difficulty obtaining. Because such equipment is unfamiliar and difficult to obtain, political scientists may sometimes decide not to engage in small-group research because they believe that the personal and professional payoffs are not commensurate with the necessary investment of time and effort.

Possible payoffs: an example. Notwithstanding the technical demands of small-group research, such research can have importance in both theoretical and applied senses. Perhaps an example will clarify this issue. A topic of current research across several disciplines interested in small groups is a phenomenon known as the risky shift. In essence the risky shift hypothesis states that people behaving in the context of small groups will make collective decisions which involve more risk than decisions made by those same persons behaving individually. Unfortunately for the hypothesis, while there is experimental evidence in support, there is also considerable evidence that either no shifts occur or that conservative shifts occur. To a very large extent differences in conclusions result from differences in the instruments used to measure the risky shift.

Typically in a risky shift experiment, experimental subjects (usually college students) are given a series of vignettes on various topics and asked to respond to those vignettes after some specified small-group discussion. Control subjects respond without the small-group interaction. Usually the experimental subjects are required to respond to vignettes which define risk in some personal terms, even when the vignettes center on political phenomena. The risk, in other words, is a personal risk. More significant in politics are other kinds of risks, specifically systemic risks. A systemic risk is one where the decision may have no direct personal effect, but may affect public policy to a considerable degree. The Joint Chiefs of Staff, for example, might make decisions which could lead the United States into limited war, yet that war might not require any individual personal risk to the Joint Chiefs. It seems quite likely that members of small groups involved in policy decisions might well make different kinds of decisions when the risks are systemic rather than personal, or vice versa, and herein lie important methodological problems.

At least from the viewpoint of political science, a further problem is generated when college students are used as experimental subjects relative to such hypotheses as the risky shift. Namely if we are trying to simulate a court, a city council, the Joint Chiefs of Staff, or even a jury, most college students have not had experiences which would qualify them for such simulations. This criticism, while traditional, does not disqualify the use of students as experimental subjects for a wide variety of hypotheses. It does, however, raise a considerable number of questions relative to the testing of hypotheses dealing with certain systemic goals and objectives. Although there have been efforts to use experienced participants as experimental subjects, these efforts have been few and far between. With proper groundwork it is quite likely that a considerable number of existing political groups would consent to responding to a few vignettes, such as those used in the risky shift experiments, in a controlled situation. Political scientists do not, apparently, wish to make the effort involved. Indeed, the present writer is better with the advice than with the doing in this respect.

Organizing small-group research. Throughout these last few paragraphs I have mentioned the desirability of controlled situations. These controlled situations do not, of course, have to be at an academic institution; but the instrumentation involved in doing research at remote sites complicates the matter to an even greater extent, for it is often difficult or impossible to make adequate use of existing facilities. It would be fascinating, however, to identify a number of political groups, engage in sufficient background research to work out realistic vignettes for those groups, and then engage in a multifaceted data gathering effort designed to acquire a variety of different kinds of information about group interactions and the impact of the group experience on both the individual members on the one hand and the systemic implications of the group(s) on the other hand.

While the costs of such studies as those outlined above are manifest, the benefits would be considerable. From both a theoretical and applied perspective, such hypotheses as the risky shift have considerable implications for any concept of government or politics. If, indeed, decisions made by groups plot courses of action more risky than decisions made by individuals—and if those decisions relate to group dynamics rather than to an assessment of issues—then we may need to rethink the extensive use of committees in governmental and other political bureaucracies. Likewise conservative shifts with respect to risk also bear some analysis. If, however, the risky shift is not a norm of political life, then we can look to other, better, theories of group decision making.

From what has been said, it is clear that there are important—politically relevant—questions to be answered through small-group research by political scientists. The broader opportunity—beyond the testing of specific hypotheses—relates to the ability of small group methodology to "get at" behaviors taking place within the structural context of politics. As was mentioned previously, a great deal of politically relevant behavior takes place within small groups. Explanations which refer only to individual behavior or to systemic behavior solve no long-term problems in the prediction of political acts. Only when we turn the tools of scientific endeavor on all politically relevant units of observation will we be able to offer a comprehensive theory of politics. Because small group studies provide us with a means for using laboratory technologies, such studies may also provide us with the experience necessary—as a discipline—to extend those technologies to assessments of individual behavior or to systemic behavior. Finally, small-group research provides an avenue (among others) by which our knowledge of political behavior may be related to more general kinds of social and psychological behavior.

DATA GATHERING TECHNOLOGIES

Before closing this chapter we should, perhaps, look at some of the data gathering technologies available for the study of small groups and the way in which these technologies have (or have not) been applied in political science. Much of the development of data-gathering technologies has been invested in techniques used to measure social interaction among individuals in small groups. There are, essentially, two ways in which such data can be collected. First we can ask participants to fill out a questionnaire in which patterns of interaction are somehow described. Second we can train observers to watch carefully and record patterns of interaction. Both techniques are important. The first allows us to assess interaction patterns which extend beyond the specific context of a group meeting. The second allows us to explore systematically the nuances that arise out of face-to-face confrontation.

Much of the extension and development of specific techniques for gathering data of either general type noted above extend from the works of J. L. Moreno and Robert Bales.[5] Moreno, during the 1930s, developed a system labeled sociometry which was a relatively simple technique of asking small-group participants a series of choice-criterion items. Such items can be phrased to relate to almost any subject matter, in almost any group composed of people at any age or socioeconomic level. By way of contrast Bales, during the 1940s and 1950s, developed a system he called interaction process analysis, which was a set of categories used by observers for recording interactions among members of small groups. Bales and his associates have also developed various recording devices to make the task of the observer easier and more straightforward. There were earlier observational systems than Bales's, but none that so much extended and refined development of the procedure.

In addition to the techniques noted above, there have also been efforts made to develop questionnaire forms for measuring (rating) certain qualities of groups, such as cohesiveness or leadership styles. Group scores stemming from such questionnaires using rating scales are today widely used in bureaucratic structures to aid in the assessment of working conditions in circumstances where there is no direct means for measuring productive output.

As technologies for social measurement have been developed in other areas, some have been found useful as extensions of one of the techniques mentioned above. The semantic differential, developed by Osgood, Suci, and Tannenbaum, for example, has been found useful as a substitute for choice-criterion items, can be used by observers and can also be used to evaluate leadership styles or other problem areas within existing small groups.

Note that examples of the uses of several observational technologies by political scientists will be illustrated below, especially in Chapters III, IV, V, and VII.

Somewhat beyond existing uses of observational technologies in Political Science, the marked improvement of electronic technology in the recent past has also opened up potentials for small-group research, although at this writing I suspect that these technologies have not been widely used except, perhaps, in the use of media devices such as video tape recorders. An example of one such device which might be put to use is a technique for assessing stress through the analysis of the characteristics of speech (either live or with recordings). Stress has long been a variable thought to have some importance in small-group situations, and physical symptoms of stress or tension have been recorded by observational techniques. Now, however, it is possible to assess stress directly by physical processes. We could, of course, go further and record other physical symptoms, although such attempts might well reduce the spontaneity of group interaction. Improvements in the ability to enter data for computer analysis may also improve the ability of observers to record data reliably and to make it possible for observers to use more extensive observational schedules.

RESEARCH UTILITY FOR POLITICAL SCIENTISTS

In closing this section I would like to reiterate some of the opportunities political scientists have before them with respect to small groups. In the most general sense, small-group research offers a means by which we as a discipline can relate some political characteristics to both individual behavior and systemic behavior. It is, in other words, a unit of analysis which has manifest political importance relating to both individuals and systems. In a more restricted sense, small-group research offers one or more technologies by which we can move from cross-sectional analysis to research designs which allow us to assess causal relationships (if indeed such relationships do exist).

Choice-criterion tests have been used in political science to measure group behavior in legislatures and city councils. Such studies have often been directed toward an assessment of leadership, but could also be directed toward such important political and social problems as minority group prejudice, bureaucratic communications, decision making, and power structures. Studies in all these areas have indeed been done, although many such efforts are within bureaucratic frameworks and few are executed by political scientists. Indeed if a management study of a governmental agency is to be done, it is often a social psychologist or a sociologist who is called in rather than a political scientist. Nor are we limited by the number or variety of small groups. We have already suggested a research design revolving around political parties at the local level, but we could just as easily look at city councils, committee structures in legislatures, administrative committee systems in bureaucracies, or any number of other small groups. Some legislation passed in the 1970s—the so-called sunshine laws—may also aid us in being able to observe certain small groups. Certainly when governmental groups can make essential decisions in closed sessions, it is difficult for observers systematically to explore the decision-making characteristics of those groups.

It is clear that many benefits and opportunities are derived from small-group studies. The costs are generally high, however. Some of the technologies suggested above imply the gathering of data on a large number of groups over time in a systematically comparable manner. Such data-gathering activities are usually beyond the scope of a single individual—hence the organization and cost of such research might be substantial. Some of the technologies suggested above require a level of sophistication not often found among political scientists, and these problems too will have to be remedied. Finally, to use such technologies, those who control funds will have to be convinced that political scientists as well as physicists, chemists, psychologists, and others, require sometimes elaborate laboratory facilities and instruments, or at least access to such facilities and instruments—not a problem of small dimensions. When these problems can be overcome, however, the improved understanding of politics, with the requisite improvements in the ability to explain and predict political behavior, should have beneficial theoretical and applied utility.

NOTES

1. Thomas Wm. Madron, *Small Group Methods and the Study of Politics* (Evanston: Northwestern University Press, 1969), p. xii.
2. Robert T. Golembiewski, *Behavior and Organization: O & M and the Small Group* (Chicago: Rand McNally, 1962); Madron, *Small Group Methods;* and Sidney Verba, *Small Group and Political Behavior* (Princeton: Princeton University Press, 1961).
3. Elihu Katz and Paul F. Lazarsfeld, *Personal Influence* (Glencoe: The Free Press, 1955).
4. See, for example, one of the early articles in the literature: Michael A. Wallach and Nathan Kogan, "The Roles of Information, Discussion, and Consensus in Group Risk Taking,"*Journal of Experimental Social Psychology,* 1 (1965): 1-19.
5. J. L. Moreno, *Who Shall Survive?*, Nervous and Mental Disease Monograph, no. 58 (Washington, D.C., 1934); *Sociometry, Experimental Method and the Science of Society* (New York: Beacon House, 1951); and Robert F. Bales, *Interaction Process Analysis* (Reading, Mass: Addison-Wesley, 1950).

REFERENCES

Bales, R. F. 1950. *Interaction process analysis.* Reading, Mass.: Addison-Wesley.
Barber, J. D. 1966. *Power in committees.* Chicago: Rand-McNally.
Golembiewski, R. T. 1961. *Behavior and organization: O&M and the small group.* Chicago: Rand McNally.
Katz, E., and Lazarsfeld, P. F. 1955. *Personal influence.* Glencoe: The Free Press.
Madron, T. W. 1969. *Small group methods and the study of poltiics.* Evanston: Northwestern University Press.
Moreno, J. L. 1934. *Who shall survive?* Nervous and mental disease monograph, no. 58. Washington, D.C.
Moreno, J. L. 1951. *Sociometry, experimental method and the science of society.* New York: Beacon House.
Verba, S. 1961. *Small group and political behavior.* Princeton: Princeton University Press.

II. Conceptual Contexts

Increasing Specificity
about a Core Insight

Observers have long been acutely aware of the ubiquitous significance of aggregations of humans for good or ill. Given the diverse senses in which each person is sui generis, each person is nevertheless defined in intimate and subtle ways because he is in-relationship with others. Thus Aristotle noted that humans are social animals, by way of explaining what he observed everywhere around him. Similarly Le Bon noted that if they are not careful, individuals can be swept along by the compelling passions he associated with crowds. And in our own time, unions have sought and received additional compensation for alone time, for work which due to technological necessity must be done in small air-conditioned cubicles in which individuals are denied the comfort of human contact for four-hour periods. All three examples imply, if not specifically, that important things can happen when individuals are considered in interpersonal or social environments. But it is not clear what those important things are, nor is it obvious what specific environments will induce which consequences.

Now for some purposes such imprecisions might be tolerable, but not for people interested in understanding one another or concerned with understanding nature. Consider such elemental embarassments. If humans really are social animals, how do we explain those many cases in which they respond in antisocial or even inhumane ways? And no doubt crowds can be observed waging war on one another, and they can be seen encouraging a fellow human threatening suicide from a tall building to: "Do it!" But the attendees at the Last Supper also qualify as a crowd.

This book is addressed to those intent on understanding one another and concerned with comprehending reality. Hence the focus here is on greater conceptual specificity about the group concept, first in two parent disciplines and then in Political Science.

TOWARD GREATER SPECIFICITY IN SOCIOLOGY AND PSYCHOLOGY

The group concept from its earliest days reflected awareness of the existence of a number of functionally important units of social control. Aristotle, for example, recognized families, bands, villages, and states. But precision in this regard was slow to develop, and real progress is a product of the last few decades.

Illustrating this progress toward precision is the immediate goal. Specifically the focus will be on general approaches to—and roughly on three successive stages in—the study of man's unity in social aggregates. The approximate locus of demonstration will be the disciplines of sociology and social psychology (Golembiewski 1962, 9-18).

The Simple-and-Sovereign-Principles approach to man's unity in social aggregates sought the single basis for unity. Thus Aristotle explained man's unity in terms of human nature: man was social or political. Other students employed similar monolithic explanations. For Trotter and others human unity was the result of the herding instinct; for Freud it was the fruit of the compelling force of Eros, or man's love for men; and for many it was the product of a regulative group mind which existed in large social units just as the mind exists in the individual human being.

These similar explanations can be similarly evaluated. They sometimes brilliantly rephrased the question for study. But they contributed little to the systematic study of social microunits. To suggest the point: (1) The microunits usually were considered to be mere conditions, not behavior-regulating units (Strachey 1955, 92); (2) The direct study of the microunits was at least discouraged, if not precluded, by the general fixation of attention on the individual and/or on the positive regulative aspects of macroscopic social units, that is, of society or the state. The bases for unity emphasized in the Simple-and-Sovereign-Principles, then, were the individual with his natural endowments and the society or state. These macroscopic units were envisioned as holding more or less successful rein on man's base instincts.

The deficiencies of the first approach are implied in its designation. The monolithic picture of the social process involved is too simple. And the theoretical nets of individual and society are too fine and too coarse, respectively, for the task of social analysis. The most elemental difficulty of the Principles, however, is an implicit logical problem. That problem: how one principle can serve as the basis of unity for the macrounit as well as for smaller groups, for these smaller groups were mere conditions. But they were also conceived as (always or often) at odds with society.

A way out of this dilemma was provided by a second approach to social organization: that there might be two bases of unity. One basis derived from a sentimental bond between persons who are essentially homogeneous. The other derived from a quasi-mechanical integration of complementary differences, that is, a practical organization in which mutual bonds of sentiment are minimal or unnecessary. These two bases of unity are designated by such terms as "Gemeinschaft" and "Gesellschaft," or organic solidarity and mechanical solidarity, respectively (Tönnies 1887).

Early versions of the distinction were used in a revealing way. In the half-century following the introduction of the Gemeinschaft concept, the rational development of the properties of the Gesellschaft society was emphasized. There were two basic reasons for this emphasis. First, students were still so intent upon macroscopic phenomena that the study of primary groups was considered an evasion of important issues, as a focus on vestigial formations that at best impeded the evolution of macrosociety (Lerner 1951, 45). Second, the emphasis upon the rational development of the properties of the Gesellschaft society was a curious result of the early studies of various exotic peoples. Such studies were important empirical antidotes to earlier speculative approaches. The picture of these comparatively small human aggregates tended, however, to be a little too definite. This misinterpretation guided the efforts of many students intent upon designing the new integrated, or Gesellschaft, society (Maunier 1929). Gemeinschaft elements, at best, thus were considered as a kind of fallout of the attainment of the Great Society (Thomas 1971). Consider Durkheim's "disorganized dust of individuals." This disorganized dust was conceived as the human debris left in the wake of the creation of Gesellschaft quasimechanization of social relations resulting from industrialization and urbanization (Durkheim 1902).

With few exceptions, then, the emphasis in the second developmental view of social organization was on the individual as deprived of Gemeinschaft anchorages, not of the anchorages per se (Thomas and Znaniecki 1927).

A third emphasis in social organization, the Positive Gemeinschaft approach, finally succeeded in breaking up such global concepts of social organization into handier units of study. An important preliminary element in this specification of the Gemeinschaft concept was the development of the concept of the primary group (Cooley 1909).

The primary group was first stressed by Cooley, and its development has largely been the work of American students. Small informal groups were nominally defined in a general sense by example, i.e., as family, children's, or work groups. They were primary for Cooley in that they developed and sustained in two ways the consensual framework which must underlie any broader society: as the agencies which are the childhood sources of the behavior norms which operate in adulthood; as the agencies which in later life serve to reinforce and support the adult in his relations with primary groups other than those few to which he belongs or with which he is acquainted. Cooley also suggested certain rough operational indicators of such groups. The most important of these operational indicators was a feeling of psychological closeness reflected, for example, in the use of the term "we." Cooley's conceptual and operational awareness, if rudimentary, was unusual in the study of social organization.

American social scientists did not quickly take Cooley's lead. However, a rash of community studies in the twenties and thirties reflected both a general recognition of the limitations of macroscopic study as well as the necessity for more microscopic work. The dialectic was under way. Basically awareness grew that the enormous range of behavior and thought observed in any large social unit could only be explained by postulating the existence of multiple existential bases for behavior.

This set the stage for the exploitation of the long-neglected implications in the work of Durkheim and Thomas as well as Cooley. Early work investigated reference groups (or hypothesized units of social control intermediate to society or state and individual) such as Jewry and Catholicism. However, this did not solve the problems of nominal and operational definition, which set significant limits on the research utility of the concept and resulted in slackened interest in reference groups. The research ambiguity of the mother concept, finally, led to an emphasis on the membership group. The concept of membership group did not solve the problem of specifying the research unit either. It did, however, encourage small-group analysis, the most marked research trend in the post-World War II social science revolution. On the transition from reference group to small group research, see Hartley and Hartley (1952).

This Johnny-come-lately boom in small-group analysis is a composite of many elements. Perhaps the most important element has been the usefulness of the small-group concept in explaining behavior incomprehensible in terms of an individual psychology or in terms of the influence of a macroscopic social unit. This research attractiveness derives from the possibility of the scientific treatment of the small group, which has contributed to and gained from the momentum of the natural science approach in the social sciences. Moreover, as Moreno (1941, 19) noted, the study of the small group permits concern "with the patterns of social structures which actually exist in human society." In contrast the global approach to societies, states, or communities in terms of patterns which actually exist presents a far more complicated problem. This difficulty is reflected in the nonempirical nature of much of the social organization literature.

Size is, of course, the key to the usefulness of the small group. Small size permits the intensive study of meaningful social units. But it also opens the way to the creation and observation of experimental groups under more controlled conditions than usually prevail in the natural state. The experimental test of a few relations, holding others constant, is one of the most powerful tools of the physical sciences. The exploitation of such potential depends, of course, on the degree of development of the skills necessary to describe and create groups. This is a substantial order. But the promise is an enticing one.

TOWARD GREATER SPECIFICITY IN POLITICAL SCIENCE

A similar history of growing specificity in exploring the group concept also applies to Political Science. This chapter introduces the concern of four political scientists to make themselves understood while they seek to understand nature more clearly. Specifically these observers are seeking to refine increasingly precise concepts for describing an important set of relationships in nature, based on the common perception or observation that interpersonal and social environments really do matter. Conceptualization is no simple matter, for it seeks nothing less than to isolate the major dimensions necessary to describe meaningfully some portion of reality. Epigrammatically, counting the leaves on trees is but a small start down the road toward an adequate conceptualization of the leafing and deleafing processes. Appropriate concepts include temperature, photosynthesis, seasons of the year, etc.

David B. Truman begins for us this difficult process of conceptualization in his "The Group Concept," a selection from a major book of the 1950s that influenced many political scientists. Truman's interest has a patent source. "The justification for emphasizing groups as basic social units," he notes, "is the uniformities of behavior produced through them." But groups differ in a wide range of characteristics even as they share this generic commonality. That much conceptual refinement was necessary beyond that provided by Truman is manifest in the concluding two sentences of the selection. He notes: "In addition to the category 'institution,' . . . various subcategories have been designated on the basis of fairly obvious differences of function—the family, economic groups, political groups, and religious groups. On somewhat different bases distinctions are drawn among crowds, publics, assemblies, organizations, mobs, primary groups, secondary groups, in-groups, out-groups, and a host of others."

There was much potential for progress and mischief in such common but unspecific usage, and the mischief tended to win, by a very large margin indeed. This summary is amply supported by two selections below: Peter H. Odegard's "The Group Basis of Politics: A New Name for an Ancient Myth" and Peter Loveday's "Group Theory and Its Critics."

Odegard's magisterial selection reflects a number of flash points at which many varieties of the early group approach rankled political scientists, two of which deserve special mention here. First, Odegard noted that early interpreters of Bentley took to heart only a part of his argument—the most troublesome portion. Specifically Bentley emphasized the concept of process of government far more than he did the role of groups, a critical point of neglect which had powerful consequences (Kress 1970). However, political scientists neglected the implied richness and fixated on the theme that a group is a group is a group. Odegard was not pleased by this casual simplification. More or less, he saw the group literature through the 1950s—stripped of its persiflage and waffling—as not advanced far beyond Aristotle's ancient conclusion that man is a social animal. Second, and relatedly, the neglect of process encouraged truncated attention to politics, as Odegard understood it. To many group theorists, he charged, politics was unfortunately static versus dynamic, devoid of ideas and values and full of vectors of force and interests. "Group theorists," he concluded, "have all but banished reason, knowlege, and intelligence from the governmental process." That was too much for him.

The mischief inherent in many early group interpretations also may be illustrated profitably via a brief contrast, specifically the contrast with how a scientific effort might proceed from the basic but very general observation that uniformities of behavior are induced in interpersonal and group situations. Schematically, scientific efforts should follow such a schema:

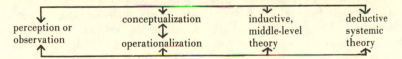

Figure 2.1. A schema for the process of scientific development

Briefly, the thrust of the Political Science literature basically shortcircuited this complex interactive schema. The literature tended to jump from gross observation or perception to broad systemic theory.

Loveday's "Group Theory and Its Critics" provides details about this short-circuiting, using Bentley's *The Process of Government* as a benchmark. Things got very complicated in the literature, as Loveday documents. But two points are indisputable about the development. First, Bentley's interpreters tended to express his argument about the ubiquitous significance of all manner of groupings—both large and small, public and private, etc.—in a group theory of politics that focused only on the role of pressure groups or interests in the political process. Second, interest groups were defined and characterized mostly by example, even as they referred to only a part of the group phenomena to which Bentley drew attention.

This first start toward exploring the basic insight of the significance of human groupings was faulty in both central particulars. Let us neglect nuances and qualifications. Basically most versions of the group theory of politics were vulnerable to the charge that they did not constitute a general theory of the political process, given their common fixation on pressure groups. Relatedly, even in versions that were truer to the conceptual fullness of Bentley, the universal tendency of the literature to skip over the arduous processes of conceptualization/operationalization left it vulnerable after the first blushes of discovery wore off. Loveday gently observes: ". . . the vagueness and confusion of important concepts in the general theory of groups can be demonstrated without difficulty." As other critics took pains to emphasize, the group concept often was so broad and undifferentiated that it became synonymous not only with politics but with all of life.

Significantly, in addition, many versions of the group theory were simple hydraulic models that left little or no room for the impact of man's values or for the impact of the determined man or the central idea. Public policy became the resultant of a sterile process of pushes-and-pulls by pressure groups. This was a major weakness as the mass of political scientists came to see it, perhaps <u>the</u> weakness. Thus many traditional disciplinary interests were devalued by many versions of the group theory, and were even excluded from the disciplinary turf by some versions. This was the case with public interest, for example. Relatedly a hydraulic view of policy—however realistic a description it was of what actually happened—ran the risk of falling into the trap: What is, should be. Political scientists simply were unwilling to give up their rich prescriptive tradition and resisted such tendencies to define "ought" in terms of "is."

One concluding selection seeks to keep the baby separate from the bathwater, as it were. Sidney Verba provides detailed perspective on the value of the study of groups, especially with respect to that variety called primary or small group. Verba's "The Small Group and Political Behavior," for convenience, may be said to take a dual course. Overall it documents how small-group membership can impact on individuals so as to influence important aspects of their political lives. Specifically Verba demonstrates how small group experiences can (1) help mold personality or behavioral traits that will influence if not determine political behavior,

(2) serve as a training ground for political participation, in the sense that an individual's success in influencing his "primary" relationships may generalize into attitudes and skills for influencing secondary associations such as political parties or the electoral system, (3) provide experience in small-group roles that have politically relevant analogs such as leadership, and (4) help determine a broad range of attitudes that will impact on political processes and institutions.

Beyond these impacts on the individual, Verba also seeks to relate small-group experiences to two central features of political systems: the amount of conflict, including the style in which it is managed and resolved; and the degree of political instability. There is no need to re-do Verba's cogent analysis here. Suffice it to note that he sees the small-group perspective as a valuable one in looking at both conflict and degree of stability in political systems.

REFERENCES

Cooley, C. H. 1909. *Social organization: A study of the larger social mind.* New York: Scribner's.

Durkheim, E. 1902. *La division du social travail.* Paris: F. Alcan, especially the Introduction, 4-6.

Golembiewski, R. T. 1962. *The small group.* Chicago: University of Chicago Press, 9-18.

Kress, P. F. 1970. *Social science and the idea of process: The ambiguous legacy of Arthur F. Bentley.* Urbana, Ill.: University of Illinois Press.

Lerner, D. 1951. "The study of the primary group." In *The policy sciences: Recent developments in scope and method,* eds. Daniel Lerner and Harold D. Lasswell, p. 45. Stanford: Stanford University.

Maunier, R. 1929. *Essais sur les groupements sociaux.* Paris: F. Alcan.

Moreno, J. L. 1941. "Foundations of sociometry,"*Sociometry,* 4: 19.

Strachey, J. R. 1955. *The standard edition of the complete psychological works of Sigmund Freud.* London: Hogarth.

Tonnies, F. 1887. *Gemeinschaft und Gesellschaft: Abhandlung des Communismus und des Socialismus als emperischer Culturformen.* Leipzig: Fues' Verlag.

Thomas, W. I. 1917. "Persistence of primary group norms in present-day society and their influence in our educational system." In *Suggestions of modern science concerning education,* ed. H. S. Jennings. New York: Macmillan.

Thomas, W. I., and Znaniecki, F. 1927. *The Polish peasant in Europe and America.* New York: Knopf.

The Group Concept

DAVID B. TRUMAN

If the uniformities consequent upon the behavior of men in groups are the key to an understanding of human, including political, behavior, it will be well to specify somewhat more sharply what is involved when the term "group" is used. An excessive preoccupation with matters of definition will only prove a handicap. "Who likes may snip verbal definitions in his old age, when his world has gone crackly and dry." Nevertheless, a few distinctions may be useful.

We find the term "group" applied in two broad senses. Both popularly and in much technical literature it is used to describe any collection of individuals who have some characteristic in common. These are sometimes known as categoric groups. In this sense the word is applied to persons of a given age level, to those of similar income or social status, to people living in a particular area, as Westerners, and to assortments of individuals according to an almost endless variety of similarities—farmers, alcoholics, insurance men, blondes, illiterates, mothers, neurotics, and so on. Although this sense of the word may be useful, it omits one aspect of peculiar importance. The justification for emphasizing groups as basic social units, it will be recalled, is the uniformities of behavior produced through them. Such uniformities do not depend immediately upon such similarities as those mentioned above, but upon the relationships among the persons involved. The significance of a family group in producing similar attitudes and behaviors among its members lies, not in their physical resemblance or in the proximity, as such, to one another, but in the characteristic relationships among them. These interactions, or relationships, because they have a certain character and frequency, give the group its molding and guiding powers. In fact, they are the group, and it is in this sense that the term will be used.

A minimum frequency of interaction is, of course, necessary before a group in this sense can be said to exist. If a motorist stops along a highway to ask directions of a farmer, the two are interacting; but they can hardly be said to constitute a group except in the most casual sense. If, however, the motorist belongs to an automobile club to the staff of which he and the other members more or less regularly resort for route information, then staff and members can be designated as a group. Similarly, groups in the first sense—collections of people with some common characteristic—may be groups in the proper sense if they interact with some frequency on the basis of their shared characteristics. If a number of mothers interact with one another as they tackle problems of child training, whether through a club or through subscription to a mothers' periodical, they have become a

Reprinted from *The Governmental Process* (1951), 23-33 by permission of Alfred A. Knopf. Copyright 1951 by Alfred A. Knopf, Inc.

group, though the two forms differ in structure and frequency of interaction. If the members of any aggregation of blondes begin to interact as blondes, alcoholics as alcoholics (or former addicts), people over sixty as aged—they constitute groups. That is, under certain recurring conditions they behave differently with each other than with brunettes, teetotalers, or the young. In fact, the reason why the two senses of the term "group" are so close is that on the basis of experience it is expected that people who have certain attributes in common—neighborhood, consanguinity, occupation—will interact with some frequency. It is the interaction that is crucial, however, not the shared characteristic.

These groups, or patterns of interaction, vary through time in a given society, and they obviously differ sharply in different societies. Why this variation occurs has been only incompletely ascertained, since comparative studies of simple cultures are relatively few and competent comparative analyses of complex cultures are virtually nonexistent. The most satisfactory hypothesis, however, indicates that the relative complexity of such interactions depends upon the degree of diversity in the everyday business of living. The latter in turn reflects refinement in the techniques by which the society adapts to its environment and the degree of specialization and division of labor that these techniques involve. In a simple society in which all activities—economic, religious, political—are carried on within the family, the division of labor is rudimentary, the techniques are simple, and the patterns of interaction are few and standardized. The latter become more complex as the routine activities of existence alter in conformity with altered techniques for dealing with the environment.

Variations in the division of labor are nowhere more striking than in the activity of house building. An Eskimo igloo is usually constructed by a single family, each man erecting the structure of snow block with the aid of his wife and sons. Division of labor is slight, and the interactions among the participants—the patterns of superordination and subordination—are simple. Frequently among a sedentary farming people, however, such as the Riffians of North Africa, relatively elaborate and permanent dwellings are constructed by work parties in which a fairly complex division of labor occurs, based upon more developed techniques and differences in the skill with which particular individuals can perform the various operations:

> Among Riffians, some of the men will bring stones, others will nick them into shape and set them in the walls, while still others puddle clay for the mortar. When the walls are up, two men . . . climb up and set the ridgepole and rafters in place. Meanwhile other men have been cutting young alders and other small saplings near the stream; they peel these and hand them up in bundles. Most of the men have now climbed to the roof, and they tie these sticks to the rafters to form a foundation for the clay.

It is a considerable step from this moderately complex division of labor to the elaborate activities necessary in the construction of an ordinary American house. The collection, preparation, and transportation of materials, the elaborate behavior involved in procuring and readying the site, and the welter of specialties that contribute to its erection bespeak a series of complicated interaction patterns.

The complexity and variation of group life among human cultures apparently grow out of the daily activites of their participants and reflect the kinds of techniques that the cultures have developed for dealing with the environment. These techniques, however, are not confined to those directly utilized in providing food, clothing, and shelter. The invention of a written language and its diffusion through a population include techniques of at least equal importance. Similarly, group patterns in a culture in which the priest, or "shaman," deals with the crises and problems arising from birth, sickness, death, flood, drought, earthquakes, thunderstorms, and eclipses of the sun and moon will be far simpler than the group patterns of a culture where these crises are separately dealt with by various specialists. The activities of the shaman, and those of his functional descendant, the specialized scientist, consist of techniques for adjustment to the environment fully as much as do those of the farmer, the weaver, and the bricklayer. The skills of shaman and scientist are parts of different group patterns and their resulting attitudes and behavioral norms.

In any society certain of these group patterns will be characterized by "a relatively high degree of stability, uniformity, formality, and generality." These are customarily designated by the term "institution." The word does not have a meaning sufficiently precise to enable one to state with confidence that one group is an institution whereas another is not. Accepted examples, however, include the courts, legislatures, executives, and other political institutions, families, organized churches, manufacturing establishments, transportation systems, and organized markets. All of these, it will be noted, are rather highly organized (formality); examples of the same type of institution show the same patterns (uniformity); and these patterns are characteristic of, though not necessarily peculiar to, a particular society, such as the American (generality).

The institutionalized groups that exemplify these behavior patterns, and the patterns themselves, represent almost by definition an equilibrium among the interactions of the participants. In a typical American family, for example, it will be accepted almost unconsciously and without discussion that the male parent will almost always make certain kinds of decisions for the family group, such as what kind of automobile tires to purchase, whether they can afford a new washing machine, and how much money can be spent on the family vacation. He will be expected to take the lead in such actions, and the rest of the family will accept his decisions. The mother will make many more decisions affecting the children than will the father. The husband, moreover, will follow her lead in such things as home decoration, the color of a new car, and the guests to be included at a dinner party. These and the other expected patterns of interaction that make up the in-

stitutional group are normally in balance, or in a state of equilibrium. The
same situation applies to any institutionalized group, although perhaps in a
somewhat more complicated fashion, whether political, economic, or
religious.

An equilibrium of this sort must be worked out within an institutionalized group or an institution if it is to survive. That is, the
equilibrium must be achieved along standardized lines if the pattern is not
to be radically altered or if the particular group is not to be irrevocably disrupted, as, for example, in the case of a family by the separation or divorce
of man and wife. It is characteristic of such balanced groups that if the
equilibrium is disturbed by some event outside the group, the equilibrium
will be restored when the disturbance is over. This tendency to maintain or
revert to equilibrium is what is meant by the stability of an institution. The
existence of the equilibrium and its stability presumably can be measured
by observing the consistency of interaction patterns. Although such observations have been made for simple groups and in a general way for more
complicated ones, the possibilities in this area are largely still to be explored. The basic propositions, however, have been sufficently tested to
give them strong presumptive validity.

Although institutionalized groups are characterized by stability, that is,
by the tendency to revert to an equilibrium among the interactions of the
participants following a disturbance from outside the group, not all disturbances are followed by a return to such a balance. If the disturbance is of
great intensity or if it persists over a long period of time, a quite different
pattern of interactions is likely to be established in place of the previous
one. How serious the interruption must be and how long it must last in order to produce an alteration of the pattern are matters for careful observation, precise or approximate depending upon the use to which the observations are to be put.

An obvious example can be seen in the case of a family that loses one of
its members through death. Since the remainder of the group can no longer
interact with the deceased, any subsequent stable interaction pattern in the
group will differ sharply from the preceding one. The possibilities of establishing a new and stable pattern will depend in part upon the role of the
deceased in the previous balance. That is, it will be far more difficult if a
parent or an only child has been withdrawn from the group, since
relationships with a parent or only child will have constituted a very large
segment of the total behavior pattern of the remaining members of the
family. The death of one of eight or ten children, however, may be far less
disruptive, since almost inevitably a major portion of the total interactions
in the group will not have depended upon one of eight or ten children.

If the removal of one member of a family group is not permanent, but
temporary, a quite different situation will result. If the male parent is
obliged to be away from the rest of the family for a short period of time or if
his breadwinning activities temporarily require him to spend less time in
the family than has been customary, the equilibrium of the group will be

disturbed. The pattern and frequency of interactions will be altered. When the husband-father has returned from his travels, however, or when his duties permit him again to participate in the group with normal frequency, the previous balance probably will be restored.

In the strictly political sphere there are obvious parallel instances of the effects of disturbances in established patterns of interaction. Thus the death or unexpected resignation of the boss of a highly organized political machine constitutes a serious disturbance to the group. It will be followed by a more or less prolonged tussle among aspiring successors. Unless some stable new pattern is established under the leadership of one of the previous boss's henchmen, the group will disintegrate into competing factions. Similarly, take the case of a trade association whose principal function is the fixing of prices. If it finds its methods outlawed as a result of government action, this disturbance will result in the disappearance of the group unless equilibrium is re-established in one of three ways. First, the group may secure the repeal of the disturbing decision. Second, new methods of performing the function may be developed. Third, an entirely different set of functions may be developed. The first of these results in a restoration of the disturbed pattern, whereas the second and third produce new patterns of interaction.

An important point must be kept in mind in talking of patterns, equilibriums, and the like. These terms do not refer to a mystical entity like a "group mind" that suffers, changes, and dies. A group is "real" in the sense that the interactions that are the group can be observed, and these terms are convenient ways of describing interactions. But one is dealing with the activities of individuals too. To draw any other inference is to become involved in the literally false and disastrously misleading distinction between "the individual" and "society." When men act and interact in consistent patterns, it is reasonable to study these patterns and to designate them by collective terms: "group," "institution," "nation," "legislature," "political party," "corporation," "labor union," "family," and so on. Similarly, it is reasonable for some purposes to study particular individuals, as do the clinical and individual psychologists. But these are merely two approaches to the same thing, not separate entities. Men exist only in society; society is the interactions of men.

It follows, therefore, that when one speaks of a disturbance in an institutional pattern, one refers as well to a disturbance in the individual organisms whose activities have made up the pattern. One of the features of an institutionalized group, as has been noted, is its persistence. It may be thought of as a habit and as being made up of certain habitual activities of a number of individuals. When the pattern is interrupted, there is disturbance or frustration in varying degrees of the habits of the participants, a circumstance that is always unpleasant and may be extremely painful. One may study the consequences for the affected individuals or the changes in the interaction patterns or both, but "the equilibrium of the internal environment (the organism), the equilibrium of the individual in relation to others, and the equilibrium of the group are similar and related phenomena."

When the equilibrium of a group (and the equilibriums of its participant individuals) is seriously disturbed, various kinds of behavior may ensue. If the disturbance is not too great, the group's leaders will make an effort to restore the previous balance. As we shall see in more detail later, this effort may immediately necessitate recourse to the government. Other behaviors may occur if the disturbance is serious to the point of disruption. These may be classified in various ways for different purposes. In the present context three broad types of behavior may be distinguished on the basis of their effect upon the existing or potential groups involved. In the first place, the participants may individually engage in various kinds of inappropriate or aberrant or compensatory substitute activities: complaining, rumor-mongering, phantasies, alcoholism, drug addiction, indiscriminate aggression, and the like. Thus in a revolutionary situation where the equilibriums of a wide range of institutions have been disturbed or disrupted, there is a constant possibility that large segments of the populace will engage in undisciplined loafing, irresponsible violence, or other activities useless to a successful revolutionary movement. It is the task of revolutionary leadership to limit such behavior by providing new and constructive forms of interaction in the place of those that have been disrupted. Similarly, a sudden change in the relations (interactions) between management and workers in a factory, initiated by the former, may at first result in gossiping, griping, and picking on scapegoats.The adolescent, whose roles are in a highly fluid state alternating between those of an adult and those of a dependent child and necessarily involving disequilibrium, will frequently indulge in daydreams and phantasies. These substitutive activities may be harmless or may have neurotic consequences, depending on the situation.

Second, the disturbed individuals may increase their activities in other groups in order to restore some sort of personal balance. Thus a state of disequilibrium in the family group may be compensated for by increased interaction in the work group (longer hours at the office) or in a recreational group (increased attendance at meetings of a bowling league, woman's club, and the like).

The third type of behavior that may result from a serious disequilibrium is the formation of new groups that may function to restore the balance. For present purposes this type is the most important of the three, especially if a considerable number of individuals is affected, since these new groups are likely to utilize political means of achieving their objectives. They are likely to become political groups, although they need not do so. Adolescents who cannot establish a stable set of relationships in family groups may join others of the same age level in informal or formal clubs or gangs. This behavior is particularly likely where the adolescent adjustment is made more difficult by special problems such as arise for American-born children of immigrant parents, or for young men and women who are unable to establish stable and satisfactory relationships in an economic group. Among adults new groups are likely to develop or old ones to grow and increase their activity where a serious disequilibrium is produced in family and work groups by a depression or similar economic crisis. Farm movements throughout American history have developed and reached their peaks of strength in times of great economic distress, such as the 1870s and the early 1920s.

When Japanese Americans and Japanese aliens resident on the West Coast were ruthlessly uprooted from their homes in early 1942 and sent to relocation centers, the disruption of established equilibriums was profound. In his distinguished study of the relocation camp at Poston, Arizona, Leighton found ample evidence to this effect: "Although social patterns did exist, some new and some old, more prominent was disarticulation and the absence of the accustomed habits of human relationship. People were strangers to each other in a strange situation and did not know what to expect." This imbalance involved not only the family groups, work groups, and neighborhood groups but more inclusive institutions such as the nation itself. That is, the attitudes and behavior of wide segments of the American people, especially in the West, with whom Niseis in particular had been accustomed to interact peacefully and on a basis of considerable equality, sharply contradicted what most of the victims had been accustomed to expect. The imbalance was not temporary or minor, but persistent and inclusive: "Most aspects of life were lived with acquaintances made since coming to Poston and every individual and every family was trying to adjust to a society that had no framework and no stability. Hardly anyone had a confident expectation as to how anybody with whom he worked or had contact would behave from week to week." Out of this situation a series of new groups emerged, some spontaneously and some under the guidance of the camp's administrators. Among the former were gangs that administered beatings to alleged informers.

Examples of the emergence of new groups in compensation for disturbances in the equilibrium of existing institutionalized groups can be drawn from simpler societies as well as the more complex. When government officials and missionaries arrived in the Papua Territory, New Guinea, in the 1920s, they attempted to alter the ways of the natives and particularly to keep them from holding some of their customary religious ceremonies. The resulting disturbance in the established patterns of interaction was followed by the development of a series of religious movements that spread over New Guinea.

When one views any society as a sort of mosaic of groups, one is confronted with a bewildering array of groups that may be classified in different ways. Thus various characteristic activities seem to be carried on in one group that make it different from another in that particular respect. The examples used in the preceding paragraphs are sufficient illustration. Similarly, although it is an observable fact that all groups involve the same fundamental process, the interaction of individuals, they seem to differ from one another in the form that this process takes—for example, in the degree of formality. In the pursuit of meaning and understanding, students of society, particularly sociologists, have classified groups on these and other bases, distinguishing and defining classes of groups. These efforts have varied with the purposes, skills, and insights of the classifiers. In addition to the category "institution," which has been examined briefly above, various subcategories have been designated on the basis of fairly obvious differences of function—the family, economic groups, political groups, and religious groups. On somewhat different bases distinctions are drawn among crowds, publics, assemblies, organizations, mobs, primary groups, secondary groups, in-groups, out-groups, and a host of others.

A Group Basis of Politics:
A New Name for an Ancient Myth

PETER H. ODEGARD

Perhaps the most familiar of all political aphorisms is that which says, "man is a social animal." This statement helped Aristotle, as it has helped his successors, to demonstrate that political communities, like other forms of social organization, have their roots in the inherent needs of human nature. Only a beast or a god can live outside society.

As a social animal, man enters into social relations of almost infinite variety. Whether as an infant "mewling and puking in the nurse's arms," a schoolboy "creeping like snail unwillingly to school," a lover "sighing like furnace," or as soldier, statesman, butcher, baker, candlestick maker—men seem forever and everywhere to be found in groups of one kind or another.

So universal is this group phenomenon that one is tempted to say, with *McCall's* magazine, that life is "togetherness" and "togetherness is life." So deep indeed is the hunger of the individual to attach himself to others—i.e., to belong—that it is surely one of the most powerful of all human drives. There is a touching story that illustrates the point:

A well-dressed lady riding the New York subway was annoyed by the conduct of a grimy, ragged boy of six who insisted on sitting as near to her as he could. So long as the train was crowded, she endured his presence by her side in painful silence; but when the crowd thinned out, she moved to the upper end of the car away from the unwelcome ragamuffin. But he, nothing loath, followed her, seating himself again as close to her as possible. If she moved to another car he followed. Finally, her patience exhausted, she turned to him and said, "What on earth are you doing, following me this way?"

"I ain't doin' nuthin', lady. I'm just pretendin' I belong to you."

This passion for belonging has posed no end of problems for students of man and society. What are the actual and what are the desirable relations between individual man and the myriad groups to which he belongs? What are the actual potential and desirable relations of groups to each other and to the political community? Are all groups free and equal? Is the political community to be viewed simply as another group of the same level as the family, church, corporation, and trade union, or is it a superior kind of association with rights and powers that transcend other inferior or subordinate groups? Has the individual human being any rights, powers or privileges—or indeed any meaning or existence apart from the groups to which he belongs? What is the nature of the groups in general or in particular? What are the dynamics or statics of group behavior?

Reprinted from *Western Political Quarterly*, Vol. 20, No. 3 (September 1958) by Peter H. Odegard. Reprinted by permission of the University of Utah, copyright holder.

Political and social philosophers from Plato and Aristotle to John Dewey
and Bertrand Russell have struggled with these and other related questions.
"The question is," wrote Floyd Allport, in commenting on Dewey's
analysis of this problem, "how to reconcile personality as an ethical end
with the inevitable increase in the number of special publics that include
mere segments of the personality and never the whole." Endless quotations
might be cited to indicate the kinds of answers that have been suggested. A
crude scale might be contrived to classify them in terms of the relative importance which they assign to the individual or to the group in the political
process. It is not my purpose here to construct such a scale or to examine
the history of group theory in Western culture. What I should like to do is
examine some of the statements made by fairly recent protagonists of what
may be called the Group Theory or the Group Basis of Politics. This theory
has been most clearly stated in summary form by Arthur Bentley, whose
book, *Process of Government,* appeared in 1908, and who has a considerable following among political scientists in the United States.

According to Bentley, the raw materials for the study of politics are acts,
not legislative acts alone, but action itself, activity, "something doing."
Government and politics invariably involve "the shunting by some men of
other men's conduct along changed lines, the gathering of forces to overcome resistance to such alterations, or the dispersal of one grouping of
forces by another grouping." This action, this shunting of men's conduct,
is always and invariably a group process. "The raw material we study," he
says, "is never found in one man himself, it cannot even be stated by
adding men to men. It must be taken as it comes in many men together."

Ideas, thoughts, feelings, laws, proceedings of constitutional conventions, essays, addresses, "diatribes on tyranny and democracy" are important only when related to action. In this context they "seem to give the individual man his orientation in the social (or group) activity in which he is
involved. . . . There is no idea which is not a reflection of social activity.
There is no feeling which the individual can fix upon except in a social
form." Groups of people pushing other groups and being pushed by them in
turn—this is the process of government—this is the raw material of
politics.

Bentley is an early exponent of quantitative methods in politics,
although he recognizes that political measurement is primitive at best. If
one is to study politics scientifically rather than sentimentally, he argues,
one should look for significant measurable quantities in action. Ideas cannot be measured except when they are related to activity. Acts and acts
alone produce measurable results—whether "purer food, safer insurance,
better transportation facilities, or whatever else." Political power can be
measured in terms of force, as, "when one nation defeats another in war,"
or by acts of revolution. Force or potential force can also be measured by
votes, provided one goes behind the votes to "examine the quantities that
have been in play to produce the given results." Indeed, says Bentley:
"There is no political process that is not a balancing of quantity against

quantity. There is not a law that is passed that is not the expression of force and force in tension."

This force or force in tension is at all times exerted by masses of men, i.e., by men in groups. The nation is properly to be conceived not as a mass of individuals but as "groups of men, each group cutting across many others." In one context we see them as citizens of New York City; in another as citizens or residents of New York State; or in another as directors of a corporation, members of a trade union, a church, trade association, or civic league. But always we see them as groups. Individuals appear only as members of groups. When a "man belongs to two groups . . . which are clashing with each other" that which represents his dominant interest will claim his loyalty and allegiance. Nor is this an uncommon experience—for multiple group membership is virtually universal in modern society. Groups arrayed against one another as North and South would be quite differently arrayed when viewed as workers and employers, creditors and debtors, Catholics and Protestants.

"If," says Bentley, "we take all the men of one society, say, all citizens of the United States, and look upon them as a spherical mass, we can pass an unlimited number of planes through the center of the sphere, each plane representing some principle of classification, say, race, various economic interests, religion or language." Various classifications will be useful in various contexts depending upon the issues and the actual groups involved.

The important thing for the student of politics is "the analysis of these groups. (For) when the groups are adequately stated everything is stated. When I say everything, I mean everything. The complete description will be the complete science in the study of social phenomena, as in any other field."

To Bentley all legislation and indeed all politics and administration are the products of group conflict. In the words of Earl Latham, "The legislature referees the group struggle, ratifies the victories of the successful coalitions, and records the terms of the surrenders, compromises, and conquests in the form of statutes. . . . The legislative vote on any issue (represents) . . . the balance of power among the contending groups at the time of voting. What may be called public policy is actually the equilibrium reached in the group struggle at any given moment."

Administration, on the other hand, is simply a name for the process of carrying into effect the "treaties that the legislators have negotiated and ratified." The bureaucrats "are like armies of occupation left in the field to police the rule won by the victorious coalition."

There is little or no room in this theory for the individual. Instead of the Rosseauean idea that the relation between the state and the individual is and ought to be direct and immediate, the group theory insists upon the group as a necessary and inevitable intermediary. Indeed, according to Bentley, the "individual stated for himself and invested with an extra-social unity of his own is a fiction."

These quotations do not represent a complete statement of the group theory of politics. They do, however, convey a sense of what the so-called group theorists are driving at. At the risk of being accused of bias and partiality, I shall take them as the basis for some comments to which I invite attention and criticism.

Let me begin by admitting the reality and the importance of individuals acting together, as members of social and political groups, to any comprehensive theory of political behavior. Nearly every political scientist from Plato and Aristotle to John C. Calhoun and John Dewey has recognized this. To assume that Arthur Bentley discovered or invented the group as a vital factor in government and politics is, to say the least, something of an exaggeration. Plato's apparent "willingness to impose order and value on human life at the expense of moral liberty and dignity," as John Chapman has said, arises directly from his theory that justice is essentially a state of equilibrium among various groups or classes, an equilibrium maintained and enforced by another group—the guardians. And the most notable characteristic of the guardians is their emancipation from all other group loyalties such as those of family, neighborhood, property, or occupation. Even Aristotle, who saw the political state as primarily a community of individuals, recognized the importance of other groups and especially of the family.

Among the Romans, both Polybius and Cicero sought to rationalize the Roman constitution as a system of countervailing powers—or group pressures—expressed respectively through the consuls, the Senate, and the people. And as Otto von Giecke has told us, medieval society was composed essentially of a hierarchy of more-or-less autonomous groups, each of which was, in effect, an island of peace and security in an otherwise turbulent and dangerous world.

Within these groups and among them, it was argued, the Platonic ideal of justice was realized—an ideal of social equilibrium with each man and each group in its proper place with the rights and duties appropriate to its rank and station. In this society, as in Bentley's, the individual was a fiction—not so much subordinated to the group as merged with it in an "unbroken series of living ties." It was a cooperative society of which the manor, the monastery, the church, the guild, the corporation, and ultimately the Empire and the Papacy were the constituent parts, each with a personality and an existence quite independent of its individual members.

With the passing of medieval corporative society, the relationship of organized groups to one another and to the state was complicated not only by the dissolution of old groups and the emergence of new ones, but also by the emancipation of the individual from the authority of the groups to which for centuries he had been subject. A new freedom and a new allegiance was established in a new and transcendent group, the sovereign territorial state.

There is no time to review the complex factors involved in the group conflicts from which the state ultimately emerged victorious. Nor can I recount the elaborate arguments by which Popes and princes and feudal lords, merchant adventurers, burgesses, and nonconformist believers, sought to rationalize their own claims to power and freedom. The point is simply that all recognized the importance of group loyalties and interests in the political process. And this is as true of Thomas Hobbes, the great protagonist of the sovereign absolutist state, as of John Locke and Rousseau, philosophers of the modern democratic state. Everyone is by now familiar with the classic statements of group theory in Article 10 of *The Federalist,* the *Communist Manifesto,* de Tocqueville's *Democracy in America,* Calhoun's *Disquisition on Government,* and the writings of political pluralists from Figgis and Maitland to G. D. H. Cole and Harold Laski. The importance of organized groups in the process of government has long been recognized. Nor are contemporary students of pressure politics and group theory the first to note the influence of group interests on American government and politics. Alexander Hamilton and Thomas Jefferson, John Adams, James Madison, John Taylor of Carolina, O. G. Libby, Charles Beard, and Arthur Schlesinger, Sr., to name but a few at random, have made the point as effectively if not as pretentiously and dogmatically as Arthur Bentley and his acolytes.

But none of these—excepting possibly Karl Marx and Calhoun—regarded group interests and group conflicts as a complete account of the process of government and politics. And it is to this aspect of the so-called Group Theory of Politics that I wish to take exception. Let me, then, as briefly as I can, summarize some of my reasons for regarding the Group Basis of Politics as somewhat less than adequate as a theory of Political Behavior.

In the first place, I am troubled by a general lack of any clear definition of the terms used, including the term "group" itself. Bentley and some of his disciples are impatient with those who ask for such definitions. David Truman, for example, says that "an excessive preoccupation with matters of definition will only prove a handicap." But is it asking too much to insist upon knowing what is meant by "interest group" when this term is made the center of what is offered as a complete theory of political behavior?

Bentley offers no satisfactory definition of the term "group" except to say that it refers to a "relation" between men, a process of adding man to man. He also says that groups vary in size, i.e., the "number of men who belong"; in intensity, i.e., the degree of concentration of interest which gives the group its effectiveness; and in techniques, i.e., whether it employs propaganda, reasoning, bribery, threats, assassination, or other forms of violence. But just when "relations" between men constitute a group, or how many there must be or how intense their concentration, he doesn't say. If every casual relation, direct or indirect, between individuals constitutes a group, then virtually every human act is a group act, and the term becomes tautological and useless for scientific purposes. Not even St. Simeon Stylites on his desert pillar would fail to qualify as a group.

Bentley identifies the terms "group" and "interest." "There is no group," he says, "without its interest. An interest . . . is the equivalent of a group." As to whether the interest is responsible for the group or the group responsible for the interest, Bentley says, "I do not know or care." A group without an interest is nothing and presumably an "interest" without a group is inconceivable. But I find no very clear explanation of what is meant by "interest," except that the term, as Bentley uses it, is broader than economic interest. Bentley does say that common interest is more important in constituting a group than other common characteristics. Blondes and brunettes, as such, presumably do not constitute groups until they assert some common interest, which I assume means some common goal or purpose. Presumably no individual apart from a group can have a politically significant or relevant interest.

It is dangerous, according to Bentley, to assume that a group's interest is what its members or leaders say it is. Presumably we judge group interests by group behavior, i.e., by action rather than words, even though verbalizing is also an important form of behavior. What, then, would be the interest of a wet Congressman who votes dry or a dry Congressman who votes wet? Does this simply mean that he is at the same time a member of two conflicting groups pulling in opposite directions? Bentley is aware of these conflicts but argues that the most intense interest will prevail. In the case cited, however, it is by no means clear which is the more intense interest—the dry voting or the wet drinking? Does the individual play any role in resolving this dilemma or is he but a pawn of rival groups?

Bentley has a good deal to say about the complexity of group loyalties. If all United States citizens, he says, are regarded as a spherical mass, "we can pass an unlimited number of planes through the center of (the) sphere" and each plane will represent "some principle of classification, say, race, economic interests, religion, or language." But does this help us in our search for a definition of "interest" or "group"? Presumably if one were to pass an unlimited number of planes through the center of the sphere, he might conceivably end up with one person in each plane and not with groups at all, unless, or course, individuals are also groups. But this, again, smacks of tautology.

Nor are other group theorists much better at defining their terms. David Truman offers as one definition of a group "any collection of individuals who have some characteristic in common" but admits that this is not helpful. More important, he says, is a common interest. If, then, a common interest is the key, what kind of interest may it be? Would a common interest in good health, or in peace and security constitute a group and, if so, wouldn't such a group embrace mankind? Do definitions which admit of categories so broad add substantially to our understanding of political dynamics?

Moreover, when Congress and the courts and the President and all other institutions or aggregations, including majorities and minorities within them, are defined as interest groups, the term becomes synonymous not merely with politics but with human life itself. One is led to wonder whether under these circumstances the Group Theory of Politics adds anything to Aristotle's aphorism that "man is a social animal."

I am willing to proceed without sharp definitions of "interest" or of "group" if the group theorists will allow me a similar latitude in my use of such terms as "individual," "state," "government," "general will," "public interest," and so forth. If political scientists flub these definitions—so do the sociologists. According to Florian Znaniecki, for example, an examination of forty-eight textbooks in sociology revealed that eleven had no definition or classification of groups, the other thirty-seven "differed so much that not a single logical class was included in all of them."

I am aware that more exact definitions of these terms have been proposed, as, for example, by Homans in his *The Human Group* and by Donald Campbell in his article, "Common Fate, Similarity and Other Indices of the Status of Aggregates of Persons as Social Entities" in *Behavioral Science*, January 1958. Unfortunately, neither the sociologists nor the political scientists have examined with any care the implications of these more precise definitions for students of political behavior.

The pseudoscientific use of fuzzy terms or the fuzzy use of pseudoscientific terms is, I realize, not confined to those who espouse the Group Theory of Politics. Nevertheless those like Bentley who take special pride in rigorous methods of scientific analysis ought to be more careful in avoiding the most common of all logical fallacies.

There are other terms used commonly by group theorists that require clarification: "Equilibrium," for example. Just what this means is not clear to me nor whether (assuming we know what it means) it is necessary or desirable. Is it a synonym for what the Physiologists call homeostasis? "In an organism," says Professor Sluckin, "homeostasis represents the equilibrium level of activity. If a homeostatic condition is upset, activity increases or decreases as necessary until equilibrium is restored. This happens because information regarding the amount of unbalance is fed back by the autonomic nervous system to the mechanisms which regulate bodily activity....The regulation is automatic in that the amount of unbalance determines the level of activity directed towards the restoration of balance." Is this what is meant by political equilibrium? If so, what are the political terms corresponding to temperature, blood pressure, nervous tension, and so forth which mark the limits within which equilibrium is maintained?

Equilibrium is an essential condition of survival in living organisms. Perhaps it is a condition of survival also for groups of living organisms and even for political communities—but what, in this context, does it mean? Is it, as Earl Latham says, "the balance of power among contending groups at the moment of voting"? Is public policy "the equilibrium reached in the group struggle at any given moment"? If so, who are the contenders in this struggle? Are they the pressure groups outside but having access to the decision makers? Are they the rival factions or groups forming and reforming with bewildering fluidity and frequency among the decision makers themselves? Are they the relatively small company of "leaders" or "oligarchs" among both outsiders and insiders? And in what forum does this struggle occur and at what point is "equilibrium" achieved? Is it in the subcommittee, the full committee or a plenary session of the Legislature? Is it in the "deliberations" of "task forces," consultants, ad hoc experts, or staff specialists?

Does it make any difference to the group theory of politics whether equilibrium is attained at one point or in one forum rather than another? It is at least possible that it could make a profound difference since group pressures as distinguished from individual influence may operate decisively in one context and not at all in another. Moreover, the forum in which decisions are made (not merely formally but actually) may profoundly affect the factors which are decisive in the process. In one forum, group interest, propaganda, organized pressure, even violence, may be the controls which produce political equilibrium, as temperature, blood pressure, or nervous tension produce organic homeostasis. In another forum, argument and debate carried on at a high level of logic and rationality may be decisive. In the first case the group basis of politics may account for what occurs. In the second case I am not so sure.

In another sense the term "equilibrium" is used by group theorists to refer to the adjustment which every group must make to its environment "if it is to endure and prosper." This is done by "putting restraints on its environment," "neutralizing it," or "conciliating it and making it friendly." But this can be said of individuals even more realistically than it can be said of groups. For groups are not only instruments by which the individual seeks to effect this adjustment. They are also part of his environment which he in turn hopes to restrain, neutralize, or conciliate and from which he not infrequently seeks to free himself. Indeed a not unimportant problem—often ignored or neglected by group theorists— is the progressive encroachment upon the individual's privacy by organized groups seeking to absorb more and more not only of his time, energy and money, but of his personality.

There are still other terms in contemporary writing on group politics that, to say the least, harbor Promethean ambiguities. Reference, for example, is often made to the "rules of the game," general "systems of belief," or an underlying "consensus" in terms of which the group struggle is carried on. Are these simply the "ideas," "principles," "rules," or "beliefs" concerning which there is no significant controversy? Are they to be taken as synonymous with Wilhelm Bauer's "static" as distinguished from "dynamic" opinion? Are they Sumner's "folkways" in a new dress or an example of Pareto's "persistence of aggregates" or perhaps even "residues"? If so, how are they applied or enforced? How and by what means do they give "orientation" or establish limits to group action which Bentley assures us is all there is to politics? Is it simply that all groups believe in and act upon them without reference to any special mechanism or group for their application and enforcement? Or are they the rules to be applied by what Hobbes called public groups, i.e., those having "officiality," to the conflicts arising among private groups, i.e., those not having "officiality"? And if this is what they are, how are they to be applied or enforced in the case of conflicts among public groups and between public and private groups? Is officiality an attribute, right, or privilege won by a certain group or groups in competition with other groups—as, for example, by Henry and his associates in their conflict with Thomas à Becket and the Church—or by Philip the Fair in his quarrel with Boniface VIII? If this is so, doesn't it amount simply to a reassertion, in new terminology, of the supremacy of law and the State—with their various attributes and organs—over private rules and private or subordinate associations? And if this be the case, what does the group theory of politics add to the general body of familiar—even classical—political theory?

Bentley and his followers are impatient with those who talk of such vague things as "ideas" and "feelings," of the "character of the people," "the general will," the "general welfare" or even of "law" and "justice," of "right and wrong." These things, these "spooks" Bentley would say, are of little if any concern to the man "who is settling down to study the phenomenon of government from the raw material." What he sees is action, pressure, force, tension, in a world composed not of individuals but of groups. A world, moreover, in which law is but a treaty of peace among transient and warring groups and administrators are armies of occupation to enforce its terms on the vanquished. Yet consider such concepts as "latent groups," "unorganized interest," "rules of the game," "consensus," "officiality," "equilibrium"! To what specific sets or groups or pressures or vectors of groups in conflict do they refer "For law to have force," writes Earl Latham in his brilliant essay on "The Group Basis of Politics," "there must be popular consent and understanding to support the law. . . . The concept of officiality, then, is the sum of the technical differences which are rooted in the social understanding as to who does what to whom; and the difference between the public and private groups is the officiality of the former . . . the principal function of official groups is to provide various levels of compromise in the writing of the rules, all within the body of agreed principles that forms the consensus upon which the political community rests."

Thus the "spooks" that Bentley had banished reappear. A new mystique is born which turns out to be not so very new after all. One scarcely needs 20-20 political vision to see in all this the shades of Hobbes and Hegel, Bradley, and Bosanquet, T. H. Green and even J. J. Rousseau himself.

Space forbids inquiry into the meaning of other terms used by contemporary exponents of the Group Theory of Politics. Does "access," for example, mean physical access, or can it be access by indirection—by "stirring up the people," by transforming static into dynamic opinion? And are we to understand that only groups (assuming that term to mean something other than an individual) have significant access to decision makers? When Bernard Baruch "advises" the President and the President acts upon his advice—is this group politics or Baruch politics? When Albert Einstein writes a letter to Franklin Roosevelt that sets in motion the Manhattan

Project—is this, too, group politics? It can, I suppose, be said that although Baruch and Einstein speak as individuals, behind them are the elite groups to which they belong, vast multitudes of latent groups or unorganized interests, exerting actual or potential pressure on decision makers. But does this say any more than Aristotle said in describing man as a social animal? Unless these groups can be identified, and their quantities or pressures measured, have we said anything significantly different than that Mr. Baruch and Mr. Einstein "influenced" Presidential decision on significant issues at a time when the President, for a variety of reasons, was responsive to influence or suggestions of this kind?

As a matter of fact, do groups as such often have access to decision makers? The Anti-Saloon League used to indulge in mass or group pressure by transporting hundreds of supporters to Washington or to a state capital to appear before committees as "petitions in boots." Other pressure or interest groups on occasion use similar devices. But few sophisticated lobbyists regard this as the most effective way to achieve their ends. Group representation is normally representation by an individual whose effectiveness is by no means always to be measured by the size of the group he represents, or by the intensity of its interest, or by the specialized techniques of pressure and propaganda it employs. His status, his access, his influence may depend on group attributes of this kind, but they may also depend upon friendship or personality traits having little or nothing to do with any measurable or even discernible group interest he represents. They (i.e., his status, access, influence) may even depend upon his knowledge and intelligence.

Group theorists, like the early radical behaviorists, have all but banished reason, knowledge, and intelligence from the governmental process. Public policy and administration are regarded as vectors' of group pressures—a kind of resultant in a parallelogram of group forces. Group pressure, group force, and above all group action are the dynamic and decisive factors. The governmental process is to be understood not in terms of reason or logic but solely in terms of Newton's laws of motion and inertia. These, we are told, are more important than the laws of reason or logic. The rules of identity, contradiction, excluded middle and sufficient reason have no relevance to the process of government—only force, tension, pressure. Decision makers are regarded either as neutrals pushed this way or that by the group pressures that impinge upon them, or as active group partisans whose own group interests determine their decisions. The notion of the decision maker as a rational creature motivated by considerations of the "general welfare" or the "public interest," making his decisions in the light of logic and the weight of the evidence, is regarded as a naive residue of the romantic Heavenly City of the eighteenth-century philosophers.

My concern about this line of argument is that the group theorists, in their quite reasonable rejection of rationality as the sole or major factor in political decision making have all but banished rationality from the governmental process. They have, as the saying is, thrown the baby out with the bath water. Anyone familiar with the decision making process knows that pressure, force, intimidation, self-interest, and, heaven knows, group interests, account for no small fraction of the decisions that are made. But they do not account for them all. Reason and logic are by no means strangers to the decision-making process. Not infrequently decisions both on policy and administration are made not under pressure of rival group interests but in the light of reason and on the weight of the best available evidence. Indeed I am encouraged to believe that with the increasingly technical nature of the problems confronting modern governments and with the growing prestige and influence of scientific modes of thought, rationality will become more and not less important in the decision-making process.

Consider, for example, the nature of the problems involved in the formation of economic and financial policy in a modern industrial state. In Great Britain, for example, having determined upon a basic policy of full employment and its logical corollary, a healthy balance of international payments, British statesmen must see to it that public policies of all kinds—of welfare and defense, public works and public health, housing and education—contribute to these ends or at least do not upset the apple cart. Among the facts to be considered are the degree of technological development and productive power in the economy, the level and pattern of consumer demand, spending and saving, the general conditions prevailing in and affecting international trade, and many others. In formulating economic policy the government must foresee the impact of these factors upon prices, incomes, the supply of resources, and the balance of payments. A "high level of monetary demand will stimulate output (which is desirable)...but it will also stimulate...the demand for imports and may also reduce the incentive to seek for export markets. As a result the balance of the payments may deteriorate, the reserves may fall, and the confidence in sterling may be weakened. If these tendencies were allowed to develop too far, the objective of full employment would itself be in jeopardy and it would, therefore, be necessary to restrain the growth of demand."

Even in the United States, where laissez faire is more honored, at least in theory, the formulation of public policy has reached such a level of complexity that without the assistance of social scientists, who, I am bound to believe, at least strive for rationality, government would be even more confused and chaotic than it is. The basic objectives of national security, economic prosperity and stability, social security, education and welfare, high employment, the development and conservation of basic resources, and reasonably stable prices, require for their realization scientific and technical skills as varied and as important as those required at Los Alamos or Oak Ridge. The basic instruments to be used, the executive budget, the gross national product, taxes, price supports, subsidies, the public debt, legislation, and administrative rules and regulations, are delicate instruments requiring knowledge, skill and wisdom. To interpret this process solely in terms of group pressures is to do a disservice to both reality and reason. Increasingly, decisions of this kind will be made not under pressure of rival group interests but upon the basis of rational analysis so far as this is possible with the crude tools presently available. Speaking for myself, I should like to see political scientists exerting more of their energies in defense of reason in politics and less in providing academic absolution for what, in our days of innocence, we called the "invisible government."

In these remarks I have confined myself to but one weakness (as I see it) of the Group Theory of Politics—its ambiguity. Discussions of other questions must be deferred, although some of them may be indicated. To what extent does the Group Theory of Politics give an accurate—let alone a complete—account of the process of government? What, for example, are the implications of the Group Theory for geographic as distinguished from functional or proportional representation? Does the theory adequately or accurately account for patterns of voting behavior under a system based on the secret ballot and the single member district? How does the Group Theory of Politics avoid what Floyd Allport has called the "institutional fallacy" or what William McDougall frankly proclaimed as a "group mind"? Is the Group Theory of Politics equally applicable to every type of party system? Is it consistent and compatible with such democratic values as majority rule and individual rights? By their apotheosizing of the group and group pressures, do group theorists contribute to the devaluation of the individual, to conformity and to anti-intellectualism? To what extent does the current vogue for group theory reflect an escape from freedom and nostalgia for neomedieval corporative society? Is the *Process of Government* as described by Bentley substantially different from that described by Thrasymachus, Machievelli and Hobbes? Does it in effect defend the principle that might is right?

These are questions that cannot be discussed here, but which I believe call for more extended analysis than they have received. If politics is a process for the peaceful allocation of values in society, political scientists must take account of the values no less than the process of allocation. Among these values are rationality and freedom, freedom not only for groups but for individuals. A theory of politics which excludes where it does not frankly reject a concern for values, which denies that reason has a significant role to play in the proccess of government, and which devalues the individual by its exaltation of the group, is, I suggest, inadequate. As Professor Gail Kennedy has said, political decisions "will not be a simple mechanical resolution of claims as though they were the sum of so many vector quantities; to suppose this is to revert to the notion that a compromise is a division of the spoils, each party, including a group called the public, receiving shares proportional to their powers. To equate might with right, even where public interests are included as a countervailing force, does not produce a mutual promise to abide by a decision; what it produces is a decree requiring enforcement." By no stretch of the imagination can this be said to account for the process of government in a democracy.

Group Theory and Its Critics

PETER LOVEDAY

There has been much of discussion recently about the so-called Group Theory of Politics.[1] We need not here inquire into the origins of the theory, or theories. In one sense, political theory has always been conducted partly in terms of groups—whether in terms of "classes," "estates," "sectional interests," "factions," "voluntary associations," or what have come to be called "pressure groups" since the 1920s. It is not difficult to trace such theories to Plato and Aristotle, and they are implicit in such well-worn political concepts as "mixed government," "the separation of the powers" and the "balance of the constitution."

However, the group theorists considered here belong to the twentieth century; and the key figure in the modern development of group theory is Arthur F. Bentley, whose major work on the subject, *The Process of Government,* was published in 1908. We shall take him, for present purposes, as the founder of the line. The intellectual pedigree since then is not straightforward. Much of what Bentley said was forgotten, and he had to be rediscovered after World War II, when his work was given fresh currency (though, as we shall see, in a misleading way) by American political scientists such as David Truman.[2] In the meantime, the notion of the "pressure group" had passed into popular discussion in a way rather different from anything that Bentley himself intended; and some of the later confusions derive from this fact.

Perhaps the point may be made shortly in this way. Bentley thought of his own group theory of politics as a quite general theory applicable to all phases of the political process. His was not the pressure group theory of the modern man in the street, the theory that the formal institutions of government (Parliaments, Cabinets, public services, etc.) are importantly influenced by the activities and pressures of various private interests (employers' associations, trade unions, reformist groups, lobbyists, etc.).

It may be true that he was influenced in developing his views by the "fin de siècle waves of scandal and reform in American government, centered on privileged evasions or manipulations of the law by private interest groups."[3] But his debt to German sociology,[4] and to the early thought of the pragmatist, John Dewey, was of much greater importance in *The Process of Government.* He did not wish to draw some imaginary line between private groups, on the one hand, and the formal institutions of government on the other—or between the overt processes of public life and its covert manipulation.

Reprinted from *Groups in Theory and Practice,* (Sydney Studies in Politics No. 1), Peter Loveday and Ian Campbell, (Melbourne, Australia: F. W. Cheshire Publishing P/L, 1962) pp. 3-17. Published for the Department of Government and Public Administration, University of Sydney.

The generation of political scientists that followed Bentley on the whole retreated from this position. When, in the late 1920s, Americans began to write books about pressure groups,[5] again under the stimulus of notorious examples of the private lobby, they tended to develop a more limited group theory of politics. In this, pressure groups were recognised as an important feature of political life, operating alongside (some said to distort the operations of) other kinds of political entities, governments, political parties, courts, individual politicians and bureaucrats with their "ideals" or "conceptions of the public interest." This is still the main way in which the subject is discussed in America, Britain, and Australia.[6]

Sometimes the earlier writers went as far as to suggest that the other political bodies were so inert that they merely responded passively to group pressures. They emphasised, overemphasised in the opinion of many, the part played by the private groups in government, to the point where their influence was paramount and decisive.

This in turn produced its reaction, conveniently dated by an article by Merle Fainsod, published in 1940 (it is discussed at greater length below). Fainsod had read Bentley, but took him to be simply a pressure group extremist of the kind just described. Fainsod thought that the group theorists of his day underestimated "the independent creative force" of government. In fact, in saying this he was saying nothing that Bentley could not have agreed with; and it was part of the business of the group theorists who followed Fainsod (including Truman and Earl Latham) to point this out. Truman, in particular, rediscovered Bentley and sought to write a fresh version of the group theory. He tried once again to universalise it by recognizing that "the independent creative force" of legislatures, courts, and regulatory agencies in general put them, with private interests, in the category of "groups" which entered in a positive way into the pattern of relationships and pressures which constituted politics. Members of Congress, or members of the Supreme Court, or public servants in the Department of Agriculture, had "shared attitudes," and interests in common, in the same way as members of the American Federation of Labor, or the American Medical Association. Politics was the study of all such "interests."

It is from this point that the most recent controversies may be said to start. A large and important part of the argument between the group theorists and their critics in the 1950s and 1960s has centered on the question whether the group theory is a quite general theory, applicable to all parts of the political process. Bentley claimed that it is; the critics have denied the claim. There are certain things that neither side (with unimportant exceptions) wishes to claim. The "general" theorists do not hold that government is the mere register of the competing pressures of private groups, though this view is often attributed to them. On the other side, their critics agree that pressure groups have an important place in the political process alongside the official institutions of government political parties; but they cannot agree that the institutions and parties are them-

selves open to a "group interpretation." Most of them would agree with
Stanley Rothman that "if the group theory is to be useful, group theorists
must give up their claim to have developed a comprehensive system and
limit their scope to a more narrow, though still important, range of
phenomena."[7]

This is the verdict of commonsense. It must be admitted at once that
there is something to be said for it. Certainly texts can be quoted in abundance from Bentley, Truman, and Latham which seem to give their case
away; the vagueness and confusion of important concepts in the general
theory of groups can be demonstrated without difficulty, and attempts to
test it by applying it carefully in field situations are, in La Palombra's
words, "likely to be misleading and fruitless."[8]

Nevertheless the debate on the subject has been peculiarly inconclusive.
The critics feel that they have given forceful reasons for not treating the
group theory as a general theory of politics. As these objections have not
been met, they feel that those who persist in upholding the theory are not
responsible controversialists, but tough-minded cynics of the muckraking
kind who clothe and conceal their cynicism and toughmindedness in doctrines borrowed from Bentley.

The group theorists, for their part, are unrepentant. They think that
their opponents have missed the point and that, until they have seen it,
there is nothing to do but remain silent or reiterate the doctrine. It is
therefore not surprising that few changes have been made in the theory
since Bentley first set it out, and that confusions in his formulation of it
have persisted to the present day.

The most general argument against the group theory is that it is "reductionist," that is to say, that it explains away what its exponents claim it explains—the individual, his personality, his ideas and beliefs, his reason and
intelligence; the state, its public interest and important features of its institutions. Dowling has argued that the reductionism, in Bentley, extends
to political techniques and to the environment as well.

I believe that the group theory as usually formulated is reductionist, but
not in the way described by its critics. The inference of the critics' arguments is that the Group Theory is reductionist because it is a theory of a
particular part of the political process masquerading as a theory of the
whole process. What they have not seen is that if the theory is reductionist
it will be as unacceptable for the pressure groups themselves as for the rest
of the political process. If, for example, reason is an important factor in
governmental decisions, as Odegard claims, is it not also likely to be important in the decisions of associations of manufacturers, or trade unions? Can
one argue that individuals are effective in the one sphere and of no account
in the other, except as the bearers of "shared attitudes"? Or can one suppose that pressure, mechanistically conceived, is only part of the process at
one level of government and the whole of it at another? In short, the critics
have not carried their attack through to its logical conclusion: if the theory
is reductionist in the one field, it is bound to be reductionist in the other.

The term "pressure group" can, of course, be retained as "a handy and intelligible colloquialism"[9] for certain obvious kinds of organized private interests that regularly appear on the governmental doorstep. Pressure groups in this limited sense are part of the political process. But to say this is not to say, as the critics seem to assume, that the Group Theory is, or should be, confined to this one field.

I

Let us begin with Fainsod's statement of the case. He starts by quoting Bentley: "When we talk about government we put emphasis on the influence, the pressure, that is being exerted by group upon group. . . . . The balance of group pressures is the existing state of society. . . . Law is activity, just as government is. . . . It is a group process, just as government is. It is a forming, a systematisation, a struggle, an adaptation, of group interests. . . ."[10]

Fainsod then gives an account of the consequences of this approach for institutions and public policy. He thinks that despite its obvious attractions, "Government in this view can do little more than register the shifting balance of forces in the community; regulatory agencies become prizes in the struggle for power. That interest or group of interests which captures control of them impresses its policy upon them. . . . Government institutions thus tend to be transformed into mere pawns in a struggle for supremacy. Deprived of independent creative force, the purposes which they serve simply mirror the changing fortunes of battle. . . . The idea of public interest becomes a fiction used to describe an amalgam which is shaped and reshaped in the furnace of (interest group) conflicts."[11]

Then, buttressing the conclusion by examples, Fainsod argues that the group analysis underestimates "the independent creative force and manipulative power which the wielders" of the regulatory agencies "acquire by virtue of their special competence or their strategic position in the regulatory hierarchy. . . it is obvious that, within limits such power exists . . . independent power to change (their) environment."

The defect of this kind of criticism, often repeated since, is that it is not an argument against the group theory as stated by Bentley and quoted by Fainsod. The extract quoted gives no ground for assuming that the word "group" is to be understood to mean simply pressure groups in the common and narrow sense, pressure groups as distinguished from the parties and the institutions of government. Yet Fainsod, in setting these things in contrast to groups, assumes that this is what the word means in the passage he quotes.

Indeed, there is every reason to suppose that this is what Bentley did not mean in this text—he thought he had taken up into the group analysis the very things Fainsod thinks the group approach is committed to neglecting. Small wonder then that Gross[12] replied to Fainsod, saying that he was not contradicting Bentley, but that his discussion of the regulatory agencies was a fruitful way of restating or extending the group hypothesis.

It may be true that Bentley could not successfully give a "group" explanation of all the things Fainsod mentioned. But this cannot be demonstrated merely by asserting that "it is obvious" that regulatory agencies have power. Bentley would not have denied that fact for a minute, nor would any other group theorist. They sought to explain the power these bodies possessed. The vital question (as we shall see) is whether, in explaining it, they did not explain it away. But pointing to one of the facts which group theorists would not dispute cannot settle that question. The question can only be settled by an examination of Bentley's or Truman's reasoning, by an examination of the theory, to see whether it went astray, and if so, why. Pointing to the facts could be significant only in the context of such an examination.

Few of the critics undertake this examination. Almost without exception, they load the discussion in their favor at the outset by assuming a narrow interpretation of the group theory to begin with. They then have no difficulty demonstrating that it cannot deal with all the admitted facts. Their conclusion, that the theory should be confined to the area of pressure groups, or that it is not a general theory of political processes, is simply their first premise restated. The reference to facts in such a context, even when it is in the form of a report of field investigations such as La Palombara's,[13] is quite misleading. It gives the discussion an appearance of being empirically based, but it does nothing to support the argument.[14] There is in fact no argument but merely counterassertion.

A second group of critics accept the conclusion that the group theory can be restated in a form which secures it against attacks like that of Fainsod. But they argue that this is at the cost of making it so general that it is empty and platitudinous or even tautologous. It becomes "nothing more than a language,"[15] a new language for old terms and old myths. This is the substance of Odegard's discussion of the theory.[16] "When Congress and the Courts and the President and all other institutions or aggregations, including majorities and minorities within them, are defined as interest groups," he says, presenting one alternative, the term "interest group" becomes "synonymous not merely with politics but with human life itself." He then wonders whether "the Group Theory of Politics adds anything to Aristotle's aphorism that 'man is a social animal.' "

So, stated broadly, the theory is empty. It can have substance only if it is stated narrowly and then it ceases to be a general theory. For example, in discussing confusions about the term "equilibrium," Odegard says: "In one forum, group interests, propaganda, organized pressure, even violence, may be the controls which produce political 'equilibrium.' . . . In another forum, argument and debate carried on at a high level of logic and rationality may be decisive." The "group basis of politics" cannot account for what happens there. The same argument is repeated with reference to individuals and their adjustments to their environments. In sum, stated narrowly, the theory cannot explain them in the same way that it explains groups and pressures; stated broadly, it is empty; and if the two things are run together, the result is a hopeless confusion of concepts.

Before discussing whether a theory like Bentley's is necessarily empty we should note that Odegard does not pause to consider the implications of Aristotle's aphorism. It means at least that men and their doings should not be treated both socially and nonsocially, or that the social should not be treated as both natural and conventional, but throughout on the one level, the natural social level.

Bentley came to the same conclusion in Part I of the *Process of Government*. He considered that some of the things which Odegard and many other critics would like to see established in social theory—the individual, his ideas, his rational decision—had been treated as nonsocial factors in contemporary writing. He presented an argument, not against talking about individuals, ideas, and decisions in social theory, but against giving them a special explanatory function or status in it. His complaint was that to do so made a logical separation between two types of entities, the things whose job it was to explain, and the things which had to be explained.

If the individual man were set "in concrete contrast to society," the fictitious, and in principle insoluble, problem would arise of bringing the individual and society into relations again.[17] Likewise, the individual's ideas, faculties, ideals, will, and reasoning are all unsatisfactory as causes in social theory because they are presented as independent objects —"things," he calls them—put up to explain why men act in particular ways. He then goes on to point out that these things need to be explained even more than the actions they are supposed to explain, and that when an explanation of them is sought, it is found that they are defined by the events or actions that they are supposed to explain. They are therefore useless as explanations of these actions. One need not accept Bentley's behaviorist psychology at this point—"every bit of activity, which is all we actually know of the individual" (Bentley 215)—to see the force of the point he is making. The distinction between individuals, or ideas et al., and society meant that the explaining "things" had to have a dual status. Bentley accordingly called them "spooks" or metaphysical entities to signify, not that they were out of the social world, but that they were both in and out of it.

Another type of criticism of the group theory is directed at its supposed "scientism," or at attempts to give political studies a scientific methodology. One form of this is to accuse the group theorists of concealing value judgments behind a facade of scientific objectivity and detachment. In Armstrong's words, group theorists "obscure distinctions which are important . . . from the view point of legitimacy and desirability." "Political scientists who, vastly impressed by the second half of their title, claim to be speaking in completely value-free terms, do not realize just how ambitious their claim is."[18] He concludes that "silence about values is not the same thing as neutrality." Hale has argued that Bentley's "search for both 'realism' and a 'science' of politics may lead to a surreptitious sanctification of the actual."[19]

The implications that Hale and Armstrong profess to find hidden behind the facade of science are, however, opposed. In Hale's opinion "the implications of Bentley's cosmology are conservative"; in Armstrong's opinion, group theorists leave students "with no grounds on which to condemn" the corrupt aspects of pressure politics, and they do not ask "how true" an institution or practice is "to the nature of our political system as generally understood and desired."

It is true, of course, that some commentators[20] on the American political system have found support in group theory for their opinion that the political parties do not need reform, and that pressure groups have a necessary and desirable representative function in that system. Truman himself thought that his account of the political process had some bearing "upon the survival of representative democracy."[21] The group theory, like Marxian theory or the thought of Burke, provides many texts against voluntarist, rationalist, and optimistic schemes of reform. But a theory cannot be tested by its utility to reformers and their opponents nor discredited because it leaves students to discover that there is a gap between the political norms and the political practices of a society.

Parker claims that the group theorists' "relativist view of all moral valuations in politics . . . conceals an ambiguity." To show it, he asks: "Are we to infer from positions like Bentley's that all methods of pursuing group interest are morally neutral, or that the methods conventionally condemned by 'public opinion' are, in fact, as morally acceptable as any others ?"[22] The answer is, neither. There is a distinction, Golembiewski reminds us,[23] between empirical theory and "goal-based empirical theory," which is commonly overlooked by the critics and the defenders of the group theory alike. Parker in fact admits as much as soon as he turns to argue that "neither objective tests (of the kind supplied by a public interest) nor 'subjective' valuations by individuals . . . need be at daggers drawn with the group analysis." As soon as this admission is made, there can no longer be any question about the theory itself. It makes no recommendations, and this, in fact, is what the critics dislike about it.

Another argument against scientism, touched on by writers like Odegard and Parker, is most elaborately set out in a recent paper by Dowling. Bentley, in his opinion, can claim that his group theory is scientific only so long as he treats social processes mechanistically.[24] Dowling says that his "main objection to Bentley is his repeated assertion and implication that political science and political dynamics are equivalent, and that we ought to abstract from our political experience nothing but groups and their relating pressures." The success of dynamics, such men (as Bentley and Catlin) seem to have thought, "is evidently the result of its method, which they took to be the reduction of phenomena to the primary qualities of matter and motion."

In support of this, Dowling argues that there are "very close parallels" between Bentley's theory and Newtonian physics at three points. The groups and their pressures are conceived mechanistically and Bentley even has statements like some of the Newtonian laws of dynamics; Bentley treats of society as a whole much as the classical physicists regarded physical systems in discussing their energy; and finally Bentley rejects as "secondary" or "epiphenomenal" the things for which he has no place in his system, much as the classical physicists left colour, for example, out of their dynamics. This mechanistic approach, according to Dowling, compels Bentley to be inconsistent and reductionist in his treatment of political techniques, the environment, government, the individual and reason.

Dowling's argument acquires spurious plausibility from his "reification" of the groups, as it does in so many of the critics' discussions.[25] He thinks of them as the social counterpart of the body or particle in classical dynamics, and automatically reifies them by his analogy. This makes it easy to attack the group theory. But Bentley was strongly opposed to the "crudities which attend the extension of physical causation to the social field" (p. 83) and developed his whole discussion of individuals and other "factors" from this position. He argued that these factors were "things" that could not effect the changes that they were supposed to effect. In his theory, groups were processes, not particles; and by ignoring Bentley's discussion of these points, Dowling is not attacking his theory.

At the same time, Dowling exploits the ambiguity in the group theory about the term "groups." The features, he says, "of the actual groups (are) imported into the conceptual 'groups.' . . . This almost invariably produces something approaching a crude conspiracy view of politics, an assumption that there must be a 'they,' or a 'social force' behind everything that the individual does in the political arena."

Yet it was the crude conspiracy view of pressure groups that the group theorists wanted to transcend. They said in effect that if institutions and parties had social force, so too did pressure groups. The question whether "conspiracy" was one of the techniques of force employed by any of these types of bodies was then another and lesser question, one to be answered in any given case by factual investigation. They also held that when the question was put in this way, it was loaded with ethical imperatives that could not but add confusion to the discussion of the ways in which social change occurs.

Dowling introduces the individual into his argument at this point. "It is quite obvious," he says, "that in fact individuals participate in politics." It is. But it is not at all obvious how they participate. Dowling says that on this question Bentley has a doctrine like Marx's doctrine of "objective forces" in which, "no matter what anybody does, the group process marches on." If Dowling thinks that "anybody" is an individual without force, then there is no question that that individual is irrelevant. If he thinks that an individual is able to do something about the marching process, then he must admit that he has force, and be prepared to give the appropriate explanation of it.

That explanation must avoid setting individuals on a different level from the processes they affect. Dowling can scarcely object to this since it is part of his criticism of Bentley that, like the physicists, he made a distinction between the epiphenomenal and the underlying reality. Second, it must avoid reifying the individual. The difficulty is that the individual becomes reified as a consequence of other things the critics say about him,[26] for example, that he is a special explanatory factor, alongside other explanatory principles such as groups, institutions and ideas. Or they imply that he is self-acting or has in him a special self-replenishing reservoir of will, or an untouchable region of self or inheritance, or that part of his mind is a reserve for ideas, beliefs and principles which are not derived from his society, his culture or his physical environment, but from some other non-historical and often eternal, higher, realm.[27] If the group is reified and taken to be a fundamental unit the multiplication of reified entities is no way out of the difficulties presented by such a theory.

Dowling rounds off his discussion of this point by advising the group theorist to purify his concepts. "Starting . . . with conceptual entities (such as 'polbods' and the 'sway' they exert on each other) he would be the less likely to muddle fact with logic in the Bentleyan way, and should pretty quickly test the worth of the mechanistic approach." What would be shown, of course, is not the worth of the mechanistic approach, but the worthlessness of the advice. By such an argument any approach in political science could be discredited, including an individualistic one, which is to say that the exercise is an empty play upon words.

The critics wish to avoid false scientism by treating the group, and other concepts, simply as useful tools of analysis which can all be used together. Bentley himself, reared like many of his critics in a pragmatist atmosphere, explicitly stated that he had attempted to fashion a tool. And ever since, the various arguments which assume that theories in politics are merely methodological and conceptual are saying no more. The buried assumption is that since concepts are no more than tools of our own contrivance we can apply or not apply them at will and that we can fashion or refashion them to suit our purposes, again at will, the only test of them being their utility.[28]

The talk of tools in this context is misleading even though it makes the argument for harmony among the students plausible. The group theory, like other theories, is a good deal more than a tool; and in fact the critics give testimony that it is, in thinking that it threatens other theories. It threatens them by contradicting them and it is this which makes it, or any other theory, something more than a tool. By contradicting them it makes a claim to truth.

The critics commonly try to evade the difficulties in their position by saying that each tool must be confined to its proper field. The assumption is that the group theory may be judged not only useful but true, or false, within its field and not outside it. But then the problem has to be faced of showing how any two fields are related—for example, the fields where the individual is a useful tool and where the group is a useful tool.[29]

Of all the critics, Rothman alone approaches the alternative of rejecting the group theory in toto.[30] He observes that it is inadequate to explain even the "pattern of interest group politics, not to speak of the general pattern of social life, in any country."[31] It is true that he also says that the group theories should "limit their scope to a more narrow" range of phenomena, but his arguments in criticism of the inconsistencies in Truman's *Governmental Process* warrant the former and more sweeping conclusion if they hold good. They do hold good, but against Truman rather than against Bentley. Although Rothman takes them to be "generally applicable" he mentions Bentley only at the beginning of his paper, and, as Golembiewski has observed, Bentley's "lot has been to legitimise a subject matter rather than to inspire methodological innovation."[32] The implication is that parts of Bentley's theory were never developed by his followers, but were neglected and obscured in the additions and alterations later made to it.

Truman's notion of a potential interest group is a good example. It is, as Rothman says, one of Truman's basic concepts, and one which leads to incompatible statements in his theory. A potential interest group is defined in terms of "interests that are not at a particular point in time the basis of interactions among individuals, but that may become such."[33] He first introduces the concept as a means of explaining how the norms or rules of the game exist, on which the cohesion of a society is thought to rest. The device makes its appearance again whenever Truman is trying to explain why organised groups do not pursue their own self-interest unrelentingly against the weaker interests in society. "If these wide weak interests are too flagrantly ignored, they may be stimulated to organise for aggressive counteraction" (p. 114).

As to the first point, Truman seems quite unable to comprehend that something, it may be a society or a state, could be maintained by the tension and conflict between its internal parts. Instead, he speaks as if a society could persist as an ongoing entity only if everyone, or almost everyone, upheld certain norms or rules of political conduct that promoted the continuation of the entity.

Once this is maintained it follows (if it is to be reconciled with a group theory) that Truman must postulate a group of some sort to be the bearer of the interest in the rules of the game. He assumes that a society without such an interest "would have torn itself apart long since." We infer "the existence of such factors (as traditions of constitutionalism, civil liberties, representative responsibility) only from the behaviour and habitual interactions of men. If they exist in this fashion, they are interests. We can account for their operation and the system by recognising such interests as representing . . . potential interest groups in the 'becoming' stage of activity."[4] He does not, incidentally, explore the possibility that the traditions might be ideological patterns of belief in actual groups that exacerbate group conflict as well as mitigate it.

Truman also thinks he needs the notion of "potential interest groups" to explain why organised groups do not press all the weaker interests out of existence. The fault here lies in his assumption that all actual interest groups are shared attitude groups, which make claims upon other groups. These claims are shared attitudes about what the group needs. An actual interest group therefore says, in effect, "I believe," and "I believe I want" in Truman's theory. By definition, it can say nothing more, nor can it be anything else. The result is that the world of Hobbes, Bentham and John Mill, which Truman explicitly disowns, is reincarnated in his world of groups, as Rothman points out. "While Truman talks of groups rather than individuals," he says, "the norm is still rational groups pursuing a rational self-interest."[35] On such a theory, an actual interest group cannot be mistaken about its interest, and it cannot have beliefs or make claims that are irrelevant to its self-interest. It will always pursue its true interest to the limit. Yet groups do make irrelevant claims, and they are mistaken, in this special sense, in their beliefs. They build up ideologies, shared attitudes even, that are not statements of their claims and their needs. There is no need for potential interest groups to explain why groups do not always pursue their self-interest fully and unerringly.

It is these two assumptions, one concerning the stability of society, the other the rationality of actual groups, that make it necessary for Truman to think of a potential interest or a potential interest group. When the notion is first introduced into his theory, it is tagged on to and legitimised by texts taken from Bentley, and there is no question that Bentley says things which justify Truman in making these connections. He does, for example, talk about "wide, weak interests" checking organised groups when their activities bear too heavily upon them (Bentley p. 372), but Truman fails to do justice to other parts of Bentley's argument to which he refers, notably the parts dealing with tendencies to action (p. 184f.). Bentley insists that these tendencies to action are themselves ways of acting. He does not suggest for a moment that there is nothing "doing" in them.[36] Yet in Truman, tendencies become potential activities, and even this distorted interpretation of Bentley is forgotten when the term "potential interests" takes its place. What was in Bentley an activity becomes in Truman an inactivity, and the whole force of Bentley's analysis is lost.

Another weakness in Truman's theory is his use of the dual concept of status-role. Rothman points out that Truman "is forced to rely upon the ad hoc use of the concept of role to explain an important dimension of political action" that his theory cannot take account of. The reductionism in his analysis forces him to put much of his discussion of the structure, organization and leadership of groups in the form of a discussion of the statuses that an individual may occupy in society, and the expectations of other men about his behaviour in the offices he holds. The objective facts of structure and leadership are transmuted into sociopsychological material in Truman's theory. They are put into individuals' minds, and, as norms, they are "determinants of the ways in which . . . (he) behaves."[37]

One can imagine that Bentley would have had no time for this use of the concept of status-role. The prescriptive norms that cluster around statuses in Truman's theory are no more than devices. Truman thinks he is answering questions about leadership in groups, for example, by referring us to norms about leadership in men's minds. Transmuting social facts into sociopsychological norms does not provide an explanation of the facts. At best, it is an answer to the question why individuals act in this way or that, a question that could not arise if the individual was not surreptitiously being kept apart from and in contrast to the society of which he is supposed to be a member. The arguments Bentley used against giving ideas, ideals, faculties and the like a special explanatory status or determining role can be applied with equal force to the norms in Truman's theory. Giving the norms a social content does not save them from this criticism.

II

The group theory is reductionist, but not because its exponents claim too wide a field for it. It is reductionist because Bentley and his followers are convinced that the political process can only be explained if a fundamental basis is found for it. This alone is sufficient to destroy the generality of the theory. The actual basis chosen is immaterial: any search for a basis, for something underlying the political process is certain to be reductionist if it is carried through consistently.

For Bentley, the raw materials of politics are men and their activities. Politics "is first, last and always activity, action, something doing" (p. 176). But he pushed this to the point where nothing but masses of men have any force. He has scarcely stated his belief before he begins to qualify it in reductionist fashion: "political groups are highly differentiated groups reflecting or representing other groups, which latter can easily, and I believe for the most part properly, be regarded as more fundamental in society" (p. 209). The word "fundamental" is the clue to his difficulty. The notion of sheer aggregation, of a mass (the words are his, e.g., 203), is quite inadequate to describe an organized group of men. Yet Bentley, anxious always to be pragmatic and empirical, is unwilling to give up his belief that a simple mass of men is the datum of investigation.[38] He finds that it is inadequate to describe a group such as a political party so he introduces a distinction between the "fundamental" and the "dependent" group. Broadly speaking, organization and leadership are characteristic of the dependent group, the "representing" group, in Bentley's theory, while interest and activity characterise the underlying "represented" group.

NOTES

1. W. J. M. Mackenzie, "Pressure Groups: the Conceptual Framework," *Political Studies* 3 (1955): 247. H. S. Kariel, "Political Science in the United States," *Political Studies* 4 (1956): 113. C. B. Hagan, "The Group in Political Science," in R. Young (ed.), *Approaches to the Study of Politics* (Evanston, Ill.: Northwestern University Press, 1958). P. H. Odegard, "A Group Basis of Politics: A New Name for an Old Myth," *Western Political Quarterly* 11 (1958): 689. B. Crick, *The American Science of Politics* (London: Routledge, 1959). J. La Palombara, "The Utility and Limitations of Interest Group Theory in Non-

American Field Situations," *Journal of Politics* 22 (1969): 20. S. Rothman, "Systematic Political Theory: Observations on the Group Approach," *American Political Science Review* 54 (1960): 15. R. E. Dowling, "Pressure Group Theory: Its Methodical Range," *American Political Science Review* 54 (1960): 962. M.Q. Hale, "The Cosmology of Arthur F. Bentley," *American Political Science Review,"* 54 (1960): 955. R. T. Golembiewski, "The Group Basis of Politics — Notes on Analysis and Development," *American Political Science Review* 54 (1960): 962. R. S. Parker, "Group Analysis and Scientism in Political Studies," *Political Studies* 9 (1961): 37. R. C. Macridis, "Interest Groups in Comparative Analysis," *Journal of Politics* 23 (1961): 25.

2. Arthur Bentley, *The Governmental Process* (New York: Knopf, 1951). Bentley's book was reprinted in 1935 and 1949. The edition used is that of 1949.

3. Parker, p. 38.

4. A. F. Bentley, "Simmel, Durkheim and Ratzenhofer," *American Journal of Sociology* 32 (1926): 250. cf. *The Process of Government*, p. 83, for his praise of Jhering. Parker, p. 38, does less than justice to Bentley's indebtedness to the European theorists whom he criticised.

5. Truman, p. 539, for a bibliography.

6. Some of the more recent works of this kind, including comparative studies are: S. Finer, *Anonymous Empire* (London: Pall Mall Press, 1958); J. D. Stewart, *British Pressure Groups* (Oxford: Clarendon Press, 1958); A. Wildavsky and D. Carboch, *Studies in Australian Politics* (Melbourne: F. W. Chesire, 1958); H. W. Ehrmann (ed.), *Interest Groups on Four Continents* (Pittsburgh: Pittsburgh University Press, 1958); "Unofficial Government, Pressure Groups and Lobbies," *Annals of the American Academy of Political and Social Science,* 319 (1958); H. Eckstein, *Pressure Group Politics* (Stanford: Stanford University Press, 1960); G. A. Almond and J. S. Coleman (eds.), *The Politics of the Developing Areas* (Princeton: Princeton University Press, 1960); A. M. Potter, *Organized Groups in British National Politics* (London: Faber, 1961); H. H. Wilson, *Pressure Group* (London: Secker and Warburg, 1961).

7. Rothman, p. 16. This the main trend of Rothman's argument, but he contradicts it by saying also that the theory is inadequate for the pressure groups themselves. See below, p. 14.

8. La Polombara, p. 36.

9. Mackenzie, p. 247.

10. M. Fainsod, "Some Reflections on the Nature of the Regulatory Process," *Public Policy* (Cambridge, Mass.: Harvard University Press, 1940), p. 297. cf. K. G. Armstrong, "Political Science and the Pressure Groups Theory," *American Political Science Association News* 4 (1959): 10.

11. cf. the claim made by R. M. MacIver in *The Web of Government* (New York: Macmillan, 1947), p. 220, that "To Bentley . . . a legislative act is always the calculable resultant of a struggle between pressure groups, never a decision between opposing conceptions of national welfare." For Bentley, according to MacIver, the public interest is "nothing but the diagonal of the forces that constantly struggle for advantage."

12. B. M. Gross reviewing Bentley's *Process of Government, American Political Science Review* 44 (1950): 742.

13. La Palombara concludes, after an examination of politics in Italy, that "while the interest group approach . . . permits the orderly classification of data regarding the behaviour of many central actors in the political process, it falls short of providing a satisfactory explanation for the patterns of action and the policy outcomes . . . in the Italian political system." (p. 36). He contrasts interest groups with bureaucrats, for example, and then argues that as policy and action are not simply the resultant of group struggles, the attempt to explain them "within the general framework of interest group 'theory' is likely to be misleading and fruitless."

14. cf. Macridis, p. 27.

15. Echstein, p. 153; cf. La Palombara, pp. 30, 49.

16. Odegard, p. 693 ff.

17. Bentley, *The Process of Government,* pp. 57, 83-4, 90. Bentley was discussing Jhering's attempt to bring a wide range of social facts "into one effective system." In Bentley's words Jhering "broke away from 'pure reason' . . . from the presocial or extrasocial individual

as . . . principle(s) of interpretation. . . . He brought moral phenomena into a systematic working relation to legal phenomena, and . . . with economic phenomena. He strove to make all his interpretations in social terms. . . . But . . . his individual man, even after he had socially interpreted him, was kept in concrete contrast to society." The theory of "Zwecke" was used, an elaborate "psychological system," " to function the individual in society," that is, to overcome the separation, and it collapsed completely in the face of Bentley's examination.

18. Armstrong, p. 13, and *American Political Science Association News* 4 (1959): 11.

19. Hale, p. 955.

20. e.g., J. Fischer, "Unwritten Rules of American Politics," in F. M. Carney and H. F. Way, Jr. (eds.), *Politics 1960* (San Francisco: Wadsworth, 1960), p. 12. The argument is reviewed in A. Ranney and W. Kendall, *Democracy and the American Party System* (New York: Harcourt, 1956), pp. 481-483 and passim.

21. Truman, p. 49.

22. Parker, pp. 41-3.

23. Golembiewski, p. 963.

24. Dowling, loc cit. The argument had already been put forward succinctly by P. Sorokin in *Contemporary Sociological Theories* (New York: Harper and Bros., 1928), ch. 1, p. 29. Bentley, in "Kennetic Enquiry," *Science* 112 (1950): 775, took it to be his position that "All behavioral events are by postulation transactions," which, he explained, were "in contrast with the interactional reports obtained under mechanistic enquiry" (p. 776, his emphasis). The "mechanist" argument also appears in G. A. Schubert, "The Public Interest in Administrative Decision Making, *American Political Science Review* 51 (1957): 346, and as an objection to "crude determinism," in Macridis, p. 32.

25. This point has already been made by R. W. Taylor in Arthur F. Bentley's "Political Science," *Western Political Quarterly* 5 (1952): 218-19.

26. Hagan, pp. 43-4.

27. cf. H. Mayer, "A Comment on Mr. Truman's Note," *American Political Science Association News* 4 (1959): 17, being a reply to D. Truman's *The Group Interpretation, a Note,* loc. cit.

28. It takes little imagination to see that if concepts are treated merely as tools, to be tested by their utility and fashioned to suit our purposes, any science of politics might readily be made normative or "goal based" while still appearing to be "empirical."

29. Mayer, pp. 18, 19.

30. Macridis, pp. 26f, who advances similar arguments, does not reach this conclusion.

31. Rothman, p. 29.

32. Golembiewski, p. 968.

33. Truman, p. 34.

34. Ibid., p. 51, cf. p. 159, v. Macridis, pp. 28, 32. He observes that group theorists neglect ideology.

35. Rothman, p. 28.

36. See the discussion of pressure in Bentley's theory.

37. Truman, p. 346.

38. He was therefore led to what Dowling calls the "regrettable statement" that President Roosevelt means a certain number of millions of Americans. (Bentley 322.) Dowling is right about the reductionism, but wrong about the reason for it.

The Small Group and Political Behavior

SIDNEY VERBA

Primary group experiences influence an individual's political behavior in
several ways. In such groups individuals develop nonpolitical personality
traits and general expectations from interpersonal relations. These traits
and interpersonal expectations first receive specifically political content
when the individual faces a particular political situation. Or the influence
of the primary group can be more directly and manifestly political. Within
the primary group, individuals may learn generalized attitudes toward
government and the state. These general attitudes include trust and confidence in government, respect for the state and its symbols, respect for
law, and the like. On the other hand, the political attitudes learned in the
primary group may be quite specific. These may be support for a particular
party or issue.

THE POLITICAL PERSONALITY

The influence of personality traits on political behavior has been stressed
in political science for a number of years. The early works of Harold
Lasswell, as well as recent works on the authoritarian personality, suggest
that much political behavior is a projection of private needs and emotions
onto the political sphere.[1] What is of particular interest here is the way in
which the authority system in the primary group (what one might call the
political system of the family) influences the expectations of the individual
in regard to authority in the larger political system. Within the primary
group, the individual receives training for roles that he will later play
within society. This training consists in both the teaching of certain standards of behavior that can be applied to later situations and, perhaps more
significantly, the playing of roles in the family and in other primary groups
that are similar to roles later to be played in the political or economic
system.

The type of political structure the child experiences in the family will affect the type of participation that the child will have in other social structures. In a study of ethnocentrism among children, Else Frenkel-Brunswik
found that the degree of prejudice among children was related to the family
atmosphere. Ethnocentric children tended to come from families in which
the authority figure (the father) was strict and rigid, and in which the
parent-child relationship was one of dominance and submission. Unpre-
judiced children came more often from families characterized by a more af-

Reprinted from Sidney Verba, *Small Groups and Political Behaviour: A Study of
Leadership* (Princeton: Princeton University Press, 1961) pp. 30-45 and 49-60. Reprinted by
permission of Princeton University Press.

fectionate and less rigid relationship. It is especially significant that the prejudiced and nonprejudiced children had expectations in nonfamily role relationships similar to those developed in the family. When asked to describe the "ideal teacher," the two types of children gave quite different answers. Frenkel-Brunswik cites the typical responses of two nonprejudiced boys:

> Would carefully listen to your viewpoints and explain what's wrong and what's right about it, and let you argue it out instead of flatly telling you you are wrong. . . . If she can relate her own experiences in relation to some topic you are studying, it is interesting. Has the personality to keep order in the classroom and not afraid the pupils will dislike her if she does. Should accept a joke, but not let it go too far.
>
> Fair in her attitude toward all pupils, doesn't favor one, explains the lessons and helps you with reason.

On the other hand, a highly ethnocentric girl replied: "Someone that is strict. If she asks for homework, you have to have it done. Most teachers are not strict enough. If the assigned work is not in you should be given a zero. She shouldn't let the class get out of hand."[2] Similarly, Baldwin, in a long-term and continuing study of power structure in the home, found that where the political system of the home was an open one—free communication in both directions between parents and children, some participation by children in family decisions, "fair" (not arbitrary) behavior on the part of parents—the children were better prepared to show initiative and participate fully in other role systems.[3]

Numerous writers have attempted to trace styles of political participation and types of political expectations back to early experiences in the family. Both Mannheim and Fromm emphasize that a stable and independent "democratic" personality, upon which at least to some extent democratic government depends, develops basically in the primary group.[4] Perhaps the major body of literature dealing with the impact of family training on political behavior is that of the "national character" school.[5] A large group of anthropologists and psychologists have attempted to find certain dominant psychological patterns within national societies. The patterns that characterize the "modal" person in that society are developed during earliest childhood experiences. Early childhood experiences may result in a personality that desires a submissive relationship to authority,[6] a personality that alternates between acceptance and rejection of authority,[7] or a personality that thrives on signs of love and acceptance.[8] And these different personalities result in different political behavior in later life. Germans raised in authoritarian families, for instance, will want and expect political leaders to stand in such an authoritarian relationship to them.[9]

Many of the studies of the effects of early family experiences on political behavior have generalized too easily from childhood experiences to adult attitudes. The step from early socialization to political attitudes is a long one and, as we shall suggest below, can be fully understood only in terms of the intervening effects of other intermediate face-to-face contacts and of the political system itself.

TRAINING FOR POLITICAL PARTICIPATION

Small-group experiences in childhood not only provide certain generalized expectations from political relationships; they also provide training for participation in these relationships. Much of this training of course takes place within the family, but it takes place in other face-to-face situations as well—in the classroom and, especially during adolescence, in the peer group. Furthermore, the training for political participation that takes place in face-to-face groups continues beyond childhood and adolescence.[10]

Participation in decisions in small face-to-face groups where the individual can have some grasp of the alternatives available for choice is a preparation for participation in decisions that are more complex, less immediate, and engage only a small part of an individual's attention. According to Bryce, "An essential ingredient of a satisfactory democracy is that a considerable proportion of the people should have experience of active participation in the work of small self-governing groups, whether in connection with the local government, trade unions, cooperatives or other forms of activity."[11] Some writers have in fact maintained that democracy is possible only in situations in which relations are predominantly face-to-face in nature.[12]

Much of the literature on the authoritarian family suggests that a democratic political system is difficult, if not impossible, to achieve unless there is experience in democratic participation within the family. Levy, for instance, on the basis of his studies of Nazis and anti-Nazis, concluded that democracy could not be introduced into Germany simply by removing authoritarian controls, since there was not sufficient training for democratic participation among the German people.[13] Similarly, it can be argued that an absence of participation in decisions in other face-to-face situations outside the family will affect the level of participation in the broader political system. Crozier, on the basis of a study of administration in French governmental agencies and industrial organizations, notes a complete absence of participatory leadership. Social distance between different levels in the various organizations is great, and there is little communication. Organizational relations are characterized by a "fear of face-to-face contacts" and a "constant recourse to impersonality."[14] Charles Micaud, who cites the Crozier work, suggests that this lack of face-to-face participation is one reason for the combination of a highly centralized state and highly atomized society in France. Lack of participation leads to an "espoir millenariste" and a desire to escape from political activity. If there were greater participation in primary groups, there might be greater political participation.[15]

Participation in decisions on levels below that of the political system is a requisite or, at least, a desirable adjunct to a democratic political system. In the first place, insofar as significant political decisions are made in such subgroups, effective participation in the political system will not exist unless members can participate on these lower levels. Furthermore, participation in decisions is much easier within smaller units. In larger units, the organizational necessities associated with a larger structure make participation difficult, if not impossible. Bureaucratic structures, introduced to bring rationality into the organization, limit participation. The decision process and the effects of decisions are less visible. Communication on an organization-wide basis requires the use of formal media, more easily controlled by the hierarchy. And the complexity of decisions is likely to limit the ability of the individual members to comprehend the issues involved.[16] Evidence of the rarity of participation by members in organization decisions is found in numerous studies.[17] The proposition is also supported by the finding in numerous small-group studies that as the size of the group increases, there is a tendency toward less free participation on the part of group members and toward the concentration of group activities in the hands of a single leader.[18]

The most complete study of the relationship between the existence of small subunits in which individuals can participate and organizational democracy is that of the International Typographical Union carried on by Lipset, Trow, and Coleman. Unlike most other unions, the ITU has maintained a democratic system. This is attributed by the authors to the existence of numerous formal and informal subgroups to which the members belong. Most of these subgroups are formally apolitical and deal with social affairs, but they perform a number of important political functions. They are centers of communication about what is going on in the union. Through them members develop interest in union affairs and are drawn into participation in union politics. Participation in the subunits also trains potential leaders for union office—training that otherwise would have to take place within the organizational hierarchy. Thus a pool of potential leaders not necessarily committed to the existing leadership is developed. Furthermore, the subunits serve as possible alternate power centers to challenge the leadership hierarchy. The maintenance of democracy in the large organization—the ITU—is, therefore, highly dependent upon the existence of subgroups in which members can participate, even though these groups are not formally political.[19]

SMALL GROUP ROLES AND POLITICAL ROLES

Though experiences within primary groups profoundly influence political behavior, one cannot accept any simple primary group monism and look for the explanation of all political behavior within the family, the peer group, and other primary groups. Political behavior is not determined solely by the predispositions that an individual brings into the political process from his experiences and training in primary groups. It is also affected by the way in which the political system interacts with these predispositions. The political system can channel political behavior in a number of directions. Insofar as political predispositions are molded in childhood, they are developed in essentially nonpolitical situations. The point is obvious but significant. It means that predictions that can be made about adult political behavior on the basis of childhood experiences will be limited to a rather general set of predispositions that an individual brings into the political process—in a sense, to an individual's psychological orientation to politics. We may be able to predict some of the psychological satisfactions that he will seek from political participation, but we will know little about the political content of that participation. This content will depend, among other things, upon the position of the individual within the political structure and the alternatives that the political structure offers him. As Shils has pointed out in his commentary on the Berkeley studies of authoritarianism, similar authoritarian personality traits may be directed toward the Left (Communism) or the Right (Fascism), depending upon the political environment in which the individual finds himself.[20]

The limitation in the range of choices that any political system offers an individual means that particular predispositions and expectations developed in early primary group situations may be directed into diverse political activities, depending upon the political environment. But the range of choices within the political system may also direct the individual seeking to satisfy expectations developed in the primary group in another direction—out of politics. This situation will arise if the political system cannot satisfy the needs developed in primary groups. Much of the literature that attempts to link childhood experiences and political behavior assumes that the political system will be congruent with the patterns in the primary group and will satisfy the needs developed there. Authoritarians will find an authoritarian political system, and nonauthoritarians will participate in democratic relationships. But this assumption is not necessarily valid. This can be seen if we compare the relationship between family training and political participation in France and Germany. According to Schaffner, the political orientation of the German people is a reflection of the respect for authority learned within the family. Thus the Germans readily accepted Hitler, "whose manner was that of the traditional German father: it inspired confidence."[21] The French family system, according to Rodnick, has a similar pattern and develops expectations similar to those of the German family. "Individuals (are) conditioned to expect guidance and a dependency relationship from their authority figures."[22] But, unlike the German political system, the French system has produced (at least, until recently) no authority figures who inspire such confidence. The individual cannot find satisfaction in the political sphere for needs developed in the family. "The reaction against authority has been because it has been weak rather than because it has been strong."[23]

Similar role experience in primary groups may, therefore, lead to quite different political behaviors. The question as to whether there is pressure toward homogeneity among the various political systems to which a person belongs is still open. Do those who experience one type of authority in the family, school, and peer group desire the same type of authority in their economic and political relations? Some of the evidence we have cited suggests that such will be the case, but it may well be that in certain situations there is a high degree of autonomy among the various authority systems in which a person participates. Further research is needed on the relationship between primary group training and political predispositions.[24]

POLITICAL ATTITUDES AND THE SMALL GROUP

The impact of the primary group on politics has been discussed so far in terms of the political structure of the primary group. Participation in families, peer groups, work groups, and other formally apolitical groups influences the individual's style of political behavior by developing certain expectations of political roles and certain skills for political role playing. But the impact of the face-to-face group on political affairs can be more direct and have a more specific political content. The explicit political attitudes with which an individual comes into contact in the face-to-face group have a significant impact on his political views and behavior. This is especially so in the light of the strong influence that the primary group has on the attitudes of its members. This primary group influence does not involve the development of a political personality or of generalized role expectations that receive political content only when brought into contact with the political system, but the impact of the primary group may be on quite general political attitudes as well as on specific political opinions. Thus children may learn by direct teaching, or by observing the political attitudes and behaviors of their parents, certain general attitudes toward the state, toward law, and toward other political groups. They may learn to have trust and confidence in political figures, or to look with distrust and disdain on politics. They may learn respect or disrespect for law. This aspect of political socialization has been little explored, but there is reason to believe that it is very significant. French "incivisme" was explained by Rodnick in terms of the disappointment of the individual Frenchman at not finding in the political system the strong authority figure that he had been led to expect by his experience in the family; and by Crozier and Micaud in terms of the lack of primary group training for participation. But "incivisme" is probably also influenced by the explicit attitudes toward the political system that young people hear from the adults around them. Wylie reports that the children in the French village he studied ". . . constantly hear adults referring to government as the source of evil and to the men who run it as instruments of evil. There is nothing personal in this belief. It does not concern one particular government composed of one particular group of men. It concerns government everywhere and at all times—French governments, American governments, Russian governments, all governments. Some are less bad than others, but all are essentially bad."[25]

The development of political attitudes begins in the family. The relations between the attitudes of parents and those of their children have been most widely explored in the fields of intergroup relations and voting behavior. Studies of grade-school children as well as of college students have found that the racial attitudes of parents are a major influence on the attitudes of children.[26] Voting behavior is also influenced by early family experiences: "Indeed it would not be inappropriate to consider the family as the primary unit of voting analysis"[27] The panel studies of voting behavior indicate that between two-thirds and three-quarters of the American voters vote for the party for which their fathers voted.[28] The family may also influence the general tendency of an individual's political affiliation, rather than the specific party for which he votes. Thus members of the Communist party show a tendency to come from radical and left-wing, but not necessarily Communist, families.[29] The emphasis in much of the literature on the connection between family experience and such implicit personality-oriented attitudes as authoritarianism may have led to an underestimation of the more manifest and direct political training that an individual receives in primary groups. On the basis of an analysis of numerous studies of political socialization, Herbert Hyman concludes that socialization into party affiliation seems to take place earlier than that into ideological orientation. Similarly while there is little evidence for an implicit personality-oriented authoritarianism among children, studies have found that manifestly political authoritarian attitudes (say, opposition to civil rights) are more highly developed at a young age.[30]

The influence of the primary group on voting extends beyond that of the family during childhood. The face-to-face contact that a voter has during a campaign has a significant effect on his voting choice. This was the discovery made in the Erie County voting study: not only does one's class, religion, occupation, and residence affect one's voting choice, but the small face-to-face groups in which one participates play an important role.[31] A major finding in relation to the role of the small face-to-face group in voting and other decisions is that the mass media of communication, rather than acting directly upon the individual audience member, act upon individuals through a two-step communication process. Certain community members, it was found, are more receptive to the communications of the mass media. These opinion leaders, in turn, pass on the content of these media to those with whom they have face-to-face contact.[32] The discovery of the intermediary role of face-to-face communication between the individual and the mass media serves as a strong qualification of the conception of modern society as a mass society—a place where lone individuals stand naked and defenseless before the mass media. The two-step process of communication has been found in voting and community studies in this country. It has also been found as a major determinant of the lack of impact of hostile propaganda on the Wehrmacht and as an important technique of propaganda and agitation in the Soviet Union.[33]

The face-to-face communication groups found by Lazarsfeld and his associates in the voting studies and the Decatur study, as well as the primary group in the Wehrmacht, are informal parts of the communication process. These groups did not come together with the explicit purpose of linking the individual and the mass media. They are not planned parts of the communication process. But as was mentioned earlier, face-to-face groups are not necessarily informal. Their communication functions may be explicitly planned. One of the major sources of the strength of the Communist party, it has been suggested, is the fact that it is organized on the basis of cells, for which the optimum size is about 15-20 members.[34] The strength of the cell system lies not only in its greater adaptability to clandestine action, but in the greater influence that such small meetings can have on the attitudes of the members. For many members, Micaud points out, the cell is a substitute for primary ties in family or church. Furthermore, it performs the intermediary function in the two-step process of communication. The Party literature is available in the cell, and its transmission in the small group context gives it an especially strong impact.[35]

The process of transmitting communications from the mass media through the face-to-face group is not merely one of amplification. Communications from the group's external environment do not reach the group unchanged by the process of face-to-face transmission. The views of the opinion leader will, of course, affect the content of the transmitted message. So will the nature of the group. Communications that challenge the solidarity of the group, for instance, tend to be rejected by group members.[36]

The participation of an individual in politically relevant face-to-face groups affects not only the content of his political attitudes, but the intensity of these attitudes, as well. There are two variables to be considered here: (1) the range of primary groups in which there is political participation; and (2) the homogeneity of that participation. The wider the range of primary contacts that are politicized, the greater the intensity of political participation. In a survey in France, voters were asked: "Before voting, do

TABLE 2.1

Percentage Saying They Discuss Politics

Party Preference	With Family	With Friends	With Colleagues
Communist	68	65	69
Socialist	53	49	42
Radical	58	49	31
MRP	51	43	40
Moderates	53	53	36
RPF	58	51	32

you discuss the election with others in your circle?" The percentage answering "yes" is shown in Table 2.1, broken down into party affiliation.[37] The interesting point of these figures is that not only do the Communist supporters report discussion within the family more frequently than do the supporters of the other parties, but unlike the other parties there is no falling off in the frequency of discussion among Communists as one moves from family to friends to colleagues on the job. The political intensity of the Communist supporter is manifested in the high degree of politicization of the range of primary groups to which he belongs.

Second, the greater the homogeneity of primary group contacts, the greater the intensity of political participation. It was found that voters with friends of various political persuasions were less strong in their voting intentions than those whose friends were all of the same persuasion. McClosky and Dahlgren report similar findings, both for relations within the primary group and for those among primary groups. The greater the political homogeneity of a particular primary group—for instance, the more solid a family is in one political direction—the more likely the individual is to be a stable voter in that direction. And the greater the political homogeneity among the family of origin, the present family, and the peer group, the more likely the individual is to be a stable voter in that direction.[38]

That the face-to-face group plays a significant role in the political process is now clear. The process of decision making in small groups has been described, as has the influence of the small group on the political attitudes and behaviors of its members. What remains is to consider the small group from the point of view of the operation of the political system as a whole. . . .

THE SMALL GROUP IN CONFLICT
WITH THE POLITICAL SYSTEM

The face-to-face group may conflict with the larger political system of which it is a part in several ways. In the first place, the very existence of primary groups which have an effect on the political system may be regarded as a source of conflict with the development of a rational, efficient system. Second, the face-to-face group may support particular behaviors or attitudes that are deviant in terms of the norms of the larger system. We shall look at these in turn.

The "irrationality" of small group behavior. It was once a common view among sociologists, as Shils has pointed out, to consider the primary group and modern society ". . . logically antithetical and empirically incompatible. . . . The persistence of traditionally regulated informal and intimate relations was regarded as an archaism inherited from an older rural society or from a small-town handicraft society."[39] This view that informal relations are per se in conflict with larger structures is found among those administrative theorists who view organizations as essentially rational and formal. Though the organization planner will have to consider the informal relations that exist within an organization, he will look at them as deviations from the formal pattern and will try to minimize them. Urwick describes the process of designing an organization:

> He (the planner) should never for a moment pretend that these difficulties don't exist. They do exist; they are realities. Nor, when he has drawn up an ideal plan of organization, is it likely he will be able to fit in all the human material perfectly. There will be small adjustments . . . in all kinds of directions. But those adjustments are deliberate and temporary deviations from the pattern in order to deal with idiosyncrasy. . . .
> What is suggested is that problems of organization should be handled in the right order. Personal adjustments must be made insofar as they are necessary. But fewer of them will be necessary and they will present fewer deviations from what is logical and simple, if the organizer first makes a plan, a design.[38]

Insofar as the face-to-face groups in larger structures are informal—that is, perform unplanned functions—they are here looked on as in conflict with what is felt to be the essential planned rationality of the larger structure.

Similarly, it was pointed out earlier that the face-to-face voting groups are informal in the sense that their function in influencing voting decisions is a form of influence which has not been considered by traditional theories of the way in which a democracy operates.[39] In this sense, face-to-face contacts in voting can be considered to be in conflict with the operation of a "rational" democratic system in which voting choices are made on the basis of principle or a rational calculation of interests, or both. V. O. Key contrasts the voting decision made on the basis of party or issue with that made on a "friends and neighbors" basis. The support of a candidate by his "friends and neighbors who know him" is an indication of ". . . the absence of stable, well-organized, state-wide factions of like-minded citizens formed to advocate measures of a common concern. In its extreme form, localism justifies a diagnosis of low voter interest in public issues and a susceptibility to control by the irrelevant appeal to support the hometown boy."

In this view, personal influence in the voting decision is looked at as the antithesis of a voting decision made on the basis of party or issue; the passage cited above would seem to reflect a belief that such face-to-face influence is inconsistent with political choices made on a rational democratic basis. This view of a conflict between the primary group and the rational political system or the rational organization may, however, be more a reflection of an artificial, rational model than a reflection of actual conflict between primary and secondary structures.[40]

Deviant small groups: Face-to-face participation will also be in conflict with the larger political system if the particular norms of that system differ from those of the face-to-face group. Thus conformity to the face-to-face group, when that group is a deviant one, will mean nonconformity to the norms of the larger system.

> I . . . have been, am still, a criminal. But there is a sense in which I have been an almost abjectly law-abiding person. From my very first years I adapted myself wholeheartedly to the community I lived in, accepting its values, obeying its imperatives, observing its customs. Submissiveness could go no further. If, then, law-abidingness is acting according to the dictates of the community you were born into, there never was a more law-abiding person than myself.
>
> But, unfortunately or otherwise, the community I was born into was a small one at variance with the larger community containing it. In obeying the laws of the criminal quarter I incurred the disapproval of the law courts.[41]

Similarly, the people with radical family backgrounds who join in radical political movements will be conforming to their primary group background, though they are deviants from the point of view of the larger political system.

Conversely the absence of strong face-to-face commitments on the part of the individual strengthens the norms of the general political system. As illustrated in the Elmira voting study, in a dominantly Republican community, this dominant norm has its least effect where the face-to-face group is "solid"; that is, where one participates in face-to-face groups of homogeneous political composition. Where the face-to-face group is "solid,"

> . . . the strong community majority for the Republicans has little effect because it has little access to persons within homogeneous Democratic groups.
>
> But when the primary environment is internally divided, the effect of the distant community can be seen. Then the Republicans get a higher proportion of the vote. . . . The impact of the larger community is thus most evident among voters with discordant or disagreeing primary groups. When the voter's close associates do not provide him with a single, clear political direction—when instead they offer an alternative—then wider associations in the surrounding community reinforce one position over the other.[42]

Attachments to face-to-face groups may thus lessen the impact of the overall political culture on the individual. This fact is especially relevant in totalitarian societies. Insofar as such societies demand total loyalty to the state, loyalties to primary groups are in conflict with the dominant political norm. Attachment to a family or other primary group places an area of behavior outside government control. Thus in Soviet theory, loyalty to primary groups is "deemed intolerable."[43] "Family circles" (informal cliques of local officials) have often come under severe criticism in the Soviet Union because of the many illicit activities that go on in them. Fainsod reports the exposure of such a "family circle" in Smolensk which had been formed for the self-protection of the local leaders against the demands placed on them by Moscow. The important point about these "families" is that while they were for the central government "the mortal enemy of control," they performed significant functions for the members in providing them with a sanctuary. The main reason why the "family" system grew in the local area studied by Fainsod was an "almost desperate desire for relaxation and security" in the face of the overwhelming production demands of the central government.[44]

THE SMALL GROUP AND POLITICAL STABILITY

Face-to-face groups are not necessarily in conflict with the political system. They also perform significant supportive functions. The norms they support, for instance, may be norms that are congruent with those of the larger system. They may supply the individual member with affective outputs, the absence of which might place burdens on the political system. And they are a source of flexibility in running the system. Let us look at these functions in turn.

Socialization for citizenship. The major supportive role played by the primary group is the socialization of children to take adult roles in the political process. We have emphasized above some ways in which socialization into deviant political roles may take place. But it is highly probable that unless a large proportion of the population is socialized into behaviors that support the political system, that system will be highly unstable. In any case, even totalitarian states, afraid of competition from the family for the loyalty of their citizens, have had to revise doctrine so as to accept the basic role the family plays in socialization.[45]

Political socialization, furthermore, continues beyond childhood. Face-to-face contacts have a continuing effect on the individual's political attitudes and behavior. These face-to-face groups may, it was pointed out, support norms that are deviant from the point of view of the political system. They may, on the other hand, foster norms that are supportive of that system. What determines whether the pressures placed upon the individual in his face-to-face contacts—both as a child and later—will act to further the goals of the larger system? The question is a difficult one.

The small group as a source of affect. Just as the face-to-face group may support the political system by its furtherance of supportive norms, so may it support that system by providing affective outputs to its members. Relations in large organizations that engage only a part of the individual and that are specifically goal-oriented afford the individual insufficient emotional and affective ties.[46] The political system can offer some satisfaction for the individual's affective needs through emotional attachments to the symbols of the state, to a charismatic leader, or to some cause for which the state stands. But the specific demands that the larger system places upon the individual and the distance of the center of authority from the individual make it difficult for the system to satisfy his affective needs adequately. Argyris suggests that there is an inevitable conflict between the formal organization and what he calls the healthy personality, and that the more intimate face-to-face group in organizations is an adaptive mechanism whereby the affective gap is filled.[47] In political systems, such gap-filling face-to-face groups may also be found. Local political organizations, for instance, give the individual a feeling of attachment to the political system that is not gained from participation in the larger, more formal processes. Writing of the political clubs of New York, Peel states: "Since in the modern democratic state the participation of the individual in the actual working of government is reduced to a minimum, the (local political) clubs might give him what the primaries, general elections, initiative, referendum, recall, assembly and petition have failed to give him—the feeling that he is an important part of the self-governing community."[48]

The important point is that affective ties to the primary group have significant latent effects on the political system. Loyalty to the face-to-face group may lead an individual to behave in such a way as to support the larger system. Thus studies of wartime behavior in the American and German armies indicate that soliders were motivated to fight by loyalty to the primary group. The results as far as the larger systems were concerned were the same whether the soldiers fought for the democratic or the Nazi ideology. The affective security and emotional rewards given by the primary group were directly related to the soldier's ability to act effectively in regard to the larger system. As Shils and Janowitz point out: "It appears that a soldier's ability to resist (enemy propaganda) is a function of the capacity of his immediate primary group (his squad or section) to avoid social disintegration. When the individual's immediate group and its supporting formations met his basic organic needs, offered him both affection and esteem from both officers and comrades, supplied him with a sense of power, and adequately regulated his relations with authority, the element of self-concern in battle, which would lead to disruption of the effective functioning of his primary group, was minimized.[49] And it is important to note that though the attachment to the primary group was essentially a nonpolitical attachment, it functioned directly to support the political goal of the organization. "The solidarity of the German army was discovered by these studies . . . to be based only very indirectly and very partially on political convictions or broader ethical beliefs. Where conditions were such as to allow primary group life to function smoothly, and where the primary group developed a high degree of cohesion, morale was high and resistance effective or at least very determined, regardless in the main of the political attitudes of the soldiers."[50] Thus in this case, the unplanned functions of the small group served the purposes of the formal organization by performing functions of which the formal organization was incapable.

The proposition that satisfactory affective ties within the primary group will lead to behavior on the part of the individual that supports the larger political system finds confirmation in a number of studies that link radical behavior with the absence of such ties. Several authors have argued that one of the major appeals of participation in the Communist party is that its deep political ties satisfy affective needs left unsatisfied by the secondary relationships in an industrial society. The Communist cell often replaces weakened face-to-face ties in family or church.[51] A lack of face-to-face ties has been shown to be related to political instability in a number of other situations. Ringer and Sills found that political extremists in Iran tended to have fewer family, religious, and friendship ties. They engaged in individualistic recreation and reported that they received communications through the mass media rather than through visiting and talking.[52] Davies and Wada, in a study of the background characteristics of rioters and non-rioters, present tentative evidence that rioters tend to have fewer family and other primary group ties.[53]

Even the face-to-face group whose norms conflict with the formal organization may perform supportive affective functions. Thus Argyris has shown that even those informal work groups whose norms (limiting production) operate to hinder the goal attainment of the larger organization perform positive functions for that organization by satisfying needs of the workers that the organization itself cannot satisfy.[54] Similarly Fainsod suggests that the family group in Russia, even though it fosters behavior overtly opposed to the central regime performs a supportive function by serving as an escape valve. He suggests that the Bolshevik attempts to transform the country rapidly under harsh conditions despite the opposition of many Russians would have led to stronger negative reactions than the formation of family groups if these informal, self-seeking groups had not developed.[55]

Source of flexibility. Lastly, face-to-face communications may aid the achievement of the goals of the larger system by introducing an element of flexibility into the operation of the formal system. Over-conformity to the rules and directives of the formal system is a form of deviant behavior that can harm the larger system. And as Blau points out, the over-conforming bureaucrat—the stickler for rules—may behave in that manner because of ". . . lack of security in important social relationships within the organization."[56] The face-to-face group, often developing outside the structure of the formal organization, allows a flexibility in interpreting rules not possible within formal bureaucratic channels. Formal systems will, therefore, develop a tolerance for these informal structures. Thus, though the Soviet system is officially opposed to informal arrangements among administrators, it has become tolerant to some extent of these arrangements as a means of introducing flexibility into an otherwise highly formal and bureaucratized structure.[57] And the discovery of the importance of the informal organization in American administrative studies has led to attempts to put the informal structure to the use of the formal organization.

NOTES

1. Harold Lasswell, "Psychopathology and Politics," *The Political Writings of Harold Lasswell* (Glencoe, Ill.: Free Press, 1951); and T. W. Adorno, et al., *The Authoritarian Personality* (New York: Harper, 1950).

2. Else Frenkel-Brunswik, "Further Explorations by a Contributor to The Authoritarian Personality," *Studies in the Scope and Method of "The Authoritarian Personality,"* eds. Richard Christie and Marie Jahoda (Glencoe, Ill.: Free Press, 1954), 239.

3. A. Baldwin, "Socialization and the Parent-Child Relationship," *Studies in Motivation,* ed. D. McClelland, (New York: Appleton-Century-Crofts, 1955).

4. Karl Mannheim, *Freedom, Power, and Democratic Planning* (London: Routledge and Kegan Paul, 1951) 181; and Erich Fromm, *Escape from Freedom* (New York: Farrar and Rinehart, 1941) 287ff.

5. For a general discussion of this school, see Nathan Leites, "Psychocultural Hypotheses about Political Acts," *World Politics* 1 (1948): 102-119; and Margaret Mead, "The Study of National Character," *The Policy Sciences,* eds. Lerner and Lasswell.

6. David Rodnick, *Postwar Germans* (New Haven: Yale University Press, 1948); and Bertram Schaffner, *Fatherland: A Study of Authoritarianism in the German Family* (New York: Columbia University Press, 1948).

7. Geoffrey Gorer, *The People of Great Russia* (London: Cresset Press, 1949); and Dinko Tomasic, *The Impact of Russian Culture on Soviet Communism* (Glencoe, Ill.: Free Press, 1953).

8. Geoffrey Gorer, *The American People* (New York: W. W. Norton, 1948).

9. Rodnick, *Postwar Germans.* The same point is made by Fromm, *Escape from Freedom;* Schaffner, *Fatherland;* and Kurt Lewin, *Resolving Social Conflicts* (New York: Harper, 1948).

10. Cf. A. S. Maslow, "Power Relationships and Patterns of Personal Development," *Problems of Power in American Democracy,* ed. Arthur Kornhauser, (Detroit: Wayne University Press, 1957). The influence of the peer group is discussed in Sherif and Cantril, *Psychology of Ego-Involvements,* 156-347. John Dewey argues that democratic techniques must permeate the family, the school, and the community to be effective. *The Public and Its Problems,* (Chicago: Gateway Books, 1946) ch. 5 and 6.

11. James Bryce, *Modern Democracies,* vol. 1 (New York: Macmillan, 1921) 132.

12. G. D. H. Cole, for instance, maintains that men "can control great affairs only by acting together in the control of small affairs, and finding, through the experience of neighborhood, men whom they can entrust with larger decisions that they can make rationally for themselves. Democracy can work in the great States (and a fortiori between great States or over Europe or the world) only if each State is made up of a host of little democracies, and rests finally, not on isolated individuals, but on groups small enough to express the spirit of neighborhood and personal acquaintance. . . . Democracies have either to be small, or to be broken up into small, human groups in which men and women can know and love one another." G. D. H. Cole, *Essays in Social Theory* (London: Macmillan, 1950) 94-95. Cf. J. J. Rousseau, *The Social Contract* (London; Everyman's, 1931) 55.

13. David M. Levy, "Anti-Nazis: Criteria of Differentiation," *Personality and Political Crisis,* eds. Alfred H. Stanton and Steward E. Perry, (Glencoe, Ill.: Free Press, 1951). The importance of primary group participation as a basis for a democratic political system is stressed in Lewin, "The Special Case of Germany," in *Resolving Social Conflicts.*

14. Michael Crozier, "La France, Terre de Commandement," *Espirit* 25 (1957): 779-798; and Crozier, "Pour une Sociologie de l'Administration Publique," *Revue Francaise de Science Politique* 6 (1956): 750-769.

15. Charles Micaud, unpublished manuscript on the French Left, ch. 2. Micaud cites Charles Bettelheim and Suzanne Frere, who point out the low level of participation in face-to-face relations in *Une Ville Française Moyenne: Auxerre en 1950* (Paris: Armand Colin, 1950). Only eighteen percent of the men and 38 percent of the women of Auxerre visit each other. They do belong to a large number of interest groups, but these are centrally organized

with headquarters in Paris. This is supported in Roy V. Peel, *The Political Clubs of New York* (New York: Putnam's, 1945), who found that France had none of the diffuse, social-political local clubs found in American cities. A similar finding is reported by Lawrence Wylie, *Village in the Vaucluse* (Cambridge, Mass.: Harvard University Press, 1957). See also Edward C. Banfield, *The Moral Basis of a Backward Society* (Glencoe, Ill.: Free Press, 1958), for a similar, but more extreme, situation in a southern Italian village.

The view that the type of participation in the face-to-face group will be similar to the type of participation on other levels is supported by some findings in a different context from the one discussed above. It has been found in military and industrial situations that leaders of lower-level, face-to-face groups tend to stress participation of the group members in decisions if the leaders in the hierarchy above them also stress participation. The style of leadership in the higher levels of the organization is directly related to the style on lower levels. See Stanley Seashore, "Administrative Leadership and Organizational Effectiveness," *Some Applications of Behavioral Research*, eds. Rensis Likert and Samuel P. Hayes, (Paris: UNESCO, 1957), 57; and Edwin A. Fleischman, "Leadership Climate, Human Relations Training, and Supervisory Behavior," *Personnel Psychology* 6 (1953): 205-222.

16. These reasons why participation is difficult, if not impossible, in large organizations are essentially the ones suggested by Michels, *Political Parties*, 2-44, 130-135, 185-204, and passim. Cf. Seymour M. Lipset, Martin A. Trow, and James S. Coleman, *Union Democracy: The Internal Politics of the International Typographical Union* (Glencoe, Ill.: Free Press, 1956) 9-10.

17. Michels, *Political Parties*, is still the classic study on the German Socialist Party and trade unions. See also Duverger, *Political Parties*, 151-168; Oliver Garceau, *The Political Life of the AMA* (Cambridge, Mass.: Harvard University Press, 1941); and David Truman, *The Governmental Process* (New York: Alfred A. Knopf, 1951) 139-155.

18. Carter and his associates found that as group size is increased from four to eight members, a more restricted atmosphere develops. "In the group of four, each individual has sufficient latitude of space in which to behave and thus the basic abilities of each individual can be expressed; but in the larger group only the more forceful individuals are able to express their abilities and ideas, since the amount of freedom in the situation is not sufficient to accommodate all the group members." Launor Carter, et al., "The Relation of Categorization and Rating in the Observation of Group Behavior," *Human Relations* 4 (1951): 250.

Similar results are reported by Bales, et al., "Channels of Communications in Small Groups," *American Sociological Review* 16 (1951): 461-468; and by F. F. Stephan and E. G. Mischler, "The Distribution of Participation in Small Groups: An Exponential Approximation," *American Sociological Review* 17 (1952): 598-608.

19. Lipset, Trow, and Coleman, *Union Democracy*, ch. 4-9.

20. Shils, *Studies in the Scope*, eds. Christie and Jahoda, 24.

21. Schaffner, *Fatherland*, 75.

22. David Rodnick, *An Interim Report on French Culture* (Maxwell Air Force Base, Ala.: Human Resources Institute, 1953).

23. Ibid. This section does not necessarily agree with the accuracy of the descriptions by Schaffner and Rodnick. Their works are used merely as examples of the types of interaction that may take place between primary group training and political structures to influence the political behavior of the individual.

24. The problem of connecting roles in small face-to-face groups with roles in larger systems is a thorny one about which little is known. Roles in face-to-face groups—say, the role of participant in decisions or the role of leader—may be quite different from participant or leadership roles in larger systems. Authority patterns in a small group where all members communicate directly are clearly not the same as authority patterns in systems in which communication is indirect and authority figures are distant. The question of moving from analysis of roles on the small group level to analysis of roles in larger systems will be discussed below. See also Talcott Parsons, "The Small Group and the Larger Social System," *Toward a Unified Theory of Human Behavior*, ed. Roy R. Grinker, (New York: Basic Books, 1956).

25. Wylie, *Village in the Vaucluse*, 208. It is interesting to note that this political education is effective despite the fact that it is in direct conflict with the teachings of the school

civics textbooks. Ibid., 106-107. This is another example of the greater effectiveness of informal as against formal communication.

26. The study of grade-school children is by E. L. and R. L. Horowitz, "Development of Social Attitudes in Children," *Sociometry* 1 (1938): 301-308. The college student study is by G. W. Allport and B. M. Kramer, "Some Roots of Prejudice," *Journal of Psychology* 22 (1946): 9-39. These and other corroborative studies are discussed in John Harding, et al., "Prejudice and Ethnic Relations," *Handbook* ed. Lindzey, vol. II, chap. 27.

27. Berelson, et al., *Voting*, 93.

28. Ibid.; and Lazarsfeld, et al., *The People's Choice.* Of course since children usually share certain politically relevant characteristics with their parents—residence, class, religion, ethnic group—the relationship between vote of father and vote of child may not be due to family influence. The Elmira voting study attempted to test the relative weight of family influence and social characteristics. Among those having family influences and social characteristics that led in different political directions (members of the working class whose fathers had voted Republican; members of the middle class whose fathers had voted Democratic), family influence was found to play as large a role as social position. Berelson, et al., *Voting*, 88-93.

29. Gabriel A. Almond, *The Appeals of Communism* (Princeton: Princeton University Press, 1954) 221-224.

30. Herbert Hyman, *Political Socialization* (Glencoe, Ill.: Free Press, 1958), 47.

31. Lazarsfeld, et al., *People's Choice*, ch. 15, and Berelson, et al., *Voting*, 137-138.

32. See Elihu Katz, "The Two-Step Flow of Communications," *Public Opinion Quarterly* 21 (1957): 61-78.

33. Shils and Janowitz, *Public Opinion Quarterly* 12 (1948); and Alex Inkeles, *Public Opinion in the Soviet Union* (Cambridge, Mass.: Harvard University Press, 1950), ch. 5-8.

34. Duverger, *Political Parties*, 28-30.

35. Charles Micaud, "Organization and Leadership of the French Communist Party," *World Politics* 4 (1952): 318-355; and Inkeles, *Public Opinion in the Soviet Union* 84.

36. See Shils and Janowitz, *Public Opinion Quarterly.*

37. From Jean Stoetzel, "Voting Behavior in France," *British Journal of Sociology* 6 (1955): 119.

38. Berelson, et al., *Voting*, 98; and Herbert McCloskey and Harold E. Dahlgreen, "Primary Group Influence on Party Loyalty," *American Political Science Review* 53 (1960): 757-776.

39. Shils, *Policy Sciences*, ed. Lerner and Lasswell, 44.

40. L. Urwick, *The Elements of Administration* (New York: Harper, 1953) 36-39.

41. Berelson, *Public Opinion Quarterly* (1952); and Berelson, et al., *Voting*, ch. 14.

42. V. O. Key, *Southern Politics* (New York: Alfred A. Knopf, 1949) 37-38.

43. As the studies of Berelson and Lazarsfeld have shown, face-to-face contact is not necessarily in conflict with political choice on the basis of party or issue. Even decisions based on party or issue are made in a face-to-face context.

44. From an autobiographical novel by Mark Benney, *Low Company* (New York: Avon, 1952), quoted in Morton Grodzins, *The Loyal and Disloyal* (Chicago: University of Chicago Press, 1956), 42.

45. Berelson, et al., *Voting*, 100-101.

46. Raymond Bauer, Alex Inkeles, and Clyde Kluckhohn, *How the Soviet System Works* (Cambridge, Mass.: Harvard University Press, 1956), 81. See also Margaret Mead, *Soviet Attitudes Toward Authority* (New York: McGraw-Hill, 1951) 55-57. On the attempts of totalitarian societies to atomize interpersonal retions below the level of the state, see Robert A. Nisbet, *The Quest for Community* (New York: Oxford University Press, 1953), ch. 8; and Hannah Arendt, *The Origins of Totalitarianism* (New York: Harper, 1951).

That attachment to a primary group is a possible challenge to the state has long been realized. Thus Plato argues in *The Republic* that communal property and families will prevent the guardians of the state from having divided loyalties. They can then serve the state better. "Both the community of property and the community of families, as I am saying, tend to make them more truly guardians; they will not tear the city in pieces by differing about 'mine' and 'not mine'; each man dragging any acquisitions which he has made into a separate house of his own, where he has a separate wife and children and private pleasures and pains; but all will be affected as far as may be by the same pleasures and pains because they are all of one opinion about what is near and dear to them, and, therefore, they will all tend towards a common goal." *The Republic,* Book V, Jowett translation.

47. Merle Fainsod, *Smolensk Under Soviet Rule* (Cambridge, Mass.: Harvard University Press, 1958), 48-50, 92, 111. See below for a discussion of some of the positive functions these same groups perform. See also Barrington Moore, *Terror and Progress: USSR* (Cambridge, Mass.: Harvard University Press, 1954), 161. Moore writes: "From the point of view of the rulers, a 'good' friendship clique is one that aids in the execution of policy, while from the point of view of the population a 'good' clique is one that aids in the evasion of policy."

48. See Moore, *Terror and Progress* 158-160.

49. Gabried A. Almond and James C. Coleman, eds., *The Politics of the Developing Areas* (Princeton: Princeton University Press, 1960), 24-25.

50. See Chapters IX and X in Verba, *Small Groups and Political Behavior.*

51. Cf. Nisbet, *Quest for Community;* and Kahler, *The Tower and the Abyss.*

52. Chris Argyris, *Personality and Organization* (New York: Harper, 1957), 139 and passim. The fact that in large organizations affective satisfactions can be found within informal small groups is one of the major findings of the rediscovery of the small group.

53. Roy V. Peel, *The Political Clubs of New York* (New York: Putnam's, 1945), 136.

54. Argyris, *Personality and Organization,* ch. 4.

55. Fainsod, *Smolensk,* 450.

56. Blau, *Dynamics,* 188.

57. Bauer, Inkeles, and Kluckhohn, *How the Soviet System Works,* 79; and Fainsod, 151.

III. Natural-State Contexts

Small-Group Dynamics as Handles for Description and Foci for Research

In retrospect it seems clear enough why the early history of a group approach to politics can be described by several discovery/decline cycles. At least three interacting factors are involved. First, the early literature could not restrain itself. It leaped, without necessary methodological preliminaries and development, from the common perception of the influence of groups to the Group Theory of Politics. As several of the selections in the previous chapter detail, the leap-of-faith was far more ambitious than available research development warranted. The analytical superstructure, as it were, was built on unstable and inadequate foundations. Hence that superstructure was easy enough for determined critics to topple, once the general exhilaration of discovery had worn off, as it always does.

Second, the inability to distinguish types of groupings—compounded by the related but theoretically more troublesome inability to describe differences between specific groups within any one type—left the group approach vulnerable to either or both of two telling criticisms. To explain the point, recall that political scientists generally equated "group" and "pressure group." That their group theory was consequently even at its best not a "general theory" was perhaps the major charge against this casual usage. Although palpably true, this was a jarring criticism in that many group proponents presented the Group Theory as a general theory. Other critics noted that the group literatures in sociology and psychology typically dealt with primary membership aggregates, often quite small and face-to-face in character. These included street-corner gangs, groups sharing a profession or some social or legal deviance, ethnic collectivities, small societies and cultures, etc. Despite some generic similarities, it was at least not clear to these critics that pressure groups were groups in the same sense as those emphasized in the basic group literatures. This also was a telling criticism.

Third, however, evidence of group influence kept growing over the years in the sociological and psychological literatures, so declines in attention of political scientists to the group approach soon were followed by rediscoveries. For example, no sooner had the critics tamed the group approach of David Truman and his followers in the 1950s, than small-group research became perhaps the dominant theme in the social-psychological literatures. Small-group research was more difficult to quarrel with than the more general literature from which Truman had extrapolated. The relative impregnability of small-group analysis derives from obvious features: it was basically controlled research which often tested specific hypotheses, whose results often could be tested or extended in replicatory studies. But small-group research also was less malleable than the literature on which Truman had relied, and it resisted careless equations of this sort:

a group is a group is a pressure group

These three interacting features usefully frame the detailed consideration of the impact of small-group research on Political Science. In effect the influence of groups on politically relevant matters was so great and so ubiquitous, that the approach could be put down, but not for good. The problem was to find a specific level of group that was congenial to empirical research, as well as one significant to social and political life. The small group seemed to fill the bill in both particulars.

The intellectual leap from broad awareness of group influence to the Group Theory of Politics having sought too much too soon, whatever the full catalog of reasons, retrenchment became the general order of the day in the late 1950s and early 1960s. The retrenchment had two features. First, critics hammered at the excesses of many group interpretations, which had the effect of encouraging those in search of simple and sovereign models to look elsewhere. The group approach was no longer hot. Second, some observers began the slow but necessary task of establishing the relevance of groups with relatively specific characteristics in specific contexts of traditional concern to political scientists.

The shift can be expressed in simple terms without sacrificing accuracy. Early work on the group in politics was largely derivative and quite general. The common thrust thus could be expressed in such terms: Given the ubiquitous influence of groups in the social-psychological literatures, groups ought to be important in political matters. In contrast later work on the group in politics tended to emphasize detailed observations of specific small natural-state groupings whose activities had a patent political content. This new common thrust might be expressed as "such-and-such a group had these specific effects which are politically relevant." The difference in emphasis was slow in coming but massive.

Three selections below illustrate this more focused attention on specific kinds of groups in Political Science, beginning more or less with the very late 1950s. An early example of this genre of research is "Primary Group Influence on Party Loyalty" by Herbert McClosky and Harold E. Dahlgren.

Their work improves on preceding efforts in two important particulars. First McClosky and Dahlgren deliberately seek to avoid the "group is a group" simplicism. Their specific focus is on primary groups—"those small, face-to-face, solidary, informal and enduring coteries that we commonly experience as family, friendship and occupational peer groups." Second the authors postulate not only that primary groups are a unique kind of group, but also that they represent an especially important level of social organization. They explain, based on then-recent research, that "Primary groups, it now seems plain, are among the principal carriers and repositories of cultural beliefs and values. They are instrumental in launching and supporting class, religious and ethnic identifications, and are even thought to function as intermediaries between consumers and the mass media."

The orientation of McClosky and Dahlgren proved a useful one. They were variously able to explain differences in loyalty to, and identification with, political parties in terms of a range of differences between some of the primary group memberships of those involved in the study.

Ada W. Finifter extends the focus on primary groups in politics in important senses in her "The Friendship Group as a Protective Environment for Political Deviants." Not only do friendship groups have an influence on the behavior and attitudes of their members, she establishes, but such groups can also serve broader purposes as well. Thus Finifter learned that, in her sample, friendship groups apparently served to provide support for those with political attitudes differing from those dominant in the work environment she studied. Individuals having few worksite friendships strongly tended to reflect the dominant political attitudes, and to participate less in politics. She underscored the broad import of her findings in this way:

> The findings reported here have potentially profound implications for political democracy. Concern with constitutional and procedural protection for the rights and expressions of views of political minorities may be substantially irrelevant if basic social psychological processes act to discourage minorities from holding or expressing deviant views. . . . the group may function as a defense against the extragroup environment. In the event of threat, cohesive groups can stand and "fight," whereas unintegrated groups or isolated individuals "flee" and "disintegrate." This is obviously a primary concern of "mass society" theorists, who stress the breakdown of interpersonal association and the the consequent atomization of individuals in totalitarian societies.

Significantly, also, note that Finifter began with a different hypothesis than her data required that she adopt. This reflects one of the attractive side effects of research on primary groups. The small scale of the groups permits the testing of theoretical statements, both by the original researcher and in replications by others. This raises the probability that the researchers can develop increasingly useful biases, as they must inevitably leap from what seems relatively certain toward that which is still unclear.

Irwin Janis takes us an important step forward in this quick survey of attention to specific natural-state primary groups having political relevance. His "Generalizations about Groupthink" establishes that group effects work at lofty hierarchical levels, as well as in families and among friends. Janis analyzed a number of cases of significant public policy. He concludes that: "groupthink tendencies sometimes play a major role in producing large-scale fiascoes."

Group influence is thus shown to be multi-directional. McClosky and Dahlgren trace the impact of small groupings in the very essentials of politics—cultural beliefs and values that underlay partisanship. Finifter shows that groups can help protect those with politically deviant attitudes, with great potential value to a representative system. In contrast, Janis establishes how decision-making groups characterized by eight major symptoms of groupthink can whistle their way through obvious graveyards with great derivative danger to any system of government.

All three perspectives on primary groups patently recommend their intense analysis by political scientists. To say the same thing in other words, both Finifter and Janis establish the influence of small membership groups, even as they show that such influence can be put to very different uses. The implications are profound. From one perspective, to study small groups does not mean that one must have a low-level bias, either hierarchically or in terms of the significance of the issues dealt with. From another perspective, to study small groups implies being in touch with both conformity and deviance, and also with a unit of social control central in both.

Primary Group Influence on Party Loyalty

HERBERT McCLOSKY & HAROLD E. DAHLGREN

Political science, like other fields of social inquiry, has had an enduring interest in questions of stability and change. This interest—until now principally expressed in studies of the rise and fall of institutions—has lately been focused increasingly upon individual and group behavior, in a search for the influences that hold men to their political beliefs and affiliations or cause them to shift about. Such influences are important not only for the study of voting and party membership, but for "haute politique" as well—for the great and dramatic questions surrounding political loyalty, conformity, deviation, apostasy, and other states of membership or disaffiliation. Although the research reported below concentrates on the former, it is our hope that it may also cast light upon the latter. It is concerned specifically with primary groups—those small, face-to-face, solidary, informal, and enduring coteries that we commonly experience as family, friendship and occupational peer groups.

THE POLITICAL ROLE OF PRIMARY GROUPS

The belief that people who associate together come to think alike is now so thoroughly buttressed by research and daily observation that it has become commonplace. Studies have also shown that the more intimately we relate to our associates, the greater the correspondence between their views and ours. Since we interact most frequently and familiarly with the members of our own primary groups, it is mainly in these groups that our social and political attitudes are anchored. An impressive body of data supports the claim, earlier advanced by social theorists like C. H. Cooley, that the primary group is an essential bridge between the individual and the "great society," serving to transmit, to mediate, to interpret and, in the end, to sustain society's norms. Primary groups, it now seems plain, are among the principal "carriers" and repositories of cultural beliefs and values. They are instrumental in launching and supporting class, religious, and ethnic identifications, and are even thought to function as intermediaries between consumers and the mass media.[1]

Almost every major voting study furnishes additional proof that primary groups are essential links in the complex process by which political norms are indoctrinated and party preferences implanted.[2] They find, for example, that members of the same primary groups characteristically vote alike, think alike on issues, and affiliate with the same party; that voters in doubt about for whom to vote usually resolve their indecision by embracing the political preferences of their friends; that approximately three out of four young people vote as their parents do; and that the more uniform a group's

Reprinted from *The American Political Science Review*, LIII, (September 1959).

political outlook the firmer the voting intentions of its members. Homogeneity of opinion among primary group members also affects voting turnout and the level of political curiosity. People who disagree with their families or friends about politics are less apt to vote and less likely to develop or to retain an interest in politics.[3] But primary groups may help to reinforce habits of participation and interests as well as to inhibit them. Patterns of participation, as one study concluded, are "contagious"—likely to be active when voters belong to groups which are politically active and apathetic when they belong to one politically indifferent.

THEORY OF PRIMARY GROUP INFLUENCE

The singular influence exerted by primary groups on the behavior of their members arises from a number of attributes that distinguish them from other types of groups.[5] Compared with larger and more impersonal associations whose direct impact is felt only occasionally or sporadically, the members of a primary group enjoy unparalleled opportunities to make their attitudes known, to check, modify, or correct each other's views, and to bring dissenters into line. Their power is further augmented by their extraordinary capacity for rewarding conformity and punishing deviation, and, what is equally important, for doing so immediately, directly, and tangibly. Other associations, in contrast, must rely upon reinforcements that are often more distant in time, more dimly perceived, more ambiguous, and likely, therefore (as numerous experiments in the psychology of learning make plain), to be far less effective. Then too, primary groups enlarge their influence through being able to dispense (or withhold) rewards that are specially valued by their members: more than any other social institution, they have the faculty to satisfy fundamental needs for affection, acceptance, approval, and self-definition, for the grounding of values, and for the resolution of conflicting standards of conduct.[6] Should the use of rewards fail, a primary group may, and often does, win obedience by rejecting or threatening to ostracize the deviants—measures with a potency that increases in proportion as the latter esteem the group or find no alternative groups to turn to.[7]

   Primary groups have also been found to play an important part in defining the social reality we experience, which means that they not only structure certain of the ways in which we perceive the world—itself a powerful source of influence upon us—but that they also furnish us with many of our standards and with an image of ourselves in relation to these standards.[8] Since their portrait of us is obviously important for our happiness, it is not surprising that we usually try to behave as they would like us to. Yielding to a primary group and to its power to define social reality may also help us gain confidence in many of our beliefs. In fact, one reason we fraternize with like-minded people is to reassure ourselves of the wisdom and probity of our opinions.[9] Through the feedback mechanism of congenial primary alliances we frequently manage to soften the conflict between our opinion preferences on the one side and the empirical realities that crowd in upon us on the other. These alliances also furnish the social support we need to face and to discount the possibility that other people may consider our opinions false, foolish, or even base. The effect of these ministrations is, of course, to increase our dependency upon them and to permit them to impinge even more strongly upon our attitudes.

Some of the pressure for uniformity exerted by primary groups is unintentional, a mere incident of the tendency for people who associate together to arrive at common opinions, especially about subjects that are inherently ambiguous.[10] But much of their influence is deliberate, the result of the group's efforts to realize its goals and to survive. Since the governing of primary groups depends so heavily upon voluntary and informal incentives, they may require a greater measure of agreement than other associations. In a small, face-to-face group, differences of outlook stand out sharply, looming especially large in proportion to the size and intimacy of the group. Disagreements are, furthermore, difficult to confine: the ready accessibility of members to each other heightens the danger that any differences among them may spread to the entire group and divide it severely.

Partly to avoid such catastrophes, the members of small groups quickly set about to resolve disagreements that arise among them. Research has shown, for example, that when disagreements are first discovered, a disproportionate number of comments are addressed to the dissenters in the hope of persuading them to modify their opinions and to restore the group's equilibrium.[11] In general, the intensity of the effort to impose uniformity will depend on the felt relevance of the disputed opinions to the group's activities or goals. The presence of dissension not only interferes with the fulfillment of the group's purposes but also weakens its confidence in its own opinions and hence in its own viability. Finally primary groups set about to achieve unanimity not merely for the instrumental reasons cited, but for the simple reason that their members have learned to understand things in a certain way and find it puzzling and discomfiting to confront alternative ways of seeing them.[12]

HYPOTHESES AND PROCEDURES

We were concerned in the present study not merely to verify anew the connection between group membership and political orientation but to explore the role which primary groups play in strengthening or weakening party loyalty—in the contribution they make to life-long patterns of political support at the one extreme or to political apathy, vacillation, or defection at the other. We began our inquiry with a number of assumptions, e.g., that political preference is rooted in primary group memberships, changing as they change; that the parental family (family of orientation) functions to sustain as well as to initiate the political affiliations of its offspring; and that other primary groups, such as peers and the family of procreation (spouse and children), serve mainly as secondary or reinforcing agents to bolster or undermine the political predisposition implanted by the family of orientation.

The ability of the parental family to stabilize the party affiliations of any of its members would depend most critically, we thought, on the following considerations: (1) the strength of the family's initial political indoctrination, (2) the degree of unity with which its remaining members support its original preferences, (3) the extent to which the family continues to offer opportunities for affection and solidarity (cohesiveness), (4) the physical availability of the members to each other (physical distance), (5) the degree of exposure to certain life style influences (occupation, class, education, religion, etc.) that reinforce or counteract the family's initial preferences, and (6) the degree of correspondence between the political views of one's parental family and one's newer primary group alliances (e.g. friendship and occupational groups and family of procreation).

We anticipated that instability or shifts in party preference would most frequently occur (1) when the parental family has little interest in politics; (2) when one belongs to or enters primary groups with conflicting political norms; (3) when the groups that gave life to the original norms themselves change, experience conflict, or cease for whatever reason to reinforce their earlier views; and (4) closely related to this, when a voter has become estranged or physically cut off from the groups in which his political outlooks have been anchored.

Systematic inquiry into these and related matters was undertaken in 1953-1954 through a field project based on directed, two-hour interviews (conducted by professional interviewers) with a sample of 215 adults in the Twin City area of Minnesota. Since only a minority of voters reject their parents' party preferences, special procedures were employed to muster a sample of political changers large enough to be statistically useful. Essentially, we proceeded by first drawing a random, cross-section sample of the general population, and by then selecting our final sample from this pool, stratifying it purposely in such a way as to overrepresent the number of voters who favor a different party from their parents.

All respondents were presented with the same interview schedule and, wherever possible, were asked identical questions. The interview inquired in detail into the past and present life of the individual members of the respondent's family, friendship, and occupational groups, their social and intellectual background, their political habits and preferences, etc. A special effort was made to collect all vital information on the respondent's voting history and political attachments. From the copious data yielded by these questions we then constructed indexes for each of the variables that interested us, assigning index scores to each respondent according to the information elicited. Since we were compelled to rely heavily upon recall data—a risky procedure at best—we preferred to ask as many detailed, factual questions as possible, approaching the same core of information from several directions and combining each individual's answers into appropriate index scores. In this way we hoped to catch inconsistencies and to offset somewhat the failures and distortions of memory that time and prejudice are bound to introduce.[3]

More than a dozen indexes were worked out to assess such key variables as respondent's party stability, modal political orientation of his parental family, social distance between respondent's life style and that of his parental family, degree of family cohesion or solidarity, reinforcement by friendship groups and spouse, and so on. The elements from which these measures were fashioned will be set forth as we present the findings concerning them.

RESULTS: THE INFLUENCE OF FAMILY INDOCTRINATION

The observation that three out of four voters adopt the party attitudes of their parents merely begins the analysis of family influence on political preference. Not all voters, for example, maintain their affiliations with equal firmness. Some cling tenaciously to the same party, supporting its candidates regularly and without regard for their individual merit. A smaller number at the other extreme identify with a party but vote only intermittently for its candidates. Here we have called the former stable voters and the latter unstable voters. A third class of voters, who are less consistent than the stables but more consistent than the unstables, have been labelled moderately stable voters (or moderates).[14]

Whether a voter shifts or remains firm in his party support may depend on a number of political factors, including changes in social conditions and the impact of individual candidates and issues. The influence of these factors is, however, severely circumscribed by a voter's readiness to receive them. Many voters are so unfaltering in their conviction and so deaf to the opposition's appeals that no practical way can be found to disengage them from their habitual attachments; others are held so loosely to a party that any of a number of influences (a dramatic issue, an unfamiliar candidate, a compelling slogan, an alarming rumor, an unfavorable ethnic background, etc.) may be sufficient at the moment to dislodge them.[15] A voter's susceptibility to defection would, we thought, greatly depend on how firmly his party affiliations have been anchored in his primary groups, especially his family. As Table 3.1 shows, voters who share their parents' political orientation are far more likely to be consistent in their party support than voters who have rejected parental preferences. Although the latter have renounced the family's political outlook, they are unable to rid themselves of its influence entirely, and have difficulty embracing a new political loyalty without wavering. Only twenty-nine percent of them become stable voters, compared with fifty-three percent stable among voters who continue to support their parents' party.[6] Similarly, forty-three percent of the voters who disown the family's political loyalties are unstable in their adopted preferences, whereas among those who cling to the family party, few (only

TABLE 3.1

Percentage of Voters Agreeing with Party Preferences of Their Parents

Respondents are →	Republicans		Democrats		Total	
	Parents Were		Parents Were		Voter Supports Same Party as Parents	Voter Supports Different Party from Parents
	Republican	Democratic	Democratic	Republican		
Stable Voters	52.8	17.4	54.0	38.5	53.4	28.6
Moderate Voters	30.2	30.4	32.0	26.9	31.1	28.6
Unstable Voters	17.0	52.2	14.0	34.6	15.5	42.8
Sample Size*	53	23	50	26	103	49

*The sample sizes in this and the following nine tables vary somewhat. Some of the total sample of 215 voters have been excluded from one or another of our indexes or classifications owing to inappropriateness or lack of reliable information required by the particular index, e.g., voting record, family political background, marriage status, etc.

sixteen percent) turn out to be unstable.[17] Table 3.1 also suggests, for reasons we will later consider, that the Republican children of Democratic parents are, on the whole, slightly less stable than the Democratic children of Republican parents.

The present study proceeded on the hypothesis that the primary family not only launches but also helps to sustain the political loyalties of its offspring. Since many voters remain in communication with their families throughout their lifetimes, and since they are likely to have parallel life styles, the family's influence can be expected to endure far beyond the time of the original indoctrination. This expectation is in some measure borne out by the data presented in Table 3.2. There we have grouped our respondents according to the initial and current affiliations of their families, taking into account the modal preferences of the entire family, siblings as well as parents. Those whose family members were predominantly Democratic when the respondent was in his teens and who remain primarily Democratic today were placed in the D-D category. Republicans in the parallel condition were classified under R-R; while voters whose political backgrounds varied over time in any way were placed in the "Conflicted" column.

These percentage distributions show that a voter's party regularity is strongly affected by the consistency of his family's political preferences. Moving from the stable Republicans at the one extreme to the stable Democrats at the other, the frequency of respondents with an R-R pattern

TABLE 3.2

Percentage of Voters Remaining Consistent
To Party Loyalties of Their Parents
From the Time Voters Were in Their Teens
To the Present

Respondent's Prefer-ence and Stability	N	Family Political Preference*		
		R-R	D-D	Conflicted
		%	%	%
Stable Republicans	32	84.4	6.2	9.4
Moderate Republicans	23	60.9	13.0	26.1
Unstable Republicans	21	42.9	38.1	19.0
Unstable Democrats	17	23.5	35.3	41.2
Moderate Democrats	26	11.5	53.8	34.6
Stable Democrats	37	10.8	56.8	32.4

*R-R – Family preference has remained consistently Republican over the years.

D-D – Family preference has remained consistently Democratic over the years.

Conflicted – Family preference has varied or shifted over the years.

of family preference sharply declines, falling from eighty-four percent to eleven percent, while that of respondents with a D-D family background gradually increases, rising from six to fifty-seven percent. The more unstable the voter, in short, the greater the probability that his family has either shifted its past support from one party to the other or has consistently favored the opposition party. The data in the Conflicted column also suggest once again that stability among Democrats may be less dependent than Republican stability upon appropriate family influences.

Comparable inferences can be drawn from the data on family "reinforcement"—a term which has reference to the strength with which the family has, over the years, reinforced its initial political indoctrination.[18] As can be seen from Table 3.3, party regularity is significantly affected by the strength of reinforcement a voter receives from his family. If his family has been united and steadfast in its support, exhibiting the characteristics of a dependable, homogeneous, and politically aware reference group, he is far more likely to turn out a stable voter than if any or all of these conditions are absent. On a six-point stability measure in which a high score of 6.0 signifies stable support for the parents' party and a low score of 1.0 represents stable support for the opposition party, the strongly reinforced voters have a mean stability score of 4.77 while the weakly reinforced have a score of 3.89. Examination of the distributions and percentages in Table 3.3 will show these relationships in greater detail.

Findings from small group research also lead one to expect that reinforcement (and hence family influence) will be greater when its members like one another and are able to see each other often. A voter who is psychologically or physically cut off from his family should be less influenced than one who is frequently exposed to his family and hopes to win or keep its affection. To test this hypothesis a measure was developed for the pur-

TABLE 3.3

Percentage of Voters Remaining Stable According to Strength of Family Reinforcement, Democrats and Republicans Combined

Respondents' Stability	Family Reinforcement		
	Strong	Moderate	Weak
6 Stable voters, support family party	40.7	45.1	20.0
5 Moderate voters, support family party	27.1	21.6	25.7
4 Unstable voters, support family party	13.6	13.7	8.6
3 Unstable voters, reject family party	8.4	9.8	22.9
2 Moderate voters, reject family party	6.8	2.0	14.3
1 Stable voter, rejects family party	3.4	7.8	8.6
Sample Size	59	51	35
Mean Stability Score	4.77	4.75	3.89

TABLE 3.4

Percentage of Voters Remaining Stable and Family Reinforcement
Under Conditions Favorable and Unfavorable to Reinforcement,
Democrats and Republicans Combined

Respondents are	Respondents under Favorable Conditions Who Support:		Respondents under Unfavorable Conditions Who Support:	
	Same Party as Family	Different Party from Family	Same Party as Family	Different Party from Family
	%	%	%	%
Stable Voters	58.1	23.8	32.3	25.0
Moderate Voters	28.4	19.1	44.1	37.5
Unstable Voters	13.5	57.1	23.6	37.5
Sample Size	74	21	34	16

pose of classifying respondents into those who satisfy the conditions of high solidarity and low physical distance (the favorable condition) versus those who fail to meet either or both these requirements (the unfavorable condition).[19] Comparison of the two groups is presented in Table 3.4 and shows that the hypothesis is strongly supported. Frequent exposure to one's primary family and affection for its members thus have a substantial impact on the nature and stability of party loyalties. Voters who become alienated or separated from their families tend either to renounce its initial political affiliations entirely or to retain them more tenuously. Among voters who share the family's political attachments, fifty-eight percent of those in the favorable condition, but only thirty-two percent in the unfavorable condition, are stable party supporters.

Comparison of voters in the favorable and unfavorable conditions who have discarded their family preferences yields similar results, but, as our hypothesis would anticipate, in inverted form, i.e., for such voters family propinquity and solidarity serve to weaken rather than to strengthen party regularity. Among voters who have renounced the family preferences, fifty-seven percent in the favorable condition, but 37.5 percent in the unfavorable condition, are unstable. Family solidarity and interaction can thus either strengthen or weaken stability, depending on whether one shares or rejects the family preferences. The stronger the attachment to the family, the greater its influence and the more difficult it becomes to hold firmly to views of which it does not approve.

STABILITY, LIFE-STYLE, AND SOCIAL DISTANCE

Since disunity within the primary family discourages party regularity among its members, it seemed reasonable to expect disagreements between primary groups to beget similar consequences. To test this and related hypotheses, detailed information was collected on all individuals named by a respondent as his primary group associates, especially his spouse, friends, and occupational associates. In addition, however, we tried to ascertain, as carefully as possible, the memberships which define his life style, i.e., his educational, religious, and socioeconomic identifications, on the assumption that these categories of social stratification are also indirect measures of primary group affiliations. A voter who belongs to a church or social class, in other words, will doubtless be a member of some of the face-to-face groups which comprise the larger category. These smaller groups, furthermore, are often the vehicles that transmit the social and political norms of the larger aggregation. All such groups, it was assumed, have power to inspire loyalties, to set norms, to grant or withhold rewards for conformity and nonconformity, and thus to weaken or reinforce the family's influence on the respondent's political values. Retaining the family's life style should lead one to hold its preferences more firmly; placing "social distance" between oneself and one's family, i.e., attaining a higher or lower SES level than one's parents, switching to a different religion, etc., should cause one to become politically more unstable.

To assess the strength and direction of political influence arising from life-style associations, each respondent and his family were scored on a politically related "index of life-style," their scores ranging from 1.0 (Strongly Republican) to 5.0 (Strongly Democratic). Like the Lazarsfeld et al. "Index of Politicial Predisposition"[20] which it resembles in certain respects, our life-style index rested upon several assumptions about the political relevance of SES and religious group factors, along with a further assumption about the relation of education to party preference. To illustrate at the extremes, in the Twin City area a Catholic worker and trade union member who has not gone beyond grade school and whose income is small can safely be assumed to have encountered pressures that are overwhelmingly Democratic; a Congregationalist or Episcopalian businessman who has attended college and earns a high income can be supposed, on the basis of known patterns of voter preference, to have experienced a powerful thrust in the Republican direction.[21] Between these extremes, of course, voters with more heterogeneous life styles are to be found who are politically more cross-pressured.

The validity of these assumptions may be determined from Figure 3.1., where it can readily be seen that the index of life style has a strong bearing on both the direction and stability of political preference. Thus not only do Democrats and Republicans have life styles appropriate to their actual party preferences, but the variations in their life style scores correspond closely with the variations in their level of party stability. As their life-style scores approach 1.0, stable Republican preferences become more frequent; as they approach 5.0, Republican preferences give way to loyalties that grow increasingly and more firmly Democratic. Both the Republican and Democratic unstables tend to fall in the middle, or cross-pressured, ranges of the index. Although the data are not shown in the table, voters whose

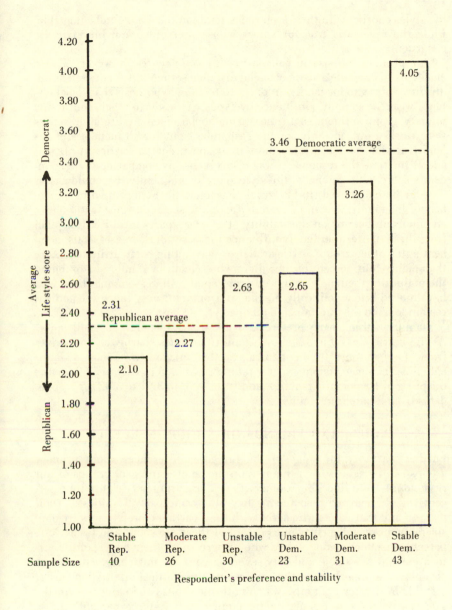

Figure 3.1. Life Style and Stability of Voter Preference

life styles conflict with their preference tend, on the whole, to be unstable, while the reverse is true for voters whose preference and life style are congruent.

Our primary purpose in calculating life-style scores, however, was to enable us to compute a score of social distance (or mobility) between an individual voter and his family, in order to test the hypothesis that social distance weakens a family's influence by exposing a voter to other, conflicting primary group influences. In measuring social distance, life style scores were worked out not only for the respondent but for all members of his family as well, taking into account their social characteristics at present and at the time the respondent was in his teens. By comparing the respondent's score with the modal life-style score of his family, we could assess how far he had moved (in his social characteristics) from the other members of his family. As can be seen in Table 3.5, social distance factors have an important bearing on the stability of a voter's party loyalties. It is plain from these figures that family influence increases or decreases as its members enter other groups with parallel or conflicting party attitudes. More than eighty-four percent of the voters who remain in a milieu favorable to the politics of the family retain its preferences, whereas among those who have moved into a politically hostile environment, only forty-five percent remain loyal to the traditional family party.

Stability within a party preference is likewise affected by social distance. As the entries in Table 3.5 show, stability declines sharply as one moves from the favorable to the neutral to the antagonistic social distance columns, the mean stability scores falling from 5.25 to 4.04 to 3.50 for the offspring of Democratic families, and from 4.90 to 3.91 to 3.32 for respondents from Republican families.

SPOUSE AND FRIENDSHIP GROUP INFLUENCE

Further warranty for some of the foregoing inferences about primary groups can be gained from the data on the spouse and peer groups of our respondents. We find, for example, that a large number (eighty-four percent) of our married respondents have the same party loyalties as their mates,[22] and that voters who agree with their partners' preferences are considerably more stable (fifty-one percent of these are stable and twenty-one percent unstable; among voters who disagree with their mates, only fourteen percent are stable and fifty-seven percent are unstable). The spouse also plays an important part in reinforcing the political orientation earlier instilled by a voter's parents. When both the spouse and parents favor the same party, the chances are overwhelming (ninety-three percent) that a voter will also favor that party; when, however, their political outlooks are diverse, the probability that a voter will remain loyal to his parents' party falls to only 28 percent.

Conflict between one's parental and acquired families also has a marked effect on the stability of voting, reducing it severely (Table 3.6). The

TABLE 3.5

Relationship Between Voter Stability, Family Preference, and Social Distance

Family Preference—Republican

Respondent's Preference	Respondent's Social Mobility Percentage (% Down)		
	Favorable (Rep)	Neutral	Antagonistic (Dem)
Republican	84.6	60.8	42.1
Democratic	15.4	39.1	57.9
Sample Size	39	23	19
Mean Stability Score*	4.90	3.91	3.32

Family Preference—Democratic

Respondent's Preference	Respondent's Social Mobility Percentage (% Down)		
	Favorable (Dem)	Neutral	Antagonistic (Rep)
Democratic	84.3	62.9	50.0
Republican	15.5	37.0	50.0
Sample Size	32	27	12
Mean Stability Score*	5.25	4.04	3.50

*The mean stability score is computed on a 6-point scale in which 6.0 represents highest party stability in the same direction as the family preference, and 1.0 represents highest stability in the direction of party opposed by the family.

TABLE 3.6

Influence of Spouse's Party Preference on Voter Stability*

Family Background	Republican Spouse's Preference			Democratic Spouse's Preference			Combined Samples Spouse's Preference		
	Strongly or Moderately Repub.	Neutral or Weak	Strongly or Moderately Dem.	Strongly or Moderately Dem.	Neutral or Weak	Strongly or Moderately Repub.	Same as Family's Strong or Moderate	Neutral or Weak	Different from Family's Strong or Moderate
Respondent's Mean Stability Scores:	5.35	4.00	2.60	5.38	4.50	2.50	5.36	4.20	2.60
Sample Size:	28	15	19	21	12	13	49	27	32

*The measure of spouse's strength of party preference is an index comprised of data on the spouse's level of political interest; frequency of voting; frequency of political discussion; intensity of party feeling; and direction of party preference. The Mean Stability Scores are computed, as before, on the 6-point scale.

stronger the political interest and preference of the spouse, moreover, the greater his or her influence on the respondent's party loyalties. But this influence can work both ways—to increase stability when husband and wife agree in their party attitudes, or to decrease it severely when they disagree. The magnitude of this influence is doubtless a function of the frequency of interactions between husband and wife, and of the solidarity ordinarily achieved by primary groups of this type. As anticipated, there was a tendency for women to switch to their husbands' preferences more often than the reverse. However, our sample of "switchers" was too small to place much confidence in this conclusion.

It should also be noted from Table 3.6 that when family background is taken into account, no difference is found between the stability of voters who marry Democrats and those who marry Republicans. A respondent from a Democratic family who marries a Republican is badly shaken in his voting habits, but no more so, apparently, than a voter from a Republican family who marries a Democrat.

Data on the friends named by our respondents, including friends at work, at church, in neighborhoods, clubs, and other social activities, furnish additional proof of the crucial role which primary groups play in stabilizing political loyalties. As Table 3.7 demonstrates unmistakably, the higher the proportion of friends who support a voter's party, the more stable his preferences: as one reads downward in the left-hand columns, from the stable Republicans through the moderate and unstable voters to the stable Democrats, the frequency of Republican peers steadily declines (from 60.8 percent to 18.8 percent) while the proportion of Democratic peers uniformly rises (from 21.2 percent to 53.8 percent). Whereas stable voters have the highest proportion of peers who share their preferences, the unstable voters draw their friends almost equally from both parties and are subject, therefore, to greater cross-pressure. But they are also politically less aware, they select their friends with less regard for political belief, and they know least about the actual affiliations of their friends; they were unable, for example, to identify the party preferences of 38.6 percent of their friends, while the comparable figure for the moderates was 30.2 percent and for the stables 23.4 percent. Whether out of anxiety or apathy, the unstables seem somewhat more inclined to avoid friendships with people who reveal strong political convictions—a practice which tends to prolong their own instability.[23]

Controlling for family background does not alter the nature or direction of these findings in any important way. Stability, as anticipated, is greatest when the loyalties of one's peers predominantly correspond with (and thus reinforce) the political outlook of one's family. However, when the majority of a voter's peers do not support the party favored by his family, the conditional probability is high (over eighty percent) that he will abandon the family's voting tradition and shift his support to the opposition. Approximately one-third of these "shifters" become stable opposition supporters.

TABLE 3.7

Relation Between Stability of Voting Preference and Percentage of Democratic and Republican Peers*

Respondents are	Total Sample		Voters from Republican Family Backgrounds		Voters from Democratic Family Backgrounds	
	Percentage of Peers Who Are		Percentage of Peers Who Are		Percentage of Peers Who Are	
	Reps.	Dems.	Reps.	Dems.	Reps.	Dems.
Stable Republicans	60.8	21.2	59.2	20.8	75.0	15.0
Moderate Republicans	43.8	21.6	47.6	21.8	50.0	26.6
Unstable Republicans	36.6	26.0	34.0	24.0	4.7	28.2
Unstable Democrats	27.4	29.2	30.0	36.6	21.4	24.2
Moderate Democrats	23.4	50.6	30.0	52.8	24.6	48.6
Stable Democrats	18.8	53.8	22.0	54.0	18.2	51.4
Sample Size	193		81		70	

*The proportions of peers named whose party preferences were unknown to the respondents have been omitted from this table. In every case, however, it would be the percentage remaining after subtracting the proportion of Republican and Democratic peers from 100 per cent: e.g., for the Stable Republicans in the total sample, the party preference of 18.0 per cent of the peers is unknown; for the Unstable Republicans, the proportion is 37.4 per cent.

The rather impressive power exerted by friends on voting behavior does not mean that they have entirely displaced the family as a source of influence. In Table 3.8, we hold friendship preferences constant and vary family background, and find the family continues under all conditions to register an impact upon the preference and stability of the offspring. As the figures show, Republican voters from Republican families are proportionately more stable than voters from Democratic families, even when the latter have as many Republican friends as the former. The same relationships hold for the Democrats when we control for the number of Democratic friends.

In considering the relative influence of family and friends, furthermore, we should keep in mind that the connection between stability and the party preferences of one's peers is not the simple, unilateral relation it may appear at first to be. Cause and effect in this matter are not always easy to distinguish. Our choice of friends is, in some measure at least, governed by our political views, and these in turn have largely been predetermined by our families. Since our families also help to fix our levels of party loyalty, they are indirectly responsible, in part, for the high correlation between voting stability and the party affiliation of friends. Unfortunately the magnitude of such indirect family influence cannot be assessed and demonstrated in studies of the type we are now considering. Its importance, nevertheless, can safely be assumed.

The data on friendship groups, it should be observed, show no significant or systematic differences in the strength of the influence exerted by Democratic or Republican peers. The correlation between voter stability and the proportion of peers with congruent preferences is .40 (sig. .001) for the Republican respondents and .37 (sig. .01) for the Democratic respondents.

TABLE 3.8

Family Influence upon Voter Stability When Frequency of Republican and Democratic Friends is Controlled

	Percentage of Stable Republican Voters			Percentage of Stable Democratic Voters	
Proportion of Republican Friends	From Republican Families	From Democratic Families	Proportion of Democratic Friends	From Democratic Families	From Republican Families
Under 20%	25.0	0.0	Under 20%	25.0	0.0
21-60%	41.6	0.0	21-60%	57.7	46.1
61-100%	69.6	50.0	61-100%	66.6	44.1
Total Republican Sample		76	Total Democratic Sample		75

PRIMARY GROUP INFLUENCES COMBINED

So far we have seen that each type of primary group registers its own separate impact on our political loyalties. What happens, however, when they are combined? Our theory suggests that their influence ought to be cumulative, becoming stronger (or weaker) as favorable (or antagonistic) units of reinforcement are added. Warranty for these expectations may be found in Table 3.9 where combined data are presented for four of the more important variables employed in the study: family reinforcement, social distance, spouse's preference, and peer group influence. Each time one of these factors supported a respondent's party preference, he was assigned a plus (+) score for that variable; each time a variable was in conflict with his preference, he was given a minus (-) score.

It should first of all be noted that group affiliations tend to be mutually reinforcing. When the total number of reinforcements was tallied for all respondents, sixty-four percent were found to be favorable (+), twenty-four percent were negative (-), and twelve percent were neutral. Regular party supporters, however, have experienced a significantly greater proportion of positive reinforcements than unstable supporters, the figures being eighty-two percent for the former and fifty-four percent for the latter.

Examination of Table 3.9 shows that seventy-four percent of the stables have been exposed to three or more positive reinforcenents (out of a possible four), while only 25.9 percent of the unstables have been so consistently reinforced. When we compute the percentages vertically, the degree to which stability depends upon the frequency and homogeneity of primary group support becomes, if anything, even more obvious. The probability that a voter will be stable if all his reinforcements are favorable is 70.5 percent; it declines sharply, however, as the number of his positive scores diminishes—dropping from seventy to fifty-eight to thirty-five and finally to seventeen percent. Similarly, if all four group reinforcements are favorable, the probability is small (only 5.9 percent) that a voter will become unstable, whereas it is quite high (64.7 percent) if only one of the four reinforcements is favorable. Clearly, party loyalty strongly depends upon the ratio of favorable to unfavorable primary group supports.

Controlling for initial family background modifies these results only in detail, for stability rises as reinforcements increase, no matter what political outlook voters have received from their families. Nevertheless, a voter who does not follow his family's preference is less likely to be stable than a voter who does, even when both have been subjected to the same number of subsequent group pressures. The impact of the family's initial indoctrination persists, in short, even if it does not always result in retention of the parents' party.

Correlations were computed which summarize and elaborate these findings somewhat. The simple correlation between family reinforcement and the level of respondent's stability is, to begin with, .27 (sig. .01). If we add social distance and compute a multiple correlation, the figure rises to

TABLE 3.9

The Combined Effect of Four Primary Group Influences (Family Reinforcement, Social Distance, Spouse, and Peer Groups) on Voter Stability

Respondents are	Number and Percentage of Favorable (+) Reinforcements*			
	1+	2+'s	3+'s	4+'s
Stable Voters	17.6	35.7	58.1	70.5
Moderate Voters	17.6	32.1	27.9	23.5
Unstable Voters	64.7	32.1	13.9	5.9
Sample Size	17	28	43	17

Respondents are	Number and Percentage of Favorable (+) Reinforcements			Voters Who Support Initial Family Preferences			Voters Who Changed from Initial Family Preferences		
	1 or 2 +'s	3 or 4 +'s	(N)	1 or 2 +'s	3 or 4 +'s	(N)	1 or 2 +'s	3 or 4 +'s	(N)
Stable Voters	26.0	74.0	(50)	18.9	81.0	(37)	46.1	53.8	(13)
Moderate Voters	42.9	57.1	(28)	36.9	61.3	(19)	66.7	33.3	(6)
Unstable Voters	74.1	25.9	(27)	66.7	33.3	(12)	78.6	21.4	(14)

* Favorable or (+) = Association with a primary group whose party loyalties are congruent with those of the respondent.

.41, with similar correlations for Republican and Democratic respondents. When spouse and peer group variables are added, the multiple correlation rises again, this time to .49.[24] Had we also been able to take account of family solidarity and propinquity (which unfortunately we could not, owing to complications involving the small size of the N), these correlations would doubtless be even higher, since family influence is increased, as we have seen, when physical and psychological distance are favorable to reinforcement.

SUMMARY AND CONCLUSIONS

The data presented in this paper largely confirm the hypotheses with which the project began and furnish additional support for some of the inferences about primary groups suggested by the Elmira study, the Maccoby study, and others. The findings make it plain that the indoctrination, retention, or shift of party loyalties is significantly related to, and often determined by, family and other primary bonds. Of course, our results do not explain stable or shifting patterns of support in particular elections; for these, as Key and Munger correctly point out, require explanations that are more immediately political, i.e., that chiefly take account of issues, candidates, or changing political conditions.[25] What the findings do show, however, is that voters differ widely in their susceptibility to political influence, and that their tendencies to shift or remain stable in response to such influence will vitally depend upon the strength and homogeneity of primary group affiliations.

Specifically, the following inferences seem warranted from our data:

1. The family is a key reference group which transmits, indoctrinates, and sustains the political loyalties of its members. Voters who support the party favored by their families develop firmer and more consistent habits of party allegiance than voters who renounce the family preference.

2. Family influence on the stability of a voter's preference increases when (a) the party outlooks of its members are homogeneous, (b) political interest and loyalty among the other members are high (this affects direction of preference more than stability, however), and (c) the same family preference has been retained over time. Family influence on party allegiance becomes stronger, in addition, when its members like and often see each other; however, these factors undermine the party loyalty of voters who have rejected the family preference. The family thus serves as a continuing agency for defining the party affiliations of its members.

3. A voter's political attachments are strongly affected by both his and his family's life style (occupation, income, education, and religion). Homogeneous life styles that are consistent with the family's political loyalties reinforce those loyalties; heterogeneous life styles, and discrepancies between life style and party preference, weaken them. Social distance, i.e., changes in life style away from the modal family pattern, diminishes family influence by placing a voter among new and often conflicting primary groups.

4. Unless they embody a party viewpoint or life style that conflicts with the family's outlook, primary groups other than the parental family, such as spouse and peer group associates, operate to reinforce the party loyalties a voter acquires from his family. The more widespread the agreement among them, and the more intense their outlook, the more stable his own party allegiance. Compared with party regulars, unstable voters are less often able to identify the political affiliations of their friends.

5. Disagreements among the several primary groups to which a voter belongs are among the most important sources of party irregularity and defection. Most voters, however, are anchored in a matrix of politically harmonious primary associations—a result, to some extent, of conscious selection and of the tendency for the social environment to bring together people of like views.

6. Democrats and Republicans were observed to differ somewhat in their response to family and other primary group influences, but the differences were neither large nor systematic enough to warrant firm generalization. If family political background is allowed to vary freely, Republican voters appear to conform more strongly than Democrats to family influence. They also appear to be less affected by changes in life style or social mobility—a result consistent with the findings reported by the Elmira study, by Maccoby, and others.[26] These inferences, which imply the greater tenacity of Republican loyalties, are misleading, however, for they overlook the consideration that some of our Republicans and Democrats were initially indoctrinated by families of a contrary political persuasion. When we took this into account and controlled for family party preference, the differences between Democratic and Republican voters either disappeared or reversed themselves: Democrats from Democratic families and Republicans from Republican families proved to be equally stable; while Democrats from Republican family backgrounds turned out, on the average, to be somewhat more stable than Republicans from Democratic backgrounds. Voters whose origins were Democratic, in short, appear more resistant to conversion than voters from Republican backgrounds. These findings could mean either that Democratic families leave a more enduring imprint on the politics of their members or—a more plausible explanation—that the balance of nonfamily forces in the Twin City community favored the Democrats. On this explanation, the apparently greater tenacity of Democratic family influence would be largely an artifact of our measurement procedures, and would arise from our inability to assess independently other important influences in the community. In any event, the belief that Republicanism is the more magnetic and enduring preference, owing to the higher status of its more visible supporters and its symbolic identification with the middle and upper classes, is not substantiated in our data. The Republican party does tend, on the whole, to be the party of status, but it is not always the preferred or prestige party. Especially since the New Deal, with its strong impact on political affiliation and perceptions, the advantage of being the prestige party belongs, in many communities, to the Democrats.

7. Reference to the role of the community environment underscores the need to observe that primary group memberships cannot, by themselves, account for all the variance in political belief and affiliation, and that other influences, such as economic interest, status needs, the mass media, the behavior of the parties themselves, etc., will often have to be considered. We should also enter the qualification that, having dealt in this research largely with party affiliations, we cannot be certain that the results can be generalized to all forms of political attachment. We have, nevertheless, proceeded on the assumption that the several forms of political support are sufficiently alike so that knowledge gained from the study of party affiliation will prove useful in the investigation of other forms of political loyalty.

NOTES

1. Cf. Charles H. Cooley, *Social Organization* (New York: Scribner, 1909), especially chs. 3, 4. For a review of current theories and research on the role of primary groups, see Edward Shils, "The Study of the Primary Group," *The Policy Sciences*, eds. Daniel Lerner and Harold Lasswell (Stanford: Stanford University Press, 1951), 44-69; Elihu Katz and Paul F. Lazarsfeld, *Personal Influence* (Glencoe: Burns and MacEachern, 1955), chs. 2-5; also Dorwin Cartwright and Alvin Zander, *Group Dynamics: Research and Theory* (Evanston, Ill.: Row Peterson, 1953), passim. Two valuable works dealing with small group influence on the formation of political attitudes have become available since this manuscript was prepared: Herbert H. Hyman, *Political Socialization: A Study in the Psychology of Political Behavior* (Glencoe: Free Press, 1959) and Sidney Verba, *The Experimental Study of Politics: The Contribution of Small Group Experiments in Leadership to the Understanding of Political Leadership*, unpublished dissertation, (Princeton University, 1959).

2. Cf. Bernard R. Berelson, Paul F. Lazarsfeld, and William N. McPhee, *Voting* (Chicago: University of Chicago Press, 1954), 88-89, 92-93, 96-97, 120-122; P. F. Lazarsfeld, B. R. Berelson, and Hazel Gaudet, *The People's Choice*(New York: Columbia University Press, 1948), ch. 15; Angus Campbell, Gerald Gurin, and Warren E. Miller, *The Voter Decides* (Evanston, Ill.: Row, Peterson, 1954), 199-206; R. S. Milne and H. C. Mackensie, *Straight Fight* (London: Hansard Society, 1954), 44-45, 123-125; Eleanor Maccoby, Richard E. Matthews, and Anton S. Morton, "Youth and Political Change," *Public Opinion Quarterly* 18 (1954): 23-29; Alice S. Kitt and David B. Gleicher, "Determinants of Voting Behavior," ibid., 14 (1950): 393-412; Mark Benney and Phyllis Geiss, "Social Class and Politics in Greenwich," *British Journal of Sociology*, 1 (1950): 324-327; Kenneth Helfant, "Parents' Attitudes vs. Adolescent Hostility in the Determination of Adolescents' Sociopolitical Attitudes," *Psychological Monographs* 66 (1952).

3. Kitt and Gleicher, "Determinants," 401-402; Berelson et al., *Voting*, 120-122; on the effects of cross-pressures of various types on the decision to vote, see Lazarsfeld, Berelson, and Gaudet, *The People's Choice*, 56-64. However, in their study of the 1952 election, *The Voter Decides*, 202-203, Campbell et al. found no connection between level of participation and membership in groups of "divided political loyalty."

4. Lazarsfeld, et al., *The People's Choice*, 142; Campbell et al., *The Voter Decides*, 202.

5. For a review of theories concerning the psychology of small group influence, see Henry W. Riecken and George C. Homans, "Psychological Aspects of Social Structure," *Handbook of Social Psychology*, ed. Gardner Lindzey (Reading, Mass.: Addison-Wesley, 1954), II: 786-832; Daniel Katz, "Social Psychology and Group Processes," *Annual Review of Psychology* 2 (1951): 137-172; C. I. Hovland, Irving L. Janis, and H. H. Kelley, *Communication and Persuasion* (New Haven: Yale University Press, 1953), ch. 5. An important attempt to elaborate and to apply a theory of group structure and influence has been made by Leon Festinger, Stanley Schachter, and Kurt Back, *Social Pressures in Informal Groups* (New

York: Harper, 1950), ch. 9; also by George C. Homans, *The Human Group* (New York: Harcourt, Brace, 1950). For summaries of small-group theory as it applies more immediately to the research problem considered below, see Henry W. Riecken, "Primary Groups and Political Party Choice,"*American Voting Behavior*, ed. E. Burdick and A. J. Brodbeck (Glencoe, Ill.: Free Press, 1959), ch. 8; and Katz and Lazarsfeld, *Personal Influence*, 34-115.

6. See E. A. Shils and Morris Janowitz, "Cohesion and Disintegration in the Wehrmacht in World War II," *Public Opinion Quarterly* 12 (1948): 280-315; also T. M. Newcomb's study of the Bennington College community in *Personality and Social Change* (New York: Dryden, 1943), and W. F. Whyte's *Street Corner Society* (Chicago: University of Chicago Press, 1943).

7. For experimental data bearing on these tendencies, see Stanley Schachter, "Deviation, Rejection, and Communication," *Journal of Abnormal and Social Psychology* 46 (1951): 196-207; Kurt Back, "Influence through Social Communication," ibid, 9-23; H. H. Kelley and E. H. Volkhart, "The Resistence to Change of Group Anchored Attitudes," *American Sociological Review* 17 (1952): 453-465; L. Festinger and John Thibaut, "Interpersonal Communication in Small Groups," reprinted in G. E. Swanson. T. M. Newcomb, and E. L. Hartley, *Readings in Social Psychology* (New York: Holt, 1952), 125-133. For evidence that group influence may be exercised even in the absence of cohesiveness see the landmark experiments by S. E. Asch and M. Sherif, brief descriptions of which are available, ibid., 2-11; and 249-262.

8. Festinger, Schachter, and Back, *Social Pressure*, 168-176; Katz and Lazarsfeld, *Personal Influence*, 53-56.

9. The theoretical statement and summary of research bearing on these processes are set forth most thoroughly by Leon Festinger, *A Theory of Cognitive Dissonance* (Evanston: Row, Peterson, 1957).

10. See Sherif, *Readings in Social Psychology*.

11. Festinger and Thibaut, *"Interpersonal Communication"*; Schachter, *"Deviation."*

12. Katz and Lazarsfeld, *Personal Influence*, 62.

13. The interview schedule is too lengthy, and the manner of constructing the indexes too complex, to be described in detail in this paper. Information concerning them may be had upon request, however, through the Laboratory for Research in Social Relations, University of Minnesota.

14. The classification of voters as "stable," "moderate," or "unstable" was determined from their responses concerning present party preference; first vote; first presidential vote; presidential candidates supported in 1944, 1948, 1952; present preferences in congressional and state elections; self-description of voting habits and consistency of party support; etc.

15. The effect of such factors on stability of preference was explored in an unpublished study by Herbert McClosky and Norris C. Ellerston, carried out through the Laboratory for Research in Social Relations. The degree to which voters responded to these factors was found to be determined largely by the stability of their party attachments.

16. Unless otherwise indicated, all differences discussed are statistically significant at or beyond the .05 level.

17. Apparently these relationships are also somewhat affected by the strength of the family's indoctrination, the more strongly indoctrinated favoring the party of their parents more frequently and consistently than the weakly indoctrinated. The differences are not large, however, and are only significant at the .07 level. Possibly our measure of "strength of family influence," resting as it does on retrospective reporting, is too insensitive to give full scope to this variable.

18. The "index of family reinforcement," which was built to measure this variable, takes into account the initial and current party outlook of each family member, siblings as well as parents. It includes the direction and intensity of the initial indoctrination and of all adult members of the family at present, all of which are scored in relation to the respondent's party preference. The "intensity" scores, in turn, take into account levels of political interest, frequency of political discussion with parents and siblings, strength of party attachment among the several family members, etc.

19. The measure of "physical distance" took into account place of residence of each family

member, the actual geographic distance between them, and the average number of times respondent saw each of them. The cohesiveness measure was comprised of a scale of items testifying to various aspects of family harmony and solidarity, which was principally developed, and generously made available to us, by Luther T. Jansen. See his "Measuring Family Solidarity," *American Sociological Review* 17 (1952): 727-733. We should have liked, of course, to allow "cohesiveness" to vary while controlling for "physical distance" (and conversely), so that we could measure the effect of each of them separately. The size of the samples did not make this feasible, however, so we paired them in this way.

20. Lazarsfeld, Berelson, and Gaudet, *The People's Choice*, ch. 3. The Index of Political Predisposition combines three criteria—occupation, religion, and rural-urban residence—in ascertaining a voter's "natural" party predisposition. Ours was an urban sample, which meant that we could not employ the rural-urban criterion at all. Our index also differs from Lazarsfeld's in that its SES rating took into account income as well as occupation. Furthermore, we did not rely on the Catholic-Protestant distinction alone, but took into account the rate of church attendance and the Republican or Democratic predispositions of the specific Protestant denominations. Finally our index also used education as a criterion. Each of these was weighed and combined into a single life style score for each respondent. In determining the weights for the index we are indebted to Angus Campbell and the Survey Research Center for making available to us in advance data on the demography of party affiliation from their 1952 election survey.

21. For voting patterns arising from religious affiliation, see W. and B. Allinsmith, "Religious Affiliation and Politico-Economic Attitude: a Study of Eight Major U. S. Religious Groups," *Public Opinion Quarterly*, 12 (1948): 377-389.

22. Cf. Campbell et al., *The Voter Decides*, 201; Maccoby et al., *"Youth and Political Change,"* Lazarsfeld et al., *The People's Choice*, 140-145.

23. The Elmira study found, for example, that voters, and especially uncertain or undecided voters, avoid talking with people who hold different views. See R. H. Baxter, "Interpersonal Contact and Exposure of Mass Media during a Presidential Campaign," unpublished dissertation (Columbia University, 1951).

24. The multiple correlation for stability, family reinforcement, spouse, and peer group preference is .49, even if social distance is omitted. This is consistent with our assumption that social distance variables can, for many purposes, be viewed as indirect measures of primary group membership.

25. V. O. Key and Frank Munger, "Social Determinism and Electoral Decision: The Case of Indiana," in Burdick and Brodbeck, *American Voting Behavior*, ch. 15.

26. Maccoby et al., *"Youth and Political Change"*; Berelson et al., *Voting*.

The Friendship Group as a Protective Environment for Political Deviants

ADA W. FINIFTER

> There is a limit to the legitimate interference of collective opinion with individual independence: and to find that limit, and maintain it against encroachment, is as indispensable to a good condition of human affairs as protection against political despotism.[1]

The importance of groups as mediators between individuals and the larger society is a persistent theme of theories of political democracy. From the perspective of the development of the individual's political role, groups are typically seen as socializing agencies, affecting the basic values, attitudes and political skills of their members.[2] At the same time groups are credited with playing a vital role in preventing political totalitarianism by insulating individuals from the direct influence of the state and by providing arenas for the development and expression of minority points of view.[3] Thus the relationship between the individual and the group may be viewed from at least these two complementary perspectives: (1) the influence of groups on the attitudes and behavior of members, and (2) the process by which individuals join together in groups to express and protect their political beliefs. Depending on the perspective adopted, the hypotheses which are important to study will vary considerably.

Drawing on the first perspective, the present research began as an attempt to specify the conditions under which small, informal, ostensibly nonpolitical groups affect the political attitudes and behavior of members. The basic assumption was that primary groups tend to transmit and reinforce the norms and values of the larger culture of which they are a part. Because the influence of groups on their members depends on the existence of affective ties among members, groups with stronger ties and more cohesive structures are more effective in transmitting norms and values than weakly integrated groups, where deviant opinions are more likely to go unsanctioned or sanctions to be ineffective because of the low psychological investment of members in the group. I therefore expected that the more highly members were integrated into their primary groups, the more they would be influenced by the group and the more their attitudes would be consistent with the norms and values of the larger cultural groups to which these primary subgroups belong. I found, however, that high integration within the primary group tended to be associated with holding deviant political opinions. This and other initial

Reprinted by permission of *American Political Science Review* LXVIII, (June 1974).

findings strongly suggested that, for the particular groups and attitudes studied, the relationship should be viewed from the second perspective, emphasizing the effect of attitudes on individual integration into social groups. Working with derivations from available theory, further exploration of the data suggested that the propensity to form small friendship groups is a function of the perception of oneself as a political deviant. That is, the relationship between attitudinal similarity and the forming of friendships is not a simple one. Political deviants, but not political conformers, were motivated to form friendships on this basis. The friendship group seems to protect the deviant from a hostile political environment. The data indicate also that the group provides social support for the active expression of minority points of view, in that deviants who are socially isolated are more likely to withdraw from political participation. Thus, while the study began with an image of the individual being acted upon by group forces, the analysis suggests, rather, that individuals are active agents in the construction of their social groups, and that these social groups are formed on the basis of prior attitudinal factors. The groups then serve as protective environments for individuals whose attitudes deviate from those of the culture around them.

PRIMARY GROUPS IN THE ATTITUDE FORMATION PROCESS

A basic way that groups influence the attitudes and values of their members is by generating a group culture which defines certain values as correct or proper. Through the selective application of sanctions, "correct" (i.e., group-supported) attitudes and values are then rewarded and "incorrect" ones are punished. Basic dependence on groups for social approval generally makes this process very effective. The threat of sanction often is not necessary to induce conformity to group norms. Numerous experiments (by Asch and others) demonstrate that the mere expression of unanimity by other group members induces conformity in most subjects even when the groups have no history or continuity and the subject's own sense perceptions tell him that the group is wrong.

In persuasive interactions, primary groups are more influential than larger groups because strong affective bonds tend to develop among primary group members.[4] Expulsion from the group or isolation from other members is then particularly painful. For example Langton and Jennings found that a major reason why mothers generally have a stronger influence than fathers in the political socialization of children is that most children feel a stronger sense of attachment to their mothers.[5] Similarly Middleton and Putney report that students who felt distant from or hostile to their parents were much more likely to deviate from their parents' political positions than students who had warm affective relationships with their parents.[6] In general, then, primary groups that develop relatively strong bonds among members are more effective in influencing them and in encouraging normative and attitudinal conformity and homogeneity. From the individual perspective, group members who develop strong bonds with others in the group should be more affected by the normative climate of that group.

Since the norms that primary groups enforce are usually those of the larger social structure of which they are a part, many large organizations establish networks of smaller, more intimate primary groups as a way of propagating organizationally supported norms. The Communist party, through the cell structure, is perhaps the ideal typical example of the use of primary groups to transmit organizational norms. The basic process also is exemplified, however, in the subcommittees, task forces, and social and educational subgroups set up by churches, unions, business firms, and other organizations in all societies.

THE DATA

The data were collected in early 1961 as part of a study of political communication during the Kennedy-Nixon presidential campaign.[7] The primary groups studied were work groups in the large automobile plants in the Detroit area. All work groups within all plants in the Western Greater Detroit Region (IA) of the United Auto Workers union were defined as the universe of interest. A "work group" was defined as all individuals supervised by a given foreman. Twenty-four work groups of from ten to forty-five members were selected for the sample.[8] We attempted to interview every member of each selected work group. The overall response rate was 79 percent; the median group rate was 82 percent. The final N was 419. Twelve individuals who did not provide sociometric data for the friendship integration index were omitted, so that the basic N for most of the present report is 407.

OPERATIONALIZING INTEGRATION INTO SOCIAL GROUPS

To some extent measures of individual integration into social groups depend upon how one conceptualizes cohesion at the group level. Once group cohesion is defined, the degree to which an individual shares in a group's cohesiveness may then be derived from the group level concept. In this study, group cohesiveness was conceptualized as the strength of interpersonal ties among group members.[9] The measure of the individual's integration into the group therefore had to indicate the extent to which he interacted with other group members.

As a part of a battery of questions on social relations in the plant, each worker received a card listing all other members of his work group and was asked, "Of the people who work under your foreman, which five would you say you are most friendly with?" These friendship choices were the raw data from which sociometric matrices were constructed for each group. The number of reciprocated choices for each individual is the operational measure of integration into the work group.[10] Since it is based on a question specifying "friendliness" as the choice criterion, the measure is designated as "friendship integration." The friendship integration scores ranged from 0 to 10, with a mean score of 1.79.

TABLE 3.10

Validation of Number of Reciprocated Choices as a Measure of Friendship Integration

	Number of Reciprocated Choices				
	None	One	Two	Three+	Total
a. Length of time on current job					
Less than three years	30%	27	27	16	100%(140)
Three years or more	20%	20	28	32	100%(267)
Gamma=.27					
b. Is this the kind of job where you can talk with people around you while you are working?					
No	29%	23	26	22	100%(121)
Yes	21%	22	28	29	100%(286)
Gamma=.15					
c. During the last campaign did you discuss politics with any of the people who work under your foreman? (Number discussed politics with)*					
None	26%	27	26	21	100%(160)
1-4 persons	15%	25	34	26	100%(116)
5 or more persons	14%	14	31	41	100%(104)
Gamma=.28					
d. Work group size					
8-16	21%	24	29	26	100%(137)
17-21	31%	22	20	27	100%(149)
22-32	17%	21	36	26	100%(121)
Gamma=.04					

*Twenty-seven individuals who came into their current work groups after the election campaign are omitted from this table.

While the number of reciprocated friendship choices has high face validity as a measure of interpersonal communication and the individual's integration into the group, further validation tests were undertaken (Table 3.10). First, the number of reciprocated choices increases as a function of time spent on the job. Second, jobs which permit talking with others tend to facilitate the development of friendships. The most directly relevant validation test, however, was the association between number of reciprocated choices and political discussion in the work group. This relationship also suggests the specifically political relevance of friendship choices, which is a central theme of this analysis. Finally, since sociometric measures may sometimes yield scores that reflect the number of people available for choice rather than substantive concepts,[11] the absence of a correlation between the number of reciprocated choices and group size was reassuring.

FRIENDSHIP INTEGRATION AND POLITICAL ATTITUDES

A basic working assumption of the study was that the more integrated an individual is into his work site primary group, the more subject he is to its political influence. In a pluralistic society, however, we need to ask with which larger social group or organization will a given primary group associate itself as a source for its political norms?[12] For the work groups studied here, political norms of the major secondary groups to which the workers belong converged substantially toward support for the Democratic party. Each such additional source of support for the Democratic position should then serve to reinforce the others. In the absence of opposing attitudes, primary group integration should therefore increase support for these consensual norms.

The workers belonged to at least two dominant subcultures favoring the Democrats. The first is the blue-collar, working class subculture in general. The historical association of the working class with the party of Roosevelt is well known, and in 1960-61, this association was still strong. For example, 43 percent of the labor sample described themselves as strong Democrats as opposed to only 21 percent of the Survey Research Center national sample of the same year. Eighty-two percent of the labor sample preferred Kennedy over Nixon in the 1960 presidential election, while the national sample split 49.5 percent to 50.5 percent. Moreover the United Auto Workers had given consistently active support to Democrats in national and local elections, donating both money and campaign workers. Media support also was strong. In addition to the national newspaper received by all union members, all locals had newspapers that supported Democratic candidates. The UAW also sponsored a twice-daily radio program (Guy Nunn's "Eye-Opener" and "Shift Break") which presented heavily anti-Nixon, pro-Democratic material. In sum the major membership groups of the respondents were strongly Democratic. Because their work groups were viewed as subgroups of this Democratic political environment, I hypothesized that the level of friendship integration in the primary group would be positively associated with pro-Democratic attitudes.

Three related indicators of pro-Democratic attitudes were used to test the hypothesis: support for the 1960 presidential, gubernatorial, and senatorial candidates of the Democratic party. In each case not only did the data fail to support the hypothesis, but the relationships were strong enough to suggest a stable pattern in the opposite direction—that is, that friendship integration was associated with decreasing support for Democratic candidates. The pattern clearly suggested that the workers with higher levels of friendship integration were simply more likely to be Republicans than the less integrated workers. This was indeed the case. For example, of workers with no reciprocated choices at all, sixty percent were strong Democrats and only three percent were Republicans, while of those who had three or more reciprocated friendships, only thirty-one percent were strong Democrats while fifteen percent were Republicans. Thus as the level of friendship integration increased, the proportion of Democrats became smaller and the proportion of Republicans larger.

The discovery that friendship integration was negatively related to identification with the Democratic party threw into question not only the initial hypothesis relating integration to political attitudes but also the underlying assumption that friendship integration should be viewed as an independent variable and political attitudes as the dependent variable. It seemed highly unlikely that basic partisan loyalties, known to be among the most stable of all political attitudes,[13] would be disrupted by friendships formed as an adult. Indeed only twenty-two percent of the total sample indicated that they had ever had some other party identification, and since this group includes independents who previously identified with a party, the amount of cross-party conversion is overstated. Moreover, of those individuals who indicated that their basic partisan predisposition had changed, only thirty-five percent said that this change had occurred in the previous seven years, the average length of time on the current job. Thus to the extent that friendship integration is associated with Republican partisanship, friendship within the work group probably did not affect these attitudes, particularly the basic party identification. Work group relationships may be capable of reinforcing dominant political attitudes, as the original hypothesis suggested, but it seems less likely that they could cause counternormative change. Rather the relationship suggests that political attitudes operate in some way to affect friendship integration.

As a check on the presumed temporal order of this relationship, a measure of past political behavior (the individual's vote in 1956) was used. Even though many more people voted Republican in 1956 than in 1960, the magnitude of the relationship between 1956 presidential vote and friendship integration was about the same as the relationships involving current political behavior, and it was in the same direction. However, forty-five percent of the sample were not at their present job during the 1956 election, so that many, if not most, of the present friendship ties could not have existed then (barring joint movement of friends from job to job). If most of the present friendship ties were not in existence in 1956, they could not have influenced 1956 voting behavior; however, the friendship ties could be a product, developed in the intervening years, of attitudes associated with a Republican vote in 1956. This relationship can therefore be interpreted as further evidence that political attitudes probably influence friendship patterns rather than the reverse.

TABLE 3.11

Party Identification and Friendship Integration*

Reciprocated Choices	Strong Democrats	Weak Democrats	Independent Democrats	Independent Independents	All Republicans**
None	32%	22%	19%	9%	7%
One	23%	17%	12%	34%	38%
Two	26%	28%	47%	20%	15%
Three or more	19%	33%	22%	37%	40%
	100%	100%	100%	100%	100%
	(174)	(94)	(59)	(35)	(40)

Gamma = .22

*Five individuals who had no or refused to state their party identification are omitted from this table.
**To achieve a more stable estimate, Strong Republicans (15), Weak Republicans (15), and Independent Republicans (10) are combined in this category.

The basic relationships between friendship integration and both party identification and presidential preference, viewed from this new perspective, are presented in Tables 3.11 and 3.12. As we traverse the party identification scale toward the Republican end, the level of friendship integration rises fairly consistently. Similarly Nixon supporters tend to have more friends than Kennedy supporters. What can account for the differences in levels of friendship integration among these political groups?

TABLE 3.12

Presidential Preference and Friendship Integration*

Reciprocated Choices	Voted for or Preferred	
	Kennedy	Nixon
None	28%	5%
One	20%	33%
Two	28%	29%
Three or more	24%	33%
	100%	100%
	(322)	(70)

Gamma = .26

*Fifteen individuals who didn't know or refused to state their presidential preference are omitted from this table.

REPUBLICAN AUTO WORKERS AS POLITICAL DEVIANTS

In viewing partisan attitudes as the independent variable in the relationship between attitudes and friendship integration, it is important to understand the meanings which political attitudes have for the individuals who hold them. By considering how attitudes are useful to individuals, the ways in which they motivate behavior can be clarified. While social psychologists have posited many needs that attitudes fulfill, two are particularly germane in this context. Smith, Bruner, and White suggest that opinions play a critical role in people's social adjustment and in facilitating their relations with others. "[I]t is by holding certain views that one identifies with, or indeed, differentiates oneself from various 'reference groups' within the population . . . The act of holding certain opinions . . . is an act of affiliation with reference groups. It is a means of saying, 'I am like them.' "[14] This act of affiliation does not merely express a need for conformity. "A wide variety of psychological mechanisms is at work, motivating us to relate our destinies to those of the concrete membership groups around us and to those of the more remote reference groups to which we adhere. Requirements of ego defense, dependency needs, drives for autonomy, hostility, drives for status, and many other dynamisms may be involved."[15]

Similarly Rosenberg posits that a prime gratification of political behavior is the use of political orientations as unification devices to affirm group cohesion, to "lubricate social relationships," and to establish interpersonal relations. Additionally politics may serve as a source of gratification by providing "personal strength by immersal in movements which give support and a feeling of belongingness to individuals."[16]

These needs that attitudes serve suggest an explanation for why Republicans and independents tend to have higher friendship integration scores than Democrats. As indicated above, the political environment of this sample is overwhelmingly Democratic. Not only is this true of the work situation, but also of the local area in which most workers live. In 1956-1960, Wayne County was fifteen percent more Democratic than the state of Michigan in virtually every election contest. The Democratic share of the two-party vote usually ran around sixty-seven percent. Even in Eisenhower's 1956 victory, in which he received fifty-six percent of the state's vote, Wayne County gave fifty-eight percent of its votes to Stevenson. In 1960, when Michigan reflected the national split by voting 51-49 for Kennedy, he received sixty-six percent of the county's votes. In this context the farther one departs from identifying as and voting Democratic, the more one objectively becomes a political deviant and the more likely one will so perceive oneself. If attitudes do serve to unite individuals to groups in their environments, this function clearly cannot be served by a Republican or independent stance in an environment where most people are strongly Democratic. Republicans in such a situation may therefore have little political contact outside the work group and attempt to compensate for this by increasing work group friendships. This seems somewhat paradoxical because the work group itself, of course, is made up predominantly of Democrats. Yet it is a social situation in which people are together for long periods of time, where there are extended opportunities for interaction, and in which individuals may therefore exert special efforts to serve a variety of personal needs.

Tables 3.13a and b show that Republicans do talk about politics much less than Democrats with friends outside the factory and in the voluntary organizations to which they belong. (Data not presented here indicate that the same pattern holds for political discussion in the family and among neighbors and relatives.) It is particularly interesting that Republicans are

TABLE 3.13

Party Identification and Extent of Political Discussion

	Strong Democrats	Weak Democrats	Independent Democrats	Independent Independents	All Republicans
a. With Nonwork Friends*					
Not much/none	61%	68%	68%	69%	82%
Some/a lot	39%	32%	32%	31%	18%
	100%	100%	100%	100%	100%
N	(174)	(94)	(59)	(35)	(40)
Gamma = .19					
b. With Members of Clubs, Groups, or Organizations**					
Not much/none	72%	82%	95%	80%	94%
Some/a lot	28%	18%	15%	20%	6%
	100%	100%	100%	100%	100%
N	(58)	(22)	(13)	(15)	(17)
Gamma = .34					
% Belonging	33	23	22	43	42
c. In the Work Group***					
No	48%	42%	27%	47%	32%
Yes	52%	58%	73%	53%	68%
	100%	100%	100%	100%	100%
N	(157)	(89)	(55)	(34)	(40)
Gamma = .17					

*"And how much did you talk about politics with your friends who aren't neighbors or don't work at your plant?"

**Body of table includes only the 125 respondents who belonged to any club, social group, or other organization. These respondents were asked, "How much do you talk about politics with the members of this group?"

***"During the last campaign, did you discuss politics with any of the people who work under your foreman?"

more likely than Democrats to belong to voluntary organizations (last line of Table 3.13b), but the relationship between partisan loyalty and political discussion suggests that these organizations are not likely to provide outlets for political expression. From these relationships we can infer that as deviance increases, opportunities for sociopolitical communication tend to decrease.

Despite the consistency of the relationship between party identification and political discussion in nonwork contexts, it does not hold for political discussion in the work group. Of the six contexts for political discussion about which respondents were queried, only in the work group did Republicans report as much political discussion as Democrats; furthermore, discussion about politics tended to increase with political deviance (Table 3.13c). This departure from the previous relationships indicating less discussion on the part of political deviants in other social contexts suggests that the work group may be serving a special function for individuals who deviate from the prevailing political norms of the larger culture. Far from reinforcing the predominant political norms, the work group apparently provides a haven and source of reintegration for those whose political views differ from others' in their nonwork social environments. While it might seem easier for deviants to find likeminded friends in contexts less Democratic than the factory, Tables 3.12a and b demonstrate that they apparently do not. Perhaps the relatively large number of hours spent at work encourages a stronger effort here than elsewhere. We will return to this general question below.

THE MOTIVATIONAL DYNAMICS OF THE RELATION BETWEEN DEVIANCE AND INTEGRATION

Given the affiliative function served by attitudes, at least three complementary theories can help explain why deviants should be more motivated than conformers to seek friends in their work groups:

1. Deviating from group norms increases anxiety and a sense of isolation because the deviant is rejected by the group.[17] He therefore seeks relationships in other groups to reduce anxiety and isolation and to increase social support.[18]

2. Deviance from a group norm leads the person to question his opinions, and motivates an evaluation of them. Evaluation is achieved through comparison of one's own opinions with those of other people.[19] Therefore the need for evaluation motivates affiliative behavior.

3. Deviance from a group norm arouses cognitive dissonance. One way of reducing dissonance is to seek additional social support for the deviant opinions, thereby adding new information consonant with one's opinions.[20] New cognitions to bolster deviant opinions might be found by increased interaction with others who hold similar attitudes.

These explanations are not contradictory in any way and all three dynamics probably operate for the political deviants in this sample. Their decreased political communication outside the work group suggests that they may be rejected by others in a variety of social contexts.[21] They are therefore likely to take advantage of the extended opportunities for interaction in the work group to satisfy their psychological needs for affiliation and social support. This is done by forming many more friendships than others not so deprived in other social groups and unencumbered by the psychological needs of the deviant.

For Democrats in this sample, the work group is politically and psychologically less important. Needs for political expression can be satisfied by talking with family, friends, and members of clubs and other groups to which they belong. But for Republicans, the work group is an important source of political association. By establishing friendship relations there, they reduce social anxiety at the same time that they can express and evaluate deviant political opinions and receive support for them.

"SYSTEMATIC REPLICATION" OF THE FINDINGS

How much confidence can we have in the ex post facto interpretations developed above to explain the relationship between political attitudes and friendship integration? Since the explanatory ideas were generated from findings on this data set (even though an extensive body of theory supports the explanation offered and presumably could have been used to generate the correct hypotheses beforehand), the data cannot then be claimed to support the ideas. The conventional solution to this problem is to collect a fresh set of data on which the hypotheses can be tested (or to implore others to do so).

Because the type of data necessary to test these hypotheses is relatively difficult to collect (i.e., individuals in natural groups), and because some immediate sense of the reliability of the findings is inherently useful, a way to replicate the findings and test the explanation on the present body of data would be particularly desirable. The method chosen is the one used so powerfully by Durkheim in his classic study of suicide, that of subgroup analysis and comparison.[22]

The explanations offered for the relationship between political deviance and friendship integration can be used to deduce hypotheses about the conditions under which the original relationship should be weaker or stronger, and in this way the hypothesis developed on the basis of the findings can be tested on the same body of data which generated it. This procedure satisfies to a significant extent the reservation mentioned above. We will be replicating by analyzing the same relationship in several different subgroups. These replications are systematic because the subgroups used are chosen on the basis of certain theoretical properties which are relevant to a test of the explanation offered for the original relationship.[23]

The logic of the explanatory propositions offered above suggests that the strength of the relationship between political deviance and number of friendships in the work group should vary as a function of the extent to which the attitudes are in fact deviant for particular individuals. If the worker belongs to social groups in which having pro-Democratic attitudes is not a strong norm, other partisan attitudes are less likely to be defined as deviant and to lead to anxiety, dissonance, or a need for opinion evaluation.

The replication strategy used here is therefore to locate especially pro-Democratic social groups within the overall sample, and to examine the political deviance-friendship integration relationship in these groups in comparison with others in which support for the Democrats is weaker. Since the explanatory hypotheses rest on the assumption that objective deviants perceive themselves as deviants and that it is this self-perception that motivates affiliative behavior, it follows that, where the pro-Democratic norm is stronger, the affiliative reaction to deviance should be greater.

This hypothesis and replication strategy can be applied to several (to some extent overlapping) groups:

Race. Since the Depression era, the proclivity of blacks to vote for the Democrats has been steady and reliable. In the 1956 election, thirty-three percent more blacks than whites living outside the South voted for the Democratic presidential candidate.[24] While the 1960 election actually represents one of the low points of black support for Democratic candidates in the postwar era, sixty-eight percent of blacks did vote for Kennedy, as compared to only forty-nine percent of whites.[25] Given this relatively strong pro-Democratic tendency, we would expect that Republicanism among blacks should motivate friendship integration to a greater extent than among whites.

Religion. While the religious polarization of the vote decreased between 1948 and 1956,[26] Catholics were still considerably more inclined than non-Catholics to vote Democratic in 1956; in 1960, when the popular vote was almost evenly split between the candidates, Catholics split 80-20 in favor of John Kennedy.[27] Therefore we expect that political deviance among Catholics will have greater effects than among non-Catholics.

Social class. The inverse relationship between measures of social class and Democratic partisanship has been demonstrated many times. Occupation, the status variable usually most strongly related to voting behavior, is virtually a constant in the present study. Formal education and income, however, vary somewhat and are also moderately related to partisan attitudes. Therefore it is hypothesized that because of their stronger pro-Democratic norms, the positive relationships between deviant partisan attitudes and friendship integration will be stronger in the lower educational and income groups than in the upper groups.

Membership in the UAW. Since the union has a history of vigorous support for Democrats, we can expect that the pro-Democratic norm grows stronger the longer one has been exposed to this union activity. It is therefore hypothesized that the relationship between political attitudes and friendship integration is stronger among longer-term than for short-term members of the UAW.

If political deviance is what leads to an intensified motivation for friendships in the work group, then for each of the social classifications mentioned above, the relationship between political attitudes and friendship integration should be stronger in those subgroups that have the stronger Democratic norm. Thus, five subhypotheses have been generated from the major explanatory hypothesis. The relationship between political attitudes and friendship integration in the work group will be (1) stronger for blacks than for whites, (2) stronger for Catholics than for non-Catholics, (3) stronger for individuals with less education than for those with more education, (4) stronger for individuals with lower incomes than for those with higher incomes, and (5) stronger for individuals who have belonged to the UAW for a longer period of time than for those who have belonged for fewer years.

The data testing these hypotheses are presented in Table 3.14. The table

TABLE 3.14

Relationships (Gamma) Between Political Attitudes and Friendship Integration, in the Total Sample
and by Selected Demographic Characteristics*

	Party Identification	Presidential Preference
Whole sample (N=402; 392)**	.22	26
Race		
Blacks (54; 52)	.38	.51
Whites (348; 340)	.19	.22
Religion		
Catholic (155; 154)	.31	.43
Non-Catholic (247; 238)	.16	.22
Education		
Non-high school graduates (277; 271)	.25	.38
High school graduates (125; 121)	.02	-.02
Hourly Rate of Pay		
Less than $3/hour (286; 279)	.24	.26
$3+/hour (112; 109)	.12	.12
Length of membership in UAW		
15 years or more (300; 292)	.25	.35
Less than 15 years (102; 100)	.05	.01

*Friendship integration, party identification and presidential preference are coded as in previous tables. Pro-Republican attitudes received higher values so that the correlations may be considered as measures of the relationship between political deviance (i.e. Republicanism) and friendship integration.
**The base Ns for the party identification and presidential preference correlations are 402 and 392, respectively. Subcategory Ns are provided in the same order. There were four cases of missing data for hourly rate of pay.

is arranged so that the more Democratically oriented group in each classification appears on the upper line. Thus for each attitude and each classification, the prediction is that the correlations will be larger on the first than on the second line of each pair. Without exception, the hypotheses are supported.[28]

TABLE 3.15

Mean Friendship Integration Scores for Republican and
Democratic Members of Groups Favoring the Democrats

	Republicans	Democrats
Blacks	1.67 (3)	1.16 (44)
Catholics	3.00 (4)	1.72 (142)
Non-high school graduates	2.75 (20)	1.60 (237)
Less than $3/hour	1.90 (21)	1.65 (240)
15 years or longer in UAW	2.44 (25)	1.59 (251)

Another way of looking at the data is presented in Table 3.15. Given that the relationships are considerably stronger in each of the Democratically oriented groups, I have computed mean scores on the friendship integration index for Republicans and Democrats in each of these groups. (This analysis omits the middle category of Independent Independents.) The mean scores perhaps make clearer than the measures of association the extent to which deviants in each group are more highly motivated to affiliate than conformers. The data reported in Tables 3.14 and 3.15 therefore suggest that the motivating dynamic in the relationship between political attitudes and level of friendship integration is the sense of deviance that accompanies attitudes that are not pro-Democratic.

MEMBERSHIP GROUPS AS REFERENCE GROUPS

A basic assumption on which this analysis rests is that the social groups I have been discussing actually do serve as sources of political norms for their members. Granted that demographic or sociological categories such as blacks, Catholics, particular educational groups, and so on, do not normally function as social groups in the way that families, committees, or work groups do. Even though these membership groups do not necessarily involve the interaction and communication with others similarly situated that defines a social group, I will argue that we can still treat them as such, at least at the minimal level necessary to support the proposition that they are identified with certain political norms that guide the attitudes and behavior of their members.

This argument is based on three related propositions: (1) many people do in fact identify psychologically with these membership groups, (2) these identifications motivate a responsiveness to normative cues coming from the groups, and (3) the levels of friendship integration between those who do identify with these groups and those who do not differ systematically. The differences referred to in the third proposition are consistent with the assumption that the membership groups function as reference groups, and with the hypothesis that perception of oneself as a deviant from one of these groups motivates affiliative behavior in the work situation. These data will be presented below.

In a commentary on the Index of Political Predisposition developed in *The People's Choice*, Berelson outlined the process by which social category groupings exert normative influences on individuals' behavior. The Index was successful in predicting voting behavior because the IPP score "ranks people according to how strongly their demographic location predisposes them to receive social influences . . . to vote for one or the other of the major parties . . . . The chances of social support for given political choices . . . vary with the distribution of such preferences in the particular segment of the community."[29] Thus my analysis turns on the notion that demographic categories (membership groups) are likely to be associated with a set of socialization and social interaction experiences that convert statistical norms (e.g., the frequency of particular behaviors or attitudes) into internalized norms, that is, felt guidelines the individual accepts as his own and responds to in forming his attitudes and deciding on his behavior. To the extent that this process occurs, membership groups are also reference groups. My treatment of membership groups as reference groups therefore depends on the frequency of occurrence of this identification process, and on showing that the behavior of identifiers differs from that of nonidentifiers in theoretically consistent ways.

Data from this study suggest that this identification process and the recognition of group norms associated with it are, indeed, frequent in these membership groups. For example, eighty-nine percent of the blacks stated that they had "quite a lot" of interest in how Negroes are getting along in this country, and eighty-two percent believed that more Negroes were for Kennedy than for Nixon. Catholics were somewhat weaker in their group identifications. Only forty-eight percent described themselves as "strong" Catholics. On the group-interest question, however, seventy-three percent said that they had "some" or a "good deal" of interest in how Catholics as a whole were getting along. With reference to the social class categories, eighty percent of the sample said that they thought of themselves as belonging to either the middle or working class, and ninety-six percent were able to so classify themselves when asked to do so. The same figures held for those in the lower education and income brackets (i.e., those who are not high school graduates, earn less than $3 per hour, or both). For those in this lower socioeconomic group who identified with the working class (eighty-three percent), fifty-four percent had "a good deal" of interest in how working class people were getting along and an additional thirty-eight percent had "some" interest. Seventy percent believed that the majority of the working class voted Democratic. Group identification was also high among individuals who had been members of the UAW for fifteen or more years, as was attribution of political legitimacy to the union. Fifty-two percent think it is all right, without reservation, for unions to help political candidates (and an additional twenty percent think "it depends"); on a different question only twenty-seven percent believe they should disregard the union's views on candidates.

These data support the assumption that social category membership groups may be treated as norm-bearing reference groups. If the individual knows that his political views are different from those of others in these membership groups, he is therefore likely to perceive himself as a deviant. Note that in this case the group does not cease to be a reference group for him. Instead, it becomes a comparative rather than normative reference group.[30] Only because Republicans do identify with the membership group and do use it as a reference group do they come to perceive themselves as deviants. Identification with the group (1) increases the likelihood of the individual's knowing the attitudes and behavior patterns of other group members, (2) simultaneously increases his dissonance, discomfort, and anxiety if his own attitudes and behaviors are different,[31] and (3) increases the likelihood of his questioning the correctness of his deviant opinion. These factors then motivate a search for friendship support elsewhere—in this instance in the work group. The proper test of this reference group hypothesis, then, is among Republicans only. The hypothesis actually explains why some Republicans do not have as high friendship integration scores as others. If the motivational dynamics implied by the explanation are correct, then among political deviants (Republicans in Democratic membership groups), as identification with the membership group increases, friendship integration should also increase. Among those Republicans who are in membership groups with which they do not identify or with whose normative standards for political action they are unfamiliar, there can be no sense of deviance. In this case it would be unwarranted to expect that statistical deviance would result in behavior motivated to increase social support and evaluation opportunities.

A practical problem in testing this hypothesis obviously is one of sample size. As it is, the number of deviants (by definition as well as empirically) is small. To further subdivide them on the basis of membership group identifications jeopardizes the reliability of the findings. Notwithstanding this difficulty, but bearing in mind the possibility of fortuitous results, the findings of this phase of the analysis are reported because of their importance to the proper development and test of the theory. Because of extremely small subgroup Ns, the findings are offered only as tentative support for the hypothesis and to suggest how more reliable tests might be performed in further studies.

Table 3.16 presents the mean friendship integration scores for the members of each social group by their level of identification with the group.[32] Where questions measuring attribution of political legitimacy to a group or

TABLE 3.16

Mean Friendship Integration Scores by Subjective Identification with Membership Group and Party Identification, for Members of Groups with Pro-Democratic Norms

	Republicans	Democrats
a. Catholics		
Strong group identification[1]	3.67 (3)	1.57 (61)
Weak group identification	1.00 (1)	1.86 (50)
b. Non-high school graduates OR earn less than $3/hour		
Working-class identifiers[2]	2.57 (21)	1.66 (245)
Middle-class identifiers	1.67 (6)	1.59 (34)
Among class-conscious working class only[3]		
1. Good deal of interest in working class[4]	3.00 (7)	1.79 (112)
Some interest in working class	1.86 (7)	1.41 (75)
2. Perceive working class as Democratic[5]	2.56 (9)	1.66 (148)
Perceive working class to be split	2.20 (5)	1.63 (54)
3. Good deal of interest, perceive working class as Democratic	33.33 (6)	1.66 (89)
Compare with middle-class identifiers above	1.67	1.69
c. 15 years or longer in UAW		
Strong group identification[6]	3.17 (12)	1.73 (138)
Weak group identification	1.77 (13)	1.42 (113)
Listen to or watch UAW programs[7]	3.11 (9)	1.68 (153)
Never attend to UAW programs	2.06 (16)	1.45 (98)
Among strong identifiers only		
Union is legitimate source of voting cues[8]	3.40 (5)	1.53 (101)
Union is not a legitimate source of voting cues	3.00 (7)	2.24 (37)

[1]This index is composed of two questions: "Would you call yourself a strong Catholic or not a very strong Catholic?" and "How much interest would you say you have (a good deal, some, or not much at all) in how Catholics as a whole are getting along in this country?" The index was dichotomized so as to yield the most nearly equal number of cases in the strong and weak categories. "Strong" identifiers described themselves as strong in answer to the first question and had at least some interest in Catholics as a whole. All others were classfied as "Weak" group identifiers.

[2]Class identification is based on the final response to the following sequence of questions: "There is quite a bit of talk these days about different social classes. Most people say that they belong to either the middle class or to the working class. Do you think of yourself as being in one of these classes?" and "Which one?" or "Well, if you had to make a choice, would you call yourself middle class or working class?"

[3]Working class identifiers who responded "Yes" to the first class identification question (see note 2 above) are defined as "class-conscious."

[4]"How much interest (a good deal, some, or not much at all) would you say you have in how working class people are getting along in this country?"

[5]"Do you think more working class people vote Republican, they are evenly split, or do more vote Democratic?"

[6]This index is composed of two questions: "How much interest (not much, some or quite a lot) do you have in how other members of the United Auto Workers are getting along?" and "And how much interest do you have in how other members of your own local union are getting along?" The index was dichotomized so as to yield the most nearly equal number of cases in the strong and weak categories. "Strong" identifiers had "a lot" of interest at one level (either UAW or local) and at least "some" at the other.

[7]"How often do you listen to or watch any programs on radio or television that are regularly sponsored by the UAW?"

[8]"In deciding how to vote, how much attention (none at all, not much, some, quite a lot) do you think union members should pay to what the union says about the candidates?" Any response except "none at all" is classfied as according the union political legitimacy.

perception of a group political standard were available, they are also used. In each instance the hypothesis predicts that, among political deviants, the stronger the identification with the group or the clearer the group's political norm, the higher the level of friendship integration.[33]

The table is arranged to contrast levels of identification within each group, by party. Attention should be focused first on the data for Republicans. In each comparison, the members with stronger identification are on the upper of the two lines, and therefore we expect that the friendship integration scores will be higher on the upper line of each pair than on the lower. For example among the lower educational and income groups (category B), the relevant reference group is the social class.[34] Since the pro-Democratic norm is stronger in the working class than in the middle class, the effect of deviance should be more pronounced among working class identifiers. Consistent with this hypothesis, the mean friendship integration score for those who identify with the working class is 2.57 as compared with 1.67 for middle class identifiers. Similar results appear for Catholics and long-time UAW members. Since the impact of group norms is strongest among strong identifiers, more refined comparisons are made among class-conscious working class identifiers (B.1, 2, and 3), and for long-time union members, among those strongly identified with the union.

The large number of tests performed in this analysis compensates, at least partially, for the likely unreliability of findings based on any one test, in view of the small subgroup Ns. In each test, among Republican identifiers belonging to pro-Democratic membership groups, identification with the membership group is associated with higher levels of friendship integration in the work groups. Presumably the subjective identification converts a mere membership group into a comparative reference group; an individual's deviance from its norms then has motivational significance for his social behavior. Perception of the pro-Democratic tendencies of the group or legitimation of the group as a political agent is also associated with higher friendship integration levels. These factors apparently increase tension for the deviant by making the group norm clearer and more salient.

CONSIDERATION OF AN ALTERNATE EXPLANATION
OF THE FINDINGS

An alternative interpretation is that these group identifications are basically measures of gregariousness and that strong identifiers will therefore tend to have more friends regardless of whether or not they are or perceive themselves as political deviants. To investigate this alternative hypothesis, I repeated on the Democrats all of the subgroup tests reported above for Republicans.

If the group identification measures are indeed measures of gregariousness, then the relationships between identification and friendship integration should be as strong for Democrats as they are for Republicans. The relationships among Democrats are reported in the final column of Table 3.13. While all of the relationships had been in the hypothesized direction for Republicans, the trend for Democrats is much less clear. Two of the relationships are in the opposite direction (i.e., identifiers have fewer friends), and all of the others are considerably smaller than the corresponding relationships among Republicans. Thus while some part of the group identification-friendship integration relationships may be due to gregariousness, this factor appears to be a relatively minor influence. The most striking message from the data is that the hypothesized relationships hold uniformly and with considerably larger differences for Republicans, as compared to the erratic and much weaker relationships among Democrats.

COMPOSITION OF THE FRIENDSHIP GROUPS

The explanations developed above for the stronger tendency among political deviants than among conformers to form friendships suggest also that deviants will choose as friends like-minded others. While much research suggests that friendships form on the basis of attitudinal similarity, the analysis already presented suggests that we may expect differential effects depending upon whether the attitudes are deviant or conforming. We therefore need to analyze the composition of these friendship dyads to see under what conditions choices do tend to be intraparty specific.

The measure of friendship integration is based on reciprocity of friendship choices within work groups. Since the number of Republicans in the entire sample is small, some groups have no or only one Republican. These work groups were therefore omitted from this analysis because they provide no possibility of homogeneous Republican friendship dyads. Of the twenty-four original work groups, nine, with from two to eight Republicans in each, remained.

In each of these nine groups, two null hypotheses were sequentially investigated:[35] H^1. There is no tendency to reciprocate choices within work groups. Once this hypothesis can be rejected, the hypothesis of more direct interest to us can then be tested: H^2. Given a tendency to reciprocate, friendship dyads tend to be uniform throughout the work group rather than being related to partisan identification.

For each analysis, a chi-square test was used to compare the expected and observed distributions of friendship dyads described by the partisan identification of the dyad members. An example, presented in Table 3.17, from the group with the largest number of Republicans (but not the strongest relationships) will make the procedure clear. There are several points of interest in this table. First, for this particular group, H^1 may be rejected (df = 4, p > .001) but H^2 may not be (p = .4). The first section of the table demonstrates that the ratios of observed to expected choices are much larger in the dyads where partisanship is homogeneous (RR, DD) than in the mixed dyads (RD and IR, ID) (where R = Republican, D = Democrat, and I = independent). Thus both Republicans and Democrats tend to overchoose one another. However, more noteworthy for present purposes is the finding, signalled by both the O/E ratios and the dyad contributions to χ^2, that once the calculation of expected frequencies is adjusted for the general tendency to reciprocate (in the bottom half of the table), it becomes clear that Democrats choose each other only about as often as we would expect by chance, but that Republicans choose each other more than twice as often as would be expected by chance.

The equivalent of Table 3.17 was calculated for each of the nine work groups with at least two Republicans. Then a pooled χ^2 value was computed for each hypothesis.[36] The pooled χ^2 for Hypothesis 1 is 208.19 (31df, p < .001).[37] The pooled χ^2 for Hypothesis 2 is 49.39 (p < .02). Thus over the work groups as a whole, both null hypotheses may be rejected. Examination of the patterns of dyads most prevalent reinforced the conclusions suggested by the illustrative example in Table 3.16; namely, that friendship dyads do tend toward partisan homogeneity, but that once the appropriate allowance is made for the general tendency toward reciprocation, choice on the basis of partisanship occurs mainly among political deviants. Table 3.18 summarizes the data supporting this conclusion by reporting the mean ratios of observed to expected choices by dyad type over the nine work groups. Note that regardless of whether we use H^1 or H^2 as the base, the largest ratios occur among the deviant homogeneous types of RR and II. Given that there is a strong tendency for reciprocation of friendship choices to occur in the work groups, the second line makes clear that the political content of these choices is produced entirely by the strong proclivity of both Republicans and independents to make choices within their own partisan groups. DD choices occur only as frequently as one would expect by chance given the tendency to reciprocate, and the heterogeneous combinations of RD and IR or ID occur about as or slightly less often than expected. Thus it is the political deviants who contribute disproportionately to the tendency toward friendship group formations in work groups and, when possible, they tend to choose as friends those with similar partisan attitudes.[38]

TABLE 3.17

Expected and Observed Composition of Friendship Dyads in an Illustrative Work Group*

a. Null H^1: There is no tendency to reciprocate choices within work groups.

Dyad Type	E (reciprocation)**	Observed	$(fo\text{-}fe)^2/fe$	O/E
RR	.73	4	14.65	5.48
RD	4.37	8	3.02	1.84
DD	5.46	13	10.41	2.38
IR, ID	2.26	4	1.34	1.77
II	.08	0	.08	0
	12.90	29	$\chi^2 = 29.50$	2.25

b. Null H^2: Given a tendency to reciprocate, friendship dyads tend to be uniform throughout the group rather than being related to partisan identification.

Dyad Type	E (reciprocation)**	Observed	$(fo\text{-}fe)^2fe$	O/E
RR	1.64	4	3.40	2.44
RD	9.82	8	.34	.81
DD	12.98	13	.04	1.06
IR, ID	5.08	4	.23	.79
II	.18	0	.18	0
	29.00	29	$\chi^2 = 4.19$	

*Work group G4-D has the following characteristics: General Motors, day shift; natural size 38, interviews attained 32; 21 Democrats, 8 Republicans, 3 Independents

** The subtables differ only in the computation of the chance expectation. The Es for the first table are based on the assumption of no tendency to reciprocate. The expected number of choices possible for each dyad type is equal to the product of the number of dyads possible for that type and the probability of a chance reciprocation in a group of that size. E.g., given 8 Republicans in the group, the number of RR dyads possible is $8(7)/2 = 28$; the probability of a reciprocated choice in a group of 32, where each member is allowed 5 choices is $(5/31)^2 = .026$; $28(.026) = .73$. More generally, the possible number of dyads of a homogeneous type is equal to the number of combinations of the type n, e.g., $\binom{8}{2}$ for Republicans. The possible number of dyads of a heterogeneous type is equal to the product of the two type ns. The probability of a reciprocated choice in a group is $(d/N\text{-}1)^2$, where d=the number of choices permitted and N is decreased by 1 because the member cannot choose himself. For the second subtable, which takes as a given the tendency to reciprocate, the expected number of choices possible for each dyad type is equal to the probability of a reciprocated choice of this type given the number of dyads possible for the type and the total number of reciprocations possible in the work group $\binom{N}{2}$, multiplied by the number of reciprocated choices actually occurring in the work group. E.g., the number of RR dyads possible is 28 (from above); the number of reciprocated choices possible in the group as a whole is $\binom{32}{2} = 496$ (this can also be calculated by summing the number of dyads possible of each partisan type); the number of reciprocated choices actually observed in the group as a whole is 29. Given a tendency to reciprocate, we would therefore expect that of the 29 choices, 1.64 would be of the RR type.

TABLE 3.18

Mean Ratios of Observed to Expected Choices for Dyad Types

	Homogeneous Dyad Types			Heterogeneous Dyad Types	
	RR	DD	II	RD	IR, ID
Null Hypothesis 1	3.32	1.61	3.15	1.90	1.68
Null Hypothesis 2	1.67	1.01	2.22	0.96	0.89

This substantive point must be stressed: the major finding of this paper is not that partisans tend to choose each other as friends, but that deviant partisans both have more friends and choose attitudinally similar friends much more often than conforming partisans. Thus the analysis goes beyond the familiar finding that people form friendships on the basis of similar attitudes to specify a condition (attitudinal deviance) under which this tendency is accelerated. This specification contributes to an understanding of why the phenomenon occurs at all in suggesting that the interpersonal attraction that follows perceived attitudinal similarity is at least partially an attempt to ward off threat from potentially hostile nonbelievers.

POLITICAL DEVIANCE, FRIENDSHIP SUPPORT, AND POLITICAL PARTICIPATION

If political deviants do indeed feel threatened by a hostile political environment, they may be dissuaded not only from the informal expression of political attitudes but also from active political participation.[39] To the extent that friendships provide supportive environments for deviant attitudes, they should serve a similar function in encouraging political participation. Thus we can expect to find a positive relationship between friendship integration and political participation among political deviants. Since friends do not serve the same supportive function for political conformers, friendship integration should not be related to participation among Democrats.

We would expect this effect on participation to occur primarily with respect to campaigning and other active types of participation where the deviant's political position becomes subject to public scrutiny. Without the psychological support of friends, a deviant should be less willing to risk this sort of public exposure. But to the extent that he feels threatened in any expression of political views and therefore accustoms himself to political withdrawal, even the secret form of participation represented by voting should be affected.

Table 3.19 presents data to test this hypothesis. Voting in the 1960 election is the indicator of participation. While the small number of cases in the Republican sample again suggests caution, the data do tend to support the hypothesis. Among Republicans voting participation is diminished unless friendship integration is at least moderate. Among Democrats, in contrast, voting is independent of friendship integration. Those in the political mainstream apparently need no special psychological support to encourage the expression of their political views.

TABLE 3.19

Friendship Integration and Political Participation,
by Party Identification

| | Friendship Integration | | | | | | | |
| | Republicans | | | | Democrats | | | |
	None	Low	Medium	High	None	Low	Medium	High
Didn't vote	33%	13%	0%	0%	10%	20%	7%	10%
Voted	67%	87%	100%	100%	90%	80%	93%	90%
	100%	100%	100%	100%	100%	100%	100%	100%
N	(3)	(15)	(6)	(16)	(87)	(64)	(99)	(77)
	Gamma = .90				Gamma = .10			

SUMMARY AND DISCUSSION

The research reported here began with the unanticipated finding that Republicans tended to have more friends in their work groups than Democrats. Since the political context of the study sample is heavily Democratic, Republicans in this environment were viewed as political deviants, whose feelings of social insecurity and anxiety, dissonance, and need for opinion evaluation motivated a search for social support, protection, and affiliation. The work group friendships Republicans are more likely to establish were interpreted as sources for filling these needs.

Since this was an ex post facto explanation of the findings, a large part of the analysis was devoted to testing hypotheses deduced from the suggested explanation in order to increase confidence in the original finding and the explanation. These hypotheses constitute a small set of interrelated propositions about the behavior of political deviants.

First, it was hypothesized that deviants tend to be isolates in their non-work social environments and utilize their work situation for political integration and self-evaluation. The supportive finding was that Republicans have fewer political discussions outside the work group and more inside the work group than Democrats.

Second, on the assumption that deviance becomes more problematic and anxiety-provoking as the opposing political norm becomes stronger, it was hypothesized that reactions to deviance increase with this condition. In support of this hypothesis was the finding that the strength of the relationship between party identification and friendship integration is more pronounced in membership groups where the pro-Democratic norm is stronger than in groups where the norm is weaker.

Since the second hypothesis assumes that membership groups serve as reference groups, it was further hypothesized that anxiety and dissonance resulting from deviance increase with subjective identification with the membership groups supporting the norm which the deviant opposes. Consistent with this hypothesis was the finding that friendship integration among Republicans (but not among Democrats) increases as a function of reference group identifications with pro-Democratic membership groups.

A fourth supported hypothesis was that deviants tend to choose other deviants for friends while attitudinal similarity has less effect on the friendship choices of conformers. The familiar relationship between attitudinal similarity and attraction therefore appears to result at least partially from threat potential from supporters of opposing viewpoints.

Finally, it was hypothesized that deviant status discourages the expression of political views unless the deviant has supportive social ties. Here it was found that among Republicans (but not among Democrats), political participation increases with friendship integration.

While Ns were small in several of the tests, the second and third hypotheses were operationalized in numerous ways and in several different subgroups. The consistency of the findings in all tests lends credence to the results in spite of the small subgroup sizes.

This paper has described several changes in the original hypothesis that integration in the primary work group would lead to support for pro-Democratic norms. First, the hypothesis was turned around causally—the independent variable became dependent and vice versa. Second, the explanatory variable, deviance, was introduced and its effects tested for in a variety of ways. In spite of these apparently extreme changes, however, the theoretical orientation remains the same, and no basic challenge is posed to the underlying theory with which I began. The original hypothesis assumed that primary groups enforce political norms through group sanctions of rejection and isolation. The new hypothesis is still predicated on this notion, but it now begins with the fact of deviance and specifies that in order to cope with their deviance and the rejection and isolation to which they are subjected in other social groups, deviants become more integrated into their work groups. The major alteration, therefore, is the identification of the outside groups as the salient ones for group pressure rather than the work group, and the work group as a residual protective environment to which the isolate can retreat under stress. The same basic theories continued to guide the research by suggesting appropriate tests for an explanation of the unanticipated finding.

Why is the work group the setting in which the affiliative needs of deviants can be fulfilled rather than an additional source of pressure toward conformity with dominant norms? In part, this may be because of the limited real social importance of the work group for most of these workers and the consequent limitation on its influence potential. For example, while seventy-seven percent of the workers have at least one reciprocated friendship in the work group, only a quarter of them ever socialized with fellow workers outside of the plant. At the same time workers spend more time in their work groups than with any other social group. This makes the work group eminently available to serve affiliative or other social psychological needs that workers bring to their jobs.

More important is the work group's capacity for political influence. If this is limited, the group is not likely to serve as a socializing agent for the union and the pro-Democratic political culture in general, as I had originally assumed. In retrospect the extent of politicization of the work group is not impressive. In the midst of a very close presidential election campaign, in which their national and local unions were all active, only fifty-eight percent of the workers reported ever discussing politics with fellow workers. Of several hundred free-answer responses to questions asking for evaluations of the international and local unions, only ten responses used nonunion politics as a basis of evaluation, and seven of these were critical of the union's political involvement. Nor is the union's political posture overwhelmingly approved on direct questioning. While most workers feel that it's all right for the union to work for laws favorable to union members, only slightly less than half approve the union's helping candidates and most disapprove spending dues money for this purpose. In general the worker's view of the union's role is limited to the traditional bargaining, grievance, and personal service functions. Moreover political penetration of the work group by the party and union elite is not particularly effective. While virtually all the workers reported speaking with their steward at least occasionally, only seven individuals reported that politics was a usual topic of conversation, and only twenty-four percent reported a political contact by their steward during the presidential campaign. Aside from such infrequent campaign contacts, it seems doubtful that the union's political position is really salient to very many workers. Thus, because the work group is not a positive source of political norms, it can be penetrated by deviant normative positions.

The work group may also serve as a contraculture[40] within the UAW. Data not presented here suggest that the more cohesive the work group, the more alienated the members are from the union and the less satisfied they are with the union's efforts on their behalf. While alienation may well be just a reflection of the stronger Republican allegiances of well-integrated groups, the analysis suggests that the groups become cohesive because of these anti-Democratic and antiunion attitudes.

IMPLICATIONS

The findings reported here have potentially profound implications for political democracy. Concern with constitutional and procedural protections for the rights and expressions of views of political minorities may be substantially irrelevant if basic social psychological processes act to discourage minorities from holding or expressing deviant views. The ways in which minorities deal with the social pressures for conformity are therefore of considerable importance.

Golembiewski has pointed out that "the group may function as a defense against the extragroup environment." In the event of threat, cohesive groups can stand and fight, whereas unintegrated groups or isolated individuals "flee" or "disintegrate."[41] This is obviously a primary concern of "mass society" theorists, who stress the breakdown of interpersonal association and the consequent atomization of individuals in totalitarian societies.[42] Much experimental evidence indicates that subjects in friendship groups are better able to resist pressures for conformity than subjects alone or subjects receiving support from strangers.[43] The present analysis, a study of natural groups, suggests that hypotheses based on laboratory research in this area may be useful for understanding real world attitudes and behavior.[44]

The apparent irrelevance of tasks frequently used in experimental research (for example, the Asch situation) may discourage generalization of the findings to attitudes which have significance for political systems. Because of this, a recent series of experiments demonstrating the operation of conformity pressures in tasks involving cruel interpersonal behavior is germane. Milgram has shown that the support provided by a social group may be vital to the individual's ability to withstand pressures for compliance with a destructive task. When instructed to administer supposedly severe shocks to an innocent person, the large majority of subjects comply in spite of cries of pain coming from the victim. However, placing a subject in a group with two confederates who defy the experimenter reduces compliance substantially. Among other reasons for this effect, Milgram reports that many subjects never even think of defying the experimenter until a confederate suggests it. The confederates also provide social reinforcement of the subject's belief that harming the innocent is wrong, and they give the subject moral support in defying the strong pressures to conform to the authoritative wishes of the experimenter.[45] All of these factors are related to my discussion of the ways in which groups function to protect deviant opinions. That the group is necessary to support even a socially approved and deeply ingrained value points to its critical importance. Group support reduces needs to gain approval from others and therefore makes people less responsive to conformity pressures. On the other hand, isolation is a punishing experience which people try to avoid by conforming to group norms.[46]

This analysis suggests the importance of the immediate environment as a social context for political behavior. Obviously Republicanism could not be considered deviant in many other social contexts or geographic areas. Similarly there is temporal as well as spatial variation in normative contexts. Democratic support among workers such as these is much less substantial now than it was earlier. In many auto factory work groups in 1972, McGovern Democrats might well have been the political deviants. The methodological import of this is that further studies need to utilize measures of deviance appropriate for the time and place studied; one would not necessarily expect that the relationships found in the present research could be replicated today if the same indicators were used. A theoretical problem highlighted by the fact that there are temporal changes in normative contexts is the need to understand more about how the political norms of social groups change over time, given the pressures for conformity discussed in the present study.

That I have cast the analysis in terms of a theory of deviance and conformity should not obscure the fact that I have been dealing here not with deviant views that are esoteric, unpatriotic, or in any way disparaged by the society at large. We are dealing with self-identified members of a mainstream political Party that controlled the executive branch of the federal government for the eight years preceding the data collection. The difference between these workers and many other Republicans lies simply in their living and working in a political environment that was heavily Democratic. That this relatively minor party difference can have noticeable behavioral effects suggests the severity of the strains and the importance of the adjustive mechanisms used by real political deviants. Understanding them seems critical to an appreciation of the social psychological bases of pluralist societies.

NOTES

1. J. S. Mill, *On Liberty*, cited in Dorwin Cartwright and Alvin Zander, eds., *Group Dynamics*, 3rd Edition (New York: Harper & Row, 1968), 141.

2. Sidney Verba, *Small Groups and Political Behavior* (Princeton: Princeton University Press, 1961), pp. 21ff. The classic statements of this position in the voting behavior literature are Paul Lazarsfeld, Bernard Berelson, and Hazel Gaudet, *The People's Choice* (New York: Columbia University Press, 1944) and Bernard R. Berelson, Paul F. Lazarsfeld, and William N. McPhee, *Voting* (Chicago: The University of Chicago Press, 1954).

3. William Kornhauser, *The Politics of Mass Society* (New York: The Free Press, 1959).

4. Communication is also greater in more cohesive groups so that there may be more explicit attempts to convert deviants to dominant group opinions. Albert J. Lott and Bernice E. Lott report positive relationships between group cohesiveness and both communication and conformity in their "Group Cohesiveness, Communication Level, and Conformity," *Journal of Abnormal and Social Psychology*, 62, 2(1961): 408-412.

5. Kenneth P. Langton and M. Kent Jennings, "Mothers Versus Fathers in the Formation of Political Orientations," *Political Socialization*, Kenneth P. Langton, ed. (New York: Oxford University Press, 1969), 67-69.

6. Russell Middleton and Snell Putney, "Political Expression of Adolescent Rebellion," *American Journal of Sociology*, 68, 5 (March 1963), 527-535. Herbert McClosky and Harold Dahlgren report similar findings in their "Primary Group Influence on Party Loyalty," *American Political Science Review*, 53, 3 (September 1959), 757-776.

7. The sample was designed and the study carried out under the direction of Donald E. Stokes and Warren E. Miller of the University of Michigan. I served as Assistant Study Director. The data were collected through the Detroit Area Study, then directed by Harry Sharp.

8. The universe of work groups was stratified by company, shift, political activity level of local union leaders, and the ability of the work group to talk informally during the working day. The work groups were then chosen randomly to balance the stratification variables.

9. This is similar to Landecker's definition of group cohesion as "communicative integration." Werner S. Landecker, "Types of Integration and Their Measurement," *The Language of Social Research*, eds. Paul F. Lazarsfeld and Morris Rosenberg (Glencoe: The Free Press, 1955), 19-27.

10. A slight source of measurement error resulted from the fact that response rates were not 100 percent for any of the work groups. This meant that some respondents gave one or more of their choices to individuals with whom we did not secure interviews, so that reciprocity was precluded. For these respondents, the number of reciprocated choices may underestimate the number of friends they actually had. An additional possible source of difficulty is that the groups varied in size. Because respondents were asked to choose five friends from the list of persons in their work group, the measure appears to favor individuals in smaller sized groups, where the likelihood of reciprocation is greater. A number of corrections to the raw score were attempted to adjust for this possibility, but none of these measures had as good construct validity as the raw score itself. And, as reported in Table 3.9d, the anticipated difficulty of a negative correlation between the raw number of reciprocated choices and group size did not materialize. This fortunate result appears to have been caused by an interesting natural correction mechanism in the sociometric question, whereby people in smaller groups tended to give fewer choices than we requested, while those in larger groups insisted on giving more (all choices were coded). Thus the probability of a reciprocated choice in the different sized groups was substantially equalized by this phenomenon.

11. Joan Criswell, "The Measurement of Group Integration," *Sociometry*, 10 (1947), 259-267. See footnote 10 for further discussion of the relationship between group size and number of reciprocated choices.

12. For a general discussion of the conditions under which primary groups support or oppose the larger organization of which they are a part, see Verba, 54-60.

13. Philip E. Converse, "The Nature of Belief Systems in Mass Publics," *Ideology and Discontent*, ed. David Apter (New York: The Free Press, 1964), 238-241.

14. M. Brewster Smith, Jerome S. Bruner, and Robert W. White, *Opinions and Personality* (New York: John Wiley and Sons, Inc., 1956), 41-42.

15. Ibid., 43.

16. Morris Rosenberg, "The Meaning of Politics in Mass Society," *Public Opinion Quarterly*, Spring 1951, 6-7 and 8. Rosenberg credits Erich Fromm, in his *Escape from Freedom* (New York: Rinehart, 1939), with identification of this last source of gratification.

17. A. Pepitone and C. Wilpizeski, "Some Consequences of Experimental Rejection," *Journal of Abnormal and Social Psychology*, 60 (1960), 359-364.

18. See especially Stanley Schachter, *The Psychology of Affiliation* (Stanford: Stanford University Press, 1959). Schachter stimulated anxiety by threat of electric shock. Further experimental research supports the positive relationship between threat and desire for affiliation using both economic and social threats. See Mauk Mulder and Ad Stemerding, "Threat, Attraction to Group, and Need for Strong Leadership," *Human Relations*, 16, 4 (November 1963), 317-334. Notable examples of the manipulative use of this relationship are reported by Franz Schurman and Edgar Schein. Schurman points out, for example, that the criticism program in the Chinese Communist study groups, designed to identify individual deviance from group norms, evokes great anxiety and insecurity, and sets up a need for reintegration with the group ("Organization and Response in Communist China," *Annals*, 321 (January 1959), 51-66). From his studies of prisoners in the Korean War, Schein ("Interpersonal Communication, Group Solidarity, and Social Influence," *Sociometry*, 23, 2 (June 1960), 8-160) argues that lack of interpersonal communication induces strong motives for reintegration and search behavior designed to reestablish communication through new social relationships. The Chinese Communists used this tendency to encourage prisoners, who were denied communication with each other, to develop relationships with the Communists or with

cooperative prisoners. The type of interpersonal isolation implied by the present findings obviously is hardly comparable to the extreme, extended, and enforced isolation endured by the prisoners of war. Nevertheless, in relative scale, the motive for reintegration may also be present among political deviants who find few people in their social environments with whom to share political communication. In a less extreme situation, Alexander and Campbell found that lack of parental support for an adolescent's attitudes is associated with a stronger network of friendships among children. They suggest that the lack of support from parents leads to an imbalance which is resolved through greater support of friends. C. Norman Alexander, Jr. and Ernest Q. Campbell, "Balance Forces and Environmental Effects: Factors Influencing the Cohesiveness of Adolescent Drinking Groups," *Social Forces*, 46, 3 (March 1968), 367-374. In the search for social support, the friendship group of two persons may be especially important, for the dyad is the only size group in which supportive interactions exceed aggressive interactions. Carl N. Zimet and Carol Schneider, "Effects of Group Size on Interaction in Small Groups," *The Journal of Social Psychology*, 77 (1969), 177-187.

19. Leon Festinger, "A Theory of Social Comparison Processes," *Human Relations*, 7 (1954), 117-140.

20. Leon Festinger and Elliot Aronson, "Arousal and Reduction of Dissonance in Social Contexts," in Cartwright and Zander, *Group Dynamics*, 130.

21. Some research suggests that deviants also reject conformers. W. F. Norrison and D. W. Corment, "Participation and Opinion Change in Two Person Groups as Related to Amount of Peer Group Support," *British Journal of Social and Clinical Psychology*, 7, 3 (1968), 176-183.

22. For a discussion of Durkheim's method of subgroup comparison as a type of replication, see Hanan C. Selvin, "Durkheim's *Suicide*: Further Thoughts on a Methodological Classic," *Emile Durkheim*, ed. Robert A. Nisbet (New York: Prentice-Hall, 1965), 113-136. For a discussion of a variety of statistical procedures for "pseudoreplication" of findings on the same data set, see Bernard M. Finifter, "The Generation of Confidence: Evaluating Research Findings by Random Subsample Replication," *Sociological Methodology 1972*, ed. Herbert L. Costner (San Franciso: Jossey-Bass, 1972). Since the basic purpose of significance tests is to suggest the degree of reliability of a finding, Finifter argues that replications serve this purpose without making distributional and other assumptions. Following this logic and because of the nature of the present sample, I have refrained from using significance tests except in Section IX below.

23. For a discussion of "systematic" and other types of replication, see Murray Sidman, *Tactics of Scientific Research: Evaluating Experimental Data in Psychology* (New York: Basic Books, 1960).

24. Even after controls for ten life situation variables were introduced (representing region, size of place of residence and social class), nonsouthern blacks were almost 12 percent more Democratic in their voting behavior than comparable whites. Angus Campbell, Phillip E. Converse, Warren E. Miller, and Donald E. Stokes, *The American Voter* (New York: John Wiley and Sons, Inc., 1960), 300-306.

25. Stanley Kelley, Jr., "The 1960 Presidential Election," *American Government Annual; 1961-1962* ed. Ivan Hinderaker (New York: Holt, Rinehart and Winston, Inc.), 57-75.

26. Campbell, et. al., *The American Voter*, 300-306.

27. Philip E. Converse, Angus Campbell, Warren E. Miller, and Donald E. Stokes, "Stability and Change in 1960: A Reinstating Election," *The American Political Science Review*, 55, 2 (June 1961), 273.

28. Technically, this is a specification analysis, in which the focus is on identifying the conditions under which the initial relationship is weakened or strengthened. However, the reader should note that in controlling for the specification variables we are also in effect checking on the possibility of a spurious relationship resulting from any association between the control variables and the independent variables. That the resulting relationships become both stronger and weaker in a systematic pattern suggests that the spurious relationship type of interpretation is inappropriate. An analysis which presented only one partial correlation for each control variable (interpretable as an average relationship in the subcategories of the control variable) would obscure this pattern.

29. Berelson, et al., *Voting*, 126.

30. Briefly, normative reference groups set standards which the individual is motivated to follow; comparative reference groups are used by the individual to evaluate himself and others. The same group may also perform both functions. See Harold H. Kelley, "Two Functions of Reference Groups," *Readings in Reference Group Theory and Research*, eds. Herbert H. Hyman and Eleanor Singer (New York: The Free Press, 1968) 77-83.

31. Festinger hypothesizes, and it has been supported by experimental evidence, that dissonance as a function of disagreement with a group increases with the importance of the group to the individual. Festinger and Aronson, "Arousal and Reduction," 130.

32. The subgroup size difficulties are amply illustrated in the fact that it was not possible to do a within group analysis of black Republicans. There were only three of these and all were highly identified with their racial group and perceived it to have a Democratic political norm.

33. Previous analyses have shown that group identification increases compliance with group norms. See, for example, Campbell, et al., *The American Voter*, 295-332. The present analysis in a sense focuses on one aspect of the unexplained variance in this relationship, i.e., what is the effect on high identifiers of not conforming?

34. Because the same reference group questions are used for both of these social categories, they are combined in the analysis. For the total sample, the gamma between income and education is .60.

35. I am grateful to Leo Katz, Director of the Statistics Laboratory at Michigan State University, for advice on this analysis.

36. The pooled χ^2 value is simply the sum of the separate χ^2 tests and the sum of the degrees of freedom, which is then evaluated in the usual way. "In effect, we are saying that if a relationship comes out roughly the same each time but the probabilities of the separate results are each greater than .05, we still may ask ourselves how likely such a combination of outcomes would be if there were no relationship in any of the tables." H. M. Blalock, Jr., *Social Statistics*, 2d ed. (New York: McGraw-Hill, 1972), 309-310. In the present case, eight of the eighteen individual relationships were also separately significant. Chi-square is, of course, highly sensitive to N and the Ns for these analyses are rather small. In fact, the use of chi-square in the individual work groups is technically inappropriate because the expected values for dyad types involving Republicans and independents frequently fall below the generally accepted minimum. Nor does any combination of categories that is theoretically meaningful solve the problem. The results should therefore be interpreted in a tentative and exploratory spirit.

37. Some work group tables had fewer than four degrees of freedom because they had no or only one independent, thus eliminating the II and/or ID, IR lines.

38. Lone Republicans in the remaining groups had slightly fewer friends than Republicans in those groups where like-minded partisans were available (although still more than Democrats); they demonstrated their partisan selectivity by disproportionate friendships with independents over Democrats.

39. Cartwright and Zander, *Group Dynamics*, argue that "public behavior is more likely to be conforming than private behavior" because of the greater likelihood of sanctions being invoked when deviance becomes known (p. 145). Some Wallace campaign activists, for example, reported in the media that during the 1972 presidential primaries there were numerous cases of individuals who covertly expressed support for Wallace but who could not be induced to participate in his campaign until they were persuaded that their "friends and neighbors" were for him too.

40. J. Milton Yinger, "Contraculture and Subculture," *American Sociological Review*, 25, 5 (October 1960),625-635.

41. Robert T. Golembiewski, William A. Welsh, and William J. Crotty, *A Methodological Primer for Political Scientists* (Chicago: Rand-McNally, 1969), 78, 81.

42. See, for example, Kornhauser, *Politics of Mass Society;* also Verba, *Small Groups*, 52-54.

43. See, for example, Nicholas P. Pollis and Joseph A. Cammalleri, "Social Conditions and Differential Resistance to Majority Pressure," *Journal of Psychology*, 70, 1 (1968) 69-76; and Vernon L. Allen and John M. Levine, "Social Support, Dissent and Conformity," *Sociometry*, 31, 2 (1968), 138-149.

44. While the experimenter's ability to control and manipulate variables is enviable, one must not forget his concern that the artificiality of the laboratory situation may severely limit the generalizability of findings. See for example Robert R. Blake and Jane S. Mouton, "Conformity, Resistance and Conversion," *Conformity and Deviation*, eds. Irwin A. Berg and Bernard M. Bass, (New York: Harper and Brothers, 1961), esp. 5-7 and 24-25. Replication of experimental findings in real-life situations is thus especially necessary.

45. Stanley Milgram, "Liberating Effects of Group Pressure," *Journal of Personality and Social Psychology*, 1, 2 (1965), 127-134.

46. Peter M. Blau, "Patterns of Deviation in Work Groups," *Sociometry*, 23, 3 (September 1960), 245-261.

Generalizations About Groupthink

IRVING JANIS

HOW WIDESPREAD IS GROUPTHINK?

At present we do not know what percentage of all national fiascoes are attributable to groupthink. Some decisions of poor quality that turn out to be fiascoes might be ascribed primarily to mistakes made by just one man, the chief executive. Others arise because of a faulty policy formulated by a group of executives whose decision-making procedures were impaired by errors having little or nothing to do with groupthink. For example a non-cohesive committee may be made up of bickering factions so intent on fighting for political power within the government bureaucracy that the participants have little interest in examining the real issues posed by the foreign policy question they are debating. They may settle for a compromise that fails to take account of adverse effects on people outside their own political arena.

All that can be said from the historical case studies I have analyzed so far is that groupthink tendencies sometimes play a major role in producing large-scale fiascoes. To estimate how large the percentage might be for various types of decision-making groups, we need investigations of a variety of policy decisions made by groups of executives who have grossly miscalculated the unfavorable consequences of their chosen course of action. The "only-in-America" question could be pursued in an examination of a substantial number of ill-considered decisions made by various European and other foreign governments, including some from earlier centuries. Among the most recent fiascoes to be considered would be the Nasser government's provocations in 1967 that led to the outbreak of the six-day Israeli-Arab war and the Pakistan government's provocations in 1971 that led to the outbreak of the thirteen-day Indian-Pakistani war.

A selection of United States government decisions to be used in further research on the incidence of groupthink-dominated deliberations should include some made during Republican administrations that might be comparable to the ones made during the Roosevelt, Truman, Kennedy and Johnson administrations. The sample might also contain representative instances of governmental decisions made by executive groups below the top level—comparable to the decisions of Admiral Kimmel's naval group in Hawaii in 1941—including some having nothing to do with war and peace. One example would be the decision made by United States Department of Justice attorneys who spent several years preparing a case against Dr. Andrew Ivy, an American scientist who was distributing a worthless drug known as Krebiozen and claiming that it was a cure for cancer. The group of government lawyers, with the concurrence of administrators in the Food

Reprinted from Irving Janis, *Victims of Groupthink* (Boston: Houghton Mifflin, 1972).

and Drug Administration, made the mistake of bringing a massive indict-
ment charging conspiracy, fraud, and a variety of related crimes that could
have put Dr. Ivy in jail for more than a hundred years. When the trial took
place in 1966, they failed to convince the jury of the truth of these extreme
charges; they undoubtedly would have had a solid case on lesser charges.
The archives of other nations might also provide evidence of groupthink
among comparable groups of bureaucrats, as in the case of the decision by
Britain's National Coal Board to ignore warnings about a coal tip slide in
Aberfan, Wales, in order to save the money and time that would have been
required for taking proper precautions. When the predicted slide disaster
occurred in October 1966, the local school was completely buried and all
the town's school children were killed.

Unwise and disastrous policy decisions made by industrial firms might
also be examined in order to investigate groupthink tendencies in organizations outside of governmental bureaucracies. Here are some likely candidates:

A lethal decision was made in 1961 by a group of nine directors and
scientists of Grunenthal Chemie, the German firm that was making huge
profits from marketing Thalidomide as a tranquilizer, to ignore alarming
reports from physicians all over the world about dangerous side effects and
to advertise that their cherished money-making drug was safe enough to be
used by pregnant women, even though the firm had not run a single test to
find out its effects on the unborn. Within less than a year after the adver-
tising decision, approximately seven thousand deformed children were
born. The German government brought criminal charges against the directors and, as a result of civil suits by parents of "Thalidomide babies," the
firm had to pay millions of dollars in damages.

During the 1950s a clique of general managers and vice presidents of
General Electric, Westinghouse, Allis-Chalmers, McGraw-Edison, and
other electric companies met together informally at golf clubs and hotels to
make illegal price-fixing arrangements, confident that their firms would
support them in the unlikely event they were caught. But caught they
were—then convicted of conspiracy, fired, fined, and imprisoned.

HYPOTHESES ABOUT WHEN GROUPTHINK OCCURS

When groupthink is most likely to occur pertains to situational circumstances and structural features of the group that make it easy for the
symptoms to become dominant. The prime condition repeatedly encountered in the case studies of fiascoes is group cohesiveness. A second major
condition suggested by the case studies is insulation of the decision-making
group from the judgments of qualified associates who, as outsiders, are not
permitted to know about the new policies under discussion until after a
final decision has been made. Hence a second hypothesis is that the more
insulated a cohesive group of executives becomes, the greater are the
chances that its policy decisions will be products of groupthink. A third

hypothesis suggested by the case studies is that the more actively the leader of a cohesive policy-making group promotes his own preferred solution, the greater are the chances of a consensus based on groupthink, even when the leader does not want the members to be yes-men and the individual members try to resist conforming. To test these hypotheses we would have to compare large samples of high-quality and low-quality decisions made by equivalent executive groups.[1]

THE GROUPTHINK SYNDROME:
REVIEW OF THE MAJOR SYMPTOMS

To test generalizations about the conditions that increase the chances of groupthink, we must operationalize the concept of groupthink by describing the symptoms to which it refers. Eight main symptoms run through the case studies of historic fiascoes. Each symptom can be identified by a variety of indicators derived from historical records, observers' accounts of conversations, and participants' memoirs. The eight symptoms of groupthink are:

1. an illusion of invulnerability, shared by most or all the members, which creates excessive optimism and encourages taking extreme risks;

2. collective efforts to rationalize in order to discount warnings which might lead the members to reconsider their assumptions before they recommit themselves to their past policy decisions;

3. an unquestioned belief in the group's inherent morality, inclining the members to ignore the ethical or moral consequences of their decisions;

4. stereotyped views of enemy leaders as too evil to warrant genuine attempts to negotiate, or as too weak and stupid to counter whatever risky attempts are made to defeat their purposes;

5. direct pressure on any member who expresses strong arguments against any of the group's stereotypes, illusions, or commitments, making clear that this type of dissent is contrary to what is expected of all loyal members;

6. self-censorship of deviations from the apparent group consensus, reflecting each member's inclination to minimize to himself the importance of his doubts and counterarguments;

7. a shared illusion of unanimity concerning judgments conforming to the majority view (partly resulting from self-censorship of deviations, augmented by the false assumption that silence means consent);

8. the emergence of self-appointed mindguards—members who protect the group from adverse information that might shatter their shared complacency about the effectiveness and morality of their decisions.

When a policy-making group displays most or all of these symptoms, the members perform their collective tasks ineffectively and are likely to fail to attain their collective objectives. Although concurrence seeking may contribute to maintaining morale after a defeat and to muddling through a crisis when prospects for a successful outcome look bleak, these positive effects are generally outweighed by the poor quality of the group's decision making. My assumption is that the more frequently a group displays the symptoms, the worse will be the quality of its decisions. Even when some symptoms are absent, the others may be so pronounced that we can predict all the unfortunate consequences of groupthink.

ARE COHESIVE GROUPS DOOMED TO BE VICTIMS?

The major condition that promotes groupthink has been emphasized as the main theme of this book: The more amiability and esprit de corps among the members of an in-group of policymakers, the greater is the danger that independent critical thinking will be replaced by groupthink, which is likely to result in irrational and dehumanizing actions directed at out-groups. Yet when we recall the case studies of the Cuban missile crisis and the Marshall Plan, we surmise that some caveats about applying this generalization are in order. A high degree of "amiability and esprit de corps among the members"—that is, group cohesiveness—does not invariably lead to symptoms of groupthink. It may be a necessary condition, but it is not a sufficient condition. Taking this into account, I have introduced an explicit proviso in the wording of the generalization, asserting that the greater the cohesiveness of the group, the greater is the danger of a groupthink type of decision. Dangers do not always materialize and can sometimes be prevented by precautionary measures. In effect, then, the hypothesis asserts a positive relationship, which may be far from perfect, among three variables that can be assessed independently: A high degree of group cohesiveness is conducive to a high frequency of defects in decision making. Two conditions that may play an important role in determining whether or not group cohesiveness will lead to groupthink have been mentioned—insulation of the policy-making group and promotional leadership practices.

Obviously the main generalization about the relationship of group cohesiveness and groupthink is not an iron law of executive behavior that dooms the members of every cohesive group to become victims of groupthink every time they make a collective decision. Rather we can expect high cohesiveness to be conducive to groupthink except when certain conditions are present or special precautions are taken that counteract concurrence-seeking tendencies.

When appropriate precautions are taken, a group that has become moderately or highly cohesive probably will do a much better job on its decision-making tasks than if it had remained noncohesive. Compliance out of fear of recrimination is likely to be strongest when there is little or no sense of solidarity among the group members. To overcome this fear a person needs to have confidence that he is a member in good standing and that the others will continue to value his role in the group, whether or not he argues with them about the issue under discussion. Social psychological studies indicate that as a member of a group is made to feel more accepted by the others—a central feature of increased group cohesiveness—he acquires greater freedom to say what he really thinks. Dittes and Kelley, for example, discovered in a social psychological experiment that when individuals in a group were given information indicating that they were highly accepted by their fellow members, they became more willing to express opinions that deviated from the group consensus. Members who were made to feel that they were not accepted by their colleagues became subdued. After being informed about the low acceptance ratings, they participated in the group discussions only half as often as they had before. When they did speak, they showed much more conformity with the group consensus than any of the other members did. However, these conformists had developed an attitude of inner detachment from the group. This was revealed in their answers to questions that elicited their private views, which showed little conformity to the group's norms and low valuation of membership in the group. Their superficial conformity appears to have been motivated by a fear of being humiliated by being expelled from the group altogether.

The unaccepted members in the Dittes and Kelley study probably reacted the way most people do in a group of high-status people who are strangers, before cohesiveness and feelings of security have developed. The highly accepted members probably reacted like members of cohesive groups. In the Dittes and Kelley study, the accepted members were more responsive than unaccepted members to new information that contradicted the group's earlier assumptions and more freely expressed opinions differing from the group consensus. This pattern of relatively independent thinking is probably characteristic of group members who have developed a relationship of mutual acceptance in which each person assumes that the others in the group want to know what he really thinks and will want him to continue as a member regardless of what he says.

When a group has a low degree of cohesiveness, there are, of course, sources of error in decision making in addition to deliberate conformity out of fear of recrimination. One that is especially likely to plague a noncohesive group of politicians or administrators is a win-lose fighting stance, which inclines each participant to fight hard for his own point of view (or the point of view of his organization), without much regard for the real issues at stake. When unlike-minded people who are political opponents are forced to meet together in a group, they can be expected to behave like couples in olden times who were forced to live together by a shotgun marriage. The incompatible members of a shotgun committee often indulge in painfully repetitious debates, frequently punctuated with invective, mutual ridicule, and maneuvers of one-upmanship in a continuous struggle for power that is not at all conducive to decisions of high quality. This is another reason for expecting that policy-making groups lacking amiability and esprit de corps, even though spared the unfavorable symptoms of groupthink, will sometimes show more symptoms of defective decision making and produce worse fiascoes than groups that are moderately or highly cohesive. When we consider the two major sources of error that beset noncohesive groups—deliberate conformity out of fear of recrimination and a win-lose fighting stance—we see that cohesive groups can have great advantages if groupthink tendencies can be kept from becoming dominant.

As the members of a decision-making group develop bonds of friendship and esprit de corps, they become less competitive and begin to trust each other to tolerate disagreements. They are less likely to use deceitful arguments or to play safe by dancing around the issues with vapid or conventional comments. We expect that the more cohesive a group becomes, the less the members will deliberately censor what they say because of fear of being socially punished for antagonizing the leader or any of their fellow members. But the outcome is complicated because the more cohesive a group becomes, the more the members will unwittingly censor what they think because of their newly acquired motivation to preserve the unity of the group and to adhere to its norms. Thus, although the members of a highly cohesive group feel much freer to deviate from the majority, their desire for genuine concurrence on all important issues—to match their opinions with each other and to conduct themselves in accordance with each other's wishes—often inclines them not to use this freedom. In a cohesive group of policymakers the danger is not that each individual will fail to reveal his strong objections to a proposal favored by the majority but that he will think the proposal is a good one, without attempting to carry out a critical scrutiny that could lead him to see that there are grounds for strong objections. When groupthink dominates, suppression of deviant thoughts takes the form of each person's deciding that his misgivings are not relevant, that the benefit of any doubt should be given to the group consensus. A member of a cohesive group will rarely be subjected to direct group pressures from the majority because he will rarely take a position that threatens the unity of the group.

Prior research on group dynamics indicates that at least three different types of social rewards tend to increase group cohesiveness—friendship, prestige, and enhanced competence. Concurrence-seeking tendencies probably are stronger when high cohesiveness is based primarily on the rewards of being in a pleasant "clubby" atmosphere or of gaining prestige from being a member of an elite group than when it is based primarily on the opportunity to function competently on work tasks with effective co-workers. In a cohesive policy-making group of the latter type, careful appraisal of policy alternatives is likely to become a group norm to which the members conscientiously adhere; this helps to counteract groupthink. But even when the basis of high cohesiveness is enhancement of task-oriented values in a well-functioning group whose members trust each other sufficiently to tolerate disagreements, there is still the danger that groupthink will become a dominant tendency. Each member develops a strong motivation to preserve the rewards of group solidarity, an inner compulsion to avoid creating disunity, which inclines him to believe in the soundness of the proposals promoted by the leader or by a majority of the group's members.

A cohesive group that on one occasion suffers from groupthink is capable on other occasions of gaining the advantages of high morale and free expression of dissent, depending on whether special conditions that promote groupthink are present. The duality of cohesiveness may explain some of the inconsistencies in research results on group effectiveness. For example, Marvin Shaw in a recent book, *Group Dynamics*, presents as a plausible hypothesis the proposition, "High-cohesive groups are more effective than low-cohesive groups in achieving their respective goals," but he acknowledges that the evidence "is not altogether consistent." A major source of inconsistency may be variation in the strength of concurrence-seeking tendencies, which counter the goals of a work group on any task requiring planning or decision making. This is how I interpret the difference between the ineffective Bay of Pigs decision and the effective Cuban mis-

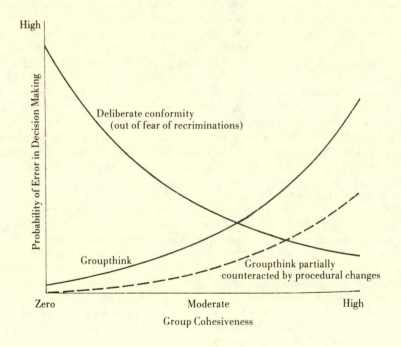

Figure 3.2. Hypothetical curves showing
expected relationships between cohesiveness of the group
and errors from deliberate conformity and
from groupthink tendencies

sile crisis decision made by nearly identical cohesive groups of policymakers headed by the same leader.

For most groups, optimal functioning in decision-making tasks may prove to be at a moderate level of cohesiveness, avoiding the disadvantages of conformity out of fear of recrimination when cohesiveness is low and the disadvantages of strong concurrence-seeking tendencies when cohesiveness is high. If, however, the latter disadvantages can be held to a minimum by administrative practices that prevent groupthink tendencies from becoming dominant, then the optimal level of cohesiveness for effective decision making could prove to be much higher.

Some of the implications of the distinction between deliberate conformity based on fear or recrimination and nondeliberate conformity based on concurrence-seeking tendencies are illustrated in Fig. 3.2.

The inverse relation between cohesiveness and deliberate conformity out of fear of recrimination is represented by the descending curve in the diagram. In contrast, a positive relation between groupthink tendencies and cohesiveness is represented by the ascending (solid-line) curve. The assumption that groupthink tendencies can be partially counteracted is represented by the dashed line, which shows the expected decrease in groupthink tendencies from various administrative changes that meet the conditions for preventing or counteracting concurrence-seeking tendencies. (The dashed line could also represent the lower degree of concurrence seeking expected when cohesiveness is based on enhancement of competence and other task-oriented values rather than on purely social rewards of friendship and prestige.) When none of the conditions that counteract groupthink are present, the combination of the two conformity curves (deliberate conformity out of fear of recrimination and concurrence seeking) will produce a U-shaped curve, with the optimal level falling somewhere in the middle range of cohesiveness, where deliberate conformity is substantially lower than at zero cohesiveness but where concurrence-seeking tendencies have not yet become very strong. By optimal level, I mean the degree of cohesiveness that gives rise to the fewest errors in decision making. The optimal level corresponds to the lowest point on the combined U-shaped curve, which, for two combinable curves like those shown in the diagram, occurs near the point where they intersect. When groupthink is partially counteracted, the combination of the curve for groupthink tendencies (the dashed line) with the curve for deliberate conformity results in a U-shaped curve whose lowest point is much farther to the right; that is, the optimal level is at a higher level of cohesiveness. Theoretically speaking, if groupthink could be eliminated, there would be nothing to add to the curve for deliberate conformity, and the optimal level would be at the highest possible degree of cohesiveness. The main point is that the more effectively groupthink is counteracted, the higher will be the optimal level of cohesiveness.

RUDIMENTS OF AN EXPLANATORY THEORY

The problem of why groupthink occurs is more difficult to investigate than the problem of who is vulnerable and when. But why is the heart of the matter if we want to explain the observed phenomena of groupthink. An adequate explanation would account for the known conditions that encourage or discourage concurrence-seeking tendencies and would enable us to predict the effects of conditions that we do not yet know about.

The search for an explanation forces us to tread through a quagmire of complicated theoretical issues in still largely uncharted areas of human motivation. For many years psychologists have been trying to formulate general psychological principles that would apply to all the observed phenomena of group dynamics, but no well-established theory is generally accepted by behavioral scientists. However, promising leads extracted from recent social psychological research may point the way to an adequate explanation of the groupthink syndrome. The evidence needed to test hypotheses about the causes of groupthink must ultimately come from field experiments and other systematic investigations specifically designed to pin down causal sequences, rather than from historical case studies, which are useful mainly for suggesting hypotheses.

The central explanatory concept involves viewing concurrence seeking as a form of striving for mutual support based on a powerful motivation in all group members to cope with the stresses of decision making that cannot be alleviated by standard operating procedures. Anxieties aroused by salient risks of material losses for themselves and for their organization or their nation will generally impel members to become vigilant, to set in motion the administrative machinery for obtaining objective information, and to institute other standard operating procedures for working out careful plans to eliminate the threat. However, other sources of stress in decision making cannot be coped with so easily. For example few if any operating procedures enable a policymaker to cope with the threat of losing self-esteem from violating ethical standards of conduct. Often the group's deliberations about policy issues generate within each participant an intense conflict between humanitarian values on the one hand and the utilitarian demands of national or organizational goals, practical politics, and economics on the other. The participant may try to reassure himself with the platitudinous thought that "you can't make an omelet without breaking some eggs." Nevertheless, each time he realizes that he is sacrificing moral values to arrive at a viable policy, he will be burdened with anticipatory feelings of shame, guilt, and related feelings of self-depreciation, which lower his self-esteem. Similar feelings are generated whenever a decision maker is faced with a perplexing choice that he considers beyond his level of competence or that forces him to become keenly aware of his personal inadequacies. For all such sources of stress, participating in a unanimous consensus along with the respected fellow members of a congenial group will bolster the decision maker's self-esteem.

Some individuals are extraordinarily self-confident and may not need the support of a cohesive group when their decisions are subject to social criticism. For example, the spirited symphony orchestra conductor Sir Thomas Beecham once said, "I have made just one mistake in my entire life and that was one time when I thought I was wrong but actually I was right." Not everybody who is accustomed to putting it on the line as a decision maker is able to maintain such an unassailable sense of self-assurance.

PSYCHOLOGICAL FUNCTIONS OF THE EIGHT SYMPTOMS

Concurrence seeking and the various symptoms of groupthink to which it gives rise can be best understood as a mutual effort among the members of a group to maintain self-esteem, especially when they share responsibility for making vital decisions that pose threats of social disapproval and self-disapproval. The eight symptoms of groupthink form a coherent pattern if viewed in the context of this explanatory hypothesis. The symptoms may function in somewhat different ways to produce the same result.

A shared illusion of invulnerability and shared rationalizations can counteract unnerving feelings of personal inadequacy and pessimism about finding an adequate solution during a crisis. Even during noncrisis periods, whenever the members foresee great gains from taking a socially disapproved or unethical course of action, they seek some way of disregarding the threat of being found out and welcome the optimistic views of the members who argue for the attractive but risky course of action.[2] At such times, as well as during distressing crises, if the threat of failure is salient, the members are likely to convey to each other the attitude that "we needn't worry, everything will go our way." By pooling their intellectual resources to develop rationalizations, the members build up each other's confidence and feel reassured about unfamiliar risks, which, if taken seriously, would be dealt with by applying standard operating procedures to obtain additional information and to carry out careful planning.

The members' firm belief in the inherent morality of their group and their use of undifferentiated negative stereotypes of opponents enable them to minimize decision conflicts between ethical values and expediency, especially when they are inclined to resort to violence. The shared belief that "we are a wise and good group" inclines them to use group concurrence as a major criterion to judge the morality as well as the efficacy of any policy under discussion. "Since our group's objectives are good," the members feel, "any means we decide to use must be good." This shared assumption helps the members avoid feelings of shame or guilt about decisions that may violate their personal code of ethical behavior. Negative stereotypes of the enemy enhance their sense of moral righteousness as well as their pride in the lofty mission of the in-group.

Every cohesive group that is required to make policy decisions tends to develop a set of policy doctrines, derived from the members' subculture, that provides the members with a cognitive map for conceptualizing the intentions and reactions of opponents, allies, and neutrals. But to be effective decision makers, the members need to exercise a certain flexibility in the use of those doctrines to take account of new information and their own feelings of empathy. They can then evolve sophisticated concepts that enable them to weigh the prospects for negotiations in the light of fresh evidence about their opponents' current objectives and strategies. During a confrontation involving the threat of open hostilities, the loss of flexibility is the price a cohesive group pays to gain the greater sense of moral righteousness from sharing an image of the enemy as intractable and deserving of punishment. Stereotypes that dehumanize out-groups alleviate guilt by legitimizing destructive and inhumane acts against them. As Donald Campbell says, "The out-group's opprobrious characteristics seem (to the in-grouper) to fully justify the hostility and rejection he shows toward it." Focusing hostility on out-groups probably also serves the psychological function of displacing aggression away from the in-group, thereby reducing stress arising from latent jealousies and antagonisms within the group.

When most members fall back upon the familiar forms of social pressure directed against a member who questions the group's wisdom or morality, they are in effect protecting a prop that helps them to keep anxiety and guilt to a minimum. If subtle pressures fail, stronger efforts are made to limit the extent of his deviation, to make him a domesticated dissenter. We have seen this clearly in the case of President Johnson's in-group when one or two of the members disagreed with the majority's position that air attacks against North Vietnam should be increased. A doubter who accepts the role is no longer a problem because his objections are confined to issues that do not threaten to shake the confidence of the group members in the reasonableness and righteousness of their collective judgments. At the same time the doubter's tamed presentation of an opposing viewpoint permits the others to think that their group is strong-minded enough to tolerate dissent. If the domestication efforts do not succeed, the dissenter is ultimately ostracized, so that the relatively tranquil emotional atmosphere of a homogeneous group is restored.

When a member is dependent on the group for bolstering his feelings of self-confidence, he tends to exercise self-censorship over his misgivings. The greater the dependence, the stronger will be the motivation to adhere to the group's norms. One of the norms that is likely to become dominant during a crisis involves living up to a mutual nonaggression pact. Each individual in the group feels himself to be under an injunction to avoid making penetrating criticisms that might bring on a clash with fellow members and destroy the unity of the group. Adhering to this norm promotes a sense of collective strength and also eliminates the threat of damage to each participant's self-esteem from hearing his own judgments on vital issues criticized by respected associates. We have seen how much painful emotion was generated in Kennan's group of critical thinkers working on the Marshall Plan and in Kennedy's executive committee debating alternative ways to get rid of the Soviet missiles in Cuba. In contrast, the emotional state of those who participated in the groupthink-dominated deliberations that led to fiascoes was relatively placid. When the mutual nonaggression pact and other related norms for preserving the unity of the group are internalized, each member avoids interfering with an emerging consensus by assuring himself that the opposing arguments he had in mind must be erroneous or that his misgivings are too unimportant to be worth mentioning.

The various devices to enhance self-esteem require an illusion of unanimity about all important judgments. Without it the sense of group unity would be lost, gnawing doubts would start to grow, confidence in the group's problem-solving capacity would shrink, and soon the full emotional impact of all the stresses generated by making a difficult decision would be aroused. Preserving the sense of unity can do more than keep anxiety and guilt to a minimum; it can induce pleasant feelings of elation. Members of a group sometimes enjoy an exhilarating sense of omnipotence from participating in a crisis decision with a group that displays solidarity against an evil enemy and complete unanimity about everything that needs to be done.[3]

Self-appointed mindguards help to preserve the shared sense of complacency by making sure that the leader and other members are not exposed to information that might challenge their self-confidence. If the mindguard were to transmit the potentially distressing information, he and the others might become discouraged by the apparent defects in their cherished policy and find themselves impelled to initiate a painful reevaluation.

CONCLUSION

The greater the threats to the self-esteem of the members of a cohesive decision-making body, the greater will be their inclination to resort to concurrence seeking at the expense of critical thinking. If this explanatory hypothesis is correct, symptoms of groupthink will be found most often when a decision poses a moral dilemma, especially if the most advantageous course of action requires the policymakers to violate their own standards of humanitarian behavior. Under these conditions each member is likely to become more dependent than ever on the in-group for maintaining his self-image as a decent human being and accordingly will be more strongly motivated than ever to maintain a sense of group unity by striving for concurrence.[4]

Until the explanation of groupthink in terms of mutual support to cope with threats to self-esteem is verified by systematic research, it is risky to make huge inferential leaps from theory to the practical sphere of prevention. Ultimately a well-substantiated theory should have valuable practical applications to the formulation of effective prescriptions. As Kurt Lewin pointed out, "Nothing is so practical as a good theory." But until we know we have a good theory—one that is well supported by controlled experiments and systematic correlational research, as well as by case studies—we must recognize that any prescriptions we draw up are speculative inferences based on what little we know, or think we know, about when and why groupthink occurs. Still, we should not be inhibited from drawing tentative inferences—so long as we label them as such—to call attention to potentially useful means of prevention. Perhaps the worst consequences can be prevented if we take steps to avoid the circumstances in which groupthink is most likely to flourish.

IV. Experimental Contexts

Creating and Measuring Aspects of Politically Relevant Reality

The experimental study of small groups signaled a major liberation from some major research problems, but it did not finesse all such issues and indeed created some new concerns. These three themes will get attention in this chapter, from general and specific perspectives. Organizationally the advantages and disadvantages of experimentation will be sketched first. Following that, five studies reflecting these several advantages/disadvantages will be introduced.

ADVANTAGES/LIMITS OF EXPERIMENTATION

The advantages of laboratory experiments with small human collectivities loom very large, in fact so large that a veritable scholarly deluge of such research has occurred in the last two decades (Hare 1972). One is tempted to observe that such a large number of researchers could not be very far wrong and let it go at that. It is useful, however, to provide some perspective on why so many researchers saw the same light, and why experimentation with small groups has gone on apace, even given the acknowledged limitations of the approach (Weick 1967).

Advantages. Four advantages of experimentation are particularly noteworthy. First, the experimenter's control over the specific processes to be studied is potentially far greater in laboratory settings than in most natural-state settings. Consequently, for example, instrumentation and/or observation can typically be more elaborate and sophisticated in experimental settings, while it is also possible to run large numbers of groups in any specific experiment. Although there is no necessary relationship between the degree of elaborateness or sophistication and the quality of derivative results, the first feature alone implies major advantages in the laborious process of testing alternative concepts cum operations, and of developing increasingly comprehensive theoretical linkages of covariants.

Second, hypothetical relationships can be tested with more certainty in the laboratory, as by studying large numbers of similar small groups that at least would be very much more difficult to assemble in natural-state settings. Two related advantages must be distinguished. Not only does the laboratory permit more facile manipulation of variables affecting a group's composition or processes or development; but the laboratory also facilitates the replication of the results of any individual study, under more-or-less specified conditions that would be more difficult to control or influence in the natural state.

Third, laboratory experimentation simplifies many problems of interpreting data, especially some nasty statistical ones (Campbell 1963). Experimentation in the natural state is possible, so this simplification is not unique to the laboratory. But natural-state experimentation is often difficult to arrange, and it typically is subject to a range of confounding variables that often severely complicate the interpretation of effects.

Fourth, laboratory experimentation facilitates the use of control or comparison groups, that is, groups which are matched to the experimental groups but which do not experience the experimental manipulation or intervention. Defining a control or comparison group is no simple or straightforward matter. In principle, however, such groups help avoid many interpretive problems, as in judging whether the effects reported by experimentals could be accounted for by such nonexperimental changes or influences as the mere passage of time.

Limits. Six limitations of experimentation also require confronting. First, experimentation implies that it is possible to create realistic small social systems in laboratory settings, and typically in a brief period of time. The evidence is convincing that laboratory groups often do become anchorages for the behaviors of their members. But care is necessary to establish this fact in individual cases so as to permit confident interpretation of results. Group effects, in brief, should hardly be expected in nongroup contexts.

Second, relatedly, laboratory experimentation implies that interpersonal processes induced therein are valid replicas of natural-state processes. Substantial confidence is warranted on this point, in general. Again, however, each laboratory manipulation must be evaluated in terms of its own success/failure ratio in inducing analogs of natural-state processes. For convincing research implies, and commonsense agrees, that significantly different effects can be expected when individuals are "ego involved" and when they are not. Both sets of effects are "real," of course. But there seems no reason to lump the two sets of effects together (Sherif and Sherif 1967, 105-121).

Third, several general types of experimental collectivities have been utilized in laboratory settings, and it is at least possible that qualitatively and quantitatively different effects can be generated by them. For example, some experimentation has involved natural-state groups brought into laboratory settings. Other experimentation has involved individuals who interact only in the limited sense that one party is somehow responding to a presumed second party, who in reality is a tape recording or a collection of handwritten notes prepared by the experimenter. Experimental groups also might differ in more subtle ways. Interpretations of results must strive to be sensitive to such differences.

Fourth, there is a temptation in much of the small-group literature to neglect the possibility (indeed, I believe, the fact) that various levels of social organization can differ profoundly. Thus some observers imply, or even state, that empirical regularities observed in a small group can be expected in a large organization and also in society. For this book's purposes, at least, the developmental model provided by small-group analysis has two basic characteristics. It illustrates the levels approach to phenomena, and it indicates the usefulness of concentrating initial research upon a level of phenomena which will permit rigorous study. It took the better part of a century for these two lessons to be learned well enough for small-group analysis to develop, be it noted.

The particle-atom-molecule-mass progression illustrates the levels analysis of a class of phenomena. No one of these levels is more basic than the others. Moreover, to variable degrees, each level may be developed independently. In physics, for example, Boyle's Law was developed without knowledge of mesons. But full theoretical development depends upon the development of all levels of organization, in physics as well as in the behavioral sciences.

While the levels of any class of phenomena are equally basic, at any point in time some levels are more amenable to research. This feature is of profound practical significance, and this feature of small-group analysis is its present trump card. In brief, small-group analysis is more amenable to research in these several senses: the small group has been found to be a useful and a relevant level in behavioral study; the concept implies that a social unit, a content-filled system, and systems can be rigorously studied; and the small group is amenable to experimentation, largely because of modest size. The small group, then, can make a unique claim for research attention.

Fifth, despite the apparent simplicity of many experiments, it is often problematic as to what is really going on. Consider an apparently straightforward case (Schachter 1959). Experimental subjects are randomly told that they will later receive either a painful but not dangerous electric shock or a very mild shock. The subjects are offered a choice: to wait alone or to wait with others. The hypothesis is that those looking forward to a painful shock will prefer company more than those expecting a mild shock. The data confirm that hypothesis. Nearly twice as many awaiting the painful shock opt for company.

At least six possible alternative hypotheses can explain the obvious behavioral differences, however. Briefly, subjects may have sought to engage one or more of six potentially overlapping processes (Smith 1973, 14-15): a process of social influence, to get together with others to seek a way out of the anticipated painful experience; a process of social comparison, to get some idea if others are reacting with as much anxiety, etc.; an information process, to seek clarification about what is going on; an anxiety-reduction process, as by talking things out with another in the misery-loves-company sense; a process of heightened gregariousness or affiliation induced by a common threat; and a distraction or busywork process, to reduce the probability of thinking about the anticipated shock. The differences between these processes are often significant ones. For example, distracting processes do not imply much groupiness in the sense of perceived membership, reciprocal influence, norms, and so on. Social influence processes, in contrast, imply much groupiness.

Sixth, and significantly, not all research in groups is about groups. The point is important to keep in mind, for sometimes it can be critical in the interpretation of the results of specific studies.

Let us illustrate the point by considering some research by William H. Riker and William James Zavoina, "Rational Behavior in Politics," which appeared in the March 1970 number of the *American Political Science*

Review. Their focus is on bargaining in 3-person groups; and their goal is to shed light on the hoary issue in Political Science of the degree of rationality in political decision making. Riker and Zavoina set out to determine which of three alternative philosophical positions most nearly accounts for the actual behavior of participants in a "3-person game" involving bargaining that requires the formation of coalitions. These philosophical positions are: (1) choosers maximize expected utility in making decisions, that is, they are "rational calculators"; (2) choosers make decisions in terms of habit and discovery rather than by an analysis of preferences; (3) choosers do not maximize expected utility, as in the psychoanalytic position that reason and will are sometimes at war, and often at odds.

The reader can consult the original source to learn which model was most likely to guide participants in the experiments, but two more general points need to be made here. One point deals with a major advantage of experimentation using small groups; and the other illustrates a ubiquitous question about such research. That is, despite the major contention in Political Science about which of the three models above is most descriptive of humans-as-choosers, Riker and Zavoina emphasize that "remarkably little effort" by political scientists has been devoted to resolving that contention. A major explanation of this lack of effort has been the paucity of the kind of work illustrated in the selection by Riker and Zavoina.

Moreover, it remains an open issue whether the Riker/Zavoina results would have been similar if they were derived from 3-person groups with long-standing norms and patterns of interaction, both of which characterize many natural-state groups. More specifically, different patterns of coalitions might develop in groups with "autocratic" climates or atmospheres than in "supportive" or "laissez-faire" climates. There is no conveniently available taxonomy for differentiating groups, but it seems clear enough that a group is not necessarily a group. All small-group experimentation must be sensitive to this critical point, and results must be qualified accordingly.

This second point implies a major shortcoming of all research like that of Riker and Zavoina. Substantial evidence suggests that at least three classes of interacting variables are necessary to describe group dynamics. They are (Golembiewski, 1962): (1) a population panel of variables, which deal with the individual characteristics of group members; (2) a structural panel of variables which deal with relatively persisting patterns which characterize how group members relate to one another (e.g., as in relative performance of leadership behaviors) or how groups relate to external persons or entities (e.g., in sanctioning or forbidding multiple memberships; (3) a style panel of variables dealing with the quality or tone of a group's processes, as in a group's norms for acceptable behavior.

In these terms, it is clear that Riker and Zavoina do not deal explicitly with any of these panels of variables, but rather with individual behavior. The moot point is whether group properties significantly influenced the behavior of their subjects. It is only clear that group properties can significantly influence individual behavior, which motivates attempts by researchers to deal with group-level analysis.

SIX EXAMPLES OF LABORATORY EXPERIMENTATION WITH POLITICALLY RELEVANT REALITY

Authority as a focus. We need not sidle up to our subject. Directly, there is perhaps no more central issue in Political Science than that addressed by Stanley Milgram in "Behavioral Study of Obedience," which is one of a long line of his studies on a critical theme. Whether in the restricted article reprinted here or in various other wider-ranging publications including a major book, the way Milgram addresses that issue constitutes an academic blockbuster. That judgment stands whatever the technical and philosophic reactions that individuals have to the research design and its consequences. Peter B. Smith observes of Milgram's work: "These experiments are among the most controversial to have been conducted by social psychologists to date." He adds: "Critics . . . have questioned whether researchers have the right to impose on their subjects the kind of stress which Milgram's subjects undoubtedly faced in deciding whether or not to disobey their orders. Furthermore, studies of such destructive forms of obedience are open to misuse by totalitarian authority" (Smith 1973, 31). If this introduction and the article below whet the reader's appetite, Milgram has detailed his experimental results and dwelled on their implications in a noteworthy book (Milgram 1964).

Political scientists have long puzzled as to how to create and maintain political systems that are lawful. Such systems walk a narrow line. They should rest on enough obedience to authorities perceived as legitimate enough to avoid anarchy. At the same time such lawful systems should not thereby induce so much obedience to authorities utilizing so much force and so much manipulation of reality/truth that the system is autocratic verging on totalitarian. Worldwide experience implies that this target-zone of relatively representative systems is a narrow one, which is achieved and maintained only under rather special conditions in today's political systems.

Milgram deals with a significant piece of the profound issue of governance sketched above. He asks, "How far can people be pushed by an authority figure before they are induced to defiance, given that the price of continuing obedience is the apparent injury of another human being?" Milgram's basic experimental set up involves three people: a scientist, a learner who is actually a stooge of the experimenter, and a subject who is at the controls of equipment that is said to administer variable degrees of electric shock to the learner. The surface explanation is that Milgram is interested in the effect of punishment on facilitating a learner's progress in mastering a task, which induces a major conflict for the subject. The experimenter demands that the subject continue; and the ostensible learner, a stooge of the experimenter, pleads even more insistently that the punishment cease. The essence of the experimental manipulation in its several forms is the same, as Milgram explains: "The crux of the study is to vary systematically the factors believed to alter the degree of obedience to the experimental commands, to learn under what conditions submission to authority is more probable, and under what conditions defiance is brought to the fore" (Milgram 1964, 60).

Nearly a thousand adults have been subjected to Milgram's procedure, and the overall pattern of results can be summarized with confidence, although only a full reading of the selection will provide vital detail. The results reflect (in Milgram's words) a "high level of obedience (which) greatly exceeded the expectations of the experimenter and his colleagues," as well as those of a panel of 40 psychiatrists. Indeed it appears that the limits to such obedience are very wide indeed. Witness Milgram's report about the results of an effort to find such a limit. He reports: "Cries from the victim were inserted; not good enough. The victim claimed heart trouble; subjects still shocked him on command. The victim pleaded that he be let free, and his answers no longer registered on the signal box; subjects continued to shock him" (Milgram 1964, 74).

Reasonable men have differed as to the implications of the results of this experimentation. Milgram himself is disturbed by the results, perhaps even despairs about them. Those results, he notes, "raise the possibility that human nature, or—more specifically—the kind of character produced in American democratic society, cannot be counted on to insulate its citizens from brutality and inhumane treatment at the direction of malevolent authority" (Milgram 1964, 75). Most observers seem to agree with Milgram and worry with him. There are exceptions, however. Thus Erich Fromm seems more surprised—and encouraged—by the fact that about a third of the experimental subjects refused to continue beyond some point. Fromm also sees the results as permitting no conclusions applicable to real-life situations. He explains, "The psychologist was not only an authority to whom one owes obedience, but a representative of Science and of one of the most prestigious institutions of higher education in the United States . . . . it is very difficult for the average person to believe that what science commands could be wrong or immoral" (Fromm 1973, 51). For Fromm, that is to say, Milgram induces processes that have few (if any) natural-state analogs.

It is not necessary here to decide between such opposed views. We know too little to begin. Moreover even Milgram's research leaves major questions unanswered on this score. In one of his experiments a group of three persons were to administer the shock. Two of the three were accomplices of the experimenter; one was a naive subject. Obedience to the experimenter dropped very sharply when the accomplices, by prearrangement, refused to go on with the shock sequence (Milgram 1965). It is not exactly clear how such an effect should be interpreted. Alternatively but not exclusively: (1) the naive subjects may have been influenced by the experimenter's accomplices to change their reactions to the experiment, and thus to resist authority; (2) the naive subjects may have received confirmation that their negative reactions were shared, and hence reasonable, which could have emboldened the subjects to trust their feelings and refuse to obey; and (3) the authority induction was weak to begin with, and was therefore easy to disrupt and not analogous to real-life authority situations.

However one reacts to the pattern of results, it is patent that Milgram is engaged in empirical research that has enormous prescriptive implications. Consider two levels of such implications. As for the subjects of such experimentation, value issues clearly are involved in how such research should be designed and implemented, and also in whether subjects should be exposed to the design at all. Milgram carefully seeks to deal with the anticipated emotional arousal in the experiment, and before and afterward as well; and guidelines of the American Psychological Association seek to delimit acceptable research. But these hardly constitute the ultimate word. Considering the results of such experimentation, in addition, profound value-relevant questions are everywhere. A sample includes: (1) Can and should such experimentation be justified on the grounds that it generates greater knowledge about the medical/psychologic reactions experienced by those put in extreme obedience situations? This knowledge might then be used to point up the moral stakes involved in extreme obedience situations, and also might provide clinical reinforcement for emphasis on alternative values in organizations or society. (2) What kinds of prescriptive safeguards, if any, do such results suggest can be developed to reduce the incidence of extreme obedience? (3) What concept of authority can and should be developed to avoid extreme obedience without risking anarchy or chaos?

These introductory notes could easily burst their britches and extend far beyond what they intend. At the very least, Milgram's article should establish two points, with plenty to spare. Thus experimental situations can be very real, even terrifying and perhaps scarring. So cautious care is often appropriate. Relatedly, politically relevant processes clearly can be induced and studied in laboratory settings. These processes will have both empirical and normative aspects.

Conformity as a focus. Frank P. Scioli, Jr., also shows how experimentation with small collectivities in laboratory situations can focus attention on phenomena that are of great relevance to real-world political issues. The title of his selection patently advertises the analysis of dynamics at the heart of much behavior historically labelled as "political": "Conformity in Small Groups: The Relationship Between Political Attitude and Overt Behavior."

The temptation will be resisted to redo here what Scioli brings off so clearly below, but two major points concerning his piece demand emphasis. First, Scioli's effort shows how laboratory designs can and should complement field studies. Given that both field and laboratory designs do imply unique and substantial research problems, the two approaches clearly have major advantages. Fortunately it is sometimes possible to have much of the best of both worlds. In this sense, Scioli's contribution is necessarily linked interactively with such natural-state observations as those reported in Chapter III. There, recall, attention was focused on three examples of natural-state observation of small groups as their dynamics related to party loyalty, voting patterns, and decision making within government. In simplified terms laboratory experimentation permits greater control over the conditions under which observation occurs, as well as over the range of variables to be observed. Natural-state observation has other advantages: it requires a test of the degree to which generalizations about behavior must be sensitive to various situational contexts, to specific histories or unique experiences; and it is crucial in establishing the relevance of networks of relationships isolated in the laboratory. Natural-state and laboratory observation cannot live in celibate isolation. They must be married, decisively and continuously.

Second, Scioli's selection reflects a complex blend of analytical caution as well as optimism. Thus Scioli patently shows that significant political phenomena can be intensively analyzed in small-group laboratories; and his article implies that the regularities are widely applicable to a vast range of political decisions as well as to a panoply of public decision making bodies. But Scioli clearly provides no comfort for small-group yahoos. Witness his cautionary conclusion: ". . . a vast amount of research . . . must be undertaken before a researcher can be confident that a particular attitude questionnaire may serve as a predictor of political behavior. Situational factors cannot be ignored when investigating attitude-behavior congruence, and many more variables will have to be isolated before a thorough understanding of the relationship between attitude and behavior is possible."

Anticipation of membership as a focus. Darien A. McWhirter III focuses on a subtle feature of the effects of small groups on individuals in his "Testing for Groupthink." He accepts as incontrovertible that group dynamics can have great impact on attitudes and behavior. But what of the mere anticipation of membership in some group whose membership is specified only generally? Will such anticipation impact on individuals who anticipate group membership, but who in fact will not really experience it?

McWhirter focuses on this intriguing issue, based on his appreciation of a substantial research tradition in the small-group literature. Patently the demonstration of the effects on individuals of a group that never has and never will exist would stand as formidable testimony of the powerful programs for behavior locked into the mind by past socialization experiences and expectations. McWhirter's research design is especially attractive in that it involves differential risk taking by individuals as individual decision makers who are anticipating membership in a group.

To say that McWhirter tackles a central and intriguing issue is not to say that he provides a definitive resolution to it. That would be far too much to expect, especially given the limited resources available to almost all political scientists for laboratory experimentation. And the state of research is at the problem-sensing stage, rather than at a more sophisticated stage where determinative and specific demonstrations are possible. Overall, given the small size of his population, the pattern of McWhirter's results implies that an anticipation effect may occur. And his results also suggest that researchable differences may exist between men and women in how anticipation of group membership effects them.

Search behavior in groups. Dwight F. Davis illustrates well both the potential and the problems of small-group experimentation for issues of historic relevance to Political Science.

Davis's approach, design, and conclusions are usefully sketched. Basically, he grounds his experiment squarely in a theory of political decision making. He quotes approvingly this basic statement: "What is done with information in a political context—that is, how it is stored, modified, retrieved, and communicated—represents the principal data of political analysis." Consistently, Davis's research design tests for the interaction of one aspect of personality with a range of information-processing activities in small groups. That is, in convenient shorthand, do individuals with differing degrees of cognitive complexity display different patterns of search behavior when confronted with a decision-making task? His results variously support the conclusion that such interaction does exist, with significant implications for a broad range of research.

Davis's work also implies some central problems of laboratory experimentation. For example, one implication of his results is that the character of search behavior is influenced in significant ways by a personality characteristic of the searchers. Political scientists are more likely to explain such search behavior in terms of the historical and institutional contexts in which they occur. Short-term experimental groups tend to lack such contexts, which is at once their virtue and their limitation.

The alternatives above are not necessarily either/or alternatives, although in debates they may often be presented as such. What we need guidance on—and about which short-life experimental activities are not optimally informative—is which is cart and which horse? Is the historical/institutional context dominant, with personality features moderating or reinforcing their basic thrusts? Or is it the other way around? Or are the two classes of variables interactive in complex ways? Whatever the case, the kind of interaction is researchable and need not be consigned to debate or personal preference. For example assume a massive change in the membership of a decision-making group which has developed stable norms about search behavior. If the new members have personality features contrary to such norms, what happens to the quality of search behavior? Do the norms change? Do the new members "play above their heads"? Or does a gap between ideal and performance develop, with consequent feelings of guilt, loss of competence, etc.?

Political discussions and decision making. James W. Dyson, Paul H. B. Godwin and Leo A. Hazlewood seek to investigate some of the questions raised in the selection by Dwight Davis. Their "Political Discussions and Decision Making in Experimental Small Groups" seeks to explore three hypotheses, the primary one of which is that the level of participation in group negotiations is influenced by a specific personality characteristic. Essentially the three Florida State University researchers reinforce the need to approach political analysis at multiple levels. In the present case the interacting levels include the policy context under discussion, the processes of decision making, and one significant personality attribute of group members.

The selection also reflects two noteworthy features that hopefully will become increasingly characteristic of various behavioral science borrowings by political scientists. The authors seek simultaneously to place their experimentation in the context of issues/problems in Political Science while also establishing the senses in which they extend the small-group tradition of research. The piece, in short, intends a kind of dual synergy. Relatedly the selection implies the development of observational facilities and sophistication about experimentation which "sunk costs" should make succeeding research efforts at Florida State both easier and more comprehensive.

Like most available work by political scientists, the present piece also evidences that progress does not come easily. The small number of cases, for example, implies much about the limitations of resources that constitute such a constraint to struggle against as political scientists seek to develop new traditions of research that will enhance the potency of the evolving empirical theory of politics. As that theory expands in breadth and depth, so also will political scientists be more able to develop goal-based empirical theories that prescribe how normative goals can be successfully approached via knowledge of empirical conditions and relationships.

Instrumentation as a focus. A final selection by Charles Walcott and P. Terrence Hopmann, "Interaction Analysis and Bargaining Behavior," illustrates another kind of contribution that political scientists can make to small-group experimentation. By way of preview, two conclusions underlay their effort. First, studies like those discussed here will provide more useful results to the degree that observers are aware of specific processes in individual groups. In contrast, as in the cases of the Riker/Zavoina study, group processes are more or less a black box from which some decision emerges. Second, Walcott and Hopmann became convinced that available schemes for classifying interaction (Golembiewski 1962, 215-223) are not optimally useful for the kind of choice-situations in which political scientists are interested, situations like diplomatic bargaining. Hence the line of work which led to the selection reprinted here.

This sketch of Walcott and Hopmann's motivation implies two special points of relevance to political scientists intent on small-group research. Thus they give needed attention to differentiating groups in terms of their specific interaction patterns, which is the only long-run approach to a comprehensive theory. Results based on contrary notions—that groups are groups, or that all three-person groups of undergraduates from the same college are more alike than not in their processes—may be convenient, but they also can be wickedly deceiving. Relatedly the final selection of this chapter is also instructive in the regard that political scientists moving into small-group analysis may have to be producers as well as users of instruments developed by others for other purposes (Madron 1969). The same spirit and level of inquiry can unite researchers with diverse substantive interests. But major differences in research design and in the character of observational instruments may be necessary nonetheless.

REFERENCES

Campbell, D. T. 1963. From description to experimentation. In *Problems in measuring change*, ed. Chester W. Harris, pp. 212-242. Madison: University of Wisconsin Press.

Fromm, E. 1973. *The anatomy of human destructiveness*. New York: Holt, Rinehart and Winston.

Golembiewski, R. T. 1962. *The small group*. Chicago: University of Chicago Press.

Hare, A. P. 1972. Bibliography of small group research, 1959-69. *Sociometry* 35: 1-50.

Milgram, S. 1964. Some conditions of obedience and disobedience to authority. *Human Relations* 19:60.

Milgram, S. 1965. Liberating effects of group pressures. *Journal of personality and social psychology* 1:127-134.

Milgram, S. 1974. *Obedience to authority: An experimental view*. New York: Harper & Row.

Schachter, S. 1959. *The psychology of affiliation*. Stanford, Calif.: Stanford University Press.

Sherif, C. W. and M., eds. 1967. *Attitude, ego-involvement and change*. New York: Wiley, pp. 105-121.

Weick, K. E. 1967. Promise and limitations of laboratory experiments in the development of attitude change theory. In *Attitude, ego-involvement and change*, ed. Carolyn W. and Muzafer Sherif, pp. 51-75. New York: Wiley.

Behavioral Study of Obedience

STANLEY MILGRAM

Obedience is as basic an element in the structure of social life as one can point to. Some system of authority is a requirement of all communal living, and it is only the man dwelling in isolation who is not forced to respond, through defiance or submission, to the commands of others. Obedience, as a determinant of behavior, is of particular relevance to our time. It has been reliably established that from 1933 to 1945 millions of innocent persons were systematically slaughtered on command. Gas chambers were built, death camps were guarded, daily quotas of corpses were produced with the same efficiency as the manufacture of appliances. These inhumane policies may have originated in the mind of a single person, but they could only be carried out on a massive scale if a very large number of persons obeyed orders.

Obedience is the psychological mechanism that links individual action to political purpose. It is the dispositional cement that binds men to systems of authority. Facts of recent history and observation in daily life suggest that for many persons obedience may be a deeply ingrained behavior tendency, indeed a prepotent impulse overriding training in ethics, sympathy, and moral conduct. C. P. Snow (1961) points to its importance when he writes:

> When you think of the long and gloomy history of man, you will find more hideous crimes have been committed in the name of obedience than have ever been committed in the name of rebellion. If you doubt that, read William Shirer's *Rise and Fall of the Third Reich.* The German Officer Corps were brought up in the most rigorous code of obedience . . . in the name of obedience they were party to, and assisted in, the most wicked large scale actions in the history of the world (p. 24).

While the particular form of obedience dealt with in the present study has its antecedents in these episodes, it must not be thought all obedience entails acts of aggression against others. Obedience serves numerous productive functions. Indeed, the very life of society is predicated on its existence. Obedience may be ennobling and educative and refer to acts of charity and kindness, as well as to destruction.

General procedure. A procedure was devised which seems useful as a tool for studying obedience (Milgram 1961). It consists of ordering a naive subject to administer electric shock to a victim. A simulated shock generator is used, with thirty clearly marked voltage levels that range from

Reprinted from *Journal of Abnormal and Social Psychology* 67 (1963), 371-378, with permission of author and American Psychological Association. A full account of Milgram's experiments is found in: S. Milgram, *Obedience to Authority*, 1974, Harper & Row.

15 to 450 volts. The instrument bears verbal designations that range from Slight Shock to Danger: Severe Shock. The responses of the victim, who is a trained confederate of the experimenter, are standardized. The orders to administer shocks are given to the naive subject in the context of a learning experiment ostensibly set up to study the effects of punishment on memory. As the experiment proceeds, the naive subject is commanded to administer increasingly more intense shocks to the victim, even to the point of reaching the level marked Danger: Severe Shock. Internal resistances become stronger, and at a certain point the subject refuses to go on with the experiment. Behavior prior to this rupture is considered "obedience," in that the subject complies with the commands of the experimenter. The point of rupture is the act of disobedience. A quantitative value is assigned to the subject's performance based on the maximum intensity shock he is willing to administer before he refuses to participate further. Thus for any particular subject and for any particular experimental condition the degree of obedience may be specified with a numerical value. The crux of the study is to vary systematically the factors believed to alter the degree of obedience to the experimental commands.

The technique allows important variables to be manipulated at several points in the experiment. One may vary aspects of the source of command, content and form of command, instrumentalities for its execution, target object, general social setting, etc. The problem, therefore, is not one of designing increasingly more numerous experimental conditions, but of selecting those that best illuminate the process of obedience from the sociopsychological standpoint.

Related studies. The inquiry bears an important relation to philosophic analyses of obedience and authority (Arendt 1958, Friedrich 1958, Weber 1947), an early experimental study of obedience by Frank (1944), studies in authoritarianism (Adorno, Frenkel-Brunswik, Levinson, & Sanford 1950, Rokeach 1961), and a recent series of analytic and empirical studies in social power (Cartwright 1959). It owes much to the long concern with suggestion in social psychology, both in its normal forms (e.g., Binet 1900) and in its clinical manifestations (Charcot 1881). But it derives, in the first instance, from direct observation of a social fact; the individual who is commanded by a legitimate authority ordinarily obeys. Obedience comes easily and often. It is a ubiquitous and indispensable feature of social life.

METHOD

Subjects. The subjects were forty males between the ages of 20 and 50, drawn from New Haven and the surrounding communities. Subjects were obtained by a newspaper advertisement and direct mail solicitation. Those who responded to the appeal believed they were to participate in a study of memory and learning at Yale University. A wide range of occupations is represented in the sample. Typical subjects were postal clerks, high school teachers, salesmen, engineers, and laborers. Subjects ranged in educational

TABLE 4.1

Distribution of Age and Occupational Types
in the Experiment

Occupations	20-29 years	30-39 years	40-50 years	Percentage of total (Occupations)
Workers, skilled and unskilled	4	5	6	37.5
Sales, business and white collar	3	6	7	40.0
Professional	1	5	3	22.5
Percentage of total (age)	20	40	40	

Total N=40.

level from one who had not finished elementary school, to those who had doctorate and other professional degrees. They were paid $4.50 for their participation in the experiment. However, subjects were told that payment was simply for coming to the laboratory, and that the money was theirs no matter what happened after they arrived. Table 4.1 shows the proportion of age and occupational types assigned to the experimental condition.

Personnel and locale. The experiment was conducted on the grounds of Yale University in the elegant interaction laboratory. (This detail is relevant to the perceived legitimacy of the experiment. In further variations, the experiment was dissociated from the university, with consequences for performance.) The role of experimenter was played by a 31-year-old high school teacher of biology. His manner was impassive and his appearance somewhat stern throughout the experiment. He was dressed in a gray technician's coat. The victim was played by a 47-year-old accountant, trained for the role; he was of Irish-American stock, and most observers found him mild-mannered and likable.

Procedure. One naive subject and one victim (an accomplice) performed in each experiment. A pretext had to be devised that would justify the administration of electric shock by the naive subject. This was effectively accomplished by the cover story. After a general introduction on the presumed relation between punishment and learning, subjects were told:

> But actually, we know very little about the effect of punishment on learning, because almost no truly scientific studies have been made of it in human beings.
>
> For instance, we don't know how much punishment is best for learning—and we don't know how much difference it makes as to who is giving the punishment, whether an adult learns best from a younger or an older person than himself—or many things of that sort.
>
> So in this study we are bringing together a number of adults

of different occupations and ages. And we're asking some of them to be teachers and some of them to be learners.

We want to find out just what effect different people have on each other as teachers and learners, and also what effect punishment will have on learning in this situation.

Therefore, I'm going to ask one of you to be the teacher here tonight and the other one to be the learner.

Does either of you have a preference?

Subjects then drew slips of paper from a hat to determine who would be the teacher and who would be the learner in the experiment. The drawing was rigged so that the naive subject was always the teacher and the accomplice always the learner. (Both slips contained the word "Teacher.") Immediately after the drawing, the teacher and learner were taken to an adjacent room and the learner was strapped into an "electric chair" apparatus.

The experimenter explained that the straps were to prevent excessive movement while the learner was being shocked. The effect was to make it impossible for him to escape from the situation. An electrode was attached to the learner's wrist, and electrode paste was applied "to avoid blisters and burns." Subjects were told that the electrode was attached to the shock generator in the adjoining room.

To improve credibility the experimenter declared, in response to a question by the learner: "Although the shocks can be extremely painful, they cause no permanent tissue damage."

The lesson administered by the subject was a paired-associate learning task. The subject read a series of word pairs to the learner, and then read the first word of the pair along with four terms. The learner was to indicate which of the four terms had originally been paired with the first word. He communicated his answer by pressing one of four switches in front of him, which in turn lit up one of four numbered quadrants in an answerbox located atop the shock generator.

The instrument panel consists of thirty lever switches set in a horizontal line. Each switch is clearly labeled with a voltage designation that ranges from 15 to 450 volts. There is a 15-volt increment from one switch to the next going from left to right. In addition, the following verbal designations are clearly indicated for groups of four switches going from left to right: Slight Shock, Moderate Shock, Strong Shock, Very Strong Shock, Intense Shock, Extreme Intensity Shock, Danger: Severe Shock. (Two switches after this last designation are simply marked XXX).

Upon depressing a switch: a pilot light corresponding to each switch is illuminated in bright red; an electric buzzing is heard; an electric blue light, labeled "voltage energizer," flashes; the dial on the voltage meter swings to the right; various relay clicks are sounded. The upper left-hand corner of the generator is labeled Shock Generator, Type ZLB, Dyson Instrument Company, Waltham, Mass. Output 15 Volts-450 Volts.

Details of the instrument were carefully handled to insure an appearance of authenticity. The panel was engraved by precision industrial engravers, and all components were of high quality. No subject in the experiment suspected that the instrument was merely a simulated shock generator.[1]

Each naive subject is given a sample shock on the shock generator prior to beginning his run as teacher. This shock is always 45 volts, and is applied by pressing the third switch of the generator. The shock is applied to the wrist of the naive subject and has its source in a 45-volt battery wired into the generator. This further convinces the subject of the authenticity of the generator.

The subject is told to administer a shock to the learner each time he gives a wrong response. Moreover—and this is the key command—the subject is instructed to "move one level higher on the shock generator each time the learner flashes a wrong answer." He is also instructed to announce the voltage level before administering a shock. This serves to remind subjects of the increasing intensity of shocks administered to the learner.

Pretests revealed that the procedure of reading words and administering shocks requires some practice before it can be handled smoothly. Therefore, immediately preceding the regular run, the teacher is given a preliminary series of ten words to read to the learner. There are three neutral words in the practice series (i.e., words that the learner answers correctly), so that shocks are administered for seven of the words, with the maximum shock at 105 volts (moderate shock). Almost all subjects master the procedure by the time the preliminary run is over.

Subjects are then presented with a second list, and are told that the procedure is the same as for the first list; the experimenter adds, however: "When you get to the bottom of the list, repeat it again, and continue giving shocks, until the learner has learned all the pairs correctly." The experimenter instructs the subject to "start from 15 volts and increase the shock level one step each time the learner gives a wrong answer."

In all conditions the learner gives a predetermined set of responses to the word pair test, based on a schedule of approximately three wrong answers to one correct answer. In the present experimental condition no vocal response or other sign of protest is heard from the learner until Shock Level 300 is reached. When the 300-volt shock is administered, the learner pounds on the wall of the room in which he is bound to the electric chair. The pounding can be heard by the subject. From this point on, the learner's answers no longer appear on the four-way panel.

At this juncture, subjects ordinarily turn to the experimenter for guidance. The experimenter instructs the subject to treat the absence of a response as a wrong answer, and to shock the subject according to the usual schedule. He advises the subjects to allow 5-10 seconds before considering no response as a wrong answer, and to increase the shock level one step each time the learner fails to respond correctly. The learner's pounding is repeated after the 315-volt shock is administered; afterwards he is not heard from, nor do his answers reappear on the four-way signal box.

At various points in the experiment the subject may turn to the experimenter for advice on whether he should continue to administer shocks. Or he may indicate that he does not wish to go on. It was important to standardize the experimenter's responses to these inquiries and reactions. If the subject indicated his unwillingness to go on, the experimenter responded with a sequence of "prods," using as many as necessary to bring the subject into line.

Prod 1: Please continue or Please go on.
Prod 2: The experiment requires that you continue.
Prod 3: It is absolutely essential that you continue.
Prod 4: You have no other choice, you must go on.

The prods were always made in sequence: Only if Prod 1 had been unsuccessful could Prod 2 be used. If the subject refused to obey the experimenter after Prod 4, the experiment was terminated. The experimenter's tone of voice was at all times firm, but not impolite. The sequence was begun anew on each occasion that the subject balked or showed reluctance to follow orders.

If the subject asked if the learner was liable to suffer permanent physical injury, the experimenter said:

Although the shocks may be painful, there is no permanent tissue damage, so please go on. (Followed by Prods 2, 3, and 4 if necessary.)

If the subject said that the learner did not want to go on, the experimenter replied:

Whether the learner likes it or not, you must go on until he has learned all the word pairs correctly. So please go on. (Followed by Prods 2, 3, and 4 if necessary.)

Dependent measures. The primary dependent measure for any subject is the maximum shock he administers before he refuses to go any further. In principle this may vary from 0 (for a subject who refuses to administer even the first shock) to 30 (for a subject who administers the highest shock on the generator). A subject who breaks off the experiment at any point prior to administering the thirtieth shock level is termed a defiant subject. One who complies with experimental commands fully, and proceeds to administer all shock levels commanded, is termed an obedient subject.

With few exceptions, experimental sessions were recorded on magnetic tape. Occasional photographs were taken through one-way mirrors. Notes were kept on any unusual behavior occurring during the course of the experiments. On occasion, additional observers were directed to write objective descriptions of the subjects' behavior. The latency and duration of shocks were measured by accurate timing devices.

Following the experiment, subjects were interviewed; open-ended questions, projective measures, and attitude scales were employed. After the interview, procedures were undertaken to assure that the subject would leave the laboratory in a state of well being. A friendly reconciliation was arranged between the subject and the victim, and an effort was made to reduce any tensions that arose as a result of the experiment.

RESULTS

Preliminary notions. Before giving an account of the experimental results, it is instructive to consider how persons predict others will perform when commanded to administer powerful shocks to another person. Fourteen Yale seniors, all psychology majors, were provided with a detailed description of the experimental situation. They were asked to reflect carefully on it, and to predict the behavior of one hundred hypothetical subjects. More specifically, they were instructed to plot the distribution of obedience of "one hundred Americans of diverse occupations, and ranging in age from twenty to fifty years," who were placed in the experimental situation.

There was considerable agreement among the respondents on the expected behavior of hypothetical subjects. All respondents predicted that only an insignificant minority would go through to the end of the shock series. (The estimates ranged from zero to three percent; i.e., the most pessimistic members of the class predicted that of one hundred persons, three would continue through to the most potent shock available on the shock generator—450 volts.) The class mean was 1.2 percent. The question was also posed informally to colleagues of the author, and the most general feeling was that few if any subjects would go beyond the designation Very Strong Shock.

Result of experiment I. With few exceptions subjects were convinced of the reality of the experimental situation, that they were administering shocks to another person, and that the most potent shocks were extremely painful. In the post-experimental interview subjects were asked: "How painful to the learner were the last few shocks that you administered to him?" Subjects were instructed to indicate their answers on a printed 14-point scale ranging from "Not at all painful" to "Extremely painful." The modal response was 14 (Extremely painful) with the mean at 13.42.

Many subjects showed signs of nervousness in the experimental situation, especially upon administering the more powerful shocks. In a large number of cases the degree of tension reached extremes that are rarely seen in sociopsychological laboratory studies. Subjects were observed to sweat, tremble, stutter, bite their lips, groan, and dig their fingernails into their flesh. These were characteristic rather than exceptional responses to the experiment.

One sign of tension was the regular occurrence of nervous laughing fits. Fourteen of the forty subjects showed definite signs of nervous laughter and smiling. The laughter seemed entirely out of place, even bizarre. Full-blown, uncontrollable seizures were observed for three subjects. On one occasion we observed a seizure so violently convulsive that it was necessary to call a halt to the experiment. The subject, a 46-year-old encyclopedia salesman, was seriously embarrassed by his untoward and uncontrollable behavior. In the post-experimental interviews subjects took pains to point out that they were not sadistic types, and that the laughter did not mean they enjoyed shocking the victim.

It had been conjectured that persons would not, in general, agree to administer shocks beyond the level designated as Very Strong Shock. The dis-

TABLE 4.2

Distribution of Breakoff Points

	Verbal designation and voltage indication	Number of subjects for whom this was maximum shock
Slight	15	0
Shock	30	0
	45	0
	60	0
Moderate	75	0
Shock	90	0
	105	0
	120	0
Strong	135	0
Shock	150	0
	165	0
	180	0
Very	195	0
Strong	210	0
Shock	225	0
	240	0
Intense	255	0
Shock	270	0
	285	0
	300	5
Extreme	315	4
Intensity	330	2
Shock	345	1
	360	1
Danger:	375	1
Severe	390	0
Shock	405	0
	420	0
XXX	435	0
	450	26

tribution of maximum shocks for this experiment is shown in Table 4.2. The obtained distribution of scores deviates radically from the prediction.

Upon command of the experimenter, each of the forty subjects went beyond the expected breakoff point. No subject stopped prior to administering Shock Level 20. (At this level—300 volts—the victim kicks on the wall and no longer provides answers to the teacher's multiple-choice questions.)

Of the forty subjects, five refused to obey the experimental commands beyond the 300-volt level. Four more subjects administered one further shock, and then refused to go on. Two broke off at the 330-volt level, and one each at 345, 360, and 375 volts. Thus a total of fourteen subjects defied the experimenter. It is instructive to reprint their remarks at the point of defiance, as transcribed from the tape recordings:

> (0124) I think he's trying to communicate, he's knocking. . . Well it's not fair to shock the guy . . . these are terrific volts. I don't think this is very humane. . . . Oh, I can't go on with this; no, this isn't right. It's a hell of an experiment. The guy is suffering in there. No, I don't want to go on. This is crazy. (Subject refused to administer more shocks.)

> (0123) He's banging in there. I'm gonna chicken out. I'd like to continue, but I can't do that to a man. . . . I'm sorry I can't do that to a man. I'll hurt his heart. You take your check. . . . No really, I couldn't do it.

These subjects were frequently in a highly agitated and even angered state. Sometimes, verbal protest was at a minimum, and the subject simply got up from his chair in front of the shock generator, and indicated that he wished to leave the laboratory.

Of the forty subjects, twenty-six obeyed the orders of the experimenter to the end, proceeding to punish the victim until they reached the most potent shock available on the shock generator. At that point, the experimenter called a halt to the session. (The maximum shock is labeled 450 volts, and is two steps beyond the designation: Danger: Severe Shock.) Although obedient subjects continued to administer shocks, they often did so under extreme stress. Some expressed reluctance to administer shocks beyond the 300-volt level, and displayed fears similar to those who defied the experimenter; yet they obeyed.

After the maximum shocks had been delivered, and the experimenter called a halt to the proceedings, many obedient subjects heaved sighs of relief, mopped their brows, rubbed their fingers over their eyes, or nervously fumbled cigarettes. Some shook their heads, apparently in regret. Some subjects had remained calm throughout the experiment, and displayed only minimal signs of tension from beginning to end.

DISCUSSION

The experiment yielded two findings that were surprising. The first finding concerns the sheer strength of obedient tendencies manifested in this situation. Subjects have learned from childhood that it is a fundamental breach of moral conduct to hurt another person against his will. Yet, twenty-six subjects abandon this tenet in following the instructions of an authority who has no special powers to enforce his commands. To disobey would bring no material loss to the subject; no punishment would ensue. It is clear from the remarks and outward behavior of many participants that in punishing the victim they are often acting against their own values. Subjects often expressed deep disapproval of shocking a man in the face of his objections, and others denounced it as stupid and senseless. Yet the majority complied with the experimental commands. This outcome was surprising from two perspectives: first, from the standpoint of predictions made in the questionnaire described earlier. (Here, however, it is possible that the remoteness of the respondents from the actual situation, and the difficulty of conveying to them the concrete details of the experiment, could account for the serious underestimation of obedience.)

But the results were also unexpected to persons who observed the experiment in progress, through one-way mirrors. Observers often uttered expressions of disbelief upon seeing a subject administer more powerful shocks to the victim. These persons had a full acquaintance with the details of the situation, and yet systematically underestimated the amount of obedience that subjects would display.

The second unanticipated effect was the extraordinary tension generated by the procedures. One might suppose that a subject would simply break off or continue as his conscience dictated. Yet, this is very far from what happened. There were striking reactions of tension and emotional strain. One observer related:

> I observed a mature and initially poised businessman enter the laboratory smiling and confident. Within 20 minutes he was reduced to a twitching, stuttering wreck, who was rapidly approaching a point of nervous collapse. He constantly pulled on his earlobe, and twisted his hands. At one point he pushed his fist into his forehead and muttered: "Oh God, let's stop it."
> And yet he continued to respond to every word of the experimenter, and obeyed to the end.

Any understanding of the phenomenon of obedience must rest on an analysis of the particular conditions in which it occurs. The following features of the experiment go some distance in explaining the high amount of obedience observed in the situation.

1. The experiment is sponsored by and takes place on the grounds of an institution of unimpeachable reputation, Yale University. It may be

reasonably presumed that the personnel are competent and reputable. The importance of this background authority is now being studied by conducting a series of experiments outside of New Haven, and without any visible ties to the university.

2. The experiment is, on the face of it, designed to attain a worthy purpose—advancement of knowledge about learning and memory. Obedience occurs not as an end in itself, but as an instrumental element in a situation that the subject construes as significant and meaningful. He may not be able to see its full significance, but he may properly assume that the experimenter does.

3. The subject perceives that the victim has voluntarily submitted to the authority system of the experimenter. He is not (at first) an unwilling captive impressed for involuntary service. He has taken the trouble to come to the laboratory presumably to aid the experimental research. That he later becomes an involuntary subject does not alter the fact that, initially, he consented to participate without qualification. Thus he has in some degree incurred an obligation toward the experimenter.

4. The subject, too, has entered the experiment voluntarily, and perceives himself under obligation to aid the experimenter. He has made a commitment, and to disrupt the experiment is a repudiation of this initial promise of aid.

5. Certain features of the procedure strengthen the subject's sense of obligation to the experimenter. For one, he has been paid for coming to the laboratory. In part this is canceled out by the experimenter's statement that: "Of course, as in all experiments, the money is yours simply for coming to the laboratory. From this point on, no matter what happens, the money is yours."[2]

6. From the subject's standpoint, the fact that he is the teacher and the other man the learner is purely a chance consequence (it is determined by drawing lots) and he, the subject, ran the same risk as the other man in being assigned the role of learner. Since the assignment of positions in the experiment was achieved by fair means, the learner is deprived of any basis of complaint on this count. (A similar situation obtains in army units, in which—in the absence of volunteers—a particularly dangerous mission may be assigned by drawing lots, and the unlucky soldier is expected to bear his misfortune with sportsmanship.)

7. There is, at best, ambiguity with regard to the prerogatives of a psychologist and the corresponding rights of his subject. There is a vagueness of expectation concerning what a psychologist may require of his subject, and when he is overstepping acceptable limits. Moreover, the experiment occurs in a closed setting, and thus provides no opportunity for the subject to remove these ambiguities by discussion with others. There are few standards that seem directly applicable to the situation, which is a novel one for most subjects.

8. The subjects are assured that the shocks administered to the subject are "painful but not dangerous." Thus they assume that the discomfort

caused the victim is momentary, while the scientific gains resulting from the experiment are enduring.

9. Through Shock Level 20 the victim continues to provide answers on the signal box. The subject may construe this as a sign that the victim is still willing to "play the game." It is only after Shock Level 20 that the victim repudiates the rules completely, refusing to answer further.

These features help to explain the high amount of obedience obtained in this experiment. Many of the arguments raised need not remain matters of speculation, but can be reduced to testable propositions to be confirmed or disproved by further experiments.[3] The following features of the experiment concern the nature of the conflict which the subject faces.

10. The subject is placed in a position in which he must respond to the competing demands of two persons: the experimenter and the victim. The conflict must be resolved by meeting the demands of one or the other; satisfaction of the victim and the experimenter are mutually exclusive. Moreover, the resolution must take the form of a highly visible action, that of continuing to shock the victim or breaking off the experiment. Thus the subject is forced into a public conflict that does not permit any completely satisfactory solution.

11. While the demands of the experimenter carry the weight of scientific authority, the demands of the victim spring from his personal experience of pain and suffering. The two claims need not be regarded as equally pressing and legitimate. The experimenter seeks an abstract scientific datum; the victim cries out for relief from physical suffering caused by the subject's actions.

12. The experiment gives the subject little time for reflection. The conflict comes on rapidly. It is only minutes after the subject has been seated before the shock generator that the victim begins his protest. Moreover, the subject perceives that he has gone through but two-thirds of the shock levels at the time the subject's first protests are heard. Thus he understands that the conflict will have a persistent aspect to it and may well become more intense as increasingly more powerful shocks are required. The rapidity with which the conflict descends on the subject and his realization that it is predictably recurrent may well be sources of tension to him.

13. At a more general level the conflict stems from the opposition of two deeply ingrained behavior dispositions: first, the disposition not to harm other people, and second, the tendency to obey those whom we perceive to be legitimate authorities.

NOTES

1. A related technique, making use of a shock generator, was reported by Buss (1961) for the study of aggression in the laboratory. Despite the considerable similarity of technical detail in the experimental procedures, both investigators proceeded in ignorance of the other's work. Milgram provided plans and photographs of his shock generator, experimental procedure, and first results in a report to the National Science Foundation in January 1961.

The report received only limited circulation. Buss reported his procedure six months later, but to a wider audience. Subsequently technical information and reports were exchanged. The present article was first received in the editor's office on 27 December 1961; it was resubmitted with deletions on 27 July 1962.

2. Forty-three subjects, undergraduates at Yale University, were run in the experiment without payment. The results are similar to those obtained with paid subjects.

3. A series of recently completed experiments employing the obedience paradigm is reported in Milgram (1964).

REFERENCES

Adorno, T., Frenkel-Brunswick, Else, Levinson, D. J., and Sanford, R. N. 1950, *The authoritarian personality*. New York: Harper.

Arendt, H. 1958. What was authority? In *Authority*, ed. C. J. Friedrich, Cambridge: Harvard University Press.

Binet, A. 1900. *La suggestibilite*. Paris: Schleicher.

Buss, A. H. 1961. *The psychology of aggression*. New York: Wiley.

Cartwright, S. 1959. *Studies in social power*. Ann Arbor: University of Michigan Institute for Social Research.

Charcot, J. M. 1881. *Oeuvres completes*. Paris: Bureaux du Progres Medical.

Frank. J. D. 1944. Experimental studies of personal pressure and resistance. *Journal of general psychology* 30: 23-64.

Friedrich. C . J., ed. 1958. *Authority*. Cambridge: Harvard University Press.

Milgram, S. 1961. *Dynamics of obedience*. National Science Foundation (mimeo).

Milgram, S. 1964. Some conditions of obedience and disobedience to authority. *Human relations*.

Rokeach, M. 1961. Authority, authoritarianism, and conformity. In *Conformity and deviation* ed. I. A. Berg and B. M. Bass, pp. 230-257. New York: Harper.

Snow, C. P. 1961. Either-or. *Progressive:* 24.

Weber, M. 1947. *The theory of social and economic organization*. Oxford: Oxford University Press.

Conformity in Small Groups:
The Relationship Between Political Attitude and Overt Behavior

FRANK P. SCIOLI, JR.

Field observational and laboratory experimental investigations conducted in sociology and social psychology have suggested that individuals with given attitudes will modify their overt behaviors when they perceive that the attitudes they hold are at variance with what is expected of them by others (DeFleur and Westie 1958, Linn 1965, Fendrich 1967, Ajzen and Fishbein 1969). This others category has been broadly defined to include family members, work associates, school friends, and peer groups. Concomitant with these studies is a substantial body of literature which has utilized small-group experimental techniques to demonstrate that a significant number of individuals have modified their attitudes and behaviors in group situations when their attitudes are at variance with the attitudes expressed by other members of the group (Asch 1956, Bennett 1955, Festinger and Thibaut 1951). There is thus a tendency for minorities to conform to the opinion of majorities.

The experimental situation of these small groups has frequently included a design in which a group of confederates working in conjunction with the experimenter attempt to induce a subject to conform to the norms of the group by acting as a unanimous majority. Using experimentally contrived groups composed of all naive subjects, this study investigated the relationship between verbal political attitudes and overt behaviors in group situations. The groups were composed so that some individuals held attitudes in accord with the majority of members of that group and other individuals held views that were in the minority, i.e., at variance with the political views of the majority of group members.

The literature on conforming behavior suggests the following propositions which were tested using experimentally contrived groups: (1) the relationship between verbal attitude and overt behavior is greatest among individuals who share the predominantly expressed attitudes of the group, and (2) the relationship between verbal attitude and overt behavior is lowest among individuals who do not share the predominantly expressed attitudes of the group.

RESEARCH DESIGN

The subjects for this experiment were student volunteers obtained from introductory courses in American Government at Florida State University. A

Reprinted from *Comparative Group Studies* Vol. 2, No. 1 (Feb. 1971) pp. 53-64 by permission of the publisher, Sage Publications, Inc.

paper-and-pencil-test attitude questionnaire designed to differentiate subjects along a liberal-conservative attitude continuum was administered to
approximately three hundred students in their classes. The questionnaire
contained four subsets of statements designed to provide a measure of a
subject's attitudinal response to the stimulus objects of each respective
subset and represented four different dimensions of the subject's attitude
system. One subset consisted of statements incorporating the subject's
racial attitude dimension and was designed to provide a measure of the subject's positive or negative response to the stimulus object, a Negro. A
second subset of statements was designed to provide a measure of a subject's favorable or unfavorable response to the expenditure of government
funds to aid persons classified as poverty-stricken, low income, poor, and
so forth. A third set of statements was designed to provide a measure of a
subject's response concerning the class of phenomena associated with the
word "censorship." The fourth set of statements was designed to provide a
measure of a subject's response to statements associated with the phrase
"law and order." Each individual's response patterns to the four subsets of
statements were then computer scaled utilizing the Guttman (1944) scaling
procedure. The individual's Guttman scale scores for each of the four attitude dimensions were then obtained and served as the basis by which individuals were assigned to discussion groups.

Of the nearly three hundred individuals who were administered the attitude questionnaire only individuals with scale scores of 1 or 2
(representing a liberal position) on any of the four subsets of statements,
or scale scores of 6 or 7 (representing a conservative position) were selected for use in the small group sessions. These scale scores represented the
upper and lower 20 percent of all responses. As a result of this selection
procedure a pool of subjects was created along the following dimensions
with no individual being used in more than one category: (1) Liberals and
conservatives on the race dimension; (2) Liberals and conservatives on the
censorship dimension; (3) Liberals and conservatives on the social welfare
dimension; and (4) Liberals and conservatives on the law and order dimension.

Subjects were then selected from this pool and assigned to a five-person
discussion group in which they discussed two political candidates running
for office in a nonpartisan election. Each candidate offered opposite platform positions (liberal versus conservative) on one of the four attitude
dimensions. As a result of this selection procedure the following sets of discussion groups were established: (1) A group of four liberals on the race
dimension and one conservative on the race dimension discussing two
political candidates offering opposite platform positions on the race dimension; (2) A group of three liberals on the race dimension and two conservatives on the race dimension discussing two political candidates offering
opposite platform positions on the race dimension; (3) A group of four conservatives on the race dimension and one liberal on the race dimension dis-

cussing two political candidates offering opposite platform positions on the race dimension; and (4) A group of three conservatives on the race dimension and two liberals on the race dimension discussing two political candidates offering opposite platform positions on the race dimension.

The above procedure (1-4) was replicated for each of the three other attitude dimensions thus producing sixteen groups of five members each.

The platforms of the two political candidates contained statements drawn from items reflecting specific attitude dimensions in the paper-and-pencil attitude questionnaire. Thus the stimulus to which the subjects were asked to respond in the group discussion situation and the stimulus presented in the paper-and-pencil attitude questionnaire were the same.

The students to be used in the small group sessions were contacted in their classes and given assignment sheets, each of which contained the student's name, an assigned identification number to maintain anonymity, and the date, time, and location of the discussion situation. To ensure the experimenter the correct composition for each group discussion, no fewer than nine subjects were assigned to each particular group.[1]

When the subjects came to the small-group discussion session (held approximately two weeks from the date the attitude questionnaire was administered) they were greeted by the experimenter, led into a waiting room, and presented with an instruction sheet stating the following:

> When you enter the other room you will be presented with the platforms of two candidates seeking office in an electoral contest in which you are eligible to vote. Please read the platform of each candidate and then as a group discuss the candidates. At the end of 20 minutes fill in the group decision form in the center of the table. The form requests that you select one of the candidates. If you as a member of the group differ with the group decision please complete the individual decision form which is also on the table. You will be notified two minutes before the decision is required.

At the conclusion of the group discussion the experimenter collected the decision form and led the subjects to another section of the building where a post-test questionnaire stating the following was administered: "Now that you have left the group discussion which of the two candidates do you prefer?" The subjects were also given the paper-and-pencil attitude questionnaire that they had completed several weeks prior to the group discussion situation. This entire group and post-group situation enabled an analysis of whether holding a political attitude at variance with a majority of individuals within the group led any individuals to conform to the decision of the group, or select the candidate that reflected the minority attitude position. Thus conformity behavior could be investigated under conditions of a majority of four against a minority of one and under conditions of a majority of three against a minority of two.

RESULTS

Table 4.4 presents the relationship obtained between attitude and behavior in the sixteen five-person, group discussion situations.

TABLE 4.4

The Congruence between Attitude and Behavior
in 16 Groups of Heterogeneous Composition

Subject's Attitude Position	Candidate Seclected in the Group	
	Liberal	Conservative
Liberal	75% (30)	25% (10)
Conservative	40% (16)	60% (24)

$\chi^2 = 10$ p < .001   N = 80

It is apparent that the congruence between a subject's political attitude (as ascertained by the paper-and-pencil test) and his selection of a political candidate is moderately strong. Seventy-five percent of the subjects with liberal attitudes chose the candidate espousing liberal views in his platform, and sixty percent of the subjects with conservative political attitudes chose the candidate espousing conservative political views. But it is also clear that the congruence between a subject's attitude and his choice of candidate is not perfect. Twenty-five percent of the subjects with a liberal attitude chose the conservative and forty percent of the subjects with a conservative attitude chose the liberal candidate. The main reason for this switching might be grasped if we consider the composition of the groups in terms of a disposition toward conformity.

The small groups were comprised such that fifty-six of the eighty subjects participating in the discussion were in a majority attitude position and twenty-four were in a minority attitude position. In Table 4.5 we see that seventy-seven percent of the individuals in a majority attitude position

TABLE 4.5

The Relationship Between Position in the Group
and Candidate Selection

Subject's Position in Group Discussion Situation	Candidate Selection	
	Voted with Majority	Voted with Minority
Majority	77% (43)	23% (13)
Minority	54% (13)	46% (11)

chose the candidate favored by the majority members of the group and twenty-three percent selected the candidate expressing political views different from their own attitude and from the majority attitude position. Thus this behavior of the majority attitude members in the group discussion is consistent with the report of another researcher (Gerard 1954) who suggests that subjects show greater resistance to changing an opinion if it is anchored in a cohesive group. We find also in Table 4.5 that fifty-four percent of the individuals who were in a minority attitude position joined the majority in unanimously selecting a candidate and forty-six percent voted for the candidate consistent with their attitude position.

When the discrepant cases (switching from minority to majority attitude position) are considered in terms of the composition of the group, the effect of the attitude of a majority on the attitude of individuals possessing an attitude shared by a minority of group members becomes clearer. Table 4.6 presents the instances where individuals in a minority attitude position went along with the political candidate selected by those subjects in the majority attitude position.

Of the sixteen group discussion situations, we find that, despite the absence of a confederate intentionally trying to persuade an individual, the minority acceded to the majority selection fifty percent of the time. This process occurred four times when the group composition was three versus two, and four times when the group composition was four versus one; thus it does not appear that the size of the majority was a major factor determin-

TABLE 4.6

Groups Where Minority Switched to Majority

Type of Majority	Dimension of Group*			
	Race	Censorship	Law and Order	Social Welfare
3 Liberals 2 Conservatives	—	x	—	x
3 Conservatives 2 Liberals	x	—	—	x
4 Liberals 1 Conservative	x	x	x	—
4 Conservatives 1 Liberal	—	—	x	—

*In one group discussing the law and order platforms three conservatives joined two liberals and submitted a unanimous decision for the liberal candidate.

ing whether the minority joined the majority. It appears also that the political issue being discussed in the group was of relatively little significance in either causing or preventing the switch from a minority to a majority since the switch occurred in two of the four groups on each political dimension.

We find, also, in Table 4.7 that of the twenty-four individuals in the sixteen groups who were in a minority attitude position, thirteen of these individuals, or fifty-four percent, joined the majority. Thus it seems that neither of the candidate platforms was more persuasive or biased since the switch from being in the minority to joining the majority occurred among nearly as many individuals with a liberal attitude position as among subjects with a conservative attitude. Thus although the switch from the minority position to the majority position did not occur in all of the sixteen groups or among all of the twenty-four possible switchers, the results obtained in this investigation take on greater significance when it is considered that a strong tendency toward conformity was found among only thirty-five percent of the naive subjects in the presence of inducing confederates in the classic conformity investigation conducted by Solomon Asch (1956).

Since it is expected that the individuals who joined the majority did so only because they conformed to what was expected of them by other members of the group, the natural implication would be that when presented with the post-group questionnaire the individual would choose the candidate more in line with his original attitude. The selection of a different candidate in the post-group session is expected particularly since the individual is isolated from the other members of the group where pressure to conform is absent and the opportunity to express privately held feelings is present. Despite these expectations only one of the thirteen switchers chose a different candidate in the post-group questionnaire than the candidate selected in the group. As a reason for this post-group candidate change the subject stated that he went along with the other four members

TABLE 4.7

The Relationship between Attitude Position of
Minority Subjects and Joining the Majority

Attitude Position Minority Subject	Candidate Selection	
	Switched to Majority	Did Not Switch to Majority
Liberal	6	6
Conservative	7	5
Total	13	11

N=24

TABLE 4.8

Attitude Change Among Switchers and Nonswitchers

	Attitude Change	No Change
Switchers	11	2
Nonswitchers	1	10

$\chi^2 = .16$ $P < .001$

of the group not because he preferred the candidate selected but solely to prevent an argument.

Due to the fact that only one individual changed his candidate selection in the post-group session, the question arises as to whether the group discussion experience produced attitude change for those who joined the majority or was merely a behavioral response to a specific situation. As a means of investigating this question, the experimenter readministered the paper-and-pencil-test attitude instrument to each subject after the group discussion situation. Although the readministering of the questionnaire was temporally close to the group experience, several interesting results emerged. In Table 4.8 we find that eleven of the thirteen individuals who joined the majority did, in fact, change their attitude position from the pre-group to the post-group situation, and one of the two showing no attitude change was the subject mentioned earlier who clearly implied that group pressure led to his candidate selection. Ten of the eleven subjects who were in a minority position but did not join the majority showed no change in attitude position from pre-group to post-group sessions. It would appear then that the individuals who switched to the majority position might have done so not merely as a response to a pressure to conform but because they were exposed to a viewpoint in the group discussion situation that they had not previously attended to and this exposure led to a modification in their original attitude. A subsequent research project in which this author is involved is concerned with questioning the above subjects several months after the group experience and ascertaining the extent to which the attitude change has persisted. One researcher (Kelman 1961) has stated that the persistence of the new attitude depends on a continuation of the relationship that produced it; it would be interesting to discern, therefore, how enduring the group experience was for each of the switchers.

SUMMARY

The research results reported above support the proposition that the relationship between verbal attitude and overt behavior is greater among individuals who share the predominantly expressed attitudes of the group than among individuals who are in the minority and at variance with the majority of group members. This was ascertained in contrived experimental groups where individuals with minority attitude positions (either one or two individuals in the minority) discussed two political candidates offering opposing platform positions with individuals with majority attitude positions (either three or four individuals in the majority). It was discovered that a conforming process occurred in half of the group discussion sessions despite the fact that confederates were not used to induce conformity in naive subjects. It was further found that there was a high rate of attitude change among individuals who switched from the minority attitude position to the majority attitude position and very little attitude change among nonswitchers.

This research project has demonstrated that political phenomena may be investigated intensively utilizing the small-group environment. It is clear that a vast amount of research in this area must be undertaken before a researcher can be confident that a particular attitude questionnaire can serve as a predictor of political behavior. Situational factors cannot be ignored when investigating attitude-behavior congruence, and many more variables will have to be isolated before a thorough understanding of the relationship between attitude and behavior is possible.[2]

Due to the fact that most political decision-making bodies such as city councils, school boards, legislative committees, and judicial bodies are in effect small groups of individuals, it is necessary to investigate questions relating to how these groups arrive at decisions and the process by which they formulate public policy. Governmental agencies do not often allow free access to their decision-making sessions, so the small-group technique provides numerous opportunities for attending to questions where major gaps in understanding exist. The small-group environment provides an excellent opportunity for investigating political phenomena such as bargaining, coalition formation, conflict resolution, decision making, and leadership emergence. These are by no means the only areas capable of investigation, but the current dearth of small-group research efforts by political scientists attests to the need for immediate investigations of political phenomena by those who employ small-group techniques.

NOTES

1. Extra subjects were isolated and presented with the platforms and told to choose the candidate they preferred. They were given the paper-and-pencil test again and were then allowed to leave.

2. For example the author is currently investigating the effect of personality traits, such as dominance and dogmatism, on attitude-behavior congruence and conformity behavior.

REFERENCES

Ajzen, I., and Fishbein, M. 1969. The prediction of behavioral interventions in a choice situation. *Journal of experimental and social psychology* 5: 400-416.

Asch, S. 1956. Studies of independence and conformity: I. A minority of the one against a unanimous majority. *Psychology monographs* 70: 416.

Bennett, E. 1955. Discussion, decision, commitment and consensus in group "decision." *Human relations* 8: 251-273.

DeFleur, M., and Westie, F. R. 1958. Verbal attitudes and overt acts. *American sociological review* 23: 667-673.

Fendrich, J. M. 1967. A study of the association among verbal attitudes, commitment, and overt behavior in different experimental situations. *Social forces* 64: 347-355.

Festinger, L., and Thibaut, J. 1951. Interpersonal communication in small groups. *Journal of abnormal and social psychology* 66: 92-99.

Gerard, H. B. 1954. The anchorage of opinions in face to face groups. *Human relations* 7: 313-32.

Guttman, L. 1944. A basis for scaling qualitative data. *American sociological review* 9: 139-150.

Kelman, H. C. 1961. Processes of opinion change. *Public opinion quarterly* 25: 57-78.

Linn, L. S. 1965. Verbal attitudes and overt behavior: A study of racial discrimination. *Social forces* 63: 353-364.

Testing for Groupthink:
The Effect of Anticipated Group Membership on Individual Decision Making

DARIEN A. McWHIRTER III

INTRODUCTION

For some time, political scientists have been interested in both individual and group decision making. Individual decision making is emphasized in dealing with topics such as voting behavior and reference group theory. Group decision making is usually the focus when considering bureaucracies and Congressional committees. The following study deals with the effect on individual decision making of belonging to a group, thinking about belonging to a group, or having reference to a group. Through the use of experimentation we will ask the question: What effect does the anticipation of group membership have on individual decision making? Although decision making in general has been an important object of study for some time, this central question has seldom been explicitly asked in an experimental setting by students of behavior. In this paper, a brief survey of the literature bearing on the question will be presented with close attention being paid to an experiment conducted by Neil M. Malamuth and Seymour Feshbach. An explanation of the experimental design will be presented, followed by the hypothesis to be tested. The exact procedure will be described, the results presented, and conclusions drawn.

This study began with the hypothesis that the mere anticipation of group membership could have an effect on individual decision making. An experiment was conducted to test this hypothesis. The instrument used was the Choice Dilemmas Questionnaire, and the results were examined in terms of the amount of risk exhibited. The results clearly suggest that anticipated group membership does have an effect on individual decision making.

PAST RESEARCH

During the past decade much interest has been shown by psychologists in the study of risk taking. The studies of individual risk taking have been mainly concerned with the effect of personality variables, with the important studies essentially beginning with the discovery by Atkinson (1957) that high achievers prefer intermediate risks and low achievers prefer either very high or very low risks. The willingness of groups to take risks has also been explored, with much interest in the fact that groups tend to be riskier than individuals. This interest originated with a study performed by Stoner at M.I.T. (1961). Stoner had a group of business graduate students make a series of decisions individually and then discuss these decisions in small groups to arrive at a group consensus. He found that groups were more willing to take risks than individuals, and triggered a long line of experiments concerned with the "risky-shift."

During the past decade hundreds of experiments have been performed and a dozen theories have been developed to account for the risky-shift. Most of these experiments follow a similar procedure, with a group of college students first completing the Choice Dilemmas Questionnaire developed by Kogan and Wallach (1964). This questionnaire consists of twelve descriptions of everyday life situations. In each case a hypothetical person is faced with a major decision. He can follow a safe course or take a chance in hopes of a greater reward. For example, a man is offered a much better job than his present one, but the prospective job is with a firm that may soon fold. Each student is faced with a series of probabilities from one-in-ten to ten-in-ten that the company will not fold, and is asked to choose the lowest probability he would consider acceptable to make it worthwhile for the person described to take a new job. After the students have indicated their opinions for each of the twelve items, they are divided into small groups where they are instructed to discuss each item and come to a consensus. After that they are asked to complete the questionnaire again. Thus we have each person's risk level before and after group membership, as well as the risk level of the group. Individuals are generally riskier after group discussion than before. Moreover the groups they form are usually riskier than one would have expected, given the individual decisions made before group formation.

An important discovery in the exploration of the risky-shift was made by Nordhoy (1962) when he demonstrated a conservative shift. He found that with some decisions, groups were actually more conservative than individuals acting alone. What Nordhoy demonstrated was that on certain items groups consistently make riskier decisions than individuals, while on other items they consistently make more conservative decisions. These findings have been replicated many times. Because of these results this area of study has come to be referred to as the study of choice-shifts rather than risky-shifts.

A variety of hypotheses have been developed to account for the experimental findings. Bateson (1966), for example, suggested that groups are generally riskier than individuals because the subjects are more familiar with the material. Kogan, Wallach, and Bem suggested that groups are riskier because group consensus decisions allow the participants to spread the responsibility among themselves with the result that everyone feels less responsibility for the decision (Bem, et al. 1965). Many other theories have been developed as well. Most, however, fail to stand up under replication or fail to explain the conservative shift as well as the risky-shift.

The theory that seems to be the most accepted is that the group shifts in a direction dictated by societal values. This theory posits that in some cases the society values risk, and in other cases it values caution, depending upon the circumstances involved. (Brown 1965, Clark, et al. 1971; Wallach and Wing 1968). This is supported by the consistency with which groups shift to caution or risk depending upon specific circumstances described in the questionnaire. More will be said later about the Choice Dilemmas Questionnaire (henceforth called the CDQ) and the shift to value hypothesis.[1]

MALAMUTH AND FESHBACH'S STUDY

Having looked at the history of risk-taking studies, let us examine the only study (to the knowledge of this author) that is directly concerned with the effect of anticipated group membership on individual decision making. Malamuth and Feshbach's (1972) "Risky-Shift in a Naturalistic Setting" sought to study the risky-shift using a method other than the Choice Dilemmas Questionnaire. They used ten subjects in the Individual Condition and ten groups of three subjects each in the Group Condition. The subjects were given ten dollars and told to reach a person named Joe by simulated long-distance telephone calls eight times, with the stipulation that each subject could keep the money not used in making the calls. They could make person-to-person calls which would cost $1.20 each if they succeeded in reaching Joe, but would cost nothing if they failed. Or they could make station-to-station calls which would cost seventy-five cents each whether they were successful or not. The experimenter acted as operator and collected the money. The subjects were told that Joe was randomly alternating between two rooms when in fact he was standing by two pay phones. Joe answered these phones in a constant manner such that each subject and each group reached Joe eight times after fourteen calls.

The safe course for the subjects was to call person-to-person, in which case forty cents was guaranteed. Each station-to-station call was a risk. The authors also figured that calling person-to-person was more rational because, given the probabilities involved, the amount of money a person could expect to receive using station-to-station calls was never very high.

This study is important because, for the first time in risky-shift studies, those making the group decisions were allowed to make individual decisions with the knowledge that they would later become members of a group. In past studies, the subjects had made individual decisions without knowing they were to become group members. Therefore the past studies simply recorded decisions made by individuals and decisions made in subsequently formed groups. In this study we have a third piece of data: the kinds of decisions individuals make when anticipating group membership.

The results of Malamuth and Feshbach's experiment are most interesting. Not only were the groups riskier than the individuals acting alone, but the individuals anticipating group membership were riskier than those subjects making strictly individual decisions. Thus Malamuth and Feshbach present the first epxerimental evidence that anticipated group membership can have an effect on individual decision making. Individuals making decisions in anticipation of group membership were almost as risky as decisions made in a group and significantly riskier than individuals not anticipating group membership.

DEVELOPING THE EXPERIMENT

Experimental design. It seemed to this author that it would be useful to test the effect of anticipated group membership (a new finding) by using the CDQ (an old method). After some consideration, a Posttest-Only Control Group Design was chosen. In this design there are two groups, an experimental and a control group. At time one the manipulation is given to the experimental group. At time two both the experimental and control groups are tested to judge the effect of the manipulation. Premanipulation equality of subjects is assured through randomization rather than through a pretest or matching. We could attempt to match the subjects before the experiment to assure equality, but what characteristics should be matched? How many matched factors signify equality? The simplest procedure, and for our purposes the best, is to use randomization (Campbell and Stanley 1966, McConahay 1973, Kraut and McConahay 1973).

Internal validity. Internal validity, put simply, poses the question: Did the results achieved come about because of the experimental manipulation or from some other cause? Several threats to internal validity are outlined by Donald Campbell and Julian Stanley in *Experimental and Quasi-Experimental Designs for Research* (1966), including history, maturation, and statistical regression. By using a true experimental design, we avoid these problems. Through the use of randomization, a posttest only and a simultaneous control group, any difference between the two groups is attributable to the experimental manipulation.

External validity and realism. External validity is concerned with the question of generalizability. "To what populations, settings, treatment variables, and measurement variables can this effect be generalized?" (Campbell and Stanley 1966, p. 5). The amount of generalizability is difficult to determine. Certain general threats to external validity can be minimized, however. For example, few things in nature are preceded by a pretest, and thus by not using a pretest we increase external validity. There are other problems which are not so easily minimized. The Hawthorne effect, for example, suggests that people who know they are in an experiment may respond differently than those who do not know.[2] Conducting this experiment in a classroom rather than in some more artifical setting may help reduce this possibility. Multiple treatment interference is a problem that arises when subjects who have participated in prior experiments are used for additional experiments. This problem is difficult to minimize when dealing with the student population of Yale University.

There is also the question of realism. First, two types of realism must be distinguished: experimental realism and mundane realism. Experimental realism deals with how real the experiment is to the subject. Specifically is the situation in this experiment such that the subjects will really believe they are to be put into groups at a later date? Given the fact that this experiment was conducted in a psychology class taught by a professor known to engage in research activities, there is every reason to believe that a certain amount of experimental realism was attained. Mundane realism asks the question: Is the event occurring in the laboratory similar to the real world events of interest? As in this experiment, it is certainly probable that many decisions are made by groups in which those involved have previously reviewed a written summary of the questions to be decided.

Choice dilemmas questionnaire.[3] Before discussing the hypothesis to be tested, a word is in order concerning the device to be used in this study. The CDQ has been in use for over a decade in psychological research. An early form of it was used by Stoner in his original risky-shift experiment. Since that time, close to a hundred published studies have reported results achieved using the CDQ. It has definite advantages in that it is easy to administer, it is a standardized measure, and it allows each subject to project personal decisions onto the people in the stories

CDQ has some real disadvantages, however. The fact that it is a paper-and-pencil test gives it a certain amount of artificiality. Belovicz and Finch (1971) found that if the subjects were given a continuous schedule of probabilities on each item (1 in 100 to 99 in 100), no risky-shift occurred. Most CDQs have presented the subjects with probabilities of 1 in 10, 3 in 10, 5 in 10, 7 in 10 and 9 in 10. Belovicz and Finck have suggested that this array of probabilities distorts the results. To minimize this distortion, the subjects in this study were presented with a probability array of 1 in 10, 2 in 10, 3 in 10, etc., up to 10 in 10. This array makes more sense to the author.

THEORY AND HYPOTHESIS

During the last decade many theories were developed to explain the results of the risky-shift experiments. The theory that is most accepted at present is the value-shift theory. It suggests that shifts in either direction occur because cultural values and group norms are enhanced by group discussion. We will adopt this to our needs by suggesting that the anticipation of group membership alone can cause a shift in the direction of social values and group norms. For our purposes, however, we need a more exact prediction than "some items will be riskier and others more cautious."

Cartwright (1971) examined data from several risky-shift studies which used the CDQ and found some interesting facts. On items 4, 7, and 11, the average score for those making individual decisions was from 4.1 to 4.5. On items 2, 5, and 12, the average score was from 6.8 to 7.5, and on the remaining six items the average was from 5.0 to 5.9. Bear in mind that a score of 1 on an item means the subject is willing to accept a 1 in 10 probability of the better event occurring, and thus is willing to take a great risk in hopes of a reward. A score of 10 means the subject is not willing to take any chance and wants a probability of 10 in 10 that the hoped-for reward will come about. If our experiment is analogous to past studies, those making individual decisions (the control group) should be fairly risky on items 4, 7, and 11, fairly conservative on items 2, 5, 12, and slightly risky on the remaining items. Cartwright also found that there is a correlation of .81 between the initial mean of an item and its mean after group discussion. In other words, items which elicit conservatism in individuals tend to shift to further conservatism after group discussion, and vice versa. For this minitheory to be supported, similar behavior must be forthcoming from those anticipating group membership. Thus our minitheory predicts that the subjects anticipating group membership will be more conservative on items 2, 5, and 12, and riskier on the other items than the control group.

Another relevant study was conducted by McCauley, Teger, and Kogan (1971). They ran the standard risky-shift design and found that individuals had an average score of 66.4 for all twelve CDQ items. Keep in mind that a score of 120 means the subject has been as cautious as possible on all the items, while a score of 12 means the subject has been as risky as possible on all the items. The same individuals who averaged 66.4 were then put into groups for the purpose of reaching a group consensus. After group discussion the average group total was 59.2. In other words, the groups had significantly shifted to risk. The experimenters then did something that had not previously been done. They formed groups of people who had not filled out the CDQ individually and asked them to discuss the items and come to a group consensus. The average for these groups was 62.0. If those in our experiment who anticipate group membership answer closer to what a group would (as was found to be the case in Malamuth and Feshbach's study), and if our results are analogous to those achieved by McCauley, Teger, and Kogan, then we would expect those in our experiment acting as individuals to have a mean total close to 66.4 and those anticipating group membership to have a mean close to 62.0.

Another study, conducted by Ferguson and Vidmar (1971), bears on this hypothesis. They asked subjects to fill out the CDQ and then estimate for each item what they thought would be culturally appropriate. On those items where the responses usually shift to risk, they judged a riskier response to be more appropriate; on the items where the responses usually shift to caution, the subjects judged a cautious response to be more culturally appropriate. If those subjects in our study who are anticipating group membership answer closer to what is culturally valued, they should answer closer to what a group would answer. Stoner, in a later study (1968), found that decisions on the CDQ were consistent with widely held values as assessed by a different instrument.

A study conducted in France also lends support to the value-shift theory by showing groups to be more extreme than individuals acting alone. Moscovici and Zavalloni (1969) found that Frenchmen liked DeGaulle before group discussion, and liked him even more after group discussion. The same study showed that Frenchmen hated Americans before group discussion, and hated them even more after group discussion. Charters and Newcomb (1952) found that Catholics gave responses closer to their religious group's norms when the experimenter invoked their group membership. Thus if the invoking of group membership can effect individual responses in the direction of group values, perhaps the anticipation of group membership can have the same effect.

PROCEDURE

This experiment was conducted in April 1973 in a small lecture hall at Yale University. The thirty-five subjects were students of The Psychology of Social Movements taught by John McConahay. A 10:00 A.M. lecture had been scheduled for the day of the experiment. During the first thirty minutes, Professor McConahay presented a condensed version of the lecture he had prepared. He then introduced the experimenter, who proceeded to pass out the questionnaires.

The questionnaires were passed out in a random fashion. They were identical except for one paragraph. For those subjects in the control group, the third paragraph read as follows:

> The purpose of this session is to assess your individual opinions. There are no right or wrong answers. Work as quickly as possible but give careful consideration to each question. Of course, do not be concerned with anyone else's answers and do not discuss anything pertaining to this until you have left the classroom.

For those in the anticipated group membership condition, this paragraph was replaced by the following:

> The purpose of this session is to assess your individual opinions and for you to familiarize yourself with this material. At a later date you will be put into groups of 5 for the purpose of discussing these items and coming to a group consensus. Further information about these sessions will be distributed as you leave the classroom.

Note that the dissimilar paragraphs are almost the same length, and the first line and last two words of each are the same. This was done to insure that if anyone did glance at the questionnaire of the person next to him, he would not find a discrepancy.

Before the students began filling out the questionnaire, they were instructed to pick up a sheet of paper from the experimenter as they left the classroom. It was hoped that this would add further realism to the situation by causing those in the anticipated group membership condition to assume that the sheet would contain further instructions for their subsequent group meetings. Control group subjects could simply assume that all others, like themselves, received a debriefing sheet, which in fact they did.

As the students left the classroom, they handed in their questionnaires and took a debriefing sheet. After a few days, the experimenter returned to the class and explained the results. The only difference in stimulation between the two groups was the difference between the two paragraphs discussed above. Through random distribution, fifteen males and three females were in the control group, and ten males and seven females were in the anticipated group membership condition.

RESULTS

The average total CDQ score was 64.3 for those who anticipated group membership, and 67.1 for those who did not. Thus we find those who anticipated group membership riskier (willing to accept a higher risk and thus achieving a lower score) than those who did not, with the totals being very similar to those achieved by McCauley, Teger, and Kogan in their comparison of groups and individuals (62.0 and 66.4). Our results do not reach usually accepted levels of statistical significance,[4] however, partially due to the fact that there was wide variation in the ratio of males to females in the two experimental groups. In the anticipation group, there were ten males and seven females, while in the nonanticipation group there were fifteen males and three females. Women have historically scored more conservatively on the CDQ, and that was the case in this experiment. Thus the large percentage of females in the anticipation group dampened the effect of the experimental manipulation. Recall that the value hypothesis does not predict a shift to risk on all items. It predicts that those anticipating group membership should be more conservative on items 2, 5, and 12, and riskier on the remaining items. If we compare just the nine items expected to be risky, we find that the aggregate scores are 43.08 and 46.12 respectively, which is statistically significant at the .05 level.[5] This was the case even though item 7 showed no difference, and those who anticipated group membership were more conservative on item 3.

The value hypothesis predicted that those who anticipated group membership would be more conservative on items 2, 5, and 12. In this experiment they were more conservative on items 2 and 5, but riskier on item 12. The value hypothesis predicted that those who anticipated group membership would be riskier on the other nine items. This was the case except for item 3 which was slightly more conservative. This could have occurred because item 3 is concerned with investing in the stock market. During the last decade when the CDQ was administered, the stock market was doing well; in the last two years it has been doing rather badly. Perhaps society's values concerning the stock market have changed so that caution is now valued.

When we look at individual items and compare performance on the risk-evoking items, a significant difference in the expected direction also exists. It seems warranted, given the results of Malamuth and Feshbach's study and the results of this study, to conclude that group formation is not needed to achieve the risky-shift effect. We can also conclude, given the results of past CDQ studies and the results of this experiment, that the value hypothesis best accounts for the results obtained.

DISCUSSION AND CONCLUSIONS

In terms of the risky-shift literature, this experiment reaffirms past results achieved through the use of the CDQ. It also suggests that almost as much risky-shift can be obtained without actual group discussion when such discussion is merely anticipated.

Now we must ask the question: How many decisions in government are made by groups or by individuals acting on the recommendations of groups? At the federal level there are Congressional committees, interagency committees, policy-making committees, high level decision-making committees like the National Security Council, and others. At other levels of government we find city councils, county councils, state legislative committees, commissions, and many more groups charged either with reaching a decision or setting the boundaries within which a decision can be made. It is usually hoped by those interested in public administration and policy analysis that whoever makes the decision will have a full range of alternatives before them. Yet this may be impossible, given the group aspects of high level decision making. Many alternatives may never be considered because normative constraints operate to exclude them from the very beginning. One of the major aspects of a good decision, according to Janis, is the consideration of a full range of alternatives. Many observers have suggested that the group dynamics of some situations can put constraints on this. This experiment demonstrates that other aspects of the decision-making structure, such as what might be called mental-group dynamics, can have an effect as well.

This study is extremely relevant to those interested in studying and improving decision making in both the private and public sectors. It has long been known that decisions can be the result of individual decision making in anticipation of group membership. There is a distinct difference between the two, although both are significant.

NOTES

1. I refer readers interested in learning more about this aspect of the literature to the following review articles: Kogan and Wallach 1967, Pruitt 1971, Cartwright 1971, Vinokur 1971, and Clark 1971.

2. See Kraut and McConahay 1973 for an up-to-date discussion of the Hawthorne effect.

3. For a copy of the Choice Dilemmas Questionnaire, see Appendix E, pp. 256-261 in Kogan and Wallach 1964.

4. Using an unweighted means of analysis of variance.

5. Using an unweighted means of analysis of variance.

REFERENCES

Atkinson, J. W. 1957. Motivational determinants of risk taking behavior. *Psychological review* 64: 359-372.

Bateson, N. 1966. Familiarization, group discussion, and risk taking. *Journal of experimental and social psychology* 2: 119-129.

Belovicz, M. W., and Finch, F. E. 1971. A critical analysis of the risky shift phenomenon. *Organizational behavior and human performance* 6: 150-168.

Bem, D. J., Wallach, M. A., and Kogan, N. 1965. Group decision making under risk of aversive consequences. *Journal of personality and social psychology* 1: 453-460.

Brown, R. 1965. *Social psychology.* New York: Free Press, Ch. 13.

Campbell, A., et al. 1964. *The American voter.* New York: John Wiley & Sons, Inc.

Campbell, D. T., and Stanley, J. C. 1963. *Experimental and quasi-experimental designs for research.* Chicago: Rand-McNally.

Cartwright, D. 1971. Risk taking by individuals and groups. *Journal of personality and social psychology* 20: 361-378.

Charters, W. W., and Newcomb, T. M. 1952. Some attitudinal effects of experimentally increased salience of a membership group. *Readings in social psychology.* New York: Henry Holt and Company.

Clark, R. D. 1971. Group induced shift toward risk: a critical appraisal. *Psychological bulletin* 76: 251-270.

Clark, R. D., Crockett, W. H., and Archer, R. L. 1971. Risk-as-value hypothesis: the relationship between perception of self, others, and the risky shift. *Journal of personality and social psychology* 20: 425-429.

Ferguson, D. A., and Vidmar, N. 1971. Effects of group discussion on estimates of culturally appropriate risk levels. *Journal of personality and social psychology* 20: 436-445.

Janis, Irving L. 1972. *Victims of Groupthink.* Boston: Houghton Mifflin Company.

Jellison, J. M., and Riskind, J. 1970. A social comparison of abilities: interpretation of risk taking behavior. *Journal of personality and social psychology* 15: 375-390.

Jellison, J. M., and Riskind, J. 1971. Attribution of risk to others as a function of their ability. *Journal of personality and social psychology* 20: 413-415.

Kogan, N., and Wallach, M. A. 1964. *Risk taking: a study in cognition and personality.* New York: Holt, Rinehart and Winston.

Kogan, N., and Wallach, M. A. 1967. Risk taking as a function of the situation, the person, and the group. *New directions in psychology,* Ed. G. Mander, P. Mussen, N. Kogan, and M. Wallach. New York: Holt, Rinehart and Winston.

Kraut and McConahay. 1973. Soon to be published article in the *Public opinion quarterly* 37: 398-407.

Levinger, G., and Schneider, D. J. 1969. Test of the risk is a value hypothesis. *Journal of personality and social psychology* 11: 165-169.

Madaras, G., and Bem, D. J. 1968. Risk and conservatism in group decision-making. *Journal of experimental and social psychology.* 4: 350-365.

Malamuth, N. M., and Feshbach, S. 1972. Risky shift in a naturalistic setting. *Journal of personality* 40: 38-49.

McCauley, C., Teger, A., and Kogan, N. 1971. Effect of the pretest in the risky-shift paradigm. *Journal of personality and social psychology* 20:379-381.

McConahay, J. 1974. Experimental research in political psychology. In *The handbook of political psychology,* ed. J. Knutson. San Francisco: Jossey-Bass.

Moscovici, S., and Zavalloni, M. 1969. The group as a polarizer of attitudes. *Journal of personality and social psychology* 12: 125-135.

Nordhoy, F. 1962. *Group interaction in decision-making under risk.* Unpublished master's thesis, School of Industrial Management, MIT.

Pruitt, D. G. 1971. Choice shifts in group discussion: an introductory review. *Journal of personality and social psychology* 20: 339-360.

Stoner, J. A. F. 1961. *A comparison of individual and group decisions including risk*. Unpublished master's thesis, School of Industrial Management, MIT.

Stoner, J. A. F. 1968. Risky and cautious shifts in group decisions: the influence of widely held values. *Journal of experimental and social psychology* 4: 442-459.

Vinokur, A. 1971. Review and theoretical analysis of the effects of group processes upon individual and group decision involving risk. *Psychological bulletin* 76: 232-250.

Wallach, M. A., and Wing, C. W. 1968. Is risk a value? *Journal of personality and social psychology* 9: 102-106.

Search Behavior of Small Decision-Making Groups: An Information-Processing Perspective

DWIGHT F. DAVIS

INTRODUCTION

An emphasis on information search and processing in a theory of political decision making is justified in part by the fact that decision making in general can be described almost exclusively in communication terms, i.e., those processes by which information is transmitted, received, and used by decision makers. In other words decision making is information-dependent, whether the information is solely the product of decision makers' memories or is acquired from sources external to decision makers. Moreover this assumption appears to underlie most political research, though often implicitly. Dyson, Godwin, and Hazlewood state the argument succinctly: "It may be suggested, from the perspectives of content and methods of political research, that what is done with information in a political context—that is, how it is stored, modified, retrieved, and communicated—represents the principal data of political analysis."[1]

Because decision making is information-dependent, the study of how decision makers generate and use information is intrinsically interesting. Furthermore information search, as one aspect of decision-making behavior, is from a normative perspective of crucial interest to decision-making theorists because of the purpose of such activity in the decisional enterprise. A decision maker cannot know everything. Therefore in deciding, it is necessary to seek information in order to limit (if not eliminate) the possibility of error. Decision makers need information on the nature of the problem, the problem environment, the nature and consequences of alternative actions, and feedback from previous decisions on the problem or related problems.[2] The quality of decisions, in large measure, hinges on the ability of decision makers to obtain and process this information.

It is odd, given the importance of information search in political decision making, that few scholars have systematically addressed it in their research. Commenting on the lack of research in this area, Wilensky notes with ambivalence: "It is strange that social scientists, who are by profession devoted to the application of reason to man's affairs, have been more impressed by the use and misuse of power than by the use and misuse of knowledge."[3]

The study described below is part of a larger project aimed at helping to fill this void in decision-making research.[4] Utilizing comparative small groups, an experiment was conducted to investigate the relationships be-

An earlier version of this paper was presented at the 1974 annual meetings of the American Political Science Association; Chicago, Ill., Aug. 29-Sept. 2, 1974.

tween constraints imposed on decision makers and information search behavior by these decision makers. The fundamental assumption of this effort is that only by systematically observing under controlled conditions how decision makers store, modify, retrieve, transmit, and receive information can we begin to develop general explanations for political decision making. Hopefully, repeated efforts in this direction will aid us in escaping the tendency to explain political decisions in terms of the historical context in which they occur.[5]

CONSTRAINTS ON INFORMATION SEARCH IN DECISION MAKING

The search for information to solve a problem or reach a decision is not costless. As Downs observes: (1) "information is costly because it takes time, effort, and sometimes money to obtain data and comprehend their meaning, and (2) decision makers have only limited capabilities regarding the amount of time they can spend making decisions, the number of issues they can consider simultaneously, and the amount of data they can absorb regarding any one problem."[6] This being the case, it would seem imperative that decision-making research address the relationships between constraints imposed on decision makers and the search for information by decision makers, as well as other predecisional processes. Allison has demonstrated, for example, that decisions made during the Cuban missile crisis can be explained almost exclusively in terms of the organizational constraints on decision makers addressing the problem.[7] Simon anticipated such a research focus more than two decades ago when he suggested that organizational procedures and communication patterns largely predetermined the type and quantity of information acquired by decision makers.[8]

Situations condition search behavior also. Hermann, for example, suggests that consideration of alternatives is constrained in crisis decision making.[9] Presumably decision makers are more easily overloaded (i.e. reach information processing capacity) in crisis situations than in noncrisis situations, and consequently tend to limit search activity during crisis decision making. Though not specifically concerned with crisis decision making, Janis's work on groupthink indicates that a number of foreign policy fiascoes were the result of limited search behavior on the part of decision makers involved and a concomitant inability or failure to correct initial estimate errors.[10] Janis postulates that limited information search is associated with conformity tendencies which are present in almost all small group decision-making situations.

As Downs notes, decision makers are also constrained by their cognitive limitations. Individual decision makers can only attend to and process limited amounts and varieties of information. Moreover the processing capacity of individual members of a decision-making group is probably variable. It follows, therefore, that information search behavior by decision-making groups is affected by the cognitive limitations of the group's members. It is this kind of constraint on search behavior which provides the focus for this study.

INFORMATION PROCESSING CAPACITY
AND SEARCH BEHAVIOR

A point of general agreement among cognitive psychologists is that all acts of cognition are essentially constructive in nature. That is, we create our perceptions of our environment rather than directly reflect stimuli as a mirror reflects a physical image. According to one prominent psychologist, ". . . seeing, hearing, and remembering are all acts of construction, which may make more or less use of stimulus information depending on the circumstances."[11]

Differences in perception and information processing are not, however, the result of random distortion. If cognition is a constructive process, then it occurs according to specific rules. Indeed conceptual learning is normally discussed in terms of the rules used to combine stimulus information to give it meaning.[12] A conceptual rule which has been widely addressed in political research is that of balance. First suggested by Heider, the theory has had various formulations; but the primary thrust is that individuals seek and process information to maintain a consistent view of their environment and themselves.[13] All research on the relationship between political attitudes and behavior essentially involves the investigation of the use or nonuse of a balance rule.

Perception and information processing can be discussed in terms other than cognitive balance, however. If we conceive of cognition as the use of various kinds of conceptual rules which have been learned and stored in memory, then the fact that people perceive the same stimuli differently may be explainable in terms of the availability of conceptual rules to different individuals. One cannot assign meaning to a set of stimuli unless he has learned (or is able to learn) the necessary rules for combining stimulus information and relating it to information which he has stored in memory. Phillips and Edwards, for example, demonstrated that subjects in a simple probability estimating experiment were unable to make accurate predictions until they had learned the appropriate combinatory rules necessary for utilizing the information provided in the problems they were to solve.[14]

Additionally the interrelationships between conceptual rules also affect information processing. According to Schroder, Driver, and Streufert: "Information processing refers to the nature and interdependence of conceptual rules available for organizing dimensional values. One problem is to determine the number of dimensional attributes processed in an environment, and if two or more dimensional attributes of information are perceived, the next problem is to determine the degrees of freedom involved in the rules of combination."[15]

Using this framework then, it is clear that we can discuss information processing by decision makers in terms other than the content of beliefs of decision makers. Instead we can look at information processing in terms of the availability of conceptual rules for decision makers and the level of structural complexity of conceptual rules (i.e. the level of interdependedness of rules), or simply, cognitive complexity. In short decision makers are limited in their information processing capacity by their level of cognitive complexity.

The behavioral results of varying levels of cognitive complexity (or "integrative complexity") have been developed in detail by Schroder, Driver, and Streufert. Essentially an individual is considered to be cognitively simple if the conceptual rules available to him for the processing of information are relatively few in number and "fixed" or hierarchically arranged. Symptoms of this kind of cognitive structure are categorical thinking or perceptual rigidity. An individual is considered to be cognitively complex if the rules available to him for processing information are large in number and interdependent or arranged in a manner so that he has more connections between rules and is able to develop alternative connections and rules as the information presented to him becomes increasingly complex. Furthermore, "the more integratively complex the information processing structure, the more 'self' enters as a causal agent in generating new perspectives and new ways of relating to objects."[16] In other words, cognitively simple individuals are more "stimulus-bound" than cognitively complex individuals, and are therefore heavily reliant on situationally specific information. Cognitively complex individuals, on the other hand, are more capable of integrating information which they have stored in memory with information provided by stimuli.

The logical consequences of varying information processing capacities on information search behavior by decision makers are (1) that decision makers will consciously or unconsciously acquire only as much information as they can effectively process and (2) that the diversity of information acquired will vary according to the level of cognitive complexity of decision makers. One effort to test these propositions was conducted by Shapiro and Bonham.[17] Dissatisfied with the traditional approaches to the study of foreign policy decision making, which were almost exclusively concerned with how decision makers considered given alternatives, these scholars attempted to measure the impact of varying levels of cognitive complexity on the generation of alternatives by decision makers. Their experiment involved the presentation of identical international crisis scenarios to three recognized experts on international politics with the charge that these experts study the material and formulate information search strategies and decisional alternatives for policy makers who would address the crisis. The fields of expertise of each of their three subjects ranged from very narrow to very broad in scope, which the authors reasoned would provide a basis for classifying the subjects along a continuum from cognitively simple to cognitively complex with respect to the issues involved. The results of the experiment clearly suggested that the cognitively simple subject was much more "stimulus-bound" and consequently considered a much narrower range of information and alternatives than did the subjects who were more cognitively complex.

The experiment described below represents an additional attempt to measure the impact of varying levels of cognitive complexity of decision makers on information search. Instead of individuals, however, the units for analysis are decision-making groups. The basic hypotheses tested are:

> H_1: Decision-making groups composed of cognitively complex decision makers will acquire more predecisional information than decision-making groups composed of cognitively simple decision makers.
> H_2: Decision-making groups composed of cognitively complex decision makers will be less "stimulus-bound" in their search for information than will decision-making groups composed of cognitively simple decision makers.

Failure to falsify these hypotheses should open a host of questions for future research. Notable among them is the role of learning in decision making. If information processing is conditioned by the nature of conceptual rules which have been learned and stored in memory, then changes in informational patterns of decision-making groups with stable membership must necessarily involve the learning of new rules and/or the development of new interrelationships between available rules.[18]

RESEARCH DESIGN

Scenarios. Subjects for the experiment were thirty-six small groups of undergraduate students which were directed to act as student government budgeting committees. Preliminary scenarios provided to groups described their task as follows: "You have been asked to participate in a decision-making experiment. The problem is to decide on the student government budget for Merriwether University, a medium sized institution of higher learning. . . . " Also, included in the preliminary scenario was background material concerning the previous year's budget, expected revenue for the coming year (the same as the previous year), current budget information concerning the amounts requested by the various campus activities (all had requested a ten percent increase), and estimates of the consequences of either allocating the amount requested or allocating a marginal increase. In no way were groups limited to the four decision issues discussed in the scenario. Indeed they were informed that they could request any information which they considered relevant to make their final budget decisions.

Measurements. To measure the cognitive complexity of experimental decision makers, a modified version of a technique developed by Zajonc was used.[19] On the pretest, subject volunteers were asked to list freely all the important attributes they could think of which were important in describing a university, and based on this to compose an outline which organized the attributes into meaningful groupings and subgroupings, with headings and subheadings if necessary. Complexity scores were obtained by summing across the number of attributes which were weighted according to their level of imbeddedness in the outline. Attributes assigned to the level of main headings received a weighting of one; attributes assigned to the first level of subheadings received a weighting of two, etc.

Two points about the cognitive complexity measure employed are worth noting. First, high complexity scores result not only from attribute dif- ferentiation (i.e. the number of attributes listed), but also the degree to which subjects perceived interrelationships between attributes. This logic follows the definition of cognitive complexity previously described: that cognitive complexity involves both the availability of conceptual rules and the interrelationships between rules. Second, the stimulus specified in the cognitive complexity measure is the same as the primary stimulus object in the tasks given to groups. This strategy is suggested by the lack of scholarly consensus as to whether cognitive structures are enduring properties of in- dividuals, or are specific to the stimulus object under consideration, or the situation.[20] At a minimum it is reasonable to assume that budget decision makers are influenced by their conceptualization of the institutions being funded.

Though theoretically appealing, the cognitive complexity measure em- ployed did pose several dilemmas for the experimenter as it applied to characterizing groups. First, the distribution of cognitive complexity scores was highly skewed with approximately half the volunteer population clustering in the lowest range. (Descriptive statistics for the distribution of cognitive complexity scores are range = 1-97, mean = 19.9, median = 14.1, standard deviation = 16.8, and kurtosis = 4.4.) This led to a random assign- ment procedure rather than the creation of comparison groups which were homogeneous with respect to member cognitive complexity. A random assignment procedure seems reasonable, moreover, because there is no reason to expect that members of any given decision-making group are homogeneous with respect to their levels of cognitive complexity. Second, subject attrition, a common plague of small group experimentation, resulted in some groups which changed in terms of group size and heterogeneity of member cognitive complexity from meeting to meeting*.

*Attrition rates for the three experimental sessions are respectively, 25(13.9%), 35(19.4%), and 43(23.3%). These figures include five subjects who attended meetings but who were in groups which did not meet because they lacked the required three-member quorum at one or more meetings. Group sizes for the three meetings are as follows:

	Group Size				
	0-2	3	4	5	Total
Meeting 1	1	3	14	18	36
Meeting 2	2	7	11	16	36
Meeting 3	1	9	19	7	36

A check for systematic bias from subject attrition revealed that individuals in the low, moderate, and high levels of cognitive complexity had almost exactly the same probability of

Finally, even if groups could be consistently characterized by heterogeneity of member cognitive complexity, the potential impact of members with extreme scores would be hidden if groups were characterized strictly in such terms.

Consequently in the data analysis section of this paper, groups are characterized by their mean level of cognitive complexity. In addition to being sensitive to the impact of members with extreme scores, this measure allows comparison between groups with different numbers of members attending. Furthermore, when treated as an ordinal level variable, the measure proved to be stable over the three experimental sessions despite subject attrition. Excluding the three groups with no quorum at one or more meetings, all groups maintained the same ordinal level (low, moderate to high) of mean cognitive complexity from meeting one to meeting two. Three groups changed their mean level of cognitive complexity from meeting two to meeting three. Attention will be drawn, however, to those instances where group heterogeneity appears to explain some of the variance in search behavior by groups.

Information search by decision-making groups is treated in two ways. First a distinction is made between external search and internal search. External search is operationalized in terms of the written requests for information by groups. These requests were coded according to the number of information items requested and the number of different kinds of information requested. Sixteen information categories were possible. Internal search is operationalized in terms of information transactions between group members during their groups' discussions. Each conversational segment was coded according to the theme being discussed and the total number of themes per group meeting recorded. (Sixteen different discussion themes were possible. The information and theme categories were similar, but were not perfectly coterminous. The coding scheme used for information requests allowed for finer distinctions among categories than did the coding scheme used for themes.) While realizing that the range of topics discussed by decision makers is only part of internal information search, it was felt that at this stage of inquiry a relatively simple observer coding scheme was best. Subsequent research will involve in part the development of measurement apparatuses for investigating intensive search behavior on a narrow range of decision issues.

A second distinction is made between information search at discussion meetings or predecisional sessions, and information search at the decisional meeting. During discussion meetings decision makers are assumed to be concerned specifically with removing as much uncertainty as possible. In the decisional meeting decision makers are under pressure

---

not attending experimental sessions. Nevertheless excluding groups which did not have a quorum at one or more meetings resulted in five groups which changed their level of heterogeneity from meeting one to meeting two and four groups which changed from meeting two to meeting three. Cut points for cognitive complexity levels were as follows: low complexity=1-18, moderate complexity=20-38, and high complexity=41+.

to decide and must, therefore, devote their discussion to consideration of a few alternatives and the mechanics of recording their decisions rather than attempting to remove whatever residual uncertainty persists.

Subject recruitment. Experimental subjects were drawn from a pool of volunteers in Introductory American Government courses at Florida State University. The experimenter entered several classes and informed the students that volunteers were needed for an experimental research project and that those who participated would be given extra credit toward their final grade. The experiment itself was described simply as a decision-making experiment which would involve one evening meeting a week for three weeks. Students were told that the meetings would take very little of their time, the first two lasting twelve minutes each and the last twenty minutes. They were also informed that there would be questionnaires for them to complete, and that each meeting would be videotaped. The experimenter emphasized that all data collected would be kept in strictest confidence and that the experiment would involve no tasks which were embarrassing. From a pool of 221 volunteers, 180 subjects were randomly assigned to thirty-six five-person groups.

Experimental setting and procedures. All experimental sessions were held in a small classroom and recorded on videotape. No attempt was made to conceal the microphone or videotape camera. Controls for the recording equipment, however, were operated from an adjacent room by an assistant. This arrangement allowed the experimenter to record all verbal interactions between group members, thus providing the opportunity to code these interactions at a later time rather than make on-the-spot judgments. Additionally the experimenter was able to be absent from the experimental meeting room except at the beginning and end of each session. It is interesting to note that overt recording strategy seemed to provide almost no diversion for subjects. What few comments were made about the equipment were made at the beginning of experimental sessions. Subsequently subjects appeared to be oblivious to the fact that they were being recorded, and they concentrated on the task presented to them. This is probably due in part to the fact that only the controls of videotaping equipment emit noise, and also because no special lighting equipment was necessary. The experimenter and two trained assistants coded the tapes.

When subjects arrived at the meeting location, they were greeted by the experimenter or an assistant and given copies of the scenario. At a designated time the group was led into the meeting room and seated in a semicircle. One member of the group was designated chairperson (the selection was random) and given an information request form for the group.* The experimenter then left. One minute before the group session

---

*Formal designation of chairpersons was done to see if formal leaders affected search behavior of groups which varied in terms of the cognitive complexity of group members. No relationship was found. In fact, chairpersons were no more likely to be group leaders than other group members regardless of the cognitive complexity of group members or the cognitive complexity of the chairperson.

was to end, groups were informed that they had one minute to finish their discussion and write down any requests for information. At the conclusion of the session, subjects were directed not to discuss their task with anyone other than each other, and reminded that they would meet at the same time and place the following week. The second discussion meeting was conducted in the same manner as the first except that groups received answers to their information requests. Information provided to groups was manipulated with respect to its utility for removing uncertainty. This manipulation had no effect on search behavior.

At the decisional meeting, in addition to typed answers to information requests, each group received a decision form on which to record the budget allocations for each of the campus activities listed. A five-minute warning was provided at this meeting to insure that groups had adequate time to record their decisions.

ANALYSIS OF DATA*

External information search. While we are interested in all information requested by groups, it is informative to look at distributions of information requests at each of the discussion meetings. From Table 4.9 it is apparent that most groups never engaged in extensive search for information from sources external to the group. One-third of the groups requested few information items at both discussion meetings. Of those groups which requested few information items at the first meeting, only twenty-five percent requested more than a few items at the second meeting, and none of them engaged in extensive search at the second meeting. If we combine those groups which engaged in low search for both meetings with those groups which engaged in low search at one meeting and moderate search at the other meeting, we account for twenty-six of the thirty-six groups, or seventy-two percent.

Since there were no groups which engaged in extensive external information search at both discussion meetings, the moderate search and high search categories are collapsed in Table 4.10. Additionally, because there were only six groups in the moderate mean cognitive complexity level, the moderate and high categories for mean cognitive complexity are also collapsed. Collapsing these two levels of cognitive complexity is also justified by the fact that so few groups ever engaged in extensive external information search. If information provided in the scenario caused most groups to reach processing capacity or if the decision-making task was perceived to be sufficiently simple as to require little information other than that provided in the scenario, then there is little reason to expect differences between moderately complex and highly complex groups.[21]

* Contingency tables are used throughout this section because the distribution of data points for almost all variables deviated widely from normality and precluded the use of regression analysis or analysis of variance. Cut points used for ordering data represent natural gaps in the distributions.

TABLE 4.9

Comparison of External Information Search Levels*
at Discussion Meetings (N=36)

Search Levels	Search Levels for Meeting Two					
	Low Search		Moderate Search		High Search	
for Meeting One	%	No.	%	No.	%	No.
Low Search	75	12	25	4	0	0
Moderate Search	71**	10	14**	2	14**	2
High Search	33	2	67	4	0	0

*Low Search equals 0-10 items requested, moderate search equals 11-27 items requested, and high search equals 32 plus items requested. Descriptive statistics for external search at meeting one are: range=2-63; mean=18.4; median=14.8; standard deviation=16.9; kurtosis=0.7 Descriptive statistics for external search at the second meeting are: range=0-37; mean=9.1; median=4.5; standard deviation=9.7; kurtosis=0.9.

As Table 4.10 clearly illustrates, no relationship was found between the mean level of cognitive complexity of decision-making groups and external information search. In fact the relationship appears to be almost totally random. Further evidence for falsification of our hypotheses is provided in Table 4.11 which shows the relationship between the mean cognitive complexity of group members and diversity of information sought by decision-making groups. Theoretically we would expect moderately complex to highly complex groups to seek more differentiated information than cognitively simple groups. Again, however, no relationship was found between the mean cognitive complexity of groups and external information search. Moreover, contrary to initial expectations, groups with low mean cognitive complexity appear to have a slightly greater propensity for requesting diverse information than moderate- to high-complexity groups. Though still not statistically significant, this tendency was even clearer when the investigator looked at the relationship between heterogeneity of member cognitive complexity and external search behavior by groups. Of the twenty-eight groups which maintained a consistent level of group heterogeneity, eight were composed of all low-complexity members, eleven predominantly low-complexity members, seven of predominantly moderate- to high-complexity members, and two of all moderate- to high-complexity members. In terms of raw amounts of information requested, no pattern was found; but in terms of diversity of information requested, homogeneous low-complexity groups had the greatest probability of requesting a moderate to high level of information diversity. Eighty-eight percent of these groups requested a moderate to high level of information diversity as compared to fifty-five percent of the heterogeneous low-

TABLE 4.10

The Relationship between
the Mean Cognitive Complexity of Decision Makers
and Total External Information Search by Groups (N=33*)

Mean Cognitive Complexity Levels of Groups**	Search Levels***				
	Low Search		Moderate to High Search		
	%	No.	%	No.	N
Low Complexity	47	9	53	10	19
Moderate to High Complexity	50	7	50	7	14

Tau B= -.03† χ^2 =.04††   P= N.S.

*The N equals 33 because one group did not have a quorum at the first discussion meeting and two groups did not have a quorum at the second meeting.

**Low mean cognitive complexity equals 5.5-18.0 and moderate to high mean cognitive complexity equals 20+. Descriptive statistics for the distribution of mean cognitive complexity at meeting one are: range=5.5-49.8; mean=19.2; median=13.9; standard deviation=11.3; kurtosis= 0.1. Descriptive statistics for the distribution of mean cognitive complexity at meeting two are: range=5.5-49.8; mean=20.5; median=13.5; standard deviation=12.9; kurtosis=-0.3.

***Total external search levels were computed by summing the number of items requested at both meetings and using parallel cut points. Thus low search equals 0-20 items requested and moderate to high search equals 21+ items requested. Descriptive statistics for overall external information search are: range=5-83; mean=27.4; median=21.5; standard deviation= 22.3; kurtosis=0.4.

†Kendall's Tau B is a measure of association for grouped data. See Hubert M. Blalock, Social Statistics, 2nd ed. (New York: McGraw-Hill, 1972), 418-426.

††Chi square is corrected for continuity. This procedure is followed for all 2 by 2 tables in this analysis section. See Blalock, 285-287.

complexity groups, seventy-two percent of the heterogeneous moderate- to high-complexity groups and fifty percent of the homogeneous moderate- to high-complexity groups. Because the relationship between heterogeneity of member cognitive complexity and external information search is not consistent and also because of the small Ns involved, any generalization is necessarily speculative; but this finding is nevertheless intriguing.

It may be that groups composed solely of cognitively simple members tended to use a scatter gun information search strategy because there are no individuals in the groups who can remove decisional uncertainty without resort to wide ranging external search. This possibility underscores the need for more refined measurement techniques which can distinguish between random search over a wide variety of types of information and intensive search for relevant information.

In summary, external information search by decision-making groups in

TABLE 4.11

The Relationship between
the Mean Cognitive Complexity of Decision Makers
and Diversity of Information Sought by Groups (N=33)

Mean Cognitive Complexity Levels of Groups	Diversity of Information Sought*						
	Low Diversity		Moderate Diversity		High Diversity		
	%	No.	%	No.	%	No.	N
Low Complexity	26	5	53	10	21	4	19
Moderate to High Complexity	36	5	43	6	21	3	14

Tau C=-.07** $\chi^2=.39$ P=N.S.

*Low diversity equals 0-4 kinds of information requested. A group which requested no more than four kinds of information essentially limited itself to the issues raised in the original senario, and was therefore considered to be "stimulus bound." Moderate diversity equals 5-6 different kinds of information and high diversity equals 7+ kinds of information. Descriptive statistics for information diversity sought by groups are: range=2-11; mean=5.4; median= 5.3; standard deviation=2.2; kurtosis=0.6.

**Tau C is a measure of association for grouped data with unequal numbers of categories. See Hubert M. Blalock, Social Statistics, 2nd ed. (New York: McGraw-Hill, 1972), 421-426.

this experiment cannot be explained in terms of the cognitive complexity of group members. In part this results from the fact that most decision-making groups engaged in only limited external information search. Thus the dependent variable of interest has bounded variance. As speculated, this may be due to information overload provided by the scenario material or a perception by experimental decision makers that the task was essentially simple and did not require much information in addition to that provided in the scenario. Resolution of the first possibility requires an attempt to measure the extent to which decision makers integrate information provided to them. Testing the second possiblity involves utilizing essentially the same research design, but with a different type of decision problem in which the alternatives are not as clearcut as in budgeting. At this point cognitive complexity of decision makers does not appear to be a very useful variable for explaining external information search behavior of groups.

Internal search: Discussion meetings. In addition to acquiring information from external authorities decision makers also remove uncertainty by disseminating information and alternative perspectives to each other in discussion. Discussion focus by decision-making groups may vary from concern with a few issues to attempts by group members to remove uncertainty about a broad range of issues.

Tables 4.12 and 4.13 present the relationship between the mean cognitive complexity of decision makers and internal information search at discussion meetings. Unlike the results which were obtained with respect to external search, there is a moderately strong relationship between mean cognitive complexity levels of groups and internal search. The relationship is particularly strong at the first discussion meeting during which decision makers are first considering their decision problem. Sixty-three percent of the low-complexity groups focus on no more than four issue areas at this meeting, whereas none of the moderate- to high-complexity groups are so constrained. Content analysis of the discussions, moreover, indicated that in almost all cases those groups which engaged in a low level of internal search behavior never considered any decision issues which were not raised in the scenario material.

TABLE 4.12

The Relationship Between
the Mean Cognitive Complexity of Decision Makers
and Discussion Focus at the First Discussion Meeting (N 35)

| Mean Cognitive Complexity Levels of Groups | Discussion Focus* | | | | |
| | Narrow Focus | | Moderately Broad to Broad Focus | | |
	%	No.	%	No.	N
Low Complexity	63	12	37	7	19
Moderate to High Complexity	0	0	100	16	16

Tau B = .66 $\chi^2 = 12.70$ P = .001

*Narrow focus equals 1-4 topics discussed, a moderately broad to broad focus equals 5+ topics discussed. Descriptive statistics for discussion focus at meeting one are: range 1-11; mean=5.2; median=5.7; standard deviation=2.5; kurtosis= -0.7.

The relationship between the mean cognitive complexity of decision makers and internal search is considerably weaker at the second meeting though still in the expected direction. The weakness of the relationship at the second discussion meeting is not unreasonable, however, when we consider the fact that decision makers knew that they must reach a decision at their next meeting. Consequently discussion focus for all groups tended to narrow at this meeting as groups developed a decisional strategy. Indeed, at the second meeting only one group discussed more than six issue areas, whereas during the first discussion meeting six groups discussed seven or more topics.

Looking at Table 4.14 we can see that in terms of overall internal information search, the mean cognitive complexity of decision makers is a fairly powerful predictor variable. While all of the moderate- to high-complexity groups engaged in broad discussion focus overall, only twenty-six percent

TABLE 4.13

The Relationship Between
the Mean Cognitive Complexity of Decision Makers
and Discussion Focus at the Second Discussion Meeting (N=34)

Mean Cognitive Complexity Levels of Groups	Discussion Focus*				
	Narrow Focus		Moderately Broad to Broad Focus		
	%	No.	%	No.	N
Low Complexity	63	12	37	7	19
Moderate to High Complexity	27	4	73	11	15

Tau B=.36 χ^2=3.14   P=.08

*Cut points for discussion focus at meeting two are the same as those for meeting one. Descriptive statistics for discussion focus at meeting two are: range=1-9; mean=4.6; median =4.7; standard deviation=1.9; kurtosis=-0.5.

TABLE 4.14

The Relationship Between
the Mean Cognitive Complexity of Decision Makers
and Overall Discussion Focus for Both Discussion Meetings (N=33)

Mean Cognitive Complexity Levels of Groups	Overall Discussion Focus*						
	Narrow Focus		Moderately Broad Focus		Broad Focus		
	%	No.	%	No.	%	No.	N
Low Complexity	42	8	32	6	26	5	19
Moderate to High Complexity	0	0	0	0	100	14	14

Tau C=.72 χ^2=17.9   P=.0002

*Cut points for overall discussion focus are the same as those for overall diversity of information requested and discussion focus at individual meetings. Thus narrow focus over 11 equals 1-4 topics discussed, moderately broad focus equals 5-6 topics discussed, and broad focus equals 7+ topics discussed. Descriptive statistics for overall discussion focus are: range=1-11; mean=6.6; median=7.0; standard deviation=2.5; kurtosis=0.4.

of the low-complexity groups did so, and almost half of the low-complexity groups engaged in very narrow discussion focus overall.

It is interesting to note that six of the eleven groups with low mean cognitive complexity which engaged in a moderate to high level of internal search at discussion meetings were composed of all low-complexity members for both meetings one and two. These six groups represent seventy-five percent of the groups which maintained homogeneously low-complexity membership for discussion meetings. In contrast fifty-six per-cent of the groups with low mean cognitive complexity which were heterogeneous in terms of member cognitive complexity (i.e. had at least one moderate- to high-complexity member) engaged in moderate to broad discussion. This finding and the finding that homogeneous low-complexity groups had the greatest probability of requesting diverse information from external sources are truly anomalies, given the findings of Schroder, Driver, and Streufert, that such groups are less capable of processing com-plex information than are groups whose members have moderate to high levels of cognitive complexity.[22]

In summary, results obtained in this experiment clearly indicate that in-ternal information search by decision-making groups is affected by the cognitive complexity of decision makers. In general the results are in the expected direction with moderate to high cognitive complexity groups overwhelmingly going beyond stimulus information in their group discus-sions at predecisional meetings. Adequate explanation of the search behavior by groups with low mean cognitive complexity must await further inquiry, however. In future experiments the author hopes to measure the extent to which groups integrate information which they have generated. If it turns out that low complexity groups do not process information they have acquired as well as moderate- to high-complexity groups, then we can legitimately assume that extensive search by low-complexity groups repre-sents random behavior. Furthermore consistent reliance on diverse exter-nal information may represent a different way in which such groups are stimulus bound, in that their decisions are heavily influenced by authoritative sources external to the group.

Internal search: Decisional meeting. Discussion focus during the time established for deciding is necessarily constrained due to the pressure for reaching a decision. Accordingly groups spent little time attempting to remove uncertainty. Instead they spent most of their time recording their budgetary decisions and making marginal adjustments among budget items. In fact, twenty-six, or seventy-four percent, of the experimental groups dis-cussed less than five topics at the decisional meeting.

Table 4.15 presents the relationship between the mean cognitive com-plexity of decision makers at the decisional meeting and discussion focus at that meeting. In contrast to results obtained in discussion meetings, no statistically significant relationship was found, though moderate- to high-complexity groups were twice as likely to engage in moderately broad to broad discussion. Groups with low mean cognitive complexity evidence no pattern in their discussion at decisional meetings.

Apparently something other than the cognitive complexity levels of deci-sion makers accounts for the variance in internal information search behavior at decisional meetings. Homogeneous and heterogeneous groups with low mean cognitive complexity have almost identical proportions in

TABLE 4.15

The Relationship Between
the Mean Cognitive Compexity of Decision Makers
and Discussion Focus at the Decisional Meeting (N=35*)

Mean Cognitive Complexity Levels for Groups	Discussion Focus**				
	Narrow Focus		Moderately Broad to Broad Focus		
	%	No.	%	No.	N
Low Complexity	52	12	48	11	23
Moderate to High	33	4	67	8	12

Tau B=.18 $\chi^2 = .50$ P=N.S.

*The N equals 35 because one group did not have a quorum at the decisional meeting.

*Because discussion focus for all groups was narrowed at the decisional meeting, cut points for the discussion focus levels are modified to reflect this fact. Thus a narrow focus equals 1-3 topics and a moderately broad to broad focus equals 4+ topics. Descriptive statistics for discussion focus at the decisional meeting are: range=1-8; mean=3.7; median=3.7; standard deviation=1.7; kurtosis=0.1.

The number of groups in each of the mean cognitive complexity levels changed at the decisional meeting due to subject attrition. Descriptive statistics for mean cognitive complexity at the decisional meeting are: range=6.0-49.8; mean=19.6; median=13.5; standard deviation=12.5; kurtosis=0.4.

each of the two levels of discussion focus at this meeting. The contrast between these null results at the decisional meeting and those obtained at discussion meetings illustrates the importance of distinguishing between predecisional and decisional activity. Though always active, it is during the time designated for decision that value preferences, bargaining, coalitions, and leadership take on paramount importance in the decisional enterprise. Subsequent reports from this project will address some of these issues.

CONCLUSION

It has been argued in this study that the cognitive complexity levels of decision makers affect the search for information by decision-making groups. Specifically it was hypothesized that decision-making groups composed mostly of moderate- to high-complexity members engage in more extensive information search behavior than decision-making groups composed mostly of low-complexity members, and that moderate- to high-complexity groups are less stimulus bound in their search for information than low-complexity groups. These hypotheses were falsified in terms of external information search by decision-making groups. With respect to internal information search, however, the results were generally in the expected direction and were statistically significant, but only for predecisional meetings. An interesting finding is that groups composed solely of members with low levels of cognitive complexity tended to behave much like groups with moderate- to high-complexity members. These mixed results strongly suggest the need for incorporating additional constraint variables in future research on search behavior by decision-making groups.

Though modest in scope, this experiment does underscore the viability of conceptualizing decision-making in terms of information processing. Human beings interact with one another through symbolic communication. It logically follows, therefore, that factors which affect communication are important in the study of decision making by political groups as well as other kinds of political phenomena. If we can, through the conscious inclusion of communication variables in our research, explain variation in the reception, modification, storage, retrieval, and transmission of information by political actors, we can account for a great majority of politically relevant behavior. Adopting such a theoretical focus, however, requires that we divest ourselves temporarily from overriding concern with political outcomes. As this experiment illustrates, there is considerable variation in communication and information processing patterns prior to making decisions. Though we may observe that a set of decisions by decision-making groups are marginally different from one another, this does not explain variations in information processing and communication patterns which preceded the decisions.

NOTES

1. James W. Dyson, Paul H. Godwin, and Leo A. Hazlewood, "Political Discussion and Decision-Making in Experimental Small Groups," paper delivered at the annual meetings of the American Political Science Association, Washington, D. C. 5-9 September 1972. Also see Lester W. Milbrath, *The Washington Lobbyists* (Chicago: Rand McNally, 1963) and Karl Deutsch, *The Nerves of Government* (New York: The Free Press, 1966). For a review of writings on communication see Ithiel de Sola Pool, et al., *Handbook of Communication* (Chicago: Rand McNally, 1974).

2. Stephen S. Skjei, *Information for Collective Action* (Lexington, Mass.: Lexington Books, 1973), 9-46.

3. Harold L. Wilensky, *Organizational Intelligence* (New York: Basic Books, 1967), 7.

4. Dwight F. Davis, "Search Behavior in Small Decision-Making Groups: An Experimental Inquiry," (Unpublished Ph.D. Dissertation, The Florida State University, 1974).

5. For a discussion of this tendency see Charles Roig, "Some Theoretical Problems in Decision-Making Studies," *Political Decision Making Processes*, ed. Dusan Sidjanski (San Francisco: Jossey-Bass, 1973), 19-54.

6. Anthony Downs, *Inside Bureaucracy* (Boston: Little Brown, 1967), 3.

7. Graham T. Allison, *The Essence of Decision* (Boston: Little Brown, 1971), Ch. 3, 4.

8. Herbert A. Simon, *Administrative Behavior* (New York: MacMillan, 1947).

9. Charles F. Hermann, *Crises in Foreign Policy* (New York: Bobbs-Merrill, 1969), 133-137, 158-170.

10. Irving L. Janis, *Victims of Groupthink* (Boston: Houghton Mifflin, 1972).

11. Ulric Neisser, *Cognitive Psychology* (New York: Appleton-Century Crofts, 1966), 10.

12. Lyle E. Bourne, Jr., *Human Conceptual Behavior* (Boston: Allyn and Bacon, 1966), 73-79.

13. William J. McGuire, "The Current Status of Cognitive Consistency Theories," *Attitude Theory and Measurement,* ed. Martin Fishbein (New York: John Wiley & Sons, 1967), 401-421.

14. Lawrence D. Phillips and Ward Edwards, "Conservatism in Simple Probability Inference Tasks," Unpublished manuscript, The University of Michigan, Institute of Science and Technology, 1966; cited in Ward Edwards, "Decision-Making: Psychological Aspects," *International Encyclopedia of the Social Sciences,* ed. David L. Sills, vol. 4 (New York: Macmillan, 1968), 34-42.

15. Harold M. Schroder, Michael J. Driver, and Siegfried Streufert, *Human Information Processing* (New York: Holt, Rinehart and Winston, 1967), 14.

16. Ibid., 9.

17. Michael J. Shapiro and G. Matthew Bonham, "Cognitive Process and Foreign Policy Decision-Making," *International Studies Quarterly,* vol. 17 (June 1973): 147-174.

18. This is an established line of research in psychology. See H. F. Harlow, "The Formation of Learning Sets," *Psychological Review,* vol. 56 (1949): 51-65, and Robert Axelrod, "Schema Theory: An Information Processing Model of Perceptions and Cognition," *American Political Science Review,* vol. 67 (December 1973): 1248-1266.

19. Robert B. Zajonc, "The Process of Cognitive Tuning in Communication," *Journal of Abnormal and Social Psychology,* vol. 61 (1960): 159-167. For a discussion of alternative measures of cognitive complexity see Schroder, Driver, and Streufert, 163-204.

20. ———, "Cognitive Theories in Social Psychology," in Gardner Lindzey and Elliot Aronson, eds., *The Handbook of Social Psychology,* vol. 1 (Reading, Mass.: Addison Wesley, 1969), 320-411, esp. 327-328.

21. Schroder, Driver, and Streufert, 54-66.

22. Ibid., 107-125.

Political Discussions and Decision Making in Experimental Small Groups

JAMES W. DYSON, PAUL H. B. GODWIN, & LEO A. HAZLEWOOD

The analysis of small-group decision making is not new to political science, for the group basis of politics is extensive, ranging from city councils and commissions to school boards, and from regulatory agencies to juries and the courts. In all of these contexts the principal mode of interactions is bargaining over feasible solution sets. The relationships between participants invariably contain both common and conflicting interests, making bargaining a mixed-motive interaction. Kelley and Thibaut put the point thusly: "If the interests of the parties are totally congruent, there is nothing to bargain for; and if they are totally opposed, there is no basis for bargaining. In the bargaining relationship the interests of the parties are partly in conflict (for example, their preferences are different), but there is also at least some degree of commonality of interest (both parties lose from costly negotiations or from disruption of the relationship)."[1]

In addition to bargaining, decision-making discussions in political groups involve negotiations in the presence of others. Experimental studies in small-group behavior indicate that working in conjunction with others or simply before others tends to make members of a group increase their similarities and decrease their differences. This tendency holds when there is a shift to risk (when the behaviors of group members become more risky) or a shift to caution (when members become more cautious than any single individual was on a pretest or when there is a regression to the mean in expressions of view).[2] Natural observation suggests that these experimental findings are not without parallel in politics. Familiar examples of the shift to caution might be the behavior of liberals on a committee who follow the norm structure much the same way as conservatives. Perhaps the presence of others is important in a political context because of the realization that bargaining is the name of the game, but in any event it does appear to influence behavior.

A third factor related to behavior of experimental groups dealing with open solution sets, also present in small political groups, is the communications structure. The "comcon" communications network—a decentralized net in which each member of a small political group is free to speak to any other member of the group—is present in most of these political groups. It is generally conceded that these decentralized nets are more efficient, commit fewer errors and achieve higher levels of satisfaction than centralized nets when the problem tasks are complex.[3] Yet the advantages of decentralized nets are not what make them interesting for political scientist; they are interesting mainly because many political bodies function with this form of communication network.

A fourth characteristic which appears to link experimental groups to political group behavior is the distribution of information about a problem found among members of the group. Some group members possess more information must apply their knowledge wisely to effectively avoid an-political groups, those who believe that they possess a greater share of information must apply their knowledge wisely to be effective avoid antagonizing other members of the group. Yet even if the experts are successful in conducting themselves gracefully, they may fail to persuade; for eloquence is not equated with persuasion.

The problems our experimental groups faced did not have a correct solution or imply one or two best solutions. On the contrary the stipulated problems permitted a large number of alternative solutions, a situation which is commonly expected to create uncertainty among group members.[4] Furthermore leaving the solution set open is a primary condition of political bargaining. Members of a political group may be constrained by their own predispositions, constituency relations, appraisals of what outcomes are most viable, and individual information processing capacity, but they are seldom constrained by the correct or best solution.

HYPOTHESES

Three hypotheses are considered in this paper: (1) Levels of participation in group negotiations are influenced by personality; (2) Group decisions tend to favor compromises which lead to stand-pat or incremental choices; and (3) Groups with a single, emergent leader are more likely than leaderless or multileader groups to arrive at consensual decisions. These hypotheses involve certain expected relationships between personality and activity levels, between interaction and individual differences, and between leadership and decisional outcomes which are implicit within the small-group literature. The first hypothesis modifies the focus present in the small-group literature on the personality of leaders, and directs that focus toward the personality of small-group participants generally. We hypothesize that high-dominant personality types will be high participators and low-dominant personality types will be low participators.

The second hypothesis is based on the argument that interaction or activity in the presence of others increases the similarities and decreases the differences between individuals. We expect this tendency to be manifested in two ways. First we shall expect group discussions to reach a common and redundant level in which individual differences in decisional preferences decrease and individual similarities in decisional preferences increase. Second we shall expect this tendency toward decreasing individual differences to result most frequently in decisions which are closest to past practice. Given Bennett's finding that individuals tend to moderate their viewpoints to a compromise position in the presence of others,[5] it is difficult to imagine a condition where a great-change decision is a likely compromise decisional outcome. In short the tendency in small groups is to compromise so as to retain past decisions (stand-pat decisions) or to vary from them only slightly (incremental decisions).

The third hypothesis examines the impact of the nature of leadership on the extent of agreement among group members. With a single leader the group is provided with a simple interaction structure and a clear line of responsibility. The presence of a single leader, together with the group characteristics which this tends to produce, is more likely to facilitate consensual agreements than will those situations in which the group has no leader or multiple leaders. Here the more complex structure and the more ambiguous lines of responsibility associated with either of these leadership conditions will lead to less focused discussion, less resolution of individual differences, and lower levels of decisional agreement. Thus we expect single leaders to be associated with consensual decisional outcomes.

RESEARCH DESIGN

Four variables were controlled in the experiment reported here: personality, communications network, sex, and decisional tasks. Since previous research has shown that those who score high on a dominance personality inventory are most likely to converse in groups and to play leadership roles, we placed at least one high-dominant personality in each of thirteen groups. We also relied on a comcon net, a communications network in which every person was free to speak to everyone else. We controlled for sex by deliberately creating groups comprised only of males, only of females, and of males and females. The scenarios given to each group (to be discussed in the following section) provided an information base for the participants to use in reaching their decisions. Thus the decisional tasks were controlled.

In addition to the controlled variables, two process variables were allowed by vary in the small groups: mean ($\bar{X}$) interactions, and attitudinal presets of group members relevant to the particular political problems. Mean interactions tell us whether the groups discussed the problem in a lively or introspective way, relying on Bales' Interaction Process Analysis. From these data we hope to learn how the degree of interaction is related to leadership patterns, increasing or decreasing individual differences, and decisional outcomes. Attitude presets, describing the value systems of the participants, are intended to show how predispositions relate to the information which the participants introduced, their level of interaction, and their actual decisions.

Experimental constraints. A number of situational or structural constraints are present in any group experiment. Five of these constraints are of general importance: (1) the time frame, (2) interaction outside the experiment, (3) communication networks, (4) personalities of members of the groups, and (5) the nature of the information provided the groups. While the first four constraints can be discussed in general terms, the last constraint is contextually specific and is considered separately.

Although in almost all political situations the decisional time frame is limited and interactions outside the group context may directly influence behavior within the situation, experimental techniques are not yet sufficiently refined to assess how these conditions affect results. Typically the experimental exposure is limited to one brief meeting, and members of the experimental groups usually do not know each other. We deviated from this procedure by using multiple exposures (one twenty-minute meeting per week for three weeks) to individuals taking an undergraduate course in Political Science together. All the groups functioned in a comcon communications network, and at least one dominant personality was assigned to every group to decrease the likelihood of obtaining groups without a leader. These variations were employed not to replicate a particular political situation but simply to vary the constraints so we may eventually learn whether they systematically influence group behavior.

The fifth experimental constraint was the information provided. Each individual in the experiment was given a background factbook which described pertinent aspects of the geographical location and physical terrain, historical legacies, and economic, social, and political systems of a mythical country. Participants were informed that they were expected to become familiar with the contents of the factbook, and one class session was held to discuss these contrived data. Each member of the five-person discussion groups, instructed that he or she was a decision maker of the mythical country, was given different one-page scenarios at several time points which dealt with community development, budgetary allocations, and electoral reform. Each contained (1) basic information (including past decisions in the area) on the problem under examination, (2) some structural constraints imposed either by time, available personnel, funds for expenditure or some combination of these factors, and (3) a recommendation of some alternative courses of action by different mythical authority groups (e.g., The Special Advisory Committee, The National Commission on Social Problems).

The Ss were explicitly informed—both in pretreatment oral instructions and in the scenario—that they could accept or reject any alternative suggested in the scenario, or that they could create their own alternatives. Thus the experiment established some structurally constraining parameters while preserving the idea of open solution sets. Assignment of Ss to the groups was by random procedure except as required by the modifications discussed in this section.

Measurement. Several measurement procedures were employed to assess the variables contained in the three hypotheses tested here. First, a shortened version of Gough's dominance personality inventory[6] utilizing Guttman items was used to assess personality traits commonly associated with public activity, including the willingness to act and lead in the presence of others. Second, group interaction was assessed through the Bales Interaction Process Analysis (IPA) and the number of initiate statements given by the subjects. (Initiate statements are ones which advance a point of view about the problems the group is considering. In a sense, this type of statement is a subset of the Bales Interaction Process Analysis.) In these experimental groups both the Bales IPA and the initiate statements produced highly comparable results as the initiate categories closely paralleled the two commentary categories of Bales Interaction Process Analysis: individuals who initiate statements also interact in a variety of ways. Thus the real advantage of using the two coding procedures is that this affords a check on coder reliability.

Task leadership was assessed through the Bales Interaction Process Analysis, a procedure which has shown that members of small groups usually select those who score high on the Bales categories as leaders. As is so often the case in small-group research, however, these results were obtained by using groups meeting only once. It has not been demonstrated sufficiently whether the same individual in a group will dominate interactions with groups meeting over time. Thus repeated applications of the Bales procedure allowed us to examine any variations in task leadership from meeting to meeting.

To deal with the issue of leadership after group members become familiar with each other, the first meeting of each group was a familiarization session. At this meeting Ss were placed in the environment which they would encounter in subsequent sessions (i.e., information and tasks presented in scenarios, the presence of videotape equipment, time constraints, etc.); hence the familiarization session was not coded. The following two sessions were coded, however, to provide the interaction and decisional outcome data to be reported in this paper.

Finally decisions were coded as stand-pat, incremental, or great-change according to how closely they resembled the past decisions on the problem given in the scenario then under consideration. Stand-pat decisions were those which were roughly the same as those made in past decisions on the problem. Incremental decisions involved some minimal increases in the funding levels over prior allocations. Great-change decisions involved large increases over prior funding or large deviations from the categories in the scenario and the development of new allocation categories.

DATA ANALYSIS

The Gough dominance scale was administered to each subject after each group session and the responses were Guttman scaled. Analysis of the resulting scales showed that both CRs (first session = .89, second session = .88, and third session = .90) and the MMRs (first session = .70, second session = .69, and third session = .69) were stable.* Additionally the distribu-

---

*The fact that the coefficients of reproducibility for these time periods fall marginally below Guttman's suggested cut-off point should not be a point of concern. Hans Zetterberg (*On Theory and Verification in Sociology*. Totowa, N. J.: Bedminister Press, 3rd ed., 1965, 110) argues that there are justifications for using these results which are marginal from accepted scale cut-off points noting that some might reject a scale when the coefficient of reproducibility "is not quite the desired .90." He rejects this notion since "the reliability and statistical significance are not so far off that they subtract from the good impression the test gives."

TABLE 4.16

Dominance Distributions at Three Test Points

Dominance Level	T^1		T^2		T^3	
	n	%	n	%	n	%
High	6	08.8	6	09.7	3	04.9
Moderately High	31	45.6	28	45.2	28	45.9
Moderately Low	23	33.8	26	41.9	29	47.5
Low	8	11.8	2	03.2	1	01.7

T^1=Before first session T^2=After second session T^3=After third session

tion of subjects across scale locations was very stable at the three time points. A comparison of the second and third test points indicated that 85.4 percent of the individuals occupied the same category both times. On the other hand, Ss were disproportionately distributed in the two middle categories. At the second test point (administered after the second scenario), 87.1 percent of the Ss fell into the two middle categories and at the third test point 93.4 percent did so. Thus few high- and few low-dominant personality types participated in the experiment. Some important features of the distributions are shown in Table 4.16.

To establish task leadership we calculated mean interactions for all of the groups and selected those Ss who scored at least one standard deviation (SD) above the mean as leaders. The means and standard deviations for the two sessions—$\overline{X}$=20.0 and SD=11.9 for the community development scenario; $\overline{X}$=21.6 and SD 9.2 for the budget scenario—were comparable. Thus an interaction percentage score equal to or greater than 32.0 was required for designation as a task leader in the first session, while a score of 30.8 or greater was needed in the second session. Inspection of the distributions of interaction scores indicated the criteria did not create anomalies. The pattern of dominating group interaction was almost always clearcut when we used one standard deviation above the mean to infer leadership patterns.

With the mean and the standard deviation as criteria, four basic leadership patterns occurred: some groups had no leader for any session; some had leaders for one session only; some had leaders for both sessions; and some had a competitive leadership pattern in which two individuals scored at least one standard deviation above the mean. Since groups without a leader had at least three Ss participating around the mean level on interaction, we speak of a leaderless pattern.

Two groups exhibited the leaderless pattern across time, six had at least one leader for one of the two sessions, and five groups had a leader at both sessions. The leaderless pattern did not result from leadership competition among group members, however, as members of these groups tended toward mean interaction levels. In other words these groups may be described as participatory. Similarly there were no instances of leadership competition for those groups having a leader at only one session. In the three groups with leadership competition (i.e., dual leaders in a single session), the other group members engaged in relatively limited interactions. Relevant data are not reproduced here.

To test the first hypothesis, we compared dominance scores with levels of interaction in the groups. The data indicate that high and moderately high dominant personalities are more likely than low and moderately low personalities to be high participators. Dichotomizing dominance into high (including high- and moderately high-dominant) and low (including low- and moderately low-dominant) yields a strong positive association ($Q=.75$; $\phi=.45$) with high participation (Ss one standard deviation above the mean in either session) and low participation (Ss one standard deviation below the mean in either session).* This strong relationship between dominance and participation generalizes a previous finding that the association between dominance and leadership may be reduced by not requiring the group to come to a consensual agreement.** In other words, even though the high-dominant personalities remain active, if a group is not instructed to arrive at a consensual decision, its deliberations are less likely to be controlled by the high dominants.[7]

Although dominance is related to participation in group discussions (as Table 4.17 illustrates), the association is not perfect. Two of the three individuals who were either leaders or competed for leadership in both sessions were moderately high dominants while the other was a moderately low dominant. Moreover at least two moderately high dominants were located in each of the two leaderless groups.

On the other hand, the vast majority (eleven of fifteen) of the stable Ss who were relatively nonparticipatory had moderately low-dominant personalities. Thus we observe the same congruence between low levels of in-

---

*Given the congruence between sociometric and interaction measures of individual and group activity, we should recognize that high participation generally designates group leaders. In these groups we found thirteen single leaders, three competitive (multiple) leaders and ten leaderless groups.

Commonly experimental tests of leadership rely on sociometric responses (i.e., reponses to a question such as "who did the most to influence or guide your group?") as well as IPA. We did not follow this procedure because we did not want to produce a contamination effect for session three by asking a leadership question after session two. Obviously, asking such a question after session three would produce responses based on recollections of the three sessions (the familiarity session as well as the two observational sessions). Measuring leadership exclusively through IPA gives considerable weight to verbal interaction and insufficient weight to "sociability."

**The inclusion of chi square with these hypotheses may concern some readers. A conservative view of when to use the chi square test is expressed by Siegel who notes that "when N is between 20 and 40, the χ^2 test may be used if all expected frequencies are 5 or more. If the smallest expected frequency is less than 5, use the Fisher test." See Sidney Siegel, *Non-Parametric Statistics* (New York: McGraw-Hill, 1966), 110. Because Fisher's exact is a more stringent test with two by two tables, we have reported it in all cases.

TABLE 4.17

Relationship Between Personality and Participation*

Participation	Personality	
	High Dominant	Low Dominant
High	13	5
Low	4	11

$Q=.75$ $\phi=.45$ $\chi^2=6.789$, Fisher's exact p-value $=.01$

*In addition to the data in the tables, one high participator and five low participators were unstable on the dominance scale over the last two applications. One low participator was not tested with the dominance scale.

teraction and lower dominance as was found when high levels of interaction and higher dominance were compared. Lower dominant personalities were much more likely than higher dominant personalities to withdraw from group discussions, while higher dominants were more likely than lower dominants to participate in group discussions. Moderately high-dominant personalities were likely to participate around the mean level of interaction. Thus the higher dominant personalities played a larger role in the overall discussion patterns than the lower dominant personalities. These findings support the first hypothesis that personality is related to levels of participation.

The second hypothesis considers the types of decisions made in small groups, suggesting that compromises tend to dominate group decision making. To test the notion of what type of compromises were prevalent, we

TABLE 4.18

Relation Between Leadership in Groups and Compromise–Great-Change Decisions*

Type of Decison	Leadership	
	No Single Leader	Single Leader
Compromise	10	8
Great-Change	3	5

$Q=.35$ $\phi=.17$ $\chi^2=.722$, Fisher's exact p-value $=.33$

*In this experiment there were thirteen distinctive groups with each group meeting for two observations after each group was first exposed to the experiment through a familiarity session. Since each group considered two different kinds of budget problems, there were 26 observations. Thus, we are treating the n-size as equal to 26, even though if one looks at the issue from the view of subjects within groups, there are 13 matched pairs.

coded decisions into stand-pat, incremental, and great-change categories. The first two categories represent compromise decisions in which there was minimal deviation from previous decisions on the same problem as reported in the scenarios. Eighteen of the twenty-six groups (about sixty-eight percent) made either stand-pat or incremental decisions. These results may be interpreted as support for the second hypothesis.

Whether the pattern of leadership has an impact on the chances for a compromise decision is considered on Table 4.18 where the type of decision and the leadership patterns are reported. If the leadership pattern does influence the likelihood of a compromise decision, then we should obtain a substantial statistical relationship. In fact the nonsignificant χ^2 and the moderate Q value indicate that the tendency to arrive at compromise decisions is not a function of the presence or absence of a single leader.

In addition we hypothesized that groups with a single leader were more likely to reach consensual decisions than were those with multiple (competitive) leaders or without leaders. As Table 4.19 demonstrates, eleven of the eighteen consensual decisions (sixty-one percent) were reached with a single leader. Moreover, eleven of the thirteen decisions (eighty-five percent) involving a single leader were consensual. Multiple leadership or leaderless patterns, on the other hand, could only produce a consensual decision seven out of thirteen times (fifty-four percent). Thus while leaderless groups and groups with multiple (competitive) leaders could make consensual decisions, the presence of a single leader substantially increased the likelihood that a group would reach a consensual decision.

The data also permit us to test whether the amount of agreement among members is associated with the type of decision reached by the group. Much of the political science literature on decisional processes seems to suggest that changes in individual preferences for a particular outcome are generally undertaken to increase the attractiveness of an alternative outcome to others, thereby maximizing the chances for attaining the desired outcome and increasing the likelihood of group consensus for it. Thus compromise tends to be undertaken to achieve consensus. If there is a strong relationship between consensus and compromise, we should expect the ma-

TABLE 4.19

Relation Between Leadership and Type of Decision

| | Leadership | |
Type of Decision	Single Leader	No Single Leader
Consensual	11	7
Not Consensual	2	6

Q=.65 ϕ=.33 χ^2=.2.889, Fisher's exact p-value=.10

TABLE 4.20

Relation Between Compromise and Consensual Outcomes

	Decisional Agreement	
Type of Decision	Consensus	Majority
Incremental / Stand Pat	10	8
Great Change	8	0

$\phi = .44$ $\chi^2 = 5.136$, Fisher's exact p-value = .03

jority of our cases to fall into a consensus-compromise cell in the distribution presented in Table 4.20.

Table 4.20 suggests that proposals for great change resulted in consensual rather than divisive decisions. All of the eight majority-minority (nonconsensual) decisions occurred in conjunction with dual stand-pat/incremental (compromise) proposals, and they were never associated with great-change (noncompromise) decisions. On the other hand consensual groups were about as likely to arrive at noncompromise decisions (44 percent, $N = 8$) as to reach compromise decisions (56 percent, $N = 10$). Thus a careful reading of Table 4.20 indicates that the relationship between decisional agreement and the type of decision ($\phi = .44$) is largely attributed to the tendency of groups proposing great-change decisions to arrive at these choices in a consensual way.

SUMMARY

After discussing some parallels between the concerns of experimental social psychologists interested in small-group research and political scientists working with small political groups, we tested three hypotheses on small-group decision making under conditions of open solution sets using data from thirteen five-person groups which met over three time periods. Experimental constraints on discussion and decision time, interactions outside of the experimental setting, communications networks, the personalities of group members, and the nature of the information provided to the Ss were introduced into the design. Evidence was found to support the three hypotheses tested. First, high-dominant personalities were more likely to participate in group discussions and less likely not to participate than low-dominant personalities. Second, the decisions reached by the experimental groups were usually constrained by the scenarios, thereby reflecting compromises which resulted in stand-pat or incremental decisions. Third, single-leader groups tended to arrive at consensual decisions more frequently than leaderless or competitive leader groups.

The main findings reported from this experiment appear to have clear nonexperimental equivalents. For example, twenty-three of the twenty-six groups were either leaderless or had a single leader. Strikingly similar results were produced in Eulau's study of the San Francisco area city councils. Many of these small political groups were unipolar and over seventy-five percent were either unipolar (having a single leader) or nonpolar (leaderless).[8] Thus the experimental small groups examined here reflect the same tendency towards a harmony of leadership focus as did the city councils studied by Eulau.

Similar results appear to emerge from studies of crisis decision making in foreign affairs.[9] In most of these ad hoc small groups a single leader emerged who was important in the decisional outcome eventually reached by the decision-making group. Additionally this crisis decision-making literature appears to yield nonexperimental examples of the importance of a single leader for consensual decisions. For example narratives of the 1962 Cuban missile crisis appear to indicate that as competition for leadership (i.e., the existence of multiple leaders) in the ad hoc decision-making group declines, the chances for consensual policy recommendations increased. A careful review of studies of elite politics in single party or authoritarian states might yield additional nonexperimental manifestations of this relationship.[10]

It appears, then, that these "real political world" equivalents for our experimental findings can be generated in a number of the areas of substantive concern to political scientists. Administrative, judicial, and metropolitan behavior might provide particularly fertile grounds for the observation of these relationships. Wherever they are isolated, however, these everyday occurrences provide but one more incentive for political scientists systematically to incorporate elements of small-group research from social psychology into the ongoing research of our discipline.

NOTES

1. Harold H. Kelley and John W. Thibaut, "Group Problem Solving," *The Handbook of Social Psychology*, Gardner Lindzey and Eliot Aronson, eds. vol. IV (Reading, Mass.: Addison-Wesley, second edition, 1969), 44.

2. M. A. Wallach and N. Kogan, "The Roles of Information, Discussion, and Consensus in Group Risk Taking," *J. Exp. Soc. Psychol.*, I (1965): 1-19; D. J. Bem, M. A. Wallach, and N. Kogan, "Group Decision Making Under Risk of Adversive Consequences," *J. Pers. and Soc. Psychol.*, 2 (1965): 453-460; Edith Becker Bennett, "Discussions, Decisions, and Consensus in 'Group Decisions'", *Human Relations*, 8 (1955): 251-274.

3. A. Bavelas, "Communication Patterns in Task-Oriented Small Groups," *J. Acoust. Soc. Amer.*, 22 (1950): 725-730.

4. Kelley and Thibaut; also see, Barry E. Collins and B. H. Raven, "Group Structure: Attraction, Coalitions, Communication, and Power," in Lindzey and Aronson, 102-204.

5. E. B. Bennett, "Discussions."

6. H. G. Gough, *Manual for the California Psychological Inventory* (Palo Alto: Consulting Psychologists Press, 1957); R. F. Bales, *Interaction Process Analysis* (Cambridge: Addison-Wesley, 1950).

7. James W. Dyson, Daniel W. Fleitas, and Frank P. Scioli, Jr., "The Interaction of Leadership, Personality, and Decisional Environment." *J. of Soc. Psychol.* 86 (1972): 29-33.

8. Heinz Eulau, "The Informal Organization of Decisional Structures in Small Legislative Bodies," *Midwest Journal of Political Science* 13 (1969): 341-366.

9. For example see E. Abel, *The Cuban Missile Crisis* (Philadelphia: Lippincott, 1966); Robert Kennedy, *Thirteen Days* (New York: W. W. Norton, 1969); Graham Allison, *Essence of Decision* (Boston: Little, Brown and Company, 1971).

10. Sidney Ploss, *Conflict and Decision-Making in Soviet Russia* (Princeton, N.J.: Princeton University Press, 1965); Carl A. Linden, *Khruschev and the Soviet Leadership, 1957-1964* (Baltimore: Johns Hopkins Press, 1966).

Interaction Analysis and Bargaining Behavior

CHARLES WALCOTT & P. TERRENCE HOPMANN

Many of the phenomena which students of politics might wish to investigate in the experimental laboratory involve verbal interaction among individuals. Studies of group decision making, bilateral or multilateral bargaining, coalition formation, or influence processes of various kinds are apt to be set up in such a way that subjects are required to talk to one another or at least to communicate via written messages. Clearly the content of such communication is of central interest in the description and explanation of such phenomena. This article reports the development of an interaction analysis instrument designed for such a purpose.

Our theoretical focus in the development of this instrument has been on the phenomenon of bargaining. Specifically we have sought to study bargaining in the context of arms control negotiations, utilizing an approach which combines laboratory experimentation with analysis of transcripts from actual arms control conferences. In the interest of maximizing comparability of data obtained from these sources, we have designed the instrument to be suitable for both the coding of verbal interaction and the content analysis of transcripts.

The idea of utilizing interaction analysis in the study of the political behavior of groups is, of course, not novel. Barber (1966) has employed Bales' Interaction Process Analysis (see Bales 1950) in his laboratory study of local decision makers, while Walcott (1971) has used a simplified version of the same system to study experimentally created budgetary decision-making groups. However as Best (1971) has pointed out in discussing Barber's work, Bales' system is more suitable for coding variables of importance in traditional small-group research, i.e., leadership or integration, than for coping with concepts of political strategy or influence.

With specific regard to bargaining behavior, McGrath and Julian (1963) modified the Bales system in an attempt to deal more explicitly with phenomena pertinent to a theory of negotiation. Along the same line Zechmeister and Druckman (1973) have experimented rather tentatively with an original approach to coding bargaining behavior. These studies represent the beginnings of what we regard as a useful approach: the development of special-purpose coding systems, derived from a particular theoretical orientation (as Bales' system is from that of Parsons), and particularly appropriate to a delimited set of substantive and theoretical concerns. The system to be described below may be regarded as a further extension of this type of approach.

BARGAINING PROCESS ANALYSIS

The Bargaining Process Analysis (BPA) system represents our present attempt to measure the processes of bargaining and conflict in the context of small-group interactions. The BPA is drawn from two major sources. The bargaining variables are developed primarily from the conceptual scheme advanced by Schelling (1960), with modification and elaboration reflecting the influence of thematic content analysis instruments previously utilized in the study of arms control negotiations (Jensen 1968, Hopmann 1972). The contextual variables, that is, the measure of everything that isn't coded as a bargaining variable, are adapted from Bales.

The coding form for the BPA system is found in Appendix 1. The operational definitions of the categories in the system are as follows:

A. Substantive Behavior: Behaviors directly associated with the subject matter of the negotiations.

1. Initiations: Actor advances a substantially new proposal or states his own substantive position for the first time.

2. Accommodations: Actor concedes a point to another, retracts a proposal in the face of resistance, or expresses a willingness to negotiate or compromise his own stated position.

3. Retractions: Actor retracts a previously made initiation or concession or modifies a previously stated position so as to make the position clearly less agreeable to another.

B. Strategic Behavior: Behavior designed to affect the behavior of other actors in the negotiations, but not implying a substantive change of position on the part of the initiator.

1. Commitments: Actor takes a position or reiterates it with a clear statement that it will not change under any circumstances and/or declares his own position nonnegotiable.

2. Threats: Actor offers or predicts negative consequences (sanction or withholding of a potential reward) if another does not behave in a stated manner.

3. Promises: Actor offers or predicts positive consequences (reward or withdrawal of sanction) if another behaves in a stated manner.

C. Task Behavior: Behavior primarily designed to promote business-like discussion and clarification of issues.

1. Agreements: Actor accepts another's proposal, accepts a retraction or accommodation, or expresses substantive agreement with another's position.

2. Disagreements: Actor rejects another's proposal, refuses a concession or retraction, or disputes a substantive (including factual) issue.

3. Questions: Actor requests information, inquires as to another's position, reaction or intention, or requests clarification or justification of a position.

4. Answers: Actor supplies information, reiterates a previously stated position, or clarifies or justifies a position.

D. Affective Behavior: Behavior in which actors express their feelings or emotions toward one another or toward a situation.

1. Positive Affect: Actor jokes or otherwise attempts to relieve tension, attempts to create feelings of solidarity in the group, or expresses approval or satisfaction.

2. Negative Affect: Actor becomes irritable or otherwise shows tension, criticizes another in general terms, expresses disapproval or dissatisfaction with group performance or with the situation.

E. Procedural Behavior: Behavior designed to move the discussion along, but which does not fit any of the above categories.

1. Subject Change: Attempts to divert discussion from one substantive topic to another.

In addition to these general category definitions we have devised some special conventions for handling unusual or complex situations; these conventions may be found in Appendix 2.

Each of the categories above may require some explication. Categories A and B involve Substantive and Strategic behavior, and the distinction between these two categories is reflected in their titles. Substantive behavior refers to actions involving the substantive issues under discussion. It includes making a proposal, backing down from a proposal or position (accommodation), and toughening a previously softened position (retraction). These differ from the agreement and disagreement items in category C in that they involve taking an initiative in modifying one's position. Thus they may reflect, in virtually all cases, elements of a strategy or manipulative pattern of behavior. Agreements and disagreements, on the other hand, are reactive and often do not in fact involve significant position taking on issues as, for example, when they concern procedures or the establishment of facts. These variables, of course, may be empirically related, but they are analytically separable. Substantive behavior differs from strategic behavior in that actions in category B reflect purely strategic intent. Strategic behaviors (commitments, threats, and promises) do not represent any change in the substantive position of an actor. Rather, they represent gestures designed to manipulate the stakes involved or the subjective probabilities of events in such a way as to alter the behavior of the other party.

Categories C and D, Task Behavior and Affective Behavior, are essentially borrowed from the Bales system. They thus do not have their basis in a theory specifically dealing with the bargaining process. However, their combination with variables which do purport to tap bargaining behaviors offers some interesting possibilities for the integration of these variables into propositions relevant to bargaining processes. For instance the ratio of task to affect, a measure of task-oriented behavior, may be associated with certain configurations among the bargaining variables. In this manner the integration or "bridge building" between small-group concepts and bargaining theoretic concepts may be approached. Nevertheless we do believe that there are fundamental differences between these sets of variables. Task and Affect variables represent the kinds of behavior normally associated with problem solving, while the Substantive and Strategic categories represent the kinds of behaviors particularly likely to be associated with attempts to reach agreement or to attain a preferred outcome under bargaining conditions.

Category E, Procedural Behavior, is simply a residual category. Perhaps the need for such a category represents a weakness in the BPA system, but we have found that there are occasionally interactions which simply can't be sensibly coded into any of the usual categories in the system. Our procedure has been to code them as "procedural" and then to recheck the tape of the interaction to attempt to determine how to cope with the event in the analysis. This is not very satisfactory, to be sure, but then the interactions which have been involved in this category have tended not to be very significant.

INTERCODER RELIABILITY

The training of coders in the use of a system as complex as the BPA is a relatively demanding task. However, with adequate training it is possible to obtain fairly impressive results. The following data were obtained over twenty-four runs of a simulated arms control negotiation session involving triads, each session lasting approximately two and one-half hours. Intercoder reliability was computed as the average, weighted by frequency of occurrence in each category, of the intercoder correlation coefficients (Pearson's r) over each of the thirteen BPA categories. The reliability coefficient was .922, indicating a remarkably high degree of reliability for such a complex system. Breaking this down for each category, the following correlations were obtained, all significant beyond the .001 level:

The establishment of a satisfactory level of intercoder reliability indicates the workability of the coding system, given adequate training.

TABLE 4.21

Intercoder Correlations

Category	Correlation	Category	Correlation
Initiations	.667	Disagreements	.977
Accommodations	.659	Questions	.976
Retractions	.699	Answers	.927
Commitments	.855	Positive Affect	.920
Threats	.953	Negative Affect	.961
Promises	.859	Subject Change	.677
Agreements	.816		

However it says nothing about the utility of the system. The following data will shed some light upon that question.

CONCEPTS AND OBSERVATION FREQUENCIES

The frequency with which the behaviors defined by the coding system will occur is, of course, a function of the particular characteristics (e.g., problem, setting, attitudes, and experience of negotiators) associated with a bargaining situation. The patterns obtained in the experiment noted above, therefore, are not to be construed as normal or as baseline expectations relevant to different experimental or natural settings. However, they may be useful for comparative purposes, especially for comparisons between relatively similar phenomena found in and out of the laboratory (e.g., simulated arms control negotiations and real ones). Our findings for this experiment, based on 14,172 total interactions, were as follows:

TABLE 4.22

Frequency of Interactions Within Categories

Substantive Behavior	.081	
Initiations		.056
Accommodations		.020
Retractions		.005
Strategic Behavior	.044	
Commitments		.035
Threats		.006
Promises		.003
Task Behavior	.766	
Agreements		.066
Disagreements		.207
Questions		.227
Answers		.266
Affective Behavior	.088	
Positive		.049
Negative		.039
Procedural Behavior	.023	

Total equals more than 100% due to rounding

Clearly the bulk of the interaction recorded in this experiment fell outside those categories (substantive and strategic) that uniquely tap bargaining-relevant behavior. However, the question most relevant to an appraisal of the coding instrument is whether the measurement of such variables, whatever their frequency of occurrence, enabled us to identify regularities in the bargaining process which would have been missed otherwise. In this regard the data from the experiment give substantial grounds for optimism.

EXPERIMENTAL FINDINGS

In the study referred to above we attempted to simulate a problem in arms control negotiations (for a fuller discussion, see Hopmann and Walcott

TABLE 4.23

Significant Findings Involving BPA-Generated Variables

BPA Variable	Relationships
1. Ratio of hard to soft bargaining behavior*	1a. Higher as international environment becomes more hostile.
	1b. Higher when attitudes of negotiators toward one another are more negative.
	1c. Negatively related to ratio of agreement to disagreement (BPA coded).
	1d. Positively related to ratio of negative to positive affect (BPA coded).
	1e. Positively related to ratio of affective to task-oriented behavior (BPA coded).
	1f. Negatively related to the production of agreements at conclusion of negotiation.
2. Ratio of agreement to disagreement	2a. Lower as international environment becomes more hostile.
	2b. Lower when attitudes of negotiators toward one another are more negative.
	2c. Positively related to the production of agreements at conclusion of negotiation. (see also 1c above)
3. Ratio of positive to negative affect	3a. Lower as international environment becomes more hostile.
	3b. Positively related to the production of agreement at conclusion of negotiation. (see also 1d above)
4. Frequency of commitments	4a. Higher as international environment becomes more hostile.
	4b. Negatively related to the production of agreements at conclusion of negotiation.

*Hard bargaining is a composite variable comprised of threats, commitments, and retractions. Soft bargaining includes promises, initiations, and accommodations.

1973). Manipulating the simulated international environment as an independent variable, and employing negotiated outcomes as a dependent variable, we treated both bargaining behavior, as measured by the BPA, and negotiators' attitudes toward one another, as measured by a semantic differential instrument, as intervening variables. Our data indicate that variables derived from the BPA coding were significantly related to both independent and dependent variables as well as to attitudes and to one another. A summary of our strongest and most consistent findings appears in Table 4.23.

While these findings do not establish the BPA, or something like it, as the sine qua non of future studies of bargaining, they do at least suggest its utility. The BPA provided empirical access to a set of variables generally thought to be important but seldom quantified, and it revealed significant and interesting patterns of relationships which would not have emerged otherwise. It did, in other words, what it was intended to do.

DISCUSSION

Our primary purpose in presenting this discussion of the BPA has been to inform others who might share our general research concerns of its availability and to provide some initial evidence as to its utility. The development of such an instrument, however, also has other implications worthy of note.

An instrument such as BPA clearly maximizes the advantages of an experimental approach to bargaining phenomena. In particular it enables us to make the most of the observational capabilities associated with laboratory experimentation. We are thus given the opportunity to move beyond the confines of binary choice (e.g., Prisoner's Dilemma) and related models of interdependent decision making through the use of more complex scenarios permitting free verbal interaction. We can thereby not only increase the evident realism of laboratory models, but also examine a wider range of phenomena. Additionally the employment of BPA could lend new dimensions to the analysis of existing types of laboratory-created phenomena. For instance the study of processes of coalition formation could be facilitated greatly by a capability to observe, record, and analyze the interactions of persons in the process of attempting to form coalitions.

However, the laboratory is not the only setting in which BPA has proven useful. Hopmann (forthcoming) has demonstrated the applicability and utility of BPA in dealing with verbatim transcripts of international negotiations. Indeed the experiment reported above represents an early phase of an overall project which, as noted above, will seek to compare systematically the analyses of laboratory and real world phenomena. The existence of a common methodology for dealing with both types of phenomena permits a more thorough and ambitious approach to the validation of experiments and/or simulations than has hitherto been attempted.

Finally the development of BPA, whatever its particular strengths and limitations, suggests the opportunity for others who might be interested in different sets of phenomena, or in approaching bargaining from alternative theoretical perspectives, to develop additional instruments of this sort. While there are obvious advantages in accumulating evidence developed through common methods, there are at least equally compelling reasons for wanting to innovate. The initial development of BPA proceeded out of dissatisfaction with other available systems. BPA itself can hardly be considered fully developed—the possibility of revision is very much alive at this early stage of our research. Interaction analysis is a flexible tool, adaptable to many kinds of theoretical and substantive concerns, but no single system will be appropriate for even the majority of those concerns. If BPA only serves as a model for additional development in the area of interaction analysis, it may well be regarded as having contributed substantially to our capacity to deal systematically with the phenomena of political behavior.

REFERENCES

Bales, R. F. 1950. *Interaction process analysis*. Cambridge, Mass.: Addison-Wesley.

Barber, J. D. 1966. *Power in committees: An experiment in the governmental process*. Chicago: Rand-McNally.

Best, J. J. 1971. The use of media in small group research, *Experimental study of politics* I (February): 42-60.

Hopmann, P. T. 1972. Internal and external influences on bargaining in arms control negotiation: The partial test ban, *Peace, war, and numbers*, ed. B. M. Russett. Beverly Hills, Calif.: Sage Publications.

Hopmann, P. T. In press. Bargaining on arms control negotiations: The seabeds denuclearization treaty, *International organization*.

Hopmann, P. T., and Walcott C., 1973. The bargaining process in arms control negotiations: An experimental analysis, University of Minnesota, Harold Scott Quigley Center of International Affairs (mimeo).

Jensen, L. 1968. Approach-avoidance bargaining on the test ban negotiations, *International studies quarterly* 12 (June): 152-160.

Schelling, T. C. 1960. *The strategy of conflict*. Cambridge, Mass.: Harvard University Press.

Walcott, C. 1971. Incrementalism and rationality: An experimental study of budgetary decision-making, *Experimental study of politics* I (December): 1-34.

Zechmeister, K., and Druckman, D. 1973. Determinants of the resolution of a conflict of interest in a simulation of political decision making, *Journal of conflict resolution* 17 (March): 63-88.

APPENDIX 1

BARGAINING PROCESS ANALYSIS CODING FORM

		Substantive Behavior			Strategic Behavior			Task Behavior				Affective Behavior		Procedural
Time	Subject	Issue	Initia-tions	Accommo-dations	Retrac-tions	Commit-ments	Threat	Promise	Agree-ments	Disagree-ments	Ques-tions	Answer	Positive Affect	Negative Affect	Subject Changes

APPENDIX 2:
CLARIFICATION AND CONVENTIONS FOR CODING
ON BARGAINING PROCESS ANALYSIS FORM

1. **Threats and promises:** Sometimes these will be difficult to tell apart, as when one actor promises not to invoke or carry out a potential threat, contingent upon the behavior of another. Code all such cases involving a potential or hypothetical sanction as threats, even if offered in a tone of promising. It is a promise only if the sanction referred to is already in force, and the promise is to remove it.

2. **Initiations:** Code a statement of position by an actor as an "initiation" only the first time it is offered. Subsequent statements of the same position become "answers" (unless "commitment" is appropriate). If an actor's first statement of his own position is simply an expression of exact agreement with a position already stated by another, code "agreement." If an actor reiterates a position with only a slight modification or elaboration of his previous statement(s), code as "answer" and (on the same line) as either "initiation," "retraction," or "accommodation," as appropriate.

3. **Questions:** Leading, insinuating, or hostile questions should be coded as "questions" and (on the same line) "disagreement" or "negative affect" as appropriate.

4. **Uncommitments:** If a position to which an actor has been recorded as committed is changed (either through accommodation or retraction), code in one of these two categories, as appropriate, and circle the coding mark. (If you have time, also draw an arrow to the "commitment" space on the same line.

5. **Retractions and accommodations:** A single act can be both if it moves the actor's position simultaneously toward one other actor and away from another. Code as both (indicating toward whom it is an accommodation and toward whom it is a retraction) on the same line.

6. **Subject change:** If an attempt to change the subject is rejected passively, i.e., without explicit comment or discussion, code "subject change" and circle it. However, if the issue is debated or discussed, do not circle, but code another subject change if the original issue is returned to. Subject changes may also be troublesome in two other respects. First, some attempts to change subjects may well have strategic implications, not merely procedural. Second, you may encounter apparently procedural gestures, i.e., arguing about rules, which are not really subject changes. Simply code all of these as "subject changes." All subject change codings will be reviewed specifically in the data analysis for possible recoding. When coding a subject change that in the above or other ways seems not to conform to the simple procedural definition, circle it.

7. **Technical arguments:** Disagreements as to objective facts (e.g., the state of technology) should be coded as "questions" and "answers" unless, in your judgment, they clearly reflect substantive policy disagreements, in which case they may be coded as "agreements" and "disagreements."

8. **Affect:** Code laughter as " positive" only if designed to relieve tension or promote good feelings, or is reflective of this. Derisive laughter should be coded "negative." If you are in doubt as to what the laughter means, or if it relates to external events (e.g., excessive feedback in intercom or the collapse of a chair), don't code it.

9. **Actors:** Always code the number of the agent of the action first followed by the target(s) (e.g., 1-2). If there is no specific target and a statement is directed at the entire group, simply code the number of the agent (e.g., 1-). When two actors are discussing a third (present or not), code in the following form: 1-2/3, meaning "1 to 2 about 3." Use for both comments about the third party (e.g., "he is stubborn") and for predictions or threats concerning his behavior (e.g., "he will walk out unless we agree to that"). Always code in the appropriate category.

10. **General distress:** If you are simply uncertain as to how to code a given behavior or set of behaviors, just do the best you can and mark the codings you really don't trust with an asterisk. Consult the experimenters about all such problems. In such ways does the system (and especially this list of clarifications) grow.

V. Simulation Contexts

From Simplified Replications
to Comprehensive Theory

In addition to work in natural-state and experimental contexts, "simulation" has recently reflected multiple expressions of the group approach in Political Science. Two definitions of "simulation" can start us on our way:

— "a simplified replication in another medium of observed phenomena,"
—"to assume or have the appearance of" (Webster's *International Dictionary*)

Perhaps the most developed example of such man-system interaction, for example, is the computer-controlled simulation of the flight of a jet aircraft, which deals with relatively intricate but highly determined man/machine interfaces. A landing or an emergency, for example, can be simulated, whose effects will register on realistic cockpit instruments or even as visual images the pilot can see, as on a movie screen. In turn, "pilot" responses to these variable inputs will be fed into the "plane's" system of controls and sources of power, as represented by a computer and its programs. The record of whether pilot actions made things better or worse will be available for later study and analysis over a very wide range of possible conditions and without risking a single person or aircraft.

Even this simplified example suggests the awesome dimensions of the promise of and the problems with simulation. Specifically, for example, simulation activity deals with a critical transfer point in the transmission of knowledge, that point where pure science interacts with applied science. There, both can ideally enrich one another, reflecting two useful rules of thumb: (1) that there is nothing so useful as good theory, and (2) that all good empirical theory must be tested vigorously to establish that its anticipated effects occur, as the central factor in the escalation of theory toward increasing comprehensiveness, or in the rejection of a theory as being useful for limited purposes but as inadequate beyond some point. Hence jet simulations could be useful to test theories of, for example, what flight strategy can best adapt to specific weather conditions. Similarly war games might provide evidence of the strengths/weaknesses of particular tactics or strategies, given the complex blend of science/art issues involved. That is the good news. The bad news can be awesomely tragic. Simply, one can become "simulation bright" with disastrous consequences as well as with salubrious ones. The key factor is the quality of the works of the simulation, of the congruence with reality of the relationships or theories built into it. For example, one might do famously in a business simulation which uses a model of the economy. If that model is inadequate, the simulation might only encourage bad habits, or worse.

This brief illustration of optimism/caution implies that there are few unqualified and uncomplicated things that may be said about simulation in Political Science. Two approaches here will seek to circumscribe some of the more prominent aspects of this qualified complexity. First, the methodological advantages of simulation activity will be previewed briefly. Second, four selections from the literature will be introduced so as to provide some in-depth samples of available work.

ACCUMULATING AND TRANSMITTING KNOWLEDGE VIA
SIMULATIONS

The burgeoning of simulation implies important research and teaching advantages. Indeed, the rapidly growing fascination with simulation stems substantially from the breadth of advantages it seems to provide for Political Science. Once limited to management research and war gaming, simulation has spread to international relations, small-group research, and studies of voting behavior. And these are only the more prominent applications. Payoffs already permit at least cautious optimism regarding the pedagogic and theory-building contributions of simulation.

Principal among the research advantages of simulations are the manipulative opportunities they provide. Simulation facilitates theory-building in three major senses. First, researchers ordinarily encounter substantial difficulties in attempting to conduct experiments on natural systems. Access is commonly limited, costs are often high, and most important, the usual myriad of confounding variables cannot be controlled. While canceling, irrelevant, or additive factors usually can be identified tbrough existing field-study techniques, confounding factors cannot. When properly designed, simulation models can facilitate such identification. As Zelditch and Evan (1962, 520) explain:

> The classic ex post facto of dealing with contamination is to hold constant the contaminating factor, c. But where a and c, or b and c, are highly correlated in natural settings, obtaining a sufficient number of the necessary contrasts may be costly or even impossible. In such a case it may be necessary to create the required contrasts artificially. The contaminant may be a canceling factor, the effects of which run counter to the effect of a; an additive factor, independent of a but obscuring the relative importance of a; an irrelevant factor, unrelated to b but highly correlated with a so that the package ac requires purification; or a confounding factor, spuriously generating the correlation between a and b . . . The effects of confounding are never entirely controlled by investigations in natural settings, since randomization is the only (relative) safeguard against the indefinitely large number of relevant factors of which we are, at any moment, quite ignorant.

Second, simulation also offers advantages in generating hypotheses, whether they be predictive or verificatory. The re-creation of past events in the simulate may yield new insights into previously unexplained phenomena. And the ability to move forward in time in a controlled fashion from a set of circumstances abstracted from the contemporary real world may provide important information on future states of affairs.

Third, simulations as operating models may help refine existing verbal models. Particularly in the case of complex verbal formulations, implicit assumptions often limit efforts to apply models to reality. Indeed, some complex verbal models are so constructed that they defy testing. Their failure to generate operating models in simulations would make patent their inadequacy. Likewise, illogical (e.g., intransitive) relationships among variables may be unknowingly posited and hidden in complex verbal models. Simulation can aid both in identifying and in correcting these omissions or sloppy insertions.

Formidable research advantages notwithstanding, simulation's greatest advantages today may be pedagogic. Alger reports that undergraduate students generally responded more favorably to instructional programs in international relations utilizing internation simulation (INS) than to classes using more traditional methods. The students emerged with a keener appreciation of the informal side of diplomacy and international affairs. Alger more broadly summarizes his students' impressions of INS (1963, esp. 178-179). Simulation (1) provides vividness and understanding beyond what one gets from a textbook; (2) gives one a realization of the complexities and the lack of simple solutions to international relations problems; (3) indicates the importance of having reliable knowledge and the importance of communication in international relations; (4) develops better understanding of the problems and goals of nations not like the United States; (5) gives experience in decision making which enables one to understand better the problems of the decision-maker; and (6) demonstrates the difficulties of balancing the requirements of internal and external affairs.

Not that the issue of pedagogic usefulness can be taken for granted. It should be researched and results replicated, as it was by four scholars associated with the Northwestern Inter-Nation Simulation who reported a complex comparison of the effects of simulation and case-study methods in undergraduate international relations courses. They concluded that "the claims and expectations we had for simulation were not borne out," which is a patent sign of the work still needed (Robinson et al. 1966, 64).

Despite the gaps and conflicting data, all this is to say, simulation can hardly be neglected. Three reasons may be cited. First, social science simulations originally emerged from concern with basic methodological difficulties plaguing other approaches. In particular, social (especially political) scientists often could not manipulate the environment in ways analogous to laboratory experiments in the hard sciences. This inability became increasingly frustrating as the calls for empirical theory grew more strident. Similarly builders of explanatory models of political processes became disenchanted with static verbal structures because of their inability to handle complex, dynamic real-world relationships. Manipulable operating models were needed. Simulation was one response to this need.

Second, the complexity of most simulation enterprises almost from the beginning nurtured the image of methodological sophistication, the protection of which image in turn encouraged critical neglect. Evaluations of simulations in Political Science have been highly general, and some have been content to ascribe precision as a logical result of complexity. Hence our emphasis here.

Third, simulation assumes importance because of its constantly changing nature. The INS model, for example, has undergone frequent modifications, sometimes of substantial importance. The fluidity of applications of the technique generates both problems and promise for us. Problems exist because it is difficult to be sure that one is not evaluating a noncurrent phase of the project's development. Promise also exists, for it is likely that significant methodological questions will continue to be unearthed and examined.

FOUR ILLUSTRATIONS OF THOUGHT/RESEARCH
ABOUT SIMULATION

In important senses, the preceding section has gone too far too fast. Let us backtrack, then, so as to give these general advantages/limitations of simulation depth and perspective by four selections from the literature. Each selection will be introduced in a separate section.

Some species of simulations. Charles Walcott develops some useful distinctions between types of simulations in his "Small Groups and Large Systems: The Uses of Simulation in the Study of Public Administration." Thus Walcott distinguishes "segmental simulations," which he sees as simply "small group experiments with elaborate scenarios." In such a study, for example, Milgram's design concerning obedience to authority (see Chapter IV) might have been located in a simulated organizational context, as defined by job descriptions, statements of duties and responsibilities, organizational charts, and similar paraphernalia that provide cues to men in complex structures. These paraphernalia could constitute part of the "elaborate scenario" to which Walcott refers, a definition of the context of the behavior-to-be-observed. A segmental simulation, less content-filled, also might be focused on a role-play by students in a management course oriented around the scenario provided by a case study.

Segmental simulations are distinguished from "systemic simulations," which seek to root their target phenomena in complicated systems. For example a systemic simulation might deal with that complex of interacting systems that we call "metropolitan government and politics," as a shorthand. Or such simulations might deal with the interaction of nation-states, a very complex medium for such target phenomena as bargaining.

Despite the necessary simplifications involved, Walcott sees systemic simulations as helping remedy one major inadequacy of most of the literature in Public Administration, that it is only marginally knowledgeable about the "black box" of policy processes. At best careful scholars can work backwards and isolate those elements which seem to have supported the development of some specific public policy. But existing analysis is weak in weighting such elements as well as in tracing their interactions. For example typical research can only speculate weakly on these generic and crucial questions: (1) What would have happened if such-and-such had been the case? and (2) What elements, if varied appropriately, would or could have changed the actual policy outcome? Simulations provide one way of gaining perspective on such questions and on their underlying processes via multiple runs of a particular simulation that vary some factors to see if they influence policy outcomes. As Walcott notes of systemic simulations, limitations and all: they provide a "unique opportunity . . . for examining complex, integrated systems under controlled conditions which are conducive to detailed observation and measurement."

Some methodological perspectives on the genus. John R. Raser provides a hard look at the fundamental justification for simulation activity in his "Simulating Social Systems: Philosophical and Methodological Considerations." His base line for analysis is definite. As he explains: "Despite the extreme complexity of human behavior and of societal structure, we have reason to assume . . . that there are identifiable patterns, regularities, and laws. It is upon this assumption that social science simulations are constructed."

A number of basic dilemmas inhere in Raser's base line. To simplify, it is clear that no full simulation is possible until social scientists are in command of the relevant lawful regularities in nature. A full simulation must be built around a comprehensive theory or model of reality, and parameters of that theory could be systematically controlled or varied in multiple runs so as to observe effects or to judge their consistency in replications of any single simulation. Patently, however, such a comprehensive theory does not exist. Indeed it is a major purpose of simulation to aid in the development of the very comprehensive theory that simulation activity requires.

Raser suggests three approaches to getting started on what needs doing, which he likens "to rebuilding an airplane while it is in flight." Not that Raser prefers such a task. That is simply the way things are. Raser discusses three alternatives to full simulations: (1) piecemeal simulations, (2) skeletal simulations, and (3) gaming, as in the model illustrated by Riker and Zavoina in Chapter IV. Only a full reading of Raser's selection will suffice to establish the relative merits of these three alternatives to, and ways to progress toward, full simulations. The reader should be alerted, however, to Raser's discussion of "pattern matching vs. the quest for punctiform certainty" as the proximate goal for simulation activity. Raser's reference to "the quest" reflects that his preference is to seek pattern matching at this time. But Raser's analysis does not set up strawmen to bowl over in service to his preference. The epistemological issues he raises in the process, as well as Raser's approach to developing the logic underlying his preference, are central. They shed much light on the methodological virtues of what he refers to as the "messing around in science" required at this stage of the development of the social sciences.

Simulating negotiations between "experts" and "politicos." Allan W.

Lerner "messes around in science" by focusing on an increasingly critical interface in our public life, the interaction between experts and politicians. Simply the two roles are complementary in major senses. Thus politicians need the technical skills of the expert; and the expert requires the insight and office of the politician to mobilize public support for programs, or at least to sense broad moods or passions or needs. At its best the combination can help avoid two horns of the basic democratic dilemma: (1) rule by the technocracy, which is elite and variously unrepresentative, with a focus on doing whatever is done with optimal efficiency but with too little attention on whether what is done should be done; and (2) rule by elected politicians whose common lack of technical skills/awareness runs the risk of promising responses to public needs that are in fact improbable or impossible, with consequent raising of expectations and dashing of hopes. Lerner attempts to simulate aspects of expert/politico interaction, which is a delicate and subtle business. The stability of his results remains to be tested by replications of his research design and by extensions of that design. What is already patent is that Lerner illustrates a convenient way to get at a network of relationships that is of major significance for the political scientist.

Simulating international systems. Mari Holmboe Ruge's contribution, "Image and Reality in Simulated International Systems," does double duty here. Thus it illustrates how what Raser calls "skeletal simulations" can be applied to macrorelationships. Simply there is no more comprehensive level of earthly organization than that involving its constituent nations. Moreover Ruge uses that very large simulated stage to test the applicability of Boulding's observation: "It is always the image, not the truth, that immediately determines behavior." The concept "image" here refers to the sum of accumulated and organized knowledge that a person has concerning self and the world, a major determinant of behavior if not the sole determinant.

Ruge employed the Inter-Nation Simulation using eight "nations," each represented by a small group of decision makers. This is consistent with Boulding's distinction between the images of the small elite that typically make decisions on behalf of their nation, and the images of the mass of a nation's population who may be affected by such a decision but who usually have only a trivial role in its making. "Image" was simply measured by Ruge as the participants' estimate of the intentions toward them of other participants, using such dimensions as hostility/friendliness.

Care is necessary to place the emphasis where it belongs in this case. Ruge's results were consistent with her initial expectations, on balance, but only replications under variable conditions will establish the stability of those results and build them into a more complex network of relations. So Ruge's own careful tentativeness should be respected.

One need not be tentative about a second point, however. Ruge has established how simulations can serve to relate variables at two grossly different levels of organization—the microlevel of aspects of the self and the macrolevel of some attributes of simulated nations. Forcing such interactive tests between what we seem to know at two or more levels of social organization often will demonstrate how wrong we have been. But it also is the basic approach to achieving two requisite scientific goals: testing the adequacy of our knowledge of relationships at any one level of organization, and establishing the kind and quality of interaction necessary between aspects of two or more levels of organization.

REFERENCES

Alger, C. F. 1963. Use of the inter-nation simulation in undergraduate teaching. In *Simulation in international relations*, ed. Guetzkow, et.al., 150-189. Englewood Cliffs: N. J.: Prentice-Hall.

Robinson, J. A., Anderson, L. G., Hermann, M. G., and Snyder, R. C. 1966. Teaching with inter-nation simulation and case studies, *American political science review*, 60.

Zelditch, M., Jr., and Evan, W. M. 1962. Simulated bureaucracies: A methodological analysis. In *Simulation in social science: Readings*, ed. Harold Guetzkow, 520. Englewood Cliffs, N. J.: Prentice-Hall.

Small Groups and Large Systems: The Uses of Simulation in the Study of Public Administration

CHARLES WALCOTT

Although progress toward the development of systemic, empirical theory in the field of public administration has been marked in recent years, major gaps in our understanding still remain. Most conspicuous in this respect has been the relative lack of attention paid to the behavioral processes of administration—what systems theoretical conceptualizations often refer to as the "conversion process" or "throughput function" of social systems. This is the proverbial black box which has generally been the aspect of social systems that has proved most difficult to deal with empirically. The reasons for this appear to involve primarily the difficulty of obtaining access for the observation of such processes as they occur, and the commensurate difficulty of adequately conceptualizing and measuring the structural and interactional components of these processes. The development of research strategies for overcoming these difficulties represents perhaps the major methodological challenge in the contemporary study of public organizations.

One possible approach to the gathering of data and the development of theory concerning behavioral processes in administration is the utilization of laboratory experimentation. In this vein Golembiewski, for instance, has suggested the application of relevant findings obtained through small-group experimentation in cognate disciplines to problems of public management (Golembiewski 1962). Similarly students of organizational behavior in several disciplines have utilized the findings and the techniques of small-group experimentation fairly extensively (Weick 1965). However there are obvious problems inherent in a strategy of borrowing extensively from the findings of other disciplines to shed light upon our own particular black box. In general these difficulties stem from the fact that such findings have been developed with reference to a set of theoretical concerns and substantive interests which are often only tangentially relevant to the central issues which have emerged in the study of public bureaucracies and public policy-making processes. For example much of the empirical small-group literature is based upon studies of the behavior of cooperative problem-solving groups. As Best has pointed out, even the most widely accepted technique for measuring small-group interaction processes, Bales' Interaction Process Analysis, is strongly oriented toward the kinds of theoretical issues involved in the study of such groups (Best 1971). And, while cooperative problem solving is indisputably a component of most organization processes, an exclusive focus upon such phenomena tends to exclude the consideration of highly relevant political variables such as goal and value conflict, bargaining processes, and the impact of structural and environmental constraints upon group decision making.

The implication of this is that adequate experimental treatment of the central concerns of public administration is most likely to come about only in work done in cognate fields, supplemented with experimental work explicitly directed toward those concerns. The purpose of this paper is to direct attention toward this possibility through an examination of the laboratory technique known as simulation.

Simulation models: Two major types. In using the term "simulation" here, we restrict our meaning to that class of laboratory models in which human actors (experimental subjects) play roles which, in their relationships with one another and with an artificial environment, comprise some form of presumed analog with a real-world interaction system. This, as Dawson (1962) points out, amounts to a dynamic model of the real world, or referent system. In adopting this definition we exclude not only all-machine (i.e. computer) simulations, but also educational games (because they have different purposes) and many conventional laboratory experimental models. The latter are excluded where the relationship between the laboratory model and any particular referent system or well-defined class of systems is either not obvious or not intended. However, this definition still subsumes at least two distinctive approaches.

Perhaps the best-known simulation model is the Inter-Nation Simulation, a comprehensive representation of the international political system including formal representation of such features as domestic political systems, foreign policy decision-making processes, and national force capabilities (Guetzkow, et al., 1963). this model represents a macro, or systemic approach to simulation construction. It is an attempt to encompass within the confines of a laboratory the most salient aspects of a total, complex, integrated social system. The INS and other systemic models, such as Ray and Duke's METRO simulation (Ray and Duke 1968) are the usual referents when terms such as "man-machine" simulation are employed, with the term "machine" referring to the fact that the environmental constraints within which the human actors must function are programmed decision-rules.

There is another approach, however, which is quite different and which is sometimes, if not always, identified as simulation. This type of model—illustrated in the works of Evan and Zelditch (1961), Zelditch and Evan (1962), and Barber (1966)—focuses not upon the operation of a total system but rather upon the behavior of a few individuals operating within the context of a larger system. Such models are simulations to the extent that the interactions of role-playing subjects are analogous to the roles and interactions of real-world actors and also to the extent that the larger system and its environment are in some sense represented and are salient to the goals and activities of the role players. Such models may be said to represent a micro approach to the analysis of the behavior of organizations or social systems.

The key to understanding the differences between such models lies in the fact that a simulation model, if it is to be feasible and useful, must reflect some kind of analytic simplification of its referent system. What is crucial is the decision as to what must be simplified and how this is to be done. In systemic simulations the simplification process is one whereby complex organizational or group phenomena, such as foreign policy decision systems, are reduced to roles which may be played by one or a very few actors. This involves conceiving of such groups or organizations as single actors which produce a clearly identifiable and presumably coherent output. Such a conceptualization is far from unknown in the literature of organization theory (Feldman and Kanter 1965). The relationships among such actors, while simplified to some degree, may nevertheless be sufficiently numerous and complex that much of the richness of behavior found in the referent system can be reflected in the operation of the simulation. It must be stressed, however, that while systemic patterns of interaction may be plausibly reproduced by such simulation models, processes that occur within the acting units or subsystems (e.g. states or agencies) are either not represented at all or are at least greatly reduced in complexity and simplified in content. This is necessary in view of the objective of such models, which is to provide a comprehensive, dynamic representation of a total system, the behavior of which may, over time, at least grossly approximate that of the referent system in major respects.

The Zelditch-Evan "simulated bureaucracy," on the other hand, provides an example of an alternative approach to simplification. This model, which was designed to investigate the behavior of the supervisor-employee dyad within the simulated context of a larger organization, does not concern itself with the overall behavior of a total system except for the purpose of providing structure and incentives to the roles of the actors whose behaviors are under investigation. In such segmental simulations the environment, which may consist wholly of programmed decision-rules, can either be held constant or manipulated as an independent variable. The relevant data produced in this fashion refer not to overall system functioning, but to individual behavior. The model of the larger system which is employed in such simulations need not be precisely analogous to any particular real-world system, but needs only to approximate the kinds of constraints and incentives which may be imposed by some real-world system or type of system. The real referent of such a simulation is any individual or small-group behavior which is similarly motivated and similarly constrained in any real-world setting. What is simplified in segmental models, then, is the total context within which behavior occurs. The details of role and task within the small group of subjects may assume a generalized form, but they need not be simplified in any important sense.

Systemic and segmental simulations share a common purpose—to abstract and simplify important phenomena so that they may be intensively scrutinized under controlled laboratory conditions. However, the two approaches clearly differ substantially with respect to their specific purposes and techniques. These differences are extremely important in evaluating the potential contribution of each approach to the development of data-based theory in public administration.

Simulation and theory. A major distinction may be drawn between systemic and segmental simulation models with respect to the potential role of theory in each type. Systemic simulation models are developed on the basis of existing system-specific theories and commonsense ideas about the operation of the referent system. Thus the INS incorporates into its basic structure numerous hypotheses concerning the structure and behavior of the international system, some of which are drawn from the theoretical literature of international politics and others of which are created out of the necessity to make some assumptions in order to complete the model (Guetzkow 1963). While the main purpose of such models is to examine systems-level propositions, studies of individual behavior or small-group behavior are also possible (see, for instance, M. Hermann 1965 and Burgess and Robinson 1969).

When systemic simulations are employed to develop or test propositions about individual personality or behavior, however, the generalizability of such findings to the referent system becomes debatable. The Hermanns' (1967) study of the outbreak of World War I indicates that at least under special circumstances it may be possible to gather simulation data on such variables as personality types, then generalize these findings usefully to the referent system. However, since systemic models have the effect of requiring a single individual to stand for a complex collectivity, this type of generalization might be limited to circumstances where the real-world behavior of such collectivities is dominated by the personality of a single individual. To go beyond this, one would seemingly have to argue that organizations or groups have personalities which are closely analogous to the personality structures of single individuals—a proposition which is at least debatable. A similar argument applies to the use of systemic simulations for the study of small-group behavior.

The primary purpose, and most significant advantage of systemic simulations, then, is the unique opportunity which they afford for examining complex, integrated systems under controlled conditions which are conducive to detailed observation and measurement, and for manipulating the conditions under which such systems can be made to operate. Regarding theory development at this level, however, a possibly important limitation must be noted. As Allison (1969) has pointed out, policy outputs can be explained in at least three ways: (1) as the products of deliberate, rational, strategic moves, (2) as the products of preprogrammed organizational procedures or routines, and (3) as the outcomes of intraorganizational political struggles. However, since segmental simulations of necessity represent organizational processes in highly simplified forms, they seem to preclude effectively explanation of the second and third types. Individuals or small, ad hoc groups would seem incapable of reproducing complex organizational routines, especially decision-making sequences, and the kinds of intragroup disagreements which might occur in the course of a simulation would seem unlikely to adequately reproduce the kinds of bureaucratic politics to which Allison refers. Rather it would appear that participants in systemic simulations would of necessity define their tasks in accordance with the rational-policy model, and the behavior of such subjects would have to be explained in these terms. This is a theoretical limitation or, if you will, a built-in bias of systemic simulations. It would seem to restrict the applicability of such models to situations in which the rational policy model offers the most adequate explanation of policy outputs and, therefore, of patterns of interaction within the system. The seriousness of this limitation is apparent, although theorists may vary in their reactions to it according to the amount of faith which they are willing to place in the rational-policy mode of explanation.

Segmental simulation models differ considerably from those of the systemic type in both their advantages and limitations. In most applications segmental simulations are simply small-group experiments with elaborate scenarios. As such they afford opportunities for application of the considerable range of theoretical models and techniques of measurement which have been developed in the study of small groups. The purpose of the scenario is to structure the experimental small group in ways which approximate the structure of natural-state groups. The importance of this is that it enables the experimenter to address directly the questions raised earlier concerning the applicability of small-group findings to settings which occur within administrative organizations. Propositions previously developed in other settings may be checked, and new and perhaps more promising theoretical lines may be explored.

The referent system in a segmental simulation is more apt to be a general class of real-world settings and tasks than any particular interaction system, if only because the latter type of matching would presumably involve attempting to replicate not only general features of the real-world setting, but also personality characteristics and factors idiosyncratic to the referent. Attempts to match at this level of detail would appear dubious, and the findings which would result might be difficult to generalize. However, in adopting the more general approach, the researcher is making at least one significant sacrifice—he is trading off the apparent relevance to particular events which is characteristic of systemic models in return for generality and theoretical precision.

The role of theory in segmental models is thus essential. The choice of models and hypotheses for segmental simulation should be dictated by explicit theoretical notions rather than policy considerations or a concern with predicting real-world events. The interpretation of findings thus obtained must therefore stress their contribution to the development of pure theory rather than their immediate applicability to the understanding of events in the real world. This in turn raises a question: at what point, if any, do such findings and theories become relevant to those real-world processes which, after all, we have claimed to be primarily interested in all along? There is no pat answer to this. Confidence in the long-run potential of theory building is to some extent an article of faith, and it is for each scholar to decide whether and to what extent he is a believer.

One further possible limitation of segmental simulation deserves mention. In confining analysis to the group-process level, one implicitly assumes that an important part of the variance in policy output and system performance can be accounted for in terms of group-level phenomena. While this is a plausible supposition, it is far from proven, especially with respect to policy-making (as opposed to work-group) processes. Here again it is difficult to be completely convincing, and one must lapse into platitudes by pointing out that answers will only develop out of further research.

Systemic and segmental simulations, then, differ with respect to purposes, levels of theory, and types of theory. These differences also make for important differences with respect to the question most commonly asked about laboratory studies of social processes: the question of validity.

Validity. The validity of a simulation is dependent upon the satisfaction of two related sets of criteria. First the operating model must accurately incorporate and reflect the major variables of the theoretical paradigm on which it is based. Moreover these variables must be amenable to reasonably accurate measurement. Second, simulations, more than other forms of laboratory research, must be demonstrably representative of referent-system phenomena. This ultimately must involve some form of comparison between real-world observations and simulation results.

Verba (1961) has noted two sets of problems which might arise with regard to the first (or internal) set of criteria. On the one hand there may be a problem involving the absence in the experimental model of variables assumed in the theoretical paradigm. On the other hand, the model might inadvertently manifest variables which the experimenter did not intend. The first of these considerations may be seen to bear directly upon the second (or external) set of validity criteria as well, since it raises the question of whether experimental models can adequately incorporate certain kinds of variables which may be of considerable importance in the real world but are hard to represent in the laboratory.

Problems concerning the omission of variables could relate to the structure of the operating model (e.g. representation of resources, communication channels, environmental constraints, etc.), or to the motivation and expectations of individuals (e.g. the seriousness with which the task is undertaken, the expectation of further contact, the experience of anxiety or fear of sanctions, etc.). The basic question raised here is whether it is possible to design a laboratory game which is a useful reflection, rather than a misleading distortion, of any important real-world political behavior.

These questions have been asked often by laboratory experimentalists and, in response, a number of techniques have been developed for representing in the laboratory scenario equivalents of such variables as group size, time membership and career orientation, feedback, and task interdependence (Weick 1965). While the efficacy of such techniques will undoubtedly vary from one model to another, the resources available to the experimentalist in this regard are considerable. The development of techniques, however, does not completely solve the problems of omission. These problems, as might be expected, differ according to type of simulation model.

In segmental simulations, which are usually based upon a relatively simple and explicit theory, such omissions are likely to be attributable to theoretical inadequacy. The more technical problems of representing the theory as an operating model become less severe as the model is more abstract, simpler, and free from the necessity of making it look like a particular referent system. The latter is true because a very abstract model may be tested in a large number of contexts and the experimenter thus has considerable latitude in selecting operational representations of his theoretical variables. A good example of this is the experiment by Mintz, wherein mob behavior is simulated by having small groups of subjects simultaneously try to pull paper cones out of a bottle (Mintz 1951). The operating principle here is the rule of genotypic similarity, which holds that the properties of a simulate need not look like the properties they represent; what is required is that they obey the same laws (see Zelditch and Evan 1962, 53).

With respect to systemic simulations, the problems of omission and representation of variables are different, and more difficult. The models upon which such simulations are based tend to be system-specific, and the complexity of such models may lead to problems. When rendering even the outline of a complex model into an operating model, it is difficult to discern whether anything important has been left out. This is especially the case with emergent variables, which are by definition the product of particular kinds of interactions among other variables. In the absence of very good descriptive theory, the process of modeling may tend to become tentative and even almost arbitrary.

Moreover in a system-specific model, the simulator is constrained to make the operational environment look like the referent system insofar as possible. This reduces the range of creative techniques available and tends to accentuate the seriousness of questions of equivalency, i.e. whether a particular representation really functions exactly as its real-world counterpart. Since that counterpart itself is seldom understood in precise theoretical fashion, establishing such equivalency is difficult. Perhaps the best approach to questions such as these is a data-matching approach whereby one ascertains whether the simulate produces outputs similar to those of the referent system. If it does, one may infer tentatively the validity of the model.

The most important problem which arises regarding the presence in a simulation model of variables not intended by the experimenter concerns the characteristics of experimental subjects. When one uses inexperienced subjects such as college students to perform tasks which supposedly represent the kinds of tasks performed by real-world actors, it is plausible to suspect that performance will be significantly affected by characteristics which differentiate subject populations from their real-world counterparts. Such characteristics might include lack of a good understanding of the simulation scenario and therefore the consequences of behavior, lack of experience in complex interactions such as political negotiation, and the carryover of behavior patterns learned in quite different contexts.

Some investigation of the effects of subject types on simulation outcomes has been done (Guetzkow 1967), but the results to date must be considered inconclusive. However, one general speculation may be advanced for what it is worth: the more highly structured, abstract, and logically simple the experimental setting, the less difference population variables will probably make. Conversely the more complex or rich the experimental environment, the more numerous and more subtle the behavior options, and the less structured the interactions involved, the greater will be the differences among subject populations. To illustrate, we would expect an experienced administrator to perform differently (and better) from a college sophomore in tasks involving analysis of decision options for political feasibility, persuasion, coalition formation, complicated information processing, etc. Moreover we would expect considerable variation among sophomores on such tasks, but somewhat less among administrators. On the other hand in a relatively simple scenario, such as a prisoner's dilemma game, such differences should be relatively smaller, as the range and subtlety of options is reduced, and relevant experience is acquired fairly readily in such tasks.

Another intrusive factor which causes some concern is the effect of the artificiality of the experimental setting and of the fact of being observed on subject behavior. Simulation researchers commonly report high levels of subject involvement, and they seem unanimous in their conclusion that this compensates for any disturbing effects of artificiality and intervention. It seems reasonable to accept these reports. Additionally we might guess that the richer systemic simulations might have something of an advantage in this respect.

As noted above, the external validity of systemic simulations can be confirmed tentatively by comparing simulation outputs with outputs from the referent system. Such confirmation is tentative since the production of similar outputs does not guarantee that similar processes have occurred. Over time, however, such matching can lead to considerable confidence. Guetzkow (1967) has summarized the results of such comparisons for the INS model, and these indicate that some success has been achieved, although neither the number of cases nor the consistency of the results is sufficient for great confidence at this time.

Segmental simulations do not afford the advantage of validation with reference to referent-system phenomena as readily. The processes modeled in segmental simulations are somewhat harder to observe in the referent system, and such observations may be complicated by idiosyncratic factors which could not be represented in the simulation model. The ultimate validation of segmental simulations would seem to rest primarily upon the kind of development and validation of theory which was referred to above. The crucial test, in other words, is not the ability to generate data which resemble real-world data, but the ability to generate theory which proves helpful in understanding the referent system, possibly through giving orientation to field research.

However, validation of simulations of either type has one common characteristic: it is finally dependent upon natural-state research. Simulation is not, except in occasional circumstances involving prediction, a substitute for direct research on the referent system. One cannot simply study public administration, for instance, in a laboratory. The measure of the success of a simulation is, for the most part, the extent to which it helps to direct and to stimulate useful natural-system research.

Conclusion. We have been discussing here two ideal-type simulation models, labeled segmental and systemic respectively. These pure types hardly exhaust the range of options open to the simulation researcher. Rather they represent end points on a continuum of possible models. For example it would be possible to develop hybrid models which are systemic but not system-specific (if the goal were research on the general properties of systems), or which are segmental but system-specific, or to invent models which deviate from ideal types in degree, e.g. which are segmental and general, but somewhat more obviously relevant to one particular system than to any other. The possibilities are numerous. However, the general kinds of theoretical and methodological considerations which this paper has sought to identify will be relevant in some fashion whatever the model.

We have tended to dwell upon the difficulties associated with simulation models as much as upon their advantages. This approach seems necessary at this point if simulation is to be employed judiciously. Such models do in fact have serious limitations as, unfortunately, do all research techniques in the social sciences. The drawbacks to simulation are not particularly more severe than those associated with any other approach. However, discussions of simulation seem to have tended to polarize into uncritical advocacy on the one hand and blanket rejection on the other. In our view neither position is especially appropriate. Simulation is not a cure-all for the problems of data gathering and theory development in public administration or any other field. It can, however, be a useful adjunct to other forms of empirical research.

REFERENCES

Barber, J. D. 1966. *Power in committees: An experiment in the governmental process.* Chicago: Rand-McNally.

Best, James J. 1971. The use of media in small group research. *Experimental study of politics* 1: 42-60.

Burgess, Philip M., and Robinson, James A. 1969. Alliances and the theory of collective action: A simulation of coalition process. *Midwest journal of political science* 13: 194-218.

Dawson, Richard E. 1962. Simulation in the social sciences. In *Simulation in social science: readings*, ed. Harold Guetzkow. Englewood Cliffs, N. J.: Prentice-Hall.

Evan, William M., and Zelditch, Morris, Jr. 1961. A laboratory experiment on bureaucratic authority. *American sociological review* 26: 883-899.

Feldman, Julian, and Kanter, Herschel E. 1965. Organizational decision-making. In *Handbook of organizations*, ed. James G. March. Chicago: Rand McNally.

Golembiewski, Robert T. 1962. *Behavior and organization: O and M and the small group*. Chicago: Rand McNally.

Guetzkow, Harold, et al. 1963. *Simulation in international relations: developments for research and teaching*. Englewood Cliffs, N.J.: Prentice-Hall.

Guetzkow, Harold. 1963. Structured programs and their relation to free activity within the inter-nation simulation. In *Simulation in international relations*, ed. Harold Guetzkow, et al.

Guetzkow, Harold. 1967. Some correspondences between simulations and realities in international relations. In *New approaches to international relations*, ed. Morton A. Kaplan. New York: St. Martin's Press.

Hermann, Margaret G. 1961. Stress, self-esteem and defensiveness in an inter-nation simulation, China Lake, Calif.: Project Michelson, U.S. Naval Ordinance Test Station.

Hermann, Charles F., and Hermann, Margaret G. 1967. An attempt to simulate the outbreak of World War I. *American political science review* 61: 400-416.

Mintz, A. 1951. Non-adaptive group behavior. *Journal of abnormal and social psychology* 46: 150-159.

Ray, Paul H., and Duke, Richard D. 1968. The environment of decision-makers in urban gaming simulations. In *Simulation in the study of politics*, ed. William D. Coplin, Chicago: Markham.

Verba, Sidney. 1961. *Small groups and political behavior*. Princeton, N.J.: Princeton University Press.

Weick, Karl E. 1965. Laboratory experimentation with organizations. In *Handbook of organizations*, ed. James G. March. Rand-McNally.

Zelditch, Morris, Jr., and Evan, William M. Simulated bureaucracies. In *Simulation in social science*, ed. Harold Guetzkow.

Simulating Social Systems: Philosophical and Methodological Considerations

JOHN R. RASER

> ...just as we have been able to derive laws about the physical universe, it is becoming possible to posit "laws" of individual and social behavior—but as yet only in an often <u>primitive</u> and <u>probabilistic</u> way.

PRIMITIVE AND PROBABILISTIC SYSTEMS

I put the word "laws" in quotes and use the word "primitive" because most of the "laws" pertaining to human behavior can be stated only in terms of rough relationships indicating direction or trend or tendency, but not in terms of degree or causality. For example we can say with some certainty that raising the educational level of the population will increase rather than decrease citizen involvement in political matters. But we cannot determine by how much political involvement will increase, nor can we say with certainty that the raised educational level in itself directly causes increased political involvement. Our difficulties arise partly because there are so many intervening factors that we cannot control in order to test the hypothesis, and partly because we have neither the resources nor the tools to measure, in a meaningful way, either educational level or political involvement.

I used the word "probabilistic" because most of our laws are based on statistical probability and therefore must be qualified. There are many reasons for such qualification. In the first place, even in studying purely physical events, the mere taking of measurements changes the phenomenon to some degree, however slight. This distortion by measurement occurs to a far greater extent in dealing with social and behavioral events—to such an extent, in fact, that the researcher may be in danger of creating self-fulfilling or self-denying prophecies. The mere enunciation of a principle—such as, "the higher the educational level, the greater the political involvement"—may change the behavior with which we are dealing. Also, there may simply be more randomness in social systems and in human behavior than there is in physical systems. In any case, we cannot (yet?) systematically account for such randomness in the social-behavioral universe as we can, for instance, in the case of the laws describing the behavior of gases.

The best we can do is to state that some relationship in the social world

Reprinted from John R. Raser, *Simulation and Society: An Exploration of Scientific Gaming,* (Boston: Allyn and Bacon, Inc., 1969) pp. 23-43. Reprinted by permission.

holds "most of the time," or "if all other things are equal," or "allowing for the way we have made the concepts or entities operational in our study, it holds—but of course one cannot be certain that these results can be generalized . . ." and so on. We state our conclusions with a given level of confidence, not with certainty. There are too many unknowns.

The point, however, is that we do achieve something better than sheer guesswork. A sociologist may conduct a study and find that middle-class white juveniles have a lower incidence of arrests than do white juveniles in the slums of the same city. He may repeat the study enough times and in enough cities to become confident that this is generally true—even though there may be exceptions. Now he knows something. He knows that there is a relationship of a certain kind between (A) the class background of white juveniles, and (B) the arrest records of white juveniles. He has a law. He may even make gross predictions, even though he may have no theory to explain his predictions. He may find that the law frequently does not hold true, and he may know little about the other factors that determine whether or not it holds, but he is not simply shooting in the dark. This is the condition of most social science.

Despite the extreme complexity of human behavior and of societal structure, we have reason to assume, then, that there are identifiable patterns, regularities, and laws. It is upon this assumption that social science simulations are constructed. These laws are different in degree, not in kind, from those that physical engineers use in the construction of their simulations. B. F. Skinner illustrates both the problem and the assumption regarding its solution by reference to the British physicist Sir Oliver Lodge, who once asserted:

> "though an astronomer can calculate the orbit of a planet or comet or even a meteor, although a physicist can deal with the structure of atoms, and a chemist with their possible combinations, neither a biologist nor any scientific man can calculate the orbit of a common fly." This is a statement about the limitations of scientists or their aspirations, not about the suitability of subject matter. Even so, it is wrong. It may be said with some assurance that if no one has calculated the orbit of a fly, it is only because no one has been sufficiently interested in doing so. The tropistic movements of many insects are now fairly well understood, but the instrumentation needed to record the flight of a fly and to give account of all the conditions affecting it would cost more than the importance of the subject justifies. There is, therefore, no reason to conclude, as the author does, that "an incalculable element of self-determination thus makes its appearance quite low down the animal scale." Self-determination does not follow from complexity.[1]

In addition to the problem of sheer complexity, social scientists may be confounded by a host of other difficulties. For instance there is the problem of the self-fulfilling or self-denying prophecy—the problem that changes in society or in individuals often come about as a result of statements about that society or those individuals. To illustrate: one of the surest ways to turn a person into the leader in a small group is to tell him (even if it is not true) that tests show he is fitted for leadership.[2] Or note that the mere publication of income statistics will push the average income upward, for all those whose income is below average will exert the pressures at their command to increase their income.

Another difficulty for the social scientist is that there are so many pseudolaws of human behavior—bits of conventional wisdom that often are not true. For example there was a widespread belief a few years ago that if people were thrifty and built up savings accounts instead of spending for luxuries, national prosperity would follow on the heels of individual prosperity. All the developments of recent economic experience and theory tell us that this is nonsense, or at least naive, since mere blind thrift could result in idle cash deposits, idle men and resources, and a spiral of deflation and depression.

But despite these problems of complexity, inadequate measures and concepts, self-fulfilling or self-denying prophecy, and the blinders of conventional wisdom, simulators in the social sciences believe that they are dealing with a true system containing information, rather than with a nonsystem or a state of entropy; their scientific problems are the same as those of physical scientists—merely more difficult. But their practical problems are enormous. It is impossible to simulate a system unless one has an adequate understanding of how it operates. If simulation is defined as the simplified replication in another medium of observed phenomena, then it is clear that such phenomena cannot be fully replicated until social scientists fully observe and describe them. So our inability to replicate is due less to limited simulation engineering skills than to the lack of adequate social science theory and data. But despite incomplete understanding of the phenomena they are trying to model, and because they are convinced that trying to simulate the phenomena is worthwhile for a variety of reasons, scholars take a stab at it. They turn to piecemeal and skeletal simulations and games.

PIECEMEAL SIMULATIONS

A piecemeal simulation is one in which the researcher attempts to simulate a small segment of social behavior and study it intensively. The choice of the segment is usually based on a conviction that the nature of the units composing this segment and the relationships among them are fairly well established; that is, that there is an "island of theory" or a "microtheory," which describes this particular segment of social interaction with a fairly high degree of confidence. For example certain types of economic behavior such as those simulated by Orcutt, Greenberger, Korbel, and Rivlin[3] are reliably described by theory; so is the behavior of committees faced with political decisions,[4] or the conflict and cooperation behavior of two persons in a prisoner's dilemma game or one of its variants.[5] These are only a few examples of those segments of behavior which could be simulated; Berelson and Steiner[6] have documented several hundred reasonably well-established principles of human behavior, most of which would lend themselves to simulation treatment.

For example, Hovland, Janis, and Kelley[7] have explored the relationship between communications and human behavior—specifically, the conditions under which a persuasive communication is or is not effective in modifying beliefs. . . . The principles governing persuasive communication can be further analyzed through the use of simulations. Parameters such as personality characteristics, group structure, and communication flow can be systematically varied to study the impact of various configurations on the communication outcomes.

There is a difficulty with such piecemeal studies, however. Scientific knowledge of the sort I have described usually has been purchased at the price of narrow encapsulation. That is, experiments are performed in a laboratory under essentially sterile conditions, with all other factors besides the one under study presumably being held equal. But the principles derived under such conditions may not hold in the nonsterile and richly complicated world to which we wish to generalize them. We may establish in a laboratory, for instance, that in a two-person prisoner's dilemma game, women are more competitive than men; but we can never be certain that it isn't the nature of the laboratory situation itself that creates this effect. Outside the laboratory in the world of real life, something different may be true. We are probably entitled to assume that findings in one setting are more apt to hold in another than their opposites, but this probability is little comfort if we have reason to believe that the fact of extreme simplification of the situation, of holding other things equal, may produce an effect that confounds—even if probably not reverses—the results of the experiment. The unreality of the laboratory, the fact that behavior in the laboratory has no real-life consequences, also may vitiate the usefulness of knowledge gained in such piecemeal simulations. The problem is inherent in more intricate and complex laboratory games and simulations as well. There is reason to believe, however, that the problem is less severe because the subjects, or participants, become deeply involved, are subjected to more complex stimuli, and are given more avenues of response.

It should be noted at this point, however, that the assumption that a richer environment and greater involvement decreases the disparity between human laboratory behavior and natural behavior is just that — an assumption based on the impressionistic observations of social scientists and fortified by growing evidence as to the discrepancies between laboratory and field observations of animals. Systematic evidence about human beings has yet to be gathered.

SKELETAL SIMULATIONS

Another approach is to use a skeletal simulation. The researcher does not try to narrow his focus to one small segment or aspect of human social behavior; instead he tries to simulate a large and complex system, such as international relations. But he knows that he cannot identify all the units of the international system, much less the nature of the relationships among them. So he selects those units and those relationships about which his information is greatest and, using them as a framework—as the bones—he builds a skeleton of international relations. He hopes that by continually gathering more data in the field, by operating the simulation over and over and thus learning what is pertinent, he slowly will be able to flesh out the bones of his skeleton until someday he has a more complete simulation of the system in which he is interested. In the meantime, he must be aware that he has abstracted and cruelly abbreviated, that his simulation is to real life what a skeleton is to a living man.

It is here, in the abstraction and abbreviation, that danger lies. The skeletal simulation is particularly vulnerable to the danger that I might call the "excluded variable." Previously we saw that the very core of simulation is abstraction. But what to abstract from reality and include in the simulation must be determined by an intelligent evaluation of what is crucial to the operation of the system. And when the scholar is under social, financial, and intellectual pressures to create a product—to devise an operating simulation—his rules for abstraction may become less rigorous. The variables embodied in the simulation are likely to be those about which he knows the most, rather than those he has determined to be most crucial. Thus availability of information is apt to be a more powerful selection criterion than appropriateness.

Assume that you are trying to construct a simulation of international relations. You have detailed information about the comparative military hardware levels of two nations in the system. You know nothing about the personalities of the two chiefs of state. So the temptation to ignore decision-maker personality variables and to include the military variables in detail is almost overwhelming—simply because the information is available, and not because you have assessed the relative importance of the two variables as determinants of the relations between those states. Such errors arise, not because the scientific process is weak, but because the human and social pressures to take the easier path are great. One advantage of using simulations in research, however, is that if you have neglected important variables, the outcomes of your simulation are apt to be absurd. This is why simulation plays so important a role in theory building, as will be discussed more fully later.

A second danger applies to piecemeal as well as to skeletal simulations, and like the first, arises from human frailty rather than from any weakness of the scientific process. It is often heuristically useful to operate an admittedly inadequate simulation based on a limited or erroneous model; the danger lies in forgetting that the outcomes also are likely to be inadequate. Since a simulation has face validity—since it is called a simulation of human conflict, committee decision making, or international relations—it is easy to forget that it may not simulate any of those things and then to be tempted to give more weight to the results than they deserve.

In his book *Deadly Logic*, Philip Green discusses this danger in detail[8] by arguing that game theorists have fallen into just this trap. Game theorists, says Green, begin by suggesting that international strategic interaction contains certain elements of game theory. The theorists then list the assumptions and limitations essential to a game-theoretic analysis, such as known utilities, rationality of decision makers, and the ability to predict the particular outcomes of particular behaviors. They proceed to explore the game-theoretic model and then arrive at a set of heuristic recommendations based on the model. But the theorists conscientiously point out that these recommendations cannot be applied to real international strategic problems, for since real-world decision makers are not necessarily rational, since utilities are not known, and so forth, the assumptions necessary for the game-theoretic analysis are false when applied to international politics.

So far, so good. But Green goes on to demonstrate that all too often, when one reads the nontechnical writings of some game theorists—the policy recommendations they put forth as experts on strategy rather than as game-theory analysis—one finds that their real life recommendations are identical to those derived from their game-theory work. The game theorists seem to have been insidiously convinced by results obtained from a model admittedly based on false assumptions, even though they have verbally recognized the danger. This is the error of placing more stock in findings derived from a model than the quality of the model warrants. It is an error to which any model designed to look like the real thing makes a researcher as susceptible as does armchair philosophizing! But this question of the proper use of results from incomplete simulations is extremely complicated, so we shall return to it later.

THE GAMING APPROACH TO SIMULATION

We saw that due to lack of theory and supporting data, social science simulators are limited in their ability to construct adequate simulations of the systems in which they are interested. Consequently they often have recourse to piecemeal and skeletal simulations, with their attendant dangers. Another, and many think more profitable, approach is to drop the idea of simulating in the strict sense, and to turn to games.

What is a game? I implied one definition by indicating that when human players enter a simulated system (such as the simulation of medieval warfare called chess) and begin to manipulate the units and relationships in the structure, the simulation acquires the characteristics of a game. Other definitions are more elaborate, but do not essentially alter this definition.

Combining the definitions of E. W. Martin, Jr., Martin Shubik, J. M. Kibbee, and Richard Dawson suggests that the term "gaming" can be applied to simulations in which human actors participate in the simulated system, generally in a competitive situation.[9]

A more formal and at the same time more general distinction between simulation and gaming is one I have derived from sociologist Erving Goffman's analysis.[10] In a simulation the rules for translating external variables into simulation variables are highly formal; in more colloquial language, the rules are tight and tough. All substitutions and analogies must be defended; the relations between variables must be carefully specified; the operation of the simulation must be governed by mathematical rules. Clearly, the translation of variables must be based on adequate theory and data.

In a game, according to my definition, there is more leeway with respect to analogical consistency and strictness. The rules for translating real life variables into simulation variables are less demanding, so it is possible to play around a bit and make do, as we shall see in the illustration below. On the surface it does not seem that my distinction, based on the amount of strict and formal resemblance between simulation and referent, is related to the distinction suggested earlier, which is based on the insertion of human players. As we shall see, however, the use of human players is only one example of the informality that defines a game in terms of my general statement, for human players can serve as a surrogate for a missing or inadequate variable.

To illuminate the difference in formality between a simulation and a game, let us see how a researcher might go about building a game. His thinking goes something like this:

> I want to construct a simulation of a social system—international politics. But I don't know enough about this system to build an accurate analog, so I am not going to claim that I can simulate it. I may be able to build good simulations of small subparts of the international political system, or I may be able to include some of the major variables and relationships pretty adequately; but there are immense gaps in my knowledge, and there may even be gaps I don't know enough to know are there. So I'll do the best I can. I'll use the best theory and data at my disposal and see what I come up with. Where there are gaps—missing variables, or ill-defined relationships between the variables I've included—I'll admit it, and I'll leave the space empty or the linkages open. In some cases, however, I do have a rough idea of what should go in the space, but I don't know enough about it to simulate it. So I'll either use the thing itself—put it into the simulation bodily—or I'll use the closest substitute for it that I can get, even though I don't know much about the substitute either. I'll consider the substitute a "black box" to be studied as I operate the game.

For example in this game of international politics I'm building, I know that culture (whatever that means) must have an important impact on the behavior of national decision makers, but I don't know just what impact. So I'll leave an open space, and plug in culture when we know more about it. In the meantime, I'll see what difference it seems to make if I leave culture out. Perhaps the game will operate as our observations of the real world suggest it should. In that case I can conclude either that (1) culture is not an important variable and I can afford to ignore it, or that (2) the cultural effect is being cancelled out in the real world by another variable I've also left out; in this latter case I can continue to ignore both culture and the other variable, or worry about culture again when I get that other variable built in.

On the other hand (3), I can conclude that even though the game seems to operate as I think it should and its outcomes are not clearly absurd, I don't know enough about the real world to make an adequate comparison, and so I can't come to any conclusion about the culture variable. In this case, I'm better off with a game than with the real world. I can't study culture very well in the real world; I can't get access to decision makers; even if I could, I can't impose experimental controls on their behavior. With a game, however, I can use surrogate decision makers, such as college students of different nationalities. I know they're not really analogs of national decision makers, but they do give me a way of finding out something about the impact of culture on the decision-making behavior. I can study the behavior of American students in a simulation and compare it with that of Mexican, Japanese, and Norwegian students in the same simulation. At least the decisions of these students from different cultures will be more like those of their national leaders than are the a priori decisions fed into a computer.

From what I learn about the decision-making behavior of real people with different cultural backgrounds, I can start to build a theory about the culture variable in international decision making. So I can use my soft game as a laboratory: I can study certain important aspects of human behavior, and at the same time I can work towards the day when I can explicate the cultural variable with confidence, build it into my game, and take another step towards having a true, hard simulation.

This is not a hypothetical conversation, by the way; it is one I once had with myself that partially determined the direction of my current research. Note that in this illustration I translated the external variable, culture, and its linkage with decision making into a simulation analog in a loose or makeshift way; the transformation rules were extremely informal. Thus when good theory and reliable data are available for all the relevant variables, we can translate the variables according to strict rules for analogizing, and construct a simulation. But where theory is weak or data scanty, we can either leave the space open (omit the variable) or fill the space with a substitute that will itself then become an object of study so that, eventually, the space can be filled accurately.

Thus, the game can serve as a presimulation, to be used both as a laboratory for studying basic principles of human behavior and as an admittedly inadequate framework for conducting research leading to improvement of the framework itself.

This gaming approach to simulation building is one that a colleague refers to as messing around in science. This is not a disparaging phrase; "messing around" is a legitimate way to increase knowledge. In fact some philosophers of science have argued that this approach to building a body of knowledge about human social behavior is sounder and more productive than the more traditional methods. To understand why this is so, we must turn our attention directly to some questions of scientific method about which we have been hinting for several pages.

PATTERN MATCHING VERSUS THE QUEST FOR PUNCTIFORM CERTAINTY

> "Truth is found more often through error than through confu-
> sion."
> —Sir Francis Bacon

The gaming approach to simulation construction is similar to lifting oneself up by one's bootstraps or, perhaps more accurately, to rebuilding an airplane while it is in flight. Although this may at first seem like an exercise in absurdity, there are sound reasons for advocating it as a research strategy. But whether we turn to games as presimulations—as a means of elaborating and refining theory that can then be embodied in a simulation devoid of human participants—or whether we use games as a laboratory for studying the behavior of human subjects, we confront certain basic epistemological questions.

Let us first consider simulation construction and the elaboration, testing, and refining of theory. It is basic to science that tests of a theory or a hypothesis do not prove it true, but improve its credibility by failing to prove that it is false. One way of going about this is to state the theory explicitly, establish some hypotheses about the phenomenon that should occur if the theory is correct, and then determine whether the predicted phenomenon does in fact occur. If in repeated observations the predicted phenomenon does not occur, then we doubt the validity of the theory; if it does occur, then confidence in the theory is increased. To take an absurdly simple example, we may state explicitly the theory: "The world is flat, not round." We then establish an hypothesis about what will occur if our theory is correct: "If the world is flat, not round, then any object traveling in a continuing straight line in any direction will eventually fall off." If it cannot be shown through adequate observation that an object does not fall off, this constitutes failure to prove the hypothesis false, and confidence in the theory is increased. If, on the other hand, it can be shown that an object does not fall off the earth, the hypothesis is disproved, and confidence in the theory is shaken. The more tests of this kind that the theory passes, the more confidence we have in it.

Confidence in a theory is further increased if we can devise competing or alternative theories to explain a phenomenon, extract hypotheses from them, test these hypotheses, and find that they fail. By disproving the alternative theories, we increase confidence in the original theory. An illustration may be helpful. Suppose I notice that when I am getting dressed I always put on my right shoe first; I see that my wife does the same, and I begin to wonder why. Then I realize that we are both right-handed, and I tentatively set up the theory that "shoe priority" is a physiological phenomenon related to right- or left-handedness. I establish the hypothesis that "Right-handed people will put the right shoe on first; left-handed people will put the left shoe on first." I then devise an experiment, or test of the theory, by surveying many right- and left-handed people to determine the order in which they put on their shoes. My studies show that in a large percentage of the cases, shoe priority is indeed related to handedness—a high enough percentage to give me confidence that my findings are not just chance. Confidence in my theory is increased, since the hypothesis was confirmed.

However, there may be another explanation. Perhaps right- or left-handedness is not a physiological but a cultural phenomenon; if this is the case, my theory that "shoe priority is physiologically determined" is wrong. So I study many cultures. I find that right-handedness predominates in approximately the same proportions of each of them and that the relation between shoe priority and right- or left-handedness prevails in their cultures as it does in mine. So my confidence in the theory is further increased. Now I discover that some primitives, such as the Onges of Little Andaman Island, are completely ambidextrous; so again I question the physiological basis of handedness; (of course, since it never occurred to the Onges to wear shoes, it will be somewhat difficult to add them to my sample). Additional challenges can be put to my theory; there is no point at which I can say for certain that I have eliminated all possible alternative explanations for what I have observed. But as the challenges become more and more farfetched, the confidence I have in my theory increases. This is the process of science.[11]

I have intentionally used the term "farfetched," since it is precisely in the decision as to what is a farfetched and what is a reasonable explanation or theory that a difficult epistemological question arises. In simple terms, a theory is judged reasonable to the extent that it fits in with other theories that have also inspired a high degree of confidence. The more complex the network of theory into which any given theory fits, the less evidence we think we need for accepting the given theory as valid. In other words the more a given theory is consistent with what we already know, the more confidence we have in the theory. Conversely, the better that new bodies of data-supported theory fit into the existing network, the more confidence we have in the web. And the more complete and rich is the known, the more completely are we able to judge whether the theory in question is compatible with it. In short, as the network of explanations about phenomena grows more detailed, internally consistent, and complex, the more confidence we have that the explanations are accurate—even without added data to support any given single explanation.

The internal logic of the network itself is a kind of proof of the validity of any given section of it. Thus a number of theories have been put forth to explain the path of the planets around the sun. But since only one theory is consistent with all the other theories explaining phenomena that are part of the system such as gravity, and the age of the solar system, we place our confidence in that theory and reject the others. We look at the whole network or pattern, and to the degree that bits of data or theories match the pattern, our confidence in the accuracy of data, theory, and pattern is increased. Pattern matching has become a powerful epistemological tool in dealing, first, with discrete, punctiform, or proximal bits of isolated data whose significance is not evident; and second, with problems of measurement error.

The conventional, logical positivist, inductive approach to science involves gathering isolated, punctiform bits of data in a specific area of interest, fitting them together into part-theories and, in one-step-at-a-time fashion, trying to construct more comprehensive theory. In an illuminating discussion of pattern matching as a scientific approach, Donald Campbell contrasts the quest for punctiform certainty with distal knowledge derived from a prior identification of the whole. "Both psychology and philosophy," says Campbell, "are emerging from an epoch in which the quest for punctiform certainty seemed the optimal approach to knowledge. To both Pavlov and Watson, single retinal cell activation and single muscle activations (punctiform data) seemed more certainly reidentifiable and specifiable than perceptions of objects or adaptive acts."[12]

But, says Campbell, we can identify any single particle, or bit of data only because we have previously identified the complex whole. As he implies, we can single out and identify single retinal-cell activation only because we have previously identified the complex phenomenon, perception. Rather than recognizing and identifying the complex whole through identification of its particles and establishment of their relationship, it is the complex whole about which we can have the more certain knowledge, and that enables us to know something about elements or particles of which it is composed. As another example:

> Imagine the task of identifying "the same" dot of ink in two newspaper prints of the same photograph. The task is impossible if the photographs are examined by exposing only one dot at a time. It becomes more possible the larger the area of each

print exposed. Insofar as any certainty in the identification of the single particle is achieved, it is because a prior identification of the whole has been achieved. Rather than the identification of the whole being achieved through the firm establishment of particles, the reverse is the case, the complex being more certainly known than the elements, neither of course, being known incorrigibly.[13]

Campbell's contention is clearer if we think of the difficulty of identifying a particular star on a clear summer night. No single star is identifiable by itself without the pattern of stars around it to give it its identifying context. The frame of other stars, each of them also unidentifiable in isolation, provides the information necessary to give meaning to what would otherwise be uninterpretable.

This point is further demonstrated in the recent work of Nobel laureate H. K. Hartline, in his studies of primary chemical and physiological visual processes in the eye. He devised methods for recording the nerve impulses from single cells of the eye of the horseshoe crab and cold-blooded vertebrates. He and his associates demonstrated that "individual nerve cells in the retina never act independently; it is the integrated action of all units of the visual system that gives rise to vision."[14] Kepler's attempt to chart the orbits of the planets by using musical intervals as the basis is an approach based on an assumption of natural order and all things fitting together.

Again, research into basic cognitive processes mathematically demonstrates that at the most primary level of perception and cognition, no sense impression can be understood without a pre-established frame of reference—a set of rules for translating that sense impression into a meaningful message. This is the pattern a child's learning follows. He slowly builds an interpretive structure—a context for evaluating information—which is elaborated and modified with each new perception.

This kind of knowing, which comes from the recognition of patterns and thus of the subunits of those patterns, is called distal knowledge. We confront a collection of fragments—bits of punctiform data, each of which is uninterpretable—and suddenly we see the entire pattern or context. Common expressions used to describe this experience include "insight," "revelation," "seeing how it all fits together," and "having it suddenly all make sense." They all express the recognition that when an entire context or pattern is grasped, each part of the pattern is also more clearly apprehended. In a sense, we may say that the whole is greater than the sum of its parts.

Pattern matching, then, enables us to make sense of punctiform data. It also enables us, as Campbell further points out, to cope with the problem of measurement error—the fallibility of meters—and with the associated problem of explicitly relating theory to experimental data.

A fundamental problem of epistemology revolves around the argument that, in essence, all knowledge is indirect, all sense data incorrigible, and all

meters or measuring instruments are fallible. We can never hope to purify
knowledge of all faults, errors, and deviations. Since any meter involves
"many physical laws other than the construct-relevant one, . . . (e.g. iner-
tial forces in a galvanometer)," Campbell argues, we can never completely
or specifically compensate for these sources of meter fallibility. A certain
amount of error is inevitable. Hence, says Campbell, we must reject a
"purely 'proximal' science in which scientific constructs [are] defined in
terms of [exhaustively known through] specific meter readings."[15]
Punctiform certainty is a mirage.

But the inevitability of measurement error or observation error implies
that there cannot be a perfect fit between theory and data. For example,
says Campbell, take the case in which we

> graph together a set of empirical points and a theoretically
> derived curve and achieve a good correspondence. Some of the
> points lie above the line, others below, but in general they fit
> well, and some lie "exactly" on the line. If there is no
> systematic deviation, we interpret the point by point deviation
> where they occur as error, and would expect such error to oc-
> cur on some of the "perfectly fitting" points were the experi-
> ment to be replicated. While an over-all fit has been required,
> no single observation point has been taken as an infallible
> operational definition of a theoretical value. . .[16]

Thus, the points graphed together give us a pattern by which we can
match theory to data and can "distribute the fringe of error over all of the
observational points, potentially. . . . A priori . . . any of the points could be
wrong." It is through a process of this sort, says Campbell, "that physicists
can throw away 'wild observations'." At any period, physicists have
assumed that most of their knowledge is correct, and paradoxically, it is
from "this floating platform of over-all pattern," that they have been able
to question and reexamine a particular measurement process and refine
their measurement instruments. "The 'anchoring' of theory to data," says
Campbell, has not at all been achieved through a perfect correspondence at
any particular point, but rather through a pattern matching of the two in
some overall ways.[17] Furthermore a network or pattern of theory, even if it
is not absolutely accurate, provides a standard—Campbell's "floating platform of pattern"—against which to check observations that are always subject to measurement error.

We have seen the importance of looking at the whole to understand its
parts better, instead of trying to understand each part in isolation, and then
from piecemeal understanding to build up a whole. We have seen that to
the degree a theory fits (matches) a network of theory (a pattern), we may
have confidence in the theory. And we have seen that because the measurement of any single phenomenon is subject to error, the pattern-matching
model of relating theory to data allows us to assume that any meter reading
is in error without requiring us to impeach the theory. Moreover, and even

more important, it is extremely difficult to interpret the measurements in the absence of an overall framework or pattern.

Now we can use pattern recognition not only in understanding concrete physical phenomena, but also in handling abstractions—in testing concepts and in building theory. An idea acquires new meaning when it is set in the context of other ideas; then both idea and context enrich and illuminate each other. Scientists increasingly recognize that the inclusion of theories and part-theories in a larger construct is a powerful technique for enhancing data gathering and theory testing, even though the scientists may lack confidence in the absolute validity of many of the theories included in the construct. As Campbell observes, the certainty of identifying any single part is facilitated by a prior identification of the whole, even if the prior identification is uncertain and partially erroneous.

We are now back to our starting point; this is the process in science we referred to earlier as messing around. It is the process involved in constructing a game that you hope eventually to develop into a simulation. Instead of waiting to build a construct (simulation) until you are certain of the nature of all its elements, you build a game that requires tentatively postulating the entire model. By watching the behavior of the operating subparts of the tentative model and by noting how they fit with its other parts, you can check and refine both the subparts and the model as a whole. Thus, as Bacon implies and Campbell argues, establishing an uncertain and partially erroneous framework may be a way of generating the subtheory and data from which complete and well-validated theoretical constructs can eventually emerge.

REPRESENTATIVE SAMPLING:
GAMES AS COMPLEX LABORATORIES

The second sound rationale for constructing a tentative but complete model for study rather than waiting until all information is available for each subpart is that such a model can be a man-machine game providing a rich laboratory for the study of human behavior. By building a game that incorporates the central features of what we wish to study, even if those features are only rough approximations of the real world, we can provide a wide range of stimuli for the human subjects, thereby offering the subjects opportunity for a wide range of possible behaviors. In such a game situation, as in the real world, everything is complicated, messy, and tangled.

Despite the assumption to the contrary, the complex laboratory that a game can provide is superior to a more simple laboratory, such as a study of decision making in which the subject simply manipulates two sets of lights. My argument for the superiority of a complex laboratory is based on Spinoza's dictum that the pattern of research should be the same as the pattern of what is being studied. This dictum may be applied to the design of research, the organization of data analysis, or the search for theory; it also may be applied to the design of laboratory experiments. This dictum is pattern matching of a different sort and in a different context. The argument for matching the pattern of the research design or laboratory experiment with the pattern of that being studied is based on some assumptions about the uniformity of experience.

One way of gaining information about the world is by inference. Under controlled conditions we measure the behavior of some sample of a population. We then infer that the findings about the sample can be applied to the whole population, subject, of course, to the limitations imposed by the sampling techniques. For example, public opinion pollsters question only about 1500 persons in the United States, carefully selected so that the composition of this sample closely resembles the composition of the population as a whole in regard to relevant characteristics. It is then inferred that the responses of the total population would be similar to the responses of those in the sample—with, incidentally, extremely reliable results.

Alternatively we may measure the behavior of some entity (not an actual sample) thought to resemble the population in question, and then infer that the behavior of the entity tells us about the behavior of the population. For this reason comparative psychologists study the learning behavior of rats in cages and mazes. From their studies, the psychologists draw inferences about the learning process in humans. In this kind of study, the psychologists are using substitute entities, or surrogates.

It is generally assumed that the more closely the surrogate resembles the population of interest, the more confidently inference can be made. The experimental psychologist more confidently extrapolates from primate behavior to human behavior than from rat or fish behavior. The game approach we are considering here goes a step further: it suggests that the more closely the laboratory used in the study resembles the situation to which inferences are made, the more valid the inferences. The technique of representative sampling of subjects is extended to representative sampling of situations.

To illustrate the reasoning, a basic tenet of Freudian theory may be false and is at least suspect because Freud failed to take the nature of his laboratory into account and ignored the interaction between behavior and environment. Freud studied apes in the London zoo, concluded from their behavior that they are primarily dominated by sexual drives, and extrapolated to human beings. Even though he argued that his surrogates (the apes) were similar to the population in which he was interested (human beings) and thus showed awareness of the first technique for narrowing the inferential gap, he ignored the situational context—in this case the problem of environmental contamination. Recent field studies of apes have demonstrated that in the natural environment, their sexual activity is far below the level displayed in the zoo, where most activities that dominate their normal existence are impossible. Similar findings could be cited for rats, wild mice, and other common laboratory animals. Freud's inference was incorrect because the nature of his laboratory distorted the behavior of his subjects. The same problem arises when human subjects are placed in a laboratory setting that severely restricts their range of behavior.

If, for example, one is interested in learning about the decision-making behavior of chiefs of state as a function of personality, but cannot study them directly and must use surrogates, two rules should be followed: (1) The surrogates should be as much like chiefs of state as possible; and (2) The situation in which each surrogate is placed should be as much as possible like that in which the chief of state operates. Both rules are often broken for a good reason. Understandably, given the limits on resources, research subjects must be chosen on the basis of availability, not suitability. And laboratory environments are usually made as austere and simple as possible because such simplicity makes data gathering easier, because social scientists often do not know enough about the characteristics of the environment to which they wish to generalize to recreate it with fidelity in the laboratory, and because they have accepted as an article of faith that the physical science paradigm applies to social science; hence they believe that results are more reliable if all variables but the particular one under study are not allowed to vary except in exactly known ways.

The result of such studies, however, is a repetition of Freud's error. The studies neglect the fact that our subjects are human. In the stilted and restricted laboratory environment, the situation of the human subjects is like that of Freud's apes: they have little opportunity to display the richness and complexity of behavior that characterize their normal existence. The laboratory does not sufficiently resemble the referent situation. Thus, for example, in studying the relation between personality traits and decision-making behavior, we are justified in generalizing our laboratory results to real-life chiefs of state according to the degree that (1) the subjects can become intellectually and emotionally involved in the situation, (2) they can become goal oriented, (3) they can have at their disposal a variety of means as much as possible like those available to chiefs of state for reaching their goals, (4) the communication system in which they are enmeshed has the same characteristics of overload and uncertainty as does that of a chief of state, and (5) they are operating in ambiguous, threatening, and probabilistic situations.

In brief, the greater the extent to which the laboratory provides a physical, social, and psychological environment identical to that in which a chief of state operates, the greater the extent to which we are justified in inferring that these laboratory results are valid with respect to chiefs of state. Perhaps the clearest available statement of these issues is made by Donald Campbell in an unpublished paper called "The Principle of Proximal Similarity in the Application of Science," which I shall quote nearly in full.[18]

These paragraphs are an attempt to make explicit an advantage which the experimental use of manned simulation has over simpler small-group reseach when one's goal is the development of principles to be applied to a complex social situation.

This advantage has no doubt motivated the development of manned simulation, but is apt to be overlooked because it is not made explicit in current philosophies of science.

Proximal similarity. Whatever epistemology we may choose in interpreting the laws of science—even if as realists we regard science as iteratively asymptoting on truth—we recognize that the science we have today is only approximate . . .

This predicament is well known, and gives rise to the caution scientists show in applying their knowledge to new situations. It is one aspect of that caution which is central here—there is more caution the greater the extrapolation required, or the more dissimilar the situation of application from the laboratory of generation, for the greater the dissimilarity, the more likely are these as yet unknown variables to affect the outcome . . .

Extrapolating about extrapolations. The process of science consists in positing totally general laws and then qualifying them as our experience in extrapolating them to new situations shows the qualifications and exceptions to be needed. In each new application we are again going in some degree beyond the conditions under which the law has been tested. The confidence with which we do this depends upon our previous experience with this particular law and with the general domain of laws. In some domains of physics and astronomy, the experience in extrapolation has been remarkably sanguine, general laws holding without qualification in wide ranges of application. Such a background lends credence to any specific new application of one law from such a domain.

Our experience in extrapolating social-psychological principles from the experimental laboratory of undergraduate psychology courses is much poorer. Repeatedly, efforts to replicate experimental findings fail, although our publication policies (both the self-policing of authors and the preferences of journal editors) are such as to cover over a good part of this failure. Some of the failure is due, no doubt, to sampling vagaries. But a good deal of it is probably due to supposedly irrelevant differences in the experimental procedures, topics, or populations. Such failures warn us that we do not have a law which can effectively be generalized in disregard of the specific conditions on innumerable other variables.

More direct evidence comes from the usual presence of significant interaction effects in complex experiments. If in experiments in which there were two or more treatment dimensions we regularly got significant main effects with no interactions, our experience would encourage extrapolation. We would have found, for example, that the relationship between A and B was constant over all levels of C, that an A-B law unqualified with regard to C could be stated. Instead, it is our usual experience that the A-B relationship is different for levels of C, occasionally to the point of a reversal in direction. If such multiple factorial experiments be regarded as experiments in generalization, they give us great grounds for caution, particularly when we generalize the expectation that had we included in our experiment dimensions F, G, and H, or X, Y, and Z, the A-B relationship might well have shown interactions with all or some of them too. The high rate of interactions on the variables we have explored must make us expect such for the many unexplored ones . . .

Clear-cut pure-variable small group experiments vs. manned simulation as a basis for generalization to international negotiation. There is at present a tendency on the part of some to regard the results of laboratory social psychology utilizing plain settings, simple tasks and treatment differences which vary in only one pure dimension, as superior in generalizability to the products of manned simulation. For example, an early draft of a most competent review of simulation in the social sciences stated: "In this light, inter-nation simulation is not a new technique, but a very ambitious extrapolation of the usual techniques of the social psychological experiment. There are hazards in generalizing to the real world even the simplest behaviors of small laboratory groups, and these hazards clearly increase when laboratory subjects are required to play unfamiliar elite institutional roles." The implications of the principle of proximal similarity exactly contradicts this: a complex simulation is a better base for generalizing to a specific natural situation than a simple experiment if the greater complexity provides greater similarity to the natural situation in question....

Variables held constant. The differences between simple small group experimentation and simulation may be discussed under these two aspects: 1. variables held constant, 2. variables experimentally manipulated, if any. It will be argued that the main difference is, or should be, in the variables held constant. Any experiment or simulation manipulates at most three or four variables. All the other conceivable variables are held constant at some one level. This is just as much so for the "simple" experiment in which they are totally neglected as in the manned simulation in which the elaborate scenario and non-experimental inputs build up specific common values for at least a number of them. Insofar as the background is held constant, values achieved in simulation, however "artifically" established, are closer to the setting of application than are the settings of the "simple" experiment; the simulation is the better basis for generalization. Such greater similarity probably ex-

> ists for these variables: degree of involvement, group-identification, future responsibility for outcomes of decisions, type of tasks and problems faced, time spent in role, etc. When we look at the task of generalization in this light, we are overwhelmed with the petty degree of similarity achieved on these variables, and the innumerable other variables neglected entirely. Surely this is a sorry base for generalization, better only by contrast with the "simple" and "pure" small group experiment. The absolute degree of similarity will not be argued. All that is claimed is that given our many poor bases for making generalizations into the important arena of application, this is a better one. From this stance, the error of the quotation above is not its disparagement of the manned simulation, but its naive faith in the still more irrelevant simple small groups experiment. In our predicament, we must work with the best of those poor tools available to us, and manned simulation . . . seems one of them.

There is another way in which manned games narrow the gap between the data we gather and the processes to which we are interested in inferring. In the behavioral sciences we often attempt to learn about an individual by obtaining his verbal responses to a questionnaire. That is, a psychologist will infer aspects of personality from a subject's verbal reports or interpretations of a projective test. A sociologist will infer real attitudes from attitudes expressed on paper or in an interview. A political scientist or pollster will infer political beliefs and predict political behavior on the same grounds. But the inferential road is filled with pitfalls. There is a wealth of evidence that there may be little relationship between expressed feelings and true feelings, that the analysis of projective tests may be more dependent on the personality of the analyst than of the subject, that opinion and attitude surveys have little value in predicting behavior.

Gaming enables us to shorten that inferential road for some types of behavior. If we are interested in subjects' bargaining strategies, orientation towards competition as opposed to cooperation, reaction to stress, and other basic personal and interpersonal processes, these can be studied directly in a game—without the possibly contaminating intermediary of a questionnaire. In addition if we are interested in individual qualities such as political, social, economic, and military philosophy, concepts of role and status, or overall ideology, we can study this also in a game—not as directly as a more basic process—yet a good deal more directly than by interviewing a subject or asking him to respond to a questionnaire. The written messages and the minute-by-minute recorded decisions he produces as he acts within his particular simulated social system provide a detailed record of his behavior that is more illuminating than a less direct method could possibly be.

There is still the problem of analyzing these data, and this can be more difficult than analysis of a structured questionnaire, though probably not more difficult than analyzing an open-ended questionnaire, an interview, or a projective test. (Some have even gone so far as to say that a game is indeed just that—a very elaborate, rich, and unstructured projective test.) There also is the problem that whereas we can argue the greater accuracy of games as an indicator of those behaviors that are usually measured by test or interview techniques, it is virtually impossible to prove or disprove. Even though we can compare behavior in a game with responses on a test, it is usually far less feasible to compare either of these with behavior in a completely natural setting. We cannot get access to the natural behavior because we have no control over time and events and no adequate observational techniques. In short, demonstrating the validity of either tests or games is terribly difficult, whereas examining the intermethod reliability might be quite easy. I am currently undertaking just such an effort by comparing the responses of American, Mexican, Japanese, and Norwegian students on a "Modes of Strategic Thinking" questionnaire with their behavior in an Inter-Nation Simulation on political, military, and economic matters. At this point, it is too early to give results. However, the predilection of most who have used both games and verbal response tests extensively would be, I believe, to place greater faith in the validity of game responses should there prove to be a discrepancy between the two measures.

NOTES

1. B. F. Skinner, "Is a Science of Human Behavior Possible?" in *Philosophical Problems of the Social Sciences*, ed. D. Braybrooke (New York: Macmillian Co., 1965), 24.

2. Richard E. Farson, James Johannson, and Lawrence Solomon, "Studies in Group Leadership" (La Jolla, Calif.: Western Behavioral Sciences Institute, 1965).

3. Guy H. Orcutt, et al., *Microanalysis of Socio-economic Systems* (New York: Harper & Row, 1961).

4. James Barber, "Government Committees in the Small Group Laboratory," prepared for delivery at the 1963 Annual Meeting of the American Political Science Association, New York, Sept. 4-7, mimeographed, Yale University. Or, Wayman J. Crow and Robert Noel, "The Valid Use of Simulation Results" (La Jolla, Calif.: Western Behavioral Sciences Institute, June 1965).

5. Morton Deutsch and Robert M. Krauss, "Studies of Interpersonal Bargaining," *Journal of Conflict Resolution*, 6 (1962): 52-76. Anatol Rapoport and Carol Orwant, "Experimental Games: A Review," *Behavioral Science*, 8 (1962): 1-37.

6. Bernard Berelson and Gary Steiner, *Human Behavior: An Inventory of Scientific Findings* (New York: Harcourt, Brace and World, 1964).

7. Carl I. Hovland, Irving L. Janis, and Harold H. Kelley, *Communication and Persuasion: Psychological Studies of Opinion Change* (New Haven: Yale University Press, 1953).

8. Philip Green, *Deadly Logic: The Theory of Nuclear Deterrence* (Columbus, Ohio: Ohio State University Press, 1966).

9. Richard E. Dawson, "Simulation in the Social Sciences" in *Simulation in Social Science*, ed. H. Guetzkow (Englewood Cliffs, N. J.: Prentice-Hall, 1962), 9.

10. Erving Goffman, *Encounters: Two Studies in the Sociology of Interaction* (Indianapolis: Bobbs-Merrill, 1961).

11. cf. discussion by Karl Popper, "Unity of Method in the Natural and Social Sciences," in Braybrooke, 33-41.

12. Donald T. Campbell, "Pattern Matching as an Essential in Distal-Knowing," *The Psy-

chology of Egon Brunswick, ed. K. R. Hammond (New York: Holt, Rinehart & Winston, 1966) 83.

13. Campbell, 83.

14. "Science and the Citizen," *Scientific American*, Dec. 1967, 48.

15. Campbell, 99-102.

16. Ibid., 100-102.

17. Preliminary Research Memorandum: JWGA/ARPA/NU. Advanced Research Projects Agency, SD-260, Northwestern University, July 1966.

18. For another compelling statement of this position, see Wayman J. Crow, "Simulation: The Construction and Use of Functioning Models in International Relations," in Hammond, 341-358.

"Experts" and "Politicos" in Negotiating Situations: An Experimental Analog to a Critical Class of Encounter

ALLAN W. LERNER

Laboratory experimentation is a powerful technique for investigation in political science, but its full potential has hardly been realized. One reason for this, I suspect, is that experimentation has rarely been linked to more conventional modes of research—conventional from the perspective of current political science at any rate. The conviction that political science research could generally be enhanced by linking experimentation to other, more popular techniques, figures prominently in this paper because the laboratory study I would like to discuss here can be best understood when viewed as part of a larger enterprise I recently undertook. This larger enterprise with its laboratory component sought to suggest, as a kind of microrestatement of the linkage-of-perspectives issue, how a comparatively weak spot in the policymaking literature might be reinforced and better related to stronger sections of the literature.[1] Let me first describe the broader policymaking issue I am concerned with so that I can indicate the reason for my use of experimentation, how it relates to more conventional inquiry, and what I found in the experiment I devised.

I am interested in authoritative decision making in the technological society. I believe that individuals enter the circle of authoritative decision makers either through what are broadly called political career patterns or through the display of technical expertise. Those who enter authoritative decision-making circles through political career patterns I call "politicos." Those who enter by virtue of technical expertise I call "experts."[2]

Experts constitute a new class of political actors because (assuming decision making is an arena for politics) decisions to be made in the technological society involve a technological component of sufficient complexity to prevent politicos from mastering all the key decision issues. Thus experts often enter decision circles to translate technical problems for politicos who have final administrative authority to decide issues but insufficient technical skill to master them intellectually.

I make the additional assumption (hardly novel) that nominally apolitical experts have their own decision preferences and broader value preferences which together lead them to politicking within decision circles. It is thus appropriate to consider the relationship between experts and politicos in major decision circles as a mixed competitive-cooperative relationship.

Experts and politicos cooperate when their decision biases coincide, and they compete when their biases diverge. The context of the relationship is a decision-making group populated by experts, politicos, and any unspecified others. Assuming some degree of collegiality in all decision-making groups for reasons I have developed elsewhere, an element of consensus politics—of jockeying for support within the group—always appears.[3] This jockeying becomes the central political process within the group. It represents the competition between factions for the support of others in support of the option the given faction would prefer to see as the final decision recommended (or chosen) by the group. In a context such as this, maintenance of a competitive-cooperative relationship entails an emphasis on strategic interpersonal behavior. Expert-politico interaction involves substantial smoothing or stroking. It involves brinkmanship, tactical withdrawal, dissembling, and the like. From the microperspective, the intensity of politicking may rival the most intricate dealings of diplomats.

The expert-politico question seems worth investigating because it is often dealt with in fragmented fashion by those who do not name it, but deal with one or another of its manifestations. The role of consultants in urban planning, the political consequences of PPBS, the McNamara syndrome in defense policy, the "tyranny of whiz kids" in major decision-making institutions, the apolitical scientific approach to local government, the case for multiple advocacy in foreign policy, and the Halberstam genre of expose — all these issues have the expert-politico question at the core.[4]

The major question is: In a decision-making group, when given experts and politicos join to neutralize the impact of others, or when they compete because they are on opposite sides (within the group), what variables determine who has the upper hand in the intragroup jockeying, in the haggling, in the political struggle?

To begin to answer this question, I tried to develop a conceptual framework of the expert-politico relationship. The strategy in constructing the framework was to accept the notion that the relationship is played out on many dimensions. The assumption is that each dimension contributes variables which in toto determine the relationship. I have tried to develop (reconstruct) the relationship on each dimension and name variables detectable for each dimension. Then within each dimension my interest was to indicate how changes in variables might favor experts or politicos.

The five dimensions of the expert-politico relationship that frame my thinking on the subject are:

(1) The role dimension: Are there any differences in the style of expert and politico behavior which vary with their perceived differences in role?

(2) The personality dimension: To what extent might the role differences between experts and politicos be mediated by personality differences?

(3) The task-parameter dimension: To what extent are expert and politico differences and agreements bounded by perceptions of the task per se facing any given group?

(4) The organizational dimension: How do various organizational condi-

tions such as the degree of hierarchical stratification, explicit or implicit voting procedures, decision unit autonomy, and so on, affect the tactical position of expert or politico regarding conflicts and agreements within the group?

(5) The societal dimension: What social values and what institutional trends influence the relationship over the long run? What precisely is the nature of such influences?

The role dimension—the question of whether expertise per se changes one's behavior in negotiating for support of particular decision-making options—seemed the most difficult to explore. The literature on experts and decision making, or experts in politics, is slight and heavily anecdotal. It is mostly case-study material which often does not justify significant generalization. When the aim is to proceed toward a conceptual framework which must be by its nature devoid of topicality, an anecdotal literature is a difficult context from which to begin.

Moreover the development of a conceptual framework usually entails a meta-analysis of existing views with an eye partly to controlled and selective integration. This is often associated with reorganizing the problem in a novel way, introducing new taxonomies, new at least in application to the particular problem at hand.

The anecdotal mode of what is available, combined with the demands of undertaking a conceptual framework, led me to the controlled laboratory experiment, or analog study, in dealing with these role-level considerations that were part of my larger study. I make these points to underscore my view of when the analog study can be useful for political scientists who are not necessarily interested in small-group study per se.

I believe that while the controlled laboratory study has its generic weaknesses,[5] as well as weaknesses the analyst may introduce, it does things other research techniques cannot. This is not to deny that the technique is deficient where others are strong. The point is that the controlled experiment can fill a gap in analysis technique. As I will try to indicate later, it can be particularly useful in triangulation, in reinforcing a line of inference through the use of several independent modes of investigation. In this sense, it is at the very least an under-used supplement to many research approaches that are more monistic than we might wish. To me, the major advantages of the analog study are as follows:

Where it is suspected that real-world relationships are governed by a complex interaction of variables or dimensions of variables, the freedom to control, or selectively sanitize the laboratory environment can greatly help to trace the individual effects exerted dimension by dimension. While advantages such as this are in some senses obtainable with computers, the laboratory technique also allows for the retention of live human action. And while many facets of subject behavior may not be formally monitored according to the particular research design adopted for the laboratory, the heuristic value of experimenter exposure to this live human action of subjects should not be underestimated.

Also the laboratory study obviously allows for the generation of new data, often at comparatively low cost, in a form easily replicable and amenable to sophisticated quantitative analysis when that is deemed necessary. Further, compared to the case study, the advantage on control, on sequential measures for isolating confounding factors, and of distinguishing evidence from impression are substantial. Additionally, in terms of what my own experience has indicated, the use of laboratory studies often serves as a vehicle for interdisciplinary consultation because it is a tool with which sociology and psychology are familiar. Last the laboratory study (though it is not unique in this) strongly encourages the analyst to be honest with himself about the focus, biases, and weaknesses of his thinking. I believe that the clear articulation of assumptions that the preoperational search for confounding demands is more easily mumbled. over in the more conventional, discursive approaches than in the laboratory study, which seems to me more syllogistic.

I will try to illustrate some of these advantages by detailing my own experiment on experts. My perspective on expert-politico interaction dictated that the experimental design exhibit the following properties: expert-politico encounter in a decision-making group, a collegial setting, mutal role recognition, greatest individual reward for group success, initial disagreement on best solution, insufficient power of individuals to invoke their own preferred solutions without group acquiescence, a group-decision rule approaching consensus, a problem amenable in principle to expertise, and opportunity to communicate in attempts to co-opt, by bargaining, compelling logic, trickery, or whatever. To reflect these conditions expert-politico encounters in the laboratory were structured in the following fashion.[6]

Fifty male undergraduate volunteer subjects were randomly assigned to either a test group (henceforth experts) or a control group (henceforth laymen). Subjects selected for the test group were led to view themselves as experts as a result of exposure to a preconditioning procedure administered prior to the actual test condition. This preconditioning procedure was designed to convince such subjects that they possessed a specified inborn skill. The strategy of the experiment was to mix such experts with presumed politicos to form triads charged with negotiating a problem within the province of the preconditioned subjects' expertise.[7] The negotiating behavior of such expert subjects in this context would be compared to the behavior of control group nonexperts (laymen) exposed to the identical triad experience.

Fifty triads were run. In the twenty-five expert triads, an expert negotiated with the two politico confederates. In the layman triads a layman negotiated with the same two politico confederates. (The use of confederate politicos is described below.) Significant differences in behavior between the two groups would be attributed to the effects of internalizing the expert role.

Experts were produced by assembling all subjects assigned to this category for a slide showing. Such subjects were informed that the purpose of this assembly was to isolate individuals from the population at large who possessed what research on blindness has shown to be an inborn or infancy-acquired visual cognition skill. The skill was supposedly manifest in the ability to comprehend the array of simple objects on a blank two-dimensional field with a rapidity and accuracy beyond the normal individual's capabilities. Subjects were told that to isolate individuals with this skill, all would be exposed to five slides depicting an abstract pattern of black dots on a blank background. The dots would be flashed too briefly for anyone to count them. The task was to estimate the exact number of dots on each slide and record the answer in the interval between each slide and the next.

The experimenter was to score the answer sheets according to a preestablished sliding scale of accuracy which would yield percentile ratings for all participants. Participants falling within a previously determined expert percentile range would be notified and used in what experts now took to be a second phase of the experiment. This phase was described as involving negotiation in a group format on a visual problem identical to the type presently to be used to identify natural experts. In fact, all subjects who completed this bogus expert-discovering procedure were notified that they were experts. Scores in this procedure were in fact never evaluated and the experimenter was himself unaware of the number of dots on any slide. Thus experts were recruited for participation in negotiating triads involving politicos on a dot problem identical to the type used to establish expertise.

Control group subjects, or laymen, were simply volunteers recruited for what was described as an experiment in group problem solving involving persons paired to yield groups with various combinations of skills. Both expert and layman subjects were assigned to triads whose two other members were described to the subjects as established politicos. Subjects were told that politicos were so labeled because they met two conditions. First, they were supposedly recommended to the experimenter by local political groups who were asked to name people who had participated extensively in the recent electoral campaigns. Second, in addition to being so recommended, a battery of psychological tests supposedly administered to them indicated that they conform to the test profile of the political-personality type.

The politicos were in fact confederates, with the same confederates employed in all triads. Both experts and laymen were told that they would be working with these politicos in a problem involving estimation of dots flashed too quickly to be counted. Experts were told this was a type of problem identical to that in which they showed expertise.

All subjects were told that the purpose of the experiment was to see how effectively groups composed of members with different combinations of skills could work on a given problem. All subjects were told that all members of their triad knew that each would be aware of the other's expert, layman, or politico status, as the case might be. Experts were told that each triad member would be aware that politicos did not possess the skill enjoyed by experts. Laymen were told that each triad member would be aware that none possessed any special skill regarding the dot problem at hand.

Information given to subjects about the nature of the experiment and the profile of participants was provided privately in an anteroom briefing prior to meeting politicos. Instructions on the rules of triad interaction were given in the presence of politicos and subjects. With all other information given to subjects beforehand, politico-confederates were blind to subject test status. In addition, confederates were told that pilot studies had indicated that both experts and laymen would feign expertise and/or inability regardless of actual self-perceptions, in attempts to gain strategic advantages. This was designed to blind confederates even though subjects might disclose their expert or layman status during triad negotiations.

The task for the triad was to offer a single accurate-as-possible estimate of the number of dots on a slide flashed before the participants. In addition to a standard payment of two dollars to all participants, twenty-five dollars would be paid to each member of the triad whose estimate was more accurate than that offered by any other triad. Participants were separated by partitions which obscured vision of each other during the test interval, with communication confined to written messages but otherwise unrestricted. Message slips were coded beforehand to allow reconstruction of the sequence, identification of the source, and analysis of the content of all messages sent in each triad.

Participants were permitted to communicate freely for ten minutes and then cease on experimenter signal. If no agreement was reached (a certainty as a result of instructions to confederates to be described shortly), communication would continue for approximately one minute, according to a set of prepared instructions designed to facilitate closure. Any participant was free during the ten-minute period to withdraw from (opt out of) the group at any time, if he felt that the group effort was no longer productive. In this event the experimenter would poll the group for individual estimates and any winning individual answer would earn its owner fifteen dollars instead of the twenty-five dollars payable for winning group answers. By promising that the option to opt out would be available in the eleventh minute as well, the game was structured so as to make actual opting during the free exchange period irrational, while allowing reference to the rule for strategic purposes. This insured a standard time of exposure to the test situation for all subjects.

Confederates were previously instructed to avoid making any number-estimate offers until the subject sent one to either confederate. Confederates then responded with counter estimates that were fifty percent higher and fifty percent lower than the first estimate. Confederates were allowed free rein in negotiation beyond this point, with the condition that they not reach agreement. At the end of the ten-minute free-exchange period, the experimenter ascertained that there was no agreement and then instructed each participant to send a single, identical final offer to each of his counterparts. Confederates stalled until receiving the subject's final offer, and then returned identical final offers which were twenty percent higher than the subject's.

After this exchange of final offers, the experimenter ascertained that one participant (invariably the subject) was a group holdout. The subject was then instructed to select one from the following options: agree with counterparts, earning each participant twenty-five dollars if the now unanimous answer were indeed a winning one; stick to his own final offer earning any participants fifteen dollars if their answers were winning ones; offer a new number different from the joint counterpart offer and different from the subject's own final offer, again for fifteen dollars. With the subject's response, the experiment was concluded. This procedure for closure as well as the opting rule were designed simply to allow for later measures of several negotiating behaviors and do not reflect any hypotheses of special concern in the design.

In a sense the dependent variable was negotiating behavior in the presence of perceived politicos, hypothesized to be a function of internalizing the expert role. Operationally, negotiating behavior was defined as scores on a collection of forty-two separate measures applied to communications recorded for the triad. The measures may be grouped as concerning, broadly: volume of communication, references to role and ability, interest in specificity, sense of overview of the proceedings, coalition and concession behavior, handling injection of personal issues, and mediating behavior.[8]

Five tables at the end of this report summarize the results. Table 5.1 provides a list of all variables measured in the laboratory. Table 5.2 reports the variables found statistically significant at the .05 (two-tailed) level or better. Table 5.3 reports the means and standard deviations for experts and laymen. Tables 4 and 5 report the rotated factor matrices for experts and laymen. (Any additional data of interest will be provided on request so far as possible. Similarly, for the sake of convenience given considerations of length, all charges to subjects including recruitment presentations, verbatim presentations at the expert preconditioning session, anteroom briefings, triad instructions, debriefings, etc., will be provided on request.)

Data were obtained by coding all subject messages for content, reflecting behavior measured by any of the forty-two dependent variables and then arriving at a score for each subject on each variable. Except for two variables, these scores were frequency scores. A multiple coding system was used whereby a given message could be coded for scores on more than one variable if the coder judged this to be appropriate in light of the message content.

Coder reliability was calculated at ninety percent. One coder scored all messages and then a second coder scored fifty percent of all messages, selected randomly. The reliability figure represents the percent of coder agreement on both items and frequency. Coders were blind as to subjects' status.

Expert and layman scores on each dependent variable were compared by applying the t-test for significant mean differences and the f-maximum test for significant differences in variance. Orthogonal (varimax) factor analysis was also undertaken for test and control group scores separately, to ascertain differences in the way dependent variables were orchestrated for each group. The strategy in data interpretation was to focus on the factor analysis for clues as to what patterns of role interpretation (if any) could be expected in the absence of self-images of expertise (that is, for laymen, the control group), and what new or different patterns were produced when expertise was internalized. This line of analysis responds to the question of how internalizing expertise alters behavior in negotiation with presumed politicos. Statistical analyses were valued primarily as checks on the inferences drawn from the factor analysis. Thus when factor labeling implied that certain types of behavior would be suppressed, increased, or undertaken erratically, statistical results could be examined for consistency with such inferences. (Again material detailing the logic of factor labeling, the relation to statistical findings, etc., will be provided on request wherever possible.)

This approach to data interpretation was chosen though the statistical tests proved some variables significant in themselves because of (1) the belief that the style or orchestration of all behaviors and not isolated behavior measures should be of primary interest; and (2) the belief that some factors—or styles of role interpretation (and I will clarify that association presently)—while evidenced in the laboratory, are unlikely real-world postures where career choice is voluntary. Statistical measures of data that incorporate the behavior of subjects with no real-world referents (in short, artifact) ought not to be relied on in inferring from results.

The factor analysis was used in the following way. Four significant factors were found for laymen and four for experts. For each factor, principal variable components were "eyeballed" in an arm-chair exercise which sought to infer the sense, or essence, or style of behavior that could reasonably be deemed to absorb all the behaviors represented by these principal variable components. While this is admittedly a process of aggregating inferences, it seems advisable because (1) the heuristic value of the study is enhanced by such an emphasis; and (2) unlike traditional political science uses of factor analysis, the variables here do not have a conventional meaning that gives their loadings any obvious meaning.

It is not feasible here to undertake what would be a lengthy presentation of the logic of factor labeling or factor components. Suffice it to note that each factor generated for laymen or experts was taken as a pattern, as a collection of behaviors that represented a style within the role (of laymen or expert). Each factor may be viewed as a posture within the role. The assumption was that depending on personality differences—on individual patterns of interpersonal orientation—individuals would adopt one or another posture as their orientation within the larger role of expert or layman. Of course only the expert postures are of interest in generalizing to most other levels of expert-politico interaction with which I was concerned. The postures distinguished for experts were: (1) participating broker behavior marked by consensus-building, a solution-orientation, a commitment to the group format, avoidance of confrontation even after provocation, interest in compromise for the sake of unanimity, and structuring and monitoring counterpart behavior; (2) leader (dictatorial) behavior marked by rejecting any actions that might appear subordinating, an overview awareness, extensive monitoring of counterparts, evaluation of counterparts, belligerency, order giving, and clear expectations of feedback on orders; (3) nonhostile, independent behavior marked by pronounced lack of overview and a commitment to format but aversion to alignment or submission; and (4) insecure expert behavior marked by intense communicating and seeking direction. Laymen exhibited only what were taken as varieties of follower behavior: tromped-on follower behavior, company-man behavior, cooperative-contributing follower behavior, and conditional-follower behavior.

Sinking futher into the armchair by seeking commonalities not within a factor but among factors, it appears that two additional inferences tentatively may be drawn from the data. These cannot be proven correct by the data treatments reported here; they can only be proven useful by further work, part of which I undertook when dealing with aspects of expert-politico interaction beyond the role level.

First, the laboratory findings appear to suggest that experts tend to generalize their expertise. It would appear that experts may play active parts in expert-politico groups not by retaining narrowly defined sovereignty over substantive issues, but by assuming authoritative roles that involve most group processes. There is a tendency to broaden the scope of participation. This is consistent with early public administration literature;[9] and so this line of speculation seems that much more promising.

Second, it seems that expertise per se tends to encourage assertiveness in interpersonal interaction (here, in negotiation). This line of speculation is based on the view that while the laymen patterns were all varieties of follower behavior, usually in marked degree, three of the four expert patterns emphasized either leadership, pivotal actions, or independence. This line of speculation seems broadly consistent with the literature contending that expectations affect performance (if we assume that expertness is a more positive expectancy than naivete).[10] The speculation is also consistent with a recent study suggesting that expectancies may even be more powerful than actual, untampered, predilections for interpersonal activity in determining performance in problem-solving groups.[11]

Briefly, the following additional points seem in order. Controlled laboratory experimentation can be especially useful for treating subproblems that arise within multidimensional studies when a relationship is masked by its interaction or overlapping with relationships on other problem dimensions. This was the case with my multidimension approach to the expert-politico problem. Also definitional problems at the operational level can often be eased by resort to the laboratory because of its power to define problem elements that could prove unmanageable in other contexts. In this vein the freedom the laboratory offers to discard analytically the secondary problem elements, based on the assumption of randomization, is extremely valuable. Perhaps more than any other analytical technique the controlled analog study can help to insure the integrity of ceteris paribus conceptualization. In the experiment reported here it was possible, for example, to avoid the problem of defining a politico by simply presenting confederates as politicos, assuming that whatever it meant to a subject to be faced with a politico—though I could not specify that meaning—would enter into subject peformance.

Ultimately the greatest advantage of controlled laboratory experimentation for the methodologically eclectic political scientist, or for the disipline at large, lies in the use of experimentation in triangulation, in achieving stronger tests for generalization by aggregating independent modes of analysis. For example the notions suggested here concerning expert role postures could be tested by content analyses of memoirs and oral histories. Specifically it might be determined whether certain politicos actually perceived the experts whom they encountered to behave in any of the ways that the results of the experiment reported here would suggest. Memoirs are readily susceptible to the use of independent coders and content analysis, and could in principle provide a powerful check on, as well as stimulus for, concurrent laboratory investigation on a variety of problems.

NOTES

1. My unpublished dissertation, "A-Political Experts in Politics," Department of Political Science, University of Oregon, 1973. The specific experiment reported here was supported by the National Science Foundation, and I am grateful for that support.

2. I am dealing lightly with definitions here to get on with the business at hand, but have dealt with definitions at greater length in my "Experts, Politicians and Decisionmaking," General Learning Press, (Module Series), forthcoming.

3. I have defended this notion of an inevitable intrusion of collegiality in even the most bureaucratized decision settings in "Institutionalization, Collegiality, and Decisionmaking," presented at the 1974 meeting of the American Society for Public Administration, Syracuse, N. Y., May 1974.

4. The literature of greatest prominence that is most closely related to the expert-politico question is the science and politics literature. A few examples: Herbert F. York, *Race to Oblivion* (New York: Simon and Schuster, 1971); Joseph Haberer, *Politics and the Community of Science* (New York: Von Nostrand Reinhold, 1969); Donald A. Strickland, *Scientists in Politics* (West Lafayette, Ind.: Purdue University Press, 1968). The works of Gilpin, Jacobsen and Stein, and of C. P. Snow are perhaps some of the best known here.

5. On this subject see Rosenthal and Ronson, *Artifact in Behavioral Research* (New York: Academic Press, 1964).

6. Laboratory studies of negotiation would hardly appear novel; however, I believe the available experimentation in negotiation represents a far smaller collection than is generally assumed. It seems to me that much of what passes as studies of negotiation is really studies of auctioning behavior. "Negotiation" in this view is devoid of language content. Subjects ex-

change single number offers according to some bidding scale with the experimenter usually the intermediary. The implied referent is more nearly the auction podium than the bargaining table. See as examples W. H. Starbuck and D. F. Grant, "Bargaining Strategies with Asymmetric Initiation and Termination," *Applied Social Psychology* 1 (1971): 344-363; R. M. Liebert, W. P. Smith, and J. H. Hill, "The Effects of Information and Magnitude of Initial Offer on Interpersonal Negotiation," *Journal of Experimental Social Psychology* 4 (1968): 431-441.

7. Triads were used because it has been shown that a threesome offers the best climate for isolating minority views or forming majority coalitions. See H. H. Kelly and T. W. Lamb, "Certainty of Judgment and Resistance to Social Influence," *Journal of Abnormal and Social Psychology* 50 (1957): 137-139.

8. The conventional political science literature on negotiation is no help here. Consider the contrasting wave length of works such as John Kaufman, *Conference Diplomacy* (New York: Oceana Press, 1968); Arthur Lall, *Modern International Negotiation* (New York: Columbia University Press, 1966); Thomas Schelling, *The Strategy of Conflict* (Cambridge, Mass.: Harvard University Press, 1960); or Fred Ikle, *How Nations Negotiate* (New York: Harper and Row, 1964).

9. See L. H. Gulick, "Notes on the Theory of Organization," *Papers on the Science of Administration*, eds. L. H. Gulick and L. Urwick (New York: Institute of Public Administration, 1937).

10. On the power of expectancies generally, see for example: L. Lasagna, et al., "A Study of the Placebo Response," *American Journal of Medicine* 16 (1954): 779; S. R. Clemes and V. J. D'Andrea, "Patients' Anxiety as a function of expectation and degree of initial interview ambiguity," *Journal of Consulting Psychology* 29 (1965): 222-226.

11. On expectancy overriding actual compatibility see L. Lerner and R. Weiss, "Actual vs. Expected Need Compatibility in the Problem-Solving Dyad," a paper presented at the meetings of the Eastern Psychological Association, Philadelphia, April 1974.

TABLE 5.1

List of All Variables Measured in the Laboratory

Variable No.	Description
1	Number of messages subject received
2	Number of messages subject sent
3	Number of threats to opt out
4	Number of messages against desirability of opting
5	Number of positive references to own role
6	Number of negative references to own role
7	Number of positive references to politico role
8	Number of negative references to politico role
9	Number of subject requests for specific numbers
10	Number of offers of specific numbers on request
11	Number of offers of specific numbers without immediately preceding request
12	Number of references to group condition
13	Number of references to group progress
14	Number of references to own tactics
15	Number of references to counterpart tactics
16	Number of initiations of open coalitions

17	Number of initiations of secret coalitions
18	Number of passive responses, open coalition
19	Number of passive responses, secret
20	Number of rejections of coalitions, all types
21	Number of personal insults received
22	Number of challenging responses to insult
23	Number of low-key responses to insult
24	Number of insults initiated
25	Number of uses of deception
26	Number of positive references to own ability
27	Number of negative references to own ability
28	Number of positive references to counterpart ability
29	Number of negative references, counterpart ability
30	Number of explicit mediator remarks
31	Number of implicit mediator remarks
32	Number of technical messages sent
33	Number of positive references to grand coalition initiated
34	Number of passive, positive responses to grand coalition references
35	Number of negative references to grand coalition, subject init.
36	Number of negative responses to grand coalition references
37	Number of instructional messages
38	Number of identical messages
39	Number of requests for report on other dyad
40	Score on independence scale of final game answer
41	Number of concessions made
42	Net concession value of final offer

TABLE 5.2

Behaviors Individually Affected by Expertise: Grouped by Nature of Affect and Test Used to Isolate

Suppressed Behaviors (t-test, lower expert mean)
  Var. 12: References to group condition
  Var. 17: Initiating secret coalitions
  Var. 18: Accepting open coalitions
  Var. 25: Deception
  Var. 33: Initiating positive references to grand coalition

Stabilized Behaviors (f-maximum test, less expert variance)
  Var. 9: Requests for specific numbers from politicos
  Var. 19: Accepting secret coalitions
  Var. 25: Deception
  Var. 33: Initiating positive references to grand coalition
  Var. 34: Positive responses to grand coalition
  Var. 42: Net concession value of final offer

Destabilized Behaviors (f-maximum test, more expert variance)
  Var. 26: Positive references to own ability
  Var. 29: Negative references to politico ability

TABLE 5.3

Means and Standard Deviations for Experts and Laymen

Variable	Experts		Laymen	
	Mean	Standard Deviation	Mean	Standard Deviation
VAR001	13.6400	2.1579	13.6000	2.1213
VAR002	10.8800	2.5710	11.6800	2.8243
VAR003	0.2000	0.5000	0.1600	0.4726
VAR004	0.2000	0.5000	0.3200	0.6272
VAR005	0.2400	0.4359	0.0800	0.4000
VAR006	0.0400	0.2000	0.0800	0.2769
VAR007	0.0000	0.0000	0.0400	0.2000
VAR008	0.0800	0.2769	0.0800	0.4000
VAR009	0.8000	0.8165	1.0400	1.5133
VAR010	1.6800	1.3454	1.8000	1.3229
VAR011	3.3200	2.2121	4.3200	2.3402
VAR012	0.5200	0.8716	1.1200	1.0536
VAR013	0.5600	0.9165	0.4800	0.6718
VAR014	0.8800	1.6155	1.1200	1.5362
VAR015	1.2400	1.3000	0.9200	1.2220
VAR016	0.3200	0.6904	0.4000	0.7071
VAR017	0.0000	0.0000	0.2000	0.4082
VAR018	0.0000	0.0000	0.1600	0.3742
VAR019	0.0800	0.2769	0.3200	0.6272
VAR020	0.2000	0.5774	0.5200	0.8226
VAR021	1.2400	1.0116	1.4800	1.0847
VAR022	0.3600	0.7572	0.2400	0.5228
VAR023	0.4000	0.6455	0.4800	0.5059
VAR024	0.5200	0.9626	0.4800	1.0456
VAR025	0.0400	0.2000	0.4800	0.9626
VAR026	0.7200	1.1000	0.1600	0.4726
VAR027	0.2800	0.6137	0.2000	0.4082
VAR028	0.0000	0.0000	0.0400	0.2000
VAR029	0.1200	0.4397	0.0800	0.2769
VAR030	0.0400	0.2000	0.0000	0.0000
VAR031	0.1600	0.3742	0.3200	0.5568
VAR032	2.2800	1.8376	1.6800	1.9038
VAR033	0.1200	0.3317	0.6000	0.9574
VAR034	0.1200	0.3317	0.2400	0.5228
VAR035	0.0000	0.0000	0.0400	0.2000
VAR036	0.0400	0.2000	0.0800	0.2769
VAR037	0.6400	1.1504	0.7200	0.8907
VAR038	1.0000	1.0408	1.0000	1.1547
VAR039	0.1600	0.4726	0.2000	0.5000
VAR040	0.7600	0.8794	0.8800	10.536
VAR041	3.9600	1.8138	4.4000	1.8484
VAR042	15.1480	15.8218	26.5080	26.8199

TABLE 5.4
Rotated Factor Matrix for Experts

Variable*	Factor 1	2	3	4
1	-0.02485	-0.12402	0.02960	**0.72455**
2	0.41330	0.21284	0.07003	0.62511
3	**0.53055**	0.20268	-9.51567	-0.00355
4	0.34004	-0.21552	-0.44759	-0.13322
5	-0.21281	0.30009	**-0.54703**	0.45699
6	-0.07145	-0.25207	0.02990	0.92728
8	0.09330	-0.07488	0.09078	-0.39032
9	-0.11866	-0.08254	0.41854	**0.67625**
10	-0.28259	-0.21974	0.16328	0.34375
11	0.30516	0.24472	0.35067	**0.47907**
12	0.05167	0.38627	**-0.69268**	0.13105
13	-0.03625	**0.63078**	0.25482	-0.42822
14	-0.22302	**0.83004**	0.03824	-0.04511
15	-0.31965	-0.02652	-0.27426	-0.01467
16	**0.60946**	0.44306	0.11713	0.00117
19	-0.19553	-0.05308	**-0.63759**	-0.00829
20	-0.15060	**0.50323**	0.05376	0.41149
21	0.29841	0.36382	0.02710	0.20506
22	0.00591	**0.65702**	-0.19491	-0.96821
23	**0.72282**	0.92287	-0.15289	-0.15370
24	-0.24870	**0.73546**	0.17161	0.03007
25	0.43830	0.15904	0.09848	-0.27377
26	0.17185	0.25464	-0.19222	0.03944
27	-0.49775	0.04909	-0.05395	-0.15286
29	-0.45569	0.08481	-0.00514	-0.09964
31	-0.26881	0.06855	-0.06092	-0.35820
32	**0.54582**	-0.08330	-0.11149	-0.04074
33	-0.03226	0.06866	0.28187	**-0.49015**
34	0.25728	-0.24797	**-0.65975**	0.04145
36	-0.28190	0.01155	0.22707	-0.19544
37	0.00885	**0.65247**	0.30613	-0.02277
38	**0.54641**	0.22112	0.12902	0.36221
39	**0.55170**	**0.54409**	-0.13456	0.09161
40	-0.14751	0.25618	**0.53152**	0.22879
41	0.23769	-0.08096	0.48229	0.39963
42	**0.50585**	-0.16214	-0.24985	0.22315

Cumulative Proportion of Total Variance

0.13034	0.24565	0.34481	0.43027

*Note that variables 7, 17 18, 30, and 35 are excluded from the factor analysis because of zero means for one or both groups.

TABLE 5.5
Rotated Factor Matrix for Laymen

Variable*	Factor			
	1	2	3	4
1	0.10957	-0.06723	0.30674	**0.58550**
2	-0.17252	0.02678	0.43329	**0.78615**
3	-0.42459	-0.42977	0.24634	-0.03951
4	0.96872	**0.69003**	0.11664	-0.18661
5	**-0.95049**	-0.10429	-0.01353	0.08900
6	-0.05882	0.26543	0.30328	-9.31425
8	**-0.95049**	-0.10429	-0.01353	0.08900
9	0.11237	0.12798	-0.00185	0.58508
10	0.00620	-0.13786	**0.53551**	-0.00873
11	-0.06808	0.21679	**0.58271**	0.20637
12	-0.23371	**0.61437**	-0.30881	0.22486
13	-0.64638	-0.24253	0.42958	-0.02657
14	**-0.85554**	0.05007	0.12429	0.04699
15	-0.31678	-0.49306	0.03233	-0.06704
16	0.07264	0.47033	-0.09829	0.10621
19	0.12759	0.18253	-0.23074	0.68013
20	**-0.66509**	0.01589	0.15744	-0.24993
21	-0.41250	0.12161	-0.05081	-0.48027
22	**-0.76735**	0.09624	-0.21690	-0.14823
23	0.03363	0.14726	0.03153	-0.36021
24	**-0.67678**	-0.20837	-0.13944	0.00796
25	-0.65888	0.25553	-0.27897	-0.21409
26	**-0.87932**	0.12317	-0.10454	-0.11712
27	0.00060	**0.66430**	0.34052	-0.09001
29	-0.00535	-0.09657	**-0.66874**	-0.17996
31	0.11219	-0.15970	**0.59241**	-0.09741
32	0.35982	-0.45370	-0.16799	0.07073
33	0.13917	0.25162	0.36846	-0.26587
34	0.00509	**0.68353**	0.22806	0.05740
36	**-0.71646**	-0.14838	-0.37823	-0.08029
37	0.10806	0.59392	-0.13267	0.62935
38	-0.00336	-0.17610	0.28642	0.18132
39	0.08239	**-0.50750**	0.19207	0.18378
40	0.21308	-0.14622	-0.28584	0.04942
41	0.33998	0.13943	**0.75130**	-0.12790
42	0.25588	-0.22892	0.27810	-0.01320

Cumulative Proportion of Total Variance			
0.20478	0.31368	0.41571	0.49944

*Note that variables 7, 17, 18, 28, 30, and 35 are deleted from the factor analysis because of zero means for either or both groups.

Image and Reality in Simulated International Systems

MARI HOLMBOE RUGE

It is always the image, not the truth, that immediately determines behavior.   —Kenneth Boulding

INTRODUCTION

The concept of image has been discussed and used by numerous social
scientists who are concerned with what might be called actor-oriented
analysis. It is a basic assumption in this field of reasoning that no individual is ever able to perceive objective reality. One always selects certain elements from the environment and then structures the elements into
a coherent pattern of some kind. The organizing factor is what is usually
called 'image.' A good definition of the image concept is the following: "All
the accumulated, organized knowledge that the organism has about itself
and the world" (Holsti 1969, p. 544). Image thus emerges as a central concept in social behaviour on the personal level as well as on the
organizational and the national level.

This paper is concerned with images held by decision makers on the
national level, using perceptual data generated during a simulation experiment. The analysis is to a large extent inspired by and partly based on Kenneth Boulding's stimulating discussion of the effects of images held at the
national level on the relations and temperature of the international system.
In his article Boulding concentrates on the role of images on the national
level in particular. He identifies the nation as a complex decision-making
organization and argues that "in a system in which decision-makers are an
essential element, the study of the ways in which the image grows and
changes, both of the field of choice and of the valuational ordering of this
field, is of prime importance" (p. 423).

Boulding goes on to distinguish between "the image of the small group of
people who make the actual decision" (on behalf of their nation) and "the
image of the mass of ordinary people who are deeply affected by these decisions but who take little or no direct part in making them" (p. 423). He
identifies the elite image as being of the most direct importance to the understanding of a nation's major political decisions.

The problem of how to make the concept of image operational has been
discussed by Sprout and Sprout who sum it up as follows: "The first step in
linking environmental factors to policy decisions is to find out how the

Reprinted from J. A. Laponce and Paul Smoker's *Experimentation and Simulation in
Political Science* (Toronto: University of Toronto Press, 1972), pp. 293-314. By permission
of the author and University of Toronto Press.

given policy-maker, or policy-making group, conceives the milieu to be and how that unit interprets the opportunities and limitations implicit therein with respect to the ends to be accomplished. This task presents formidable difficulties. The task is to construct at second hand, from what the decision-maker says and does, a description of his image, or estimate, of the situation and his orientation to it" (p. 49). In the following an attempt will be made to discuss one way of empirical image analysis: by using data generated during a simulation experiment.

PROJECT AND DATA

The project on which the present analysis is based represents an effort to gather data relevant to decision-making behaviour on a cross-national basis, through the use of InterNation Simulation. The data consist of records of behaviour and interpersonal perceptions gathered during two INS runs conducted in Norway and two in the United States.[1] A "standard" INS model with a simulated international system of eight nations was used.

The focus of this study, however, is not so much on the structure of the simulated world at various stages of the simulation as on how the players perceive and evaluate the structure, the events occurring during the course of a run, and their fellow players. We do not consider the worlds created by the simulation participants primarily as a more or less probable sample from a range of all possible international systems. Rather, our concern is with the simulated international system as a reflection of the participants' way of thinking and acting in politics in general—their political culture. Consequently problems of validity relating to the structure of the INS model are not essential for the present analysis. The most comprehensive discussion of validation problems in connection with simulation has been made by Harold Guetzkow (1968).

The test factor in this experiment is closely tied to the participants. Consequently efforts were made to make the teams of players as comparable as possible concerning such factors as age, sex, and field of study (they were all students of political science).[2]

The data gathered during the four INS runs were endogenous as well as exogenous. Endogenous data are generated as a result of simulation activities, such as trade relations, investment and armaments, and patterns of communication. In a previous article (Ruge 1970) some of these data have been analyzed to study the different perspectives on foreign policy displayed by the participants from a small power (Norway) and a big power (United States).

Exogenous data are attitude tests and other subjective data generated by having the participants fill in questionnaires before, during, or after the simulation. Such data are not directly related to activities in the simulation, but may perhaps be regarded as a kind of by-product. During the runs, at the end of each of the nine periods, the participants filled in an evaluation form. The purpose of this form was to record the players' reactions to and evaluation of internal and external developments in the simulated system during the last period. In addition they had to estimate the degree of friendly or hostile intentions on the part of each of the other nations towards their own during the previous period, as well as to state the intentions of their own nation towards each of the other seven. The data from the evaluation forms are the basis for the present discussion. Contrary to the previous analysis made on data from this cross-cultural simulation project (Ruge 1970), the nationality of participants is not used as an independent variable in this case—the perception data are pooled.

The purpose of setting up an experiment like the InterNation Simulation is, of course, to generate data on phenomena which are unobservable in the real world for one reason or another. In this case data on the images which the actors held of each other's intentions were simply produced by having the participants estimate the intentions towards them from each of the others. In this way the images can be studied directly, whereas in the real world, as mentioned above, image is an inferred construct. It is conceived of as an intervening factor between perception and decision. In this respect our experimental data represent an advantage over real data on perception because they permit direct measurement of the images.

We shall make an attempt in this direction by reformulating some of the main arguments raised in Boulding's article into hypotheses. The hypotheses are then tested using perceptual data generated during the simulation runs.

The participants in the simulation are requested to evaluate their partners as well as to state their own intentions towards their partners. We have chosen to regard this as simple expressions of their image of the environment (evaluation of others) and of reality (their own stated intentions). By comparing these two measures we hope to be able to indicate which kinds of variables seem best suited as image determinants in the real world.

HOSTILITY/FRIENDLINESS

In his discussion of effects of various kinds of images held by nations of themselves and of their environment, Boulding places a special emphasis on the hostility/friendliness dimension: "At any one time a particular national image includes a rough scale of the friendliness or hostility of, or toward other nations. The relationship is not necessarily either consistent or reciprocal—in nation A the prevailing image may be that B is friendly, whereas in nation B itself the prevailing image may be one of hostility of B toward A; or again in both nations there may be an image of friendliness of A toward B but of hostility of B toward A" (p. 426).

The above discussion of the hostility/friendliness of intentions among nations contains two different elements which in the following will be analyzed separately: (1) the intentions which nation A has towards B and vice versa, and (2) the perception which A has of B's intentions and vice versa. If one wants to obtain some kind of measure of the overall friendliness or hostility of the system (p. 427), one has to decide whether to look at stated intentions or at perceived intentions.

In his discussion Boulding does not explicitly distinguish between the self-images of A and B on the one hand and their images of the environment on the other. He suggests that the intentions which each of the members of an international system has towards the other system members may be placed on some kind of hostility/friendliness scale and inserted into a matrix of the following kind (Figure 5.1).

Intentions to

	a	b	c
a	X		
b		X	
c			X

(left side label: Intentions from)

Figure 5.1. Type of matrix used to relate hostility/friendliness scales

He summed up the properties of this matrix as follows: "The sum totals of the rows represent the overall friendliness or hostility of the nation at the head of the row; the sum totals of the columns represent the degree of hostility or friendliness toward the nation at the head of the column. The sum of either of these sums is a measure of the overall friendliness or hostility of the system" (p. 427). However, this is the point at which the problem of perception arises. What the scores in the matrix indicate is the overall degree of friendliness or hostility of intentions from one nation in the system to another. The matrix contains no information on the degree to which the intentions are being adequately perceived and understood by the target nation.

The image which the matrix conveys is the image held by the actors (nations) about the other system members. This self-image, as it will be called in the following discussion, may or may not be transmitted and adequately received by the target nations. A different matrix would be needed to show

how actors perceive intentions from other actors—in other words, their image of the environment.

This is not an attempt to discuss which of the two matrices is more realistic—the one which shows scores of stated intentions or the one containing perceived intentions—but according to the reasoning referred to above, decisions and behavior are closely related to one's perception or image of the environment. If the matrices are identical, then the intentions are being correctly perceived by the targets. If they differ, then it is probably more important to analyze the perception matrix than the intention one.

The problem of perception among actors in internation relations has been discussed by Robert Jervis, whose main concern is precisely misperception and the factors which contribute to it. His list of hypotheses of misperception contains a variety of possibilities for systematic empirical testing along the lines suggested here (Jervis 1968).

The following discussion is organized into three main parts: (1) presentation and analysis of stated intentions of the simulation decision makers in terms of their self-images; (2) comparison of self-images with estimates of intentions (other images) and measure of the degree of misperception, if any; (3) measure of the tendency to over- or underestimate degree of friendliness in terms of the direction of misperception.

STATED INTENTIONS AMONG SIMULATION DECISION-MAKERS

To establish a base line for the analysis of image-related variables we shall first present reality in the form of an expressed degree of friendliness of intentions towards other nations. The intentions were recorded on a seven-point Likert scale which runs from "extremely hostile" (score 1) via "neither hostile nor friendly" (score 4) to "extremely friendly" (score 7). The scores presented in Table 5.6 are mean scores for all nine periods of a run. The table does not distinguish between individual runs or between Norwegian and American respondents. An independent variable, alliance membership, distinguishes three categories: within alliances (six nation-pairs in each run); between alliances (nine nation-pairs + the pairs consisting of the two nonaligned nations); and the neutral nations versus the allied (twelve nation-pairs).

The distribution of intention scores on the H-F scale falls almost exclusively on the "friendly" end, with a median score a little above 5 ("somewhat friendly"). Only four of the 112 scores fall below the neutral point of 4.[3]

Our scores support Boulding's assumption that there is a tendency for mutually friendly nations to form alliances (p. 427) insofar as they show a tendency for allied pairs to have friendly intentions towards each other when compared with interbloc pairs. However, such a finding does not reveal the causal direction of the relationship, because the nations are bloc members at the start of the simulation and presumably set their intention levels accordingly.[4]

TABLE 5.6

Intention Level and Alliance Membership Among Simulated Nation-Pairs

	1.0-3.0	3.1-4.0	4.1-5.0	5.1-6.0	6.1-7.0	Sum
Intrabloc	0	0	4	14	6	24
Interbloc	1	3	22	12	2	40
Bloc/Neutral	0	0	16	25	7	48
Total	1	3	42	51	15	112

INTERNAL VS. EXTERNAL IMAGE COMPONENTS

Having stated the level of intended friendliness between actors in the simulated system, the discussion now turns back to the problem of perception. The image which an actor has of any particular environment consists of internal and external components. By internal components is meant the collection of personality factors, internalized cultural and social norms, and experience from previous similar situations which have been accumulated in the mind of the actor. Internal image components could also be termed self-based. By external image components is meant those elements from the environment which are perceived and included in the image. This section reports on an effort to find some empirical ways of measuring the relative importance of external and internal components of the image which the participants hold of one another.

Experiments in social psychology have shown that persons who are asked to evaluate others often make use of projective techniques. They use their self-image as a frame of reference for interpreting their environment (Brown 1965). Presumably one knows oneself better than one knows anything—or anyone—else. The function of a frame of reference is precisely to bring new impressions into a familiar context, make them consistent with the established image, and thus give them meaning to oneself.

At time 0, when a relationship is initiated, the actors have no accumulated experience in dealing with one another. At this point internal factors will by definition play a decisive part in determining the actors' perceptions of the others. To the extent that the actors are members of a common group—be it a primary relationship, a nation, or a culture—the internal components of their mutual images will to a large extent be identical. As the relationship develops, external factors should increasingly contribute to the image, thus making it more realistic or accurate in an objective sense. If this were not the case no learning or socialization would take place. However, with the lag and all the constant factors which are inherent in an established image, it will never reach the level of complete realism. A completely realistic image of the environment in the sense that the total environment is reproduced with no distortions is an impossibility.

The function and purpose of an image is precisely to select, simplify and interpret the environment to the actor. Thus the tendency is for actors to prefer information which supports and strengthens their image and to reject or reinterpret information which might distort it. This tendency to cognitive and evaluative consonance contributes to the high level of stability over time which is an important characteristic of images.

We tried to construct a measure of the relative importance of internal and external determinants of images which the participants in the simulation held of their fellow players by comparing their answers to the questions recorded on an evaluation form where three different scales (labelled I, II, III in the appendix) gave us (1) a measure of a given player's intentions towards another player, (2) a measure of that player's perceptions of the other's intentions towards him, and (3) a measure of the actual intentions of the other players. An image completely dominated by external factors is indicated by identical answers on scales II and III. On the contrary, the similarity of scores on scales I and II indicates that it is the image of the self which is projected on the environment.

To test the relative importance of these factors, the image scores (scale II) were compared with the self-image (scale I) and with reality (scale III), respectively, for each of the eight simulated nations. The sum of scores for all nine periods was ranked for all three categories, and rank-order correlations computed between the images on the one hand and self-image and reality on the other. By using rank correlations we are measuring not the players' ability to guess the correct intention scores from the others, but whether they could estimate correctly which of the others was most friendly, second most friendly, etc.

The main reason for using rank correlations was that we wanted to be able to compare different sets of data. Amount of trade or communication, economic or military power, etc., cannot be compared with evaluation scores directly. By converting scores as well as behavior and structural data into ranks, it became possible to run intercorrelations. The null hypothesis for this comparison of relative importance of image components is that there is no difference between self-based and environmental factors. Table 5.7 gives the distribution of rank correlation coefficients for self-intent/image and for image/reality respectively.

With $N = 7$, Spearman's rho has to be at least 0.71 to be significant at the 0.05 level, while the 0.01 level requires a correlation of at least 0.89. As correlations decrease below 0.70, the probability for accidental results increases. The distribution suggests that self-intent is more closely correlated with the way participants perceive their environment than reality. As many as twenty-one of the correlations for the first column are significantly higher than 0, while only eight of the second column are equally high.

To test whether the two distributions of correlation coefficients are significantly different, the Wilcoxon matched-pairs signed-ranks test was used (Siegel 1956, pp. 75-83).[5] The result was a value of $z = -3.3$, which has

TABLE 5.7

Distribution of Rank Correlation Coefficients for Self-Intent-Image
and Image-Reality for Thirty-two Simulation Participants

Magnitude of Rho	Self-Intent-Image	Image-Reality
−0.10-0	1	2
0.01-0.10	1	2
0.11-0.20	0	1
0.21-0.30	2	2
0.31-0.40	0	0
0.41-0.50	1	7
0.51-0.60	4	2
0.61-0.70	2	8
0.71-0.80	5	6
0.81-0.90	8	1
0.91-1.00	8	1
Sum	32	32

a probability of occurring of 0.0005. Thus the two sets of correlations are differently distributed. The participants have used themselves rather than external factors as a reference when asked to evaluate the others.

This of course will be the case the more similar the perceiver and his object. A young boy is unlikely to attribute elements from his own self-image to the object when asked to evaluate an old woman whom he does not know well as a person. Chances are that differences in background are seen as more important than they in fact are, and serve to blur the factors which any two human beings have in common. In our experimental situation, however, with actors all belonging to the same subgroup of students roughly the same age, etc., a transfer from self-image to other-image should be rather common.

Actors in real-life situations who face each other for the very first time, and who have no experience of what to expect and how to behave in that particular situation, will still have some kind of experience from similar occasions, perhaps with holders of the same status, which can help them along. This cumulative experience in turn becomes a part of the internal component of their image, as noted above.

In the artificial simulation situation with the absence of a significant past, projective evaluation will obviously be more prominent than in real-life relationships. Consequently projection should be more easily identified than in the much more complex referent system. However, we assume that the difference between the experimental and the real-life situation is merely a matter of degree, not of substance. Further general social psychological research confirms the tendency among our simulation partici-

TABLE 5.8

Distributions of Rank Correlation Coefficients (rho) for Self-Intent-Image
and Image-Reality for Thirty-two Simulation Participants
in Periods 1 and 2 and Periods 8 and 9

Magnitude of rho	Self-Intent-Image		Image-Reality	
	1 and 2	8 and 9	1 and 2	8 and 9
–0.39-0.30	0	0	0	1
–0.29-20	0	0	1	0
–0.19-0.10	0	0	0	0
–0.09-0	0	1	0	2
0.01-0.10	1	0	2	0
0.11-0.20	0	0	1	1
0.21-0.30	1	1	2	3
0.31-0.40	1	1	3	2
0.41-0.50	0	3	4	7
0.51-0.60	3	4	2	1
0.61-0.70	5	2	5	4
0.71-0.80	7	8	7	8
0.81-0.90	4	3	4	3
0.91-1.00	10	9	1	0
Sum	32	32	32	32

pants to use their self-image as a basis for judging others. In a discussion on
"contact with the object," William A. Scott sums up the results of interpersonal perception studies as follows:

> . . . interaction between two people leads to increasing
> correspondence between each person's image of himself and of
> the other's image of him. In fact, one would suppose that inter-
> personal interaction can be stable and mutually rewarding only
> insofar as this condition develops with respect to attributes
> relevant to the interaction. Such an increasing consensus is
> only in part due to changes in one person's impression of the
> other. It often happens that, in crucial respects, one's own self-
> image is molded by the reactions of those around him, which in
> turn are based on their view of him (p. 94).

Roger Brown discusses "determinants of accuracy in response-
predicting" and concludes that three factors increase the likelihood of
realistic perception of others: projection, knowledge of (the perceived)
group, and response sets. It seems that our findings result from projection
rather than from group knowledge, although the participants had much information available about their fellow players. This response set factor will

be discussed in connection with the tendency to consistent under- or overestimation.

The results in Table 5.7 are based on the sums of scores over all the nine periods of a simulation run. They convey no information on whether duration and contact had any effect on the relative importance of internal and external image components. As the simulation develops, the contacts established and the communication between the nations should provide the participants with better clues to realistic perception of each other. Toward the end of a run's intensive activity, after the exchange of hundreds of written communications, one would expect the decision makers to be quite well informed about the behavior of their fellow players. They should be better equipped to make realistic estimates than at the start of the experiment. The hypothesis in this case is that the image scores at the end should be more closely correlated with reality than at the beginning.

To measure learning effects over time during the simulation we used the estimate scores from the two first and the two last periods of each run. The sum of scores for two periods were used to cancel accidental deviations in a single period. Table 5.8 shows the development from beginning to end for both sets of correlations.

Our primary concern in this table is with the two right-hand columns. Note that the number of correlations significantly different from 0 does not increase from the start of the experiment to the end. There are twelve correlations above 0.71 in periods 1 and 2 and eleven in the last two periods. There does not seem to be a change in the predicted direction. The Wilcoxon test used to test significance between the two distributions gave a value of $z = -0.4$, whose probability of occuring is 0.34. A hypothesis of a difference existing between the two distributions is not supported. There is no tendency for the participants in the simulation to make more realistic estimates of each other at the close of the experiment than at the beginning.

But what about the self-centered perspective? Does it change over time? As Table 5.8 shows (in the two left columns) there is a high proportion of significant correlations at the beginning as well as at the end of the experiment. This indicates persistence of the established self-image as a yardstick. This time the hypothesis states that there should be no significant difference between the two distributions. The test yielded a z-value of -1.14, which has a probability of 0.13. The hypothesis of self-image stability cannot be rejected. There is no evidence of a decrease in self-image dominance as a result of time alone.

Does this self-image dominance hold up not only over time, but also during major changes in the actors or their environment? "Actor" in this connection may mean "self" as well as "other." Changes in the situation or position of either of the two partners in a relationship may produce changes in their image of each other, or of themselves. Our results so far suggest that only a change in the self-image will in turn lead to actors' perceiving their environment differently.

Structural characteristics of the simulation nations which might serve as indicators of the actor-based variables are military power, economic position, and alliance membership. Changes in the environment can be measured on communication and trade patterns, changes in alliance membership, etc. However, when tested against image stability, none of these factors appeared to have any significant effect. The changes which took place in the actors or in the system around them have not been perceived as important enough to override the primacy of the self-image.

A study of interpersonal perception in international relations by Dina Zinnes, "Expression and Perception of Hostility in Prewar Crisis, 1914," relates to the theme discussed in this chapter. Using as data the documents circulating among top decision makers in the major European powers involved in the outbreak of World War I, she found positive correlations between perceptions of hostility (from others) and expressions of hostility in general. Perception of hostility from a specific actor was also positively correlated with expressions of hostility towards that actor. In other words, a decision maker who perceives himself to be the object of hostility from another decision maker will in turn express hostility towards the other party. However, Zinnes did not find empirical support for the related hypotheses that (1) expressed hostility will be adequately perceived by the object, and that (2) expressed hostility will lead to the object expressing hostility back. The findings of Zinnes seem to support our results on the importance of the internal components of an image.

If an actor X feels persecuted or threatened, he is likely to act on the basis of his perception. If his behavior is not adequately perceived by his object Y, then Y's response may be very different from what X expected. But it may also be that X, in his need for consonance, misperceived Y's behavior. Other studies based on the 1914 crisis have shown that self-based perceptions are more common the higher the amount of stress in the situation (Holsti, North, and Brody 1968).

Dina Zinnes has also compared her own analysis of the 1914 data and the data produced in Brody's simulation experiment. She concludes from the comparative analysis that "a decision maker's perception of a hostile environment is a function of . . . the international alliance structure and the extent to which the decision-maker received hostile communications." Further, "there are at least three variables that can account for a state's hostile behavior: its perception of a hostile environment, its receipt of hostile messages, and the international alliance system" (Zinnes 1966, p. 495).

Brody's and Zinnes's results place more importance on expressed hostility as related to perception of hostility than our data do. It may be that in their analysis the focus is specifically on hostility, while our perspective has been on the influence of external events in general. Further analysis is needed to understand the amount of impact different kinds of external events will have on actors' images of others.

Our discussion of image components will be concluded with the following tentative hypothesis: self-based image components are more important in determining perception of the environment the more structurally similar the object is thought to be, and the more ambiguous the information from the environment.

PARANOIDS AND BLUE-EYED OPTIMISTS: DIRECTION OF MISPERCEPTION

In the previous section it was shown that the estimates of intention tended to be more influenced by the participants' self-image than by external factors. We were able to observe this because the intention scores given by the participants differed. Had they all been on the same level, the correlation coefficients for self-image/other-image and for other-image/reality would also have been of the same magnitude. In other words, the matrices of intentions and perceptions would have been identical.

In this section the direction of misperceived intentions will be explored. In his article, Boulding places a particular emphasis on what he sees as a destructive tendency in international relations: "Most nations seem to feel that their enemies are more hostile toward them than they are toward their enemies. This is a typical paranoid reaction: the nation visualizes itself as surrounded by hostile nations toward which it has only the nicest and friendliest of intentions" (p. 426). Boulding outlines the paranoid reaction as an exception to a presumed general tendency to consistency and reciprocation between national images. He thinks, in particular, of the way in which enemies by definition perceive each other. Accordingly, we should expect that a nation which feels hostile towards other nations will perceive the object of its hostility to be even more hostile towards itself.

To test this hypothesis in our simulated system, estimate-intention difference scores for each nation were developed. The sum of intention scores, over all nine periods, of one nation towards each of the others was subtracted from the sum of estimate scores recorded by each of the target nations towards the first nation. A negative E-I difference score means that the intending nation is considered less friendly than it professes to be. Conversely a nation which is considered more friendly than it actually is will get a positive difference score. Difference scores between 3 and -3 were classified as zero, because within their limits the estimates were considered to be realistic. Table 5.9 presents the distribution of pessimistic, realistic, and optimistic estimates for different intention levels. 'Optimistic' stands for the number of times a simulated nation was seen as more friendly than it actually was (positive E-I differences score); 'pessimistic' records the number of negative E-I scores. The vertical variable shows the distribution of stated intentions on the different levels of the hostility-friendliness scale. There are fifty-six units for each run, since each of the eight partici-

TABLE 5.9

Intention Level and Intention Estimates Recorded by
Thirty-two Participants During Four Simulation Runs

	Optimistic	Realistic	Pessimistic	Sum
1.0-4.0	7	8	3	18
4.1-5.0	22	33	27	82
5.1-6.0	3	38	56	97
6.1-7.0	1	4	22	27
Total	33	83	108	224

pants estimated the seven others. The intentions are mean scores for all nine periods.

Looking at the marginals first, the sum column shows that on the whole the participants have rather friendly intentions towards each other. The median score is 5 (fairly friendly). The "total" row shows that the great majority of misperceived intentions are on the pessimistic side. Only fifteen percent of the estimates are too optimistic.

The immediate technical reason for the difference in the distribution pattern of estimates compared to intentions is that the participants have made use of a smaller part of the scale when estimating other nation's intentions than when recording their own intentions towards each other. They have hesitated to believe that their partners had less friendly intentions towards them, as well as to make extremely optimistic guesses. But, as noted above, there is a striking difference between the proportion of optimistic versus pessimistic estimates. The general direction of misperception is towards scepticism.[6]

The large group of pessimistic estimates contains the special cases of paranoia which are characterized by a tendency to perceive one's environment as being more hostile than oneself. A pessimistic estimate clearly involves a certain element of distrust, and hence it could be argued, as stated in Boulding's hypothesis, that this will particularly be the case between enemies. However, the distribution in Table 5.9 suggests that the opposite is actually the case. The majority of pessimistic estimates are given to nations which feel very friendly towards their partners, while the optimistic estimates are located on the lower end of the friendliness scale. The realistic estimates are more evenly distributed between high- and low-intention friendliness.

Before discarding the hypothesis predicting a positive correlation between hostility and paranoia, however, we want to study the circumstances under which a negative discrepancy between actual and perceived intentions can occur, because not all such instances can be said to result from paranoid tendencies on behalf of certain actors.

SENDERS AND RECEIVERS OF DISTRUST:
MISPERCEIVERS AND MISPERCEIVED

It seems fruitful to distinguish between actors who tend to distrust their environment in general and those who are the objects of general distrust from the environment. Only the first type could be called paranoid. This would be the actor who does not differentiate within his environment out of cautiousness and suspicion. In the simulation we have defined as paranoids those participants who estimate pessimistically five or more of the seven others. There is a total of nine such cases out of the thirty-two possible in our four runs. These nine simulated nations made fifty-one pessimistic estimates, or about half of the total. Of these fifty-one, thirty occurred with the estimating actor noting his own intention to be lower than score 5. According to Table 5.9 there are exactly thirty cases of pessimistic estimates coupled with average intention scores below 5. The hypothesis based on Boulding's discussion cannot be rejected.

This result also ties in well with the self-based perception of the environment demonstrated in the previous section. The paranoia hypothesis sees the actor as expressing hostility because he perceives hostility. The self-image hypothesis assumes that an actor with hostile intentions will perceive his environment the same way to preserve his established image. However, there is no reason to assume a one-way causal relationship.

The misperceived. The objects of general distrust are different from the paranoids. They are the victims of low credibility, not being able to convince their environment of their friendly intentions. The reasons for lack of credibility may be of two kinds: active or passive. In the active case a nation is being distrusted because "deeds speak louder than words." The nation in this category may conduct a policy which leads its environment to estimate it as less friendly than it sees itself (and presumably would like others to see it as well). The relationship between a large number of powerful nations and their satellites (United States-Latin America, USSR-Czechoslovakia) may illustrate this phenomenon.[7]

However, distrust has been defined in a relative manner as a difference between two sets of scores. Therefore a nation may experience low credibility not only because of hostile behavior, but as a result of its own unrealistically high levels of intentions. For instance, in the simulated system there are actors who list almost uniformly maximum intention scores towards all the others but who, through inactivity, fail to convince their partners of this intention.

We would expect passive rather than active low credibility to be more frequent in an interaction system, because active behavior will be estimated differently by different members of the system. An act appearing friendly to one may look like (and of course actually be) a threat to another. Nonbehavior, or passivity, will probably be more consensually estimated as either potentially friendly or hostile. Whether such an actor is estimated positively or negatively by others may possibly be related to how much power he possesses—or how powerful the environment perceives him to be.

Another reason why active low credibility occurs rarely is precisely the fact that real intentions are communicated through activity. The environment thus gets cues on which to pin their estimates, and the result should be E-I difference scores closer to 0. The passive interaction partner provides the environment solely with his initial image. In the simulation, the initial information which the participants get of their own and the other nations comes from the "World History," a source of information which is almost solely concerned with struggle, conflict, and war as characteristics of the internation relations in the simulated system.

It should also be pointed out that this pattern occurs especially when maximum intention scores are used (6 and 7). It follows that extremely friendly behavior would be needed to induce decision makers to make sufficiently optimistic estimates to obtain a zero E-I difference score. The failure to make adequate guesses of intentions as high as 6 or 7 is one reason why low credibility is so frequent in friendly relationships. However, there is a total of eight actors in the simulated system who have received distrust from five or more of the others. Of these only two have listed such high intention scores throughout the run to all other partners. The rest differentiate between actors in addition to giving fluctuating scores from one period to another. However, they are unable to convey their self-image to the others.

The misperceivers. How do low-credibility actors estimate their partners' intentions? It has been postulated above that it is primarily a lack of contact with the environment which leads to unrealistic self-upgrading. According to the self-image hypothesis, lack of such contact will cause internal components of the image held of others to dominate. In other words, the low-credibility actors should be the ones who have a tendency to overestimate others. Table 5.9 shows that there are very few overestimates occurring in the simulated systems—an average of only 1.0 per actor. However, the eight low-credibility actors made an average of 2.3 overestimates. They see themselves as friendly and perceive the world in the same way. In Norwegian political jargon this pattern is called "blue-eyed optimism."

While the low-credibility actors overestimate the friendliness of others, the paranoids, who consistently distrust others, are often seen as more friendly than they actually feel. Overestimates cluster around them: the average number of overestimates given to the paranoid actors is 2.3 compared to the general level of 1.0.

The analysis so far indicates that wrong estimates or misperceptions are closely correlated with the self-image held by the actors. Those who have been defined as paranoids and who see the other members of the system as more hostile than they are also have rather unfriendly intentions towards the others. On the other end of the intention scale are the low-credibility actors. They picture themselves as more friendly than the environment is willing or able to accept, and they tend to perceive their coactors as more friendly than they profess to be. Thus the paranoia hypothesis becomes a special case of the self-image hypothesis. We can thus explain the misperceptions at the lower as well as at the upper end of the hostility-friendliness intention scale. However, when Boulding describes the paranoid nation as one which "visualizes itself as surrounded by hostile nations toward which it has only the nicest and friendliest of intentions" (p. 426), he seems to contradict his former postulate of paranoia as a pattern of perception peculiar to relations between enemies. Our data do not support his interpretation.

The previous section concluded with a hypothesis on the conditions under which an actor's self-image will dominate his perception of the environment. Here two patterns of misperception have been analysed, and they have both been found to be related to the way the actors picture themselves. This apparent consonance between image components and paranoid-optimist estimates leads to another hypothesis: actors who record unrealistically pessimistic and/or optimistic estimates of other actors will also have a close correlation between their self-image and their perception of others. The hypothesis was tested by the Mann-Whitney U-test, which indicates whether two independent samples have been drawn from the same population (Siegel 1956, pp. 116-127). The result was a lower correlation between paranoids-optimists and self-based estimates than for the rest of the actors, but the difference is too small to be significant. Thus the hypothesis is not supported or clearly rejected by our data. More complex models are needed to understand the relationships between the structural factors in the environment, the actors' self-images, and the way the environment is perceived.

IMAGES OF THE SIMULATED SYSTEM

The two previous sections concentrated on the perceptual relations between pairs of actors. In this section the focus is on the way participants perceived the entire simulated system, in particular the effect of events in the system.

Again scores from the evaluation form make up the dependent variable. The answers to question IV which asked the participants to estimate the degree of tension or cooperation in the world in general during the last period shows that the tension-cooperation dimension is closely related to the hostility-friendliness dimension on which the participants estimated their own and each of the others' intentions. Let us try to compare the scores on the two dimensions to show the way in which self-image influences the participants' perception of events in the system, even though we cannot this time measure the effect of self-image on perception, as it was done in the two previous sections. The reason for this impossibility is that we have no independent information on which events may have influenced the actors in their estimates. We can, however, infer from our general knowledge of the simulation and from the inspections of the changes in score levels, that the participants in the simulation tend to interpret the state of the entire system in terms of their own situation. Again the actors' self-image seems to be a major factor. Decision makers whose simulated nations had great problems saw the environment as very conflict-filled. On the other hand the optimist who started a disarmament on his own saw a world which was much more cooperative than it appeared to any of the other participants at that time.

CONCLUSION

Our simulation observations are supported by studies made in the real world, especially our major finding on the predominance of subjective actor-related over structural factors as determinants in decision making. The stability of the strategic image of John Foster Dulles has been demonstrated by Finlay, Holsti, and Fagen (1967). Philip Burgess (1967), who analysed public policy statements to relate the strategic image held by the two Norwegian foreign ministers during the nine-year period 1940-1949 to subsequent policy choices, found that the major changes in Norway's foreign-policy orientation, from an essentially neutral position at the outbreak of the second world war to the decision to join NATO in 1949 were the result not of modification in established images held by particular politicans, but were the result of the substitution of decision makers.

APPENDIX: EVALUATION FORM

Hostility/friendliness scale

1	extremely hostile	5	fairly friendly
2	very hostile	6	very friendly
3	fairly hostile	7	extremely friendly
4	neither hostile nor friendly		

Write zero in boxes corresponding to own nation

I Other nations' present intentions towards this nation

LA	UA	ERGA	INGO	OMNE	UTRO	RENA	SORO

II Estimate of how other nations see intentions of this nation towards them

LA	UA	ERGA	INGO	OMNE	UTRO	RENA	SORO

III This nation's present intentions towards other nations

LA	UA	ERGA	INGO	OMNE	UTRO	RENA	SORO

IV Degree of tension or cooperation in the world in general during the last period:

1   extreme tension   5   some cooperation
2   much tension   6   much cooperation
3   some tension   7   extreme cooperation
4   neither tension nor cooperation

NOTES

1. Originally researchers from five nations participated in the project: Japan, Mexico, Korea, Norway, and the United States. However, because of a variety of difficulties, only the data from two of the research teams were completed in time for inclusion in the present analysis. Further analysis, particularly on the Japanese data, is planned. The planning conference was held in September 1966 and the runs completed in January/February 1967.

2. Norway: of the forty-eight participants (forty-four male and four female) forty-seven were Political Science students of an intermediary level (mellomfag), twenty to twenty-four years old. One was a Sociology major with Political Science as a minor subject. To secure recruitment they had been told that participation in the simulation was compulsory. However, as these students in fact have no compulsory courses, they did not believe this but seem to have registered mainly out of curiosity. They were allowed to choose the run which suited them best, but were assigned to nation and office on a random basis, immediately prior to the start of the first period. US: forty-eight Political Science majors at the third- and fourth-year university level, forty-five men and three women. They were all students in a World Politics course who signed up voluntarily, choosing the run in which they wanted to participate, but were assigned to nation and office at the end of orientation on a random basis. The present analysis is based on data from one-third of the participants: those performing as central decision makers.

3. However, the intention levels ranged from "extreme hostility" to "extreme friendliness" from period to period, reflecting quite well the type of events occurring during the simulation. Thus the whole scale of intention scores was used by the participants.

4. For a discussion of alliance-related behavior in the simulate see "Small-power versus big-power perspective of foreign policy" (Ruge 1971). The most significant thing in this connection was the difference between the Norwegian and the United States' runs. A number of alliance changes were made by the Norwegians and none by the United States participants.

5. Seigel notes that such a test requires ordinal measurement of differences both within pairs and also between pairs. We have assumed that it is meaningful to consider rank correlation coefficients as ordinal data.

6. Preliminary analysis of a part of the Japanese data suggests that there may be a higher frequency of optimistic estimates among the participants in the Japanese runs. Of fifty-six nation-pairs in these two runs, three were optimistic. Previous pair analysis of the Norwegian and the United States runs showed no optimistic pair relations. These figures were not directly comparable with the figures in Table 5.9, which are based on individual nations.

7. The problem of deception in international relations is discussed in detail by Robert Jervis (1970).

REFERENCES

Boulding, Kenneth, 1969. National images and international systems, *International politics and foreign policy*, ed. James Rosenau. New York: Free Press.

Brown, Roger. 1965. Determinants of accuracy in response-predicting. *Social psychology*. New York: Free Press.

Burgess, Philip M. 1967. *Elite images and foreign policy outcomes: A study of Norway*. Columbus: Ohio State University Press.

Finlay, David J., Holsti, Ole R., and Fagen, Richard R. 1967. *Enemies in politics*. Chicago: Rand-McNally.

Guetzkow, Harold. 1968. Some correspondences between simulations and realities. In *New approaches to international relations*, ed. Morton Kaplan. New York: St. Martin's Press.

Holsti, Ole R. 1969. The belief system and national images: A case study. In *International politics and foreign policy*, ed. James Rosenau. New York: Free Press.

Holsti, Ole R., North, Robert C., and Brody, Richard. 1968. Perception and action in the 1914 crisis. In *Quantitative international politics*, ed. David Singer. New York: Free Press.

Jervis, Robert. 1969. Hypotheses on misperception. In *International politics and foreign policy*, New York: Free Press.

Jervis, Robert. 1970. *The logic of images in international relations*. Princeton: Princeton University Press.

Kelman, Herbert. 1965. Social psychological approaches to the study of international behavior. In *International behavior*, ed. Herbert Kelman. New York: Holt, Rinehart and Winston.

Ruge, Mari H. 1970. *Decision-makers as human beings: An analysis of perception and behavior in a cross-cultural simulation experiment*. University of Oslo, Institute of Political Science. (Mimeographed.)

Ruge, Mari H. 1971. Small-power versus big-power perspective on foreign policy, *Proceedings from the Third IPRA General Conference*, Karlovy Vary, 1969. Van Gorcum, Assen. PRIO publication number 1-14.

Scott, William A. 1965. Psychological and social correlates of international images. In *International behavior*, ed. Herbert Kelman. New York: Holt, Rinehart and Winston.

Siegel, Sidney. 1956. *Non-parametric statistics for the behavioral sciences*. New York: McGraw-Hill.

Sprout, Harold, and Sprout, Margaret. 1969. Environmental factors in the study of international politics. In *International politics and foreign policy*, ed. James Rosenau. New York: Free Press.

Zinnes, Dina. 1968. The expression and perception of hostility in prewar crisis: 1914. In *Quantitative international politics*, ed. David Singer. New York: Free Press.

Zinnes, Dina. 1966. A comparison of hostile behavior of decision-makers in simulate and historical data. *World politics* 18:474-502.

VI. Social Engineering Contexts

Inducing Change/Choice in Political Actors and Systems

This chapter treads on critical but treacherous territory: the complex exchanges between pure and applied aspects of any body of knowledge. Globally the issue is a critical one for Political Science. Indeed observers such as Garson (1974) see the failure to integrate theory and practice as the critical factor in the cycling that characterizes the discipline. Thus Garson distinguishes two sets of forces acting on Political Science: "the intellectual modes and ideological needs of the times (which periodically) sweep over the discipline"; and "a 'scientific' reaction seeking to insulate political science" from such modes and needs, with their dominant preferences and values. The resolution of such forces is unhappy, with Political Science vacillating between the two poles due to the failure "to seek a wedding of theory and practice, necessarily requiring a base in normative theory." Garson describes the resulting circularity: "In this process the hopes for 'scientific' advance are surrendered to the gradual encroachment of ideas, each of which in turn is treated as if it were better than the last, and the fittest theories are equated with those which have survived" (Garson 1974, 1506).

This unsatisfactory recycling was introduced in somewhat different terms in Chapter II, especially in the selection by Loveday. It creates a sense of deja vu, of the literature having been there before. The overall effect is one of a going-nowhereness, if not a cynicism about intellectual trends and modes. It is one of the small group's major virtues that it promises one convenient but hardly cost-free way out of this enervating circularity.

FIVE PAYOFFS AND CONFLICTS

More specifically, seeking the wedding of theory and practice in areas of Political Science involves five sets of payoffs and conflicts, which can be introduced briefly.

First, it is in principle a healthy sign if any body of knowledge permits or (better yet) encourages a lively interaction between its pure and applied aspects, between the accumulation of knowledge and its effective dissemination or application. Ideally the accumulation of knowledge will permit more effective use of natural and human resources. Moreover the dissemination/application of knowledge can variously serve knowledge accumulation by indicating gaps in available knowledge, by helping set priorities for further accumulation of knowledge, and by evolving extensions of available knowledge that significantly expand what is known, or even induce major changes in the paradigms which science had heretofore accepted as the guide for inquiry. These factors, among others, imply the myopia of propositions such as knowledge for its own sake. Moreover there is practically no question that effective dissemination or application of knowledge often is the critical factor in determining the amount of resources that will be devoted to further development of any body of knowledge.

Second, however, there are few issues which in practice induce as much mischief or dissipate as much energy as pure/applied exchanges. The underlying reasons are both compound and complex despite substantial agreement with the position of Argyris and Schon that "exciting intellectual problems are related to integrating thought with action." Important among these reasons is that knowledge gathering has tended to be organized in terms of disciplines or fields or university departments, foci for analysis that permit finer resolution at the expense of a narrowing of the field of vision. That is, the barbs about "knowing more and more about less and less" touch raw nerve endings because they describe some (but hardly all) reality. Any such tendency, to complete the point, implies bad news for pure/applied exchanges. As Argyris and Schon note: effective action "requires the generation of knowledge—with as much competence and rigor as each discipline usually demands." The task is difficult, these two observers conclude, "not only because scholars rarely cross disciplines but also because few scholars are inclined and educated to generate such knowledge. The few hardy souls who plunge into cross-disciplinary waters find that their colleagues view the effort with skepticism." (Argyris and Schon 1974, 3)

Third, pure/applied exchanges often imply profound moral and ethical issues. The decision to apply knowledge about atomic physics to making a hydrogen bomb is a monumental case in point.

Fourth, the moral and ethical issues are likely to be especially profound when man is the subject of pure/applied exchange. Witness the dilemma of a military psychiatrist during the Vietnam war, who (as Lifton explains) "often finds himself in a cooling role." Lifton (1973, 434) deftly isolates the psychiatrist's dilemma. Such cooling, on the one hand, can "head off destructive patterns, give people a chance to reassess . . . behavior, and stave off social or even military holocaust." On the other hand, however, that very cooling can "be a means by which those in power maintain their exploitation and their various forms of violence."

Fifth, pure/applied exchanges are particularly problemmatic when, as is patently the case with small-group analysis, the accumulation/application of knowledge involves some relatively conscious change in the attitudes and behaviors of human beings. For there, as Peter B. Smith so forcefully explains, "the gulf between understanding a phenomenon and being able to change it" is especially awesome. He establishes a contrast with the physical sciences. "In chemistry," he explains, "if one understands the properties of a certain compound it is a relatively simple task to use that knowledge to transform it into something else." However, understanding why conflict occurs between two groups, in illustrative contrast, does not necessarily make it any easier to affect the outcome of that conflict. Smith develops the point (1973, 3):

> To intervene in a situation effectively may require quite different skills from those required to understand it. This is partly

true also in the physical sciences; one needs not only knowledge of the properties of particular compounds but also the practical skills of carrying through a particular experiment. But in chemistry it is the theoretical problems which are difficult and the practical skills are relatively easily acquired. In the social sciences the theoretical models are not so difficult to grasp, but the implementation of change is a major problem.

The reasons for the greater significance of the applied approach in the social sciences need only be illustrated here. For example the situations studied by physical scientists are more easily controlled or compared, which permits greater certainty about what factors lead to which consequences. Hence application is more direct and straightforward. Relatedly the subjects of physical analysis and the conditions of their interaction are relatively deterministic. People can and do learn to vary their behavior, to put the point in a precious way, perhaps. Atoms, in contrast, keep behaving in similar ways under similar conditions. Applying knowledge about atoms is consequently easier and has more consistent effects, given the necessary knowledge about such units and the conditions of their interaction.

This much having been said of the value of easy trading betwixt-and-between the pure and applied, between accumulation and dissemination/application, much also requires saying about the temptations and the dangers of the interaction. For example many are concerned that some narrow applied interests of elites with ample funds to support research will dangerously skew priorities toward the episodic or superficial. Indeed moral considerations might even be swamped by the boosterism or enthusiasm to get some of the action. Thus huge volumes of money and time might be spent on pacifying Vietnamese villagers, or manipulating industrial workers, or whatever, and all the activity might be too little burdened by such serious questions: (1) Is this the best way to spend our resources? Or is it a good way of accumulating knowledge? or (2) Should we be pacifying Vietnamese or industrial workers in the first place, as contrasted with seeking to modify their condition? Relatedly the accumulation/application interface raises tough issues about which is dog and which is tail. Concerns about personal ambitions and institutional funding often complicate attempts to provide working approaches to such issues (Walton and Warwick 1973).

It is revealing to view the issues of accumulation/application as centering around two ethical dilemmas. At one level of the development of a body of knowledge, the basic concern is that too little is known to warrant major applied effort. Here the ethical issue is the lack of power or development of the body of knowledge, which makes applications too risky. At another level of development the ethical concern is that knowledge is so powerful that applications are unwise because their impact is so awesome. This was the case with knowledge about nuclear energy and, more recently, with brain control (Valenstein 1973).

THE LABORATORY APPROACH AS ONE APPLICATION
OF SMALL-GROUP KNOWLEDGE

Small-group analysis pleads guilty to both major potential and ample temptation involving a broad range of accumulation/application interfaces. The small group is a ubiquitous social unit, and often a critical one for controlling/influencing behavior. Hence the small group at once attracts the attention of the pure scientist, and also has great allure for the applied scientist seeking some way to reinforce or induce changes in attitudes or behavior or values. The latter facet of small-group analysis is called "social engineering" here, perhaps an inept usage but a descriptive one at least.

The significant linkages between the accumulation/application of knowledge relevant to small groups will be suggested here by one long line of research that has clear applied implications. Consider the bare observation that the mere presence of others typically has an impact on performance or behavior, an observation published as early as 1898. Early experiments suggested a social facilitation effect. For example cyclists tended to race faster against one another than against a clock. But accumulating evidence implied that the effect was not unidirectional; the presence of others also could hamper performance. It remained for Zajonc (1965) to suggest a conceptual integration of the opposed findings. He introduced "familiarity of task" as a kind of reconciling variable. As Smith (1973, 67) explains:

> . . . on a familiar task, the subject has little need of social comparison and is easily able to obtain what data he needs from others on how well he is working. The fruits of such comparisons will frequently be confirmatory, which will enhance his performance. On unfamiliar tasks, on the other hand, the subject will find it more and more difficult to engage in social comparison. The less familiar the task, the less clear will it be to him how he can evaluate his success or failure on the task. The less clear the data he gets from others, the stronger will become his need for social comparison. Consequently, his performance will suffer as he devotes an increasing proportion of his time to seeking adequate comparison data. Thus social comparison can both augment and inhibit performance.

The laboratory approach, in a broad sense, seeks to take advantage of such a regularity. Basically it uses small groups so as to meet needs for social comparison in direct ways, with the goal of enhancing performance on complex and unfamiliar tasks. In addition the laboratory approach engages powerful forces of social influence that do multiple duty. These forces can help develop and support norms that facilitate inquiry, choice, or experimentation; provide an environment of low defensiveness cum high emotional support and safety; and serve to reinforce learning or change. Several examples below will illustrate the technology for inducing intense social comparison and influence in small groups. In brief the laboratory approach seeks to provide data that is both significant and often unavailable to individuals: data about how they are perceived by others, and about the character and quality of the processes of their interaction with others.

But this risks getting ahead of the story. To step back a little, efforts at social engineering using small groups have been attempted in a huge variety of settings—in organizations, for personal growth and development, in therapy, in race relations, ad infinitum. The purpose here is to illustrate this range of applications with article-length selections, which deal with three contemporary problems: (1) a boundary dispute between nations, (2) intergroup conflict between Arabs and Jews, (3) police/community relationships in a city experiencing racial conflict. The selections were chosen for three reasons. They deal with tough problems, which are of great interest to political scientists, and about which efforts many political scientists are likely to be unaware. Readers interested in more standard organizational applications of the small-group approach can consult Chapter VII in this volume, as well as any number of standard sources (French and Bell 1973; Golembiewski 1972).

Two preliminary points require brief statement prior to introducing the three illustrations of small-group applications. First, based on the discussion in Chapter I, the development of small-group research may be described in terms of three stages: (1) the small group as influential in influencing behavior, (2) the small group as a target of change, which context was worked on by some external change-agent seeking to use group influence to reinforce or accept some external need, such as management's desire for increased productivity, and (3) the small group as a vehicle of change or choice, in which its members play crucial roles in determining the specific character of choice/change, as well as in reinforcing any decisions, sometimes with the help of a resource person who helps group members improve their functioning.

The three illustrations below exemplify the last stage. The typical group decision-making project, in contrast, is a product of the second stage. In one such project, for example, small groups were used to encourage mothers to feed their children orange juice. Note that mothers were free only to implement or not implement a preformed decision, which was set for them by medical authorities.

Second, the three illustrations below are diversely patterned after the laboratory approach, which includes a broad family of learning designs such as sensitivity training and T-Groups. Revealingly the laboratory approach has been attacked as an application that falls prey to both dilemmas of applied science introduced above. Thus some observers have argued (Odiorne 1963) that too little is known to legitimate major applications of the body of knowledge underlying the laboratory approach. Others have argued (Steinbacker 1971) that applications should be limited because of the potency of the technology to induce a range of specific but undesired behaviors. For example the power to brainwash participants is sometimes attributed to the technology.

The three selections below also all reflect variants of the process orientation that receives its most dramatic and impactful expression in a T-Group. A start toward understanding process can be made by contrasting it with content and structure. Thus process deals with how a decision is made and implemented; content refers to the what of a decision, its logical or technical quality; and structure relates to issues such as who will formally implement a decision, what the procedures will be, and so on. Somewhat more fully, the process orientation operates simultaneously at three levels—individual, interpersonal, and intergroup—and deals with such dimensions as communication, member roles and functions, the kind and quality of problem-solving and decision-making norms for behavior, stages of growth and development in human relationships, actual leadership and authority as contrasted with formal structural position, and the patterns and quality of intergroup collaboration/competition (Scheim 1969, 15-75).

The laboratory approach and its associated process orientation is based on a relatively-elaborated normative commitment. One set of such undergirding values is presented in Table 6.1. Note that those values do not have universal acceptance by proponents of the laboratory approach, but consensus about them is quite broad (Golembiewski 1972, esp. 19-155).

THREE EXAMPLES OF APPLICATIONS
OF THE LABORATORY APPROACH

How the values of the laboratory approach can be approached will be illustrated by three selections that are basically similar in their conflictful quality, as well as in the tragedy implied for their participants if no amelioration is possible. To the degree that the laboratory approach can provide some of the amelioration, it is a welcome addition to man's helping technologies.

A problem-solving workshop and border dispute. Richard E. Walton describes the design and consequences of an ambitious small-group application based on the laboratory approach in his "A Problem-Solving Workshop on Border Conflicts in Eastern Africa." He distinguishes two phases: Phase I—developing communication relationships among a small number of representatives of three countries, generally by encouraging an awareness of process issues, eliciting a growing receptivity to process analysis, improving skills useful for diagnosis of process issues. And Phase II—seeking viable solutions to a border dispute involving the three countries, where problem-solving will profit from any improvements in process generated by Phase I.

The format for the problem-solving workshop owes much to the laboratory approach, as it builds on the concept of the group as a vehicle for change. Note that the members play an influential role, as in control of

TABLE 6.1

Three Sets of Normative, or Value, Constraints on Applications of the Laboratory Approach

(A) Meta-Values of Laboratory Approach	(B) Operating Values of Laboratory Approach	(C) Immediate Goals of Laboratory Approach

1. An attitude of inquiry reflecting (among others):
  a. a hypothetical spirit
  b. experimentalism
	1. Emphasis on here-and-now occurrences	1. Increased insight, self-knowledge

2. Expanded consciousness and recognition of choice	2. Emphasis on the individual act rather than on the total person	2. Sharpened diagnostic skills at (ideally) all levels, i.e., the levels of the:
		  a. individual
		  b. group
		  c. organization
		  d. society

3. A collaborative concept of authority having as two core elements:
  a. spirit of collaboration
  b. open resolution of conflict via a problem-solving orientation
	3. Emphasis on feedback that is nonevaluative in that it reports the impact on the self of other's behavior, rather than feedback that is judgmental or interpretative	3. Awareness of, and skill practice in, creating conditions of effective functioning at (ideally) all levels

4. An emphasis on mutual "helping relationships" as the best way to express man's interdependency with man, or man's basic social nature and connectedness	4. Emphasis on "unfreezing" behaviors the trainee feels are undesirable, on practice of replacement behaviors, and on "refreezing" new behaviors	4. Testing self-concepts and skills in interpersonal situations
5. An emphasis on "authenticity" in interpersonal relations, a high value on expressing feelings and their effects	5. Emphasis on "trust in leveling," on psychological safety of the trainee	5. Increased capacity to be open, to accept feelings of self and others, and to risk interpersonally in rewarding ways
	6. Emphasis on creating and maintaining an "organic community"	

Adapted from Edgar H. Schein and Warren G. Bennis, *Personal and Organizational Change Through Group Methods* (New York: John Wiley, 1965), 30-35; and Leland P. Bradford, Jack R. Gibb, and Kenneth D. Benne, *T-Group Therapy and Laboratory Method* (New York: John Wiley, 1964), 10, 12.

the agenda and in the extreme importance to the process orientation of the members' reactions to and assessments of the workshop. The resource persons play significant roles, but they are limited to designing the flow of major phases, intervening in interaction to illustrate the nature and importance of ongoing process, and providing theoretical statements that can give participants at least some tentative handles on the reality they are experiencing.

The Fermeda Workshop seemed a relative success in Phase I, and a relative failure in Phase II. But only replications of the design can help determine how much of that was the fault of the underlying technology, how much was due to the recalcitrance of this particular dispute, and how much was due to features of the Fermeda experience (like the twenty-eight hours of numbing bus rides to get to and from the resort) that can be easily eliminated or finessed in future replications.

Small Group Training and Jew/Arab Conflict. Martin Lakin applies a version of the laboratory approach to another of the world's sore spots. His "Arab and Jew in Israel: A Case Study of a Training Approach to Intergroup Conflict" is an impressive reflection of both the assumed power of the small group, as well as of the confidence that Lakin and others have in the laboratory approach. Lakin explains: "Our goal was to discover ways to diminish 'we-they' feelings and to establish other loyalties which would, at least transiently, overarch in-group loyalties. Since we wished group members to develop alternative perspectives on the conflict situation, we sought to involve each as much as possible in interactions with a member of the countergroup."

Lakin's article can be consulted for details of the design, which basically utilized an agendaless dialog between members of two ethnic groups who were living more or less side by side but in a state of definite tension. A process orientation and its underlying values provide the basic technology and moral guidance for this dialog. The design also implied expectations about the useful effects to which the technology-cum-values would be likely to lead. The implication was that whatever issues existed between Arabs and Jews would surface without any prodding from an agenda. Further the conviction was that the process orientation would permit meaningful exploration of these issues, and perhaps even help begin to build bridges of acceptance and understanding between people calling themselves Jews and others who were Arabs. The extended transcripts of the dialog make fascinating reading about the false starts and progress toward such acceptance and understanding.

Lakin is guardedly optimistic about the value of such training in similar conflictful situations, based on a variety of data. He sees these assumptions of the laboratory approach as useful, but partial, truths: (1) that expression of true feelings leads to their detoxification, (2) that honesty in communications between groups will tend to increase as a consequence of extended interaction, and (3) we-they perceptions will be replaced by more differentiated percepts of persons as a result of sharing and mutual disclosure. Lakin stresses the importance of an overarching or superordinate goal in energizing such dynamics in groups whose members have experienced long and bitter-end conflict.

Police/Community Relationships. A third application of the small-group approach—"Small Group Dialog and Discussion: An Approach to Police-Community Relationships," by Robert L. Bell and his associates —also hunts very big game. It seeks to deal with "the most pressing domestic problem . . . rising urban tensions," which in large degree "means increased friction between the city police force and segments of the black community." The application occurred in Houston, Texas, where 1967-1968 was punctuated by racial explosions, both real and threatened, as was the case in much of the country.

The Houston learning design was based on the laboratory approach, more specifically on the "concepts and techniques of T-Group theory and sensitivity training." The training groups had some twelve-fifteen members each, composed of equal numbers of police and citizens. Each training cycle of eighteen hours was considered a separate laboratory. The overall goal was to promote a heightened cooperative relationship between the police and the community residents they served. The derivative growth in mutual respect and understanding were then expected to facilitate communication. In the more distant future the experience also might generate some margin of good will to buffer somewhat the explosive situations that can develop in police work, even under the best of conditions and given the best of intentions. More specifically the authors describe their design as having four central features:

> . . . the group sessions are structured so as to have the police and community first examine the damaging stereotypes they have of each other; second, to consider the extent to which these stereotypes affect their attitudes, perceptions and behaviors toward each other; third, to look at the ways in which each group reinforces these stereotypes in the eyes of the other; and fourth, to develop a cooperative, problem-solving attitude directed toward resolving differences and reducing conflict to a level where both groups can work together constructively.

The effects of eighteen hours of work in small groups composed of police and citizens cannot be evaluated in any simple or indisputable way. Major measurement problems always complicate any such evaluation. And the target for change is no sitting duck. Moreover not every laboratory had similar consequences. Indeed some individual laboratories apparently were considered failures by the authors. Most critically the stereotypes dealt with had been developing for long periods, and they are variously reinforced by massive networks of memories and acquaintances.

The authors try their hand at several levels of evaluating the training effort, and they come up decidedly positive about the program, on balance.

Their own words best convey this balanced optimism: Despite setbacks in the program and sometimes contrary results of individual laboratories, the consensus of the participating staff, the city administrators, and the business patrons providing financial support has been cautiously affirmative in proclaiming the program a success. No claim is made that 18 hours of discussion will sweep away years of rancor and distrust. But it is a necessary beginning.

OTHER CONCERNS WITH SOCIAL ENGINEERING
IN POLITICAL SCIENCE

The examples above merely illustrate the impact of one approach to social engineering on several areas of historic concern to the political theorist. This is not to imply, however, that the laboratory approach is the only viable one. Nor does it mean to convey the impression that only the illustrated areas in Political Science are amenable to social engineering.

To counteract somewhat the narrowness of this chapter in the two central regards above, reference is here made to a major line of work which has involved many political scientists over the last decade or so. This tradition of work can be variously identified, but "Institution Building" is as revealing a usage as any. Esman has described that tradition of work in these terms (Siffin 1972, 116):

> The Institution Building approach has a pronounced social engineering bias. Its root proposition is that a very large proportion of the most significant contemporary changes, especially in the developing countries, are deliberately planned and guided, and can be distinguished from those that occur through gradual evolutionary processes, or as the consequences of political or social revolution. It further presupposes that the introduction of changes takes place primarily in and through formal organizations. These organizations symbolize, promote, sustain, and protect innovations, and it is these organizations as well as the new normative relationships and action patterns they foster which must become "institutionalized," meaningful and valued in the societies in which they function.

REFERENCES

Argyris, C., and Schon, D. A. 1974. *Theory in practice: Increasing professional effectiveness.* San Francisco: Jossey-Bass.

Charms, R. 1968. *Personal causation.* New York: Academic Press.

French, W. L., and Bell, C. H., Jr. 1973. *Organization development.* Englewood Cliffs, N.J.: Prentice-Hall.

Garson, G. D. 1974. On the origins of interest-group theory. *American political science review* 68: 1505-1519.

Golembiewski, R. T. 1972. *Renewing organizations.* Itasca, Ill.: F. E. Peacock.

Korten, David C. 1974. Beyond accustomed territory. *Journal of applied behavioral science* 10: 53-60.

Lifton, R. J. 1973. *Home from the war.* New York: Simon and Schuster.

McClelland, D. C., and Winter, D. G. 1969. *Motivating economic achievement.* New York: Free Press.

Odiorne, G. 1963. The trouble with sensitivity training. *Training directors journal* 17: 9-20.

Schein, E. H. 1969. *Process consultation.* Reading, Mass: Addison-Wesley.

Siffin, W. J. 1972. The institution building perspective. In *Institution building: A model for applied social change*, eds. D. Woods Thomas, Harry R. Potter, William L. Miller, and Adrian F. Aveni. Cambridge, Mass.: Schenkman Publishing Co.

Smith, P. B. 1973. *Groups within organizations: applications of social psychology to organizational behavior.* New York: Harper & Row.

Steinbacker, J. 1971. *The child seducers.* Fullerton, Calif.: Educator Publications Inc.

Valenstein, E. S. 1973. *Brain control.* New York: Wiley-Interscience.

Walton, R. E., and Warwick, D. P. 1973. The ethics of organization development. *Journal of applied behavioral science* 9: 681-699.

Zajonc, R. 1965. Social facilitation. *Science* 149: 269-274.

A Problem-Solving Workshop
on Border Conflicts in Eastern Africa

RICHARD E. WALTON

INTRODUCTION

Early in July 1969, I received a telephone call asking me to serve as a staff member in a workshop outlined as follows: At the initiative of three Yale University social scientists, and with the support of a United Nations agency, six Somalis and like numbers of Kenyans and Ethiopians were to participate in a workshop which would try to find solutions to the tension-laden border disputes between Somalia and her neighbors. The workshop, which was to begin August 2, had just received the necessary green light from the last of the three governments. The participants were drawn from the elite communities in their countries and were to attend as private individuals, not as delegates of their governments.

Elements of the whole plan—ranging from logistics to the basic concept—seemed fraught with difficulties and uncertainties. But it was acknowledged as an experiment in informal diplomacy, where formal diplomacy had thus far failed to produce any stable accommodation in the area. I agreed to serve on what became a team of four consultants. The four consultants shared expertise in group dynamics and sensitivity training; but they also had complementary individual specialties, including familiarity with Africans in training settings, experience with formal diplomacy, and expertise in third-party conflict resolution. The workshop took place from 2-14 August in a ski hotel (Hotel Fermeda) in the mountains of northern Italy.

I consider the workshop for problem solving intersystem disputes a potentially important social invention.[1] Admittedly, the pilot venture reported here was a mixture of technical successes and failures. This paper will document and analyze the Fermeda Workshop and then explicate some of the general principles which should guide the application of the concept and the design of future workshops. Part I presents some background to the dispute. Part II provides a chronological account of the workshop. Part III interprets and evaluates the workshop—its outcomes and its design.

PART I: BACKGROUND ON THE DISPUTES IN THE HORN

The primary dispute between Somalia and Ethiopia involves the areas of the Ogaden and the Haud, areas within the de facto borders of Ethiopia but largely inhabited by Somali tribes. The dispute between Somalia and Kenya

Reproduced by special permission from *The journal of applied behavioral science*, (1970), 6: 453-477.

involves a district in northeastern Kenya which is heavily populated by
people of the Somali culture. The map in Figure 6.1 shows the Somali
ethnic limits reaching beyond the de facto borders of the Somali Republic
into the Ogaden, the Haud, French Somaliland, and northeastern Kenya.

The Somali constitution states the goal of "Greater Somalia," which
would unite the ethnic Somalis living in the adjacent areas of Ethiopia,
Kenya, and French Somaliland (Thurston 1969). The Somali state itself
was born in 1960 in an act of union between the ex-British and ex-Italian

Figure 6.1

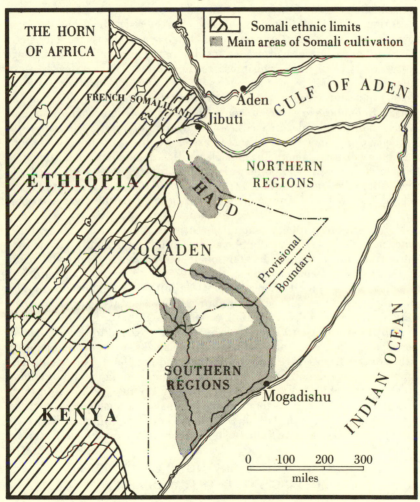

Adapted from I. M. Lewis, *The Modern History of Somaliland.*
London: Weidenfeld and Nicholson, 1965. p. 204.

Somalilands, thereby providing a historical achievement which serves to bolster the Somalis' aspirations for the larger union.

The decade since the birth of the Somali Republic has been marked by innumerable border incidents, each involving the killing of small numbers of men and as a whole promoting heavy military expenditures by the countries. Twice during this period the tensions in the border areas have erupted into war—first in the Ogaden of Ethiopia in 1963 and then in northeast Kenya in 1966-1967. During the mid-1960s Somalia began to accept large-scale arms and training assistance from the Soviet Union, complicating the military-political situation in the Horn because Kenya received military aid from the British, and Ethiopia was assisted by the United States.

During 1967-1969 detente policies characterized relations between Somalia and each of her two neighbors. The governments issued joint statements intended to normalize relations, including agreements to exchange ambassadors, lift trade embargos, resume direct air service between capitals, and refrain from subversive activities against each other. Both the Communist and Western powers welcomed the detente initiatives of the Somali Republic. However, no sooner would a new joint communique be issued than new border incidents would disturb relations, especially with Ethiopia. For example in 1969, just weeks before the workshop, two serious incidents occurred, reminding Somali politicians of their commitment to irredentism. The incidents, in which about fifty persons were killed and one hundred wounded, resulted from Ethiopian officials' efforts to collect a head tax on the livestock of Somali tribesmen in the Ogaden (Apple 1969).

Moreover none of the steps to relax tension touch the basic issues in dispute. Somalis believe that the Somali-speaking people and the lands they inhabit should be united. In addition to moral and sociologically based arguments, the Somalis contest the 1897 treaty between Britain and Ethiopia, upon which Ethiopia bases its definition of the northern border with the Somali Republic (*Africa Report* 1967). They also cite an impartial investigation by the British in 1962 which showed that five of six residents in Kenya's northeastern district wished to leave Kenya to become part of Somalia (Doob 1967). For their part, Ethiopians assert legal and historical rights to the disputed areas in the Ogaden and the Haud. Both Kenya and Ethiopia invoke the principle of respect for the sovereignty and territorial integrity of states. They do not want to give up any territory, not only because of the value of the territory itself but also because to cede territory to Somalia's claims makes the multinational, multilingual states of Ethiopia and Kenya more vulnerable to other claims or secessionist movements.

PART II: THE WORKSHOP FOR PROBLEM SOLVING INTERSYSTEM DISPUTES

The organizers. The initiator of the workshop idea was Leonard Doob, professor of social psychology at Yale University, who had developed a particular interest in this part of Africa. He enlisted the assistance of two Yale colleagues—Robert B. Stevens, a lawyer who had been involved in legal problems facing East African countries in creating a viable economic community, and William J. Foltz, a political scientist who had a special interest in the possibilities of federation in Africa. These three consulted another Yale colleague—Chris Argyris, a well-known consultant on social change. Together they developed the concept early in 1966 which was finally to be implemented in 1969.

The three-year effort of the Yale group to bring the workshop idea to fruition was exhausting and often frustrating. They met numerous obstacles in raising the necessary funds and in securing the cooperation of all three governments. For example, in 1967 the Ethiopian government declined; and in 1968 the Somali government withdrew its consent. Finally in 1969, for the first time all three governments agreed and funds were secured.

The participants from Ethiopia and Kenya were drawn from universities, including the faculties of Law, Political Science, History, Geography, Anthropology, Engineering, Mathematics, Philosophy, and Education. The six participants from Somalia, which does not have a major university, included a member of the opposition in Parliament, an educator, an editor, and high-level officials in the Institute of Public Administration, the Ministry of Education, and the Ministry of Planning.

Preplanning. The staff of consultants and organizers met in Rome on August 1. The consulting team was comprised of William J. Crockett, Charles K. Ferguson, Thomas A. Wickes, and myself, all associated with the NTL Institute for Applied Behavioral Science. The planning of the workshop design was conducted under poor circumstances. The consultants were meeting for the first time; although several of us were acquainted, none of our number had met the Yale organizers. All were fatigued from the overnight transatlantic flight, and we were pressed for time. The lack of planning time resulted from busy schedules of the consultants and the scheduling decisions of the organizers.

We readily reached unanimous decisions regarding the first three of the following major areas of design:

1. Phasing. In Phase One the emphasis would be on developing communication relationships and promoting receptivity toward and skill in diagnosis of group process—conditions which we assumed would promote more effective treatment of the border issues. Phase Two emphasizes search for viable solutions to the dispute.

2. Activities. We would utilize a mixture of techniques to facilitate the work, especially during Phase One. These would include simulations, theory seminars, and critiques of meetings.

3. Schedule. The typical work schedule would involve two morning sessions, an early afternoon session, an afternoon break followed by a social hour, and an evening session. We planned a two-day break in the middle of the workshop.

	Working Group I			Working Group II		
Somali participants	S_1	S_2	S_3	S_4	S_5	S_6
Kenyan participants	K_1	K_2	K_3	K_4	K_5	K_6
Ethiopian participants	E_1	E_2	E_3	E_4	E_5	E_6
American organizers		O_1	O_2	O_3		
American consultants		C_1	C_2	C_3	C_4	

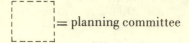 = planning committee

Figure 6.2. Makeup of Working Groups

4. Groupings. This issue was not so easily resolved. All four consultants believed that the community should be divided into two working groups comprised of one-half of the contingent from each country. However, differences centered on whether they should become the dominant grouping from the beginning. My colleagues believed they should. I urged a design that began with participants meeting in national groups for much of the time the first day or two. The majority view prevailed.

5. Operational goal. The Yale organizers stated that a goal for the two weeks was to achieve a consensus for some proposal to solve the border dispute. It was presumed that the proposal would be committed to writing, but undecided whether it would be released to the press at the end of the conference or treated confidentially by individual participants.

Phase one of the workshop. The three national groups arrived in Rome, and we all boarded a chartered bus to northern Italy. The fourteen-hour overnight bus trip was numbing. The Somalis sat together, the Ethiopians were more dispersed, and the Kenyans most dispersed. (This clue to amount of cohesion within teams proved to be predictive of the workshop social structure.)

On Saturday evening and Sunday the participants were introduced to the methods of the workshop and to one another. After a general session on Saturday evening the participants were assigned to two working groups. Each group contained approximately half the population of the community. (See Figure 6.2.) My account will draw heavily on the experience of Working Group II, usually referred to here simply as the "Group." (The experience of Group I generally can be assumed to be similar, unless a contrast is specifically drawn.)

These working groups were intentionally unstructured in two important respects. First, the consultants who announced the group assignments and scheduled time for them did not specify any substantive agenda or any mechanism for deciding upon such an agenda. Second, the consultants did not provide for any chairmanship for discussions. Instead we stressed that the time allotted to the groups could be used in any way each group chose; but that however they used the time, they were urged periodically to discuss their individual reactions and assessments of the group process in order to sharpen their skills in diagnosing process and to improve upon the functioning of their respective groups. Also we provided illustrations of process analysis and generally facilitated the development of authentic communication and positive relations among members.

The response to the emphasis on "process" was a mixture of acceptance and resistance. The inevitable floundering occurred as members endeavored to evolve some modus operandi. Members declined to accept one another's influence and effectively canceled one another's initiatives. Frustration in the group mounted. Finally on Sunday night a climax of frustration precipitated the group's first planning decision. Members agreed to form a committee to select a topic of discussion for the next group meeting on Monday.

The Monday afternoon session illustrates the concurrent development of (1) increasing capacity for coherent group discussion and (2) increasing awareness, tolerance, and respect for individual differences. The discussion centered on the role of the Organization for African Unity (OAU), the topic initiated by the previously appointed committee.

This discussion was more disciplined than preceding ones. After the topic was introduced, one speaker from each country was heard from before a second person from a country spoke. This occurred by tacit understanding. Eventually every member participated. In fact, although the formally allotted time had run out, there was general insistence that the last man have his say.

Significantly the difference in views on the OAU did not follow country lines. Thus the discussion reflected and reinforced growing individuation among Group II members. For example, K_4 outlined a pragmatic position that the OAU does not have effective power nor any intent to exercise its power in such disputes, and that the only hope to end the border dispute in the Horn depends upon the parties' calculating the costs and coming to terms. E_5 disagreed in principle, reflecting somewhat more optimism about the role of the OAU. Still his faith in the OAU was more qualified than that of his countryman, E_6. Dissenting sharply from the views of both E_5 and E_6, E_4 deplored the corruption of existing institutions such as the OAU and stressed the need for revolutionary solutions. K_5 took a position closely related to E_4. S_5 dismissed the OAU on grounds of ineffectuality.

During this discussion many individuals telegraphed philosophies and interpersonal styles that would govern their approach to future discussions of the border disputes. For example, agitation developed between E_5 and K_4, but it appeared to be as much stimulated by interpersonal rivalries as by substantive disagreement. Both persons were intellectually keen; both spoke in paragraphs rather than sentences, developing several points each time they participated. Their similarities in style fostered competition for air time and for intellectual primacy.

Late Monday afternoon the community paused to review the past twenty-four hours and assess progress. Several subgroups of four (two from Group I and two from Group II) discussed and compared individual reactions. This was followed by a brief report from each subgroup. Participants expressed uniformly positive feelings about the morning's simulation and the afternoon discussion. The earlier frustration was being replaced by a sense of progress and optimism. The organizers read a telegram they had just received from the United Nations expressing encouragement for this experiment in international problem solving.

From Monday evening to Wednesday morning can be described as a period of consolidation and preparation. There was a general building toward a confrontation of the border issues. The period was preparatory in the sense that the content of the discussions was related to but not directly focused on the dispute. Participants learned about the politics and cultures of the other two countries. For example they explored the degrees of diffusion and concentration of power in each country and the probable causes and consequences of power concentrations. It was consolidating in the sense that interpersonal relationships were being strengthened and the group was developing a more effective modus operandi.

On the first day, working without an appointed chairman and without a prior agenda was productive of only disjointed discussion and was highly frustrating for members. But soon the group was learning how to exploit the potential of low structure. Participants demonstrated their flexibility not only in managing the agenda but also in adapting the group's structure. For example, during the Tuesday afternoon session when it was decided to engage in more systematic education about the internal problems faced by each country, participants spontaneously agreed to caucus briefly by country trios and then organized to do the job efficiently.

Generally the group became more effective in handling differences. As differences arose, there were attempts to clarify them; often a person would change his position on an issue when he considered a different factual assumption offered by another participant. When differences were not subject to easy resolution, there was neither pressure to smooth over them nor any emotional outbreak.

There was a discernible increase in the ease with which participants interacted with one another. For example, on Tuesday evening the group began in a joking mood. E_4 entered the room and moved toward the couch where three persons were already seated, indicating by his actions that he wanted to sit on the far end. This would have required S_5 to move over toward the center of the couch. Thus S_5 and E_4, who had been verbal combatants on many previous occasions, were now in a face-off over who would occupy a space which they both preferred. For a while S_5 made no effort to move in either direction to make room for E_4; when he finally did move, it was toward the end of the couch, thereby denying E_4 the place he had tried to claim. Both had enjoyed the sparring match. Other group members also engaged in horseplay, frequently with a fraternal overtone that combined friendliness and rivalry.

Trust-building initiatives occurred and were reciprocated. In one instance tears came to the eyes of a person as he described his doubts and fears about the capacity of his government to meet the great needs of his people for economic and social development. Others responded with respect and quietly urged him and his fellow countrymen to continue. Later other participants responded by describing some of the weaknesses of their own countries. There was no disposition within the group to exploit revealed cracks in the national images. The mood was one of respect and understanding.

One brief interchange illustrates the attempts by participants to improve their patterns of communicating. K_4, who was prone to making lengthy contributions to an ongoing discussion, had just finished one such dissertation. S_4 asked K_4 a simple, clarifying question to which K_4 could have provided a one-syllable answer. Again K_4 gave a lengthy reply. When he finished, E_4 said to K_4, quietly but pointedly, "Your answer was 'yes'?" K_4 replied "Yes" and fully appreciated the point.

Frequently during or at the conclusion of a session one of the process consultants would initiate a critique of the way the group was functioning, which would lead to some interpersonal feedback or diagnostic insight into group process, e.g., how the topical theme of the discussion has some relevance to dynamics of the group and vice versa.

On each of the first three days of the workshop a simulation exercise was used. It lasted from one and one-half to four hours. These experiences illustrated certain theories presented either before or after the simulation. One simulation involved alternative group leadership styles and their effects on group members. The two remaining simulations structured situations in which participants were offered the choices of either competing or cooperating with other players in striving toward their goals. These experiences allowed the workshop community to explore ideas such as interdependency, reciprocity, perceptions, expectations—to mention a few. These simulations were designed with dual purposes: (1) to help improve the processes of managing interpersonal conflict and of building collaboration within the two workgroups, and (2) to provide diagnostic concepts relevant to the border disputes. In addition, because these simulations were played in subgroups comprised of at least one Ethiopian, one Somali, and one Kenyan (and usually one American), they had the intended effect of accelerating the development of interpersonal bonds across national groups.

Wednesday midmorning until Thursday afternoon was a period of transition to Phase Two. Late on Wednesday morning the consultants announced a procedure (to be discussed later) designed to promote a relatively complete and efficient preliminary airing of the issues. Participants were to meet that afternoon as national groups and prepare statements of the issues to be presented in a general session the following morning. Meetings of working groups I and II were scheduled for Wednesday evening.

All three national groups met during the afternoon, although the Ken-

yans and Ethiopians met only briefly. On the basis of the consultants' observations there seemed to be some avoidance behavior (clustering in
social activities and procrastination on the task), indicating negative feelings about the task and/or tension within the national groups. When the
working groups met that evening, the staff learned that the Somalis had not
finished the tasks and that at least some Somalis preferred to continue
working on the task as national groups rather than meet as working groups.

Before adjourning the evening session, the participants discussed their
feelings about the task which the consultants had designed. First, one Kenyan objected to forming national groups, explaining that, "After all, the
idea is that we are individuals, speaking for ourselves, not our countries."
There was only mild support for this view, and it came from other Kenyans. Second, an Ethiopian objected to the format of the presentation. He
was supported by a second Ethiopian and a Kenyan. A third complaint was
that participants should have been consulted in planning the task. This dissent received general support. Later that night the staff worked out a
mechanism for transferring power to the total community.

During the first five days the consultants had allocated time to activities,
such as the working groups, and had structured some educational experiences. They had sought evaluative reactions to each element of the
design and considered these reactions; nevertheless they had preserved the
initiative in design decisions. Now a representative committee would
assume the authority and responsibility heretofore exercised by the four
consultants.

The idea for broadening responsibility for the planning was accepted by
the total workshop community Thursday afternoon. The representative
planning committee was balanced both by working group and national affiliation. (See Figure 6.2.) These representatives were named in meetings
of the national groups. Two consultants and one Yale member were on the
planning committee which finally evolved.

The planning committee appeared to have immediate legitimacy and
functioned effectively as a group. It opted to have a permanent chairman
for the committee itself; but it decided to have the assembly (general
assembly of the community) chaired by participants not on the committee,
generally changing the chairmanship for each session by rotating the position among Somalis, Ethiopians, and Kenyans.

Phase two of the workshop. Let us return to the tasks which the consultants had assigned to the national groups on Wednesday morning:

Tasks for National Groups

Task I. As individual $\left\{\begin{array}{l}\text{Somalis}\\\text{Kenyans}\\\text{Ethiopians}\end{array}\right\}$ list on newsprint (large
sheets of paper) key grievances or disputes your people have
with each of the other countries.

Task II. On a second sheet of newsprint list your predictions of the grievances or disputes that the individuals from each of the other two countries will bring regarding your country.

Be prepared to bring these written lists for Task I and Task II to a diagnostic general meeting in the main session room at 9:00 Thursday morning, with a representative prepared to explain your lists.

The tasks generally were intended to provide a consistent format within which to identify the conflict issues and their symptoms. Beyond identifying points of friction from one's own view, the approach was intended to induce each national group to attempt to "take the role of the other" and to anticipate how one's own country is viewed by the people of the two other countries.

The total community met Thursday morning. The Somalis led with their presentation, followed by Ethiopians, then Kenyans, and finally the Yale group, who had tried to predict the grievances which would be identified by each of the other national groups. The Somalis followed the format and attempted to state the views toward Somalia which they predicted were held by people from the other countries. They were quite facile in articulating the views of others. Rejecting the suggested format, the Ethiopians presented a single listing of the issues. The Somalis objected to the Ethiopian list because it never mentioned the Somali Republic and thereby raised questions for Somalis about whether the Ethiopians were laying some historical claim to the whole of the Horn. The Kenyans likewise presented only one view of the dispute, a view which the Somalis believed was clearly biased. Reflecting on the morning presentations, one Somali was critical.

> I was disappointed that the Ethiopians and Kenyans did not follow the approach as we did. We are a free people. You can see that from how we presented both views. We appointed a lawyer for Ethiopia and for Kenya. We not only could see it from their view, but also we were free to express it from their view. But Ethiopians could not present our views. Nor could the Kenyans. This illustrates an important difference. In our land, two men may go to court—at great expense—because one claims a camel in the possession of the second. Then if the first is awarded the camel, he may allow the second to keep it. Why? Because it was an exercise for them. We can view disagreements in this way.

Interestingly this Somali was able to view the morning's presentation as a product of cultural differences rather than seeing it strictly as tactical exercise.

In its initial meeting on Thursday afternoon the planning committee had decided that future work on the border issues would generally occur in the Assembly. The committee had developed an agenda for subsequent discussion which is presented below.

Main Issues
Diagnosis and Solution

I. A. What is—
      1. a nation?
      2. a nation-state?
      3. the principle of self-determination?
    B. What is the nature of the problem?
    C. What are the implications of redrawing the map of
       northeast Africa?

II.   How do these disputes hinder—
    A. internal development?
    B. regional development?

III.   External influences on these disputes:
    A. Role of great powers.
    B. Role of other nations.

IV.   What is the significance of the disputed areas to the par-
       ties concerned?

V.   Summary of solutions and possible actions.

On Thursday evening during the first meeting of the assembly, participants failed to engage one another over the substantive issues outlined
above. Again, as earlier in the day, process issues prevented substantive
discussion. This time the stated process issue involved how much formality
should characterize the assembly meetings, with the chairman asserting
strict parliamentary procedure and one or two members challenging his
authority. A related implicit issue was how to handle deviant and obstruc-
tionist behavior. One member had disrupted the meeting by preventing any
constructive dialog. The assembly ended with a decision to resume discussion on Friday morning in Working Groups I and II. In one sense the participants were retreating to their more familiar workgroups.

The two-day break from Friday noon to Sunday noon allowed for some
rest and/or diversion after an intense week of discussion. After an
organized, staff-arranged bus trip to Venice, which most of the participants
took, all were able to return to the activity with renewed vigor.

However, a bit of disconcerting news reached members of the workshop
over the weekend. Tribal tensions in Kenya had increased during the
month before the workshop with the assassination of Tom Mboya, a leader
of the Luo tribe. Mboya had been considered a possible successor to Jomo
Kenyatta, a Kikuyu and present head of the government. The Kenyan
group included members of both tribes. Over the weekend in question, the
London *Times*, 9 August, reported developments in the apprehending of a
Kikuyu charged with slaying Mboya. It also reported that a leading Luo,
Odinga Oginga, had charged that the Kikuyu were taking tribal oaths. Two
Kenyans were especially upset by the continuing unrest which this chain
of events promised for their country.

During the Sunday afternoon session Group II picked up the discussion where it had stopped Friday noon. In addition the issue of ethnic prejudice finally was acknowledged and treated briefly. Overall the discussion revealed significant diversity within the three national groups in terms of conciliatory versus adamant views on the conflict issues.

Later Sunday evening, the consultants introduced the technique of brainstorming and practiced it on solutions to the Biafra war. This was designed to familiarize participants with the technique so that it could be employed if and when it was deemed useful to our problem-solving effort.

The committee had planned to convene the assembly after the brainstorming session to proceed with the substantive discussions of the dispute. Most participants felt the need to engage issues in the total community. However, when the assembly convened, a serious tone could not be maintained; nervous joking was heightened by the chairman's strict adherence to parliamentary procedure. After a few unsuccessful efforts to initiate a serious discussion, a move to adjourn carried. Participants and staff were unhappy about their ineffectiveness in this assembly.

Monday's morning and afternoon sessions were marked by a cooperative effort to generate and then to organize ideas that might contribute to a solution of the border problems. Working Group II started in the morning by quickly deciding to break up into two subgroups and to brainstorm for possible solutions to the problem. Some 150 ideas were developed. The group then categorized solutions into political, economic, military, and social types, which it next assigned to three subgroups.

That evening the group discussed the progress of the subgroups. Although two were progressing well, the third subgroup had hit a snag when dealing with the problem of development and administration of the disputed areas. This group had explored methods for implementing one political strategy, namely, freezing the question of sovereignty for ten years, during which free movement would be guaranteed. The snag was the question of what territories would be included in the free movement zone. Several possibilities had been debated.

When this third subgroup report was presented to the Group II members, S_5 became adamant on the Somali position. Several emotional interchanges ensued between S_5 and two Ethiopians. Because the stance taken by S_5 seemed to admit of no solution other than the one he preferred, one consultant urged S_5 to ask himself whether political compromise might not be required in any conceivable outcome. In what seemed to be an effort to offer some hope, S_5 replied that he could visualize compromises but ones that took other forms. The discussion ended on that note.

Participants generally expressed the feeling that the day (Monday) had been the most productive thus far. They also preferred to continue in the small groups within Group II and to meet in the assembly only when the group had worked through to some operational delineation of the basic controversial issues.

The Yale and consulting staffs met later that evening after a long and exhausting day. Group I's day had been less productive, and the staff from that group was depressed: although it had used many of the same procedures for working the problem, dissident members had frustrated the work.

The planning committee met Tuesday morning to review the status of the work and plan the day. Group II wanted to continue uninterrupted. There was some interest among Group I members in exchanging information between groups. It was decided to have one member from each group report to the other group for fifteen minutes at the beginning of the morning session.

After these presentations the two subgroups of Group II continued their work until they finished their respective reports. Then they joined forces and integrated their plans. The task groups had functioned well and had put in long hours hammering out one difference after another. Now members of Group II expressed considerable pride and satisfaction as they reflected on the products of their efforts.

The planning committee met Tuesday evening to integrate the proposals that had emerged from Groups I and II. (Other participants did not meet.) Group II's proposal was elaborate and typewritten. In contrast, Group I's proposal was more sketchy. The committee tried to resolve as many differences between the documents as possible; but when this failed, it stated the alternatives for floor debate in the assembly on Wednesday.

Thus, the major differences were identified: (1) Should there be recognition of ultimate right of self-determination and provision for a plebiscite? Group II included this proposal; Group I clearly avoided such recognition and provision. (2) Should the neutral or buffer zone be wholly from within the disputed territory as Group II had recommended or include territory clearly now within the Somali Republic as recommended by Group I? These differences were treated as alternatives within an otherwise consolidated document—largely the language, format, and content of Group II's proposal.

Comparing the two documents, Group I's proposals were relatively closer to the general views of the governments of Kenya and Ethiopia; and Group II's were relatively closer to those of the Somali Republic. We learned that a few of the Somalis in Group II had voiced disappointment with one or more of their brethren in Group I for going along with the proposal that emerged from that group; and that a few Kenyans and a few Ethiopians in Group I disapproved of the positions taken by their fellow countrymen in Group II. There were reports that national groups had caucused Tuesday evening. There were no grounds for optimism that the workshop participants would reach unanimous agreement on a specific proposal. On the other hand, each of the two working groups, with its multicountry membership, had been able to generate a proposal generally supported by its membership.

A Kenyan, K_4, had been selected by the planning committee to chair the

Assembly on Wednesday. He had emerged as one of the most gifted, articulate, and serious participants; also his views on the border disputes were intermediate in terms of the spectrum created by the Workshop participations. Very early in the Wednesday morning assembly session, one Somali sensed the likely direction of the day's development and was prompted to give the warning contained in a Somali proverb, "One must not follow his footprints back." He was correct in sensing that in some respects we were to retrace—backward—our steps of the past few days. The following excerpts from this meeting illustrate the tone:

E_1: (With disgust) I object to this merged document.

E^1 went on to express disapproval: first, that the documents had been merged; second, that Group I's proposals were incorporated into Group II's format rather than vice versa; third, that the committee failed to incorporate all of Group I's ideas into the merged document. Finally, he disagreed with the content of most of the proposals in the document.

O_2: The two conflict issues are self-determination and the scope of the region.

K_1: The mere reference to the right of self-determination will signal an intention ultimately to cede the disputed area to the Somali Republic. This is completely unacceptable.

K_4: The spirit was to reduce direct confrontation between our states. Therefore, we ought to stick to the idea of a buffer zone.

S_5: Let's state right of self-determination as a right of the peoples involved. We should not use the criteria of what is acceptable to the governments.

E_1: I speak both as an individual and an Ethiopian. The particular regime is not important. I am going to have to live with any position I take here. The fact that I am an Ethiopian is a reality for me.

Some differences of opinion were then expressed by persons from the same country: e.g., E_6 differentiated his view from that just expressed by E_1.

E_1: (Turning to confront S_1) By what right, by what idea of justice do you ask us to give up people and territory to the Somali Republic?

S_1: We are talking about self-determination, not annexation.

K_1: In this situation, they are the same! . . .

K_1: I am growing very angry. Somalia is like a woman who is asking for something, but with nothing to give.

C_2: Our two groups were microcosms of this larger assembly. We were able to reach agreement in them. Why can't we here?

K_4: There are areas of agreement on which we can build: (1)

We all want a solution. (2) We agree on some buffer zones. (3) We all want unity eventually. The areas of disagreement are the right of self-determination and its exercise.

S_1: The man who dies in the first clash of the fighting is deaf to reason. This is not meant as a threat to K_1. We should—in our emotional state—turn to a positive proposal of federation, lifting boundaries. Our problems are with our own governments.

There followed a futile attempt to rebuild some sense of common purpose among participants, based on the idea of larger schemes of cooperation. Unfortunately when the assembly reconvened in the afternoon, there was no change in sentiment or patterns of participation. The following are excerpts from the Wednesday afternoon meeting.

E_1: It is not becoming to a sovereign state to abrogate its rights of administration in its own territory. I accept only a small buffer zone that is free of armies, but that is all.

S_4: The arms are a consequence of the real problem. The real problem is one of sovereignty. Dealing with arms won't solve the problem.

S_2: Unless there is recognition of the underlying problems involving land, life patterns, territorial claims, we are wasting our time.

E_2: (Taking a more conciliatory stand than E_1) I'd go a step further than a buffer zone and have us pour resources into the development of the neutralized zone.

S_5: (Continuing the debate tone) That would acknowledge that there is a sovereignty issue!

E_3: (Trying to recapture the incentives for searching for an accommodation) Let us focus on the costs of continuing the dispute.

K_1. : I agree with E_1. As a Kenyan nationalist, I state we are not prepared to compromise our boundaries. We are not prepared to compromise on our nationals. I do accept a buffer zone as an experiment in cooperation, but. . . when a nation flouts international boundaries. . . . I've been called a warrior by my group. Maybe the Somalis are suffering from ethnocentrism. . . .

E_1: I'm beginning to be suspicious of the underlying sinister motives of my Somali brothers.

At this point, C_3 observed that they had reached apparent impasse in the discussions, but also noted that not everyone had been involved in the discussions. (The antagonism and debate had involved exchanges primarily among members of Group I.) C_3 raised the question of whether some regrouping or some other approach to the subject might not allow for movement. He made no formal recommendation for regrouping, but moved that the assembly break and allow the planning committee to consider ways of getting by the impasse.

After some debate, the assembly decided to take a break. Members of the committee agreed that the discussion had turned to reiteration of extreme nationalistic views and had become less and less compromise-oriented. The planning committee decided to suggest that the Assembly focus on short-run solutions and avoid the issue of self-determination, which most members agreed had stimulated much of the suspicion.

When the assembly reconvened, and after K_4 presented the idea of focusing on short-run solutions, K_1 reiterated his adamant no-compromise stand. S_2, E_2, S_1, and E_4 tried to initiate some positive note but failed. Hostility increased still further when E_1 asserted that the planning committee was not neutral because in combining the proposals it had omitted two possible outcomes from the plebiscite: namely, voting to remain with Ethiopia or Kenya and neutralization. E_3 tried to reassure him that it was an oversight.

The meeting ended on a confused note. Many were reluctant to agree to return to the assembly to continue work. The assembly adjourned on a note of general pessimism.

The assembly met after dinner but soon adjourned the substantive meeting. In urging adjournment one Somali reminded others that he had been called a cheater earlier in the day and he did not want to suffer any further such statements. "Besides," he said, "Somalis are warriors and I am likely to become violent." (Earlier in the day his facial expression had revealed extreme distress, although he was not participating verbally in the discussion.) A second Somali feared that continued discussion could only damage the many friendships which had developed over the two weeks.

One of the organizers made a brief speech to the effect that it had been a high-risk, high-payoff enterprise and that the eventual outcome was still in question. He went on to say, "Maybe the conference will have sparked an idea that leads to some resolution of the dispute. Maybe methodologically this approach will be better understood and therefore applied in other international situations. One simply can't evaluate the workshop at this point in time. In any event, we cannot afford not to keep trying." He expressed thanks to everyone participating.

The final morning, participants left Hotel Fermeda in various groupings, with plans to go back to their respective African nations either directly or indirectly.

PART III: OUTCOMES AND STRATEGIC ISSUES IN THE WORKSHOP DESIGN

The Fermeda Workshop ended on a sour note. But the developments late in the meeting were not inherent in the workshop concept. They resulted in part from very knotty issues at the heart of the border disputes and in part from features of the design of this particular workshop. More importantly the Fermeda Workshop represented technical successes as well as failures.

I assume that similar workshops focused on international disputes will be conducted in the future—in my opinion the method has significant potential. Moreover, the stakes of war versus peace are so high that any plausible strategy deserves a good trial. Therefore I intend not only to critique the Fermeda experience but also to suggest general principles that should be considered in designing future workshops.

Outcomes. Our ultimate purpose was to have some positive influence on the resolution of the border disputes between Somalia and both Kenya and Ethiopia. Defined in these terms, the effectiveness of the workshop cannot be determined in the short run; and can be only loosely inferred in the longer run if and when some accommodation is reached among the governments. I understand that the workshop participants were debriefed by their governments. Also during the month following the workshop a meeting occurred in Addis Ababa between the Prime Minister of Somalia and the Emperor of Ethiopia.

On the one hand, there were clear failures in terms of two of the staff's criteria for measuring the immediate effectiveness of the workshop. First, the workshop was unable to reach a consensus about a proposed solution. Second, the workshop community did not transfer to the assembly the trust, confidence, and problem-solving process it had developed earlier in the groups. These assessments are discussed below in connection with the design decisions that affected them.

Results of questionnaire. On the other hand, the workshop had succeeded in creating productive processes and positive results in the two working groups. There were further positive by-products reported by participants. The planning committee had approved the development and administration of a questionnaire to help evaluate aspects of this experiment. The questionnaire was administered when the mood of members was basically depressed on the last evening of the assembly and it was to be returned, completed but unsigned, to a staff member's mailbox later that evening or the next morning. Fourteen of eighteen participants returned their questionnaires. Since not returning a questionnaire might have been an expression of negative feelings toward the workshop, a conservative interpretation of the results is appropriate.

1. Mutual education. The substantive discussion during the first week included cross-cultural comparisons. The questionnaire results confirm that these earlier discussions were indeed educational. Participants were asked, "To what extent have you become better acquainted with the culture and internal problems of the other countries participating in the workshop?" Of the fourteen respondents, five scored their own learning as "moderate," five as "large," and four as "very large." None scored the two lower categories: "small extent" or "not at all."

2. Understanding others' views. Better understanding of one another's

views was essential to problem solving in the workshop and is conducive to accommodations between states in the longer run. The questionnaire asked, "To what extent have you gained a better understanding of the views of other countries toward the dispute?" All responses attested to a "very large" or "large" extent. Again, the three lower categories were not used.

3. Openness toward solutions. One question asked, "To what extent do you believe members of the workshop have developed more open attitudes toward possible solutions of the dispute?" The responses were well distributed on the five-point scale ranging from "very large extent" to "not at all"—except that the latter category was not used. The median response indicated that a moderate increase in the amount of openness toward alternate solutions had been achieved. These participants' responses tended to confirm what the staff had assumed: namely, that while the polarization of nationalistic views, the dissolution of earlier areas of agreement, and the expressions of hostility and suspicion characterized the behavior in the Assembly, they did not represent a generalized pattern of movement in the attitudes of the majority of individuals. Thus the majority of participants probably continued to feel in themselves and perceive in fellow participants increased openness toward alternate solutions despite the fact that reaffirmations of these attitudes were almost completely driven out of the last day's discussion.

4. Innovative ideas about solutions. Participants were asked: "To what extent do you believe the workshop has produced innovative ideas relevant to solving the problems between Ethiopia and Somalia and between Kenya and Somalia?" Half of the fourteen respondents reported "small extent," and four reported "moderate extent." Each of the other possible responses—"very large extent," "large extent," and "not at all"—was checked by one respondent.

5. Insight into process. Participants were asked: "To what extent did you gain any additional insights into your own communication skills or other aspects of group process?" The results provided approximately a normal curve around the "moderate extent" response.

Arab and Jew in Israel:
A Case Study of a Training Approach
to Intergroup Conflict

MARTIN LAKIN

Together with my two colleagues, Jacob Lomranz of Duke and Tel Aviv Universities and Morton A. Lieberman of the University of Chicago, I designed a training approach to be employed with Arabs and Jews in Israel during the summer of 1968. Our goal was to discover ways to diminish we-they feelings and to establish other loyalties which would, at least transiently, overarch in-group loyalties. Since we wished group members to develop alternative perspectives on the conflict situation, we sought to involve each as much as possible in interactions with a member of the countergroup. Accordingly, we paired roommates across group lines; we structured exercises so as to have members of one group act (and be reacted to) as alter egos for members of the countergroup, at specified points in the experience; and we held agendaless dialog sessions throughout. For evaluation of in-process effects, we tried to establish criteria of change which will be detailed below.

As this pilot investigation was launched, a year had passed since the Six-day War in June 1967. The hopes of the Israelis for a cessation of Arab hostility and for peace were shattered by continuing enmity on all fronts. Arab terrorism through El Fatah and other Arab groups was beginning to take a toll in lives, and the earlier professions of magnanimity among the Israeli population were becoming rare. Even before the war, the Arab-Israeli conflict was considered to be one of the most flammable in the world. Arab-Jewish competition over territory is interlaced with differences in religion, world outlook, life style, and temperament. Because armed conflicts had been so visible, the problem of creating understanding between Israeli Arabs and Jews within Israel itself had been obscured. Foreign pressures deterred many Arabs from making friendly contact with Israelis. For others, there were few communication channels outside the government and military establishments.

The project involved training programs for mixed groups of Israeli-Jews and Israeli-Arabs, one in Jerusalem and one in Haifa. The Hebrew University in Jerusalem and officials of the Arab-Jewish community center in Haifa aided in recruiting participants. There were eleven participants in the Jerusalem group; ten in the Haifa group. Because we were obliged to accept any who were willing to come from among those who had been invited, the groups could not be matched. The Jewish participants in Jerusalem were all

Reprinted from Martin Lakin, *Interpersonal Encounter: Theory and Practice in Sensitivity Training* (New York: McGraw-Hill, 1972) 249-276. Used with permission of McGraw-Hill Book Co.

	Age	Occupation

Jerusalem Series

Arab Participants

Gamal	24	student
Ibrahim	55	public official
Yussef	39	student
Amin	27	law student
Rashid	42	bank clerk

Jewish Participants

Yaron	23	student
David	21	student
Moshe	25	student
Nahum	24	student
Aharon	24	student
Mordecai	25	student

Haifa Series

Arab Participants

Abdul	34	lawyer
Saoud	26	teacher
Omar	37	public official
Hemdi	29	teacher
Abdullah	39	government worker

Jewish Participants

Dov	67	government official (retired)
Amiram	47	professor
Yaakov	50	businessman
Shmuel	49	educator, social worker
Natan	42	community center director

Figure 6.3

Description of participants in Arab-Jewish training groups in Israel

students and were less mature than the Arabs; in the Haifa group, this was reversed. The living arrangement in Jerusalem allowed for cross-ethnic pairing of roommates; the Haifa participants returned to their own homes in the evenings. The training design included (1) pretraining measures of participants' perceptions and anticipations; (2) the dialog; (3) skill-training exercises designed to improve communication in specific areas, including a cross-group project; and (4) posttraining assessment. A description of the participants, recording ethnicity, age, and occupation, appears in Figure 6.3. All were male.

On their arrival, participants were presented with two open-ended questions and a short sentence-completion form, and they were requested to describe any problem they had ever experienced with an Arab or Jew. The questions were (1) What do you expect to happen this week? and (2) What are your feelings upon entering this experience? The sentence completion items were (1) As an Arab one would feel . . . , (2) As a Jew one would feel . . . , (3) When I think about Israel, I . . . , (4) When I think about Arab states, I . . . , and (5) Arabs and Jews . . .

The problem description was as follows: "Describe one problem incident in the past six months involving yourself and Jews (Arabs). This should be a problem in which there was an emotional involvement for you and in which you were not fully satisfied with the outcome. What was the situation? What happened? What led up to it? How did it end? Can you think of ways you might have acted to change the outcome? What ways?

The questionnaire and sentence-completion responses indicated that Jews and Arabs came with different expectations. The Arabs hoped to inform the world through their participation, to tell their story, whereas the Jews sought to understand the Arab mind or to come to know Arabs as persons as a means of decreasing hostility.

AN INTERGROUP DIALOG

The dialog group met for several hours daily over a period of six days, and participants were free to structure it as they wished. The trainer's emphasis on inquiry into group process was intended to train participants to be sensitive to the effects of their own communication and to distinguish between debate and fruitful exchange. The participants were encouraged to think of themselves as potential moderators of such groups and to learn what they could from these procedures to enable them to fulfill such a role. The participants' facility with English was uneven, and at times they lapsed into their native languages (Hebrew or Arabic). The sense, if not the style, of each participant's contribution is reflected in the excerpts I have chosen to illustrate the dialog. The excerpts illustrate the problems in communication between these people and the issues to be worked through in the future.

The dialog took place, it will be recalled, under the tense conditions of neither full-scale war nor peace settlement. Arab national feeling had been rekindled by contact between these Israeli-Arabs and their relatives, who were allowed freedom of movement by Israeli authorities. The Arabs were suspicious and angry, the Israelis frankly distrustful. The Arabs bitterly complained they were not trusted (which was essentially correct; they weren't), despite their demonstrations of loyalty (some had given blood or had volunteered to help in agricultural settlements). The Jews acknowledged the mistrust and sought to explain its basis—the multiple Arab states, most hostile to Israel—and pointed to their own efforts to maintain friendly relations with the Arabs.

The opening session had been taken up with a good deal of parrying with the trainer and with each other over the demands of the schedule, which the Arabs complained were excessive. They were ultimately joined in this by the Jews, and both groups appeared delighted to join together against the trainer in negotiating for shorter hours. Let us tune in at a point where this cohesion seems to have been established, but where the trainer first begins to query the basis for it.

Trainer: How come the schedule problem came up as the first thing?

David: I don't know if it is the most important problem, but we have to settle this in order to go further.

Gamal: Through talk on the schedule, we came to know each other, and we will be interested to see in the future if the same people disagree with each other like on this topic.

David: The problem is we do not know what we are supposed to do. What do you think is the purpose of these two groups meeting here?

Yussef: Let us not consider ourselves as two different groups, Jews and Arabs. We are all citizens of Israel. We are only one group and one team working together.

Aharon: But I think that there are different opinions here.

Yaron: (To Yussef) What makes you fight so much for the idea that we are one group?

Yussef: Let me ask a question. Do you think that Arabs and Jews have different opinions?

Rashid: Am I speaking to Jews as a whole or am I talking to a person who is a Jew? I am Rashid, born in Jaffa, a Moslem, and I am Rashid, a complicated package. (Laughter.) I am not talking for the Arabs.

Yussef: He is talking as an individual and not as an Arab.

Gamal: (To Nahum) How can you ask him to talk for all the Arabs? Maybe I don't agree with him. You don't know if I agree or disagree with him.

Rashid: You are here as a person, you represent your ideas and I represent my ideas and no more.

Moshe: But a person also represents his background and history. I represent myself, but also the Jews here.

(Silence.)

David: Yussef gave the signal when he said we are one group and not two groups. He gave a signal not to discuss our differences.

Yaron: The thing is that Yussef tried to avoid a discussion of the problem that we are all thinking about.

Rashid: What's this about a problem? There is no problem! Say that there is a question to discuss and don't say that there is a problem. If you make everything a problem, then my existence here will also be a problem!

(Cries of "no, no!" "Let it be called 'subject' and not a 'problem'!")

Yaron: I think it is a problem...

When we consider this segment of dialog, we see that the Arabs who speak take a rather surprising line. They insist that "we are all Israelis here," and that "we have no problems." The Jews, by contrast, want to tackle the issues they came to deal with—issues between the peoples. Why do the Arabs identify themselves as Israelis quite so determinedly at this point? Why do they insist that there are no problems? Indeed, they appear allergic to the word "problem"! By the same token, they point out that they do not speak for other Arabs. The answers to these questions may be in the ramifications of the issue of trust. The Arabs were themselves mistrustful of each other as well as of the Jewish participants. The next segment illustrates how complex this mistrust is. It has an almost bizarre climax as one Arab, after accusing another of being a plant, discloses that he himself recommended the latter's selection for participation.

> **Gamal:** (Suspicious of selection procedures) And that is how most...that is how some of our friends are here. Some got invitations from the Prime Minister's office. All the Arab friends got such invitations, and I am asking, does this throw any light on the direction of the discussion that will be held here?
>
> **Trainer:** Aren't we really exploring how far Gamal trusts others here?
>
> **Moshe:** Maybe he is afraid of what...that whatever he says will be held against him.
>
> **Rashid:** Gamal, what do you think? You are not telling us. What are your fears or thoughts? What don't you want us to discuss?
>
> **Gamal:** I can only talk for myself, and I will tell you that I will not be afraid to say anything that I feel.
>
> **Amin:** Ah, very good.
>
> **Aharon:** I think that the problem is, "Can we rely on each other?" We know that we can rely on (trainer), but we don't know that we can rely on each other.
>
> **Yaron:** Gamal didn't yet tell exactly what he thinks. Do you think that most of the people here will express only positive ideas toward the state of Israel?
>
> **Gamal:** Let me give you a concrete example. Take the Six-day War. Some people might think that the Israeli-Arabs should have intervened in the war against Israel.
>
> **Ibrahim:** This is hypothetical only! Right?
> (Laughter.)
>
> **Yaron:** Gamal, you said that you were chosen instead of somebody from the Communist party. Why do you think that this happened?
>
> **Mordecai:** Do you think the Prime Minister's office is afraid of something?
>
> **Gamal:** I can assure you that they are.

Yussef: I think we are jumping from point to point.

Aharon: I think we are following a certain logic. We start out with the schedule, and then how we are selected and we are coming nearer to the problem we want to talk about.

Yaron: (To Gamal) Do you have any basis for saying that the Arab members here will not express their opinions openly?

Gamal: I know some other Arab students who have different ideas.

Yaron: I hope you won't hesitate to tell those ideas that you know about.

Gamal: Well, we will see in the discussion. For instance, I know many Arab students that are saying that the solution is to take all the Jews and ship them to Uganda.

(Shouts of protest, especially from the Arabs. "No, No! That's not true; that's not true, you are talking nonsense!")

Amin: I don't think Arabs say that!

Ibrahim: I think that you are extremely wrong, extremely wrong!

Amin: Is this your idea?

Gamal: No, it is not.

Rashid: You are not a megaphone for ideas of others, are you?

Yaron: He himself has certain ideas that he knows he will not express in this setting.

Amin: Is he threatened?

Yaron: I don't know. But whatever we hear from him, I think, will be more positive about Israel and the Jews than what he really believes.

Gamal: Oh, yes, I will say what I think, but many are afraid to say what they think!

Amin: Gamal, I want you to tell why you raise this question. Speak frankly!

Mordecai: Who selected you, on what criteria were you selected?

Gamal: I don't know, I don't know.

Ibrahim: Selected or not selected, everybody can say whatever he wants.

Amin: Open and frankly!

Ibrahim: I never said I was coming here to be a parrot.

Amin: Believe me, I don't know who recommended me.

Gamal: (To Amin) I recommended you.

Amin: You recommended me?

(Silence.)

Finding that the level of trust among themselves is so low consternates the members so that they seek a breather while they collect themselves. A poll of the group by the trainer elicits brave assertions of trust and con-

fidence in everyone present, which cannot have been sincere. More revealing of their actual lack of confidence in face-to-face confrontation is that
they seek for safer topics. One that is almost accepted is the then-current
police-student confrontations and rioting in Paris! The here-and-now is
almost jettisoned in favor of the there-and-then; i.e., the escape hatch
would be to discuss other people's troubles, outside the dialog room.

Eventually, of course, the focus returns, as it must, to the central concern of these two groups about the fears and suspicions which divide them.
We pick up the dialog where the issue of army service for Arabs has
become focal as an illustration of the mistrust toward them. (On account of
the unique situation of Israeli-Arabs, with their kinsfolk serving in hostile
armies on Israel's borders, they are not obligated to military service, as are
other citizens of the state.)

> **Moshe:** I want to ask a question. Ibrahim said that he wants
> rights, and he also mentioned duty. I want to consider the
> duties. Would you go and serve in the Israeli army?
>
> **Amin:** We anticipated this question! We anticipated this
> question!
>
> **Rashid:** Let me answer, let me answer.
>
> **Ibrahim:** I'll answer, I'll answer.
>
> (There is joking in Arabic among the Arabs. This makes the
> Jewish participants uneasy, since they become very serious
> about this issue.)
>
> **Ibrahim:** Is your government ready to send us to fight?
>
> **Yaron:** Are you ready to fight?
>
> **Ibrahim:** I asked you first.
>
> **Moshe:** Look what he is doing. He is answering by asking
> questions! I don't know whether the government of Israel will
> accept you or not, but I am ready to send you to fight!
>
> **Ibrahim:** I want to know what the government thinks about
> this. I think there should be one law for all citizens. If the
> government would have asked me to fight, I would have gone.
> They didn't ask me or other Arabs because it was for their
> benefit not to ask; or maybe it was for our benefit. The fact is
> that I am rejected. If I am asked to fulfill my duty, I shall fulfill
> it.
>
> **Moshe:** Look, I know a lot of Arab students and most of them
> said that they wouldn't fight in the Israeli army.
>
> **Gamal:** Who said this? How many students have you met
> that said that they won't go to serve in the army? Nahum here
> won't go either.
>
> **Moshe:** Gamal, don't compare Nahum with the Arabs who
> don't want to fight. He is a pacifist. The Arabs are not pacifists.
> You have families over there.
>
> **Rashid:** Can my son become a pilot? That is his dream. He

would like to fly an airplane. He tells me, "Father, I want to be
a pilot." Can my son be a pilot in Israel? If you answer "yes," I
will send him to the army. If you cannot answer "yes," ask
yourselves if you give him full rights. Are the Jews trusting the
Arabs? Ask yourself that!

    Yaron: I want to answer you!

    Rashid: Don't answer me. Ask yourselves!...

    Yaron: I want to say that the distrust between Jews and
Arabs is natural. I wouldn't accept Arabs in the army although
personally I trust Amin.

    Ibrahim: Amin and not Ibrahim?

    Yaron: I mean that I can't trust Arabs as a whole. I couldn't
trust them to enter the army. I could never believe that an Arab
would fight another Arab; therefore, I wouldn't trust them in
the army either.

The question-and-answer format—the charges, denials, and coun-
tercharges—seems to be heading in a fruitless direction, so Mordecai tries
to change the subject. But he hasn't reckoned on the investment of affect
built up in an emotionally charged topic. It serves as an opportunity to take
readings on each one's feelings about the state of the group.

    Mordecai: Why do we become so emotional? I believe the
main difficulty is the relationship between Arabs and Jews. The
army question is only something derived from it. You, Ibrahim,
won't convince me, and I won't convince you. All that happens
is that you get very emotional. (Pause.) Let's talk about Arab
students in the university.

(Calls from all around, "You are suggesting a different topic!
That's another issue! No! No!")

    Yaron: Ibrahim, do you mind if we continue to talk about
this?

    Ibrahim: I don't mind at all.

                         (Silence.)

    Rashid: It is quiet but not peaceful.

(Laughter, then extended silence again. Trainer says that in the
previous talk participants didn't distinguish between debate
and communication.)

    Trainer: Are we satisfied about the previous discussion?

    Nahum: At the beginning I was interested, but later on
everybody stated things that we already know.

    Ibrahim: It is natural that some people lose their patience,
but I am satisfied.

    Amin: For me the discussion is interesting and I am satisfied.

    Rashid: I am satisfied. I think we are deepening our un-
derstanding and talking freely about important problems.

    Moshe: I think our comprehension and understanding are

greater. I want to make two points. First of all, I think we have progressed since yesterday; second of all, I think everyone wants to state his own view. It might be that the next step will be a sense of dialog.

The issue of loyalty or disloyalty, now out in the open, has marshaled primary group loyalties. Personal emotional reactions are admixed with group political standpoints. Yaron confesses his own mixed feelings and reveals how his attitude is influenced by, but differs from, his mother's hostile one. The personal elements become submerged in polemics on both sides. The Arabs once again charge the Jews with unfairly limiting their freedom of movement, with inflicting indignities on them, while the Jews recall Arab student taunts and threats about how the Arab armies would drive the Jews into the sea and destroy the state.

The discussion grows sharper and more acrimonious. It shifts from abstract issues of loyalty to alleged instances of spying and sabotage. The shadow of collective guilt and collective responsibility hangs over the dialog. Actually the members act upon the assumption that each Jew and each Arab represents all Jews or all Arabs. The Israelis are challenged by the Arabs to indicate what territories they will yield in return for a peace settlement, and each Jewish member is interrogated as though he could answer for the government of Israel. By the same token, in the arguments over loyalty and the reasons for mistrust, the Jews query each Arab present as though he represented all Arabs. Let us again enter into the dialog room and follow the verbatim discussion.

> **Moshe:** The fact is that in the last year, two Arab students were found guilty of spying. My initial attitude is to trust, but you aren't making things easier for me. One of them was my friend. I had never suspected him. Till now, I didn't see much effort on the Arab side. What are the Arab-Israelis doing in order to reach peace?
>
> **Mordecai:** We heard from Moshe that he was very astonished that his classmate was accused of being a spy. What causes the Jewish students to suspect Arab students?
>
> **Ibrahim:** They are thinking according to their feelings and sentiments and not according to their common sense. There were some Arab spies caught, but there were also Jewish spies. One shouldn't generalize from then to the total population. For example, if my twenty-year-old son is picked up by the police for belonging to El Fatah, it doesn't mean that I, as his father, am to blame.
>
> **Yaron:** Parents, especially until a certain age, are always responsible for children.
>
> **Ibrahim:** Not in our days! The same overgeneralization applies when one student at the university tells a girl that she has to learn to swim because the Arabs will occupy the country. You say that all the Arabs hate this country.

(Angry arguments in Hebrew and Arabic; statements that the topic is exhausted are countered by assertions to the contrary. There is a request to play back some of the foregoing discussion. Fifteen minutes is played back.)

Ibrahim: I see that a year has passed since the Six-day War, and we didn't come closer to peace. Some say we should keep all the occupied areas. They base this on what they call the "original Israel." Others say we should retreat, but have some boundary changes. Still others say that we shouldn't do anything at all until the Arabs proclaim peace agreements. Others talk about the possibility of creating a new Palestinian state on the western bank of the Jordan. I would like to ask your opinions.

Moshe: What is your opinion, Ibrahim?

Yussef: He asked you first.

Rashid: Let us hear what Mordecai thinks. What are Mordecai's opinions?

Mordecai: The question for me is acceptance of the state of Israel. To tell you the truth, I don't know if Herzl did right in rejecting a British suggestion for Uganda as a state for the Jewish people. However, this was rejected. I was born here, raised here, fought here, and I feel this is my homeland. I personally am tired of fighting. (Mordecai had been wounded in the war.) I want to keep on living. The Arabs should recognize my right to exist. I realize that the Arabs will not be ready to make a peace agreement and leave us in the occupied areas and essentially I am not...I wouldn't argue for keeping them. I am willing to give back all of it. All I want to do is to live in this country which is my homeland, to live here in peace, and be secure. I am sick and tired of killing. Jerusalem should be under Jewish rule but there should be special guarantees and special rights for the other religions. I don't trust Syria; therefore, I agree with the Defense Minister, Dayan, that we should not give back Golan Heights.

Moshe: I believe that Arab citizens of Israel are equally interested in peace coming to this area. One should realize that after the Six-day War, things have changed. The Arab countries must realize this. I think we should keep everything until we go to the table to negotiate. I don't believe we could give back everything. Jerusalem is not negotiable. Regarding the Golan Heights, the Syrian government hasn't said a word. Therefore, we just keep them until they start talking. It might be a demilitarized zone. I agree with my government's policy.

Rashid: It is not so clear. The government itself gives different opinions regarding the borders.

Amin: I have no opinions on this point.

Yaron: Wait a minute. You are not sure about it, or you don't have any opinion?

Mordecai: He just waits.

Rashid: It may be that he really doesn't have an opinion on this.

Amin: I said that I don't have an opinion on this subject!

Yaron, Mordecai and Moshe: We don't believe you!

Moshe: Actually, we can't trust you.

Yussef: Perhaps later he will express his opinion.

Nahum: What interests me most is the feeling and aspirations of the Arabs in the occupied areas. I hear talk about a Palestinian state, and I wonder if they really want it...

Midway through the sessions on June 5, which was the first anniversary of the war's beginning, the discussions had become sequences of angry recriminations. The announcement of the assassination of Robert F. Kennedy had a profound effect. Discussion became more somber, and as it continued, the spectre of continuous and unremitting warfare against Israel was raised by the Arabs. The ominous quality of the interaction was underscored by an outburst by Amin which continued as a military jet flew overhead. Moshe is speaking as we follow the discussion:

Moshe: We heard everyone, but Amin didn't want to talk.

Amin: I think that peace is very, very far from us. For a number of reasons. First of all, the coexistence of Jews and Arabs in this state is Gamal's dream only.

Yussef: What?!

Ibrahim: Are you saying it is a dream?

Amin: (As he goes on, he talks louder till he shouts.) It is a dream! It sure is a dream! Arab nationalism cannot exist together with Jewish Israelis. (Caustically) Israel declares, "We want peace, but Jerusalem we can never give back. The Gaza Strip never was legally Egyptian territory; therefore, it is now ours. The Golan Heights is too dangerous to give up. In the West Bank, we need security." If I am saying all those things, how can I expect the other person to talk peace with me? Israel says she will enter direct negotiations, but it seems to me the person who really wants peace, seeks peace in all ways. I am not saying that the Arab leaders' attitudes are good, but I, as an Israeli, want to gain peace. From the conditions we are putting forward now, one can be sure that peace will never come. The Arab attitude is, "What has been taken by force will be liberated by force." We are very, very far from a peace settlement. I said what I think.

(The other Arabs nod and agree emphatically.)

Rashid: You are right!

(The noise of jet fighters almost drowns out the discussion.)

Amin: We are speaking about peace, and war is over our head!

Yaron: Do you want to hear me now? When the Jordanians occupied the old city of Jerusalem, they made roads through Jewish cemeteries and holy places. The monuments were taken to build army camps. Synagogues were used as stables. That is why the Old City will never be given back.

Ibrahim: Yaron, I agree with you, but the government of Israel did similar things.

Rashid: They destroyed an Arab cemetery in Tel Aviv to build a hotel.

(Shouting and argument, accusations of "lies.")

Ibrahim: The Hilton Hotel in Tel Aviv is built on an Arab cemetery! A mosque is used for a stable for horses.

Moshe: I don't believe you.

Ibrahim: I can take you now in a taxi at my expense to show you. And you will see in another mosque they are selling alcohol. Near Haifa they also built a settlement for new immigrants on an Arab cemetery.

(Pause.)

Yaron: If you transfer someone's bones from one grave to another, it is not really insulting.

Rashid: But the people didn't agree to this transfer!

Yaron: There is a High Court of Justice, and if the court decided to give permission, then it seems reasonable.

Ibrahim: You want to go according to the law? Have you gone to the High Court of Justice to appeal the annexation of the Old City of Jerusalem?

Symbols of national pride and religious loyalties are invoked to recall injustices and indignities on both sides. When the Jews complain that access had been barred to the Old City of Jerusalem and its historic Wailing Wall, that their ancient cemeteries had been desecrated, the Arabs responded by bitterly listing graveyards which had been displaced to make room for modern hotels. More rational members of the groups see the fruitlessness of this line of accusations and counteraccusations and try to redirect it.

The discussion switches to considerations of process, with the help of the trainer, i.e., of where the group stands in terms of its capacities for communication. It is agreed that truth and frankness have become greater, but it seems unclear where greater truth will lead. Indeed, it is feared that it could lead to even more intense feelings of antagonism and thence to violence, as we see from the following segment.

Mordecai: Yaron, he is right! You have to agree.

Moshe: Yaron, I think that you shouldn't argue here. We heard some facts that we didn't know.

David: Yaron, of all the important things that Ibrahim

brought up while talking for ten minutes, you picked up graveyards! The one point that you picked up is very emotional and you have aroused everybody's emotions. This won't get us anywhere, so just leave it!

Moshe: But many holy places are not used for a long time already!

Ibrahim: (Screaming) Does it become less holy? If we want to change holy places, we Moslems should change it, not you!

Trainer: Process is a little tense, right? (Agreement from all sides.) We have another ten minutes; we would certainly want to look at this process, because we all saw that we had some difficulties in communication.

Ibrahim: Here and now and now and then! (Laughter.)

Nahum: I think that communication is worse now. Trust and frankness are higher. I don't think anybody has changed his ideas, and I don't expect that in a few days we would have changed them. I myself may have listened to certain ideas which in the future might influence thinking and maybe bring me to some change, but not at this point.

Aharon: I think that our communication is better, but together with that more difficulties arise because suddenly you have got people jumping on words and getting overemotional.

Gamal: The communication becomes better, but still there are ups and downs. There is a principle at stake and we stick to it. The level of frankness seems to be increased. I don't think that there is any change of ideas.

The dialog continues through more confrontations. There are also lighter moments and even signs of agreement or at least mutual understanding on some issues. The talk that takes place is shaped not only by the intense feelings on the issues between them as peoples, but also by extrinsic factors such as the mood in the country as reflected in the media at that time. Thus the undercurrents of violence on the anniversary of the war and the shock waves of the assassination of R. F. Kennedy had effects upon the group process.

The reader will recall that specific exercises were deliberately employed for the overall purpose of empathy training and in an effort to bridge the intergroup gulf. These exercises were, of course, intended to affect the process of the group in conflict-ameliorating ways. Let us consider these in some detail, to see how they were applied and how well they worked.

Skill Development in Intergroup Communication. Skill sessions were intended to elicit empathic reactions and to improve communication. Participants were asked to identify with one member of the countergroup in a variety of exercises and to restate his views and feelings to his satisfaction. An example of such an exercise is one where a Jew is asked to express his ideas on Arab-Jewish relations to an Arab listener who must help him express his views as well as his underlying thoughts and feelings. Their interactions, viewed by two observers (one Arab, one Jew), are fed back in the form of process reactions. The roles are then rotated, giving each participant a chance to practice being a speaker, a listener, and an observer.

Another skill-training device was the cluster, in which paired participants observed and coached each other in interaction. Half the group sat in a circle; the other half made a larger circle around them. Each person seated on the periphery observed a designated partner in the inner circle. The purpose was to develop skills in observing and in helping a person communicate more effectively. Cluster feedback resulted in some changes in mode of participation in the dialog sessions.

Team Proposals for Conflict Resolution. An effort was made to build cross-ethnic teams. These teams were asked to develop specific proposals for improving Arab-Jewish relations in Israel, which were presented to the total group for critique. The aim was primarily to substitute team competition for intergroup competition and to practice cross-group collaboration (rather than the creation of feasible plans).

Team Proposal Evaluation. The project provided an opportunity for collaborative involvement for which participants in both series were eager, partly because of the frustration of so many preceding negative exchanges. Subgroup cohesion was replaced temporarily by team cohesion, but this resulted in much intrasubgroup hostility; that is, subgroup members became more critical of one another. Though there was a breakup of the prior unyielding division between the Arabs and Jews, competitiveness between the mixed teams developed an emotionalism of its own as intense as any aspect of the intergroup communication. One by-product of the cross-group exercise was that group boundaries became less distinct in the minds of some participants. These individuals therefore took risks of "trespass," i.e., agreeing with the positions of the other group which elicited furious censure from their own group. The advantage to collaboration gained from a mixed team project increased a concern about disloyalty, i.e., deviation from some implicit in-group norm or policy.

If we view interethnic team construction as one part of the task, the other (in which little progress may be claimed) was to get participants to accept a norm of nonpunitiveness for deviations from accepted group policy. The threat of in-group sanctions fostered aggressive and regressive behavior. This was apparent in both series, but particularly in Jerusalem, where obvious rivalry for leadership, personal squabbles, obdurateness, and uncontrolled shouting during the project reached higher levels than at any other time in the dialog sessions.

We drew some tentative conclusions about requirements for the success of such a project: (1) It should not arouse excessive competitive feelings among the in-group; (2) The participants should have positive conviction about its desirability; (3) A specific project should be within bounds of the expertise at hand; and (4) A norm of allowing in-group policy deviation should be fostered to encourage openness to new possibilities.

The actual proposals developed ranged from general suggestions to detailed plans; all aimed at ensuring the participation of Arabs at all levels of community life and government. They included such things as integrated schools in mixed centers of population, teacher training toward a joint curriculum, the establishment of more Arab-Jewish community centers, integrated housing schemes, competence in Arabic for all teachers and civil servants, enlisting the mass media in public education to improve intercommunal relations, and making Arabic the official second language of the state.

To assess effects of the training design, we tallied instances of key behaviors and recurrent themes, asked for sociometric ratings, and administered projective tests and posttraining interviews. We also observed interactions during meals and recreation periods. One of the investigators, acting as observer and process recorder, counted instances of the following behaviors during dialog sessions in order to assess changes in the participants' modes of communicating with one another along the following dimensions: hostility, affection, guardedness, trust, humor, specificity, and polemics.

These dimensions were used as indicators of change in the atmospheres of the groups. I have presented excerpts from the Jerusalem group, and some "feel" for that group may have been generated by the segments of dialog. The Haifa group differed in certain important respects—age and maturity—and had only half the number of sessions that the Jerusalem group had. Its processes may be expected to reflect these differences. Let us see how the groups compared in relation to the aforestated dimensions.

Hostility. Despite professions of friendships and unity, mainly by Arabs, hostile statements increased steadily and peaked on the third and fifth days in the Jerusalem group. Arab hostile statements were collective—aimed at all the Jews. After the second day, Jews began to respond in kind. In the Haifa group, whereas hostility was high initially, it diminished sharply as it progressed. It is noteworthy that the quality of the interactions differed too. The Haifa group started by being much more direct and outspoken; this may have been a factor in the high-then-low hostility count.

Affection. Expressions of affection were sparse in both groups. Playful slaps, friendly teasing, and supportive remarks took place more frequently outside sessions than in them. The Arabs' insistence in the Jerusalem group that "There is no problem!" and "We are all one group!" seemed to raise tension rather than reduce it. In Haifa, where hostilities had been more openly acknowledged from the beginning, outside-the-group affection steadily increased. In both groups it is noteworthy that signs of affection were mainly from more youthful participants toward the elders of the countergroup.

Guardedness. As trust rose gradually, guardedness diminished correspondingly. In the Jerusalem group, guardedness sharply escalated, however, on the war's anniversary date. Arabs were generally more guarded than Jews in both groups; however, in Haifa the Jews seemed protective toward and understanding of the Arabs' concern about confidentiality.

Trust. Trust was difficult to identify in both groups, as it was indicated only subtly, in more accepting statements by countergroup members or in less tension. Our tally did not reflect the signs of increasing trust for both groups in those interactions which took place outside dialog sessions.

Humor. It was difficult to discriminate whether some humorous remarks really belonged in the category of "hostility." Humor was caustic in the main and seemed to occur most frequently in the Jerusalem group. In Haifa it was restricted to in-between periods or free time, when personal talk and gossip also flowed freely. In the Jerusalem group humor decreased as time went on. Joking among the Arabs was largely political and in-group in character. Jokes were carefully translated at first so that all could understand, but later they did not bother to explain the Arabic. At the time we speculated that Haifa participants needed less humor because they were less guarded and/or less hostile to each other.

Specificity. Most assertions or questions were addressed to the groups in general even where they seemed to be directed to specific individuals. Comments by Jewish participants were more often to a specific person at the beginning in both groups, but they ended up being directed to all Arabs. Arabs addressed their comments to all Jews, but they used their Jewish colleagues as listeners and even addressed them individually, as though a conversation were being held. We concluded that the global responses of both groups were essentially position statements. In this neither group showed a positive change.

Polemics. The dimension of polemics is related to the foregoing one and shows the same pattern. The general form of communication was in fact polemical. Speeches drew rebuttals. Trainer interventions intended to focus upon communication processes were resented. Indeed, to offset his purpose in Jerusalem, "chairmen" were used (in each case an Arab), and they encouraged rhetoric by giving turns for speeches. In retrospect it is understandable that polemics were so frequent. They are cathartic, establish in-group loyalties and policies more clearly, and comprise attempts to score points in verbal competition. It is noteworthy that by contrast with Jerusalem, polemics in Haifa were issue-specific and were less associated with hostility.

Certain themes were recurrent in the discussions, exercises, and free periods. The Arabs wanted to air grievances and to use the exchange as a means of achieving redress. While the Jewish participants were more diverse in their motives, their common theme was the desire to conciliate the Arabs. Although the Arabs disclaimed a unanimity of viewpoints, the patterns of their complaints were almost identical. They resented being distrusted and all associated restrictions. There was no common positive policy among them on such issues as the question of an independent Arab Palestine, return of territories, or peace negotiations. The complaints, however, were domestic with irredentist overtones.

Jewish participants responded by attempting to rationalize restrictions as due to unremitting hostility by surrounding Arab states. They contended Arabs' rights had to be contingent on security considerations, and in explanation, pointed to the Arabs' kinships with hostile Arabs beyond the borders. When the Arabs complained of mistreatment, the Jews blamed it on those elements of the Jewish population whose enmity to Arabs stemmed from their memories of being terribly persecuted by Arabs.

The Jews' view of the Israeli-Arabs was, in fact, suspicious and distrustful. Although they had enormous self-confidence as a result of their military successes, moral aspects of Zionism did not permit casual indifference to the hardships of the Arabs. Two dilemmas were repeatedly apparent—how to be just while remaining strong, and how to diminish the suffering of innocent people resulting from the conflict of interests. Accommodating the Arabs, easing restrictions, and reducing suspicion, but without loss of security, were major preoccupations for the Jews, who were uncomfortable as victors who could not be magnanimous without endangering their survival.

For the most part, Arabs seemed to vacillate between passive resignation and active resistance. Repeated Arab references to the military and other masculine or martial aspects of the culture emphasized their feelings of impotence. They felt caught "between the anvil and the hammer," awaiting some ill-defined deliverance. The desire to pass, to be assimilated into Israeli culture and society, was hinted at by several Arabs. For them the dominant culture held some attraction. On the other hand, the frustration of this attraction and their own ambivalence fed their irredentist fantasies.

Free Interaction. In the Jerusalem group, there seemed to be a gentleman's agreement from the beginning to spend as much time as possible with members of the opposite group. Thus it was noted that most of the Arabs sat together in dialog sessions but mingled with Jews during free periods and at meals. As a matter of fact, the Arabs were careful to speak Hebrew at first and spaced themselves during meals so as to sit with Jewish participants. We took it as a sign of relaxation that they grew less self-conscious about cross-group seating—began to join each other freely and to joke in Arabic without bothering to translate.

Sociometric Choice. Three times in Jerusalem (days 1, 3, and 5) we were able to assess sociometric choices and shifts. These attributes were used: likeable, trustworthy, and wise. We wanted to see whether rankings would be along group lines or whether cross-group favorable rankings over the course of the experience would increase.

In both groups, the subgroups complimented each other by highly ranking other-group participants on likeability. Arabs became more popular for the Jewish participants over time. The Arabs appeared to agree with the Jews that the Arabs were the more likeable. The Arab elders, especially Ibrahim and Rashid, grew in popularity with the younger Jews.

The Jewish subgroup initially designated two Jews and one Arab as most trustworthy, two Arabs and one Jew as least trustworthy. Arabs also ranked a Jew first and an Arab lowest. Suspiciousness of one another's motives was marked among the Arabs from the outset. One Jew (Mordecai) and one Arab (Amin) were given low trustworthy rankings consistently. Moshe, who was early ranked high, was downgraded by the Arabs because he considered Arab society backward and justified preferential treatment for the Druze (a separatist sect which has ambivalent relations with Arabs). Nahum, low-ranked by Jewish participants as "Arabophile," was for this same reason highly regarded by the Arabs. In general Jews ranked their Arab roommates higher than they themselves were rated by Arab roommates.

The older Arabs were ranked highest on wise. The Jewish group apparently equated age with wisdom and gave the lowest rankings to their own younger fellows. In general, there was a tendency among the Arabs to give the noncombative Jewish participants higher rankings, which suggested a political criterion for "wise."

Thematic Apperception Results. In this procedure, the individual is asked to respond to a picture with an original story. The story reflects personal characteristics of the teller. Such responses are used to reveal personality factors. Our concern was not with personality per se, but to examine members' responses to the intergroup situation. After several days' interaction, participants were shown a picture of a group. Responses from all reflected the difficulties of communication; mutual suspicion was reported as the primary obstacle. The faces in the picture were carefully scrutinized for signs of hostility; the stories described strategy signals and antagonistic alignments. An underlying pessimism regarding the possibility of communication was revealed in statements such as, "There is no communication," "The Arab does not agree," "He is afraid to give in," "They are afraid of this other side," or "His opinion will not be accepted." For most of the Arabs a positive outcome could result only from a judgment by some outside authoritative body (a judge who gives a just verdict). Jewish participants, although no more optimistic in their stories, were less bitter and showed fewer disorganized responses, and the conflicts they described were less intense.

Personal Problem Test. Participants were asked to use the same interpersonal problem they had described earlier and to state any differences in the way they now perceived the problem. The Arab participants in Jerusalem so disliked this exercise that we did not even attempt it in Haifa. We were able to obtain pre- and postresponses only from the Jewish participants. The following give an indication of the reactions: One reported that his prejudiced attitude was now apparent to him and that he would behave differently in the future. Another reported that he learned "better strategies of communication." But a third concluded gloomily, "I learned that things reach a certain point where neither side listens any longer. Continuing to argue beyond it only increases tension."

Evaluations by Participants. Each participant was asked to imagine how he might describe the training experience to a friend. The assessments of our participants are subject to the limitations of all self-reports. It may be that the slight changes in outlook reflected in these interviews should be dismissed as mere testimonials. On the other hand, slight alterations in one's perspective can have practical consequences. I shall present only two of these here. They have been edited for brevity and where the respondent's terms would be incomprehensible to the reader.

Gamal: This was a very interesting experiment. I think everybody came out with certain specific things. Some of us have negative opinions about the others. I don't say hate . . . on the other hand, I won't say I am very fond of . . . any . . . (What do you mean?) Well, take Amin, I had the opinion that he is pompous. He really got on my nerves. I just couldn't tolerate him. His behavior was childish. Well, maybe I am more pessimistic about the Arab members. I figured that they might be too worried to come out frankly. Things were so, in the beginning, but then they were very frank. (How do you feel about the experience?) Well, I think it was a success because it really became a group. In the subgroups, the lines of division were only according to the issue. Personally I have also learned to look rationally at things and not so much from an emotional point of view. I thought I wouldn't be so frank, but I was frank here. However, my opinions about Arab-Jewish relations and problems haven't changed. You can't change attitudes of Arabs and Jews by having those kinds of discussions. Everyone sticks to his guns. The discussion here was mainly an outlet for emotions. This is a catharsis. You didn't train people to accept other points of view. Maybe you trained them to listen, but you didn't train them to change their views. What happened here is a compartmentalization. You see, the Jews say to themselves, "These are not Arabs, but this is Yussef, and this is Rashid" and so on.

Yaron: It was a surprise to me to find out that there is a serious problem of Israeli-Arabs. Most Israelis really don't think about it at all. I just read something in the paper that an Arab was hit in Natanya and so on; it is gone after I finish reading it, I don't think about it any more. What I really needed was a real push to make me aware . . . For myself, I can tell you that up till now I had a very superficial approach to Arabs in Israel. I looked upon Arabs in Israel as close to the Arab states around us, and I really didn't believe that they want to be loyal citizens. I thought that they were quiet and don't rebel just because they don't want trouble. I heard Rashid, for instance, talking about army service as a right. Or when he described how his village was bombed by Arab planes. We shouldn't raise two kinds of citizens. Those problems are

criteria for how one looks at the state. I don't think that my
views have changed. I have gotten a push to think from the information I have received here. (Have you learned anything
about yourself?) Sure, I tell you I am very intolerant. I just lose
my patience. And I express this impatience to the people in the
group who express their stupid views. But those people also
sense my attitude to them and realize that I am impatient
towards them . . . Another important lesson I have learned is
that people listen to you if you yourself really listen. Suddenly
you realize that your views are not so far from the other person
after all. I knew this before too, but again not as fully as I have
become aware of it in this experience here.

Some Problems in Intergroup Training. For the most part the Arabs
reported they were gratified by the opportunity to voice their complaints;
the Jews felt they had come to understand more about the Arabs' condition
and feelings. Most of the Jews had an abstract faith in the value of coming
to know the Arabs and in reducing tensions through mutual understanding. Some elements of the design were valued more. The
freewheeling dialog, with topics left to group choice, was easily understood,
but skill exercises were resisted. How may we account for this resistance?
It may be sheer suspicion of malevolent intent or feared consequences; on
the other hand, it could also be due to nonfamiliarity with a psychological
approach to problems.

"Psychological-mindedness" usually describes some habitual interest in
thinking about psychological factors, for example, viewing oneself with
some detachment and being curious about one's own response tendencies.
We did not see much evidence of this among these participants. Furthermore the issues that divided them were conflicts which have life-and-death
consequences. Thus it was difficult for them to achieve even a transitory
objectivity about these issues. In any event the skills associated with
psychological-mindedness—listening, empathy, sensitivity to the needs of
others—need to be developed over time. The trainer had to intervene firmly to turn participants' attention to process considerations: to how rather
than to what they were communicating. Listening for understanding rather
than listening to score debating points required repeated demonstration.

We ended our pilot groups by deciding that there were grounds for
further efforts along these lines, although these results could not be con-
clusive in any sense. We recommended training for personally effective
Arabs and Jews who hold key positions where cooperation is necessary for
the achievement of concrete goals. We hypothesized that key individuals
committed to cooperation would be better able to lead mutual cooperative
economic and social efforts on the basis of this kind of training experience.
If they were recruited on a team basis from recognized organizations and
could be trained with the assurance that their proposals would be actualized, their actions might increase the scope and impact of intercom-

munal cooperation. The form of the training would approximate the one we developed for the initial effort in that it would include dialog, skill training, exercises in communication, and a joint project for mixed teams of Jews have presented examples of the kinds of intergroup efforts that may be made using training methods or derivatives, it is important to assess the "state of the art." What has been established in this area, and what is still open to question? How should the training movement proceed in the area of intergroup conflict amelioration? Does it have a significant role to play, or are its efforts misguided or irrelevant to the serious quarrels among groups?

We appear to be on the threshold of training efforts to affect social problems. No effort in the area of sensitive and volatile group relationships should pass uninspected. This is perhaps one area in which the assessment of effects of training may not be premature. In other words, if it should be ascertained that more harm than good results from specific types of intergroup encounters—especially since we do not thoroughly understand the dynamics of such groups at this point—they should be processed through field experiments before being further applied.

It is easy to conceive that a training approach can produce an exchange of invectives and verbal assaults between already hostile groups, resulting in catharsis at best, or even in a worsening of relations. The catharsis aspect is an important element of conflict amelioration, but it is insufficient in itself. A pattern of assault and catharsis seems to repeat itself whenever representatives of a majority and a minority group in contention meet in verbal confrontations. The majority listens to the complaints or accusations of the aggrieved minority and responds with condescension, with veiled resentment, and frequently with guilt. We are, of course, talking about confrontations in which a modus vivendi is sought. Since there was a somewhat similar trend in the intergroup dialog just illustrated, one is tempted to speculate that contending groups generally take up psychological positions and roles relative to each other in terms of such majority-minority, dominant-submissive, oppressor-oppressed, powerful-weak, or some similar divisions. If such is the case, then the result of a confrontation which is only cathartic might be a confirmation of mutual antipathies or a feeling of release which ends at the close of the group sessions. The final result might be retrenchment in antagonism or a false and insincere propitiation. These are extreme possibilities, but the process of guilt induction may arouse anger as well as remorse.

In the present use of intergroup encounters, some sort of conciliation usually occurs, but no one knows whether such conciliations lead to actual cooperation under more conventional circumstances. There are instances where cooperation in areas of education and housing was impaired by mismanaged confrontations. One would want to check on subsequent results. In any event the goals of training in intergroup conflict should go beyond cathartic exchange. Clearly it is intended in all such approaches that members of one group should come to understand better the attitudes, feelings, and goals of members of the other group. Mere exchanges of intense feelings and mea culpas do not change the conflicts that exist. Collaboration in some joint concrete project seems promising, but even such collaboration necessitates a successful crossing of group boundaries which is sooner or later legitimated by the contending groups.

Why is such boundary crossing so delicate? In considering intergroup training experience, it is necessary to keep in mind that an individual's sense of esteem is partially, at least, based upon his identification with his group. Self-esteem is often purchased by the demonstration of group adherence, and that means keeping to group policies. Slogans, calls to self-sacrifice for the group's sake, and even normative changes in clothing or hairstyles establish group pride. Unfortunately feelings of satisfaction from mutual understanding with other groups are pallid by contrast. Even in an intergroup training experience designed to reduce intergroup tensions, it is often observed that a member clings to the very differences which define his membership in his own group but make it difficult to reach out to the other one. In an interethnic dialog, when cross-group alliances begin to develop, they threaten subgroup cohesion and thus shake the more fundamental loyalties of the person. Despite this obstacle, superordinate goals and loyalties need to be established for members of both groups to work toward. Unless these develop, preferably in the form of concrete tasks and actions, primary loyalties quickly reclaim their partisans.

Once again we must take note of a group effect which acts as a primary motivator. Cohesiveness, the strength of the bonds that unify a group, is also important in intergroup phenomena. The same process which gives the person a sense of belonging to a specific group is also an exclusionary phenomenon. ("We are in! They are out.") Thus, the élan developed by the spirit of togetherness and through loyalties to some group or social unit is furthered by differentiation from some other group. In such effects there is a troubling paradox for trainers. One works very hard to help group members develop the kind of group to which they can feel committed. Yet the dilemma for intergroup problems is that the valued group membership and belongingness may also constitute significant obstacles to intergroup cooperation where group identities depend upon exclusiveness or chosenness. Group self-definition typically becomes "they" exclusion.

It is an old story that hostilities and feelings of frustration find easier outlets against outgroup members. Some individuals even prefer a combative intergroup relationship with its characteristic tensions to calmer and less exciting interactions. Many persons feel at their best only when they are "on the barricades" in preparation for defense against attack. The problem for training is how to succeed in inducing the kinds of sensitivity and flexibility which are important for psychological approaches to intergroup conflict without sacrificing essential feelings of belongingness.

PROSPECTS FOR INTERGROUP TRAINING
IN CONFLICT AMELIORATION

To recapitulate, the use of training-derived techniques for conflict amelioration rests upon several assumptions. They are (1) Expression of true feelings leads to their detoxification. Cathartic release clears the air, creating the possibility for less hostile communication. (2) Honesty in communication will tend to go up between groups as a consequence of face-to-face interaction over time. (3) Perceptions of one another as differentiated human beings rather than the "they" opposed to the "we" will result from sharing and mutual disclosure. The exposure of stereotypes and being jarred loose from habitual perceptions parallel the destructuring, exposure, and feedback which generates novel perceptions in regular training groups.

Can one really adapt this model of learning to arenas where conflicts result from long-reinforced, mutually hostile imagery and deeply divided interests? We are left with the tentative conclusion that the characteristic confrontation and analytic procedures of the typical training experience are insufficient in themselves to ameliorate severe intergroup conflict. Other factors must also be taken into account. Among them are the motivations of the participants and their readiness to consider constructive collaboration rather than conflict. Their capacities to benefit from a training effort may be decisive. Some psychological mindedness (belief in the importance of understanding oneself and others and a willingness to learn new ways of doing so) is necessary, as we have seen. We could ask, do intergroup participants value objectification of the conflict and are they curious about their own parts in it? Willingness to explore one's own identification with his group is a motive which is not found in abundance among people. Perhaps this explains why not many people try to reach a better modus vivendi with an opposing group. Partly it is for fear of punishment from their own group, because to be objective and to attempt to understand the point of view of a rival group requires a unique willingness to risk in-group esteem. It is either a very strong individual or a very careless one who crosses group boundaries without apprehension.

"Understanding" in this area is an unsatisfactory term in the sense that it does not comprehend the kinds of acceptance and empathy required to ameliorate conflict. Similarity in attitudes does not prevent conflict. The most vicious warfare is often waged against those who are most similar in certain attitudes. Self-insight and insight into the other's group do not generate empathy unless they affect one's identification with one's own group or alter one's dependence for self-esteem upon one's membership in it.

What can be done to bring groups together for conflict diminution? The reader is reminded of the importance of an overarching or superordinate aim or goal for which they are willing to submerge their differences. The aim may be a negative one—such as fear of mutual destruction—or it may be the need to act jointly to avert some other catastrophe which will otherwise overwhelm them separately. The old and sad truth is that such common emergencies generate collaboration more quickly than the positive aims of improved standards, better services, or some other betterment of the common welfare. In any event whether the amelioration of conflict be positively or negatively motivated, what must be done is to reduce the salience of old boundaries and substitute new ones which either diminish or at least do not underscore the differences in interests between the previously quarreling groups.

In applying training and encounter methods to groups with a long history of quarrels, it is important to recognize that such barriers are deeply rooted in cultural practices. It is also important to realize that part of the self-esteem of a member of one group derives from putting down those of another group, particularly if the other group is either envied or greatly feared. As I have indicated above, one cannot hope to diminish intergroup tensions through the use of training-derived techniques without bringing into question one's adherence to one's own group. This arouses anxieties which not all members of a group are able to deal with. Unconditional affiliation reduces tensions, even if one's own group exhibits pathological behavior, whereas the anxieties of uncertainty about belonging are difficult to tolerate. Some individuals are more able than others to tolerate such anxiety in questioning their own group's position or actions. Why some individuals adapt to marginal status more easily than others, whether they are more secure or simply less stable, we do not know.

It may be that a democratic group tolerates marginal affiliation better than an authoritarian group. What kinds of societies allow their members to bridge intergroup cleavages, and what types of personalities are most able to do so? We know too little of the interaction of group parameters and personality factors. But we should know more about them in order to specify what effects can be expected from applications of training with various groups for ameliorating conflict.

A clearer, more accurate image of the other group probably does not in itself create sufficient conditions for acceptance and empathy. It might even become the justification for the statement, "I thought I disliked them because I didn't understand them; now that I understand them better, I hate them!" Obviously, such "understanding" will do little for intergroup collaboration. The research on cross-cultural contact has not been very reassuring for the hypothesis that contact per se enhances mutual acceptance and understanding. The commitment required from the contending parties has to be toward mutual benefit.

What is most needed at this time is careful experimentation and documentation of a number of conflict-amelioration training experiences and follow-up to see how graduates of such group experiences feel and act toward members of countergroups. I have reviewed some beginning efforts at intergroup conflict amelioration through uses of training methods or by techniques derived from such methods. While I cannot say that the situation calls for great optimism, I do not feel that such efforts should be abandoned. Our world is desperately in need of vehicles for increasing mutual understanding. Training initiatives offer us some hope; and while we may not proceed wishfully without scrutiny and evaluation, we cannot fail to try what methods we may devise or adapt from what we know of intragroup relations. What is of lasting and solid benefit will emerge from daring, but rigorous experimentation. Such experimentation should be well documented and take account of what is already known about group dynamics.

Having considered the possible potential of training methods for dealing with intergroup conflict, let us inquire into the future of the training movement and its methods. What does it offer in the years ahead? What is the prospect that it can be developed as a useful learning tool? Are there dangers involved in its spreading social applications? What can it mean for individuals in their daily lives and for smaller and larger groupings? The final chapter tries to put the purposes and practices of training into some perspective for the future, and asks the two-edged question, "What does the future hold for training, and what does training hold for the future?"

Small Group Dialog and Discussion: An Approach to Police-Community Relationships

ROBERT L. BELL, SIDNEY E. CLEVELAND,
PHILIP G. HANSON, & WALTER E. O'CONNELL

INTRODUCTION AND BACKGROUND
TO THE PROBLEM

There seems to be general agreement that the most pressing domestic problem confronting the country is that of rising urban tension. To a large degree urban tension, "The Urban Crisis," means increased friction between the city police force and segments of the black community. Resentments and frustrations nursed for years by the previously complacent black community find a target in the urban police force. Since for many members of minority groups, the police represent the status quo and all that is feared and hated in white society, it is the police officer who becomes the object of hostility whether deserved or not by his actual behavior. The President's Riot Commission report by the National Advisory Commission on Civil Disorders found that "almost invariably the incident that ignites disorder arises from police action."[1] Usually the police action giving rise to the outbreak of violence is in itself routine and innocuous, but for the black community it may symbolize a long history of injustice and legitimate grievances.

Until May 1967, Houston, Texas, the nation's sixth largest city, had enjoyed relative calm as far as any widespread racial disturbance was concerned. Although numerous incidents involving blacks and the police pointed to rising tension, no overt violence had erupted. But on May 16-17, 1967, four hours of gunfire occurred between the police and students at Texas Southern University, a predominantly Negro institution in Houston. One officer was killed by a bullet of undetermined origin. Student rooms and belongings were ransacked by the police, ostensibly in search of hidden weapons.

This incident alerted the city administration to the fact that a racial crisis was at hand. Many feared another Watts or Detroit. A study by Justice,[2] a psychologist, and an assistant to the mayor for race relations found that Negro antagonism toward the police had increased significantly over the pre-TSU riot period. A team of interviewers had studied attitudes of 1,798 Negroes from twenty-two different neighborhoods, concerning jobs, wages, the police, etc., prior to the TSU outbreak. Following the TSU incident the study was repeated in the same neighborhoods to assess attitudinal change. Results of these surveys indicated a significant rise in hostile feelings toward the police following the outbreak of violence.

Reprinted by special permission of *the Journal of Criminal Law, Criminology and Police Science*, copyright © 1969 by Northwestern University School of Law, (1969), 60:242-246.

The results of these surveys were influential in persuading the city administration that some type of educational or advisory program was needed to reduce existing tensions within the city. Originally the city advisors had in mind a lecture series on community relations to be presented to the police.

However a lecture series seemed inappropriate and ineffective since it provided no opportunity for badly needed exchange between the police and community. Instead a small group interaction program involving police and community members seemed more promising, since such a program would provide full opportunity for exchange of attitudes between officers and the participating community. Dr. Melvin P. Sikes,[3] then a clinical psychologist on the staff at the Houston VA Hospital, was asked to organize such a program.

Human relations training for police and community. The model employed to serve as a structural and procedural guideline in devising the police-community program was that provided by the Houston VA Hospital Human Relations Training Laboratory.[4] This Laboratory also supplied the police-community program with a majority of the professional group leaders with experience in human relations training.

The Houston VA Human Relations Training Laboratory applies the concepts and techniques of "T" group theory and sensitivity training to the problems of psychiatric patients. Departing from the traditional psychiatric treatment emphasis on the medical model, the Laboratory stresses a learning approach in the acquisition of new techniques to solve problems in living. Human relations training techniques have also been applied to the successful resolution of conflict between union and management groups, in community interracial strife, and in industry to cope with departmental friction. Accordingly it was felt that the human relations approach would be suitable for dealing with police-community relationships.

Program design and format. A series of human relations training laboratories were devised, each lasting six weeks with about two hundred police officers and an equal number of community members attending. The officers and citizens meet for three hours once a week over the six-week period. Approximately forty officers and community members are scheduled for a three-hour session each of the five work days. These officers and citizens are further divided into three smaller groups meeting concurrently. The program will continue until the entire police force of approximately 1,400 men has been involved.

Meetings are held in the neighborhood community centers and at the Police Academy.[5] An effort is made to recruit a cross-section of the community but especially representatives of minority and poverty groups and dissidents.[6] Most of the officers attend in uniform but outside their regular tour of duty and receive extra salary from the city for their eighteen hours of participation. Police are required to attend, but community participation is, of course, voluntary. Doctoral level psychologists with experience in human relations training and group therapy serve as group leaders. Financial support is entirely from private and local groups. Fees for the psychologists' professional services and funds for incidental expenses supporting the program are met through voluntary contributions from Houston business and industry. The cost for one six-week session is approximately $20,000 with half this amount going to police salaries.

The major goals of the program are to promote a cooperative relationship between the community and police and to effect greater mutual respect and harmony. To achieve these ends the group sessions are structured so as to have the police and community first examine the damaging stereotypes they have of each other; second, to consider the extent to which these stereotypes affect their attitudes, perceptions, and behaviors toward each other; third, to look at the ways in which each group reinforces these stereotypes in the eyes of the other; and fourth, to develop a cooperative, problem-solving attitude directed toward resolving differences and reducing conflict to a level where both groups can work together constructively.

In the initial session police and community first meet separately to develop images of their own group and the other group. This strategy was taken from an exercise used successfully by Blake, Mouton, and Sloma[7] in resolving conflict in a union-management situation. Police are asked to develop a list of statements as to how they see themselves and a second list of their view of the community. Community members do likewise. The groups are then brought together and these images compared and discussed. Subsequent sessions are devoted to correction of distortions identified in these lists, diagnosis of specific areas of disagreement, identification of key issues and sources of friction and, finally, devising methods for conflict resolution.

The resulting self- and other images developed by the police and community groups are far too numerous to be listed. However, a summary of some of the more salient images serves to present the flavor of this aspect of the sessions:

Police self-image. As officers we are ethical, honest, physically clean and neat in appearance, dedicated to our job, with a strong sense of duty. Some officers are prejudiced, but they are in the minority, and officers are aware of their prejudice and lean over backwards to be fair. We are a close-knit, suspicious group, distrustful of outsiders. We put on a professional front; hard, calloused, and indifferent, but underneath we have feelings. We treat others as nicely as they will let us. We are clannish, ostracized by the community, used as scapegoats, and under scrutiny even when off duty trying to enjoy ourselves. We are the blue minority.

Police image of community. Basically the public is cooperative and law-abiding, but uninformed about the duties, procedures, and responsibility of the police officer. The upper class, the rich, support the police, but feel immune to the law and use their money and influence to avoid police action against themselves and their children. The middle class support the police and are more civic-minded than upper or lower classses. The major share of police contact with the middle class is through traffic violations. The lower class has the most frequent contact with the police and usually are un-cooperative as witnesses or in reporting crime. They have a different sense of values, live only for today and do not plan for tomorrow. As police officers we see the Houston Negro in two groups: (1) Negro—industrious, productive, moral, law-abiding, and not prone to violence; (2) "nigger"—lazy, immoral, dishonest, unreliable, and prone to violence.

Community self-image. We lack knowledge about proper police procedures and do not know our rights, obligations, and duties in regard to the law. There is a lack of communication among social, geographical, racial, and economic segments of the community. We do not involve ourselves in civic affairs as we should, and we have a guilty conscience about the little crimes (traffic violations) we get away with, but are resentful when caught. We relate to the police as authority figures, and we feel uncomfortable around them. The black community feels itself second class in relation to the police. The majority of the community is law-abiding, hard working, pays taxes, is honest and reliable.

Community Image of Police. Some police abuse their authority, act as judge, jury, and prosecutor and assume a person is guilty until proven innocent. They are too often psychologically and physically abusive, name-calling, handle people rough, and discriminate against blacks in applying the law. Police are cold and mechanical in performance of their duties. We expect them to be perfect, to make no mistakes, and to set the standard for behavior. The police see the world only through their squad car windshield and are walled off from the community. Our initial reaction when we see an officer is "blue."

PROGRAM EVALUATION

In an attempt to determine to what extent this community action program was achieving its stated goal of increased mutual respect and harmony between police and citizens, a number of procedures were followed.

Police and community participants were asked to complete a questionnaire at the close of their final session, inquiring about their reaction to the program. Results from about eight hundred police and six hundred citizens completing the program indicate enthusiastic acceptance by the participating community and grudging to moderately good acceptance by the police. For example, ninety-three percent of the community rate the program either Good, Very Good, or Excellent; only seven percent rate it Poor. For the police, eighty-five percent rate it between Good and Excellent with fifteen percent rating it Poor. However, where eighteen percent of the community rate it Excellent, only four percent of the police do so. Moreover, sixty five percent of the community say that as a result of the program their feelings about the police are more positive, thirty-one percent unchanged, and four percent more negative. For the police, thirty-seven percent reflect a more positive community attitude, sixty-one percent report no change, and two percent more negative.

For the community the most frequently expressed reaction to the program is increased recognition and appreciation of the police officer as an individual and a human being rather than a member of an undifferentiated group, "the blue minority." Citizens most often comment on their tendency to dehumanize the police and see them as unfeeling, authoritarian robots, rather than real people who sometimes make honest mistakes, get angry, or behave unwisely.

For their part the police most often record a sense of gratification that as a result of the program the community gains some appreciation of the policeman's role, what he can do and cannot do. The police seem surprised as to how misinformed the public is regarding police procedures and limits of authority.

Later evaluation of the program included administration of a questionnaire especially designed to assess attitudes about the poor, minority groups and the community at large.[8] As might be expected, the police and black community differ widely on social issues involving poverty and minority groups as measured by this questionnaire, with the police scoring at the high prejudice end of the scale. However, participation in this program serves to attenuate to a significant degree the extreme attitudes held by the police. There is one exception to this latter statement in that one police group increased their prejudice scores following participation in the program. However, these officers were tested the week following the fracas between Chicago police and demonstrators at the Democratic National Convention when feelings were running high among the police about the issue of "law and order."

Problems inherent in a community action program. This police-community program did not proceed evenly or without problems. Consistent community participation has been a major problem. Although recruitment of the community was effected through announcements by the news media, social clubs, churches, and even door-to-door solicitation, citizen cooperation often failed to materialize. Inconsistent community participation disrupted the continuity of group discussions. Many citizens turned out for the initial sessions, largely to express grievances and blow off steam. Having accomplished this, they often did not return for subsequent sessions.

Extremist groups from the community attended, often for other than constructive purposes. For example, an organized group of black militants descended on one meeting and engaged the police in a heated recitation of complaints and verbal abuse. However, when the group leader finally called a halt to the harassment and suggested the group now consider possible constructive solutions to these complaints, the militants abruptly departed. These hit-and-run tactics employed by some community participants were especially difficult to control.

Extreme right-wing white political group members came apparently only to maintain the status quo, "Support their local police" and take copious notes for the purpose of publishing slanted and captious articles about the program. For example a local newspaper with strong right-wing political bias published an article describing the "brainwashing" techniques, self-criticism and confessional approaches used by the Communist Revolution and left the reader with the impression that this police-community program was similar in goals and procedure.

Some of the police were not sympathetic either to the goals or substance of the program and attempted to sabotage the program where possible by refusing to participate in the group discussions or by adopting a hostile and belligerent stance. Both the police and community tended to be suspicious of the program and its real intent and purpose.

Retention of effective group leaders for the program proved difficult. Leaders for a program such as this need personal attributes that would tax the resources of an Eagle Scout, including having poise and maturity, being experienced and skillful in handling difficult groups, intuitive, inventive, and resourceful. A third of the group leaders were, themselves, minority group members, and these leaders appeared to enjoy a decided advantage in working with both the police and community. But attrition among group leaders was high. Many reasons were given for resigning from the program, chief among them being the emotionally exhausting strain of the sessions and lack of visible reward from either police or community in the form of recognition as to the positive contribution made by the program. The repetitious and monotonous character of the sessions was another frequently mentioned detraction. Each six-week session carried a deadly encore of issues already dealt with in preceding laboratories. It was difficult for group leaders to build up interest in still another round of self-righteous accusations by the community and massive denials by the police. Some group leaders withdrew because they could not take the hostility expressed within their group, hostility they assumed to be directed at them personally. These leaders failed to recognize that the hostility, whether expressed by police or community, was not a personal attack on them, but rather for what the leader represented as an agent of change. Experienced leaders were able to interpret this phenomenon to the group and focus their attention on their own resistance to change.

SUMMARY

Has the exposure of 1,400 police officers and a corresponding number of community members been worth the time, money, and effort expended? One can point to the fact that there has been no further rioting and neither the assassination of Martin Luther King, Jr., or Robert F. Kennedy was followed by racial incidents. Houston police characterize 1968 as a "cool" summer in contrast to 1967. Another encouraging sign is that the Mayor's office reports a seventy percent drop in citizen complaints about police behavior for the seven-month period following inception of the program.[9] Also there are other suggestions of improvements in police-community relations: a white police officer organizes his own group of blacks and whites for continuing discussions in his home; officers stop their squad cars to talk with black people in their neighborhood for no other reason than to meet them.

Despite setbacks in the program and the sometimes contrary results of individual laboratories, the consensus of the participating staff, the city administrators, and the business patrons providing financial support has been cautiously affirmative in proclaiming the program a success. No claim is made that eighteen hours of discussion will sweep away years of rancor and distrust. But it is a necessary beginning.

NOTES

1. U. S. Riot Commission, *Report of the National Commission on Civil Disorders* (Kerner Commission, New York: Bantam Books, 1968).

2. B. Justice, *Detection of Potential Community Violence*, Dissemination document—Grant 207 (5.044) (Washington, D.C.: Office of Law Enforcement Assistance, U. S. Department of Justice, 1968).

3. Now with the U. S. Department of Justice, Houston, Texas. Dr. Sikes is administrative director of the Houston police-community program.

4. P. G. Hanson, P. Rothaus, D. L. Johnson, and F. A. Lyle, "Autonomous Groups in Human Relations Training for Psychiatric Patients," *Journal of Applied Behavioral Science* 2 (1966): 305-323.

5. Particular credit is due Inspector C. D. Taylor, Commanding Officer, Bureau of Personnel and Prevention, Houston Police Department, for his unceasing support of the program.

6. The Reverend John P. Murray, Director, Houston Council on Human Relations, was untiring in his efforts to obtain community participation.

7. R. R. Blake, Jane S. Mouton, and R. L. Sloma, "The Union-Management Intergroup Laboratory: Strategy for Resolving Intergroup Conflict," *The Journal of Applied Behavioral Science* 1 (1965).

8. This questionnaire is called the Community Attitude Survey (CAS). It contains thirty-eight items requiring response to each statement on a six-point continuum from strongly agree to strongly disagree. The scale yields a General Prejudice score and four subscores touching on special aspects of community relations.

VII. Organizational Contexts

The Total Paradigm Illustrated

This chapter attempts to put it all together, in today's no-think parlance. That is, the intent is to illustrate how the small group approach helps activate the full scientific paradigm, from the conceptualization/operationalization of pure science to the amelioration of man's condition that should be the goal of applied science. To put the intent in other terms, the goal here is to establish double-barrelled relevance to scientific processes and to human needs.

Hence, with equal justice, this chapter might be subtitled either "Science in the Service of Social Engineering" or "Social Engineering in the Service of Science."

One point is certain: the target here is definitely big game. The focus here is on the application of a technology of organization change that is based on small-group dynamics. The big-game quality of the focus is patent in Smith's observation (1973, 106) that "Planned changes in organizational behavior are by no means easy to achieve. . . . there are so many determinants of an organization's existing performance that any change is likely to be detrimental to someone or to some aspect of the organization. Thus it need not be surprising that attempts at organization change quite often fail." By the same token it should be very encouraging and indicative of the power of available technologies if even a smallish percentage of such attempts succeed, as they variously do.

Focusing on large organizations, this chapter will show how the small-group approach generates broad ranges of effort that should characterize a viable and vital area of inquiry. Seven interacting classes of effort will be distinguished. Briefly, these classes indicate how the small-group approach (1) helps enrich the understanding of dynamics in natural-state organizations, especially at such critical times as startup or when organization members experience unusual stress; (2) serves as the basis for an applied behavioral science technology for change and development in public agencies while also reflecting a basic concern with values and the quality of life in organizations; (3) promises some relief for a variety of problems facing units of government, while it challenges a broad range of political institutions, traditions, and notions; (4) provides learning designs that can help ameliorate some trauma experienced by individuals in organizations; (5) implies an internal logic that can basically reshape public administrative systems, as well as those in business organizations; (6) encourages pure research on a variety of central issues such as an appropriate model of change; and (7) requires an explicit choice between alternative value-sets, which provide a critical if often implicit foundation for all organizations, and which are vital in determining the quality of life generated by any organization.

To put it briefly, the small-group approach generates effort that applies to the total paradigm of scientific effort, conceived broadly as the accumulation as well as the application of knowledge.

The choice of the focus on organization rests on an uncomplicated rationale. Basically the fullest exploration of the small-group approach has

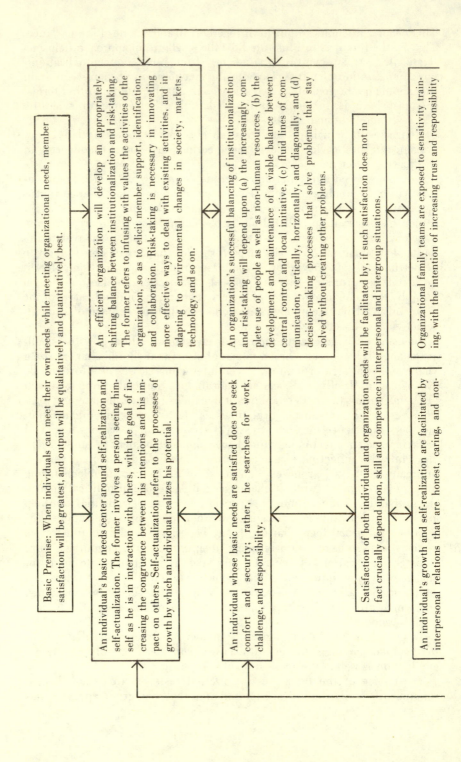

Basic Premise: When individuals can meet their own needs while meeting organizational needs, member satisfaction will be greatest, and output will be qualitatively and quantitatively best.

An individual's basic needs center around self-realization and self-actualization. The former involves a person seeing himself as he is in interaction with others, with the goal of increasing the congruence between his intentions and his impact on others. Self-actualization refers to the processes of growth by which an individual realizes his potential.

An individual whose basic needs are satisfied does not seek comfort and security; rather, he searches for work, challenge, and responsibility.

An efficient organization will develop an appropriately-shifting balance between institutionalization and risk-taking. The former refers to infusing with values the activities of the organization, so as to elicit member support, identification, and collaboration. Risk-taking is necessary in innovating more effective ways to deal with existing activities, and in adapting to environmental changes in society, markets, technology, and so on.

An organization's successful balancing of institutionalization and risk-taking will depend upon (a) the increasingly complete use of people as well as non-human resources, (b) the development and maintenance of a viable balance between central control and local initiative, (c) fluid lines of communication, vertically, horizontally, and diagonally, and (d) decision-making processes that solve problems that stay solved without creating other problems.

Satisfaction of both individual and organization needs will be facilitated by, if such satisfaction does not in fact crucially depend upon, skill and competence in interpersonal and intergroup situations.

An individual's growth and self-realization are facilitated by interpersonal relations that are honest, caring, and non-

Organizational family teams are exposed to sensitivity training, with the intention of increasing trust and responsibility

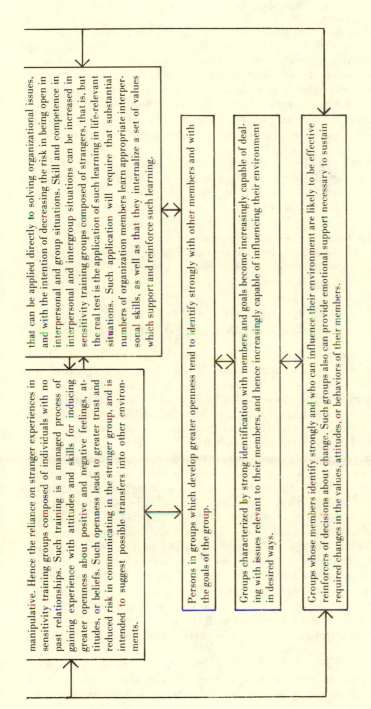

manipulative. Hence the reliance on stranger experiences in sensitivity training groups composed of individuals with no past relationships. Such training is a managed process of gaining experience with attitudes and skills for inducing greater openness about positive and negative feelings, attitudes, or beliefs. Such openness leads to greater trust and reduced risk in communicating in the stranger group, and is intended to suggest possible transfers into other environments.

that can be applied directly to solving organizational issues, and with the intention of decreasing the risk in being open in interpersonal and group situations. Skill and competence in interpersonal and intergroup situations can be increased in sensitivity training groups composed of strangers, that is, but the real test is the application of such learning in life-relevant situations. Such application will require that substantial numbers of organization members learn appropriate interpersonal skills, as well as that they internalize a set of values which support and reinforce such learning.

Persons in groups which develop greater openness tend to identify strongly with other members and with the goals of the group.

Groups characterized by strong identification with members and goals become increasingly capable of dealing with issues relevant to their members, and hence increasingly capable of influencing their environment in desired ways.

Groups whose members identify strongly and who can influence their environment are likely to be effective reinforcers of decisions about change. Such groups also can provide emotional support necessary to sustain required changes in the values, attitudes, or behaviors of their members.

From Robert T. Golembiewski and Stokes B. Carrigan, "Planned Change in Organization Style Based on the Laboratory Approach," *Administrative Science Quarterly*, 15 (March 1970), 81.

Figure 7.1. The Basic OD Schema Seeking a Congruence of Individual Needs and Organization Demands.

been made in organization contexts. Comparatively the two other areas in Political Science that have seen a substantial emphasis on the small group—legislative behavior in committees and the analysis of panels of judges—have generated only a small fraction of the effort expended on the small group in organizations. In addition, political scientists—both ancient and modern—have maintained a lively interest in the control of behavior in organizations (Kaufman 1964). Finally, and of major personal significance, this editor has an especial interest in research on organizations.

From another point of view, the organizational emphasis is intended not to imply exclusivity. Rather the guiding hope is that the present emphasis will serve as a model of what can be done, and will consequently help motivate comparable exploration of the small-group approach in other areas of interest to political scientists. These areas include voting analysis and associated training for citizenship; the design and development of alternative units of social and political control or governance; legislative behavior, with an emphasis on committees; the behavior of judges, as on the Supreme Court; and many others.

THE LABORATORY APPROACH
TO ORGANIZATION DEVELOPMENT

How an emphasis on small groups can energize the full scientific paradigm will be illustrated by an introduction to the laboratory approach to organization development, or OD. Figure 7.1 presents a broad schema for OD, emphasizing how its values-cum-technology strive to increase the congruence between what the organization demands of the individual, and what the individual needs to function in satisfying and growthful ways. The basic model is one of elemental exchange. The overall theme is that it is not necessary to pose the issue of collective life in polarized terms: individual or organization. In contrast, indeed, the more appropriate conclusion for many kinds of organizations is that, increasingly, the issue of collective life must be individual and organization. Briefly many organizations now demand so much of so many of their members—so much effort, dedication, tolerance for stress, and so on—that active efforts are now underway to seek ways of variously heightening the payoffs for individuals that are built into their work. These payoffs include not only the more or less traditional range of economic incentives. They also especially include those features associated with a more satisfying quality of life in organizations, with the design of jobs that are more psychologically engaging (Myers 1970, Maher 1971), as well as with changes in various policies that are sensitive to differences in the life styles of organization members (Golembiewski, Hilles, and Kagno 1974).

The schema in Figure 7.1 presents a rationale for why it increasingly must be individual and organization, of how and why a heightened mutual exchange is both necessary and possible. That figure reflects what is often referred to as the humanist alternative for organizing work (Chitwood and Harmon 1971), and two optimistic souls also once saw that alternative as signaling the death of bureaucracy and the inevitability of democracy in organizations (Bennis and Slater 1968). The position here is a more limited one and reflects three emphases. Bureaucracy is unlikely to die in any immediate future, and organizational democracy will only be more or less tentatively approached; but the schema clearly does provide an alternative for organizing work, whatever that alternative is called. Notably, a growing number of organizations are experimenting with that alternative, albeit with variable intensities.

FIVE PERSPECTIVES ON OD

The aptness of the three guiding emphases here will be suggested by five illustrations of the kind of work generated by the small-group approach in the accumulation and application of knowledge about organizations. The range is broad: from observing an organization in the act of becoming, to a comparison of the values underlying OD with the values implicit in the dominant system of thought about organizing.

Small groups and organizational start-up. Amrit Baruah provides an arresting analysis of a small group of officials as they struggle with their emerging sense of mission and role. His "An Interstitial Political Institution in the Act of Becoming" develops three critical points. First, a variety of forces are encouraging the increasing development of "interstitial organizations," that is, organizations that develop in the spaces between existing organizations and institutions to serve as integrators and linking pins. Second, however, doing what needs to be done generates a range of intense pressures for these organizations and for their members as well. Thus the organizations have missions and roles that change kaleidoscopically; and their authority inheres less in legal mandates than in getting others to accept some guiding concept. Adding to the stress and uncertainty, such organizations are more collegial than hierarchical; specialists work with a variable range of other specialists in ever-changing combinations; and members of such organizations must derive their satisfactions from intense but on-and-off relationships, both with fellow organization members and diverse outsiders.

Thus in more or less extreme form, what is true of interstitial organizations is true of a broad range of contemporary organizations. The derivative catalog of challenges is a familiar one by now. We need only sample that catalog here. Thus intense relationships must be quickly developed and often terminated just as quickly. Agreement about mission and roles is more critical than ever, but any agreement cannot become a barrier to the cascade of modifications and even radical departures that are more or less certain to follow. And so on.

Two major points inhere in these brief descriptions of what organizations are increasingly coming to be. More than ever before, that is, organizations are becoming a shifting set of small groupings, intense yet temporary, with an influence pattern that often must ideally shift to meet the variable demands of evolving problem situations. Knowledge about small groups consequently becomes critical; and the success of its application will determine in important ways the shape of the quality of life in our organizations. Relatedly, especially given the impermanence of so much of organization life, the quality of interpersonal and intergroup relations constitutes one of the important motivators an organization can supply. Patently, small-group analysis is central from this perspective also.

Small-group technology applied to public organizations. In addition to such descriptive enrichment as that illustrated by Baruah's contribution, the small-group approach also has generated a technology for facilitating choice and change in large organizations. That technology—often called organization development or, more broadly, "applied behavioral science"—basically rests on a critical linkage, that values rooted in small-group training contexts can influence the climate and style of larger units. The transfer process is but incompletely understood, although the character of the linkages seems clear enough in general principle. Table 6.1 in Chapter VI sketches the values consistent with the laboratory approach, whose application was illustrated there. Those values in Table 6.1—which emphasize interpersonal or small-group contexts—also imply a set of important norms for the quality of life in large organizations. This set prescribes that organizations be characterized by (Slater and Bennis 1964): (1) full and free communication; (2) reliance on open consensus in managing conflict, as opposed to using coercion or compromise; (3) influence based on competence rather than on personal whim or formal power; (4) expression of emotional as well as task-oriented behavior; and (5) acceptance of conflict between the individual and his organization, to be coped with willingly, openly, and rationally to help make organization members more effective and satisfied participants shaping their own work environment. Relevant learning thus deals with the public, here-and-now data available to all members. The range of these target data is very broad, and can deal with (1) the specific structures members develop in their interaction, such as the leadership rank-order; (2) the processes of their group life, with special attention to getting a group started, keeping it going, and then experiencing its inevitable "death"; (3) the specific emotional reactions of members to one another's behavior and to their common experiences; and (4) the varying and diverse styles or modes of individual and group behavior, as in fighting authority figures or in fleeing some issue that has overwhelmed group members. Relevant learning also can take place at many levels, three of which are especially central. These central levels are personal learning about the self in group situations, transfer of personal learning to a worksite, and restructuring the broad organization in ways that make it more satisfying and more rewarding to its members.

In sum, the scope and reach of the laboratory approach to OD can be expressed in terms of a 4-by-3 matrix, four types of target data at three levels of organization.

This 4-by-3 matrix implies lofty ambitions, to be sure, but accuracy requires an early owning of the advantages and limitations of the laboratory approach to OD. For example, the OD ideal is to affect simultaneously behavior, task, and structure. But that ideal is often out of reach, and OD in fact usually stresses behavior and interaction only. Behavior/interaction often is critical. Indeed, especially toward the top of an organization, interpersonal trust and effectiveness are of awesome significance. At lower hierarchical levels, however, the technology often induces specific patterns of behavior/interaction, which patterns will be difficult or impossible to change as long as the technology remains in place. In the latter case, applications of the laboratory approach may be less effective, if not indeed counterproductive.

Two summary evaluations of OD are safe enough, however, by way of summary introduction. Certainly the OD technology contains many gaps in both its science and art. However, what is known now can be helpful in doing what must be done, if all contemporary societies are to have any reasonable chance of avoiding a kind of latter-day dark ages because of our inability to keep pace with the trauma that progress has brought.

To become more specific, organizational extensions of the small-group approach got their start and most substantial development in business firms. Three waves of applications can be distinguished, in fact, corresponding to the three developmental stages in the small-group approach. First, beginning in the late 1920s, the power of the small group as a major behavioral influence in organizations was solidly established, as in the descriptions of the Bank-Wiring Room of the famous Hawthorne studies. For example such descriptions reveal how the level of productivity was influenced, perhaps even determined, by group norms, and how it was maintained by complex social and physical sanctions.

The implied lesson was not lost on those intent on reinforcing the influence of formal authorities in organizations. Second, major efforts were made to use the small group as a vehicle for change desired by some formal authority. The basic approach was to seek group help in determining how or perhaps only whether some desired action would be implemented. Thus the early studies in group decision making sought to mobilize the influence potential of the small group to develop and maintain norms considered desirable by some external authority. Major successes were reported in the literature (Coch and French 1948), although some groups made use of the opportunity to build greater cohesiveness only to resist more effectively that authority.

Third, the contemporary emphasis—as in OD—is to use the small group as the agent of change. The underlying rationale is straightforward. Such an approach maximizes the potential for group influence for two basic reasons. Thus group members can more easily own any choice or change since they initiate and not merely reinforce or implement the goals of an external authority. Relatedly, as in Figure 7.1, OD rests on the assumption that very basic complementarities exist between individual needs and organization demands. This basic complementarity explains why it is in the laboratory approach to OD that over the long run, at least, groups in organizations are trusted to be the agents of change.

There are some very good reasons why OD specifically, and applied behavioral science more broadly, got their earliest and deepest development in business organizations. Basically William Eddy and Robert J. Saunders develop a long list of such reasons in "Applied Behavioral Science and Urban Administrative/Political Systems." Despite the relevance of OD to a broad range of problems faced by public agencies, these students argue, a variety of institutional and historical factors limit such applications of the small-group approach there. For example Eddy and Saunders point out some potential incompatibilities between political systems and the kind of organizations congenial to OD. They explain:

> Political systems are by nature distributive—or at least are usually operated that way. They function to divide a finite amount of resources among various interest groups. This "cutting of the pie" is a win/lose game in which a variety of tactics are used to increase the rewards to one group—which frequently means they are decreased to others. The well-functioning administrative system aims at being integrative. Emphasis is placed on communality of purpose, collaboration, and win/win relationships. Ways are sought to minimize win/lose competition among operating units, and to enhance shared problem solving and planning.

OD Interventions for Individuals and Small Groups in Public Agencies. Accumulating evidence establishes the potency of the laboratory approach to organization development, despite the special challenges to OD posed in public agencies and despite the very real problems faced in all organizations. A first illustration of this accumulating evidence involves an intervention with a trinity of intentions: to help facilitate adaptation by individuals to new jobs, to legitimate individual participation in shaping their jobs, as well as to build consciously ab initio an organization with relatively specific characteristics. Hence the selection's title: "MARTA: Toward Building an Effective, Open Giant." The authors are Robert T. Golembiewski and Alan Kiepper, who is the General Manager of MARTA, the Metropolitan Atlanta Rapid Transit Authority.

In sum, the study implies the substantial potency of the underlying small-group technology. More specifically the study has two central themes, both relevant to applications of the behavioral sciences in real-life situations. First, the study implies the value for individuals in key groups of increasing the percentage and the intensity of "regenerative interaction sequences" in their public agencies. The point can be illustrated by sketching a "degenerative interaction sequence" between two individuals A and B, and by detailing some of the organizational consequences of such a degenerative sequence. Figure 7.2 does the job and seeks to highlight a

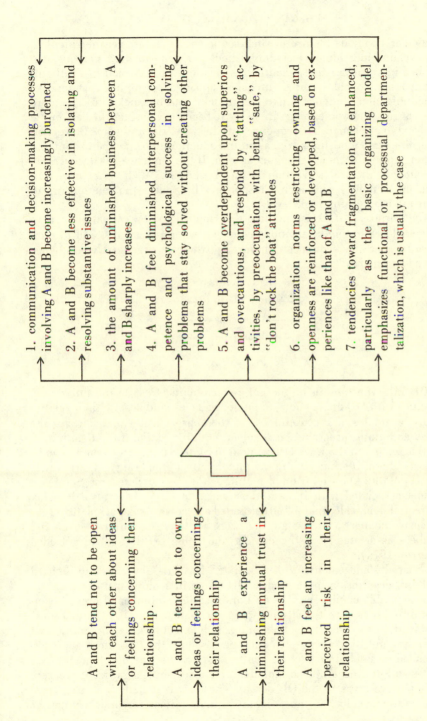

1. communication and decision-making processes involving A and B become increasingly burdened

2. A and B become less effective in isolating and resolving substantive issues

3. the amount of unfinished business between A and B sharply increases

4. A and B feel diminished interpersonal competence and psychological success in solving problems that stay solved without creating other problems

5. A and B become overdependent upon superiors and overcautious, and respond by "tattling," activities, by preoccupation with being "safe," by "don't rock the boat" attitudes

6. organization norms restricting owning and openness are reinforced or developed, based on experiences like that of A and B

7. tendencies toward fragmentation are enhanced, particularly as the basic organizing model emphasizes functional or processual departmentalization, which is usually the case

A and B tend not to be open with each other about ideas or feelings concerning their relationship.

A and B tend not to own ideas or feelings concerning their relationship

A and B experience a diminishing mutual trust in their relationship

A and B feel an increasing perceived risk in their relationship

Figure 7.2. A Degenerative Interaction Sequence and Some of Its Postulated Organizational Consequences

particularly vicious feature of such sequences: they are self-heightening. To explain, individuals feel diminished and demeaned as persons, enmeshed in an increasingly inauthentic relationship in which it is difficult or impossible to make desired outcomes happen. A person in a degenerative communication sequence is like the unlucky soul in quicksand. The more he struggles, the worse things are likely to become. Consider the case of the husband in a degenerative sequence with his wife. He buys some flowers on returning from a business trip, as an introduction to being open about and owning up to his tender feelings about her. If the sequence has degenerated far enough, the wife's reaction to the flowers is: "Well, what have you been up to now?" And such a response will escalate the relationship to more intensely unforgiving levels.

The purpose of OD designs like that applied to MARTA, patently, is to reverse degenerative interaction sequences where necessary, and to reinforce regenerative sequences wherever possible. A regenerative sequence can be outlined as:

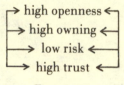

Figure 7.3

OD interventions in municipal governments. Despite the unique difficulties with OD applications in public agencies, and despite their relative rarity, examples of the usefulness of the approach do exist. Perhaps the most ambitious program was Project ACORD (Action for Organization Development) in the U. S. Department of State, which is too complex to be reported here. It seems safe to say that despite a broad range of difficulties Project ACORD knew its triumphs, although it was cancelled and State personnel associated with it went their separate ways. It is also probably correct, if debatable, that ACORD provided a necessary take-off platform for extensive changes within State that were accomplished after the fuss and feathers associated with the coming and going of ACORD had subsided (Marrow 1974).

"Shared Management: An Innovation," by Chris Cherches and Richard E. Byrd, describes a more modest OD effort in a municipal organization with some 225 employees. The authors describe a number of preintervention difficulties with the city management that, with only little qualification, could characterize the bulk of our public and business organizations. Cherches and Byrd also sketch a design based on the laboratory approach intended to ameliorate such difficulties. Given that the development project is still in process, the authors feel free to attribute significant progress in important areas to the OD design. These areas include increased trust and confidence in the chief administrative officer, greater feelings of responsibility by department heads for achieving overall goals, greater teamwork and more effective lateral communication, increased delegation, and clarification of the bases of differences in organization goals.

The results of studies like that by Cherches and Byrd permit optimism that our future is not as gloomy as some observers maintain. The conventional wisdom has long maintained that humankind is locked in a losing struggle with its own organizational creations. Thus Marx saw no real improvement in the human condition until the state, and presumably all other units of social control, "withered away." Small chance of that occurring, of course. Other observers gave the world not even such a slim hope. In contrast, the OD literature permits substantial hope, if much research is still required to establish the specific conditions under which this hope is justified. As Golembiewski and Carrigan (1973, p. 27) conclude:

> It is still too early to build organizations to order. But (a growing body of research implies) that the science/art of planned change in organizations has developed sufficiently to provide major hope that individual needs can be made more congruent with organization demands. At the risk of being melodramatic, . . . the success in increasing this congruence in organizations will significantly determine the degree of freedom that man will experience in contemporary life.

OD and issues of value. Of major significance, finally, OD applications clearly are value-filled, and no qualifications about it. Basically OD rests on a vision of the social order which meets both individual needs and organization demands to a greater degree than traditional notions for organizing. The OD technology and derivative designs, in turn, rest on a set of values that define this proposed social order. Hence the issue of values must be up front in any analysis of OD.

James M. McDuffie, Jr., provides one expression of the patent relevance of the normative in his "A Clash of Values: OD and Machiavelli's *Prince*." McDuffie takes a number of major OD properties and contrasts them and their implied values with major themes in Machiavelli's classic of political philosophy. People may make different choices as between the values underlying OD and those in *The Prince*. But choice it will have to be, McDuffie implies, and that choice will be a momentous one.

REFERENCES

Bennis, W. G., and Slater, P. E. 1968. The temporary society. New York: Harper & Row.

Chitwood, S. R., and Harmon, M. M. 1971. New public administration, humanism and organizational behavior. *Public management* 53: 13-22.

Coch, L., and French, J. R. P., Jr. 1948. Overcoming resistence to change. *Human relations* 1: esp. 519-520.

Golembiewski, R. T., and Carrigan, S. B. 1973. Planned change through laboratory methods. *Training and development journal* 27: 18-27.

Golembiewski, R. T., Hilles, R., and Kagno, M. 1974. A longitudinal study of flexi-time effects. *Journal of applied behavioral science* 10: 503-532.

Kaufman, H. 1964. Organization theory and practical theory. *American political science review* 58: 5-14.

Marrow, A. J. 1974. *Making waves in foggy bottom.* Washington, D. C.: NTL Institute of Applied Behavioral Science.

Maher, J. R. 1971. *New perspectives in job enrichment.* New York: Van Nostrand Reinhold.

Myers, M. S. 1970. *Every employee a manager.* New York: McGraw-Hill.

Slater, P. E., and Bennis, W. G. 1964. Democracy is inevitable. *Harvard business review* 42: 51-59.

Smith, Peter B. 1973. *Groups within organizations.* New York: Harper & Row.

An Interstitial Political Institution in the Act of Becoming: Early Dynamics of a Council of Governments

AMRIT BARUAH

The mix of political realities, social turmoil and a 'cultural revolution' of America in the 1960s made it unavoidable that new types of organization should appear because existing organizations were not in a position to take on the challenge. The focus here is on one of these new types, the interstitial organization. Simply, these are organizations which appear in the interstices or spaces between other organizations.

An interstitial organization is not any new organization. To qualify, an organization must satisfy the following requirements. Broadly, an interstitial organization arises out of the new social gestalt of the times. It addresses itself to some unmet needs, its preoccupations are distinctive, and the personnel attracted to it have distinctive concerns and attributes. These are the case even though interstitial organizations include examples in both the square world of business and government, as well as in various countercultures. Thus defined, a council of governments, a community controlled neighborhood corporation, and a free clinic run by and for counterculture are three examples of interstitial organizations. There are differences between these examples, of course, but their commonalities are compelling.

ORGANIZATIONS AND BOUNDARIES

An organization is an entity that gives a form and framework to an idea. It embodies certain objectives; it mobilizes resources and personnel. An organization encompasses a certain area of concern and enterprise which it circumscribes with a sense of boundary.

The overall impression is a galaxy with rules of orbit where ideally each organization fulfills itself while delicately managing its clashes with other organizations. Even substantial conflict is not to be viewed as a cause of disintegration. In fact the strains and stresses between organizations can generate much energy for internal organizational life. Such strains and stresses, in other words, need not be dysfunctional; often these provide a mirror in which some of their own contradictions can be viewed. Similarly they can also highlight the strengths of an organization, thereby increasing the morale of its participants and making them come to terms with the organization's destiny.

A central theme here is that organizations create fences and spaces between themselves and then go on with their business. These fences are not necessarily to close themselves in, but serve to distinguish between the enterprise and its environment. In fact the spaces between organizations are necessary for them to be better interacting systems.

In this paper we will take a look at the peculiar destinies of one variety of interstitial organization which is springing up in these spaces between other organizations. Interstitial organizations deserve special study and attention because they represent a whole new wave of organizational life.

A COUNCIL OF GOVERNMENTS AS AN INTERSTITIAL ORGANIZATION: CHARACTERISTIC FEATURES

This paper is based on an in-depth study of one council of governments. The council of governments represents a new approach to tackle metropolitan problems, and this approach has become popular after many reformers have had to accept the reality that the idea of metropolitan government is not popular. Municipalities voluntarily become members of a council of governments and maintain their existing legal powers and identities while working together to confront metropolitan problems. Municipalities as members of a council establish a central policy through the actions of a board of elected officials. The council has a central professional staff that carries out the coordinating and essential administrative work involved in area-wide programs.

The federal government has been a major source of financial support for the councils. Grants have been made for a wide range of activities—organizational, fiscal, planning, regional planning for land use, transportation, housing, economic development, community facilities. Although the thrust of the Great Society has become weaker, the influence of the councils has not appreciably diminished.

We believe that the issues which are paramount in such organizations are not necessarily the same as in other public bureaucracies; they definitely differ from those with which one has to grapple in industrial organizations. The often-mentioned distinction between open and closed systems is relevant in this connection, but by itself it does not sufficiently explain the work and destiny of an organization such as a council of governments which faces unique problems with values, ideology, and boundary. These issues have received little attention.

The council represents an innovative and intentional type of organization where different kinds of clientele, value and boundary questions are present to an extent which is not true in most other public systems. It is also an organization which falls between the neat dichotomy of politics and administration—with the crucial difference that it does not have the advantage of a third party which, in the case of the usual public bureaucracy, is the client constituency which in times of crisis can help a bureaucracy in its fights with the executive or the legislature.

In addition the council of governments represents a system which has to work out its identity in a diffused, fluid environment with conflicting and contradictory environmental forces impinging upon it. Some of these forces stem from conflicting life-style values of member communities. These life-style values are continuously changing through the underlying cultural (and recently counter-cultural) demands. Through our study, we also had an opportunity to obtain a look at the peculiar methods, restrictions, and promise of organizations like the council of governments, which can be termed marginal while being relational. Interstitial organizations can be characterized in terms of these features:

Administrative ideology.

1. An administrative ideology becomes a major concern in such organizations.

2. The distinction between politics and administration becomes hazy in these organizations.

3. There is an effort to remain ideologically pure. There is considerable introspection about values embodied in such issues: Did the leader sell himself out by becoming established? Is the tone of the organization becoming more autocratic and less power-sharing?

4. There is a search for institutional integrity (Selznik 1957). The truth system in these organizations is central. Most organizations have a truth system which provides operating values and guidelines and gives rise to a raison d'etre for the organization. However, in an interstitial organization it seems that there is a heightened awareness of its truth system.

Boundary-galactical concerns. Issues of boundary become important to these organizations. An interstitial organization becomes a unit in a galaxy, and much of its time and energy is spent working out galactical relationships with other units. These relationships cover the range from conflict to cooperation. There is also an acute awareness of the diverse political cultures beyond the organization.

Identity ambivalence.

1. Search for a central theme is especially intense in these organizations. Since usually an interstitial organization is a creature of grants—either government or foundation—its staple business consists of a series of projects or programs. And so a council can become a number of projects in search of an organization, instead of the other way around. This situation creates a special kind of strain. Staff members have to get oriented around different projects, which results in continuous change.

2. The fate of always becoming and never being generates discomfort in these organizations, and this cannot be explained away by saying that the organization is not very old and is naturally growing up. There is something intrinsic to such organizations which makes them one continuous potentiality.

3. Interstitial organizations are ambivalent in their relationships with established organizations. On the one hand, there is a conscious attempt to avoid becoming replicas of such organizations, as well as a desire to preserve unique values, special destiny and priorities. On the other hand, interstitial organizations recognize they cannot conduct their affairs without support and linkage with established organizations.

4. There is a shared feeling of persecution and double bind.

Technology.

1. In some interstitial organizations definitions of roles and accountability are unconventional. It is not unusual to find in a community-controlled corporation or in a free clinic, for example, that clients are also becoming service deliverers. There are some such organizations where credentialed professionals are serving under nonprofessional superiors whose basic contribution is to ease entry and provide credibility for the professionals. In other cases confidentiality between regular colleagues which normally reinforces a degree of organizational autonomy is either ignored or diluted by unplanned inclusion of consumers.

2. The process becomes more important than the product. Sometimes the product itself is lost sight of. Much of the activities are about matters which are not directly related to the product of the organization. Goals are vague, and consequently it is difficult to acquire proper machinery for goal implementation. Change becomes a continuous feature of the organization. Although there is much talk about planned change, it often turns into changed plans.

3. The major thrust of the organization becomes one of development and generation of an ethos rather than efficiency.

4. These organizations rest on a subtle technology or, perhaps better, a need to raise consciousness. Their requirements are not specific discipline-based skills, but models for dealing with ambiguities, for assistance in living with puzzlement and discomfort. The need goes beyond the usual cry for coordination. Often in these organizations, there are not enough specifics to be coordinated.

Staff uniqueness. 1. The leadership group in an interstitial organization has a maverick quality. These are people who have outgrown their own disciplines, who are looking for enlarged scope for work, or whose aspirations are not properly satisfied through usual roles. As a result they do not receive the familiar colleague support in their own professional circles. In a sense interstitial organizations attract interstitial people.

2. Staff in these organizations belong to worlds which are overlapping and sometimes even contradictory. This situation has certain advantages along with the difficulties. Such staff members use the image of one of their backgrounds to gain entry into and status in another. Thus the black militant uses his constituency support not only to become director of the community-controlled agency but also to make his case with colleagues. In a group of social scientists, the lawyer who is a team member often receives a special status which will not be his in his own professional circle.

3. Goal formulation cannot be confined to the top-leadership, unlike many other organizations.

THE STUDY

I held a series of depth interviews with the key group of eleven professional staff members of a certain council of governments. There were six sessions each of about three hours held at intervals of approximately one month. Each session was taped, and the transcriptions ran to nearly 350 pages. The data which resulted from these depth interview sessions are classifiable chiefly into four conceptual areas. An examination of these areas is vital to an understanding of the unique nature of interstitial organizations. These conceptual areas are Administrative Ideology, Boundary (Galactical Concerns), Identity Ambivalence, and Technology.

THE WORLD OF AN INTERSTITIAL ORGANIZATION: DEPTH INTERVIEWS IN A COUNCIL OF GOVERNMENTS

Administrative ideology. The place of ideology in administration is receiving increasing attention from some scholars. There is a growing recognition that technical skills, the legal structure of authority, and even harmonious interpersonal relations within organizations are not enough to make organizations really effective.[1] Press and Arian state: "But if the administrator is to be effective in his efforts, he must attempt to forge an ideology which will synthesize the values and norms of his organization and society. The result of this synthesis we have termed the 'appropriate ideology.'"[2] In contrast much literature—especially in public administration—implies that administrators not only need not be concerned about their own values, but should be neutral implementers.

It may be that in the past such an attitude was not a great handicap. One could also make a convincing case for neutrality in administration. However, beginning with the sixties, the public administrator is increasingly called upon to provide leadership in ways which should be difficult unless there is an ideological dimension in his repertoire in addition to possession of administrative skills.

It is our argument that this dimension has mainly to do with values, norms, and an ideology. To illustrate, Philip Selznik explains that the "cult of efficiency" tends to stress techniques as well as organizations which are essentially neutral. This bias, however, does not distinguish those methods which should be adapted to a distinctive type of organization or stage of development.[3]

Increasingly the new kind of organization of which the present council is an example will be called upon to deal with issues which are more controversial, uncertain, and nebulous than those issues which organizations were called upon to handle in the past. And such a situation will further call for a viable administrative ideology which can provide a sense of direction through the ambiguity. Singular allegiance to a neutral, efficient, and antiseptic pattern will work as a deterrent and will tie the hands of the leadership groups in these interstitial organizations. We discovered that some of the ambiguities and frustrations of this group engaged in significant metropolitan planning resulted from unresolved ideological, value-laden issues.

The thrust of the argument here has gained significant recent support. Thus Philip Jacob states that the attitudes of planners towards values require special consideration because planning has become established as a central and discrete function of organizational decision making in modern societies.[4]

David Ranney has expressed a similar opinion regarding the value premises of planners. He states that while making recommendations based on technical criteria, the planner also makes value judgments. Questions arise as to what and whose values a planner will seek to implement. In the allocation of land in a city plan, for example, questions of such a nature arise. How much land should be devoted to low-income housing? Low-income families will favor this priority, but downtown merchants will prefer middle- or upper-income housing or parking garages so as to have wealthier clients. Some choice must be made,[5] often by men rather than by data.

Considerable attention was devoted in our sessions to exploring the area of values of the council of government executives as this is often an ignored subject.[6] The council is an organization whose top leadership has been nourished on the principles of professionalism and rational objectivity. This group has also drawn professionals from a few of the hard engineering fields like transportation planning, data management, computer science or system analysis. An awareness that one may indeed have been influenced by one's ideology came slowly and crystallized as a result of the depth-interview sessions. Witness this quote from one of the executives during our sessions: "I think it is a fact that there is room for a lot more administrative ideology than we have talked about. The primary set of motivations for the local jurisdictions are not the ones to which we play, that we can handle during the first three days of the year and the remaining 362 days are ours to play with for the most part."

We also had the opportunity of looking at the way power is shared between the council executives and the local municipalities. We found evidence of significant ambivalence in this matter. What in fact seems to happen, at least as it surfaced in our sessions, is an emotional tug of war between the two contradicting forces. One can be a center of power, or one can abandon this position in order to be a neutral executive who only implements programs which are decided by the local municipalities.

Similar ambivalence has been observed in other complex organizations. In their study of the Yale Psychiatric Institute, for example, Rubenstein and Lasswell detected this problem while analyzing the performance of therapists. They record the discovery of latent value conflicts between specific practices. On the one hand, most of the therapists felt committed to the democratic goals of power-sharing. But they also felt that the welfare of patients was best served if the therapists took major responsibility for decisions. The authors go on to propose that "Individuals who are reared in societies that make articulate the demand for power sharing mature into persons who suffer conflicts of conscience when they behave in ways that they perceive as contradicting the norm."[7]

The members who made up the present population of council executives are of high intelligence, and are nurtured in the cosmopolitan and progressive professional atmosphere where consensus, sharing of power, and collaborative decision making have been respected values. They find themselves in a situation of metropolitan politics as cosmopolitans versus locals. The latter guard their prerogatives to decide matters considered vital to them—especially those matters where some of the executives have worked out value-oriented opinions. Contrast and conflict are inevitable.

Boundary-galactical concerns. Political participation is an important life force in the council. Since there is no set pattern for participation, and since it may vary from project to project, the boundary preoccupation becomes a continuing one for council executives.

Any treatment of the boundary question would not be adequate without dealing with issues of suspicion, fear, and conflict. This is because boundaries reflect the tentative arrangements or agreements across which transactions take place. Oftentimes these boundaries are more functional and attitudinal than physical or geographical. The following quote from our session is one example of such a situation: "To the extent that we get away from just that function, of providing information and perhaps analyses, to the extent that we leave that area and go into the area of making policy, of making decisions, or evaluating plans, to that extent the organization is jeopardized."

One can say that part of the emerging boundary arrangement is a result of interaction of two sets of fears—one of the locals, and the other of the council executives. The interaction is exacerbated because this group of council professionals is not merely involved with tangible projects but is increasingly getting into controversial matters which threaten or at least influence the lifestyles of these municipalities. It is in this crucible of fears and doubts on both sides that the boundary question must be resolved so as to provide operating guidance for all parties.

Because the nature of the product of an interstitial organization is not as clear-cut as in much industry, and because the outside social forces at times have a role in decision making about the nature of that product and yet at times withdraw and leave the implementation to the interstitial organization, ambiguities and confusion about boundaries are common. The sense of the point is well illustrated by the history of local community action programs, which many have tried to dismantle but which persist because of their useful middle role. Thus Jonathan Spivak notes such agencies "stand as an independent buffer between the poor, whose needs are insatiable, and (established) government, whose response was bound to be inadequate."[8] The present population of council executives has become increasingly conscious of their inherent power vis à vis other organizations in their galaxy. It also seems that they are engaged in drawing new boundaries based on their power, which new arrangements with other galactical forces may prove satisfactory to them. The following point made by Rice and Miller seems to be applicable to the present situation in the council: "We have seen that any transaction across enterprise boundaries, an essential process for any living system, involves the drawing, temporarily at least, of new boundaries. And the drawing of new boundaries will prove stronger than the old."[9] The following quotes from interviews are also relevant:

> I think to a great extent it is true that the local politicians are not thinking of the council all the time. They have other more vital and direct interests—their constituencies, their local problems, the ballot box, etc., but I think it is beginning to change. For one thing the availability of organized information by an advisory group like this one is a very potentially strong tool for getting in touch with people that are making decisions that you would like to influence.

> Also the latter officials are not so much interested in 1990 as they are in what you can do politically for them today and in what way will further our own efforts today.

The sense and source of council power is implicit in a response about whether executives generally gain acceptance from the local municipalities once they initiate programs for which the locals did not ask. One executive spoke for the majority when he said: "As a rule, yes, because we generally can wave a federal law at them saying 'you got to do it.'"

Such comments imply the gradual growth of power in an interstitial organization which started in a tentative manner. It is credible that interstitial organizations have been tolerated in their infancy by other members of their galaxy of organizations because of pressing needs, and will gradually grow into powerful bargaining entities. But as we will also see when discussing Identity Ambivalence, such a bargaining position is not solidly based because there is a satellite quality about these organizations.

In an interstitial organization, derivatively, adherence to the distinction between administration and politics is not possible because of the galactical relationships with which these organizations have to become involved. This is also so because administrators in these organizations feel the need to work out a proper administrative ideology. During our sessions we found that there was considerable uncertainty expressed by these administrators about the proper way in which they ought to interact with boundary forces—in this case mainly the local municipalities. Often the issues which they are dealing with have overtones which cannot be handled from a purely administrative point of view. These are tied up with the political concerns and life of local municipalities. Council executives reflect caution and hesitancy in approaching such issues. One executive expressed both themes in these words: "Well, I think the question arises because who judges whether or not it is going to have a political impact. You never quite know. I think it is pretty generally thought that you should err on the side of saying it is political rather than it is not."

In interstitial organizations , in any case, galactic relationships have to be carefully nurtured. Councils at once are satellites and yet strive toward independence. The tug of war is between the forces which have created and still dominate the councils and the growing forces of independence, visibility, and support from the public and other levels of government. This situation is vividly portrayed by the following quote.

> You must have been at our last board meeting. It is very true that there is a feeling that the dog, in this case the council, that they have been feeding has been growing every day, you know. And now he demands to be fed and now when you hand him that steak, you pull your hand back. The Transit Authority, the Public Service Commission and several others said, "Things we have done have been great and we have been very cooperative and well coordinated and you have never stepped on our toes; but we are not so sure that next year it is still going to be that way. And they are nervous.

Identity ambivalence. The council, like many interstitial organizations, is a creature of grants. Its executives are acutely aware of this fundamental condition, and hence must trade back and forth between this reality and their own values. One council member said during an interview: "I think if the federal government came out with a massive new program for library planning and spending, that we could get involved. And being an intelligent organization, I think we would probably get involved in a big way; and if you looked at our budget, we might be spending a hundred thousand a year on libraries and ten thousand dollars a year on say housing." Even as the council member made this statement, this interviewer could detect an attitude of partial helplessness and partial distaste.

To further complicate their own quest for direction and identity, council executives cannot unequivocally follow the lead of the federal government. The harder fact is that these administrators have to work out their ideology in an environment which is a composite of different points of view and of various pressures. Our council executives are generally comfortable with the federal approach. While the federal presence acts as a source of legitimacy and support for the council, it also complicates council relationships with the locals and their professional counterparts in the local municipalities if the council is viewed simply as an extension of the federal government. The federal approach also happens to run counter to the prevailing political values of some local actors and organizations.

This interviewer sees ambivalence in many of the interstitial organizations which have sprung up during the last decade. They are pulled by their clientele in definite directions, with more force than the usual customers of a public agency. In the case of the community-controlled agencies, in fact, the clientele is represented directly in the leadership circles. Nor can professionals in interstitial organizations always be up front concerning their differences of opinion with the client system. In the council of governments focal here, this particular strain does not appear in as heightened a form as in some other interstitial organizations. But it does show itself in the way the council executives at once identify with the federal government and yet play down that identification in their dealings with locals.

It is safe to assume that in the case of the council, reliance on the federal government does not result in dependence/hostility as is the case with some other interstitial organizations. Such hostility is especially likely in organizations with few professionals and a dominant community leadership. In these cases, one common tactic is to denounce publicly the government system in order to assert one's independence, while simultaneously wishing for and resenting such dependence.

The life of a group with identity ambivalence becomes full of strain and ambiguities. A group which is in the limelight, which is brought into existence by the same forces which do not want to give it real power, is in a tenuous position. There are parallels for this in the field of traditional organizations where certain units or divisions are tolerated by a top management which cannot do without them. Industrial relations, personnel, community activities, or community relations departments are examples. Sometimes these are subsystems which the system can fall back upon during times of crisis. Their managers are often in a double bind. They are not allowed to have a high profile but, if things go wrong, they are accountable. In these cases accountability, mandate, and privileges are not clearly defined, sometimes intentionally. They often are not given the necessary support, opportunities, or resources. At the same time they are held accountable.

Employees in such positions try to impress others—at times out of a sense of desperation—with their expertise. At the same time much energy and attention are turned inwards. Members of our group discussed at length, directly or indirectly, issues such as how they can improve their profile, what they have been doing that can be done better, etc. Most organizations question their goals, their direction, and procedures, of course. But the search for one's identity is particularly intense in interstitial organizations. Witness this revealing comment:

> We can talk about the frustrations consisting of not having any chips to play with. We don't have anything to offer except concepts, and the frustrations revolve around our not being able to offer anything tangible or very much tangible to cause someone to change his way of operating. We have tried to get around this by always trying to have something to offer, but the frustration comes in when maybe it is not enough, maybe what we offer him is not enough to cause him to change his own operation.

> We're really not sure what the local governments want or need. We are assuming that they want this or that, assuming that they don't want that. But we don't know directly, we are just assuming.

Paradoxically, the problem grows if the council is potent. Were the council at the mercy of the local municipalities, its members probably would experience less identity ambivalence. They would have gradually accepted their passive position, perhaps grudgingly. But we found in these interviews that council experience is more complicated. Council members are aware that in some matters they have the upper hand, or at least a strong one.

This situation is not unusual in the case of interstitial organizations which have come to be supported by a sizable segment of the public and the government. Some of these organizations have also become the tangible forms of social conscience. As a result of this, these organizations have either real or moral power. Thus on the one hand they are dependent on the local establishment, and on the other hand they are in controlling/influencing positions. This contradiction feeds their identity ambivalence.

The typical condition that an interstitial organization is always becoming and never being keeps its employees from setting down roots. It is quite possible that certain types of individuals are drawn to such organizations because of this feature. Of course any developing organization generates a touch of instability until the organization has arrived. This instability has to be distinguished sharply from the instability which inheres in the very nature of interstitial organizations. Given common feelings of persecution and isolation, it is easy to comprehend why such organizations have a shaky sense of identity.

The employees of interstitial organizations share the common task of formulating goals and charting the direction for goal achievement, as contrasted more or less sharply with the pattern in traditional organizations where the crucial decisions are made by the leadership circle. In the case of interstitial organizations, the organization becomes like a fraternity, especially in the case of counterculture organizations and those which are sustained emotionally by forces in the community. The differences between the leader and the led are minimized as a consequence. While this produces a heightened form of morale and interest in the organization, it also can have the side effect of creating major authority issues. As the leader's role is diminished, for example, members may come to miss the presence of a figure around whom some of their negative feelings can crystallize. Thus much that is frustrating is projected outside, and already-existing feelings of persecution by the outside world can be heightened. The entire organization, including the leader, may huddle together for warmth as they feel (or believe they feel) the cold of the alien environment.

Technology. The crucial technological needs of an interstitial organization are not the ones which usually keep other organizations preoccupied. The central concerns expressed by this group of executives are expressed in terms other than those which frequently appear in the literature on organizations.

Since the council lacks many precedents, one formidable task is the charting of effective and manageable goals. This is further complicated by the shifting nature of these goals taking place in an environment where there is also pressure on the executives not to move too far away from the thinking and the articulated interests of the municipalities which are to a considerable extent in the controlling position. There is patent discomfort in this ambiguity. As one council professional expressed his concern:

> Should an organization's goals be to optimize its own existence or should it be the organization's goals to serve the people who support it and hired it? And to orient these people into what are truly useful goals? Should the government set a goal, let us say of 10 percent Negro integration in the suburbs? Should we not try to design programs and get grants and attempt to influence other agencies to achieve that goal?
>
> But this point, I think, is a critical one and one that makes me nervous; that is that we will follow the grants. That our definition of a problem may very well be that area which has been funded that week.

It is generally considered that the task of setting goals is a prerogative and function of top leadership, of course. In this case, this would mean the executive director, after consultation with the board. The high-caliber professional group in this council, however, is not content with a set of goals decided upon and handed down by top management. Such goals would make their task less strenuous and frustrating. But there is a strong motivation to participate in the task of setting a direction for their organization.

Implied in the acceptance of a set of goals is the responsibility to work out the decision-making machinery or tradition whereby these goals can be put into action. The present group of council members express a wish that they would like to see proper decision-making machinery in operation. But members also sense a trap here. To explain, Etzioni has referred to the situation where because of the pressures to be rational, organizations are eager to measure their efficiency. Some aspects of an organization's outputs are more measurable than others. Attention, therefore, gravitates towards such aspects of an organization's activities.[10] Similarly an organization's thinking may shift to more tangible parts of its activities when it gets bogged down in defining those forces that are less concrete.

Several times during our depth-interview sessions, we found that when the discussions continued about issues such as values, administrative ideology, and goals, group members could neither let go of the topics, nor could they achieve any resolution. In such cases the discussion would shift to an examination of what, for example, the transportation planning department of the council was doing. This permitted talking about matters that were more tangible and measurable, and for which data existed. (When this was pointed out to the group, a few of the interviewees were frank in acknowledging the fact that they were doing so to slack off the strain a little).

Given an interstitial organization's uncertainity about goals, moreover, the amorphous nature of its environment also means that guidelines for bargaining are missing, and precedents do not exist. Gradually attention is diverted to internal processes of work. Concern for the product takes a secondary place.

There were quite a few occasions during interviews when this preoccupation with internal process surfaced. Because other forces in the situation are not manageable, council members scrutinize their conduct in a way that is comparable to an individual who feels blocked and who begins the process of self-scrutiny. This phenomenon has more applicability than just to a council of governments. Actually this council is more organized, thoughtful and product-oriented than some other interstitial organizations. This is because the council is staffed by people who have come out of the tradition of looking for tangible achievement. Nonetheless many activities in this organization are exercises in analyzing the processes of work. Witness these revealing interview responses:

> There is probably a conflict between the thoughtful process that develops in taking the time to figure out which goals you want and what you are going to do with them and the opportunism which is necessary at this level to grab hold of programs wherever you can to build your base.

> I am at a loss to know how we tackle this problem of why we are at a loss to know what we are supposed to be doing. We brag that we are a multidisciplinary organization, yet we sit across the table and we hear once a week what he is doing in a report so we know something. But are we really contributing?

> So you are caught between the horns of a dilemma. Do I finish the project in the time that I told you I would do it? Or do I use the multidisciplinary approach until termination and then run the risk of not satisfying you?

> You say you want to be in at the beginning. But in the conceptual process that goes on in planning it is very difficult because sometimes you are discarding things and ideas. When you reach the point in your own shop that you think that it is time to tell—then you probably couldn't have come sooner. It is really a problem to decide at what point in the conceptual process of an idea we should get to you.

SPECULATIONS FOR THE FUTURE

Based on analysis of this council of governments and profiting from our experiences with other interstitial organizations, I make the following statements:

1. Established organizations directly or indirectly will continue to encourage the growth and activities of interstitial organizations. There will, of course, be some resistance by established organizations. But the domi-

nant reaction will be that the smooth and untroubled functioning of established organizations within their own boundaries becomes more assured if these unique organizations appear in the cracks.

2. Because of this, traditional organizations will continue to look at interstitial organizations with a mixture of permissiveness, criticism, support, opposition, seriousness, and amusement. If the interorganizational set can be compared with a family, the traditional organizations will treat interstitial organizatiions as a family treats its rebel member because of whom the rest of the family can continue to function in their accustomed manner without having to untangle the twisted family dynamics. As a result the interstitial organization will gradually assume a controlling role just as the rebel member of the family comes to control the lives of the other members. There will thus be a love-hate relationship between the established members of the galaxy of organizations and the interstitial members.

3. These organizations will be used to send aloft trial balloons, as by leadership of more traditional organizations who may not want to risk being innovative or who might not have the confidence or resources to tackle certain problems.

4. Interstitial organizations may receive encouragement from traditional organizations, in specific cases, because the former can diffuse and dilute environmental demands thereby enabling the latter to keep their boundaries fairly impermeable.

5. Members of interstitial organizations will remain confused and uncomfortable to some degree. Such an outcome may not be desired consciously, but members of interstitial organizations may help produce such outcomes because of their perceived self-interest in being known as integrators and innovators.

POST SCRIPT

Since completion of the study of the particular interstitial organization which served as the main example in this paper, there has been a notable change in atmosphere in this country. The exuberance of the Great Society has gradually subsided, variously yielding to the cynicism of a more cautious country.

One may therefore be tempted to compose an epitaph for interstitial organizations, so many of which blossomed during the decade that saw America greening. But reasons to resist temptation clearly exist. Grants did not always prepare the soil for such organizations, grants merely gave a push and at times provided a shortcut. With grants drying up, if anything, the trend towards interstitial organizations may become more pronounced and less conflictful. For example interstitial organizations may be successful in creating or finding sources of funding which are more consonant with their ideologies, and which have remained untapped because of readily available government grants. We may see less identity ambivalence as a result.

NOTES

1. Charles Press and Alan Arian, *Empathy and Ideology: Aspects of Administrative Innovation* (Chicago, Ill.: Rand McNally, 1969) 3.

2. Ibid., 8.

3. Philip Selznik , *Leadership and Administration* (Harper and Row, 1957) 135.

4. Philip Jacob, "The Influence of Values in Political Integration," in *Integration of Political Communities* (New York: J. B. Lippincott, 1964) 239.

5. David C. Ranney, *Planning and Politics in the Metropolis* (Columbus, Ohio: Charles E. Merrill) 110.

6. Press and Arian, 17.

7. Robert Rubenstein and Harold Lasswell, *The Sharing of Power in a Psychiatric Hospital* (New Haven, Conn.: Yale University Press, 1966) 12.

8. "No Funeral Wreaths for OEO," *Wall Street Journal* (1973): 14.

9. E. J. Miller and A. K. Rice, *Systems of Organization* (London: Tavistock Publications, 1967) 268.

10. Amitai Etzioni, *Modern Organizations* (Englewood Cliffs, N.J.: Prentice Hall, 1964) 9.

Applied Behavioral Science
in Urban Administrative/Political Systems

WILLIAM EDDY & ROBERT J. SAUNDERS

It is legitimate, if not novel, to assert that local government institutions must find ways to increase their effectiveness if they are to solve the pressing problems of this urban society. One of the aspects of government that needs improving is the administrative system. A variety of avenues to upgrading administration are being proposed and tested. These include accounting and decision-making tools based on computer technology, infusion of professional and technical expertise into problem areas, and federal support to create new ancillary organizations such as neighborhood organizations, metropolitan area coordinating groups, and pollution control agencies. The establishment of this latter variety of new organization is apparently based at least in part on the assumption that existing local government structures cannot be relied on to do the job.

Each critic of local government generates his own description of what is wrong—depending upon his own orientation and the perspective from which he views the community. From the point of view of applied behavioral science the problem looks something like this: Most governmental organizations were built upon and still fit reasonably well the traditional bureaucratic model. This form is characterized by an emphasis on efficiency and rationality, a pyramidal authority system (or command system), functional units clearly separated on the basis of mission, and a system of rules and procedures to direct and control the behavior of employees. This kind of system is a rational design for the accomplishment of order, reliability, accountability, and precision as basic outcomes. But for all its rationality and reliability, the bureaucracy has distinct disadvantages in attempting to deal with the dynamic and complex urban scene. Some of the organizational problem areas that require attention include the following: (1) the need for increased flexibility and adaptation to change; (2) the need to shift from major emphasis on control, structure, and compliance to a focus on problem identification, problem solving, and innovation; (3) the need for more effective teamwork and collaboration within and among operating units; (4) the need to develop managerial approaches which utilize the full potential of employees and enhance motivation and commitment; (5) the need to develop more open organizational systems which are more in touch with and responsive to external as well as internal factors.

One approach to the resolution of these kinds of problems has been to leave the basic model of the organization intact, but to beef it up by increasing the rationality through the use of control systems, structural

Reprinted from *Public Administration Review*, (Jan./Feb., 1972) 33:11-16.

redesign, and more qualified professional experts. An alternate, though not incompatible, approach to organizational improvement has emerged from the field of behavioral science. There is no one term nor single set of techniques which define this area. The term "applied behavioral science" is broadest and subsumes within it such approaches as planned change, organization renewal, organization development (OD), and grid organization development. The purpose of this article is not to describe nor argue for the application of behavioral science in public organizations. These issues have been discussed in detail elsewhere. The present purpose is to identify and address some issues related to the fit between the behavioral science change model and urban agencies where the political/administrative mix may pose problems different from those encountered in private business.

When evaluating the applicability of behavioral science in specific kinds of systems, it is important to review the norms, values, and principles proposed in the new model which may differ in significant ways from those inherent in the traditional approach. Many applied behavioral scientists take a position about appropriateness or inappropriateness of certain kinds of organizational behavior based on a combination of values, insights, and empirical evidence. The following are illustrative.

Openness and authenticity. Communication about perceptions, ideas, and feelings should be free and open in all directions. People should be encouraged to level with each other—to be frank about their reactions. Feelings are viewed as important and appropriate aspects of interpersonal relations and should not be covered up.

Trust. A necessary component of effective collaborative relations is a level of mutual trust which will support openness, acceptance of others' positions, risk taking, and mutual support.

Shared influence and participation. Unilateral authority is not always the best approach to management. Organizations may function more effectively if employees at all levels are allowed a sense of ownership through opportunities to influence decisions and plans that affect them.

Development of people. The organization has a need and a responsibility to help its members continue to develop themselves as fuller, more competent, and actualizing total persons.

Confrontation. Traditional norms stressing avoidance of direct confrontation are dysfunctional. Avoiding conflict, keeping feelings out of it, and compromising differences may prevent problem solving.

Interpersonal competence. Substantive technical knowledge is not enough. Organizational members need to gain greater self-understanding and operational skills in such areas as communication, teamwork, and conflict management.

Change and renewal. Organizations should devote time and resources to the development of mechanisms that assure a continuing review and renewal process. Evaluation and change rather than fixed procedures should become the organization's way of life.

APPLICATION OF BEHAVIORAL SCIENCE IN GOVERNMENT

Organization development programs utilizing applied behavioral science have been tried extensively in business firms.[1] There is less direct experience in public agencies. Golembiewski[2] and Eddy[3] have discussed some of the problems in applying OD programs in government. Golembiewski's analysis emphasizes the federal government and focuses on organizational characteristics which differentiate it from business. He lists the major differentiating characteristics of government as: (1) multiple access—the system is more open to influence at many levels; (2) greater variety of interests, reward structures, and values at subgroup levels; (3) more competing command loci or influence centers rather than a clear-cut management group; and (4) weak linkages between political and career levels, which may mean between executives and operating managers.

Golembiewski also discusses the unique habit background of public agencies. These are patterns within the institutional environment which may inhibit the process of change. Phenomena discussed include reluctance to delegate because of the need to maximize information and control at the top—where responsibility is affixed; legal specification of appropriate work behaviors; greater emphasis on security; stress on procedural regularity and caution; and a less strongly developed concept of professional management.

Eddy identifies several possible reasons for the current minimal utilization of behavioral science in government: (1) alternative change programs such as systems and procedures methods are more consonant with the legal-rational bureaucratic approach and may be perceived as less threatening to the status quo; (2) some political scientists and public administrators are natural enemies of behavioral science—particularly in regard to its challenges to traditional notions about the need for strong leadership; (3) behavioral science is often seen as tenderminded with an undue focus on keeping employees happy; (4) participative approaches are suspected as cover-ups for management by committee or turning the organization over to the subordinates; and (5) the values underlying applied behavioral science (discussed earlier in this article) may be in conflict with values inherent in some agencies.

Other authors have, of course, discussed differences between public and private organizations which affect management behavior. A paper by Costello is particularly relevant because it describes unique characteristics of public agencies which may affect the ways in which change takes place.[4] His list which refers to local government includes: (1) sudden and drastic changes in leadership; (2) goals and outcomes which are less amenable to measurement; (3) more heterogeneous constituency—subgroups have conflicting interests; (4) decisions and policies are more highly visible and more subject to critique; (5) local governments are subjected to more legal constraints and can make fewer of their own decisions than other institutions; (6) it is much more difficult to go out of business—to shut down a facility or withdraw a service; and (7) programs which have immediate visibility and seem to demonstrate progress may receive political priority over slower and less dramatic—though more meaningful—efforts.

POLITICAL ISSUES RELATED TO
BEHAVIORAL SCIENCE IN LOCAL GOVERNMENT

Our experiences in carrying out organization development programs in local government agencies have made us aware of several other potential problem areas that need further attention and understanding. Most relate in one way or another to the political environment.

1. There are, of course, the usual problems of interfacing any administrative system and political system. These include public mistrust of bureaucracy and bureaucrats' mistrust of the public, politicians vs. administrators in policy formation, concerns about keeping the technocrats publicly accountable, generalized resistance to change, and political pressures in relation to specific programs. While these certainly are not unique to behavioral science applications, they may well be important factors.

2. There is a potential incompatibility between political systems and the ideal organization from a behavioral science point of view. Political systems are by nature distributive—or at least are usually operated that way. They function to divide a finite amount of resources among various interest groups. This cutting of the pie is a win/lose game in which a variety of tactics are used to increase the rewards to one group—which frequently means they are decreased to others. The well-functioning administrative system aims at being integrative.[5] Emphasis is placed on communality of purpose, collaboration, and win/win relationships. Ways are sought to minimize win/lose competition among operating units, and to enhance shared problem solving and planning. A highly integrative organization at the local government level may not serve the felt needs of politicians whose own goals require special output from a particular segment within the organization—to the possible detriment of other units.

3. Trust and openness may not be possible (or at least not perceived as possible) in situations with political implications. An official in NASA is quoted as saying ". . . we never punish error. We only punish concealment of error."[6] This policy is, of course, intended to reinforce openness and disclosure. Many local government officials may feel they cannot afford this much risk, and may be much more concerned about concealing errors than whether or not errors were made in the first place. In an "Affairs of State" editorial in the Saturday Evening Post, Stewart Alsop castigated behavioral scientists for their attempts to "unfreeze" the Foreign Service Office and create more openness and candor. He argued that secretiveness was functional. Instead of this "final humiliation" he urged, "Just let the poor old Foreign Service alone. . . ."[7]

4. Some of the techniques of the application of behavioral science involve recognizing and dealing with the feelings, attitudes, and personal styles of participants—a departure from Weberian "formalistic impersonality." There is considerable misunderstanding and suspicion regarding approaches such as sensitivity training and team building which are designed to promote communication and learning about interpersonal relationships. Many laymen, politicians included, do not have the information to distinguish between legitimate programs for personal learning and growth and various so-called thought control schemes. The protestations of the far right and the wild turn-on and nudie groups have not helped the image either.[8] One of the authors recently conducted a brief team-development program for members of a city council. The methodology involved confidential interviews with individual councilmen regarding intracouncil and council-management concerns, followed by a retreat at which generalized interview data were fed back and discussed in some depth. There was no sensitivity training involved. One council member refused to participate in the program and was quoted in the press as follows:

> I feel that the presence of a psychologist, regardless of what his title may be, is somewhat insulting to members of the council. I am quite sure that neither President Nixon nor Governor . . . would suggest such a thing to members of Congress or the Legislature.
>
> The role of the city councilman is to serve the people who elect him. I believe that rather than attending retreats we ought to be out in the districts conferring with the people, not psychoanalyzing one another.
>
> I personally do not believe in the techniques of group therapy, sensitivity training, or any other device which would reduce our individual thinking to the thinking of a group; that is, making the individual feel he is committing a mortal sin to have a thought of his own. . . .
>
> There is no substitute for training a councilman, and that is basically what these retreats purport to do, like conferring and meeting with the people in the districts and then reporting their views on the council. In other words, there is no substitute for "government of the people, by the people, and for the people." The administration needs to look no further for a philosophy nor do we need a psychoanalysis of the job we have been elected to do than to adopt the philosophy of government of, by, and for the people.[9]

5. Conventional wisdom, political thinking included, views good leadership, assertive-authoritarian leadership, and masculinity as essentially synonymous. Approaches to leadership which assert that subordinates should have upward influence, that dissident points of view should

be listened to, and that solving problems is preferable to discipline are seen as weak and ineffectual. Two articles in the *Buffalo Evening News* illustrate what may happen.[10] Behavioral scientist Warren Bennis resigned his position as executive vice president of the State University of New York at Buffalo in protest against the way in which police were involved in dealing with a student disturbance. He was quoted in the article as follows:

"I have throughout the sequence of disturbances remained firmly convinced that police occupation could do nothing but exacerbate the troubles, that they were and are unnecessary," Dr. Bennis said in an interview.

"I did not approve that decision then and do not approve of it now."

Dr. Bennis, who retains his post as vice president for academic development, also criticized what he termed "a lack of candor" and an unresponsiveness to student concern by the Regan administration since a clash between police and students Feb. 25 set off a student strike and a week-and-a-half of disorders on the Main St. campus.

"I thought we hadn't done enough to demonstrate either sensitivity to the reactions on our campus, to the events on Feb. 25, particularly the police actions in Norton Union, nor did I feel that we had as an administration adequately communicated a responsiveness to the issues facing this campus," he said.

"If I felt we had done the best we could on these latter issues, and the violence had still continued, I might have then—but only as a last resort—called for police occupation."

In a subsequent meeting of the city council, a councilwoman criticized the university administration. "The campus disorder," she said, "is separating the men from the boys. One of the boys has just resigned, thank goodness."

6. Organization development proposes that work time is legitimately spent working on relationship issues. Terms such as "team building," "working the problem," and "processing" refer to situations in which administrators do not do "work" in the traditional sense, but meet to talk about how they might work more effectively together. Politicians and the public may feel that this is wasted time and that people paid to manage local government ought to know how to work. The fact that human systems require maintenance in much the same way that machines do is not widely understood, and training which is not technical training is not valued. The fact that working on relationships requires getting together in meetings heightens the problem—since meetings are often viewed as a waste of time.

7. Special problems may be caused by a press which maintains a traditional view of organizations and of local government. There is

pressure for all official meetings to be open, and everything to be on the record. This condition reinforces closed, safe discussions ("you have to watch what you say") and discourages sound problem solving in groups. For groups to solve problems effectively, work out relationships, explore ideas, manage conflict, and make good decisions, an atmosphere of non-defensiveness, provisionalism, exploration, and trust must prevail. This cannot be accomplished in a fishbowl. Members of the press need to gain insights which allow them to differentiate between "dealing with policy" and "dealing with each other" meetings. Some newspapers are willing to accept a few closed meetings so that personal issues may be worked, but in doing so imply that secrecy is necessary out of good taste because the administrators are at each other's throats.

8. Laws and policies relating to accountability take a "Theory X" position regarding human motivation—as described by McGregor.[11] They grow out of assumptions that people in general are not to be trusted, they are not responsible, they must be closely watched. Applied behavioral science tends to assume different motives—most people want to work, to develop, to assume responsibility and contribute to the system. Shared decision making, less rigid controls, decentralization, and delegation are seen as improving, not damaging, the organization.

9. The reform movement of the early part of this century has left strong tendencies to value local government structures which provide for strong authority figures, centralization, control, and accountability as defenses against potential spoilers. In essence it may be perceived better to run a highly controlled system whose members care less and accomplish less individually and collectively, but which runs less risk of scandal.

10. The hard sciences have managed to gain the trust of many people. The soft sciences of human behavior have not reached that point. They have no easily visible "better things for better living" or men on the moon to win friends. Further, the application of the medical model to the analysis of behavior has tended to associate psychology with the sick and the flawed—not a positive association in political terms.

There are doubtless other issues related to behavioral science in the political/administrative mix. And those listed probably apply differentially according to a variety of factors not presently understood. It is hoped that the listing will alert behavioral scientists and public administrators to avoid snags in the implementation of change programs.

OVERCOMING RESISTANCE

Although it is risky to propose solutions before the problems are clearly defined, several possibilities for coming to grips with some of the difficulties listed above can be offered.

1. The authors have been involved in several efforts to utilize organization development in the interface between administrators and politicians. One was the council-manager retreat mentioned earlier. Although it was a

very short-term program and was boycotted by one council member, it was deemed useful by most who attended. Another was a longer-term effort to help elected and appointed officials in an urban county government develop better understanding and collaborative skills. The program is described by Murphy.[12] Experience indicates that such efforts are feasible and worthwhile—but one must proceed carefully. Learnings for us that have come from these programs include the need for clear prior acceptance by all parties of the relevance and validity of the problems to be attacked and a commitment to facing and solving them. Also it is important to clarify norms that can allow trust to develop. For example, that conversations be kept confidential within the training groups, that participants attempt to view feedback as an attempt to be helpful and not to be resented later, and that major conflicts and disagreements be acknowledged and worked through—rather than avoided and allowed to fester. This further suggests that some continuing attention should be paid to the contract between client and consultant so that expectations and roles of both parties will not stand unnecessarily in the way at some critical point in the change process.

2. Behavioral scientists and administrators know much more about overcoming resistance to change than they tend to utilize in implementing their own change programs. For example, involvement in planning the program by those likely to be affected by changes—both within and outside the organization—is often helpful. The greater the degree to which those involved are informed, allowed to contribute to the effort, and feel able to exert influence on the process (sometimes in order to increase their own safety), the less they are likely to resist or sabotage the effort. Other strategies for preventing resistance include building a climate of trust between the client and the change agent, not violating important organizational norms, and beginning the change with problems that the client feels are most important and most pressing.

3. Organizational change efforts may need to be preceded by thorough informational and educational programs conducted both within and outside the organization. The need for change and development, the rationale, and case examples can be usefully pointed out. It is particularly important to help the public understand that ways of viewing and evaluating organizations are changing—along with the rest of the urban scene. Elected officials are not likely to encourage different models of administrative behavior in the organizations they oversee until they feel constituents will accept such approaches.

4. Costello asserts that the principal coin in the realm of politics is power, and that behavioral scientists have written more about the process of power equalization than about acquisition and effective use of power.[13] The implications of this state of affairs may be that behavioral scientists are either uncomfortable or unknowledgeable in regard to one of the major dimensions of government, and that they may be ineffective in dealing with those who seek and use power. Costello asserts that the behavioral scientist

who would bring about change in municipal affairs must build a power backing. He may do this by (1) direct political activity in support of sympathetic candidates, (2) relating to strong community action organizations, or (3) personal cultivation or reaching out to men in power to gain understanding and personal acceptance. Although only (2) is usually acceptable to the scientist, (3) is most promising.

In the long run behavioral scientists and public administrators may have to move from a defensive to an offensive stance. Frequently the political system is accepted as the one which is fixed, and conventional wisdom is presumed to be indisputable. Those who think they know a better way to view the conduct of urban government may have to press for changes, rather than simply study and write about the problems.

NOTES

1. See, for example, Sheldon Davis, "An Organic Problem-Solving Method of Organizational Change," *Journal of Applied Behavioral Science* 3 (1967): 3-21, and Warren G. Bennis, *Organization Development: Its Nature, Origins and Prospects*, first volume in a six-volume series (Reading, Mass.: Addison-Wesley, 1969).

2. Robert T. Golembiewski, "Organization Development in Public Agencies: Perspectives on Theory and Practice," *Public Administration Review* 29 (1969): 367-378.

3. William B. Eddy, "Beyond Behavioralism? Organization Development in Public Management," *Public Personnel Review* 31 (1970): 169-175.

4. Timothy W. Costello, "Change in Municipal Government," *Emerging Patterns in Urban Administration*, ed. F. G. Brown and T. P. Murphy (Lexington, Mass.: D. C. Heath, 1970) 13-32.

5. The distinction between distributive and integrative situations is developed by Richard E. Walton and Robert McKersie in *A Behavioral Theory of Labor Negotiations: An Analysis of a Social Interaction System* (New York: McGraw-Hill, 1965).

6. Marvin R. Weisbord, "What, Not Again? Manage People Better," *Think* 36 (1970): 7.

7. *Saturday Evening Post* (11 March 1967): 14.

8. For analyses of the criticisms of sensitivity training, see American Psychiatric Association, *Encounter Groups and Psychiatry*, Report of Task Force on Recent Developments in the Use of Small Groups (Washington, D.C.: American Psychiatric Association, 1970), and W.B. Eddy and B. Lubin, "Laboratory Training and Encounter Groups," *Personnel and Guidance Journal*.

9. *Kansas City Star* (7 February 1969): 1.

10. *Buffalo Evening News* (11 March 1970).

11. Douglas McGregor, *The Human Side of Enterprise* (New York: McGraw-Hill, 1960) chs. 3 and 4.

12. Thomas P. Murphy, *Metropolitics and the Urban County* (Washington, D. C.: Washington National Press, 1970) 134-135.

13. Costello, pp. 22-23.

MARTA: Toward An Effective, Open Giant

ROBERT T. GOLEMBIEWSKI & ALAN KIEPPER

Experience at MARTA (Metropolitan Atlanta Rapid Transit Authority) can be instructive to public managers, both those contemplating start-up efforts of their own as well as those managers interested in specific applications of "organizational humanism" in public agencies.[1] Authorized by a 1971 referendum, MARTA sought to gear-up quickly to launch a program whose estimated cost was $1.3 billion, and whose developmental phase was projected to cover the better part of a decade. MARTA thus qualifies as "the biggest game in town," and is in fact the largest regional public project since the early TVA days.

THE FORCE FIELD AT START-UP

MARTA was born in a context that was both intense and uncertain, with no prospect that things would get easier or more definite. Specifically the challenges facing MARTA in 1973 reflected many aspects of both opportunity and danger, as well as of "hurry up" and "wait." Illustratively MARTA more or less simultaneously had to: (1) manage and enlarge an existing bus company, using technologies that are well-established and straightforward, in general; (2) monitor and coordinate the design and construction of sixty-nine miles of rapid-speed rail lines with associated stations, park-and-ride facilities, etc., involving technologies of sometimes substantial indeterminacy and complexity; (3) develop a broad range of design, development, and operating capabilities as a strong central staff, in contrast to a staff with a narrower mission, as is the case at BART; (4) aggressively develop a transit system when funding was highly dependent on grants from federal agencies whose levels of appropriations were uncertain; (5) develop fluid working relationships among a senior staff recruited nationwide only over the past few months, none of whom had experience with projects of the scale or pace of the MARTA program, and some of whom no doubt would learn relatively early that MARTA was not their cup of tea; (6) respond constructively to multiple constituencies—as represented by a MARTA Board whose directors were appointed by political bodies from four counties and from the city of Atlanta, with two counties having representation even though local elections there had rejected referenda to authorize a sales tax increment earmarked for MARTA—as represented by the entire state legislature, which authorized a local sales tax increment to get MARTA started, as well as a blue-ribbon committee to oversee MARTA operations—as represented by federal agencies who were variously regulators and dispensers of grants for mass transportation projects; (7) to be open to

A later version of this article appeared in *Public Administration Review* (January 1976) 36:46-60.

the broadest range of local inputs as to design features, etc., within the context of the basic plan that was voted on in the referendum; (8) organize so as to design effectively and build a $1.3 billion system by 1978; and (9) live within the limits of three awesome facts: (a) that the MARTA system would significantly determine major aspects of the development of metro-Atlanta for decades, physically, economically, as well as in terms of the quality of life; (b) that any delay in developing the MARTA system would be costly, with as much as $250,000 per day in additional system costs attributable to inflation alone, not to mention the growing economic and psychologic costs of moving more people and more things with less dispatch; and (c) that MARTA had neither taxing power nor the right of eminent domain: only the state legislature could authorize taxes; and only the several local governments could condemn property needed by MARTA.

TOWARD AN ORGANIC MANAGERIAL SYSTEM

Overall, the MARTA force field patently was not congenial to a standard operating procedure approach. Considerable expenditure of socioemotional energy at start-up thus was expended to help prepare MARTA officials to cope with certain uncertainty and permanent temporariness. The guiding model was an organic one, of MARTA as a dynamic and evolving organization with which its members and several publics could identify as an open and effective managerial system. There was no practical alternative, given that at least seven stages were envisioned in MARTA's development over a decade, beginning with the late-1972 appointment of its general manager. These stages are (1) immediately MARTA would operate and radically expand an already extensive set of autobus routes; (2) as soon as possible, MARTA must develop its unique style and character, reflected not only in staff, policies, and procedures, but also in the way MARTA business was conducted; (3) over its first two years MARTA would develop detailed designs of its integrated rail/bus system, evaluate any additions to the basic referendum plan, etc.; (4) in its second year MARTA would get heavily into real estate acquisition, relocation of families and businesses, and possibly even into construction for such relocation; (5) within three years, MARTA would transition to an emphasis on overseeing massive construction projects; (6) within six to eight years MARTA would begin an equipment-testing phase; and (7) shortly thereafter, MARTA would have to develop into an integrated operating system of rail and bus transit. In short there would have to be several MARTAs whose development would be compressed in a brief time frame. The smoothness of the unavoidable transitions would significantly influence the project's successful completion.

To help prepare for these necessary transitional shocks, learning designs based on the "laboratory approach to organization development"[2] were used to accelerate the development of the MARTA managerial team, as well as to influence the style in which that team would conduct its public business. The goal had aspects of both avoidance and approach. As much as possible, the startup goal sought to avoid the closedness and ponderousness of large-scale bureaucratic programs which tend to be hierarchy-serving and emphasize stability, and to approach the openness and agile proactiveness of an organic system which is oriented toward problem solving and emphasizes timely change of complex, temporary systems. Figure 7.4

Coercive-Compromise System	Collaborative-Consensual System
Superordinate power is used to control behavior, reinforced by suitable rewards and punishments	Control is achieved through agreement on goals, reinforced by continuous feedback about results
Emphasis on leadership by authoritarian control of the compliant and weak, obeisance to the more powerful, and compromise when contenders are equal in power	Emphasis on leadership by direct confrontation of differences and working through of any conflicts
Disguise or suppression of real feelings or reactions, especially when they refer to powerful figures	Public sharing of real feelings, reactions
Obedience to the attempts of superiors to influence	Openness to the attempts to exert influence by those who have requisite competence or information
Authority/obedience is relied on to cement organization relationships	Mutual confidence and trust are used to cement organization relationships
	Structure is task-based and solution-oriented
Individual responsibility	Shared responsibility
One-to-one relationships between superior and subordinates	Multiple-group memberships with peers, superiors, and subordinates
Structure is based on bureaucratic model and is intendedly stable over time	Structure emerges out of problems faced as well as out of developing consensus among members and is intendedly temporary or at least changeable

Based on Herbert Shepard, "Changing Interpersonal and Intergroup Relationships in Organizations," in *Handbook of Organizations*, ed. James G. Marsh (Chicago: Rand McNally, 1965), 1128-1131.

Figure 7.4.
Dominant Characteristics of Two Opposed Ideal Managerial Systems

provides substantial illustrative detail about what is to be avoided and that which is to be approached. The anti-goal was a "coercive-compromise" system of management, and the thrust was toward enhancing the "collaborative-consensual" features of the MARTA managerial team.

Movement in MARTA toward the collaborative-consensual system of management was seen as requiring a long-term effort, the success of which was dependent upon behavior consistent with five basic ethical orientations characteristic of the "laboratory approach to organization development and change." These orientations could not only be espoused, in Argyris' terms; they also had to be operating guides for behavior. Briefly the five orientations require:[3]

(1) Deep acceptance of inquiry and experimentation as the norm in relationships with others. "It is what we don't know that can destroy our relationships" could well serve as a motto. The opposed meta-value is perhaps more common and is reflected in such maxims as: "Familiarity breeds contempt." The difference between these guiding values is profound. The true acceptance of inquiry and experimentation involves a mutual accessibility of persons to one another. Such accessibility also implies a potential vulnerability to each other, as well as a real commitment to the possibility of being influenced by the other. The opposed meta-value legitimates a more distant relationship and, if only in a superficial sense, a safer one.

Such an orientation is no mere humanistic luxury in organizations like MARTA, at least in its early stages of designing and constructing a system which has numerous one-of-a-kind features. An agency with a mass-production mission could well do with far less of this spirit of inquiry and experimentation.

(2) Expanded consciousness and recognition of choice. Inquiry and experimentation would be sterile in the absence of a consciousness of the diversity of choices that exist. The linkages are direct: an expanded consciousness or awareness generates wider choices; choice permits experimentation that could lead to change or more informed decisions; and freely made choice also helps assure that the individual will own the change or decision rather than (at best) accept its imposition.

These subtle processes were seen as essential in MARTA. To suggest the point by contrast, many management teams have too narrow a view of the choices open to them, based on faulty feedback and disclosure processes. They can generate decisions that have to be constantly policed, enforced, or even continually re-decided because of low commitment to them by the very decision makers who superficially acquiesced in them.[4] This implies a human tragedy, and only trouble for projects like MARTA.

(3) Collaborative concept of authority. This is meant in two senses. In laboratory learning situations, first, the role of the participant is a far more influential one than in traditional learning situations. Second, laboratory learning situations provide an experience with collaborative authority relations that can later be approached in the real world. Even though extreme

forms of mutual influence may be seldom applicable outside of designated learning situations, more or less extensive sharing in power and authority is usually possible and is often necessary.

Experimentation with collaborative authority is no mere curiosity. Complex projects typically require substantial and subtle sharing of power and influence, by wide ranges of contributors at many levels of organization. The goal is that the problem and who has the competence to deal with it will be major determinants of who seeks to influence, and whose attempts will be accepted.

"Collaborative authority" has a pleasant sound to many nowadays, but it raises a serious potential contradiction. In this case, for example, the general manager of MARTA stressed his personal responsibility for seeing that his general preference for collaborative authority did in fact work. But he also might sometimes act unilaterally—even against the consensus of those reporting to him—for various reasons, including the failure of collaborative efforts to bear timely fruit. The balance is clearly a delicate one, with intent being likely to differ from performance and with definitions of "timely" and "collaborative" probably differing in complex ways at various points in time.

(4) Mutual helping relationships in social settings. Helping is seen as perhaps the distinctive human attribute that requires cultivation and development. Relatedly the social setting—in contrast to a one-on-one setting—is seen as an optimal (perhaps even natural) locus for mutual helping. This world view assumes the classical concept of man as a social animal. In addition the emphasis acknowledges the extraordinary and perhaps unique capacity of groups to induce massive forces to reinforce learning or change.

Numerous social adhesives reinforce the helping relationships stressed by the laboratory approach. For example its learning designs tend to generate substantial (even unparalleled) exchanges of warmth, or support, between members. Such exchanges can help cement a community of learners. Similarly the laboratory approach rests on acceptance of the other person, on what has come to be called "unconditional positive regard." Acceptance does not imply approval, but rather a concern for the person. Relatedly, designs based on the laboratory approach attempt to stress the psychological safety of participants. As two careful students note: "People must certainly differ greatly in their ability to accept the guarantee of psychological safety. To the extent that the feeling of safety cannot be achieved—and quickly—the prime basic ingredient for this form of learning is absent. Its importance cannot be overemphasized, nor can the difficulty of its being accomplished."[5]

To be sure, much of life in organizations is narrowly self-interested and even destructive, rather than helping. The goal was to encourage greater attention to helping in MARTA than is common in many organizations. More specifically, the dual objective was to test the limits of psychological safety possible among MARTA managers, as well as to determine whether these limits could be expanded. The practical result is the exchange of minimally distorted communication which is the life blood of effective managerial action. The main ethical product is a more humanistically oriented workplace.

(5) Authenticity in interpersonal relationships. A final value emphasizes the expression of feelings, as well as the analysis of the behaviors inducing them. The rationale for the meta-value of authenticity has two kinds of roots. First, there are the clearly moral precepts on the theme: "To thine own self be true; thou canst not then be false to any man." Second, authenticity is seen as critical in communication. Failure to be authentic in the sense of "leveling" and "expressing feelings" so as to elicit similar behaviors from others can accumulate so much interpersonal garbage as to overburden interaction and impair rational-technical performance.

Note that being "congruent" or "authentic" is a two-way street, to contrast these notions with the cruel narcissism associated with extreme forms of "doing your own thing." Specifically, Argyris urges thinking of authenticity as an interpersonal phenomenon rather than a personal state or characteristic.[6] He conceives of human relationships as "the source of psychological life and human growth," especially because such relationships are then those in which an individual enhances personal awareness and acceptance of self and others, in ways that permit others to do the same. Consequently, for Argyris, it is no more possible to be authentic independent of others than it is possible to cooperate with yourself.

In MARTA, the costs of inauthenticity could be enormous. For any derivative lack of communication and trust would be reckoned in terms of suspicion or overcaution, delay, and eventually huge costs of lengthening schedules. Witness the related emphasis in NASA on "zero defects" at the same time that the organization gospel was that mistakes were understandable in complex projects, up to a substantial point; that mistakes could provide valuable learning opportunities; and that in all cases it was intolerable to hide an error, for the consequences could be profoundly serious.

LEARNING DESIGNS AND SOME CONSEQUENCES

This paper basically details the early learning designs used in MARTA to move toward a collaborative-consensual system, and also sketches some of the consequences of those designs over the first year. Three major elements in the learning design can be distinguished: (1) a team-building experience for the general manager and seven aides who comprised the senior staff, a linkage between the first and second tiers of management; (2) an interface experience between the senior staff and the third tier of management; and (3) an interface experience between senior staff and the MARTA Board. Each design element was the focus of a separate three-day session held at a university center for continuing education, and each element also involved various follow-up activities.

Team-building by senior staff. Just as the last member of the senior staff had been recruited, and while others were still settling into new homes and offices, a team-building experience was held. Its thrust is suggested by Figure 7.5.

1. Any management group can improve its operations

2. Such improvement can be critical even for a management group that is well satisfied with its present performance, as in preparing for unpredictable stress situations

3. An audit of interpersonal and group processes is an important way of testing for existing effectiveness, as well as of inspiring improvements. Such an audit can:

    —aid in increasing mutual understanding and empathy

    —heighten awareness of interpersonal and group processes, and so generate more realistic and detailed perceptions of "what's going on"

    —help build identification, mutual goodwill, and comradeship borne of a sometimes-intense experience

    —facilitate the development of shared perspectives and frameworks that facilitate communication

    —emphasize the importance of reality testing based on the fullest possible expression of information, reactions, and feelings

    —build norms encouraging openness, candor, and face-to-face confrontation

Figure 7.5. Brief Rationale for Team Building

Basically the first learning design encouraged senior staff to acknowledge and deal with the products of their interactions as persons and officials. The senior staff had only a brief interactive past, so there was little unresolved socioemotional "garbage." The focus was on the present and the future soon-to-be-present. Team-building at once encourages almost nonstop interaction between participants, and also seems to speed up psychological time. One official reflected both aspects of the impact of team-building designs on time:

"I've learned more in three days about you guys, and more about my place on the senior staff, than I probably would have learned in three weeks back at the office, for sure, or even in three months.

"I also feel like I've been here forever, even though my

calendar tells me it's only been some fifty hours spread over three days."

There is ample reason to believe that such speeded-up psychological time is particularly well spent around start-up. Simply, start-up implies a set of issues having a substantial potential for polluting the rational-technical performance of an executive team. Illustratively these characteristics include: (1) substantial confusion about roles and relationships; (2) fairly clear understanding of immediate goals, but lack of clarity about longer-run operations, which cumulatively induce wicked double-binds: a strong desire to get on with the task; and yet a pervasive concern that precedents may be set which can mean trouble over the long run; (3) fixation on the immediate task, which often means that group maintenance activities will receive inadequate attention and individual needs will be neglected; and (4) a challenge to team members which will induce superior technical effort, but which may also have serious longer-run consequences for personal or family life and which in any case probably will generate an intensity in work relationships that requires careful monitoring.

The team-building design for the senior staff—which was based on a well-known technology for behavioral change—had two basic features: confronting and contracting.[7]

Confronting refers to a complex of attitudes and behavioral skills that are seen as enhancing a management team's rational-technical performance in two basic ways. Thus such attitudes and skills can make members more aware of their socioemotional processes, as well as more effective in their management.

"Confronting" often has a colorful press, as in versions that advertise "telling it like it is" or "letting it all hang out." As used here, however, confronting is a two-way exchange expressable in terms of four complex emphases: (1) team members become more aware of their own reactions and feelings, as well as those of other members; (2) team members become more aware of the stimuli inducing particular reactions and feelings in themselves and others; (3) team members accept and maintain a norm which sanctions the expression of the full range of applicable information, reactions, and feeling; and (4) team members develop skills to share their concerns in ways that encourage similar expression by other members.

The basic vehicle[8] for focusing on confronting attitudes and behavioral skills is a simple one based on the development and sharing of three-dimensional images. In this case, the general manager prepared three lists in response to these questions: (1) How do you see yourself in relation to the assistant general managers? (2) How do you see your assistant general managers? and (3) How do you believe they see you? As a group, the AGMs collaboratively also developed lists in response to three similar questions. The lists were prepared separately, and then shared. Figure 7.6 contains the two sets of 3-D images, edited here to clarify points unintelligible to outsiders.

3-D Image Prepared by Assistant General Managers

I. How AGMs See General Manager

1. Unapproachable (closed door)
2. Not open
3. Dedicated
4. Determined
5. Cool under fire
6. Hard working
7. Priorities (not ordered)
8. Meticulous
9. Procrastinator
10. Too detailed
11. Sensitive
12. Organization above people
13. Tough
14. Poor delegator
15. Aloof
16. Formal
17. Highly structured personality
18. Programmed
19. Too busy
20. Violates chain of command
21. Fails to pinpoint responsibility

II. How AGMs See Selves In Relation to GM

1. Insecure
2. Ineffective
3. Frustrated
4. Unable to perform effectively
5. Wasted and unimportant
6. Inhibited
7. Too willing to please

III. How AGMs Believe GM Sees Them

1. Relies on group (reluctantly)
2. Trusts us, with reservations
3. Does not see us as team
4. Naive (and sometimes we are!)
5. Sees potential in us
6. As less effective than we should be, and less effective than we can be

3-D Image Prepared by General Manager

I. How General Manager Sees AGMs

1. Reluctant to share concerns and opinions, especially with GM
2. As disregarding opinions of others
3. Reluctant to take initiative
4. Dedicated to MARTA
5. As wanting some answers where none exist
6. As frustrated

II. How GM Sees Self In Relation to AGMs

1. Spread too thin personally
2. As spending too little time with AGMs as group
3. As emphasizing brush fires, without breathing room to focus on key issues
4. As too lenient with AGMs as to assignments, deadlines

III. How GM Believes AGMs See Him

1. As cautious, indecisive
2. Not trusting, due to newness of relationships
3. Expresses lack of trust via deadlines, detailed reviews
4. Busy-busy, not having time for at least some AGMs

Figure 7.6. 3-D Images that Facilitated Confrontation

Extended discussion of the two 3-D images, with the aid of a consultant, constituted the basic early experience with confronting and also provided substantial skill-practice with appropriate attitudes and behaviors. Mechanically the procedure is simple. The two sets of 3-D images, written on large sheets of newsprint, are taped to a wall, side-by-side. Participants survey the lists, and are urged to ask for examples where the meaning of some item is obscure or confusing. The basic ground rule to participants is that they seek to understand the image, and to acknowledge any feelings of defensiveness or resistance but not dwell on them. Such discussion and analysis can be both varied and intense, but it is typically accompanied by periods of explosive laughter and friendly commiserating, as in a mutual reduction-of-tension.

Such designs tend to work for several reasons. First, basically, participants need such information, discomforting or even initially hurtful though it may be. The senior staff's compelling concern about "the project" is implied in their agreement, even enthusiasm, to build a better team.

Second, participants typically understand that the best—indeed perhaps the only—way to raise the probability of receiving such needed information in the future is to be accepting of the 3-D images in the present. Acceptance does not necesarily mean agreement, be it noted. "I can understand how you see it that way," might go such a case of acceptance without necessary agreement, "but I hope you recognize there are many things about which reasonable people can and do differ."

Third, confronting with 3-D images is a shared experience that can build mutual identification and understanding, which is what many participants are seeking. The design is accepted and valued, consequently, and in a sense made to work.

Fourth, most individuals are uncomfortable if their verbal or nonverbal behavior is at some substantial variance with what they really know, believe, or feel. That lack of comfort increases sharply if the person suspects that relevant others are being similarly incongruent. The analysis of 3-D images usually helps to reduce such variance by encouraging a mutual escalation toward openness and owning. Participants typically are much concerned about what the other group or person is writing on their 3-D image in that other room, for example, for they realize that too much varnishings of the truth on their part will be painfully apparent when the 3-D images are compared. The intent is that this greater but still-tentative openness and owning will free for productive use sometimes substantial energies previously needed to repress information shared in the confrontation.

Hence confrontation designs usually leave participants with a sense that barriers are being lowered, and things are really happening with less effort. Consider the symbolism in these common reactions to a 3-D image exchange. "Well, that took the cork out of the bottle, and about at the right time," reports one participant. Another participant had this insightful perspective on the exchange of images: "That's quite a load off my mind, although I didn't quite dare to put down on paper all that concerned me. I'll look for an early opportunity to make some further mileage. It was a good start, and not as tense as I had expected. I guess all of us really wanted to get over the hump of mannerly closeness, but none of us knew how or was willing to risk starting what we all were clearly eager to do. We were off-and-running on the images almost before the instructions were completed."

Fifth, substantial agreement typically exists between pairs of 3-D images, as is the case in Figure 7.6. This agreement almost always increases the participants' sense of mutual competence and acceptance by confirming that one person or group shares perceptions with another as well by signalling that a real process of exchange has been begun. Especially for a managerial team, it is both critical and comforting that its members see some important issues in similar ways, and that they also characterize the same processes in similar terms. Moreover the resulting mutual enhancement of self-esteem can provide powerful impetus toward, as well as a solid foundation for, future communication and collaboration. In sum, the inevitable areas of major agreement on pairs of 3-D images signal that the confronted other is like the self in significant ways, which can build a sense of identification and empathy. And these in turn can encourage further attempts to reach and understand the other in areas where agreement or even awareness does not exist on 3-D images.

Contracting is the vehicle that seeks to assure that the sharing of 3-D images does not merely dissipate into a kind of warm glow that is quickly forgotten. Based on the 3-D images, the general manager and the group of assistant general managers each prepared "shopping lists" directed at the other. The three lists constituted responses to three questions: (1) What should you keep doing about as now? (2) What should you stop doing that you now do? (3) What should you start doing that you do not do now? Participants were encouraged to be as specific as possible about the behaviors or attitudes in question. Not particularly helpful are such global injunctions: Be smarter!

The three lists become the bases for a complex exchange process. The key generic process follows such a form: If you want me to stop X behavior, are you willing to do more of Y which is on my list of behaviors that I would like you to start performing?

The intent of contracting is transparent. The intent is to model a process that can be used back home. More immediately the goal is to build agreement among participants about a few exchanges for openers. The process of reaching this agreement often induces forces that can later reinforce any trade offs that are decided upon in the contracting period. The potential social power implicit in such group decision making has been amply documented by much behavioral research, beginning with such classic experiments as that by Coch and French.[9]

The specific contracts entered into by the MARTA senior staff will not be

Group Behavior Inventory Dimensions	Expected Effects of Team Building	Summaries of Actual Effects	
		Short-run Effects	Longer-run Effects
I. Group Effectiveness. This dimension describes group effectiveness in solving problems and in formulating policy through a creative, realistic team effort.	I. Increase in effectiveness is expected, but may be slow to build	I. 5/8 participants report increases	Ia. 5/8 report increases
II. Approach to vs. Withdrawal from Leader. At the positive pole of this dimension are groups in which members can establish an unconstrained and comfortable relationship with their leader — the leader is approachable.	II. Increase in approachability is probable, but may be slow to build	II. 6/8 report increases	IIa. 4/8 report increases
III. Mutual Influence. This dimension describes groups in which members see themselves and others as having influence with other group members and the leader.	III. Substantial increase even in the short-run, which should persist; note that GM may perceive inroads on personal authority and power	III. 6/8 report increases	IIIa. 5/8 report increases

IV. Personal Involvement and Participation. Individuals who want, expect, and achieve active participation in group meetings are described by this dimension.	IV. Substantial increase even in the short-run, which should persist	IV. 7/8 report increases	IVa. 6/8 report increases
V. Intragroup Trust vs. Intragroup Competitiveness. At the positive pole, this dimension depicts a group in which the members hold trust and confidence in each other.	V. Increase is expected, but may be slow to build	V. 3/8 report increases	Va. 6/8 report increases
VI. General Evaluation of Meetings. This dimension is a measure of a generalized feeling about the meetings of one's group as good, valuable, strong, pleasant, as contrasted with bad, worthless, weak, unpleasant.	VI. Increase is expected, but may be slow to build	VI. 4/8 report increases	VIa. 6/8 report increases

Based on Frank Friedlander, "The Impact of Organizational Training Laboratories upon Effectiveness and Interaction of Ongoing Work Groups," *Personnel Psychology*, Vol. 20 (Autumn 1970), 295.

Figure 7.7. GBI Dimensions, Expected Effects of Team-Building Design, and Summarized Actual Effects.

reported here, but they focused around more substantial freedom of action for the assistant general managers, which was exchanged for several items on GM's START list. Overall, senior staff became more aware of how their past experiences in more stable and structured local government administrative situations limited their early and resourceful responses to the novelty and quick-silveredness of the MARTA program.

The effects of the confronting and contracting among the senior staff were judged by a series of semistructured interviews as well as by periodic administrations of a paper-and-pencil test, the Group Behavior Inventory (GBI).[10] Only the GBI will be discussed here.

The GBI, whose basic dimensions are sketched in Figure 7.7, proved useful in two basic ways. First, several administrations of the instrument permitted a test of whether the expected consequences of the team building did occur, for specific members of the senior staff as well as for the aggregate. Figure 7.7 details the effects anticipated as results of a successful team-building effort, and also summarizes the actual results, using the GBI dimensions. Note that "short-run effects" compare GBI responses immediately before the team building to responses obtained two weeks later; and "longer-run effects" involve comparisons of the benchmark GBI scores with an administration of the instrument some seven weeks after the team building began, at which time the effects of the team building become increasingly confounded by the rush of workday activities.

The GBI results are generally consistent with expectations about the effects of a successful team-building experience. Overall, that is, approximately two-thirds of the changes reported by participants are in the expected direction, and seven of the twelve aggregate comparisons achieve usually accepted levels of statistical significance. Note also that these substantial effects, if anything, understate the impact of the team building. The weeks following the initial offsite session were traumatic and difficult ones that severely stressed all members of the senior staff. In addition, benchmark administrations of instruments designed to measure team-bulding effects often seem to reflect a kind of "rose-colored glasses" effect, either because respondents are truly optimistic, or are cautious in being open, or are simply not fully aware of the variety and magnitude of issues facing them. Post-experience scores thus often will understate actual change when they are compared to such cautious/optimistic/uninformed benchmark scores. Reinforcing this surmise is the general opinion of participants about one year later. One participant noted, to illustrate the dominant and probably universal reaction: "You didn't promise us a rose garden, I know. But it was quite a shock to confront an array of issues so early in the game. It violated all my governmental experience, where such confronting was done at greater leisure, and probably not at all. But I'm increasingly glad we did the team building. MARTA cannot afford to let nature take its course. There is too much to be done in a short period to risk getting sand-bagged by hoping that issues will go away if they are neglected long enough."

Second, the GBI results were also used to indicate where follow-on activity might be appropriate for individual participants. To explain, all members of the senior staff identified their completed GBI forms, which were returned to the consultant at his university address. Only aggregate results would be discussed publicly. In the two cases in which senior staff indicated by their GBI responses that the short-runs effects of the team building were for them ineffectual or negative, however, the consultant contacted the respondents and sought to verify their "deviant" GBI scores.

The GBI proved sensitive in both cases. In one case the respondent saw the initial experience as more hopeful than impactful, but certainly not harmful to his relationships with other senior staff. The second respondent reported a significant worsening of his relationships with the GM over the interval between the first and second GBI administrations. The team-building session reinforced the AGM's perception of this rift and did nothing to resolve what was to him a one-on-one issue not amenable to discussion in that group setting. Consultant suggested a third-party design[11] to explore these issues, which suggestion the respondent accepted. Subsequently the two parties got together at an early date to deal with their relationship.

Note that such transactions imply significant ethical issues. In this case, basically, the consultant sought to create the sense and reality of his independence in that his commitment was to facilitate MARTA's effectiveness rather than to serve as an agent of the general manager. It is easy to be self-deluding in such matters, of course. Were the subordinates under duress to accept the consultant's proposal? It is at least a good sign that one AGM felt free to reject that proposal. And it is the fact that the general manager, the co-author of this paper, still is unaware of the identity of the AGM who advised that consultant's suggestion was not appropriate. Finally both the GM and the AGM who "dealt with their relationship" perceive the outcomes to have been positive, especially so in the case of the AGM whose performance until then was unsatisfactory to him and the GM because of the growing issues between them. That AGM is now a solid performer on the senior staff, perhaps in part because of the timely suggestion to both executives which was induced by the broader OD design.

Two Levels of Interfaces with Department Directors. Approximately one month after the team building among senior staff, another three-day experience sought to concentrate on two sets of interfaces: (1) between some twenty-five department directors and the senior staff, and (2) between each assistant general manager and the cluster of directors he directly supervised.

3-D images were used to explore the interface between the senior staff and the directors. Six sets of images were prepared: one by each of the five clusters of directors reporting to individual AGMs, and one by the senior staff. These were prepared in private, and then publicly shared in a large common meeting.

The sharing of 3-D images was an intense experience, in large part due to several major issues that had been generated in the early days of assembling a work force and of developing personnel policies and procedures. Illustratively these items were included by one group of directors in their list of perceptions of the senior staff:

Some autocratic elements—dictatorial

Secretiveness—lack of communication

They have a tough job, in a rough environment, and are making good progress

Question competence level of some—admire competence of some

They earn their money

Examples illustrating these descriptions were emphasized in an extensive public sharing period, and the associated discussion centered around several major substantive issues, mostly issues introduced by the directors.

Contracting took place at two levels. Thus the senior staff agreed to study a long list of issues, many of which were criticisms of newly instituted personnel policies and procedures. Parenthetically some quick changes in policies and procedures were made soon after; and other issues were studied over longer periods, with some changes being made later. This responsiveness no doubt reinforced the impact of this second design element.

—Moreover, substantial time also was provided so that each of the five AGMs with directors reporting to them could begin some rudimentary team building in the organization cluster each supervised. Again mutual 3-D images were developed and shared in each of the five clusters of AGMs-cum-directors. Consistently, also, contracting was encouraged between the several clusters of directors and the individual AGMs to whom each cluster reported. In addition each cluster was mandated to provide any additional detail about the substantive issues raised in the large public meeting.

—The effects of this second-level effort to develop an effective and open system in MARTA were estimated by the two administrations of the Likert (1967) "Profile of Organizational Characteristics,"[12] a simple and useful instrument. The benchmark administration was immediately before the organization-building session, and the post-experience administration was approximately two work weeks later. The form of the instrument used contained eighteen items.

The Profile has several interesting features. First, its several items can be scored along a continuum of twenty equal-appearing intervals, which are differentiated into four major systems of management:

Scores	System Descriptions	
(1-5)	System I.	Exploitative-Authoritative
(6-10)	System II.	Benevolent-Authoritative
(11-15)	System III.	Consultative
(16-20)	System IV.	Participative Group

Second, each item is anchored by four brief descriptive statements, one statement for each system. For example one of the eighteen items is: At what level are decisions made? The System I anchoring statement is: "mostly at the top"; and the System IV statement is "throughout [the organization] but well integrated." Intermediate statements anchor Systems II and III emphasizing "some delegation" and "more delegation," respectively.

Third, the eighteen Profile items are intended to tap six broad phenomenal areas of organizational relevance. They are:

Leadership (items 1-3)
Motivation (items 4-6)
Communication (items 7-10)
Decisions (items 11-13)
Goals (items 14-15)
Control (items 16-18)

Fourth, each Profile item is scored twice. A Now score reflects an estimate of the existing level on each item; and an Ideal score on each item provides data about the preference of the respondent. In addition to providing useful data, the exercise is seen as meaningful for the respondent in a team-building experience. Its goal, simply, is to alert organization members to any gaps between their preferences and the interpersonal and group relationships that actually exist in their organization. This alerting can help motivate early remedial action.

Figure 7.8 presents data from the directors reporting to one AGM, the criterion for selection being that the design seemed least impactful in this case. Overall, a successful experience should move respondents' scores toward System IV, whatever their starting point.

Four points about Figure 7.8 deserve highlighting. First, existing interpersonal and intergroup relationships fell substantially short of where the directors preferred. See the contrast between Ideal scores and the Now scores on the benchmark administration of the Likert Profile. A contrast of Ideal scores with post-experience Now scores gathered some two weeks after the team-building supports a similar conclusion, although the gap has been narrowed somewhat.

The pattern is understandable. Most directors had been hired only recently; some had been on the job only a matter of days; and a few had just been hired. These were very early days, indeed, and hectic ones.

Second, the team-building seems to have moved interpersonal and group relationships in the direction preferred by the directors, even in the least-impactful case illustrated in Figure 7.8. No statistical tests were run due to small sample sizes of the directors reporting to each AGM, but the conclusion holds for a variety of approaches to comparing scores. Grossly, fourteen of the eighteen Now mean scores more closely approach the benchmark Ideal scores after the training than before. The pattern is

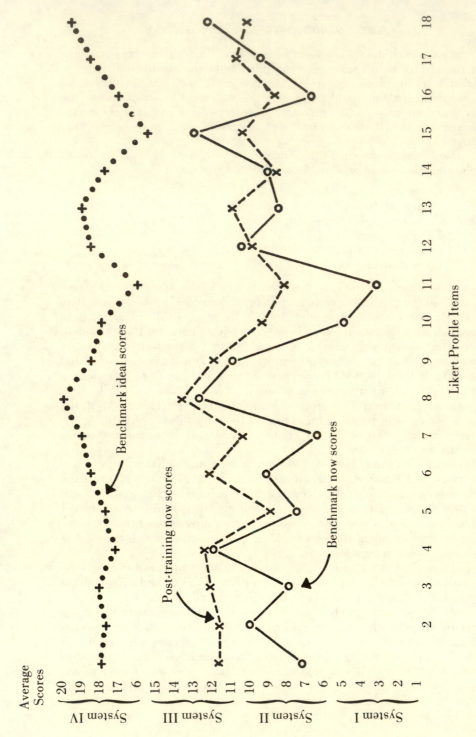

Figure 7.8. Changes in Likert Scores Among Directors (N=6) Reporting to One Assistant General Manager

similar for "large changes," defined arbitrarily as plus or minus 2 points. There are seven such large changes that move closer to the Ideal scores after the training than they were before training. Only one large average change moves away from the Ideal.

Third, the zigs-and-zags in Figure 7.8 probably understate the degree of change if anything, for at least three reasons. As was noted, Figure 7.8 presents data from AGM/directors cluster for which the design was least impactful. Moreover there apparently is a tendency for some respondents to provide benchmark self-reports that reflect the somewhat varnished truth, as they perceive it. Alternatively or even simultaneously, team building can make participants more aware of existing disagreements or unclarities. Illustratively the largest deviant change in Figure 7.8 is for Item 15, which solicits information about the degree of resistance to organization goals. This change can be explained in terms of the two possibilities above, or in terms of an actual increase in resistance generated by the team-building design. The last explanation of course, is less credible in this case because of the overall pattern of changes.

Linking the Board and the Senior Staff. The final design element in this first pass at institution building involved MARTA's board of directors and the senior staff. The board's members were appointed by elected officials in four counties and the city of Atlanta. The board of nine members—including two blacks—was clearly in transition. Earlier boards had been peopled by macro-prominents with independent power bases and a collective regional orientation. Over time appointments were made from other tiers of leadership in the five jurisdictions whose political bodies named directors. Consequently there was over time a growing responsiveness by board members to more local needs and aspirations. At the time of this OD design, the board had a quite substantial independence from local politics, but that relative autonomy clearly was being tested and would be substantially reduced as MARTA signed agreements with local governments and otherwise moved toward actual construction.

The board's style was to become increasingly active and involved in MARTA business as staff were selected and policies developed. Hence the special importance of directly exposing board members to the kind of developmental experiences to which MARTA management had devoted some time and effort, with board knowledge. Moreover the board had until then uneven but typically brief and sporadic exposure to the MARTA senior staff other than the GM. Board members desired far more contact with AGMs as a prime way of developing first-hand information about those AGMs whose policy recommendations and detailed design and construction proposals would increasingly come before the board for its action as MARTA moved toward construction. The importance of an early and mutual getting-to-know-one-another provided significant motivation for the third design element.

The design of the third stage in institution-building had three prime elements, each lasting perhaps two-thirds of a day. Sequentially, the design emphasized: (1) separate meetings for board members and the senior staff, during which data about their respective internal dynamics were fed back by consultants who summarized interview and questionnaire information to serve as stimuli to encourage the two groups to evaluate their ways of relating to one another; (2) two integrative experiences, the first relatively gentle and the second far more threatening—(a) board members and the senior staff independently developed verbal statements describing their concepts of MARTA's mission in some detail, which statements became objects for public sharing and comparative discussion, and (b) board members and the senior staff independently developed 3-D images, and these became central stimuli for public confronting and contracting activities; (3) a work session, in which matters to be publicly presented in the immediate future were discussed by the board and the senior staff in common session.

The flow of the design involving the board is direct, then. The first element stresses internal dynamics; the second encourages limited integration, consistent with the differing roles of the board and the senior staff; and the third seeks to test the usefulness of the outcomes of the first two elements in a more-or-less normal work context. There were major elements of risk and threat in dealing with the board in the confrontive spirit with which the MARTA managers sought to deal with one another. But there seemed no viable alternative to the risk and threat, given the active board role and given the style which earlier design elements had sought to foster among MARTA management.

No major effort was made to measure the effects of the third design element, but two conclusions are safe enough. First, the experience was a far more critical one for the senior staff than for the board, for obvious reasons. Basically staff was still concerned that its concept of their job might conflict with the board's view of its responsibility; and staff was unclear as to board reaction to their overall performance.

Second, reactions of participants to the design were uniformly positive, and typically emphasized the useful beginning or acceleration of processes that required nurturing over the long run. The responses of the board chairman and vice chairman are typical. They were initially positive, and remained so after nearly a year. One official observed: "Unquestionably, I considered the experience worthwhile. It afforded us an opportunity to know one another better." The other board official had a similar reaction, but stressed the need for determined follow-up after the team-building experience.

> In general, because of the difficulty in getting most people to listen, much less understand, I feel that such sessions are constructive, beneficial and desirable. . . .
>
> Specifically, I feel that this particular meeting gave me an opportunity to know our board and staff members better and to more fully appreciate the special relationship between the two groups.

I'd very much like to see these sessions repeated on an annual basis for two reasons: one, there are almost always personnel changes each year; and two, it appears that some participants have a tendency to forget the vital issues discussed and generally agreed upon.

CONCLUSION

There is a revealing way of summarizing the thrust of the three-design effort toward making MARTA an open and effective giant. First, the goal was to help build more effective teams at several levels of organization: in the board, on the senior staff, and among directors reporting to the same AGM. This team building has an internal thrust, and seeks to make members of small, formal groups more cohesive and more aware of their own dynamics. The goal is to encourage members of these groups to be more willing to confront the differences that will inevitably exist among themselves, with encouragement deriving from the similarities of experience and identification that are highlighted by successful team building.

Second, each of the three design elements had a major relational thrust. Directly, team building can be pernicious if it merely creates strong bonds of experience, identification, and affection between the members of some group. Team building in this sense can develop an intense sense of we-ness only at the expense of highlighting and perhaps manufacturing a they-ness to be distinguished from, or even opposed to. Hence the conscious effort to build cross-walk experiences into the design for a more open and effective MARTA, to utilize any forces deriving from successful team building to help bridge social and psychological and hierarchical distance rather than merely to exaggerate that distance which is variously normal or necessary or convenient.

This relational thrust is vital in MARTA for a very practical reason. Given its lack of taxing and independent condemnation power, MARTA had no reasonable alternative but getting and staying in the frame of mind that doggedly seeks the elusive reality of a complex sense of us-ness, not only inside MARTA but also (perhaps, especially) with various units of government and a wide range of interests.

Third, the three elements of the design also reflect an institutional or contextual thrust, in the form of a set of values which condition both the internal and relational thrusts distinguished above. In Selznick's terminology, the team-building experiences and the cross walks between them sought to infuse MARTA with a specific set of values. These values imply partial answers to this critical question: To what social or moral purpose does the team building and cross walking contribute?

This set of values is reflected at several levels. Thus the expectations that the design would have relatively specific consequences, as measured by the GBI or Likert's Profile, are at once predictions about what can be encouraged to exist as well as value judgments about the conditions whose existence is desirable in both instrumental and ethical senses. For example, movement toward System IV is desirable in at least three distinct senses. Thus participants overwhelmingly prefer System IV, as the ideal scores in Figure 7.8 testify, hypothetically because respondents conclude that System IV will meet their needs more than System I. Moreover, evidence seems to indicate that successful large-scale projects in fact require substantial doses of System IV philosophy and relationships.[13] Finally, System IV more closely approaches a variety of ethical guides than does System I.[14]

Care is necessary to avoid overrepresenting the narrative above. Consider the success of the efforts above. Several indicators imply that expected things did happen: (1) changes in the Group Behavior Inventory, overall, were not only expected but imply that a range of more effective relationships among senior staff were developed and maintained over time; (2) changes in the Likert Profile, overall, were not only expected but also move in the direction of presumptively greater effectiveness of the organization level reporting to senior staff; and (3) interviews with both directors and managers, overall, indicate that most personal definitions of success were met.

But this paper is also limited in basic ways. It does not report on a "complete OD experiment," but rather a description of the character and some of the consequences of initial steps to develop a team consciousness. Relatedly the results of the OD interventions are not expressed as direct management or administrative results; those results are not related to the bottom-line context of work. Those management or administrative results have to be inferred from statements of how people feel about their work and each other.

So this study reflects a pervasive in-betweenness. Some results imply that OD as a social technology has a range of predictable consequences, and hence is potent. But much still needs to be learned about the fuller range of work-related consequences of OD interventions.

NOTES

1. Stephen R. Chitwood and Michael M. Harmon, "New Public Administration, Humanism, and Organization Behavior," *Public Management* 53 (November 1971), 13-22.

2. Robert T. Golembiewski, *Renewing Organizations* (Itasca, Ill.: F. E. Peacock, 1972).

3. Golembiewski, 60-68.

4. For some chilling details, from the highest governmental levels, see Irving Janis, *Groupthink* (Boston: Houghton-Mifflin, 1972).

5. John P. Campbell and Marvin D. Dunnette, "Effectiveness of T-Group Experiences in Managerial Training and Development," *Psychological Bulletin* 70 (August 1968), 73-104.

6. Chris Argyris, *Interpersonal Competence and Organizational Effectiveness* (Homewood, Ill.: Dorsey Press, 1962), 21.

7. For details and supporting rationales, see: Golembiewski, *Renewing Organizations*, esp. 142-155, 327-386, and 455-484; Wendel L. French and Cecil H. Bell, Jr,. *Organizational Development* (Englewood Cliffs, N. J.: Prentice-Hall, 1973), esp. 112-146; and Newton Margulies and John Wallace, *Organizational Change* (Glenview, Ill.: Scott, Foresman, 1973), esp. 99-121.

8. As important preliminaries and reinforcers, members of the senior staff spent approximately forty hours at off-site learning experiences being exposed to exercises/concepts rele-

vant to group dynamics, as well as to appropriate skill practice. Most of this learning time was scheduled in one three-day period. The exercises/concepts dealt with decision making, interpersonal openness; giving and receiving feedback, functional roles, and interpersonal orientations of senior staff. In addition a process observer attended approximately ten worksite meetings of the senior staff during the three-month interval following the three-day session to help reinforce real-time effort consistent with the off-site experiences.

9. Lester Coch and John R. P. French, Jr., "Overcoming Resistance to Change," *Human Relations* 1 (December 1948), 512-532.

10. Frank Friedlander, "The Impact of Organizational Training Laboratories upon Effectiveness and Interaction of Ongoing Work Groups," *Personnel Psychology* 20 (Autumn 1970), 289-307.

11. Richard E. Walton, *Interpersonal Peacemaking: Confrontations and Third-Party Consultation* (Reading, Mass.: Addison-Wesley, 1969).

12. Rensis Likert, *The Human Organization* (New York: McGraw-Hill, 1967).

13. Leonard R. Sayles and Margaret K. Chandler, *Managing Large Systems* (New York: Harper and Row, 1971); and Harvey M. Sapolsky, *The Polaris System Development* (Cambridge, Mass.: Harvard University Press, 1972).

14. Robert T. Golembiewski, *Men, Management and Morality* (New York: McGraw-Hill, 1965).

Shared Management: An Innovation

CHRIS CHERCHES & RICHARD E. BYRD

In 1970, the administration of the City of St. Louis Park began discussing with the City Council steps which should be taken to improve the organization of the city to develop and more fully utilize the human resources of the city staff. To this end interviews were conducted with several firms in the field of organizational management and a decision was made to institute a program for developing a team approach to city management and operation by engaging the services of Richard E. Byrd, Inc., a Minneapolis-based consulting firm.

At the outset of the discussion between the city manager's office and the consultant, several conclusions were reached regarding the present traditional, vertical operating style of city management. These were (1) the present vertical operating style was tending to reenforce community planning and problem solving being done in isolation from the whole political and technical picture. The result was unilateral decision making and a lack of correlation of city functions; (2) problems arose which no staff member saw as his department's responsibility. This led to fixing blame for omissions on the city manager or another department head rather than joint problem solving; (3) one of the results of the stratification of the organization was that interpersonal relations were often strained and, therefore, unsolicited contributions from one department to another were not always appreciated; (4) too many department-level operational decisions were being shifted to the manager's office; and (5) while the routine work on a daily basis continued to be dealt with ably, there was a general absence of creative enthusiasm.

From the outset industrial management concepts and practices were rejected in favor of the more experimental approaches of the behavioral sciences. These approaches emphasize the interdependence between the social processes, interpersonal processes, and the operations of the organization. They examine such factors as motivation, communication, openness to new ideas, leadership processes, decision-making processes, cooperation, etc. While these were the softer side of management, it was also recognized that city employees operate in the softer side almost all the time as they seek to administer codes, implement council decisions, and deal with the public.

It was also recognized that a one-time confrontation meeting of department heads and the city manager's office would not achieve long-lasting results and, in fact, might be destructive. Therefore a long-range plan of

Reprinted from *Minnesota Municipalities* (The League of Minnesota Municipalities, Nov. 1971) 56: 11, pp. 344-345, 360.

organizational development was prepared that allowed for stops and starts, depending on the progress made in each phase. This decision is based on the behavioral science findings that habits, attitudes, and prejudices of long standing change only when people can test and retest new ways of working together, learning to trust the changes, and finally establishing greater credibility with one another.

Finally it was concluded that this city organization (225 employees) was small enough to utilize its staff across department lines, gaining maximum flexibility because of less necessary bureaucracy than is often the case in much larger cities.

GOALS OF THE PROJECT

To develop a program to eliminate effectively these problems, the staff began working with the consultant in January 1971 to achieve the following four long-range goals:

1. To develop a team approach where each division and department head is concerned with the entire operation of the city rather than just his departmental responsibility. Under such a system, everyone gains a stake in everyone else's performance.

2. To institute the practice of having operating and supervisory decisions made by those closest to the problem. Under such a system, the city manager and his office would be consultant, catalyst, and a source of final appeal.

3. Creating an atmosphere of innovation, creative thinking, and sharing that will challenge present personnel as well as attract bright, aggressive professionals to St. Louis Park.

4. To create an organizational climate where openness and confrontation are more the norm than hidden agendas or fear of losing face, status, or job. The result would be effective communication.

As in Torrance, California (see p. 23, "How It's Done in Torrance," *Public Management*, March 1971), the first phase of our organizational development process was focused on the actual working relationships of the city manager, his staff, and department heads which we call the manager's team. The process began by having the consultant meet with the team that would begin working on the goals outlined above. They were shown the proposal, including the diagnosis and goals, and were asked to participate cooperatively in the first phase. The first phase included having each member of the team individually interviewed by the consultant, and data gathered, using the Likert Organization Characteristics Questionnaires; William Schutz's FIRO-B questionnaire and the Rokeach Dogmatic Scale, to form the basis for the first off-site team meeting. The off-site meeting was held in January 1971. It was clearly understood that if the department heads or the city manager, for any reason, did not wish to proceed beyond this weekend, there would be no further phases.

TEAM-BUILDING ACTIVITIES

The team met in a hotel off-site meeting for three days. The actual content of the meeting was discussion of the written data, prepared from the interviews in a collated form, with recommendations, and presented to the team on Friday evening. The team explored each item and openly discussed both their differences and their affinities. Some people had harbored misunderstandings and misinterpretations for some time. Many of these were aired and clarified. In some cases issues of policy differences were only able to be identified, not resolved. In every case people were encouraged to express their feelings as openly as they felt it was appropriate to do. For, while perhaps often based on inaccurate data, negative feelings may still be considered part of the facts of a situation and may be a silent blocker and demotivator to getting the city's work done.

During this time the team decided (1) to improve staff meetings, (2) to initiate a cross-department, all-day meeting of many city employees representing various areas of enforcement and, (3) to explore the use of an innovative system of lateral coordinating sections; and to pursue the increased openness they found together during the three days.

The general results were so positive that the city manager's team was strongly in favor of continuing with the process. Thus, the short-term projects agreed upon were initiated. One such project was the all-day meeting of two key enforcement divisions with members of other interfacing departments to confront some differences occurring because of different personal styles, ordinances, and an unequal sense of responsibility for enforcement. While the direct outcomes were mixed, at first blush, the indirect benefits of the group looking more closely at their joint concerns had an almost immediate impact, for example, when Health people got in on Building Code problems and vice versa. There was also an increased sensitivity to a need to help each other by representatives of other departments represented at the meeting.

As a result of these off-site meetings, and the off-site meeting for department heads, some real changes were in evidence when six months later a second retreat was held, again preceded by interviews with department heads by the REB consultant. This meeting was somewhat different from the first. The consultant had each department head, the city manager, assistant city manager, and the administrative assistant work with him individually to develop a list of the gains they had individually experienced, as well as the future concerns to which that individual wanted the off-site meeting addressed. The Likert questionnaire was once again administered to discover what changes in attitude may have occurred along the organizational characteristics earlier examined.

This three-day off-site meeting focused on four goals: (1) evaluating the progress toward team management; (2) developing further communication skills in dealing with each other; (3) solving immediate organization problems and planning organizational development for the next six

months; and (4) gaining increased responsibility for continual development of the organization.

SUMMARY OF PROGRESS TO DATE

The following assessment which represents both the manager's team and
the consultant's observation, is a summary of the achievement and needs
after seven months of team building organizational development:

1. We find that although we have answered many operational problems,
there will continue to be some which need to be dealt with. It has become
easier to identify these problems because of increased openness in the
group and a willingness to bring out the problems as they occur, rather
than permitting them to build over an extended period of time.

2. We have discussed an innovative type of lateral organization to
provide more interdepartmental understanding and cooperation and, after
many hours of planning and discussion, have agreed to proceed with the
concept; the first section was initiated in August 1971.

3. We have been able to recognize growth and development within the
organization such as:

a. **Leadership**—Significant gains have been made during the last six
months in the amount of confidence and trust placed in the department
heads by the city manager's office.

b. **Motivation**—Without exception, department heads feel more responsible for achieving the overall organization's goals.

c. **Communication**—Greater teamwork and lateral communication have
developed and department heads feel the manager's office has greater understanding of day-to-day problems.

d. **Decision-making**—Increased delegation has been experienced, and
this has filtered down through the organization and can be seen in the
department heads' supervision of their individual departments.

e. **Clarity**—Disagreement on the nature (and articulation) of organization goals has been clarified.

WHERE TO NOW?

The organization has progressed significantly toward achieving the original
goals of the program; however, a substantial amount of work needs to be
done to fully achieve the goals.

Some of these future organizational development activities being considered are (1) to continue the periodic off-site meetings of the manager's
team. For example, disagreements over goals have not been resolved.
Recognition and utilization of organization goals still require considerable
effort. There is also some residual fear of being personally exposed or hurt,
and this keeps them from being as spontaneous as might be desired.
Through continuation of the development process of increasing credible
relationships, it is hoped that this fear can be reduced so that more

openness can be achieved. Furthermore the team needs concentrated practice in decision-making group skills and in analyzing its own difficulties as a
decision-making group; (2) to begin teamwork training activities
throughout all divisions. Delegation is still a problem within several departments. But more importantly, newer work patterns with greater attention
to personal communication factors will increase department responsiveness to other departments and to the public; (3) to implement, test, and
research four lateral sections as a better communication device. The result
should be a more even application of ordinances and policies across departments. Also the majority of the organization would still not be motivated to
do anything but their job. Effective lateral sections, each with a mix of employees from various functional and supervisory levels, should increase
employee "ownership" of city rather than department goals; (4) get group
skills training for key personnel. Team skills are learned, not built in.
While training of teams is the primary target, it is also recognized that
special skills are also needed. Various management workshops which
emphasize group skills will be recommended; (5) develop a management
seminar for department heads and their deputies on the classical management functions as particularly appropriate to a city management, using a
team approach.

It is the consensus of the team that significant gains have been made by
utilization of the team-building program and that a continuation of the
process is highly desirable. At present the team is on the threshold of making significant progress toward achieving the solutions to problems which
have become apparent and needs only additional time to work out the
techniques.

A Clash of Values:
OD and Machiavelli's Prince

JAMES M. McDUFFIE, JR.

Kaufman (1963:36) points out that parallels between political theory and organizational theory are totally unexpected for reasons of antiquity of the former and relative recentness of the latter. Furthermore there seems to have been a significant lack of communication between the two. However, a number of parallels do emerge. For example, Antony Jay (1967:5) has contended that management theory and political theory are "two branches of the same subject" and Kaufman (1963:37-38) has compared political theory and organizational theory as two different species of the same genus in that both treat human phenomena that encompass vast areas, if not all, of life. Consequently it seems that organization theory and political theory have much to learn from each other (Kaufman 1963:46).

The intent of this paper is to delve briefly into the comparison of political theory and organization theory, at least on one dimension. Specifically the political theory of Niccolo Machiavelli as expressed in *The Prince* and the organization theory of the Laboratory Approach to Organization Development will serve as focal points. Hopefully some small contribution can be made toward furthering the cause of Organization Development in producing viable and organic organizations by pointing out, in the opinion of this writer, a set of sometimes opposing values contained in what has come to be known as Machiavellianism. However, a number of surprising similarites do emerge which can only lead to a deeper understanding of both theories. More specifically the above design will be executed by comparing nine objectives of Organization Development with applicable organizational objectives as propounded in Machiavelli's *The Prince*.

The purpose here is not to analyze Machiavelli in toto but to recognize the fact that some have lived, and presently live, by many of the premises set forth in *The Prince*. It is true that posterity should not condemn the scientist for his findings being utilized by others in evil ways, as some have so condemned Machiavelli. But the fact that they are utilized and therefore deserve scrutiny is of central concern here. The problems of Machiavelli are "living and burning problems, and it is by reason of their continuing urgency that the present-day study of Machiavelli is worthwhile" (Hearnshaw 1925:111).

Attention may now be focused on the comparison of Organization Development (OD) objectives and Machiavelli's *The Prince.* For the most part it will be seen that Machiavelli's *The Prince* is incongruent with the major goals of OD programs which seek to "release the human potential within an organization" (Golembiewski 1972:128). The focus here is to provide a foundation from which the reader may conclude that the modern Machiavellian either presents a salient obstacle to realization of these OD objectives or possibly utilizes them in a manipulative manner for personal gain.

The nine objectives to be dealt with are drawn from the NLT Institute article (1968:343) entitled "What is OD?"

1. **To create an open, problem-solving climate throughout the organization**—Machiavelli fully realizes the value of truthful openness in the following excerpt:

> A prudent prince therefore should (choose) for ministers of his government only wise men, and to these only should he give full power to tell him the truth, and they should only be allowed to speak to him of those things which he asks of them, and of none other. But then the prince should ask them about everything, and should listen to their opinions and reflect them, and afterward form his own resolutions. And he should bear himself toward all his advisers in such manner that each may know that the more freely he speaks, the more acceptable will he be. But, outside of these he should not listen to anyone, but follow the course agreed upon, and be firm in his resolves (Machiavelli 1965:114).

Machiavelli clearly advises openness only insofar as it generates information to the prince for his decision-making activities. Furthermore this sense of openness is tainted by the fact that it is permitted with only a few select individuals and is generally based on solicitations by the prince. The fact that information should be given only in areas in which requests are made, in itself, serves to inhibit an air of openness. Distinct limits are placed upon the practice of openness with the advice that the prince should "ask them about everything," (an impossibility within itself), and should not listen to anyone else.

Machiavelli's fear of general openness is clearly expressed in a number of other instances, for example: ". . . as soon as you divulge your plans to a malcontent, you furnish him the means wherewith to procure satisfaction. He must indeed be a very rare friend of yours, or an inveterate enemy of the prince, to observe good faith and not to betray you" (Machiavelli 1965: 90-91).

The implications that this viewpoint smacks at the open, problem-solving climate are abundant. The implication for generation of information for decision making is but one. Also this viewpoint assumes that there is indeed a limited population of "very rare friends" or "inveterate enemies" who could be trusted with the knowledge of one's plans. Patently Machiavelli exhibits tendencies toward closedness for fear of the consequences of openness.

2. **To supplement the authority associated with role or status with the authority of knowledge and competence**—Machiavelli's opposition to

this OD objective is fundamental as a reading of *The Prince* will attest. *The Prince* recommends a theory of maximal power and leadership to the prince (Jay 1967:26, Mazzeo 1964:145). (The prince) "has merely to see to it that (a foreigner does) not assume too much authority, or acquire too much power; for he will then be able by their favor, and by his own strength, very easily to humble those who are really powerful; so that he will in all respects remain the sole arbiter of that province" (Machiavelli 1965:19). At another point Machiavelli alludes to the possibility of some degree of authority residing in other than the prince by his permission. A state may be ruled ". . . by one absolute prince, to whom all others are as slaves, some of whom, as ministers, by his grace and consent, aid him in the government of his realm. . ." (Machiavelli 1965:25).

The above implicitly indicates that Machiavelli considers authority associated with role or status to be generally of supreme importance to the authority of knowledge and competence in respect to both foreigners and ministers. Reference is made that the prince may "humble" foreigners who are powerful by his "strength" rather than by virtue of his knowledge or competence. Likewise ministers are allowed to retain a certain degree of authority by his "grace and consent" rather than their knowledge or competence. Admittedly, though, authority of knowledge and competence is recognized at other points. For example advice is given that a prince should choose only "wise men" (Machiavelli 1965:114) as ministers of his government.

Clearly then, the authority of the role and status of the prince existing within foreigners and ministers by his "consent" is given priority while the authority of knowledge and competence is attended to almost as an afterthought.

3. **To locate decision-making and problem-solving responsibilities as close to the information sources as possible**—Since the apex of any organization is not the source of all information for decision making, this objective would allow decision locations to permeate all levels of the hierarchy. It also calls for fluidity rather than stability of decision locations. This would be incongruent with any theory of centralized power and Machiavelli's is no exception. The fact that *The Prince* is viewed as a theory of maximal power to the prince has already been cited. That amount of power and decision authority not personally practiced by the prince is allowed to be practiced by others only by his explicit "grace and consent," (Machiavelli 1965:19). If possible the prince should command in person rather than by the means of magistrates. For "in the latter case, the state is more feeble and precarious" (Machiavelli 1965:52).

At another point Machiavelli deals with information flows and decision locations and, unsurprisingly, it is again centralized in the organizational apex. "The prince should be an extensive questioner, and a patient listener to the truth respecting the things inquired about. . ." (Machiavelli 1965: 115). But all is not to be believed ". . . when we conclude that good counsels, no matter whence they may come, result wholly from the prince's own sagacity; but the wisdom of the prince never results from good counsels" (Machiavelli 1965:116). The flow of information and the keen sense of sagaciousness required of the prince surely encourages stability rather than fluidity in the locus of decision-making authority.

4. **To build trust among individuals and groups throughout the organization**—Machiavelli not only advises that some men are not to be trusted but extends this to the prince himself when he states ". . . as men are naturally bad, and will not observe (their) faith toward you (the prince), you must, in the same way, not observe yours to them; and no prince ever yet lacked legitimate reasons with which to color his want of good faith" (Machiavelli 1965:86)—a perfect recipe for a degenerative system of relations.

A specific consequence of blind trust on the part of the prince is alluded to when Machiavelli (1965:114) states that the only way to guard against adulation, is "to make people understand that they will not offend you by speaking the truth. On the other hand, when every one feels at liberty to tell you the truth, they will be apt to be lacking in respect to you."

The former teaches that some people are to be allowed to speak the truth, and the latter that this principle must be extended to a limited number for fear of a reduction in respect. The reader probably detects a note of conflict in Machiavelli's thought on this point thus far, and rightly so. Above he has observed that ". . . men are naturally bad and will not observe their faith toward you. . . " (Machiavelli 1965:86). Elsewhere (1965:114) he observes that the prince should choose wise men as ministers and "to these only should he give full power to tell him the truth." But further on Machiavelli (1965:114) advises the prince to "listen and reflect (upon their advice), and afterward form his own resolutions." The implication here is that the ministers are rarely, if ever, to be believed. Machiavelli clearly allows a high trust level to exist within a limited section of the hierarchy, mainly his ministers, but this is done in a manipulative manner as the ultimate decision authority rests with the prince.

At another point Machiavelli (1965:52) encourages the prince to rule authoritatively in time of peace as well as war, for he cannot depend on what he sees in time of peace to hold true in times of adversity. Thus people are willing and loyal subjects when death and trouble are far away, but when such troubles are at hand the people will flee from the prince and he would be without citizens. Consequently the low trust level maintained by the prince serves as sufficient criteria for a war-like style of leadership even in times of peace. This is a far cry from the benign, regenerative organizations that OD has among its goals.

5. **To make competition more relevant to work goals and to maximize collaborative efforts**—The incongruence between this OD objective and *The Prince* is definitive. Throughout *The Prince*, Machiavelli consistently attempts to suppress competition displayed by others and gives little credence to collaborative efforts. More specifically he advises to suppress possible competition from "powerful foreigners" by "humbling" them

(1965:19) from his own counsels (1965:116), and from the people themselves. However, in respect to the prince, competition is a never-ending endeavor. It is never explicitly stated, but Machiavelli favors a one-sided, sort of internal-external view of competition. Machiavelli implies that others should forcefully not be allowed to compete with the prince, but he has every right to compete. Advocating the right of competition borders on self-ridicule when Machiavelli (1965:85) states: "You must know . . . that there are two ways of carrying on a contest; the one by law, and the other by force. The first is practiced by men, and the other by animals; and as the first is often insufficient, it becomes necessary to resort to the second."

It seems reasonable that the collaborative spirit implies a possible reduction in authority of superordinates. That is, the superordinate should be willing to concede the point or stand neutral to subordinates when it is demonstrated that he is relatively unqualified in a certain area. In Machiavellian theory the possibility of the superordinate conceding the point or standing neutral to competent subordinates does not exist. This is demonstrated when Machiavelli (1965:108) advises that ". . . when, regardless of the consequences, (the prince) declares himself openly for or against another, (it) will always be more creditable to him than to remain neutral." Competition from others and collaboration are viewed as impairments to furthering authoritative control.

6. **To develop a reward system which recognizes both the achievement of the organization's mission (profit or service) and organization development (growth of people)**—Machiavelli is fully cognizant of reward systems which recognize achievement of the organization's mission but reward systems directed towards growth of people are given little attention in *The Prince*. When conquering a state, the prince should execute his moves with a single blow and then ". . . assure himself of the support of the inhabitants and win them over to himself by benefits bestowed" (Machiavelli 1965:48). The importance and consequences of rewards properly bestowed are further illustrated by this excerpt: "The prince who in person leads his armies into foreign countries, and supports them by plunder, pillage, and exactions, and thus dispenses the substance of others, should do so with the greatest liberality, as otherwise his soldiers would not follow him" (Machiavelli 1965:80).

Machiavelli (1965:113) provides lip service to the individual growth and development side of reward systems when he advises that the prince should bestow riches upon his ministers, and should "share the honors as well as the cares with him." This should not be taken to constitute congruence with OD, however, by virtue of the emphasis given to the concept in the two theories. Such a reward system is at the very heart of OD but Machiavelli mentions it only in passing. Furthermore it is recognized by Machiavelli solely for the purpose of maintaining the ministers of the prince in his service rather than specifically for their growth and development.

It has been recognized in the Public Administration literature that organizations should support and sponsor periods of festival and spectacle for their members (Combs 1972). The intent of this action is, of course, to stimulate the individual and aggregate growth of organization development. Machiavelli too provided that the prince (1965:110) "should at suitable periods amuse his people with festivities and spectacles." However, the intent here is assuredly to provide an occasional rewarding respite from work well done rather than being specifically designed for the growth of people. This seems reasonable from the context from which this sentence was drawn and the very brief attention paid to the matter. On the other hand, a fairly convincing argument could be structured to indicate that Combs (1972) and Machiavelli were writing of the same phenomenon and therefore exhibit a point of congruence.

7. **To increase the sense of ownership of organization objectives throughout the work force**—The prince is taught not to own many of his personal actions and that the people will not own his organizational goals at all times. Demonstrably on the former point, ". . . for the purpose of removing the feeling of (hatred) from the people's minds, and to win their confidence, that, if any cruelties had been practiced, they had not originated with (the prince), but had resulted altogether, from the harsh nature of his minister" (Machiavelli 1965:40).

A blatant inconsistency occurs here as Machiavelli favors shifting the blame in the event of cruelties but, as cited above, Machiavelli (1965:113) teaches the prince to "share the honors as well as the cares" with his ministers. This serves as further evidence to somewhat tarnish Machiavelli's aforementioned consistency with OD in respect to the individual growth and development side of reward systems.

Machiavelli's viewpoint of manipulating the actual locale of action away from the prince when it may prove damaging to his image serves to reduce a full sense of ownership. Clearly, in view of Machiavelli's incorporation of deceit one must rule him incongruent with the OD ownership viewpoint in respect to the prince. On the other hand, when attention is focused on the people, quite a different attitude toward ownership is expressed by Machiavelli. That the people will not own their allegiance and actions is set forth with: ". . . they offer you their blood, their substance, their lives, and their children, provided the necessity for it is far off; but when it is near at hand, then they revolt" (Machiavelli 1965:82).

Therefore the lack of ownership is abundant in respect to the prince and his actions; however, at the other extreme of the hierarchy, Machiavelli teaches that organizational goals should be fully owned in times of adversity as well as of beneficence. However, rather than dealing with this problem through actions directed toward change, Machiavelli chooses to deal with it through a forceful leadership style.

8. **To help managers to manage according to relevant objectives rather than according to past practices or according to objectives which do not make sense for one's area of responsibility**—Perhaps too often our organizations are allowed to remain unchanged over time, staring a

fluid society in the face as if it did not exist. Many OD adherents have accordingly propounded this objective which, given a changing society, would indicate changing organizational patterns and processes. Chabod (1960:50) tells us that Machiavelli was keenly aware of the frequent incongruity between men and their surroundings. That is, Machiavelli is incessantly seeking change in the status quo existing at the time *The Prince* was written, and once this is done stability is the goal above all else. Once a new order has been established, Machiavelli offers a specific suggestion for maintaining it, even for those who have been accustomed to liberty:

> Conquered states that have been accustomed to liberty and the government of their own laws can be held by the conqueror in three different ways. The first is to ruin them; the second, for conqueror to go and reside there in person; and the third is to allow them to continue to live under their own laws, subject to a regular tribute, and to create in them a government of a few, who will keep the country friendly to the conqueror. . .
>
> A city that has been accustomed to free institutions is much easier held by its own citizens than in any other way, if the conqueror desires to preserve it (Machiavelli 1965:29).

Of course, the prince is taught not to abandon such control even in times of peace (Machiavelli 1965:75) and

> . . . the prince, by way of securing the devotion of his minister, should think of him and bind him to himself by obligations; he should bestow riches upon him, and should share the honors as well as the cares with him; so that the abundance of honors and riches conferred by the prince upon his minister may cause the latter not to desire either the one or the other from any other source, and that the weight of cares may make him dread a change, knowing that without the prince he could not sustain it (Machiavelli 1965:113).

Evidently Machiavelli is not teaching managers to manage according to past practices, but whether he is teaching them to manage according to relevant objectives is certainly open to question. This is true due to the nature of the organizational style posed by Machiavelli—rigid hierarchy, maximal control by the prince, etc. The more kaleidoscopic aspects of organizational life are not recognized, or at least they are not mentioned.

9. **To increase self-control and self-direction for people within the organization**—Kaufman (1963:40) poses two sides of this control question. Men who believe that other men take advantage of each other believe that central direction is necessary. On the other hand, those who assume the interests and tendencies of men to be harmonious "emphasize the possibility and desirability of coordination through reciprocity."

For whatever reason, Machiavelli clearly is in favor of central direction. "We have said how necessary it is for a prince to lay solid foundations for his power, as without such he would inevitably be ruined. The main foundations which all states must have, whether new or old, or mixed, are good laws and good armies" (Machiavelli 1965:61). The emphasis is directed away from self-control and self-direction.

To maintain consistency with the concept of central direction, Machiavelli (1965:61) lays the question of reciprocity, in respect to good laws, to rest when he states ". . . as there can be no good laws where there are not good armies, so the laws will be apt to be good where the armies are so. The existence of good laws is dependent upon the existence of good armies." To the extent that OD efforts adhere to the present objective under consideration and recognize such entities as expert power, referent power, and value power (Golembiewski 1972:537) existing throughout the organization, an incongruence between this and the power theory of Machiavelli is patent.

In summary, a number of harmonious as well as discordant points emerge when comparing OD objectives with Machiavelli's *The Prince.* The lessons to be derived from this may point toward further research in the area of relating sensitivity training to attitude change, an area that has received little attention thus far (Holloman and Hendrick 1972:177). On the other hand surprising parallels emerge between the theories—surprising in light of the popularly held attitudes that OD is a more benign approach to organization theory and that Machiavelli represents the "Devil's Disciple." Consequences of this point might indicate a general reexamination of OD objectives and attitudes concluding, hopefully, in a reaffirmation of the principle that OD seeks to bring about "the good life" in an objective manner and not just for present OD practitioners and certain select consultees. Even if no significant breakthrough is stimulated by this comparison nor any definite reaffirmation of OD attitudes is brought about, hopefully this effort will prove to have been worthwhile by providing some small contribution to the much needed dialog between political theory and organization theory. Aside from all this, given the fact that the modern Machiavelian does live and breathe, it could not have been totally in vain.

REFERENCES

Burnham, James. 1943. *The Machiavellians.* New York: The John Day Co., Inc.

Chabod, Frederico. 1960. *Machiavelli and the Renaissance.* Cambridge: Harvard University Press.

Gilbert, Allan H. 1941. *The Prince and other works.* Chicago: Packard & Co.

Golembiewski, Robert T. 1972. *Renewing organizations.* Itasca, Ill.: F. E. Peacock Publishers.

Hearnshaw, F. J. C. 1925. *The social and political ideas of some great thinkers of the Renaissance and the Reformation.* London: George G. Harrap and Co., Ltd.

Holloman, Charles R., and Hendrick, Hal W. 1972. Effect of sensitivity training on tolerance for dissonance. *Journal of applied behavioral science* 8: 174-187.

Jay, Antony. 1967. *Management and Machiavelli.* New York: Holt, Rinehart and Winston.

Kaufman, Herbert. 1963. Organization theory and political theory. In *Managerial behavior and organization demands*, eds. Robert T. Golembiewski and Frank K. Gibson, pp. 36-53. Chicago: Rand McNally and Co.

Machiavelli, Niccolo. 1965. *The Prince.* New York: Airmont Publishing Company, Inc.

Mazzeo, Anthony Joseph. 1965. *Renaissance and seventeenth century studies.* New York: Columbia University Press.

NTL Institute for Applied Behavioral Science. 1968. What is OD? In *Sensitivity training and the laboratory approach*, eds. Robert T. Golembiewski and Arthur Blumberg. Itasca, Ill,: F. E. Peacock Publishers.

Ridalfi, Roberto. 1963. *The life of Niccolo Machiavelli.* Chicago: University of Chicago Press.

Sabine, George H. 1961. *A history of political theory.* New York: Holt, Rinehart and Winston.

Seidman, Harold. 1970. *Politics, position and power.* New York: Oxford University Press.

VIII. Toward Future Development of the Small-Group Emphasis in Political Science:

The Experience of Allied Disciplines

Every silver lining has its dark cloud, and vice versa. That is the simple theme of this chapter, if it needs some translation into direct language. That is to say, sociologists and psychologists have made more progress on small-group analysis than have political scientists. But the practical fact is that one effect of this advantage has been that sociologists and psychologists made understandable mistakes, and discovered some analytical cul-de-sacs the hard way. Being there first in effect implied the expenditure of considerable misdirected energy by sociologists and psychologists, which costs their less-developed brethren may be able to avoid or at least moderate. So this chapter searches for leverage for political scientists in the context of considerable disadvantage.

The two selections below seek to faciliate learning from the past by political scientists as the only alternative to repeating that history, wrong turns and all. In rough terms the first selection below on the experience with the small group in Psychology is more distal to the present developmental stage of Political Science, and the chapter on Sociology is more proximate. The dual perspective is both intended and revealing, suggesting as it does the issues that political scientists can expect to encounter over the next decades in their efforts to apply small-group perspective to traditional disciplinary concerns.

CARL WEICK AND THE EXPERIENCE IN PSYCHOLOGY

Writing from the perspective of the mass of work on small groups by psychologists, Weick provides two sets of guidelines for those newly embarked on the serious study of groups, their covariates, and their consequences. In sum Weick isolates and illustrates (1) eleven things that he would not do if he were to begin studying groups de novo, and (2) fourteen things that he would emphasize if he were to begin a program of serious inquiry concerning groups.

Much of what Weick emphasizes is relevant to existing work on groups in Political Science, indeed to some of the selections reprinted above, even though some of Weick's thrust is against lines of research favored by political scientists. Thus Weick advises against "categorizing talk" in groups, which—in Political Science as well as Psychology—has attracted so many early students. It is not comforting to have the probable error of one's ways highlighted, even when done as gently as Weick does the job. Similarly it is the straight if double-edged gospel when Weick observes: "Backward groups can borrow the successful mutations of the advanced society and ignore most of their false starts, and this is especially true within science." Hence the prudence of carefully evaluating the history of small-group experience in Psychology, which Weick calls as he sees, even where it implies to him the limited value of lines of investigation and analysis already begun in Political Science.

Noteworthy to political scientists, and far more comforting, is Weick's emphasis on the virtues of staring at one or a few groups rather than glancing at a hundred. The virtues of "small sample size" are not frequently heard, and Weick's argument is a happy one, especially to political scientists who often find themselves unavoidably focusing on one or a few groups "in the field"—a Supreme Court, a legislative committee, a city council, and so on.

Political scientists concerned with groups also are well-advised to note Weick's reference to the tides of interest in group phenomena by psychologists. One of Weick's distinguished colleagues sees a definite pattern, in fact, looking back over perhaps seventy-five years of attention to groups. Interest in groups is seen as varying with the times, plus eight-ten years. Turbulent times inspire increased attention to groups, albeit eight-ten years after the peak of the turbulence. Similarly interest in groups falls when times are more serene again, bottoming out approximately a decade after the good times really started to roll. From this point of view group-oriented political scientists would seem well-advised to get ready for a near-future round of newly intensified interest in groups. Where we are today seems rock bottom in multiple senses, and every direction is up from the position in which we presently find ourselves.

CLOVIS SHEPHERD AND THE EXPERIENCE IN SOCIOLOGY

The stock of the small group in Sociology is down, Clovis Shepherd tells us, and he details an explanation that is not only plausible for his discipline but also resonates with the overall experience in Political Science. There is no intent here to repeat Shepherd's argument. Broadly, however, the foundations of group research by sociologists were substantially eroded by some powerful tides of the times, he explains. In large part the vulnerability of work in the small-group tradition derived from several limiting features of the existing literature, which burgeoned during the decade following the mid-1950s. Large trees with shallow roots are particularly vulnerable even to temporarily high winds. Thus Shepherd emphasizes contributors to the substantial decrease in attention to small groups by sociologists: the lack of field research on groups by sociologists, the limited applicability of available findings to pressing social problems, and a range of other features.

While Shepherd clearly reflects that in recent years the trend-line of sociological interest in groups is sharply down, he also emphasizes a variety of central functions associated with groups that inevitably must motivate a rebounding share of sociological attention. If the present state is a "holding action in Sociology regarding theoretical models and hypothesis-testing," Shepherd notes, the multiple significance of behavior in small groups implies to him that the holding action cannot last much longer. He emphasizes a number of significant processes that occur in groups, some at the heart of human development. For example Shepherd stresses the continuing belief by sociologists that groups "are very important for one's social identity, self-concept, and level of self-esteem." As such, major attention must soon be redirected to small groups.

In addition to sketching and explaining his sense of the state of the present group orientation in Sociology as one of relative inattention and substantial significance, Shepherd devotes about equal space to two themes on which many political scientists can usefully go to school. He emphasizes several major foci of current sociological work on groups; and Shepherd also suggests the kind of group emphases that are likely to characterize the revitalized attention to groups that he sees as surely coming in his discipline. The latter emphases—given that the developmental stages of Political Science and Sociology are quite similar—are no doubt of especial relevance to political scientists. For example Shepherd predicts as well as prescribes growing attention to "field work," and greater use of simulation contexts as a matrix for observing group processes. As the chapters above indicate at various points, appropriate movement in Political Science has already begun in variable degree on these two critical fronts for analysis.

Some Challenges For Future Group Research: Reflections on the Experience in Sociology

KARL E. WEICK

Imagine looking at a clock to see what time it is. Now imagine that the clock you are watching is strange. Not only can it be misread, but there are also these possibilities: "(1) that the frequency with which the clock is consulted may modify the time it reports; (2) that the time the clock is expected to show may modify the time it actually reports; (3) if the observer dislikes the clock (let us say from an aesthetic viewpoint), it will report time differently than if he is fond of it; (4) if the observer sends someone else to consult the clock, it will report differently; (5) that the time indicated by other clocks adjacent to the one being consulted or the position of this clock relative to other clocks might influence the time the clock in question reports" (Wallerstein and Sampson 1971, 45).

Observing groups is not simple, as the example of the strange clock implies. In this essay I will discuss briefly some of the things that I would and would not do if I were starting out to study groups. Although the title of this essay suggests that it will reflect "the experience in psychology" it obviously represents only the summarized experience of a single fallible observer. That being the case, I would urge any reader to ask other investigators what they would and would not do if they were starting to study groups, and then use these several contradictory lists to forge a set of interesting concepts and methods to be used.

The readers of this essay are in an enviable position, and I hope to maximize that advantage. The position is enviable because they have "the privilege of historic backwardness." This privilege—which has been described by Trotsky, Mao Tse-Tung, and Service (1960)—suggests that underdeveloped groups have an advantage over advanced ones. "Although compelled to follow after the advanced countries, a backward country does not take things in the same order. The privilege of historic backwardness—and such a privilege exists—permits, or rather compels, the adoption of whatever is ready in advance of any specified date, skipping a whole series of intermediate stages" (Service 1960,99-100).

Backward groups can borrow the successful mutations of the advanced society and ignore most of their false starts, and this is especially true within science. "Young scientists tend to surpass their elders, when other things such as brains, of course, are equal. The well-established individuals ordinarily do not go on making successive important contributions because they become so committed, adapted, to a particular line of thought. The young are generalized and unstable, in a sense, and have the privilege of

Preparation of this paper was supported by the National Science Foundation through Grant GS-33247.

backwardness' which enables them to appropriate only the more fruitful and progressive of the older generation's accomplishments, disregarding or discarding as useless debris much of the work that went on before them" (Service, 104).

The reader should not make the mistake of thinking that chronological age is intended by phrases like "young scientist." "Young" can also refer to amount of experience or familiarity with a field. Thus political scientists, being relative newcomers to the small-group area, are in the enviable position of potentially avoiding some of the problems of the older group people in Psychology and Sociology. It is this sense in which this essay attempts to magnify their advantage.

THINGS I WOULD NOT DO IF I WERE TO STUDY GROUPS

Here are eleven things that I would not do if I were to begin a program of research on groups.

1. I would not categorize talk. The group literature is loaded with valiant attempts to categorize what people say in groups. I'm convinced that what people say is less important than how they say it (e.g., Watzlawick, Beavin, and Jackson 1967). That being the case, tedious categorization of sentences probably means that the investigator is studying some of the least important things that happen in a group.

To illustrate the point, suppose that five of us are seated at a faculty meeting, a trivial decision is to be made, and a large amount of talk is going on among us. It is misleading to pay especially close attention to the content of that talk because the more crucial thing is that we are talking with some vigor and frequency. Basically this abundance of talk signifies (metacommunication) that nothing special is up. By engaging in a "usual" quantity of exchange we signify to one another that everything is normal and we can proceed. If, however, the meeting had been characterized by silence, spurts of talk followed by silence, simultaneous talking, interruptions, hushed voices, or any deviation from the normal pattern of frequency, amount, and volume of our talking, then this deviation would have spoken much more powerfully to the state of our group process. How our talk proceeds in that meeting seems to signify more about the nature of our relationship and what our problems are than do the words themselves.

Another way to demonstrate this point is to have people write suicide notes. If you compare these simulated suicide notes with real suicide notes (Osgood and Walker 1959) you will find that what people talk about does not differentiate sharply between the two kinds of notes but that the expressive style does. Long sentences, elaborately constructed with lengthy explanations are a tip that the note is simulated. What is difficult for a simulator to capture is the heightened state of arousal characteristic of a person about to commit suicide. This heightened state of arousal simplifies the kinds of sentence constructions that are available to the troubled author. His writing style becomes primitive rather than eloquent. But the crucial point is that the content of the note and what he says is a poorer diagnostic indicator than the way in which he says it.

So the first thing that I would avoid if I even decided to categorize group process would be category systems that encode the content and substance of the talk. Instead, I would look for categories that encode metacommunication.

2. I would not let the group literature proliferate unsummarized. This point is obvious, but it needs to be stated. Too many pieces of group research accumulated in psychology before anyone tried to discover common threads among them. Group research in psychology never did have a strong body of theory controlling it, nor did its several fragments ever seem to lend themselves to a compact set of propositions. It's conceivable that if more people had more frequently written state-of-the-art papers, the fragmented quality of group literature might never have developed. Unfortunately the literature on groups is now so large that only a fool would venture to summarize it, and some people are even asking, "Is the literature worth reviewing?" What I'm suggesting is that political scientists might avoid similar outcomes if they ruthlessly summarize frequently what they have and have not learned about groups.

3. I would not assume that group members are good listeners. The concept of interaction conveys the image that people fashion their remarks in response to what other people say and that this is a sensitive ongoing process with multiple contingencies. When I watch groups function, I don't see nearly this degree of tracking of other people's behavior; nor do I see people shaping and reshaping their replies in such a way that they develop, elaborate, and link up with preceding comments.

There is an old stunt sometimes used by group leaders in which they require that before any individual can make a comment he must restate the preceding comment made by another individual to that individual's satisfaction. Over and over the sobering discovery is that people are quite inaccurate in restating what happened just before them. This has been found more formally in the "Next-in-line" paradigm developed by Marshall Brenner (1971). This demonstration repeatedly shows that people in groups have the poorest memory for those remarks that immediately precede theirs—and also for those that immediately follow. The picture that begins to emerge is one in which a group often consists of individuals acting in a parallel but noncontingent manner, and the most they are doing is trying to take turns (Duncan 1972) in an orderly fashion.

I realize that's a rather harsh view of what goes on in groups. The point is that if you start your research presuming that preferences will change substantially within a group, you may be wrong because (a) people don't listen that closely to what goes on, (b) they intend to persuade other individuals of the validity of their viewpoint, and (c) this set of individual performances is orderly only because it is controlled by norms on turn taking. Notice that if this is plausible, then you don't need the concept of a group to understand what is going on.

4. I would not use large samples. When I get to my positive recommendations it will be clear that I am more favorable toward a clinical, idiographic, ethnographic, and sit-and-stare approach than I am toward the accumulation of large amounts of data where minor statistical differences gain spurious significance. My hunch is that one of the things that has made group psychology so bland has been the usage of simple situations that tempt the investigator to administer the situation to large numbers of subjects.

In particular I have in mind the prisoner's dilemma, the minimal social situation, and communication networks. While each of these situations has added to our understanding of groups, their very simplicity may prevent the investigator from staring intently at any one group of people when they perform in this simple situation. Thus the apparent barrenness of situations like the prisoner's dilemma is not necessarily inherent in the demands imposed on people, but rather is the result of investigators not watching with sufficient imagination and intuition to see some of the subtle dilemmas that are being faced and resolved by the participants. What has replaced the noticing of these subtleties is observation of gross differences which tell us only the most trivial things about groups.

So my recommendation would be that no matter how simple or complex the exercise you finally choose, avoid the temptation to run lots of people through it so that you can see trends. All you need are two groups so that you can make a comparison. Comparison is the basic act of inquiry, and as long as you have a datum and a relatum (Boring 1954) you're in business.

5. I would not videotape my groups. This is a tricky recommendation and is hedged by several qualifications. From my experiences with grant review panels and observational techniques, I repeatedly find cases in which people think that making a permanent videotape record of their group's activities will give them data that suggest patterns. To reiterate a familiar but important point, videotape is nothing but a record, and a great deal of activity must occur before these records become data that have any value (Weick 1968, 361). Find a group investigator who owns videotape equipment and I guarantee you will find he also owns unanalysed tapes of groups. There appears to be a mystical belief that videotapes supply knowledge without human intervention, and it's best to notice the fallacy of that position at the start.

I would not be against videotapes if they portrayed a very small number of occasions and permitted the observer to know intimately what went on in those occasions by looking at the same tapes over and over. I continue to be amazed and humbled by a book entitled, *The First Five Minutes* (Pittenger, Hockett and Danehy 1960). This book contains an exhaustive analysis of only the first five minutes of only one clinical interview, an analysis which required several months to complete. What is surprising is that some rather powerful inductions and potential generalizations emerged from that intensive staring at a single instance. Whenever I feel tempted to watch several groups in a cursory fashion and say something of

consequence about them, I find the example of five minutes a welcome'
constraint.

Just as large samples often preclude thinking and contemplation, it looks
as if large amounts of videotape may have the same consequences. And
since I think one of the big things that hurts the study of groups in psychology has been an absence of intellectual capital, it would follow that
anything perceived as an impediment to powerful thinking would be
something I would avoid in future research.

6. I would not call a group a group. I think part of the problem in
previous psychological work on groups is that people called some of the
strangest entities groups. Having attached a noun to what was basically a
free-floating, ill-formed assemblage, investigators reified this noun and
treated the assemblage as if it had properties of its own. If these same investigators had been more stingy in their use of this label, they might not
have mixed together such dissimilar entities.

Several points could be made relative to the assertion that people should
be stingy in their use of nouns (Weick 1974, 358-360). First, there is a
possibility that members conclude that they are a group late in the history
of an assemblage. They arrive at this conclusion retrospectively and,
therefore, the perception of "group" controls very minor amounts of the
activity that is observed (Weick 1971, 19). Second, there is a subtle
emphasis in Gordon Allport's original definition of social psychology and
in much of the writing of Cooley that most observers miss. This oversight
can be illustrated if we look at a portion of Allport's definition: social psychology is "an attempt to understand and explain how the thought, feeling,
and behavior of individuals are influenced by the actual, imagined, or implied presence of others." (Allport 1968, 3). The crucial words are "implied" and "imagined." There may be a vast difference between those individuals that a group member takes into account whenever he says,
thinks, or does anything and those individuals who are merely physically
present at the time of his performances. It seems to me that investigators
often accord too much importance to those who are physically present and
too little importance to those whose imagined or implied presence is more
influential. Thus I think it is often the case that group members, that is
people who are physically present, may be seen but unnoticed by any individual and therefore are of minor consequence to explain what he does. I
further think that the way to hedge your analysis against this possibility is
to be stingy in labeling any gathering a group. Third, it is obvious that any
researcher needs to have some kinds of words to signify and categorize a
gathering, so what I would urge is that you get the greatest number and
variety of nouns possible so that you can preserve some of the fine gradations in interdependence that are found in most gatherings. Joe McGarth's
fifteeen gradations found in the *Encyclopaedia Britannica* (15th Ed., 16:
960) are a good starting point for proliferating your nouns and reducing
the tendency to reify.

7. I would not regard the members of groups as whole people. If you ex-

the essential point that there is a threshold beyond which interaction is unendurable for both parties. It is because people frequently take leave of one another that the interaction-liking proposition maintains itself" (Schwartz 1973, 4).

I think group researchers should stay more alert to the possibility that under some conditions people are trying to cut their losses, minimize their costs, and abbreviate as much as possible their time spent with and commitments made to some of the groups in which they find themselves. Group members may be more motivated to minimize their dissatisfactions than to maximize their satisfactions when they are inside a group. If a researcher watched group activity for signs of disengagement and the reduction of interaction, he might find that a substantial portion of group activity can be understood in these terms. The resulting portrait would be rather different from most of the conventional and rather glowing portrayals of what groups can accomplish for individuals.

11. I would not have a group design group research. While I have not personally been involved in a large number of group experiments, I have been involved in group experiments that had a variable number of coinvestigators ranging from one through nine. Reflecting on these experiences with teams of different size, I see a clear trend: the greater the number of coinvestigators, the more uninterpretable the resulting study.

Notice the intricacies in this observation. You have a group of investigators studying the group dynamics of another group, but the dynamics among the watchers affect the conclusions drawn about the watched even though the watchers may not realize it. As the size of research groups increases, accretion rather than deletion seems to be the predominant decision rule for questions of design. For example in the case of our nine-person research team, we tried to simulate an organization in which the ideas of Emery and Trist (1969) could be tested. The components of that simulation increased in number and complexity because each person on the team made good suggestions that had not been thought of by the other individuals about what important things to model, to measure, or to vary. The resulting simulation, which I feel is one of the richest I've ever seen, is also one of the hardest to run and interpret. Our research team took so much time designing the simulation that the subject pool was depleted before we could get to it. Furthermore it took all nine members of the research team to do a single run of the simulation. This meant that if any team member was absent, we couldn't run.

There is an interesting sense in which that experience supports a proposition in the small-group field concerning group composition. The general pattern of findings is that as groups become more heterogeneous, their problem-solving resources increase, but so too do their difficulties in establishing good interpersonal relationships (Collins 1970, 220-221). Our large research group was heterogeneous and loaded with ideas, and to manage the interpersonal relationships, we basically took the best ideas each individual had and aggregated them. The net result was a rather un-

amine the work of people like Allport (1962), Steiner (1955), Wallace (1961), and Weick (1969), you will find that all of them argue that a crucial component in any group is the fact that some actions of individuals are influenced by their group membership but most are not. Thus it is less accurate to say that a person is a member of a group than to say, for example, that his fantasy-generating behavior is produced in the presence of and released by specific behaviors produced by other individuals in the group. The crucial questions relating to groups may involve rather specific issues, such as which behaviors does an individual allow himself to be influenced by and in which particular groups? The individual allows the group to have some influence over what he will do, but this influence is probably confined to rather specific behaviors, values and attitudes. To understand what makes a group function and why people tie themselves to groups, one should look for the specific issues and behaviors on which the individual member allows himself to be influenced rather than assume that the group has equal and high impact on all of his qualities.

8. I would not assume that groups solve problems rationally. I'm becoming more and more convinced that the real payoff in group research will not come from studying how groups solve problems that are clearly stated. Instead it will come from investigating how groups find problems and how they solve these possibly real or possibly spurious problems with poor knowledge of their problem-solving resources, vague ideas concerning when the problem has been solved, and with a rather large amount of chance, coincidence, and accident determining the outcome. Said more crisply, I am convinced that models such as the garbage can (Cohen, March, and Olsen 1972) and organized anarchies (Cohen and March 1974) capture a greater proportion of the crucial dynamics in groups than is true of those models which seem to portray a "thinking man's primary group." It is certainly nothing new to assert that the nonrational often swamps the rational in group activities, but we now seem to have better conceptual tools to talk about some of these nonrational activities. I would argue that two of Graham Allison's (1971) models, organizational routines and organizational power, are beginning to suggest a language for talking about some of these nonrational properties.

The main point I want to make is that in studying groups it is tempting to invoke the simplifying assumption that groups solve problems in the same way individuals do. This was one of the original assumptions in Bales' work (1950, 62), and proved to be a heuristic assumption even though it does have drawbacks. Researchers of groups who start from a political science standpoint could leapfrog sole reliance on a rational view of group processes and incorporate from the beginning such notions as (a) groups negotiate rather than perceive reality, (b) groups operate with unclear goals and unclear technology, (c) groups have fluid participation, (d) groups often contain solutions in search of problems rather than problems in search of solutions, (e) groups make themselves up as they go along, and (f) groups appreciate the "wisdom of divination."

To illustrate the point let me elaborate on the phrase "wisdom of divination." This phrase refers to Moore's (1957) analysis of a band of hunters in Labrador called the Naskapi Indians. Every day the Naskapi face this question: "What direction should the hunters take to locate game?" They answer this question by holding dried caribou shoulder bones over a fire. As the bones become heated they develop cracks and smudges that are then read by an expert. These cracks indicate the direction in which the hunters should look for game. The Naskapi believe that this practice allows the gods to intervene in their hunting decisions.

Whether you believe in divine intervention or not, the interesting feature of these practices is that they work. To see how they work, think about some of the characteristics of this decision procedure. First, the final decision of where to hunt is not a purely personal or group choice. If no game are found, the gods, not the group, are to blame. Second, the final decision is not affected by the outcomes of past hunts. If the Indians were influenced by the outcomes of past hunts, they would run the definite risk of depleting the stock of animals. Their prior success could induce subsequent failure. Third, the final decision is not influenced by the inevitable patterning of choice and preferences that is true for all humans. And it is these very patterns that enable the hunted animals to take evasive action and to become sensitized to the presence of human beings.

Given these general characteristics of the practice of scapullimancy, we can now say something about the utility of this practice. The use of scapula (bones) is a very crude way of randomizing human behavior under conditions where avoiding fixed patterns of activity may have an advantage. Restated in Moore's own words: "It seems safe to assume that human beings require a functional equivalent to a table of random numbers if they are to avoid unwitting regularities in their behavior which can be utilized by adversaries" (p. 73).

Whether or not seemingly nonrational practices have rational consequences is beside the point. The point is that coincidence, uncertainty, accident, timing, and other sporadic events may be the rule in groups. If so, then rational models will explain very little of the variance. If I had the privilege of backwardness, one of the first things I would dispense with is the presumption that rationality is the predominant mode in which groups operate.

9. I would not use deception if I studied groups in a laboratory. If I were to start out fresh in group research I would do everything possible to avoid deception for two reasons. First, there is the ethical question of whether an investigator should lie to people who agree to participate in his research. I think a sound argument can be made that under some conditions an investigator has no alternative but to deceive his subjects, but I personally find this a difficult strategy to use. For the sake of completeness, however, I should indicate that I think there is one ethical principle that supercedes the issue of lying. This is the principle which states that a poorly designed study is unethical (Rutstein 1969, 524). If from the beginning there was no

chance that a particular study could yield any solid information, then it is unethical to waste the time of participants. Thus good design, good controls, and the ability to draw specific conclusions are themselves ethical principles. For that reason, whether an individual uses deception is to me less crucial as an ethical issue than whether the study is one from which people could learn something in the first place. If deception is needed to learn something, then deception could be ethical because it does make these studies interpretable. If, however, the study was uninterpretable from the beginning due to its design, and if the investigator further compounded the problems by deep deceptions, then that is the worst of all possible worlds. I realize most group researchers are already aware of these points, but I personally feel a growing squeamishness about using deception in experiments for ethical reasons and have tried to avoid it as much as possible.

I think the second reason for my reluctance to deceive is more crucial than my reservations based on ethics. I think deception is lazy research. If you want to study a phenomenon, I think it is much easier to study that phenomenon by deception than by nondeceptive means. A common deception in group research is to induce cohesion by giving individuals a bogus test after which you tell them that they really have quite similar backgrounds and therefore they should work well together in the task. That's easy to do. Now ask yourself how an investigator could create cohesion without false feedback. To do this the investigator will have to be much more resourceful, imaginative, and crisp in his thinking. He'll have to devise some cohesion-inducing experiences that can be applied across groups, that can produce varying degrees of cohesion, and that have external validity. I personally think that one of the advantages of using parlor games as group tasks (for example, see the usage of Password by Goodman and Ofshe 1968), is that these games do not involve deception. The experimenter can present such games as what they are, but then he must also do the more difficult job of tying the game to group phenomena that are of general interest. If, for example, he wants to argue that Password is a reasonable exercise to capture empathy, then he has to be clear in explaining how guessing words on the basis of cues has anything to do with the observation in everyday life, "I know just how you feel."

The statement that I would try to avoid deception in group research m[ay] be one of the more controversial and personal ones in this essay. I wo[uld] simply urge each investigator, before he starts making research comm[it]ments and defending them, to make his peace with the issue of how far [to] go to get an answer and what consequences flow from that decision.

10. I would not forget that people get tired of groups. People get f[ed up] with groups, they get bored with groups, and they sometimes want [to es]cape from groups to an oasis of privacy. As Schwartz has put it, [care] must therefore be taken with Homans' proposition, 'Persons who [interact] frequently with one another tend to like one another' (provi[ding the] relationship is not obligatory). The statement holds generally, b[ut]

manageable simulation which activated more phenomena of relevance to the Emery and Trist formulation than we could ever hope to keep track of.

The basic point I'm making is that if you plan to study groups, use whatever you know about groups as both topic and resource. Groups will be a topic in the sense that groups are the object of your study, but that same information can be used as resource to understand the kinds of problems that might arise among your colleagues in designing a group study. Since group dynamics are complex and difficult to understand, I would hesitate to have a very large research team when I first started to work on groups. The topic is difficult enough without having also to manage immediately those problems of group process that go along with large research teams. The testable proposition in the preceding remarks is that there is an inverse relationship between the importance of a piece of group research and the size of the group that obtained it.

THINGS I WOULD DO IN STUDYING GROUPS

To offset the possibly discouraging tone of the preceding points, I would like to indicate several things that I would do if I were beginning to study groups. Before elaborating this list I should make the obvious point that each of the eleven proscriptions mentioned earlier could be stated positively. For example, the statement, "I would not categorize talk" could be stated positively as, "I would categorize metacommunication." I urge the reader to restate each of the eleven earlier points if he finds it easier to digest positive than negative statements.

If I were to begin a program of inquiry into groups I would do some of the following things:

1. I would complete the Desert Survival exercise with four friends. The Desert Survival Problem (Lafferty, Eady, and Elmers 1974) is a straight-forward exercise in which a group of five people have crashed in the desert, they have salvaged fifteen items from the wreck and they are to rate the importance of these items for their survival. Members individually rank the items after which they convene to arrive at a group ranking that each member could live with. Finally both lists are scored against an expert's ranking that is the correct listing for the importance of these items.

I have several reasons for making this my first positive recommendation. First, the presence of a set of correct answers provides a clear indication of whether individual resources within a group are being used well or poorly. If an individual's prior rankings are closer to those of the expert than is true for the group rankings, then it is clear that the group is somehow underexploiting the information it has available. Second, this survival problem is sufficiently novel that even though you are a researcher on groups it does not take very long before you get caught up in defending your own rankings and trying to figure out how other people could have ranked the items differently. This problem seems to evoke most of the dynamics we usually associate with groups. That's why I am urging group researchers to get some first-hand information about groups in a rather compact form by experiencing this exercise. And third, what is interesting about this exercise is that the answers seem to be purely a matter of opinion. This appearance leads the individual to defend certain choices and rankings beyond the point where they make sense. It is not uncommon to influence others to adopt your own position only to find in the end that you have actually reduced the group's chance of surviving. If this influence had occurred in the real world, you would have placed your group in more danger than if they had questioned your advice. Because of the vividness and intensity of the group discussions, the as-if quality of the role playing recedes and the realism of a real survival situation comes into prominence.

Consistent with several points made earlier, the essence of this first recommendation is simply that you immerse yourself in the phenomenon of interest quickly and vigorously, after which you study carefully and imaginatively what went on. A particularly good vehicle to gain this first-hand experience seems to be the Desert Survival Problem.

2. I would make participation in groups fluid rather than stable. Earlier I mentioned that fluid participation is one of the characteristics of an organized anarchy. Fluid participation with frequent replacement of people has been used by Ziller (1965) as the primary characteristic that differentiates open from closed groups. My hunch is that the kinds of groups political scientists will be interested in do not have stable membership. That being the case, it becomes crucial to distinguish what leaves a group in terms of lore and resources when an individual exits, and what stays behind and transcends the presence of any one individual. A common assertion in the group dynamics literature is that in many kinds of groups members are substitutable (e.g. Steiner 1955). This means that the particular person occupying a position is less crucial than the function he performs. If that person leaves and a newcomer enters and performs the same function, the group continues just as it had before. Undoubtedly that picture is oversimplified, but the question is in precisely what ways has it been simplified? When a person leaves, some portions of the group are lost and need to be supplied by the remaining members or their replacements whereas other portions don't. The essential point is that external validity in group research may be enhanced if the personnel being studied are transient rather than stable.

3. I would use negative explanation to gain an initial understanding of groups. Because so many of us are familiar with groups, we often find nothing particularly unusual about them or anything worth explaining. Those things happen that we expected to happen, and that's it. To undercut this tendency to normalize our observations due to familiarity, I would urge that investigators take seriously Gregory Bateson's (1972) suggestions about how to do cybernetic explanation.

Bateson notes that cybernetic explanation is always negative. By this he means that we "consider what alternative possibilities could conceivably have occurred and then ask why many of the alternatives were not followed, so that the particular event was one of those few which could, in fact, occur. The course of events is said to be subject to 'restraints,' and it is assumed that, apart from such restraints, the pathways of change would be governed only by equality of probability. In fact, the 'restraints' upon which cybernetic explanation depends can in all cases be regarded as factors which determine inequality of probability" (pp. 399-400).

Whenever you find yourself saying that a particular group or set of events are unremarkable, ask yourself why the group did not do something other than what you observed. Force yourself to specify first what equally probable events and outcomes could have occurred and then second, ask yourself what kept these other equally probable events from happening? Stated differently, ask how were the equal probabilities rendered unequal by the situation in which the group found itself. Sometimes it is hard to turn group phenomena into interesting questions and observations, due partly to familiarity with the objects of interest and partly to their complexity. To solve these problems the investigator might try using negative explanation. He should push himself to specify what did not occur within the group but easily could have, and then speculate about possible reasons and histories that generated the particular outcome which he observed.

4. Imitate Clifford Geertz' analysis of the Balinese Cock Fight. Robert Louis Stevenson, in attempts to improve his writing, would do such things as copy verbatim passages written by other authors that he thought were unusually well-written, write down conversations from memory, try to write in the style of some other author, read an author he admired and then try to write from memory the passage that he had read at an earlier time. Macrorie (1968) has transformed these practices into three forms of imitation that he urges upon writers who are trying to improve their skills. One method is to "find a paragraph or short passage you admire. Copy it into your journal. Take brief notes of what it says. Then tomorrow attempt to reproduce the passage without looking at it." The next form of imitation is to "write your own thoughts or observations into the same sentence patterns in the passage that you copied down for" the previous form of imitation. And finally, "listen to a conversation between yourself and another person or between two other persons. Take notes if you can do so unobtrusively, then try to reproduce the conversation accurately. Can a reader tell from your dialog that two persons are talking in different styles, or manners, or moods? Have you heard the uniqueness in their words? Do they sound real enough to be believable?" (Macrorie 1968, 170).

Taking a lead from Macrorie's efforts to improve writing, I think the same approach can be adapted to improve thinking, writing, and research about groups. I would further argue that if the potential group researcher absorbed and then tried to imitate Clifford Geertz' analysis of the Balinese Cock Fight (1972) he would be trying to imitate in the group field one of the most stimulating analyses of a social phenomenon that I've run across. It is my hunch that if the investigator copied portions of the Geertz manuscript, and later tried to reproduce them and/or tried to make his own analyses in the same manner and with the same sensitivities, he would benefit the field of group research handsomely.

Obviously each investigator has his own favorite example that epitomizes scholarship at its best. The Geertz work happens to be my favorite but, I would urge the reader to find the favorites that other investigators have. When you find some piece of work that you admire, I would urge that you try to think about your own problems in a similar style as the starting point of your inquiry. The imitation being urged here is not meant to stifle diversity. Instead, the intent of this initial imitation is simply to start the inquiry with a much richer set of images with the analysis being made simultaneously at more than one level using more than one discipline. These are the striking features of the Geertz work.

5. I would be suspicious of underlying structures. A substantial portion of the analysis of groups done by psychologists seems to assume that any group is characterized by some kind of underlying structure, and it is the job of the researcher to dig deep enough to uncover this structure. The structure remains there, binds the group together, and accounts for its regularities whether it is discovered or not. Much research with communication networks seems to make this assumption. In the initial stages of inquiry, I think an investigator might be well advised to make the opposite assumption. The opposite assumption would be that groups consist of superimposed rather than underlying structures. Another way to say this is, groups can be thought of as collective self-fulfilling prophecies.

The thrust of the argument is that if an individual or a set of individuals initially assume that a group exists and then concert their actions as if the group existed, then in fact a group has come into existence. But notice what produced the group. Having assumed that it was present, the members then rearranged themselves and their activities so that this prophecy became fulfilled. But the substance of a group in this view is considerably more ephemeral, fleeting, and perceptual than is the case if one starts with the assumption that there is an underlying structure waiting to be discovered. The suggestion that groups may be collective self-fulfilling prophecies largely states in somewhat different imagery a point that recurs in this essay. The main difference between group and individual situations may reside largely in what the individual singles out in his perceptual world as the crucial variables that can be linked into some kind of meaningful set of relations.

6. I would expect to find stratification, ethnocentrism, and norms whenever I looked at a group. These three concepts of stratification, ethnocentrism, and norms are standard labels in the group literature. They also happen to be three concepts that I have made very little use of in my own work. However, I now feel that they probably explain more of the variance in group behavior than I realized.

The argument in favor of stratification is based on the finding (e.g. Fromkin 1973) that people have strong tendencies to differentiate themselves from other individuals and to assert uniqueness. Those tendencies frequently get played out and concretized in groups in the form of status levels. As the Sherifs (1964) have shown, differentiations in status are some of the first issues that groups worry about. And since rewards, opportunities, influence, etc., are accorded in terms of these strata, how the strata come into being, how many layers there are and how stable the differentiations are can be of considerable consequence in the understanding of what is going on in a group.

It has been demonstrated repeatedly that minimal distinctions between two groups of people are quickly embellished into substantial presumed differences between the two groups, and these differences then affect subsequent activities within and between the groups (ethnocentrism). Evidence suggests that it does not take very much differentiation to trigger this pattern of in-group adulation and out-group deprecation (e.g. Billig and Tajfel 1973). Since political scientists will probably be looking at sets of groups rather than single groups, I think they should be alerted to ethnocentrism as a useful concept to sort out part of what may be occurring.

Finally the concept of norms is one that is commonly talked about, yet again this is a concept I haven't used in my own work. For example in our research on jazz orchestras (Weick, Gilfillan, and Keith 1973) we observed a large number of molecular events at rehearsals, but failed to consider the possibility that much of what goes on in an orchestra rehearsal is the establishment and reaffirmation of a fairly complex set of norms, some of which have quite narrow latitudes before sanctions are applied. There seem to be some fairly good models concerning norms. One that appears to be sound was developed by Jackson (1966) and has been shown to be useful by both Davis (1969) and Hackman and Morris (1976). In retrospect two factors explain our failure to utilize the concepts of norms: (1) I previously had looked at laboratory groups which were sufficiently short lived that norms did not develop, and (2) some of the orchestras we did observe appeared anomic and there may have been relatively few norms. But one does not have to be with a group very long before he gets the distinct impression that certain actions are tacitly reacted to by members saying in effect, "We simply don't do that here"or "We do more of that here than you are doing." Often these norms are slow to change.

7. I would pay more attention to minority influence. Lest the preceding remarks about norms and sanctions suggest that minorities are dealt with swiftly and decisively, I would urge the student of groups to examine closely an increasingly influential body of material which begins to describe conditions under which the minority in a group can influence the majority toward the minority position. This work has been summarized by Moscovici and Nemeth (1974, 217-249). Normally when one thinks about social influence in groups, the first images that come to mind are the Asch experiments on conformity and the Schachter experiments on communications with deviant members of a discussion group. Once these images are invoked, the accompanying view is that the majority prevails and that

minority views are either compromised toward the majority view or neglected.

My hunch is that any newcomer to group research will probably pay more attention to what the majority view is, how it forms, and around what issues it forms. And he will probably pay less attention to an equally powerful and interesting phenomenon, namely the conditions under which a minority is able to change the view of the majority. It is interesting to note that in some of Cartwright's (1971) reanalyses of the "risky shift" several of his alternative explanations suggest that minority influence rather than a diffusion of responsibility was responsible for the final set of judgments that the group agreed on. Similarly if by now you have completed the Desert Survival exercise and have recorded it on tape, you might wish to reexamine that tape to see whether some of the conditions proposed by Moscovici and Nemeth for successful minority influence occurred when the majority changed its ranking for an alternative. One of their suggestions is that an influential minority requires a combination of consistency (a content consideration) and confidence (an expressive consideration).

8. I would assume that groups are operating with confounded feedback. In the earlier discussion of nonrationality I mentioned that I would assume that groups don't know what their goals are. To that point I would now add the additional assumption that even if a group is clear on its goals, it may be unclear whether these goals are achieved and how they are achieved. This occurs because most situations of interdependence involve confounded feedback (Hall 1957, Rosenthall and Weiss 1966, Zander and Wolfe 1964). If it is assumed that most feedback to groups is confounded, then a fairly large number of group concepts (especially those that presuppose individual knowledge of results) are of questionable value. The concept of confounded feedback refers to the situation where people are interdependent, they work on a group task, they produce a product, and then the group is praised for the outcome. In this sequence of events, what remains obscure is precisely which inputs by whom and in what amounts produced that outcome. Given that ambiguity, for example, explanations of group phenomena that invoke equity theory are suspect in explaining much of the variance in groups. They are suspect because confounded feedback makes it virtually impossible for group members to compare their individual inputs and outcomes to establish whether the situation is equitable. Given this difficulty it is possible that equality rather than equity would be the prevailing norm of justice within groups.

Consider an additional complication which results if it is assumed that feedback is confounded. A distinction is often drawn between conjunctive and disjunctive tasks (Thibaut and Kelley 1959). In a conjunctive task the success of the group depends on all of the members making the proper responses (e.g. a division of labor). Given the prior comments about inequity, it could be argued that conjunctive tasks are both immune to inequity and vulnerable to it. They could be immune in the sense that even though all members have to contribute responses, it is impossible to say which inputs are more important or more effortful in determining the outcome. Thus given a conjunctive task and confounded feedback, one might assume that whatever rewards the group receives will be distributed according to a norm of equality. However, it could also be argued that a poor sequencing of contributions or a failure of one or more persons to contribute their expected response would be especially conspicuous when interdependence is conjunctive and therefore differential inputs would be highly visible. If differential inputs were highly visible, then inequity could occur, be observed, and be redressed by group members.

When one thinks about confounded feedback, a similar kind of confusion occurs in the case of disjunctive tasks. A disjunctive task is one in which the response of one person can solve the problem for everyone. It should be easier to see inequity in a disjunctive task because you can at least see which input led to the outcome and then you can reward it accordingly. But a rule of equity could be inappropriate in this task because one cannot observe the contributions of people who almost got the answer. Those who almost got the answer probably worked just as hard as the person who achieved the answer; inputs in this sense are equal, and unequal rewarding of these equal inputs should cause dissatisfaction and inequitable treatment.

The point is that feedback to interdependent individuals is often confounded. Obscured in this feedback are the inputs that produced the outcome. In the face of confounded feedback it is difficult to couple inputs with outcomes, a coupling that must occur if people are to worry about inequity. Thus it would appear that unless one can assume that feedback and inputs are not confounded, inequity will not be the primary consideration of those people who received the feedback; but equality may be. Furthermore any explanation of group behavior that presumes accurate individual knowledge of results and subsequent modification of individual responses consistent with this feedback is questionable when the responsibility for that outcome cannot be assigned to specific inputs by specific individuals.

9. I would watch for manning effect. I've gone on record (Weick 1969, 24) as arguing that size is a lousy place to start group research because when you vary size, other variables are being co-varied and this compounds the problem of explanation. I would like to amend that observation in two ways. First, Cohen and March's (1974) analyses of college presidents seem to gain considerable order when the data are classified according to the size of the college being administered. Even though I still think size is a confounded variable, I also now think that an abundance of interpretable patterns and regularities fall out of the Cohen and March data when they use this simple classification.

Second, it has occured to me that I partially smuggle in the variable of group size whenever I use the idea of an undermanned setting (Barker 1960, 1968). Barker is concerned about what happens when there are insufficient personnel to carry out the essential tasks or functions in a setting, as well as about what this insufficiency does to the performance and satisfaction of the participations. He predicts, for example, that in an undermanned setting you will find such things as harder work, participation in a greater diversity of tasks, and involvement by everyone in more important and difficult tasks. Moreover each individual will have more responsibility, people will view themselves in task rather than social characteristics, each individual is more important within the setting, there is less evaluation of difference between people, a lower level of best performance, and more frequent occurrences of success and failure. These several effects are attributed to insufficient personnel relative to the opportunities and obligations in a setting.

The reason I think manning theory is an improvement on the variable of size is that size now becomes a relative consideration. If you take under-manning theory seriously, then it is trivial to ask the question whether a ten-man problem-solving group is better than a five-man problem -solving group. What you try to establish instead is the optimal manning for a problem-solving group. Then you may find that ten is undermanned, adequately manned or over-manned and make your predictions accordingly. It is just such analyses that people such as Wicker and Kirmeyer (1975), Wicker (1973), and Wicker, McGrath, and Armstrong (1972) have begun to perform. I would imagine that there is very little information in Political Science about what the optimal manning is for the various settings in which you are interested. I say that confidently because no other field has established such a "table of elements" either. It might make sense if most of the energy that might be directed into comparisons among groups on the gross variable of size be directed instead to testing the predicted consequences of under- and over-manned settings. The theory of over-manned settings is just now beginning to be articulated on the basis of some of Wicker's work; and from the standpoint of a very naive layman, I would bet that the epitome of an over-manned setting is a political nominating convention.

10. I would get another fruit fly. Somewhere Kenneth Boulding has characterized the prisoner's dilemma as the "fruit fly of social science." As you might guess from previous remarks, I feel we've exhausted the value of that research species and need something else. If I were starting out in group research, I would treat all prior research on the prisoner's dilemma as received wisdom, I would presume that the majority of knowledge that can be yielded by the prisoner's dilemma is either already somewhere in the literature or not worth getting, and I would not put my energies into working one more variation on a prisoner's dilemma. But I would try to develop some other efficient and visible group situation in which I could try out a number of variations both swiftly and economically.

The thrust of this recommendation may seem to contradict my earlier argument that staring at small samples makes more sense than glancing at large samples. There are times, however, when one has a host of notions about what makes groups function. When that happens, you need a tool which is a swift editing device, a tool that will show quickly which are the more and less promising leads to follow up. The prisoner's dilemma may retain that status for some people, and in that sense there's nothing wrong with it.

I would urge the researcher, however, to be on the lookout for other possibilities. The next-in-line effect that I mentioned earlier might be an appropriate possibility. My favorite is an exercise mentioned by Catherine Bateson (1974). This exercise is called sideways pat-a-cake, and interested readers can pursue its details in the Bateson source.

The basic attractiveness of this simple yet fiendish exercise is that it seems to capture many of the dynamics presumed to operate in any situation requiring change. Interesting questions include: what prior history of playing normal pat-a-cake seems to facilitate rapid learning of the sideways version and which prior conditions impede change to the sideways version? One does not have to stretch the imagination greatly to argue that people who are adept at taking the role of another might perform better on the sideways version than people who have difficulty taking the role of another person. This exercise involves interlocked behaviors because it is the sequence of hand movements, not whole people that is crucial. For me at present, sideways pat-a-cake is a more profitable fruit fly than prisoner's dilemma.

I'm not hustling sideways pat-a-cake. I am hustling the idea that you should find or create two kinds of groups. One kind is a stable on-going group that you want to analyze carefully (see point 14 below). The second kind is a simple group exercise through which you could see clearly numerous group dynamics that are presumed to occur and in which you could make quick and visible changes of variables to see immediate effects.

11. I would look for individual and group switching rules. Earlier I mentioned that people seem to have considerable ambivalence about spending lots of time in groups. In the present recommendation I am returning to this point in a more positive manner. It might be valuable to look for the conditions under which people can/do signal that they are ready either for sociability or privacy, the effects of acting on such signals immediately or belatedly, what happens within a group when members are out of phase in their signaling for privacy or sociability, and the consequences of these rules on the quality of problem solution. If you think of intense discussions that you have with valued colleagues (e.g. Shelly and Hruby 1968), what often happens is that you quickly suffer a problem of overload. You get so many ideas, so swiftly, that all you want to do is go off somewhere, sort them out, and trace through their consequences. If your behavior were observed when you experienced this desire to flee, your interest in the group would appear minimal and observers might conclude you received very little from the group and gave little to it. That conclusion is wrong because what you're doing is showing the symptoms of an all too successful intersection of your mind with the minds of other individuals.

I'm arguing that the observation that people easily get overloaded be joined to the well-documented point that people prefer to alternate between sociable and private activity, and that they need both. Overload often occurs in groups. This being the case, it is possible that the most effective problem solving does not occur through skillful management of groups that stay together, but rather it may come in the successful sequencing of alone and together moments over the same duration of time.

12. I would collect an inventory of group tasks. Those reading this essay have different strengths and weaknesses than I do, but one of the biggest problems I have in group research is designing an appropriate task, or trying to recall one that I know I've read about somewhere. My recommendation here is a simple one, but I think it's crucial. Whenever you find a group task that looks like it might be appropriate for some study you're doing or anticipate doing or you simply find the task esthetically pleasing, copy the reference to it and file it in a conspicuous place. The reason I think this recommendation makes sense is that the single most dog-earred volume in my entire library is a technical report published by Marvin Shaw (1963, now out of print) in which he took one hundred group tasks that were in the literature and scaled them on ten different dimensions (dimensions such as decision verifiability, cooperation requirements). In the finished document what you have is a description of the task sufficiently thorough so that you can write the instructions for it based on the information contained in the manual. More important, you also have an idea for each of the tasks as to those characteristics on which it has the highest and lowest loadings. For example if I want to have a maximum amount of participation among the people in my group, then I merely thumb through the manual and look for tasks that load heavily on participation and that have the other characteristics that I desire. Though I do not know this for certain, I would bet that this report has been one of Shaw's most requested reprints. I am urging people in Political Science to start a similar catalog in similar detail and make this catalog widely available. If you ruthlessly start recording information about tasks, and keep this collection up to date, the quality of your research should be heightened.

13. I would expect amplification of small changes to be the rule. The burgeoning literature on cybernetics, positive feedback, and deviation amplification makes it clear that very small changes in a variable locked in a causal circuit can have consequences much larger than the size of the original change. What basically happens in a deviation amplification loop (Maruyama 1963) is that a small change in the variable, through its causal interconnections, becomes increased so that the final event bears little resemblance to the original starting conditions or the original change. A good example of this argument is found in Stephens' (1967) theory of spontaneous schooling where he essentially argues that it takes only two people and four tendencies interacting to "grow" a school. Similar kinds of arguments are found in Kenneth Boulding's (1953) theory of growth and in particular his nucleating principle (pp. 333-336). One of the important implications of this line of analysis is that if you see some current state of affairs that is puzzling, you will be very lucky if you can trace back and find out how that present state of affairs came to pass. The lesson implicit in the

deviation amplification literature is that it is extremely difficult to find the origins of current practices because their nature and magnitude are so different from the nature and magnitude of the current consequences of those originating conditions.

Originating conditions and final effects have very long causal chains, and the recent work on cybernetics and feedback convinces me that you may well have to pay more attention to the current forces and causal connections that hold a group in place and sustain its current modes of behavior and less to the potentially unanswerable question of how the group got to its present condition. It is in this sense and no other in which I feel that people who urge you to deal with groups in the here and now have something to offer. It is extraordinarily difficult to work backward and discover which small deviations in what variables got amplified into the current set of problems a group faces and its current mode of interacting. It is probably more worthwhile to spend time trying to uncover the current pattern of causal linkages that sustain the group and that members try to modify or sever.

14. I would start with those groups that I know best. I realize there is a danger that those groups which you know best are also those groups that will appear least problematic and least informative. If you can combat those kinds of blind spots, then I think you really should take advantage of some of the backstage perspectives that you commonly have in groups that you're familiar with (see Merton 1972).

For example several readers probably have access to classroom groups. Those settings are unusually rich arenas for group phenomena, as will be apparent if you read Beck (1972, 29-39) and Katz (1962, 365-395). These two articles about classroom groups can serve as both filtering and sensitizing devices because the question you want to ask yourself is whether you see your own classroom groups in the same way Katz and Beck see theirs. Either answer that you come up with will be worthwhile because either you will confirm some of their observations or find yourself alerted to new variables that you hadn't seen before.

Several people have been on grant review committees and are well aware of the robust interpersonal dynamics that occur in such deliberations (e.g. Noble 1974, 916-921). I have found in some of my own work that families and family problem solving are some of the more provocative everyday groups in which one can address the research literature in small groups to determine its relevance, emphasis, and oversights. The point is not that any one of these settings has particular advantages over the other one. The point is that settings with which one is familiar may be a good place to start.

CONCLUSION

I'd like to end these rather personal observations by explicating an assumption behind them that I have not yet mentioned. It seems to me that theories control data. Stated differently, I'll see it when I believe it. My best guess is that psychologists have not seen a lot in groups because they did not take many ideas or beliefs into those group settings. Despite all of the caveats in methodological texts to the effect that data never speak for themselves, I genuinely think it is often the case that investigators must simply put themselves in the best position to hear what the data are going to say. Obviously that's a disastrous course of inquiry. So the best advice I could give to someone starting out with the advantage of backwardness is to arm yourself with the best ideas you can find around because you're likely to see some of those ideas in operation in any group.

Recently in social psychology one of our most able group psychologists, Ivan Steiner (1974), has gained notoriety for his essay, "Whatever happened to the group in social psychology." Steiner's answer is, interest in groups recedes in times of serenity and asserts itself at times of turbulence, with an eight-ten-year lag in these reactions. I would like to offer a different answer to Steiner's question. What happened to the group in social psychology is that no one had adequate tools to see it or took the time to fashion them. Given the luxury of your backwardness, I imagine you'll remedy that.

REFERENCES

Allison, G. T. 1971. *Essence of decision: Explaining the Cuban missile crisis.* Boston: Little, Brown, & Co.

Allport, F. H. 1962. A structuronomic conception of behavior: Individual and collective. *Journal of abnormal and social psychology* 64: 3-30.

Allport, G. W. 1968. The historical background of modern social psychology. In *The handbook of social psychology,* ed. G. Lindzey and E. Aronson, 2nd ed., 1:1-80. Reading, Mass.: Addison-Wesley.

Bales, R. F. 1950. *Interaction process analysis.* Cambridge: Addison-Wesley.

Barker, R. G. 1968. Ecology and motivation. In *Nebraska symposium on motivation,* ed. M. R. Jones, pp. 1-49. Lincoln, Neb.: University of Nebraska.

Barker, R. G. 1968. *Ecological psychology* Stanford, Calif.: Stanford University Press.

Bateson, G. 1972. *Steps to an ecology of mind.* New York: Ballantine.

Bateson, Mary C. 1972. *Our own metaphor.* New York: Knopf.

Beck, B. 1972. Toward a poor classroom. In *Profiles in college teaching: Models at Northwestern,* ed. B. C. Mathis and W. C. McGaghie, pp. 29-39. Evanston, Ill.: Center for the Teaching Professions at Northwestern University.

Billig, M., and Tajfel, H. 1973. Social categorization and similarity in intergroup behavior. *European journal of social psychology,* 3: 27-52.

Boring, E. G. 1954. The nature and history of experimental control. *The American journal of psychology* 67: 573-589.

Boulding, K.E. 1953. Toward a general theory of growth. *Canadian journal of economics and political science* 19: 326-340.

Brenner, M. 1973. The next-in-line effect. *Journal of verbal learning and verbal behavior* 12: 320-323.

Cartwright, D. 1971. Risk taking by individuals and groups: An assessment of research employing choice dilemmas. *Journal of personality and social psychology* 20: 361-378.

Cohen, M. D. and March, J. G. 1974. *Leadership and ambiguity.* New York: McGraw-Hill.

Cohen, M.D., March, J. G., and Olsen, J. P. 1972. A garbage can model of organizational choice. *Administrative science quarterly* 17: 1-25.

Collins, B. E. 1970. *Social psychology.* Reading, Mass.: Addison-Wesley.

Davis, J. H. 1969. *Group performance*, Reading, Mass. Addison-Wesley.

Duncan, S. D., Jr. 1972. Some signals and rules for taking speaking turns in conversations. *Journal of personality and social psychology* 23: 283-292.

Emery, F. E., and Trist, E. L. 1969. The causal texture of organizational environments. In *Systems thinking*, ed. F. E. Emery, pp. 241-257. Middlesex, England: Penguin.

Fromkin, H. 1973. The psychology of uniqueness: Avoidance of similarity and seeking of differences. Paper No. 438. Krannert Graduate School of Industrial Administration, Purdue University.

Geertz, C. 1972. Deep play: Notes on the Balinese cock fight. *Daedalus* 101: 1-37.

Goodman, N., and Ofshe, R. 1968. Empathy, communication efficiency, and marital status. *Journal of marriage and the family* 30: 597-603.

Hackman, J. R., and Morris, C. G. In press. Group tasks, group interaction process, and group performance effectiveness: A review and proposed integration. In *Advances in experimental social psychology*, ed. L. Berkowitz. New York: Academic Press.

Hall, R. L. 1957. Group performance under feedback that confounds responses of group members. *Sociometry* 20: 297-305.

Jackson, J. A. 1966. A conceptual and measurement model for norms and roles. *Pacific sociological review* 9: 35-47.

Katz, J. 1962. Personality and interpersonal relations in the college classroom. In *The American college*, ed. N. Sanford, pp. 365-395. New York: Wiley.

Lafferty, J. C., Eady, P. M., and Elmers, B. A. 1974. *The desert survival problem*. Plymouth, Mich.: Experiential Learning Methods.

Macrorie, K. 1968. *Writing to be read*. New York: Hayden.

Maruyama, M. 1963. The second cybernetics: Deviation amplifying mutual causal processes. *American scientist* 51: 164-179.

Merton, R. K. 1972. Insiders and outsiders: A chapter in the sociology of knowledge. *The American journal of sociology* 78: 9-47.

Moore, O. K. 1957. Divination—a new perspective. *American anthropologist*, 59: 69-74.

Moscovici, S., and Nemeth, C. 1974. Social influence II: Minority influence. In *Social psychology: Classic and contemporary integrations*, pp. 217-249. Chicago: Rand-McNally.

Noble, J. H., Jr. 1974. Peer review: Quality control of applied social research. *Science* 185: 916-921.

Osgood, C. E., and Walker, E. 1959. Motivation and language behavior: A content analysis of suicide notes. *Journal of abnormal and social psychology* 59: 58-67.

Pittenger, R. E., Hockett, C. F., and Danehy, J. J. 1960. *The first five minutes: A sample of microscopic interview analysis*. Ithaca, N. Y.: Paul Martineau.

Rosenthal, R. A., and Weiss, R. S. 1966. Problems of organizational feedback processes. In *Social indicators*, ed. R. A. Bauer, pp. 302-340. Cambridge, Mass.: MIT Press.

Rutstein, D. D. 1969. The ethical design of human experiments. *Daedalus* 98: 523-541.

Schwartz, B. 1973. The social psychology of privacy. In *Social psychology and everyday life*, ed. B. J. Franklin and F. J. Kohout, pp. 4-17. New York: McKay.

Service, E. R. 1960. The law of evolutionary potential. In *Evolution and culture*, ed. M. D. Sahins and E. R. Service, pp. 93-122. Ann Arbor: University of Michigan.

Shaw, M. E. 1963. Scaling group tasks: A method for dimensional analysis. Technical Report No. L. University of Florida. See *JSAS Catalog of Selected Documents in psychology*, 1973, 3, 8 (MS No. 294).

Shelly, M. W., and Hruby, H. C. 1968. On the optimization of significant interaction. In *The research society*, eds. E. Glatt and M. W. Shelly. New York: Gordon & Breach.

Sherif, M., and Sherif, Carolyn W. 1964. Reference groups. New York: Harper.

Steiner, I. D. 1955. Interpersonal behavior as influenced by accuracy of social perception. *Psychological review* 62: 268-274.

Steiner, I. D. 1974. Whatever happened to the group in social psychology. *Journal of experimental and social psychology* 10: 94-108.

Stephens, J. M. 1967. *The process of schooling*. New York: Holt, Rinehart, & Winston.

Thibaut, J. W., and Kelly, H. H. 1959. *The social psychology of groups*. New York: Wiley.

Wallace, A. F. C. 1961. *Culture and personality*. New York: Random.

Wallerstein, R. S., and Sampson, H. 1971. Issues in research in the psychoanalytic process. *International journal of psycho-analysis* 52: 11-50.

Watzlawick, P., Beavin, Janet H., and Jackson, D. D. 1967. *Pragmatics of human communication.* New York: Norton.

Weick, K. E. 1968. Systematic observational methods. In *Handbook of social psychology*, eds. G. Lindzey and E. Aronson, 2d ed., 2:357-451. Reading, Mass.: Addison-Wesley.

Weick, K. E. 1969. *The social psychology of organizing.* Reading, Mass.: Addison-Wesley.

Weick, K. E. 1971. Group processes, family processes and problem solving. In *Family problem solving*, eds. J. Aldous, T. Condon, R. Hill, M. Straus, and I. Tallman, pp. 3-32. New York: Dryden.

Weick, K. E. 1974. Middle range theories of social systems. *Behavioral science* 19: 357-367.

Weick, K. E., Gilfillan, D. P., and Keith, T. A. The effect of composer credibility on orchestra performance. *Sociometry* 36: 435-472.

Wicker, A. W. 1973. Undermanning theory and research: Implications for the study of psychological and behavioral effects of excess populations. *Representative research in social psychology* 4: 185-206.

Wicker, W., and Kirmeyer, S. 1975. From church to laboratory to national park: A program of research on excess and insufficient populations in behavior settings. Presented at Clark University.

Wicker, A. W., McGrath, J. E., and Armstrong, G. E. 1972. Organization size and behavior setting capacity as determinants of member participation. *Behavioral science* 17: 499-513.

Zander, A., and Wolfe, D. 1964. Administrative rewards and coordination among committee members. *Administrative science quarterly* 9: 50-69.

Ziller, R. C. 1965. Toward a theory of open and closed groups. *Psychological bulletin* 64: 164-182.

Some Challenges for Future Group Research: Reflections on the Experience in Sociology

CLOVIS SHEPHERD

A sociologist is probably not in the ideal position to tell political scientists how to go about studying small groups, for their stock in Sociology has dropped sharply in recent years. This suggests that we sociologists have our serious problems with the small-group approach. If only in the sense of suggesting what features of small-group analysis are likely to prove resistant to scientific exploration, however, political scientists can profit from a review of the major factors that led to the present sociological opinion that the small group is no longer a hot research item.

THE PRESENT STATUS OF SMALL-GROUP RESEARCH
IN SOCIOLOGY

The early 1970s constitute a low point in sociological writing and published research on small groups. This is partly due to disenchantment with the study of small groups in laboratory settings, and partly to the limited utility of available findings for understanding and changing the dynamics of natural groups. The results of many laboratory studies have left researcher, teacher, and reader disappointed in their failure to provide convincing evidence for the adequacy of alternative theoretical models, as well as in the capacity of findings to guide research and application in natural-state groups.

The current low state of published works may be a precursor to a renewed vitality in sociological studies of small groups, however. If so the view here is that such work will have at least four major properties. It will probably place greater emphasis on observation as the major data-gathering procedure, and it will provide a more active role in the research process for those observed (subjects, or Ss, in common usage) than has been the case in the recent past. This possible new era of research also probably will have two other emphases that distinguish it from available work. Such work-to-come probably will take place more often in natural settings—as in field studies of existing groups—or alternatively in the context of simulations.

It is useful to consider how these predictions, and disappointments, are grounded in the development of Sociology and thus represent a continuation of some historical developments. In Sociology, and probably also in other social sciences, we seem to move through cycles of rejection, followed by renewed attention, followed by rejection of our intellectual heritage, and so on. This cyclical phenomenon is characteristic of Political Science, I am told. I know that the phenomenon is common in many spheres, as in individual development. Many persons in their 20s and 30s reject their parents' old furniture, the family Bible, and that atrocious crystal hanging lamp, only to find as they move into their 40s and 50s that such treasures are not only sought assiduously but that many will pay outrageous prices for such "antiques."

In this paper I want to trace some of the historical precursors of some current and emerging interests, and to use this base for helping to clarify future trends. Not only do I intend to point to these continuing threads of scientific curiosity and method, but I hope to generate added interest in them.

As I review where we are, I want to focus on published research of the last five years in the leading journals and in the few sociological books that have come out in this period. This will not be an exhaustive literature review but a selective survey. Then I want to trace a few concepts and methods in time to show how they represent continuing and important interests. Finally I want to outline some future developments that I think will occur and that I certainly hope will occur. Thus my predictions will turn out to be both informed with regard to published material and wishful with regard to my hopes and desires.

REVIEW OF RECENT RESEARCH

In preparing for this essay I have limited my search of the recent literature in ways that may be of interest to the reader who is a political scientist. Thus I reviewed the *American Sociological Review (ASR)* and the *American Journal of Sociology (AJS)*, the two leading and oldest general sociological journals. I also reviewed *Sociometry, Human Relations, Social Forces, Sociology and Social Research, Social Problems, Human Organization,* and the *Journal of Social Issues.* In addition, I reviewed *Contemporary Sociology: A Journal of Reviews,* published since 1972 by the American Sociological Association. The review section of the *ASR* became too lengthy, so this journal was founded.

Perhaps the dearth of published sociological work on small groups is best illustrated by the percentage of reviews of books about small groups included in *Contemporary Sociology.* This journal has reviewed between four hundred and five hundred books annually since 1972, and only three-five titles a year have small groups as their primary focus. This represents at best one percent of the reviews.

In the journals a similar paucity of work is patent. The *ASR* and the *AJS* each year publish six issues, with from ten to fifteen articles per issue, or approximately seventy to eighty articles annually. Three to five articles annually have dealt with small groups. In the other journals listed, fewer small group studies are usually reported than in *ASR* and *AJS.* Generously perhaps five percent of the published articles deal with small-group themes, a figure a bit higher than for books but still rather low for an area which in the early 1960s seemed about to emerge as one of the major areas of sociology.

Some Common Themes. With what have these studies dealt? Is there a common theme, or a few common themes, threaded through this slim recent output? As I review the studies there seems to be one general theme present: a critique of the adequacy of the descriptive data being gathered, coupled with questions about the generalizability of the results. When a study is a laboratory experiment, the usual critique has predictable themes. These include the superficiality of the measures of the variables involved, the dubiousness of treating a collection of strangers solving a problem together in thirty minutes as a "group," and the limitations of generalizing to groups in general and especially to natural groups in society. On the other hand when a study is a field report, the critique often focuses on the subjectivity of the measurements, which are primarily observations of one observer; the related questions of reliability and validity; the adequacy of the specific measurements as even representing major aspects of group reality; and the limitations of generalizing from one field study either to other natural groups or to theories about small groups.

Most of the articles that I have reviewed have been concerned with clarification of earlier research results and/or theoretical propositions. In these studies, two themes emerge as representing current sociological preoccupations with small groups as well as continuing threads of sociological thought. One theme focuses on a further clarification and analysis of the nature of status hierarchies (and related power issues) in small groups. Characteristic research questions may be illustrated. Are statuses from other contexts related to status in small groups? What do the various status hierarchies of small groups look like? What are some consequences or correlates of status hierarchies? The second theme focuses on a further clarification and analysis of the nature of consensual validation and shared biography, or common understanding, present in small groups. A broad range of research questions reflects this second emphasis. Are differences in background experiences and identities related to the type and degree of consensual validation in small groups? What do the various patterns of consensual validation look like in small groups? What are some consequences of correlated or consensual validation?

Status hierarchies. The nature of status hierarchies has been discussed in a number of articles. Lewis (1972), for example, reviews a well-known model developed by Bales on role differentiation which distinguishes task and social-emotional leadership in small groups. This model holds that not only are different behaviors involved in task activities (directed at achieving the group's goals) and social-emotional activities (directed at maintaining membership in the group and feelings of involvement and acceptance), but also that typically one member emerges as the task leader and another member as the social-emotional leader. The resulting status hierarchy places the task leader at the top, with the social-emotional leader second. Other group members occupy successive ranks on the basis of their participation and influence in the group. This line of thought has found its way into most introductory sociology and social psychology texts and seems to be accepted as theoretically meaningful and empirically established.

However, Lewis raises serious questions about the degree to which such role differentiation in activities is so crystallized around two group members as to permit identifying a task leader and a social-emotional leader. Lewis reanalyzes Bales' data, from which the initial hypothesis was developed, and finds that the data provide scanty support for the usual explanation. In addition Lewis reviews other data on role differentiation in small groups and suggests, instead, that integration of task and social-emotional activities in one group member is at least as common, if not more typical, than differentiation among two members. At the present time, then, the hypothesis may be doubted that a task leader and a social-emotional leader emerge in small groups. The functions or activities associated with task achievement and with involvement and acceptance in the group are not in question. Their attachment to two different persons is at issue.

Lewis' work typifies why research on status hierarchies in small groups is still up in the air, still needs clarification, before a general model can be widely accepted.

As an aside, it is interesting to note that the concepts of task leader and social-emotional leader have their counterparts in family stereotypes. Witness the father (task leader) and the mother (social-emotional leader). Though some support for this differentiation exists in research on families, there is also considerable support for mother as task leader and father as social-emotional leader. Moreover support also exists for the observation that considerable variation in family activities and roles exists. This is to say either that we don't know, or that it all depends. Neither alternative is attractive.

Similarly Mazur (1973) and Berger, Cohen, and Zelditch (1972) have reviewed various studies and sought to develop the general observation (proposition or hypothesis?) that status differences among members are a typical and recurring feature of small groups, true across animal species as well as among homo sapiens. Perhaps their basic position represents the most general and accepted view about status hierarchies in small groups in current sociological thought. Mazur supports the general observation that such status hierarchies as pecking or dominance-display orders are common among many animals, along with many similar correlates. For example low-ranked group members have more stress symptoms than high-ranked members; group members tend to interact mostly with near peers—with members within one or two status ranks of self; and high-ranked members have the highest participation rates in the group as well as the highest performance of service and control functions. Berger, Cohen, and Zelditch in their (1972) review conclude that "when a task-oriented group is differentiated with respect to some external status characteristic, this status difference determines the observable power and prestige within the group whether or not the external status characteristic is related to the group task." They also note that status differences perceived by group members result in a positive correlation between status and such variables as opportunity to interact, rate of performance, rate of positive rewards, and exercise of influence.

Status hierarchies in small groups remain a preoccupation of sociologists, consistent with the general sociological perspective in which socioeconomic status (SES) continues to be central. SES shows a correlation or association with a wide variety of other phenomena. Sociologists also believe that status positions are generally consistent across groups, categories, or organizations, a belief perhaps most obviously demonstrated in research on jury behavior. There it is clear that the rates of participation and degree of influence among jurors, and the concomitant status hierarchy of jurors, reflects the general SES of jurors more than any other single factor. Jury foremen, elected by their peers, are consistently chosen from among those members with the highest SES in the wider community. If one knows the jurors' general SES, accurate predictions can be made about who will be chosen foreman, who will talk the most, and who will have the greater influence. This is tempered by individual knowledge and experience, of course, but the broad correlation holds up quite well.

Consensual validation. The notion of consensual validation (shared biography or common understanding) has also been incorporated in small group research and study, persistently, though not as well nor as explicitly as status. "Consensual validation" refers to an awareness by group members who have a sense of common understanding and agreement concerning values, attitudes, perceptions, and group norms. When we refer to a group as having high cohesion, it usually means that the status hierarchy has been clarified and accepted by the members, and we also mean that members have a common understanding, a common perspective on their world, a strong sense of consensual validation. Consensual validation initially rests on group members' awareness of a similarity of background, which provides some basis for assuming a common understanding. As a group evolves to a relatively stable system, common understanding based on similarities of background becomes overlaid with common understanding based on shared experiences as a group. Bales (1970) and Dunphy (1972) incorporated such phenomena in what they call group fantasies and mythologies.

Consensual validation has not been investigated as systematically as the status hierarchy but is incorporated in the work of persons dealing explicitly with group development. Indeed perhaps the best current source of such material is a (1974) book edited by Gibbard, Hartman, and Mann, *Analysis of Groups*. In addition much of the literature on encounter groups, T-groups, self-analytic groups, and the like may be viewed sociologically as relevant to the analysis of consensual validation. Similarly studies conducted by Maier (1970) relate to this phenomenon, as do researches dealing with the risky-shift phenomenon in which groups are often riskier in their decision making than individuals. Although this section on consensual validation has been brief, it is a theme that will be discussed again in the latter part of the paper.

I conclude this brief review with two observations. First, in the last five years published work on small groups in the sociological literature has been scanty, in spite of an outpouring in the 50s and early 60s and in spite of the fact that group phenomena have from the beginning been one major interest in Sociology. Second, sociologists' current work on small groups highlights the relevance of status hierarchy and consensual validation as important in understanding what occurs in small groups.

SOME REASONS FOR
DECLINING INTEREST

Why the small-group approach has attracted such a lessened interest cannot be explained, but several contributing factors seem clear enough. First, as was the case in Political Science, empirical research in Sociology was affected by the demands of the 1960s—the demands for relevance, the calls for radical revisionism in the pursuit of social goals, the substantial emphasis on advocacy vs. analysis, and so on. The small-group approach had just got up a full head of steam, as it were, when many sociologists got caught up in an array of professionally and personally involving issues (Gouldner 1970).

Second, federal funding sources began to diminish and, in many cases, completely dry up for small-group research and training. With less money available for basic research in small groups, and with the inability to point directly to applications of small-group theory and research to the burning social issues of the day, many sociologists turned their attention elsewhere.

Third, the issues of civil rights, the Vietnam conflict, the poverty programs, and related social issues were directing sociologists more and more to root causes of inequality and other social problems. These root causes were perceived as located in the larger social structure and not amenable to change through small groups. The challenge to identify root causes and change them, thus creating change in the entire social structure, was heady stuff.

Fourth, as theory and research in small groups evolved, it became increasingly clear that the behavior of persons had to be dealt with in analyzing the characteristics of groups. This led to the awareness that psychological (or individual) as well as sociological (or collective) variables were necessary for a fully rounded explanatory system, as Homans (1964) and Golembiewski (1962) argued. Social Psychology has been defined as a profession that draws both on Psychology and Sociology. In addition, although Social Psychology is clearly identified as a social science discipline, it continues to suffer a split personality, with social psychologists generally tending to be trained in and primarily identified with either Sociology or Psychology. Perhaps the whole field of small groups will not move ahead as rapidly as it might until social psychologists have severed their umbilical cords to either Psychology or Sociology.

Fifth, the ardor of many sociologists for the small group was cooled by the dawning awareness that more field research on natural groups had to be conducted if advances in theory and research were to be made. Field research is time consuming, opportunities are unpredictable, and the involvement of the researcher in the lives of the subjects is almost inevitable. Phenomena seem too complex and contradictory, not at all as neat and controllable as in the laboratory or in a survey where the questionnaire receives the wrath of the respondent, not the researcher. Since most sociologists are professors in colleges and universities, they often cannot spend the time needed to do field research and, at the same time, carry a regular teaching load and the usual administrative duties. A clue to the time that can be involved may be found in the report of Howell (1973): to develop a portrait of two blue-collar families, he spent one full year living in a Washington, D.C., neighborhood and a second year writing his report. Although this extended time is not necessarily the only or even the ideal model, it does illustrate the fact that field research is much more costly, both in time and in one's personal life, then laboratory or survey research. Perhaps simulations will become a viable alternative, as researchers develop and test alternative models. Professor Fraser of Earlham College has successfully utilized a simulated economy for teaching and research, and similar models will no doubt be developed in the future.

SOME HISTORICAL TRENDS

Small groups have been an important part of the sociological enterprise from the beginning, and continue to be so despite the diminished interest in small groups that was sketched above. A brief survey of five major themes or threads in the literature will establish why group analysis will again receive major attention, notwithstanding the current fashion. Like MacArthur, to risk a pun, the small group in Sociology shall return to prominence.

This section will introduce these five major themes or threads by a brief review of several phases of development of the small-group literature.

Early sociologists spoke of the primary group as the crucible and basis for social organization. For a long time, "primary group" referred mostly to the family, but also to those small groups in which persons were inextricably involved especially in the work setting and in the political arena. Although small groups were often discussed theoretically, very little empirical work was carried out until the twenties and thirties. During this era small groups were studied and attempts made to generalize and develop theoretical perspectives on the dynamics of groups.

This initial research was perhaps epitomized in Sociology by the work of Thrasher (1927) on youth and young-adult gangs. He relied primarily on observation and informal interviews of natural-group members, and developed many generalizations or statements in the form of propositions and testable hypotheses. During this period there also appeared the famous Western Electric studies, showing that group phenomena were important factors in how persons worked in industry, especially on production lines.

The 1940s represent a transition from primarily field studies of natural groups to laboratory studies of contrived groups. The major contributors can only be sampled here: Lewin's work; the field studies of the Research Branch of the Army; work in England by the Tavistock group; the emergence of the NTL Institute and training in group behavior; and Bales' (1950) development of the Interaction Process Analysis scheme. All of this work (see Sofer 1972) reflected the hope that theories would provide a basis for deriving hypotheses, which in turn would generate results that could be generalized.

The fifties and sixties might be viewed as the golden age of sociological work on small groups. Primarily there was a burgeoning of experiments and laboratory studies of contrived groups, most of them based on Lewin's and Festinger's work in field theory, social comparison theory, and the theory of cognitive dissonance. For a review of this work the reader can do no better than to consult a classic book of this period. A. Paul Hare's *Handbook of Small Group Research* (1962) includes most studies published through 1961, and is still considered the best organized and most thorough review of the heyday of the small group in Sociology.

Sometimes neglected in the torrent of laboratory research, the Golden Age also saw much field work. Such work will be sampled here somewhat more fully because of its common neglect. *When Prophecy Fails* by Festinger et al. (1956) is a classic field study demonstrating the power of cognitive dissonance in reinforcing the cohesion of a group of true believers in spite of the failure of prophecies to come true. Newcomb (1961) conducted an intensive field experiment in a rooming house in Ann Arbor, testing various hypotheses about the relation between interaction, sentiments, perceived similarities, and the like. Many observational methods were tested in the laboratory and in the field, some testing the adequacy of the task and social-emotional leadership role differentiation, with equivocal findings. Fiedler (1967) conducted extensive research on natural groups of bombing crews, submarine crews, and other armed forces small groups. Maier (1970) studied decision-making and problem-solving groups, searching for clues to the emergence of creativity and the level of productivity.

In sum this period saw stereophonic attention to research and application. There was an extended search by many scholars for theoretical models, mathematical models, the development of deductive hypotheses, and the testing of such hypotheses in the field and in the laboratory. Concomitantly, there was the emergence and growth of various applications of group knowledge. These applications include group dynamics, broadly, as well as the widespread use of encounter or sensitivity groups, which culminated in the humanistic trend in social science, especially in Sociology and Psychology.

Currently we are in a holding action in Sociology regarding theoretical models and hypothesis testing. Most current small group models rely heavily on Bales and on early T-group conceptualizations (Bradford et al. 1964), along with the group dynamics heritage of Lewin and the analytic heritage of Bion. These models have lost most of their power to generate new ideas and new hypotheses, and the understanding of the dynamics of small groups seems to be in a state of holding with an adequate fuel supply to circle for some time to come. What we know seems often to be not far removed from common sense. A lot of myths have been destroyed. Some simplistic hypotheses have been invalidated, and others have been validated. Continued laboratory studies are being conducted, but application of their findings to natural groups seems very limited. Training in group process and group development has been a mixed success but is nevertheless very common.

What threads seem to be woven throughout this very cursory and selective review? The following have most impact on me. First, field study of natural groups emphasizing observation by a trained social scientist is a continuing thread. No one doubts the richness and depth of such work. Major attention needs to be given to the reliability and validity of the researchers' observations, reflecting a need for the researcher to systematize his method so that other researchers can consensually validate his findings. Dunphy's new book (1972) helps provide a basis for this development, as do the works of ethnomethodologists, sociolinguists, and field researches illustrated in the books by Lofland (1973), and by Schatzman and Strauss (1973). Observation is always an inference and a percept: we see certain things and we infer meanings based on our perception. Note that our inferences are symbolic and theoretical, based on our meaning systems. Consequently as we learn more or develop more ways of interpreting behavior, we also see different things. The fact gatherers are always limited both by what is seen and by what meanings are placed on those perceptions. As researchers become more adept in interpreting behavior, they also see somewhat different behavior. Thus a seasoned, experienced, and thoughtful observer will see different things than an amateur, as well as place different meanings on the same perceptions. In recent years in Sociology we have failed to engage in as much observation as we could use effectively, both because we were disenchanted with older methods of observation and because we have had such ready access to sophisticated methods of data gathering and processing, as in the case of computer processing of survey data. Sociologists seem to be placing such newer tools in a more balanced perspective of late, after an intense but brief infatuation with them. Much the same is true of much work in Political Science, I hear from my colleagues.

A second thread is the elusive nature of group leadership. No one doubts the fact of leadership or its importance. However there is considerable doubt that we can easily identify leadership acts or array group members on one or more dimensions of group leadership. At issue here are a number of things. For one there continues a running argument about whether leadership is too often confused with a status hierarchy or dominance-display system. So leadership discussions are not always clear about whether they refer to an act or behavior which leads the group, which exerts influence on other group members, or whether they refer to a status position or rank in the group with concomitant rights and duties. Leadership may also have been confounded with authority and authority figures, arousing feelings and attitudes among group members from past experiences with authority figures (parent, teacher, policeman, etc.) which become projected onto another group member who is exercising leadership acts. Of course leadership may pass from member to member. Indeed some scholars believe that high cohesive groups which manifest high task achievement and high commitment are also characterized by the exercise of leadership acts by all group members, even if there is a clear-cut status hierarchy and consensual validation.

Another issue associated with leadership is power: there is a current revival of interest in power, its nature and manifestations, generally focusing on access to resources and control over communication and transaction (exchange) systems (Rogers 1974). How is power related to leadership? We know that low-ranked group members can withhold their participation in a group and thus exert influence and power. But is this leadership? Many scholars also contend that power exists only so long as it is not overtly exercised and tested, but instead used primarily as a threat or a presumed quality. Finally there remains a continuing debate about leadership as a person with a set of characteristics and a set of behavior vs. leadership as a person who happens to be in the right place at the right time, thus being a leader due to the situation. Whatever the issues and concerns, leadership in small groups continues as a major focus but an elusive one with regard to our being empirically and theoretically clear about what it is and how it functions.

A third thread is the continuing belief in the power of groups, especially in the pressures toward conformity and in the ability of groups to protect members against outsiders. A belief in the potential creativity and productivity of groups also persists, a notion that the whole can be more than the sum of the parts. I use the words "potential creativity and productivity" to highlight the fact that many scholars and practitioners who work extensively with groups believe in the potential of groups, but even they often are disappointed with the results of group efforts. The power of groups is, perhaps, most dramatically illustrated in the phenomenon of "a minority of one": that situation in which all group members but one are agreed on some issue, while one member stands alone. The member who stands alone often reports feelings of fright, anxiety, doubt about personal convictions or even of what one otherwise would hold to be clear-cut facts. Such a member often reports going along with the group, rather than facing the power of the group and pressures feared as very uncomfortable.

Related to this fear of being the lone holdout is the positive side of group power. When a group has reached a high level of cohesion and is able to work interdependently and effectively on tasks and goals, group members typically express feelings of warmth, closeness, and high acceptance—feeling states that are rarely experienced in other circumstances. As teachers and managers use groups more in learning and problem solving, they continue to be impressed if not awed by the power of groups, a consequence that may lead to less use of groups as well as to more. The potential creativity and productivity of groups continues to be a belief of sociologists even though, in much of the research literature as well as in practice, groups are often not as effective in problem solving as the average individual members prior to group discussion. This low level of group effectiveness seems due either to the group being in an early stage of development, or if further along, having settled on a status hierarchy that is inappropriate to the task and perhaps even conducive to a high level of stress. Thus the degree of consensual validation is low, reflected mostly in pretense and superficial agreement. If these observations are apt, then the implication is that group members need to know much more than they typically do for group development to reach that point where it can support a high level of creativity and productivity.

A fourth thread in the small-group literature is the continuing belief that groups are very important for one's social identity, self-concept, and level of self-esteem, and also as a primary source of interpersonal confrontation and support. Indeed persons close to one can, if they so choose, provide direct and accurate feedback, where confronting with either positive or negative observations implies a deep level of caring and support. Consider members of training groups (encounter, T-groups, and the like) that reach a high level of development. When members of such groups participate in this feedback process, they often report that they experience negative feedback with minimum defensiveness and positive feedback with minimum embarassment. Members also often report that they sense an increase in their self-esteem and greater clarity in their self-concept and in their social identity.

Such effects are credible, for group experiences can touch significant and powerful processes. To suggest the point, considerable evidence supports the observation that people generally perceive groups as somewhat like the family in which they grew up. Role theorists argue that one's first role definitions are established in the family and that the role expectations experienced there are carried into other group settings, sometimes becoming highly modified as one matures, other times remaining very similar to family patterns. Perhaps some of the current popularity of Transactional Analysis training derives from a similar source, since the conceptual system involved emphasizes the key concepts of Parent, Adult, and Child, along with transactions between people reflecting these ego states. In addition in our current lonely and alienated society, many persons seem disconnected from others in any intimate sense, and rarely participate in a group that can be characterized as very far along in the process of development, as group trainers and leaders conceive that process.

Such features notwithstanding, we sociologists have nevertheless been substantially frustrated in our desire to develop adequate interpretive and predictive models of group process. There are many things we know, and there are many myths and beliefs about groups that have been destroyed or at least seriously questioned. Still we are unable to draw implications for everyday life, or to design learning opportunities that satisfy our desire to interpret and predict with a fair degree of accuracy. Despite alternative waves of analytic hope and despair, sociologists remain strong in their conviction that groups are a most important aspect of social life.

A fifth sign of the central role of groups, and the final one I will discuss, is the conception of groups as mediating between the individual and the society, between individuals and the larger social systems in which they participate. The group protects and nurtures the individual and prepares the individual for participation in larger social systems. Similarly society at large depends on groups for conveying information and expectations to the individual, for making those expectations compatible and acceptable to the individual, and for exercising influence on the individual. In studies of collective and social influence, two sets of phenomena have consistently been found to be the keys to reinforcing existing behavior or to changing behavior: group norms and values, and the role of opinion leaders or gatekeepers. But even here the ways in which groups mediate between the individual and the larger social system have not been adequately described, much less analyzed with respect to their dynamics.

What beginnings have been made in these central matters and what still needs doing can be suggested economically. Dunphy, for example, (1972, pp. 65-76) describes six types of natural groups: apathetic groups (e.g., deserter groups in armies), erratic groups (small crews and short assembly lines in industry), strategic groups (criminal gangs engaged in organized theft), cabal groups (lower officer groups in the army), organizer groups (groups of top executives in business and industrial plants), and conservative groups (upper elite families). These, Dunphy argues, represent a synthesized description of the major types of groups one may encounter, and they are discussed in relation to their characteristics and to the dominant roles involved in them. Though this seems to be a good beginning, the approach requires considerable field observation to increase its utility in understanding how these different groups carry out mediating functions between the individual and the larger society.

Related to this fifth theme or thread is the basic question as to whether or not it is possible for an individual to be linked with the larger society in ways other than through small groups, without suffering various psychosomatic symptoms, creating problems for people with whom one works or plays, or without existing at a poorly actualized level. The focal issue may be expressed in other ways. Perhaps geniuses whose creativity and productivity may be expressed individually would be inhibited by group membership, their genius might be squelched by group pressures and involvement in a demanding although satisfying set of interpersonal relations.

In any case the major point here is that groups are conceptualized as performing very important mediating functions between the individual and the larger society.

THE FUTURE

Finally I come to my predictions about the future. What I will say in the remainder of this paper has been anticipated in the earlier part. Thus these comments will be relatively brief, and their relationship to the selected review of recent published research and to the set of brief historical comments will be evident.

First, the focus of sociological work in small groups will extend from and be based on the exploration of status hierarchies and of consensual validation. These developments will rely more on system theory (a good current source is Kuhn 1974), and will concentrate on identifying and analyzing patterns of communication and transaction (exchange) among the members of small groups. Related to this will be careful efforts to identify resources available to members, about which they communicate and with which they carry out transactions. Related to resource control, and to communication and transaction, will come a more useful conception of power in small groups, what it is and how it is used (see Rogers 1974). From this type of analysis we will be better able to define leadership and to show how it functions both within a small group and in linking that small group to other groups in a larger social system (an organization or a community). Out of this type of analysis we will obtain greater clarification of the status hierarchy and of consensual validation, both concepts of a more abstract nature than those which constitute a systems analytic approach. Thus I predict that systems theory of the highly abstract and deductive sort proposed by Kuhn will turn out to be one of the theoretical models we have been looking for in recent years. It is compatible with earlier models, and it provides a basis for unification across the social sciences. In our case that means especially a unified approach across Psychology and Sociology, not to mention communications theory, information theory, and related perspectives in interdisciplinary approaches.

Second, advances developed in our theoretical model using systems theory will be tested, modified, and further developed in both field settings and in classroom, in-service training, and laboratory settings. This means a renewed interest in the development of observational models and skills, especially those that lend themselves to use in the field with natural groups. Related to this will be a more active participation by the subjects of our research, group members themselves, in contributing data and in questioning our observations and interpretations. Although Doc of the Norton Street Gang was as important as Whyte (1943) in developing insight and knowledge about street-corner gangs, the potential lessons for the methodology of research on natural groups from that experience have never adequately found their way into our lexicons of methodology. Advances will increase rapidly in the methodological bases for increasing our confidence in the reliability and validity of observational and self-report data, some already being evidenced in the work of field researchers (see Lofland and Schatzman and Strauss) and of sociolinguists and ethnomethodologists (see Dreitzel 1970). Related to this kind of field research on natural groups will come new perspectives on the various mediating function of small groups, as well as further clarification of the ties between the individual and the society and culture in which one lives.

In the classroom setting, as well as in in-service training and even in laboratory experiments, we will pursue a more careful attempt to study the process of group development and use simulations of natural groups (a la the astronauts' simulated spaceship trips in training, invaluable both for testing the adequacy of knowledge and as preparation for the flight) to highlight the qualities and effects of different types of groups as well as of different stages of group development.

The use of simulations in small-group research has not been common, yet it seems to hold much promise as both a method of testing theory and of learning about groups. An enterprising teacher in Oregon has developed a simulation of marriage and family life for students in high school: the course involves pairing a male and female student and then simulating the important events of a couple's life; such as a marriage ceremony, getting a job, finding an apartment, budgeting their income, preparing to have a baby, and eventually getting a divorce. The teacher reports that students learn a great deal about marriage and family through participating in this simulation. Other studies suggest that these students might not know more cognitively than nonparticipating students, but they do know much better how they would deal with these real-life issues and be more aware of their complexity.

Videotape has only begun to be used as a research and learning tool, and it permits subtle observation and analysis. Imagine videotaping a health services team in its natural setting as it meets to solve a problem, and videotaping the same team in a learning activity where it attempts to improve its capacity to function as a team. The team members could view the videotapes and seek to analyze the small-group processes occurring in them. It would be possible for group or team members to develop skills in self-observation and to see, over time, what changes occur (or do not occur) in the ways in which they function.

Groups will be used much more in the future in sociological work, more openly and with greater explanation of the researcher or teacher's intentions. It does seem rather strange that a discipline focused on groups finds itself in the state in which published research is scanty and the reported use of groups in teaching, learning, and working is sparse. This I believe will not continue, and younger sociologists will pursue group phenomena much more avidly than in the recent past.

Finally, as is evident in the comments above, future trends in the sociology of small groups will place greater stress on the utility of the knowledge gained, rather than on curiosity about the processes ("science for science's sake"). Increasingly the goal will be to help provide individuals with the kind of knowledge that will make them more informed about small-group dynamics, and thus more able to make informed choices from among an array of alternatives.

REFERENCES

Bales, R. T. 1970. *Personality and interpersonal behavior.* New York: Holt, Rinehart & Winston.

Berger, J., Cohen, B. O., and Zelditch, M., Jr. 1972. Status characteristics and social interaction. *American sociological review* 37: 241-255.

Bradford, L. P., Gibb, J. R., and Benne, K. D., eds. 1964. *T-Group theory and laboratory method.* New York: Wiley.

Dreitzel, H. P., ed. 1970. *Patterns of communicative behavior.* New York: Macmillan.

Dunphy, C. 1972. *The primary group.* New York: Appleton-Century-Crofts.

Festinger, L., Riecken, H. W., and Schachter, S. 1956. *When prophecy fails.* Minneapolis: University of Minnesota Press. (Also Harper Torchbook 1964).

Fiedler, F. E. 1967. *A theory of leadership effectiveness.* New York: McGraw-Hill.

Gibbard, G. S., Hartman, J. J., and Mann, R. D., eds. 1974. *Analysis of groups.* San Francisco: Jossey-Bass.

Golembiewski, R. T. 1962. *The small group.* Chicago: University of Chicago Press.

Gouldner, A. 1970. *The coming crisis of western sociology.* New York: Basic Books.

Hare, A. P. 1962. *Handbook of small group research.* New York: The Free Press.

Homans, G. C. 1964. Bringing men back in. *American sociological review* 29: 809-818.

Howell, J. T. 1973. *Hard living on Clay Street.* Garden City, N. Y.: Anchor Books.

Kuhn, A. 1974. *The logic of social systems.* San Francisco: Jossey-Bass.

Lewis, H. 1972. Role differentiation. *American sociological review* 37: 424-434.

Lofland, J. 1971. *Analyzing social settings.* Belmont, Calif.: Wadsworth.

Maier, R. F. 1970. *Problem solving and creativity in individuals and groups.* Belmont, Calif.: Brooks/Cole.

Mazur, A. 1973. A cross-species comparison of status in small established groups. *American Sociological Review* 38: 513-530.

Newcomb, T. 1961. *The acquaintance process.* New York: Holt, Rinehart & Winston.

Rogers, M. F. 1974. Instrumental and infra-resources: The bases of power. *American Journal of Sociology* 79: 1418-1433.

Schatzman, L., and Strauss, A. L. 1973. *Field research: Strategies for a natural sociology.* Englewood Cliffs, N. J.: Prentice-Hall.

Sofer, C. 1972. *Organizations in theory and practice.* New York: Basic Books.

Thrasher, F. M. 1927. *The Gang.* Chicago: University of Chicago Press.

Whyte, W. F. 1943. *Street corner society.* Chicago: University of Chicago Press.